THE **Building Christian English** SERIES

Building

Christian English

Progressing With Courage

Grade 6

Teacher's Manual

Rod and Staff Publishers, Inc.

Hwy. 172, Crockett, Kentucky 41413

Telephone: (606) 522-4348

Acknowledgments

We are indebted first and most of all to God, whose blessing made possible the writing and publishing of this book.

We express gratitude to each one who was involved in this work. The original edition was written by Lela Birky and Lucy Ann Conley, and the revision by Marion W. Leinbach. Marvin Eicher and Ernest Wine were the editors, H. Lynn Martin and various others were reviewers, and the artwork was done by Lester Miller. We are also indebted to the teachers who used the material on a laboratory basis in their classrooms, as well as to numerous people who assisted along the way by providing finances, by encouraging those directly involved in the work, and by interceding in prayer for the work.

Various reference books were consulted in accomplishing this task, such as English handbooks, other English textbooks, encyclopedias, and dictionaries. For these too we are grateful. We have chosen to favor the more conservative schools of thought that are considered authoritative in correct English usage.

—*The Publishers*

Copyright, 1994

First edition, copyright 1971

by

Rod and Staff Publishers, Inc.

Hwy. 172, Crockett, Kentucky 41413

Printed in U.S.A.

ISBN 978-07399-0525-8

Catalog no. 12696.3

9   10   11   12   —   21   20   19   18   17   16   15   14

Table of Contents

(Stars indicate Written Composition and Oral English lessons.)

Chapter 1 Understanding Sentences
Learning About Stories and Directions

Chapter 2 Working With Sentences
Understanding Paragraphs

Chapter 3 Working With Nouns
Developing Paragraphs

Chapter 4 Working With Verbs
Writing Outlines

Chapter 5 Using Verbs Correctly
Writing Reports

Chapter 6 Working With Pronouns
Writing Letters

Chapter 7 Using Correct Capitalization and Punctuation
Writing Stories

Chapter 8 Working With Adjectives
Writing Descriptions

Chapter 9 Working With Adverbs
Studying Poetry

Tests

To the Teacher

This English course is designed for approximately 120 minutes of class time per week (four classes per week of 30 minutes each). There is a pupil's book, a teacher's guide, a worksheets booklet, and a test booklet. For a schedule with five classes per week, some lessons may be divided—especially the chapter reviews—or the worksheets may be used more often.

The Pupil's Book

The lesson text explains and illustrates the new concepts. In the exercises, **Class Practice** is intended for oral practice with the class. If your schedule does not allow enough time for all the oral drill, some of it may be assigned as written work.

The written work is often divided into **Written Exercises** (on the present lesson) and **Review Exercises** (on concepts taught previously). These parts may be further divided into Parts A and B. An occasional **Challenge Exercise** provides optional work, which may be done for extra credit or assigned to able students.

A Chapter Review at the end of each chapter provides a review of the material taught in that chapter. The test booklet has a test for each chapter.

Note: In this course, lessons on oral and written composition are interspersed throughout the textbook. This is done for convenience in teaching a balance of grammar and composition throughout the year, rather than having the whole "composition load" in one large block. For simple reference, each of these composition lessons is marked by a design along the margin. The composition material taught in a given chapter is covered in the review and test for that chapter.

The Teacher's Guide

Each lesson in the teacher's guide begins by stating the **Purpose** of the lesson. A star indicates that a concept is introduced for the first time in this English series. If a concept was previously taught only to a certain degree, a note usually describes the extent of that previous experience.

Following the Purpose, some lessons have a part called **Teacher.** This is not a main part of the lesson but is rather for the teacher's information and awareness.

Beginning in Lesson 1, a part called **Oral Review** comes after the Purpose. The review questions in this part are intended for use at the beginning of the class period, both to review concepts already taught and to get the pupils' minds "in gear" for the new English lesson. If you wish, you may duplicate the questions and hand them to the students for personal study (especially if you have slow students).

Some lessons have a **Written Quiz** after the Oral Review. These quizzes give written review and drill on important concepts taught recently. Both the Oral Review and the Written Quiz are optional; see the following section for further explanation.

The **Lesson Introduction** suggests a way to introduce the lesson, and the **Lesson Outline** lists the specific points to be taught.

Drill and Review

This course is designed to provide sufficient drill and review of all the English concepts taught. If the Class Practice, Written Exercises, and Review Exercises are used, the average pupil's mastery of the concepts should be satisfactory for this grade level.

However, for thoroughly mastering the material, it is helpful (especially for slow students) to overlearn the concepts by repeated drill and review. This is the purpose of the Oral Reviews and the Written Quizzes in the teacher's guide and is also one purpose of the worksheets. If time allows, or if the pupils need further drill and review, the teacher is strongly encouraged to use these extra materials; however, they may be omitted if time is limited. **The Worksheets, the Oral Reviews, and the Written Quizzes are not required in order to teach this English course successfully.**

General Teaching Suggestions

Use the chalkboard frequently in demonstrating ideas. Keep a brisk pace, and do not waste precious class time to "major on minors." Students should follow along with open books during class discussion.

Most of the written work should be checked in class. Instruct students to use red ink pens for checking. Their checking should be done neatly, without unnecessary scribbling or doodling.

Plan ahead so that you will complete the book. Make a schedule showing the number of lessons to cover each week, and stick to it as much as possible.

Develop a grading system that provides an accurate picture of the children's progress but does not bog you down with time-consuming work. Do not give full credit when students fail to do neat work or to follow directions.

It is also a good policy to grade on class participation. Students need to pay attention, follow along in their books, show interest in what is being said, and participate in answering questions during class discussion.

Check the class average periodically. If it is higher than a B, you may be moving too slowly through the book or grading too leniently. If it is much lower, you may be moving too fast or grading too strictly. This is only a general guide; every class has different abilities. Comparing your class records with those from previous years may prove helpful.

The **Worksheets** may be used for remedial practice or simply for extra drill on various concepts. They may be reproduced as needed in teaching this course.

Subjects

Predicates

Clauses

Sentences

Fragments

Directions

Stories

Chapter One

Understanding Sentences

Learning About Stories and Directions

A
sentence is
a group of words that
expresses a complete
thought.

Study to shew thyself approved
unto God, a workman that needeth not to be ashamed.

·   2 Timothy 2:15

1. Sentences and Fragments

Imagine a school that had no teacher, or a school with a teacher but no pupils. Or what if a school had a teacher and pupils, but was without books or paper? Such a school would not be complete. It could not accomplish the work that a school should get done.

A sentence, like a school, has a job to do. Its job is to express a thought. And like a school, a sentence must be complete in order to do its work. If our writing has incomplete sentences, readers will not be able to understand our thoughts and ideas. We say, then, that a complete sentence is a group of words that expresses a complete thought.

To be complete, a sentence must have a *subject* and a *predicate*. The subject tells *who* or *what* the sentence is about, and the predicate tells what the subject does or is. Consider these complete sentences.

> Brother Luke preached an inspiring sermon.
>> This sentence is about *Brother Luke,* and it tells what he did—*preached an inspiring sermon.* It expresses a complete thought.

> The playful kittens chased a ball of Mother's yarn.
>> What is the sentence about? (the playful kittens) What did they do? (chased a ball of Mother's yarn) This is a complete sentence because it has a subject and a predicate, and it expresses a complete thought.

A group of words that does not express a complete thought is a sentence *fragment.* A group of words may be a fragment for several different reasons.

Lesson 1

Purpose: To define the complete sentence and the sentence fragment.

Oral Review:

(This reviews parts of speech from grade 5 to help prepare students for finding subjects and predicates in sentences.)

1. What is a verb? (a word that shows action or being)
2. Name all the helping verbs you learned in grade 5. (am, is, are, was, were, be, been, being; have, has, had; do, does, did; may, might, must; can—could, shall—should, will—would)
3. What is a noun? (a word that names a person, place, thing, or idea)
4. Name the part of speech described.
   a. It takes the place of a noun. (pronoun)
   b. It tells *how, when, where,* or *to what degree.* (adverb)
   c. It tells *which, whose, how many,* or *what kind of.* (adjective)
   d. It modifies a verb. (adverb)
   e. It modifies an adjective or adverb. (adverb)
   f. It modifies a noun or pronoun. (adjective)

Lesson Introduction: Read the following dialogue to the students.

> "Where are you going?"
> "To the store."
> "What are you going to buy?"
> "Candy."
> "What will you do with it?"
> "Treat the class."

Ask students which are complete sentences and which are not. Ask how they could be made into complete sentences. Tell them that in ordinary conversation we may use sentences that are incomplete. But in writing we must use complete sentences to make the meaning clear.

1. Sometimes a fragment does not have a subject.

   Fragment: Played in the sand.

   This group of words does not make sense because it does not say who or what played in the sand. It can be corrected by adding a subject.

   Sentence: <u>A little child</u> played in the sand.

2. Sometimes a fragment does not have a predicate.

   Fragment: The rich man Job.

   This group of words does not tell what the man Job did or was. It can be corrected by adding a predicate.

   Sentence: The rich man Job <u>lived in Uz.</u>

3. Sometimes a fragment does not have a subject or a predicate.

   Fragment: In the morning at 7:00.

   This example does not tell *who* or *what,* nor does it tell what the subject *did* or *was.* It can be corrected by adding a subject and a predicate.

   Sentence: <u>We were eating</u> in the morning at 7:00.

4. Sometimes a fragment has a verb, but it still needs a helping verb. Without a helping verb, the sentence does not make sense and is a fragment.

   Fragment: James running very fast.

   The fragment can be corrected by adding a helping verb.

   Sentence: James <u>was</u> running very fast.

Remember that every complete sentence must begin with a capital letter and end with correct punctuation.

- A sentence is a group of words that expresses a complete thought. It must have a subject and a predicate.

- A sentence fragment is a group of words that does not express a complete thought.

Lesson Outline:

1. A sentence is a group of words that expresses a complete thought.

2. To be complete, a sentence must have a subject and a predicate.

   a. The subject tells *who* or *what* the sentence is about.

   b. The predicate tells what the subject does or is.

3. A fragment is a group of words that does not express a complete thought.

   (1) Sometimes a fragment does not have a subject.

      Fragment: Could never jump that high.
      Sentence: I could never jump that high.

   (2) Sometimes a fragment does not have a predicate.

      Fragment: The hen and her chicks.
      Sentence: The hen and her chicks safely crossed the road.

   (3) Sometimes a fragment does not have a subject or a predicate.

      Fragment: Out in the field by the brook.
      Sentence: Out in the field by the brook, we found a wild goose's nest.

   (4) Sometimes a fragment has a verb, but it still needs a helping verb. Without a helping verb, the sentence does not make sense and is a fragment.

      Fragment: Father using the nails now.
      Sentence: Father is using the nails now.

Class Practice

A. Tell whether each group of words is a *sentence* or a *fragment*. If it is a fragment, tell what is missing.
1. On the other side of the stream.
2. We have heard about the fire.
3. Was watching the birds.
4. Large white clouds.
5. Charles was very helpful on Saturday.
6. Brother Elvin and his children.
7. Rising above the treetops.
8. Jane going shopping with Mother.
9. He will have some left.
10. In the house or outside.

B. Make complete sentences from the fragments in Part A.

Written Exercises

A. Write whether each group of words is a *sentence* or a *fragment*. If it is a fragment, write the number from the lesson that tells what is missing.
1. Can easily open the door.
2. One of my favorite pastimes.
3. I believe God.
4. Were gathering flowers along the road.
5. Took some ducks to market.
6. Always plants her peas and onions early.
7. Moses went up the mountain.
8. Around the house.
9. Louise and Ellen were singing a new song.
10. Ruth reading a book.
11. Later in the afternoon.
12. Louanne got home before dark.

B. Make complete sentences by adding your own words to the fragments in Part A. Write the complete sentences.

Review Exercises

These exercises review things that you studied in grade 5. Writing the answers will help to prepare you for Lesson 2, which is about the predicate of a sentence.

4. Every sentence must begin with a capital letter and end with correct punctuation.

★ **EXTRA PRACTICE**
Worksheet 1 *(Sentences and Fragments)*

Lesson 1 Answers
Class Practice
A. 1. fragment; no subject or predicate
2. sentence
3. fragment; no subject
4. fragment; no predicate
5. sentence
6. fragment; no predicate
7. fragment; no subject or helping verb
8. fragment; no helping verb
9. sentence
10. fragment; no subject or predicate

B. (Answers will vary.)

Written Exercises
A. 1. fragment, 1
2. fragment, 2
3. sentence
4. fragment, 1
5. fragment, 1
6. fragment, 1
7. sentence
8. fragment, 3
9. sentence
10. fragment, 4
11. fragment, 3
12. sentence

B. (Answers will vary.)

A. Write the definition of a verb and the definition of a noun.

B. Copy all the words in this list that can be used as action verbs.

1. good	7. hard	12. split
2. scurry	8. easy	13. leader
3. bounce	9. read	14. sad
4. rejoice	10. gift	15. send
5. mountain	11. hike	16. hour
6. carry		

C. Write all the helping verbs you learned in grade 5. Write them in organized groups. (Use the index to find them in this book if you have forgotten them. Memorize them again.)

2. The Predicate of a Sentence

Every sentence has two main parts: the subject and the predicate. The predicate of a sentence is the part that tells what the subject does or is. We may speak of the simple predicate or the complete predicate.

The *simple predicate* is the most important part of the predicate. It is the verb in the sentence. It may be a single-word verb or several verbs together as a verb phrase. The simple predicates are underlined in the following sentences.

An ostrich <u>runs</u> very fast.
Two beautiful white swans <u>were floating</u> on the still surface of the pond.

To find the simple predicate in a sentence, use the following steps.

1. *Look for a word that shows action,* since most verbs are action verbs. You will remember from past years that words like *watch, call, seek, drive, run, work, sing, pray, read, talk, listen,* and *move* are action verbs. There are thousands of action verbs in our language, but most of them are easy to recognize. Use a dictionary if you are not sure whether a word can be a verb.

2. *If there is no action verb, look for a form of* be. This verb shows being instead of action. You should memorize the eight forms of *be* if you do not already know them. They are listed here.

am, is, are, was, were, be, been, being

Review Exercises

A. A verb is a word that shows action or being.
   A noun is a word that names a person, place, thing, or idea.

B. 2. scurry   9. read
   3. bounce   11. hike
   4. rejoice   12. split
   6. carry   15. send

C. am, is, are, was, were, be, been, being
   have, has, had
   do, does, did
   may, might, must
   can—could, shall—should, will—would

Lesson 2

Purpose: (1) To define the simple predicate and the complete predicate of a sentence. (2) To define a verb, a helping verb, and a verb phrase.

Oral Review:

1. What is a sentence? (a group of words that expresses a complete thought)
2. What two main parts must a sentence have? (subject, predicate)
3. What things might be missing in a sentence fragment? (a subject, a predicate, both a subject and a predicate, a helping verb)
4. How should every sentence begin and end? (begin with a capital letter and end with correct punctuation)
5. What is a verb? (a word that shows action or being)
6. Name all the helping verbs you learned in grade 5. (am, is, are, was, were, be, been, being; have, has,

had; do, does, did; may, might, must; can—could, shall—should, will—would)

Lesson Introduction: A well-organized garden is much more profitable than one with peas, beans, tomatoes, and corn growing just anywhere. When you come into a garden and see everything in orderly rows, you know that it has been organized. It gives you a good feeling just to walk through it.

Sentences are organized for a purpose too. They are organized to make proper sense and to communicate ideas plainly. The better a group of words is organized, the less time it takes to accomplish the work. Since our words should be few, we want them well organized so that we can communicate clearly and concisely.

This lesson teaches about the predicate, which is one part of a sentence. Knowing sentence parts helps you to speak and write in an organized way.

3. *If there is no form of* be, *look for a verb that could be replaced by a form of* be. Here are the "sometimes linking verbs" that you learned in grade 5.

taste, feel, smell, sound, look, appear

Action verb: Janet <u>smelled</u> fresh bread.
Linking verb: The bread <u>smelled</u> warm and delicious.
(It would be sensible to say "The bread <u>was</u> warm and delicious.")

4. *After finding the main verb, check to see if there are any helping verbs.* Look at the verb phrase *were floating.* In such a phrase, the last word is the *main verb,* and the word used before it is a *helping verb.* The simple predicate is the main verb and all the helping verbs used with it. In grade 5 you studied the helping verbs in groups, as shown here.

Forms of *be:*   am, is, are, was, were, be, been, being
Forms of *have:*   have, has, had
Forms of *do:*   do, does, did
Forms of *may:*   may, might, must
Other helping verbs:
can—could, shall—should, will—would

Following the four steps, find the simple predicates in the following sentences.

Abraham believed the words of God.
His wife was an old woman.
God's promises to Abraham sounded impossible.
Many people are obeying the Bible today.

The *complete predicate* is the simple predicate and all the words that go with it to tell about the subject. In the following sentence, the simple predicate is underlined twice and the complete predicate is italicized.

Grandfather <u>*has planted*</u> *some cherry trees in the orchard.*

Has planted tells what Grandfather did. It is the simple predicate. *Some cherry trees in the orchard* goes with the simple predicate to tell more completely what Grandfather did. Thus the complete predicate is *has planted some cherry trees in the orchard.*

Lesson Outline:

1. The predicate of a sentence is the part that tells what the subject does or is. Write the following sentences on the chalkboard.

Gideon's troops | crept toward the Midianite camp.
The predicate tells what the troops *did.*

The men | were brave and diligent.
The predicate tells what the men *were.*

2. The simple predicate is the main part of the predicate.
a. The simple predicate is always the verb in the sentence.
b. It may be a single-word verb or a group of verbs.

Draw two lines under the simple predicates in the sentences on the chalkboard.

Gideon's troops | <u>crept</u> toward the Midianite camp.
The men | <u>were</u> brave and diligent.

3. Use the following steps to find the simple predicate of a sentence.
(1) *Look for a word that shows action.* Be sure it shows action in the sentence and is not used as a noun, an adjective, or an adverb.

Write the following words on the chalkboard or on flash cards. Have students tell whether each word can show action: *run, jump, speak, hot, beautiful, fly, sing, red, read, think, memorize, rest.*

Give help by telling them to think, "Is this something we can do?" We can *speak,* but who can *red*? Who can *beautiful*?

Some action verbs show physical action; others show mental action. Some do not seem to show much action. Help students recognize action verbs like *sleep, rest,* and *think.*
(2) *If there is no action verb, look for a form of* be. There are eight forms of *be:* am, is, are, was, were, be, been, being.
(3) *If there is no form of* be, *look for a verb that could be replaced by a form of* be. These "sometimes linking verbs" were taught in grade 5: *taste, feel, smell, sound, look, appear.*
(4) *After finding the main verb, check to see if there are any helping verbs.* The main verb is the last word in a verb phrase.

To find the complete predicate, find all the words that go with the verb or verb phrase to tell what the subject does or is. In most sentences, the complete predicate begins with the verb or verb phrase and the other words of the predicate come after the verb or verb phrase. In the following sentences, the simple predicates are underlined twice and the complete predicates are italicized.

The boys _were riding on horses in the pasture._
Our God _is great and mighty._
The white and pink roses _smell sweet._

Be sure to memorize the linking verbs and helping verbs listed in this lesson so that you can find the simple predicate of a sentence more easily.

- The simple predicate is the verb or verb phrase in the sentence.

- The complete predicate includes the verb and all the words that go with it to tell about the subject.

Class Practice

A. Tell which words make up the simple predicate. Then read the complete predicate of each sentence.
1. Jesus loves all the children of the world.
2. Noah and his sons were working on the ark.
3. Two Roman soldiers stood in front of the tomb.
4. The old oak tree grew very tall.
5. The little girl looked fearful and unhappy.
6. Pharaoh's army perished in the waters of the sea.
7. The meek shall inherit the earth.
8. Several lively gray squirrels are climbing up the trees.
9. The older boys built a bridge across the brook.
10. My other coat will be warmer than this one.

B. On the chalkboard, write the verb phrases from Part A. Underline the main verb in each verb phrase.

may have been   shall come
can do   is helping

Review the twenty-three helping verbs.

Forms of _be_: am, is, are, was, were, be, been, being
Forms of _have_: have, has, had
Forms of _do_: do, does, did
Forms of _may_: may, might, must
Other helping verbs:
can—could, shall—should, will—would

4. The complete predicate is the simple predicate and all the words that go with it to tell about the subject. The complete predicate usually begins with the simple predicate, and the other words in the predicate come after it. In the sentences on the chalkboard, all the words to the right of the dividing line belong to the complete predicate.

Lesson 2 Answers
Class Practice
A. (Simple predicates are underlined twice.)
1. loves all the children of the world
2. were working on the ark
3. stood in front of the tomb
4. grew very tall
5. looked fearful and unhappy
6. perished in the waters of the sea
7. shall inherit the earth
8. are climbing up the trees
9. built a bridge across the brook
10. will be warmer than this one

B. 2. were working
7. shall inherit
8. are climbing
10. will be

---

5. Be sure you can say the helping verbs and linking verbs by memory. It will help you find the simple predicate of a sentence more easily.

★ **EXTRA PRACTICE**
Worksheet 2 _(The Predicate of a Sentence)_

Written Exercises

A. Copy each complete predicate. Draw two lines under each simple predicate.
1. A little bird was singing just outside the door.
2. We shall be working here next week.
3. Your answer is correct.
4. Those little brown insects ruined the beans.
5. Amos has written us another letter.
6. These flowers have come from our garden.
7. Charlotte will be coming this evening.
8. My little dog recognizes my voice.
9. Some ants can lift a weight fifty times heavier than themselves!
10. Some ants build nests with underground rooms and passageways.
11. These flowers do smell sweet!
12. Joshua may have been there.

B. Copy each verb phrase in Part A, and underline the main verb. (Not all the sentences have verb phrases.)

Review Exercises

These exercises review things that you studied in grade 5. Answering these questions will help to prepare you for Lesson 3, which is about the subject of a sentence.

A. Write the following things.
1. The definition of a noun.
2. The definition of a pronoun.
3. The personal pronouns that are used as subjects. (See Lesson 61 in this book if you need help.)

B. Copy all the nouns that name persons. You should find twelve in all.
1. My grandfather was a farmer.
2. Her mother was a teacher, and her sister was a nurse.
3. Aunt Mary is a good cook and seamstress.
4. Brother John, our janitor, is also a good farmer.

C. Copy all the nouns that name places. You should find eight in all.
1. We didn't enjoy the large city, so we visited a farm in the country.
2. In which county of that state do you live?
3. Our family enjoyed a picnic lunch in the park.
4. On Saturday we did the cleaning at the school and the church.

Written Exercises

A. 1. <u>was singing</u> just outside the door
2. <u>shall be working</u> here next week
3. <u>is</u> correct
4. <u>ruined</u> the beans
5. <u>has written</u> us another letter
6. <u>have come</u> from our garden
7. <u>will be coming</u> this evening
8. <u>recognizes</u> my voice
9. <u>can lift</u> a weight fifty times heavier than themselves
10. <u>build</u> nests with underground rooms and passageways
11. <u>do smell</u> sweet
12. <u>may have been</u> there

B. 1. was <u>singing</u>
2. shall be <u>working</u>
5. has <u>written</u>
6. have <u>come</u>
7. will be <u>coming</u>
9. can <u>lift</u>
11. do <u>smell</u>
12. may have <u>been</u>

Review Exercises

A. 1. A noun is a word that names a person, place, thing, or idea.
2. A pronoun is a word that takes the place of a noun.
3. I, you, he, she, it, we, they

B. 1. grandfather, farmer
2. mother, teacher, sister, nurse
3. Aunt Mary, cook, seamstress
4. Brother John, janitor, farmer

C. 1. city, farm, country
2. county, state
3. park
4. school, church

D. Copy all the nouns that name things. You should find eleven in all.
1. "Get out your pencil, eraser, and tablet, and place them on your desk," instructed the teacher.
2. Use this soap and a brush to clean the floors.
3. Don't forget to polish the mirror, wash the windows, dust the furniture, and vacuum the floor.

E. Copy all the nouns that name ideas. You should find thirteen in all.
1. The Bible tells Christians to put on mercy, kindness, humility, meekness, patience, forbearance, forgiveness, and charity.
2. Proper thoughts will help you to overcome fear, gain courage, avoid evil, and do right.

F. Copy all the pronouns that are used as subjects. You should find eight in all.
1. We and they found the way.
2. He and she saw the new building.
3. You and I will fill the holes with wood putty, but he and they will do the sanding.

D. 1. pencil, eraser, tablet, desk
2. soap, brush, floors
3. mirror, windows, furniture, floor

E. 1. mercy, kindness, humility, meekness, patience, forbearance, forgiveness, charity
2. thoughts, fear, courage, evil, right

F. 1. We, they
2. He, she
3. You, I, he, they

3. The Subject of a Sentence

The subject of a sentence tells *who* or *what* the sentence is about. The *simple subject* of the sentence is the main word (or words) in the subject. The simple subject is a noun or pronoun.

Find the simple subject of each sentence.

A kind, thoughtful girl helped us in the afternoon.
Who is this sentence about? It is about a girl.
Girl is the simple subject.

The waves rolled and splashed in a constant rhythm.
What is this sentence about? It is about the waves.
Waves is the simple subject.

Review the following facts about nouns and pronouns to help you find the simple subject of a sentence more easily.

Lesson 3

Purpose: (1) To define the simple subject and the complete subject of a sentence. (2) To define the sentence skeleton.

Oral Review:
1. What is a sentence? (a group of words that expresses a complete thought)
2. What two main parts does every sentence have? (subject, predicate)
3. What does the predicate of a sentence tell? (what the subject does or is)
4. What is the simple predicate? (the verb or verb phrase in the complete predicate)
5. What part of speech is the simple predicate? (verb)
6. Give the definition of a verb. (a word that shows action or being)
7. What is a noun? (a word that names a person, place, thing, or idea)
8. What is a proper noun? (a word that names a particular person, place, or thing)

Lesson Introduction: Read the following groups of words to the students. Ask what is missing.

Vary greatly in size.
Had two coats.
Performed many tasks.

The subject of each sentence is missing. Do these sentences sound better?

Cats vary greatly in size.
Each child had two coats.
Workhorses performed many tasks.

A sentence must have a subject. It cannot express a complete thought without a subject. In this lesson we will study the subject of a sentence.

1. *A noun is a word that names a person, place, thing, or idea.* Study the following examples.

   Person: mother, farmer, doctor
   Place: barn, park, city, lake
   Thing: door, fence, horse, desk
   Idea: love, joy, cheer, faith

2. *A pronoun is a word that takes the place of a noun.* Review this list of pronouns that can be used as subjects.

   I, you, he, she, it, we, they

The *complete subject* of a sentence includes the simple subject and all its modifiers. To find the complete subject, look first for the simple subject. Then find the words that modify it. In the sentence *The white lilies are blooming now,* the words *The* and *white* modify the simple subject *lilies.* So the complete subject is *The white lilies.*

In the following examples, each simple subject is underlined and each complete subject is italicized. A line is drawn between the complete subject and the complete predicate.

> *The white <u>lilies</u>* | are blooming now.
> *The low blue <u>mountains</u>* | stretched across the horizon.
> *The hot vegetable <u>soup</u>* | tasted delicious.
> <u>God</u> | gives us many good gifts.

In the last sentence, *God* is both the simple subject and the complete subject because this noun has no modifiers.

The simple subject and simple predicate together form the *skeleton* of a sentence. To find the skeleton, always follow these three steps.

1. Find the simple predicate (the verb).
2. Ask *who* or *what* about the verb. The answer is the simple subject.
3. Say the simple subject and simple predicate together to see if they make sense.

Use the steps above to find the skeleton of this sentence.

> Our great Lord is coming soon.

1. Find the simple predicate. The simple predicate is *is coming.*
2. Ask, "*Who* is coming?" The answer is *Lord.*
3. Say the simple subject and simple predicate together to see if they make sense: *Lord is coming.* This makes sense, so it is the skeleton.

Lesson Outline:

1. The subject of a sentence tells who *or* what the sentence is about.

2. The simple subject *is the main word in the subject.*

  a. *The simple subject is usually a noun.* Review the definition of a noun.

  b. *It may be a nominative case pronoun.* Review the nominative case pronouns: *I, you, he, she, it, we, they.*

3. The complete subject *includes the simple subject and all its modifiers.* It includes all the words that tell *who* or *what* the sentence is about.

> <u>The shiny new shoes</u> pleased the little boy.
> <u>The pink scented soap</u> smelled fresh and spicy.
> <u>Their kindness</u> was greatly appreciated.

When the simple subject has no modifiers, the simple subject is also the complete subject.

> <u>Moses</u> | <u>led</u> the people of Israel.
>   *Moses* is the simple subject and the complete subject.

4. The simple subject and simple predicate together form the skeleton *of a sentence.* Use the following steps to find the skeleton.

  (1) Find the simple predicate (the verb).

  (2) Ask *who* or *what* about the verb. The answer is the simple subject.

  (3) Say the simple subject and simple predicate together to see if they make sense. This is a double check.

- The simple subject is the noun or pronoun that tells *who* or *what* the sentence is about.

- The complete subject includes the simple subject and all the words that modify the simple subject. The skeleton is the simple subject and simple predicate together.

Class Practice

A. Give the simple subject and the complete subject of each sentence.
1. The tomato seeds should sprout soon.
2. Love thinks no evil.
3. Jewish scribes copied the Scriptures carefully.
4. They counted each word and letter.
5. No word was written from memory.
6. The writer pronounced each word aloud.
7. You are the light of the world.
8. A certain poor widow came into the temple.
9. She put in only two mites.
10. Jesus was pleased with her gift.

B. Give the skeleton of each sentence in Part A.

Written Exercises

A. Copy each complete subject, and underline the simple subject.

Examples: a. The five tall spruce trees stood at the end of the yard.
           b. God is love.

Answers: a. The five tall spruce <u>trees</u>
          b. <u>God</u>

1. God gave language to man.
2. He confused the languages at the Tower of Babel.
3. The world has about three thousand different languages today.
4. Our English language comes from England.
5. Many words have been adopted into English from other languages.
6. Languages do change.
7. It is generally a slow process.
8. This change is not always for the better.

Write the following sentences on the chalkboard. Work through them with the class, following the three steps and marking the sentences with a dividing line and underlining.

I | <u>have been</u> there before.
    The simple predicate is *have been. Who* have been? The answer is *I.* The skeleton is *I have been.*
The <u>streetcars</u> | <u>are</u> slow.
The <u>group</u> | <u>sang</u> hymns on the square.

★ **EXTRA PRACTICE**
Worksheet 3 *(The Subject of a Sentence)*

Lesson 3 Answers
Class Practice
A. (Simple subjects are underlined.)
1. The tomato <u>seeds</u>
2. <u>Love</u>
3. Jewish <u>scribes</u>
4. <u>They</u>
5. No <u>word</u>
6. The <u>writer</u>
7. <u>You</u>
8. A certain poor <u>widow</u>
9. <u>She</u>
10. <u>Jesus</u>

B. 1. seeds should sprout
    2. Love thinks
    3. scribes copied
    4. They counted
    5. word was written
    6. writer pronounced
    7. You are
    8. widow came
    9. She put
    10. Jesus was pleased

Written Exercises
A. 1. <u>God</u>
    2. <u>He</u>
    3. The <u>world</u>
    4. Our English <u>language</u>
    5. Many <u>words</u>
    6. <u>Languages</u>
    7. <u>It</u>
    8. This <u>change</u>

9. Man is lazy and careless by nature.
10. We should put forth diligence.
11. Every person will answer for his idle words.
12. The Bible teaches carefulness in speech.
13. Several large bears lumbered through the woods.
14. Six wild geese landed on our pond last night.

B. Copy the skeleton of each sentence. Underline the simple subject once and the simple predicate twice. Draw a dividing line between the subject and the predicate.

> **Example:** The little dog was running after his little master.
> **Answer:** <u>dog</u> | <u>was running</u>

1. Grandfather was here at noon.
2. My two white geese have come back again.
3. I missed them this morning.
4. The school was cleaned yesterday.
5. Love is always kind.
6. Mary's lemonade tastes more delicious every time.
7. The sky is very blue today.
8. An iron key opened the wooden box.
9. The native women were weaving cloth.
10. The young boy chased the pig back into the pen.

Review Exercises

Write the correct words in parentheses. Use the index in the back of this book if you need help.

1. Where shall I (lay, lie) these packages?
2. (Set, Sit) them in a place where nobody will (set, sit) on them.
3. Those tools have (laid, lain) outside all week.
4. Their owner (don't, doesn't) seem to care.
5. Father (let, left) the children (raise, rise) some chicks one summer.
6. He (taught, learned) them how to care for the chicks.
7. The children (taught, learned) many valuable things from Father.
8. The driver (let, left) the disabled car along the road.
9. It was (setting, sitting) there all night.
10. Father (raised, rose) the hood and looked at the engine.
11. "(Can, May) I please have the keys?" he asked.
12. "I'll see what I (can, may) do to help you," Father said.

---

9. <u>Man</u>
10. <u>We</u>
11. Every <u>person</u>
12. The <u>Bible</u>
13. Several large <u>bears</u>
14. Six wild <u>geese</u>

B. 1. <u>Grandfather</u> | <u>was</u>
2. <u>geese</u> | <u>have come</u>
3. <u>I</u> | <u>missed</u>
4. <u>school</u> | <u>was cleaned</u>
5. <u>Love</u> | <u>is</u>
6. <u>lemonade</u> | <u>tastes</u>
7. <u>sky</u> | <u>is</u>
8. <u>key</u> | <u>opened</u>
9. <u>women</u> | <u>were weaving</u>
10. <u>boy</u> | <u>chased</u>

Review Exercises

1. lay
2. Set, sit
3. lain
4. doesn't
5. let, raise
6. taught
7. learned
8. left
9. sitting
10. raised
11. May
12. can

4. Writing a Story About a Problem

We all like to hear or read a good story. A story catches our attention and teaches us a lesson. The Bible uses many stories to teach men about God.

You studied story writing in other grades. Do you remember these rules for writing stories?

1. Know the facts. You can never write a good story if you are not sure what happened.
2. Put things in proper order—first things first and last things last.
3. Include all the important information. Tell who, what, when, where, why, and how.
4. Stick to the main idea of the story.
5. Vary the length of your sentences.
6. Use good grammar, proper spelling, correct punctuation, and neat handwriting.

In this chapter you have studied what makes a complete sentence. Be sure to use complete sentences when you write a story.

A good story tells about a problem or difficulty someone has. This is why stories are interesting. When we read about a problem, immediately we want to know what happened next! The problem does not need to be something great or unusual. Simple, everyday problems can make good stories. Consider this example.

> Mother sent Wilbur to the neighbors with a message. But in the neighbors' lane, Wilbur met a big, fierce-looking dog. The dog ran toward him, barking and growling.

Did Wilbur have a problem? He certainly did! And immediately you want to know what happened next. What did Wilbur do? Did he deliver the message? Did he run home again? Was the dog really dangerous? Did it bite him?

The first part of your story must show that someone (or something) had a problem. Give facts and details to show clearly what that problem was. Make your readers want to know what happened next.

In the second part of your story, you must show how the problem was solved. What did the person do? Did it work? Was anyone hurt? How did it all end? People who read your story will not be satisfied until they know that the danger or trouble is over. Then they can relax.

Lesson 4

Purpose: To introduce the concept that a story has *a problem to be solved (conflict). (*Previous experience:* General practice with telling and writing stories; see Oral Review below.)

Oral Review:

(The following questions review things taught in grade 5 to prepare students for this lesson.)

1. When you tell or write a story, in what order should you put the things that happen? (in the order that they happened—first things first and last things last)
2. What information should you give in your story? (who, what, when, where, why, how)
3. How many main ideas should your story have? (one)
4. How can you add variety to the sentences in your story? (Use a variety of sentence types. Vary the length of your sentences. Do not use too many short, choppy sentences. Do not use too many long sentences connected with *and*.)
5. What things should you look for when you proofread your story? (complete sentences, good grammar, proper spelling, correct punctuation, neat handwriting)

Lesson Introduction: Imagine that your family has been driving for several hours. You are sitting quietly, watching the trees go by, and feeling bored. Suddenly you hear a loud bang, the car begins to swerve, and Father pulls off the road. Do you still sit quietly? Are you still bored? No, you are very interested! Your family has a problem, and you cannot relax until you know how it will be solved.

You wrote stories last year, but this year you will study ways to put "a loud bang" into your stories to arouse the interest of your readers.

Before you start writing your story, make a few notes. First, write about the basic problem; second, write notes about how the problem was solved. Include interesting details. Then arrange your notes in the order that things happened.

Use your notes to write your story. They will show you what to write and how to keep things in order. Be sure to write in complete sentences. Last of all, check your story for sentence variety and the other things listed at the beginning of this lesson. Study the following example.

Notes for a story:
  1. The problem:

>   Mother wanted to send message to neighbor
>   Sent my little brother Wilbur with the message
>   He went happily
>   Big dog ran out, barking furiously
>   Wilbur was too frightened to go farther

  2. How the problem was solved:

>   Wilbur ran home
>   Mother wanted him to overcome his fear
>   Sent me with him
>   I showed that dog was harmless
>   Spoke kindly and petted dog
>   We have gone several times since
>   Glad to help my little brother

The story:

Wilbur Makes a Friend

One day Mother had an important message to send to the neighbor. She asked my little brother Wilbur to take it. Wilbur went gladly. He had forgotten about Barnie, their big dog, until he got there. Suddenly Barnie ran out at him, barking furiously. Wilbur was too frightened to take another step toward the neighbor's house. He turned and ran home as fast as he could.

Mother knew that the dog was harmless, and she wanted to help Wilbur overcome his fear. She knew that I, his big brother, had already learned not to fear Barnie. So she sent me with Wilbur to deliver the message. I showed my little brother that Barnie only had a fierce bark and that he would not bite. Wilbur was relieved when the dog stopped barking as we walked toward him. I talked

Lesson Outline:

1. A good story tells about a problem or difficulty someone has.

  a. The problem does not need to be great or unusual. Simple, everyday problems can make good stories.

  b. The first part of the story must show the problem.

  c. The second part of the story must show how the problem was solved.

2. Before writing a story, make a set of notes.

  a. Divide the notes into two parts.

  1) Notes to give the setting and introduce the problem.

  2) Notes to show how the problem was solved.

  b. Arrange the notes in the order that things happened.

3. Remember the rules for writing stories, which you learned in other grades.

  (1) Know the facts.

  (2) Put things in proper order, from first to last.

  (3) Include all the important information. Tell who, what, when, where, why, and how.

  (4) Stick to the main idea of the story.

  (5) Vary the length of your sentences. Do not use too many short, choppy sentences. Do not use too many long sentences connected with *and.*

  (6) Use good grammar, proper spelling, correct punctuation, and neat handwriting.

kindly to the dog and petted him, and finally Wilbur got up enough courage to pet him too. I had to go with Wilbur several more times before he was brave enough to go alone, but I did not mind. I was glad I could help my little brother.

Do not be too brief when you describe the problem in a story. Show how the problem was indeed a problem. Describe how things built up one upon another. For example, suppose your family was driving late one night and could not find a motel. Your story will not be interesting if you write just the bare facts, as in the following example.

Our family was traveling last summer. One day as evening approached, we began to look for a motel. Time after time we came to a motel only to see the same sign: No Vacancy. Finally we found a motel that did have room for us; and we all sighed with relief. We stopped there and spent the night resting from our long trip.

It would be much better to give details that show how the problem affected your family. Everyone was tired, the younger ones were getting fussy, and you were getting quite anxious. Show the things that made it seem like a really serious problem to your family.

Remember, the problem does not need to be something great or unusual. But it must be a difficulty that brings a feeling of concern, or the reader will not be concerned either. The following story is another version of the example above. Notice how the added details help the reader to feel what the characters felt.

Last summer our family took a trip to Virginia. As it began to grow dark, we started to look for a motel in which to spend the night. The first motel we found had a sign in large letters: No Vacancy. We drove another ten minutes before spying another motel in the distance. Hopefully we watched as we drove closer, but again we were disappointed. This motel was also full.

My little brother began crying. He was tired and wanted to stop. My mother was tired too because we had started at five o'clock that morning. Finally we saw another motel, but it also said No Vacancy. My father breathed a deep sigh as he drove on....

To write a good story, you must know the facts. You will know the facts best about things that have happened right around you. Think about something that happened to you or to someone in your family

You, the teacher, should be ready to give an experience of your own from your summer vacation, describing a problem faced by you (or someone close to you) and how it was solved. Of course it will need to be a story that appeals to the healthy interests of sixth graders.

this past summer. Maybe your father had a cow that was determined to kick off the milker. Perhaps you and your mother were left stranded along the road when the car ran out of gas. Or did someone lock the keys in the car this summer? Did the weeds grow too fast for you and your sisters who were trying to keep the garden clean?

You have already met and solved a number of problems in life. Almost any one of them could be developed into an interesting story for others to read.

- A good story tells about a problem or difficulty that someone has.

- To write a story, first make and organize a set of notes. Then write in a clear and orderly manner, using complete sentences and sticking to the main idea. Use good sentence variety, good grammar, proper spelling, correct punctuation, and neat handwriting.

Class Practice

A. Ask your teacher to describe a problem he had this summer and tell how he solved it.

B. Tell about problems or difficulties you or your family faced this summer. Your ideas may help your classmates think of something to write about.

Written Exercises

A. Write notes for a story about a problem you or a friend solved this summer. First, show what the problem was. Second, write how it was solved. Arrange your details in the order they happened.

B. Write your story. Be sure to include enough details so that the reader can feel the problem with the characters. Your story should be at least as long as the story about Wilbur in the lesson.

Review Exercises

Find the fragments in the following story. Rewrite them, making complete sentences. [1] (Turn to the lesson number in brackets if you need help with these review exercises.)

Lesson 4 Answers
Class Practice
A. (Teacher work.)

B. (Class work.)

Written Exercises
   (Individual work.)

Mother and I going to the store one day. Suddenly the car stopped. We were on a busy highway going up a hill! Had no power brakes and no power steering anymore. All we could do was let the car coast to a stop on the shoulder.

Mother breathed a short prayer. Then a kind driver in a pickup truck. Stopped and gave instructions to Mother. Told her to let the car roll back along the shoulder. Into the parking lot of a store. Mother thanked him for his kindness. Then she went inside and called Father, and he brought us gasoline. The next day. Father took the car to the garage to repair the fuel gauge, which had not been working properly.

---

5. More About Subjects and Predicates

The subject of a sentence may be a *noun phrase*. When it is a proper noun phrase, you can tell that the words go together because they are capitalized. In these examples the subject is underlined once.

> <u>Brother Paul Shirk</u> will lead the singing.
> <u>Mount Herman</u> is the highest mountain in Palestine.
> <u>World War II</u> ended in August 1945.

When *the* is used before a proper noun phrase at the beginning of a sentence, it is capitalized because it is the first word of the sentence. *The* is not usually part of a proper noun phrase any more than it is part of a common noun.

> The <u>Ohio River</u> flows between Ohio and Kentucky.
> **Compare:** The <u>river</u> flows between Ohio and Kentucky.

Some proper noun phrases contain small, unimportant words. These words are part of the noun phrase even though they are not capitalized. Study the following examples.

> The <u>Statue of Liberty</u> was a gift from the French people.
> <u>*Trouble at Windy Acres*</u> tells the struggles of a young boy.

Review Exercises

(Corrected sentences are underlined.)

<u>Mother and I were going to the store one day.</u> Suddenly the car stopped. We were on a busy highway going up a hill! <u>We had no power brakes and no power steering anymore.</u> All we could do was let the car coast to a stop on the shoulder.

Mother breathed a short prayer. <u>Then a kind driver in a pickup truck stopped and gave instructions to Mother. He told her to let the car roll back along the shoulder and into the parking lot of a store.</u> Mother thanked him for his kindness. Then she went inside and called Father, and he brought us gasoline. <u>The next day Father took the car to the garage to repair the fuel gauge, which had not been working properly.</u>

Lesson 5

Purpose: To work with sentences whose skeletons may be difficult to find.

Oral Review:

1. What two main parts must a sentence have? (subject, predicate)
2. What does the predicate of a sentence tell? (what the subject does or is)
3. What does the subject of a sentence tell? (*who* or *what* the sentence is about)
4. What is the simple subject of a sentence? (the main word or words in the subject)
5. What part of speech is the simple subject? (a noun or pronoun)
6. Name the pronouns that can be used as simple subjects. (I, you, he, she, it, we, they)
7. Give the three steps for finding the skeleton of a sentence. (Find the simple predicate. Ask *who* or *what*

about it. Double-check by saying the simple subject and simple predicate together to see if they make sense.)

Lesson Introduction: Write the following sentences on the chalkboard. Challenge students to tell which words make up the simple subjects and which ones make up the simple predicates. Underline the simple subjects once and the simple predicates twice. If students can pick out the skeletons, they will have little trouble with the lesson. If they have difficulty, give special emphasis in the areas where they need help.

> The <u>Pacific Ocean</u> | <u>is</u> the largest ocean in the world.
> The new <u>post office</u> | <u>opened</u> last week.
> <u>John the Baptist</u> | <u>was baptizing</u> at the Jordan.
> A <u>box</u> of books | <u>came</u> by mail.
> <u>I</u> | <u>do</u> not <u>have</u> a bicycle.

Some noun phrases are made of two words that are not capitalized. You studied a few of these in grade 5. The following words are noun phrases because the two words together name the object.

post office   chain saw   blue jay

Do not think that you can use just any adjective with a noun and call it a noun phrase. Consider the difference in the following sentences.

A big black <u>dog</u> <u>bounded</u> toward us.
> The subject is *dog,* not *black dog. Black* simply describes the dog. It is not part of the simple subject.

The <u>hot dog</u> <u>tasted</u> delicious.
> The subject is *hot dog.* The two words together name the thing that is eaten. *Hot* is not an adjective telling what kind of dog tasted delicious!

Noun phrases are listed as dictionary entries. Check a dictionary when you are not sure if two words make a noun phrase.

Sometimes the simple subject of a sentence is followed by a prepositional phrase. But remember that the subject of a sentence is never found in a prepositional phrase. Look at this example.

Our <u>Father</u> in heaven <u>will supply</u> all your needs.

In heaven is a prepositional phrase. The verb is *will supply.* *Who* will supply? The answer is *Father.* The subject of the sentence is *Father,* not *heaven.*

In some sentences the word in a prepositional phrase would seem to make sense as the subject. But even then it is not the subject. Here is an example.

A <u>loaf</u> of bread <u>was sold</u>.

What was sold? Either *bread* or *loaf* would make sense, but the word *bread* is in a prepositional phrase. So it cannot be the subject. The subject is *loaf.*

When you look for the subject, it is good to pick out the prepositional phrases first so that they do not confuse you. The following list has some of the common prepositions that you studied in earlier grades. See Chapter 10 for a more complete list.

Lesson Outline:

1. The subject of a sentence may be a noun phrase.

a. *Many noun phrases are proper nouns.*

Brother John Mack   Columbia River
Mrs. Pamela Owen   Civil War

b. *All the words in a proper noun phrase are part of the noun phrase.* This includes small, unimportant words that are not capitalized.

Song of Solomon
John the Baptist
Gulf of Mexico
Declaration of Independence
National Society to Prevent Blindness.

c. *Some noun phrases are made up of two words that are not capitalized.* These are also called compound nouns (open compounds).

post office   hot dog
blue jay   chain saw

1) These words are noun phrases because the two words together name the object. You may not use just any adjective with a noun and call it a noun phrase.

2) Noun phrases are listed as dictionary entries. Check a dictionary when you are not sure if two words make a noun phrase.

(*Teacher:* Some noun phrases are more obvious than others. Those that are not so obvious are avoided in the text. Do not require noun phrases to be treated as such if they do not appear as entry words in the students' dictionaries.)

above	below	in	over
across	beside	inside	to
after	between	into	toward
around	by	near	under
at	down	of	up
before	for	off	upon
behind	from	on	with

To pick out a prepositional phrase, remember to find the preposition first. Then find its object by saying the preposition and asking *whom* or *what*. All the words between the preposition and the object are modifiers of the object.

When a prepositional phrase follows the subject and modifies it, the phrase is part of the complete subject. It does not belong with the predicate. In the following examples, each prepositional phrase in the complete subject is set off in parentheses. Notice that the dividing line between the complete subject and the complete predicate comes *after* any phrase that modifies the subject.

> The <u>top</u> (of the box) | <u>has blown</u> off.
> The <u>flowers</u> (on the table) | <u>are</u> from Grandmother.
> A large <u>bowl</u> (of oranges) | <u>sat</u> on the table.
> The <u>door</u> (in the back) (of the room) | <u>closed</u> with a bang.

The simple predicate in a sentence may be made up of several verbs. We call this a verb phrase. Sometimes a verb phrase is interrupted by other words. Be sure to find all the words that make up the verb phrase, but do not include any words that are not verbs. Often verb phrases are interrupted by adverbs like the following:

> not   never   ever   often   hardly   still

In the following examples, the verb phrase is underlined twice. Notice the words between the parts of the verb phrase that are not underlined.

> One warm day | <u>does</u> not <u>make</u> spring.
> He | <u>could</u> never <u>do</u> that job perfectly.
> His answer | <u>can</u> hardly <u>be</u> correct.

2. The subject of a sentence is never in a prepositional phrase. Sometimes the simple subject is followed by a prepositional phrase. The object of a preposition is never the subject of a sentence.
   a. Review the common prepositions. Have a student read the list from the text orally. Refer students to the more complete list at the beginning of Chapter 10.
   b. Write the following phrases on the chalkboard. Have students underline the prepositions and circle the objects.

> in the house   without a hat
> on the front porch   with me
> under the table   with red hair

   c. Write the following sentences on the chalkboard, and have the students put parentheses around each prepositional phrase in the complete subject. Help them to identify the preposition and to ask *whom* or *what* after it. The answer is the object of the preposition. Any words between the preposition and its object are adjectives that modify the object.

> The girl with red hair is my sister.
> That man in the dark suit preached here on Sunday.
> A jar of fruit was brought here.

(*Teacher:* Sometimes an in-between word is an adverb modifying one of the adjectives, as in the phrase "with very dirty shoes"; then the adverb is only an indirect modifier of the object. But that is a nonessential point here.)
   d. With the students' help, mark the simple subjects and the simple predicates of the sentences on the chalkboard, and put a dividing line between the complete subject and the complete predicate. The finished sentences should be marked as shown below.

> The <u>girl</u> (with red hair) | <u>is</u> my sister.
> That <u>man</u> (in the dark suit) | <u>preached</u> here on Sunday.
> A <u>jar</u> (of fruit) | <u>was brought</u> here.

In the last sentence, either *jar* or *fruit* would make sense as the subject. But *fruit* cannot be the subject, because it is the object of a preposition.

- The subject of a sentence may be a noun phrase.

- The subject of a sentence is never found in a prepositional phrase.

- A prepositional phrase that modifies the simple subject is part of the complete subject.

- A verb phrase may be interrupted by adverbs. Be careful not to include these words as part of the simple predicate or to miss any part of the verb phrase.

Class Practice
Read the simple subject and the simple predicate of each sentence. Then, if a prepositional phrase comes in between, read it also.
1. Flocks of geese flew overhead yesterday.
2. The tree of life was in the middle of Eden.
3. Fanny Crosby wrote many of our favorite hymns.
4. The Susquehanna River is an important river of Pennsylvania.
5. The Middle Ages ended in the 1500s.
6. The post office stood near the corner.
7. A blue jay screamed from somewhere above the trees.
8. Mrs. Brown's sister did not call today.
9. The Declaration of Independence was signed on July 4, 1776.
10. The heart of Asa was perfect all his days.

Written Exercises
Copy each sentence, and do the following things.

a. Put parentheses around any prepositional phrase in the complete subject.
b. Draw two lines under the simple predicate, and one line under the simple subject.
c. Draw a dividing line between the complete subject and the complete predicate.

1. A journey of forty days was before them.
2. The men are still working in the fields.
3. The girl in the blue dress is my sister.
4. The Red Sea stood before them.

Lesson 5 Answers
Class Practice
1. Flocks | flew; of geese
2. tree | was; of life
3. Fanny Crosby | wrote
4. Susquehanna River | is
5. Middle Ages | ended
6. post office | stood
7. blue jay | screamed
8. sister | did call
9. Declaration of Independence | was signed
10. heart | was; of Asa

Written Exercises
1. A journey (of forty days) | was before them.
2. The men | are still working in the fields.
3. The girl (in the blue dress) | is my sister.
4. The Red Sea | stood before them.

---

3. A prepositional phrase that modifies the simple subject is part of the complete subject.

That box (on the table) | is mine.
A pair (of young spruce trees) | grew in his yard.

4. Sometimes a verb phrase is interrupted by another word. Often the interrupting word is an adverb such as the following: *not, never, ever, often, hardly, still.*

I | do not know the answer.
She | had never seen them before.
He | can hardly do it.

★ **EXTRA PRACTICE**
Worksheet 4 *(More About Subjects and Predicates)*

5. King Pharaoh was bringing his army up behind them.
6. The Civil War began in 1861.
7. Yellowstone National Park is mostly in Wyoming.
8. A very swift passenger train has just gone by.
9. The lookout tower could be seen miles away.
10. John the Baptist preached in the wilderness.
11. Her sister was not helping with the doughnuts.
12. The Song of Solomon is a Bible book of poetry.
13. The picture in the book will help us with our work.
14. The answer to your question is not found in the book.
15. An angel from heaven spoke to Gideon.
16. The man of Ethiopia was reading from the Book of Isaiah.

Review Exercises

A. Copy all the words from this list that could be used as action verbs.

1. stand	5. heavy	9. shout	13. slowly
2. hunt	6. walk	10. courage	14. spin
3. teacher	7. play	11. sing	15. pray
4. memorize	8. preach	12. pay	16. sleep

B. Do the following exercises.
1. Write all the forms of *be*.
2. Write the linking verbs you learned in grade 5.
3. Write the other helping verbs in groups.
4. Write the three main steps for finding the skeleton of a sentence.

---

6. Sentences and Clauses

A *clause* is a group of words that has a skeleton. It has a subject and a verb. You can easily tell whether a group of words is a clause.

Clause: The <u>Bible</u> | <u>is</u> God's written will for man.
(has a skeleton)

Not a clause: An old <u>man</u> with a worn Bible.
(has a subject but no verb)

Lesson 6

Purpose: To identify *clauses, and to differentiate between clauses and sentences.

Oral Review:

1. Give six words that may interrupt the verb phrase of a sentence. (not, never, ever, often, hardly, still)
2. What part of speech is a word like *not, never, always,* and *hardly*? (adverb)
3. How can you tell which words belong together in a proper noun phrase? (The words are capitalized.)
4. Is the subject of a sentence ever found in a prepositional phrase? (no)
5. List some common prepositions. (of, in, at, to, on, for, from, near, with, across, beside, around, behind, under)
6. What two main parts does every sentence have? (subject, predicate)

5. <u>King Pharaoh</u> | <u>was bringing</u> his army up behind them.
6. The <u>Civil War</u> | <u>began</u> in 1861.
7. <u>Yellowstone National Park</u> | <u>is</u> mostly in Wyoming.
8. A very swift passenger <u>train</u> | <u>has</u> just <u>gone</u> by.
9. The lookout <u>tower</u> | <u>could be seen</u> miles away.
10. <u>John the Baptist</u> | <u>preached</u> in the wilderness.
11. Her <u>sister</u> | <u>was</u> not <u>helping</u> with the doughnuts.
12. The <u>Song of Solomon</u> | <u>is</u> a Bible book of poetry.
13. The <u>picture</u> (in the book) | <u>will help</u> us with our work.
14. The <u>answer</u> (to your question) | <u>is</u> not <u>found</u> in the book.
15. An <u>angel</u> (from heaven) | <u>spoke</u> to Gideon.
16. The <u>man</u> (of Ethiopia) | <u>was reading</u> from the Book of Isaiah.

Review Exercises

A.			
1. stand	6. walk	9. shout	14. spin
2. hunt	7. play	11. sing	15. pray
4. memorize	8. preach	12. pay	16. sleep

B. 1. am, is, are, was, were, be, been, being
2. taste, feel, smell, sound, look, appear
3. have, has, had
   do, does, did
   may, might, must
   can—could, shall—should, will—would
4. a. Find the simple predicate (the verb).
   b. Ask *who* or *what* about the verb to find the simple subject.
   c. Say the simple subject and simple predicate together to see if they make sense.

---

7. What does the predicate of a sentence tell? (what the subject does or is)
8. What does the subject of a sentence tell? (*who* or *what* the sentence is about)

Lesson Introduction: Ask your students to define the word *clause*. Without commenting on their answers, write the following on the chalkboard.

A kitten with sharp claws.
The kitten was sharpening its claws.

Claws are what kittens have. And both of these word groups have *claws*! But grammatically, which group of words is a *clause*? Why?

Today we will compare clauses and sentences to see how they are different.

Since a *sentence* always contains a subject and a verb, every sentence is a clause. However, not every clause is a sentence because a clause does not always express a complete thought. Sometimes a clause is only a *fragment*. You can see that each of the following is a clause because the subject is underlined once and the verb is underlined twice. But one clause is only a fragment.

> **Clause that is a sentence:**
> God's prophets shared His message.
>   (Thought is complete.)

> **Clause that is a fragment:**
> When the men heard God's message.
>   (Thought is incomplete.)

In your writing, be especially careful to express a complete thought if you start a sentence with *when, since, because,* or a similar word. The following clauses sound much like sentences because they have subjects and verbs. But they are fragments because they fail to express complete thoughts.

> When they heard Jonah's warning.
> Since the people repented.
> Because God spared the city.

In each of these clauses, we need more information to understand the complete thought. What happened *when they heard Jonah's warning*? What took place *since the people repented*? What resulted *because God spared the city*? Can you see that each of these is a fragment?

We can make a sentence from each of these clauses by adding more words to complete the thought. The words can be placed either before or after the clause.

> **Sentence:**   The people feared when they heard Jonah's warning.
>   When they heard Jonah's warning, the people feared.

> **Sentence:**   God spared Nineveh since the people repented.
>   Since the people repented, God spared Nineveh.

> **Sentence:**   Jonah was angry because God spared the city.
>   Because God spared the city, Jonah was angry.

Here are several more clauses that are fragments. These can be made into sentences most easily by adding words before the clauses.

Lesson Outline:

1. A clause is a group of words that has a skeleton. It has a subject and a verb.

> **Clause:**   God | made the world in six days.
> **Not a clause:** In the beginning of time.

2. A clause is a sentence only when it expresses a complete thought.

> a. Since a sentence always contains a subject and a verb, every sentence is a clause.
> b. Not every clause is a sentence, because a clause does not always express a complete thought. Sometimes a clause is only a fragment.

> **Clause that is a fragment:**
> When God spoke.

> **Clause that is a sentence:**
> God spoke to Samuel.

> **Clause that is a fragment:**
> Because he was here.

> **Clause that is a sentence:**
> Yesterday he was here.

3. Some clauses can be made into complete sentences by adding more words.

> a. In writing, be especially careful to express a complete thought when you start a sentence with *when, since, because,* or similar words.

> **Clauses that are fragments:**
> Because Jeremiah obeyed the Lord.
> When Nathan reproved him.

Fragment: What <u>God</u> <u>would do</u>.
Sentence: <u>Jonah waited to see</u> what God would do.

Fragment: <u>That</u> <u>destroyed</u> the vine.
Sentence: <u>God sent a worm</u> that destroyed the vine.

Sometimes a clause needs a direct object to make it complete. The clause *Jane threw* does not express a complete thought. Jane threw what? A direct object must be added to make the thought complete: *Jane threw the ball.* Here are several more examples.

Fragment: I found.
Sentence: I found several Indian <u>arrowheads</u> in this field.

Fragment: Judy will bring.
Sentence: Judy will bring the <u>recipe</u>.

- Any group of words with a subject and a verb is a *clause.*

- A clause is a sentence only when it expresses a complete thought.

Class Practice

A. Say *clause* or *not a clause* for each group of words.
1. Grandmother came.
2. While the children were sleeping.
3. In the evening about sunset.
4. What did you bring?
5. After we got there.
6. At noon Clara and Janice.

B. Tell whether each group of words is a *sentence* or a *fragment*. If it is a fragment, tell whether it *needs a direct object* or *needs other words.*
1. Which Mother made.
2. Who will bring?
3. Jonathan became ill after he was out in the rain.
4. The sun is melting.
5. When you come to our house next week.
6. He cooks better than she does.

C. Add your own words to make sentences from the fragments in Part B.

Lesson 6 Answers
Class Practice
A. 1. clause
   2. clause
   3. not a clause
   4. clause
   5. clause
   6. not a clause

B. 1. fragment; needs other words
   2. fragment; needs a direct object
   3. sentence
   4. fragment; needs a direct object
   5. fragment; needs other words
   6. sentence

C. (Individual sentences.)

**Same clauses made into complete
sentences:**
Because Jeremiah obeyed the Lord,
<u>some people did not like him.</u>
<u>David repented</u> when Nathan reproved
him.

b. Sometimes a clause needs a direct object to
make it complete.

Fragments: Elisha would not take.
Mother made.

Sentences:
Elisha would not take any <u>gift</u> for heal-
ing Naaman.
Mother made <u>pies</u> and <u>cakes.</u>

★ **EXTRA PRACTICE**
Worksheet 5 *(Sentences and Clauses)*

Written Exercises

A. Write *clause* or *not a clause* for each group of words.
1. Rosalie brought the cookies.
2. In the morning at the house.
3. Before we begin.
4. While we were waiting for my brother.
5. My mother and her three sisters.

B. Write *S* if the group of words is a complete sentence, and *F* if it is a fragment. If it is a fragment because it needs a direct object, also write *DO*.
1. Because it was getting dark.
2. While it was raining.
3. After we have corrected our papers, we will hand them to her.
4. This morning Ben brought.
5. Then Brother John found.
6. Sharon will make some cookies before we leave.
7. Finally John found it in the bottom drawer.
8. Where the boys were working.
9. Before he had finished, it began to rain.
10. Why she was crying.
11. If the boys will help us.
12. That grow on these bushes.
13. Keep off the bench until the paint is dry.
14. Always thank.
15. Since the branch struck our car.

C. Add your own words to make sentences from eight of the fragments in Part B.

Review Exercises

Copy the part of each sentence from the *first* word of the simple subject to the *last* word of the simple predicate. If you write a prepositional phrase, put parentheses around it. [5] (Turn to the lesson number in brackets if you need help.)
1. Jesus was born in Bethlehem.
2. John the Baptist preached to the people about repentance.
3. The fire from heaven burned up Elijah's offering.
4. Ruth had followed Naomi to the land of Israel.
5. Ruth did choose the way of God.

Written Exercises

A. 1. clause
   2. not a clause
   3. clause
   4. clause
   5. not a clause

B. 1. F
   2. F
   3. S
   4. F, DO
   5. F, DO
   6. S
   7. S
   8. F
   9. S
   10. F
   11. F
   12. F
   13. S
   14. F, DO
   15. F

C. (Individual sentences.)

Review Exercises

1. Jesus was born
2. John the Baptist preached
3. fire (from heaven) burned
4. Ruth had followed
5. Ruth did choose

6. Ruth had been working hard in Boaz's field one day.
7. Brother Aden Zimmerman will speak to us on Sunday morning.
8. The desks at school were sanded.
9. Mount St. Helens erupted in 1980.
10. The volcano has erupted several times since.
11. The heat from the volcano melted much snow.
12. Floods washed away buildings, roads, and bridges.
13. Many crops were destroyed by the volcanic ash.
14. The volcano may erupt again from time to time.

6. Ruth had been working
7. Brother Aden Zimmerman will speak
8. desks (at school) were sanded
9. Mount St. Helens erupted
10. volcano has erupted
11. heat (from the volcano) melted
12. Floods washed
13. crops were destroyed
14. volcano may erupt

7. The Four Sentence Types

Sentences are put into four classes according to how they are used. Some sentences tell something, while others ask questions. Some sentences give commands or requests. Still others express strong feeling.

In earlier grades the four types of sentences were called statements, questions, commands, and exclamations. This year you will learn their standard English names.

A *declarative sentence* declares or states a fact. It always ends with a period. Notice the fact stated by each of these sentences.

Declarative sentences: John is here now.
Jesus rose from the dead.

A declarative sentence always makes a statement that is either true or false. If it is sensible to ask whether the sentence is true or false, the sentence must be declarative. For the sentence *John is here now,* it is sensible to ask "Is this sentence true or false?" If John is here now, the sentence is true. If John is somewhere else, the sentence is false. Use this test to decide whether the following sentences are declarative.

The sunset last evening was beautiful.
Listen to the roar of that waterfall.

The first sentence above is either true or false, so it is a declarative sentence. But the second sentence tells you to do something. It is not sensible to ask "Is this sentence true or false?" So it is not a declarative sentence.

Lesson 7

Purpose: To teach the four sentence types according to use. (*Previous experience:* Declarative, interrogative, imperative, and exclamatory sentences called statements, questions, commands, and exclamations.)

Oral Review:
1. What is a sentence? (a group of words that expresses a complete thought)
2. What two main parts must a sentence have? (subject, predicate)
3. What is a clause? (a group of words that has a subject and a verb)
4. Is every clause a sentence? (no)
5. What must a clause do to be a sentence? (express a complete thought)

Lesson Introduction: Have your students try to express themselves by using only sentences that are statements—that state a fact. Can they do it? How would they get permission to sharpen their pencils? They might say, "I would like to sharpen my pencil." That comes close to asking permission, but it does not exactly ask. They could also try "I would like you to tell me if I may sharpen my pencil."

Or how would they express their strong feelings if they could not use exclamatory sentences? After an interesting day at school, they could report matter-of-factly, "Today was an exciting day." But to show their strong feelings, they would have to add "I really enjoyed it."

How glad we are that our language has the four different types of sentences!

Before going into the lesson, write on the chalkboard the terms the students learned in grade 5. Then write the new names from today's lesson, and see if students can match them to the old ones.

statements—declarative
questions—interrogative
commands—imperative
exclamations—exclamatory

Lesson Outline:
1. Sentences are put into four classes according to how they are used.

2. A declarative sentence states a fact. It ends with a period. The fact which a declarative sentence states is either true or false. If it is sensible to ask whether a sentence is true or false, the sentence must be declarative.

The kangaroo rat is a desert animal.
Most desert animals are small.

An *interrogative sentence* asks a question. It ends with a question mark. The subject may come after the verb, or it may come between the words in the verb phrase.

Interrogative sentences:
<u>Who</u> <u>wrote</u> the Book of Genesis?
<u>Are</u> the <u>children</u> ready?
<u>Will</u> the <u>boys</u> <u>paint</u> the fence?
When <u>will</u> <u>they</u> <u>begin</u>?

An *imperative sentence* gives a command or makes a request. The subject of every imperative sentence is *you,* but it is not usually stated in the sentence. An imperative sentence ends with a period.

Imperative sentences:
Sing unto the Lord a new song.
   (you <u>Sing</u>)
Honor thy father and thy mother.
   (you <u>Honor</u>)
Please bring me a glass of water.
   (you <u>bring</u>)

Look at the next two sentences. Both seem to give a command, do they not? But the second one is declarative because it states a fact that is either true or false.

Do your work carefully. (imperative)
You should do your work carefully. (declarative)

Sometimes a declarative, an interrogative, or an imperative sentence expresses strong feeling. It is then called an *exclamatory sentence.* An exclamatory sentence ends with an exclamation point (also called an exclamation mark).

Exclamatory sentences:
The neighbor's house is on fire!
   (states a fact)
What are we going to do!
   (asks a question)
Call the fire department!
   (gives a command)

Most desert animals hide in holes during the hot daytime.
Compare: Read about the desert.
   (not a declarative sentence because it is not sensible to ask whether it is true or false)

3. *An interrogative sentence asks a question. It ends with a question mark.* The subject may come after the verb, or it may come between the words in the verb phrase.

Which <u>animal</u> <u>is called</u> the ship of the desert?
<u>Is</u> <u>it</u> the camel?
<u>Did</u> <u>you</u> ever <u>hear</u> of a cactus wren?

4. *An imperative sentence gives a command or makes a request. It ends with a period.* The subject of every imperative sentence is *you,* but it is not usually stated in the sentence.

Look at this display. (you <u>Look</u>)

Please put this in the mail. (you <u>put</u>)
Mary, <u>you</u> <u>type</u> this letter for me, please.
   (subject stated)

5. *Some sentences that appear to be imperative are actually declarative.*

You must sit up straight.
You should read your Bible every day.

Even though these sentences seem to be giving a command, they each state a fact. Each one is true and therefore is declarative.

6. *An exclamatory sentence expresses strong feeling. It ends with an exclamation point.* An exclamatory sentence may be declarative, interrogative, or imperative.

The man is driving furiously, like Jehu!
   (states a fact)
Is he coming in peace! (asks a question)
Flee for your life! (gives a command)

7. *Some exclamatory sentences have their own particular word order.*

What a beautiful day it is!
How did you find it!
If only Jesus had been there!

How can you remember these new names for the sentence types? A *declarative sentence* is one that *declares* or states a fact. An *exclamatory sentence* is one that *exclaims.* So these two should not be a problem.

What about the term *interrogative*? As you read and keep your ears open, no doubt you will hear words like the following: *interrogate, interrogation,* and *interrogator.* (Write them on the chalkboard.) They are related to the word *interrogative* and have to do with asking questions.

Some exclamatory sentences have their own special form.

What a terrible storm it was!
(skeleton last so that *what* comes first)

If only Father were home!
(sentence that would otherwise be a fragment)

Oh, how love I Thy law!
(verb before subject so that *love* is emphasized)

Learn to say and spell the name of each sentence type.

- A *declarative sentence* states a fact and ends with a period. It must be either true or false.

- An *interrogative sentence* asks a question and ends with a question mark.

- An *imperative sentence* gives a command or request and ends with a period. The subject of every imperative sentence is *you*, but it is not usually stated.

- An *exclamatory sentence* expresses strong feeling and ends with an exclamation point. Some exclamatory sentences have their own special form.

Class Practice

Tell whether each sentence is *declarative, interrogative, imperative,* or *exclamatory.* Tell what the end punctuation should be.
  1. Come
  2. Remember these instructions
  3. You must write your name on your paper
  4. Give unto the Lord the glory due His Name
  5. I will praise the Lord as long as I live
  6. Lead us not into temptation, but deliver us from evil
  7. How sweet God's words are
  8. The law of the Lord is perfect
  9. The Lord by wisdom hath founded the earth
  10. Where wast thou when I laid the foundations of the earth

Lesson 7 Answers
Class Practice
  (A sentence is called exclamatory only if it is likely to be said with strong feeling.)
  1. imperative, period
  2. imperative, period
  3. declarative, period (not imperative because it makes a statement)
  4. imperative, period
  5. declarative, period
  6. imperative, period
  7. exclamatory, exclamation point (has special word order)
  8. declarative, period
  9. declarative, period
  10. interrogative, question mark

The suspect was held for <u>interrogation.</u>
The officer who <u>interrogated</u> him was the <u>interrogator.</u>

What do you think an *interrogation point* is? (Write the term on the chalkboard for fast students to look up later.) It means a *question mark.*

Concerning the term *imperative,* you may have heard someone say something like this: "It is *imperative* that I go." That means he *must* go. What is an *imperator* (im·pə·rä·tôr)? It is a supreme commander or emperor. So an imperative sentence is one that gives a command.

It is *imperative* that you learn this. Shall I *interrogate* you from time to time? You will have to *declare* your knowledge. I may use some *exclamatory* remarks to help you!

★ **EXTRA PRACTICE**
Worksheet 6 *(The Four Sentence Types)*

11. When shall these things be
12. What a mighty God we serve
13. Is that so
14. Trust in the Lord with all thine heart

11. interrogative, question mark
12. exclamatory, exclamation point (has special word order)
13. interrogative, question mark
14. imperative, period

Trust in the LORD

with all thine heart;

and lean not unto thine own understanding.

In all thy ways acknowledge him,

and he shall direct thy paths.

Proverbs 3:5, 6

Written Exercises

A. Write whether each sentence is *declarative, interrogative, imperative,* or *exclamatory*. Also write the correct end punctuation. (Only three are exclamatory.)
1. Where did you learn to read so distinctly
2. The busy beavers worked on the dam
3. You must serve God with reverence
4. Samson's strength came from God's Spirit
5. What a terrible mistake he made
6. Please watch where you are going
7. Go and do thou likewise
8. A lion slew the disobedient prophet
9. David walked fearlessly toward the giant
10. Did the queen of Sheba visit Solomon
11. A small cloud arose on the horizon
12. How wicked Ahab was
13. Three brave Hebrew men refused to bow to an image
14. Was he wearing only a thin jacket
15. If only we had remembered the directions
16. Do your work correctly now

B. Describe a situation in which sentence 14 in Part A would probably be spoken as an exclamatory sentence.

Written Exercises

A.
1. interrogative   ?   (question mark)
2. declarative   .   (period)
3. declarative   .   (period)
4. declarative   .   (period)
5. exclamatory   !   (exclamation point)
6. imperative   .   (period)
7. imperative   .   (period)
8. declarative   .   (period)
9. declarative   .   (period)
10. interrogative   ?   (question mark)
11. declarative   .   (period)
12. exclamatory   !   (exclamation point)
13. declarative   .   (period)
14. interrogative   ?   (question mark)
15. exclamatory   !   (exclamation point)
16. imperative   .   (period)

B. (Possible answer.) Sentence 14 would probably be spoken as an exclamatory sentence if it referred to below-zero weather.

Review Exercises

Write *sentence* or *fragment* to describe each group of words. If it is a fragment, write the letter of the statement that tells why it is a fragment. [1, 6] (If you need help with any review exercise, turn to the lesson numbers in brackets.)

   a. Subject is missing.
   b. Predicate is missing.
   c. Both subject and predicate are missing.
   d. Helping verb is missing.
   e. It has a subject and predicate, but thought is incomplete.
   f. Direct object is missing.

1. Sat in the shade on a comfortable chair.
2. Last week Father built a new sled for the boys.
3. Several exciting ball games.
4. Mother baked five dozen oatmeal cookies this morning.
5. In the morning before dawn.
6. When Grandfather came, we were ready.
7. Because he saw me coming.
8. In the evening Jonathan brought.
9. She carried her Bible to church.
10. Leaves falling from the trees.
11. When we finished, Father thanked.
12. Before he left, Grandfather gave us each a little book.
13. When you have finished that job.
14. Mother washing the clothes.
15. Waited a long time.
16. In the kitchen on the floor under the table.
17. Two large black cats from the neighbor's farm.
18. The children sat on the front bench.

———————————

Review Exercises

1. fragment, a
2. sentence
3. fragment, b
4. sentence
5. fragment, c
6. sentence
7. fragment, e
8. fragment, f
9. sentence
10. fragment, d
11. fragment, f
12. sentence
13. fragment, e
14. fragment, d
15. fragment, a
16. fragment, c
17. fragment, b
18. sentence

8. Writing a Set of Directions

Think about a time when someone explained to you how to do something. Were the directions clear? Could you follow them without trouble? Did you have to ask for more explanation? We gain much help in life from the directions that others give us.

Sometimes directions are written instead of spoken. In some ways, written directions are better than oral directions because the steps are always there when you need them. You do not need to be afraid you will forget and miss a step. But written directions must be especially clear because the reader cannot ask the writer to explain something he does not understand. For that reason, you must be careful to write directions in a way that is simple to understand.

When you write a set of directions, be sure your information is correct. One inaccurate bit of information can cause the loss of valuable time, materials, or even money. One wrong measurement or ingredient in a recipe can spoil an entire dish of food. Always be sure you know how to do the thing you are trying to explain.

One of the most important things you must do to make directions clear is to tell things in the order they are to be done. Begin by making a list, step by step, of the things your reader will have to do. You might end up with a list something like this.

How to Fry an Egg

1. Get a frying pan, a pat of butter, and an egg.
2. Put pan on stove.
3. Put ½ teaspoon of butter in pan.
4. Turn burner to medium.
5. Melt butter and coat bottom of pan.
6. Break egg into pan.
7. Turn egg when clear part turns white.
8. Be careful not to break the yolk.
9. Turn off burner as soon as egg is finished.
10. Remove egg before yolk gets too hard.

Making a list of the important steps will keep you from writing mixed-up directions like this.

How to Fry an Egg

Break an egg into your frying pan. Turn the burner to medium, and place the pan on the stove. Be sure to put butter in the pan before you break the egg. . . .

Lesson 8

Purpose: To teach how to write a set of directions. (*Previous experience:* Oral and written directions.)

Oral Review:

1. What six questions should be answered in a story to give the important facts? (who, what, when, where, why, how)
2. How can you vary the sentences in a story to make them interesting? (Use a variety of sentence types. Vary their length.)
3. What does every good story include that holds a reader's interest? (a problem)
4. In addition to showing a problem, what must a story show? (how the problem was solved)
5. What other rules can you give for writing a story? (Tell things in order. Stick to the main idea. Use complete sentences. Use good grammar, proper spelling, correct punctuation, and neat handwriting.)

Lesson Introduction: How would you like to follow directions like these?

Get a piece of wood. Sand it for a while. It should be cut into a 5-inch square before sanding. Cut off a 1-inch piece along one edge. Then sand it a little more. Cherry wood works best for this project. . . .

Today we want to study the rules for writing clear directions.

Lesson Outline:

1. Be careful to write directions clearly so that they are simple to understand. It is especially important to make written directions clear because the reader cannot ask you to explain something he does not understand.

2. Make sure your information is accurate. Be sure you know how to do the thing yourself.

Using your list of points, write out the directions as a paragraph. Be sure to write complete sentences, not fragments. As you write, try to use sentences of different lengths. Beware of writing many short, choppy sentences. Also beware of writing just a few long sentences all strung together with *and*s. Both sets of directions below are unpleasant to read.

Sentences too long and stringy:
> Get a pan, some butter, and an egg, and put the pan on the stove, and put a dab of butter into the pan. Turn the burner on medium, and then break the egg into the pan, and . . .

Sentences too short and choppy:
> Get a pan, some butter, and an egg. Put the butter into the pan. Turn the burner on medium. Melt the butter. Break the egg into the pan. Let the egg sizzle a while. . . .

Your sentences should also have different beginnings. For instance, do not begin every sentence with *then* or *next*. Include other words such as *first, second, later,* and *finally*. Try to begin a few sentences with phrases like *after a while* or *in a few minutes*.

Study this example. Do the sentences have different beginnings? Do they have different lengths? Are the directions clear?

How to Fry an Egg
> Get a frying pan, a pat of butter, and an egg. Put the frying pan on the stove. Put one-half teaspoon of butter into the pan, and turn the burner on medium. Stir the butter until it melts and covers the bottom of the pan. Then break the egg into the pan. After the clear part of the egg becomes white, turn the egg with a spatula. Be careful not to break the yolk. In a minute or two, turn off the burner and remove the egg before the yolk gets too hard.

When your directions are finished, read over them carefully. Is everything clear? Is everything accurate? Will the reader have any questions you did not answer? Correct any weaknesses that you find.

Wrong information can cause your reader to lose time and money.

3. Tell things in the order they are to be done. It is helpful to begin by making a list of the important steps.

4. Write out the directions in paragraph form.
 a. Use your list of notes.
 b. Keep the steps in order.
 c. Write complete sentences.

5. Use variety in your sentences.
 a. *Use variety in sentence length.* Do not use too many short, choppy sentences. Do not string your sentences together with *and*s.
 b. *Use different sentence beginnings.* Do not begin every sentence with *then* or *next*. Include other words such as *first, second, later,* and *finally*. Try to begin a few sentences with phrases like *after a while* or *in a few minutes*.

6. Proofread your directions. Check to see if everything is clear and accurate. Are you sure your readers will not have questions you failed to answer? Also check for proper spelling, punctuation, and grammar. Correct any weaknesses you find.

- When you write directions, be sure your information is accurate. Tell things in the order they are to be done. Write in complete sentences. Use variety in sentence length and sentence beginnings.

Class Practice

Tell which one of these paragraphs gives better directions. Tell what is wrong with the poor paragraph.

Guatemalan Hot Sauce

Fry four or five bottle tomatoes in a coated pan till the tomatoes are soft. Next, fry a few hot chili peppers till they are almost black. Put the prepared tomatoes and chili peppers in a blender, and add one tablespoon coriander leaves, two small onions, and one-half teaspoon salt. Blend everything into a sauce. Try a teaspoon of the hot sauce on a plate of cooked rice. Taste only a small amount at first because it is hot! Later you can experiment with different amounts of peppers and other seasonings to suit your taste.

Guatemalan Hot Sauce

Fry four or five bottle tomatoes in a coated pan till the tomatoes are soft. Add coriander leaves, chili peppers, and onions. I think you can use garlic instead of onions if you wish. Blend the above ingredients in a blender. You must fry the chili peppers till they are black. My friend got this recipe from the natives in Guatemala. Remember to add salt, about three teaspoons. If you want it hotter, add more chili peppers. You can experiment with the amounts of other seasonings to suit your taste.

Written Exercises

A. Make a list of steps that tell how to do something. You may choose one of the following things. Be sure the steps are in the right order.
   1. How to Weave a Simple Mat
   2. How to Make a Kite
   3. How to Prepare a Garden (or Field) for Planting

Lesson 8 Answers
Class Practice

The first paragraph gives better directions. The second paragraph has the following weaknesses.
   1. The directions do not say how much of some seasonings should be used.
   2. The writer himself is not sure of the directions. He says, "I think you can use garlic instead of onions if you wish."
   3. The directions are not given in the order things must be done. They do not tell you to fry the chili peppers or add the salt before putting things into the blender.
   4. The directions are not accurate. They say to use three teaspoons of salt!
   5. One sentence does not stick to the main idea: *"My friend got this recipe from the natives in Guatemala."*

Written Exercises

(Individual work.)

4. How to Make Pancakes
5. How to Milk a Cow
6. How to Start a Lawn Mower
7. How to Clean a Paintbrush
8. How to Make Popcorn
9. How to Make Mashed Potatoes
10. How to Peel an Apple

B. Use your list from Part A to write a paragraph that gives a set of directions. Follow the instructions in the lesson, and make your paragraph clear and interesting. Write seven to twelve sentences.

Review Exercises

A. Tell which of these story beginnings is better, and why. [4]
1.   Yesterday was a beautiful day. My friends and I went for a hike in the woods. We saw several unusual birds and found a clear, bubbling spring. Everyone hopped and skipped along the trail, enjoying the fresh air. Henry climbed a tall tree and said he could see our farmhouse in the distance.
2.   Yesterday was a beautiful day. My friends and I went for a hike in the woods. We saw several unusual birds and found a clear, bubbling spring. The air was so clear that Henry decided to climb a tree and look around. When he was about ten feet above the ground, a branch broke and he fell to the ground. He landed on his right arm, and we all heard a muffled snap! Henry lay there groaning with pain.

B. Find the fragments in the following paragraph. Rewrite them, making complete sentences. [1]

The lion was only eight feet away! He glared at me with angry eyes. Slowly his tail moved from side to side. He looked fierce and wild. While he was crouching before me. I turned and walked to the next cage. Many interesting animals in that zoo.

————————————

Review Exercises

A. Number 2 is a better story beginning because it shows a problem.

B. (Answers may vary.)
While he was crouching before me, I turned and walked to the next cage.
We saw many interesting animals in that zoo.
or There were many interesting animals in that zoo.

9. Chapter 1 Review

Class Practice

A. Give the three steps for finding the skeleton of a sentence.

B. Answer the following questions about clauses.
1. What is a clause?
2. Is every clause a sentence?
3. What must a clause do to be a sentence?

C. Give the following verbs.
1. The forms of *be.*
2. The other helping verbs in groups.
3. The "sometimes linking verbs" that you learned in grade 5.

D. Give the answers.
1. What rules have you studied about story writing?
2. What rules should you remember when writing directions?
3. Name and describe the four sentence types.

E. Say *clause* or *not a clause* for each group of words.
1. The Grand Canyon state.
2. Here we found large areas of dry land.
3. Is mostly desert land.
4. Arizona is not completely desert land.
5. About one half of Arizona's land.
6. After the Spaniards came.

F. Tell whether each group of words is a *sentence* or a *fragment.* If it is a fragment, tell what is missing.
1. Many Indians still live in Arizona.
2. Because many people have come to Arizona.
3. The population of Arizona has increased almost fourfold since 1950.
4. My uncle once caught.
5. The cactus wren, the state bird of Arizona.
6. Have ever seen a giant cactus?
7. I drew a picture of Arizona's state flower.

G. Copy the following sentences on the chalkboard. Put parentheses around any prepositional phrase in the complete subject. Draw two lines under the simple predicate, and one line under the simple subject. Draw a dividing line between the complete subject and the complete predicate.

Lesson 9

Purpose: To review the things taught in Chapter 1.

Lesson 9 Answers
Class Practice

A. 1. Find the simple predicate (the verb).
2. Ask *who* or *what* about the verb.
3. Say the simple subject and simple predicate together to see if they make sense.

B. 1. A clause is a group of words that has a skeleton (a subject and a verb).
2. no
3. It must express a complete thought.

C. 1. am, is, are, was, were, be, been, being
2. have, has, had
do, does, did
may, might, must
can—could, shall—should, will—would
3. taste, feel, smell, sound, look, appear

D. 1. a. Know the facts.
b. Put things in proper order, from first to last.
c. Include all the important information. Tell who, what, when, where, why, and how.
d. Stick to the main idea of the story.
e. Use complete sentences.
f. Vary the length of your sentences. Do not use too many short, choppy sentences. Do not use just a few long sentences connected with *and*s.
g. Use good grammar, proper spelling, correct punctuation, and neat handwriting.
h. Tell about a problem, and show how it was solved.
2. a. Write clearly so that the directions are simple to understand.
b. Be sure your information is accurate.
c. Tell things in the order they are to be done.
d. Write in complete sentences.
e. Use variety in sentence length and beginnings.
3. a. A *declarative sentence* states a fact and ends with a period. It is either true or false.
b. An *interrogative sentence* asks a question and ends with a question mark.
c. An *imperative sentence* gives a command or request and ends with a period. The subject of every imperative sentence is *you,* but it is not usually stated.
d. An *exclamatory sentence* expresses strong feeling and ends with an exclamation point. Some exclamatory sentences have their own special word order.

(Parts E and F are on page 47.)

1. Some lakes are choked with algae.
2. It feels slimy.
3. Large quantities of algae may color a pond or lake.
4. Lake George should be cleaned up.
5. The Lake of the Ozarks was formed by a man-made dam.
6. The blue jays are plentiful here.
7. A sloth will not clean algae from his body.
8. Algae in the ocean are food for many sea creatures.

H. Tell whether each sentence is *declarative, interrogative, imperative,* or *exclamatory.* Also give the correct end punctuation.
1. Is Brazil the largest country in South America
2. Brazil is the sixth largest country in the world
3. What a large country it must be
4. Draw a map of Brazil
5. Label all the mountains and rivers
6. The Amazon River is the largest river in the world
7. Is it in Brazil
8. Part of it runs through Brazil

Written Exercises

A. Write *sentence* or *fragment* to describe each group of words. If it is a fragment, also write the letter of the statement that tells why it is a fragment.

   a. Subject is missing.
   b. Predicate is missing.
   c. Both subject and predicate are missing.
   d. Helping verb is missing.
   e. It has a subject and predicate, but thought is incomplete.
   f. Direct object is missing.

1. Arizona is sometimes called the Grand Canyon state.
2. Why didn't you bring?
3. Many Indians still live in Arizona.
4. Before Arizona became a state.
5. Most of Arizona's people.
6. The growing population.
7. People like the warm climate there.
8. Through the Grand Canyon.
9. So that we have time to hike down the mule trail.

Class Practice, Parts E and F

E. 1. not a clause   4. clause
   2. clause   5. not a clause
   3. not a clause   6. clause

F. 1. sentence
   2. fragment; needs other words
   3. sentence
   4. fragment; missing a direct object
   5. fragment; missing a predicate
   6. fragment; missing a subject
   7. sentence

G. 1. Some <u>lakes</u> | <u>are choked</u> with algae.
2. <u>It</u> | <u>feels</u> slimy.
3. Large <u>quantities</u> (of algae) | <u>may color</u> a pond or lake.
4. <u>Lake George</u> | <u>should be cleaned</u> up.
5. The <u>Lake of the Ozarks</u> | <u>was formed</u> by a man-made dam.
6. The <u>blue jays</u> | <u>are</u> plentiful here.
7. A <u>sloth</u> | <u>will</u> not <u>clean</u> algae from his body.
8. <u>Algae</u> (in the ocean) | <u>are</u> food for many sea creatures.

H. 1. interrogative; question mark
2. declarative; period
3. exclamatory; exclamation point
4. imperative; period
5. imperative; period
6. declarative; period
7. interrogative; question mark
8. declarative; period

Written Exercises

A. 1. sentence
   2. fragment, f
   3. sentence
   4. fragment, e
   5. fragment, b
   6. fragment, b
   7. sentence
   8. fragment, c
   9. fragment, e

10. The generators on Glen Canyon Dam producing large amounts of electricity.
11. Don't you think it was Noah's flood that carved out all these interesting rock formations?
12. The swirling waters may have laid down these layers of rock.
13. Could have carved out this deep canyon?
14. God showing us His greatness by the wonders of creation.

B. Copy each sentence. Put parentheses around any prepositional phrase in the complete subject. Draw two lines under the simple predicate, and one line under the simple subject. Draw a dividing line between the complete subject and the complete predicate.
1. Algae grows in oceans, lakes, ponds, and streams.
2. Microscopes must be used to see some of them.
3. Some kinds of algae are large plants with many cells.
4. Most algae are classified as plants.
5. Seaweeds are large marine algae.
6. You have never eaten algae?
7. The Japanese like a food called nori.
8. Nori is made from red algae.
9. It does taste delicious.
10. Some kinds of algae form slippery coatings on rocks.
11. A turtle may have algae on its shell.
12. The Lake of the Woods was named after the hills and forests around it.

C. Write whether each sentence is *declarative, interrogative, imperative,* or *exclamatory.* Also write the correct end punctuation.
1. Brazil has almost 175 million people
2. Is Brazil the sixth largest nation in the world
3. What a large country it is
4. Do many people live in the Amazon region
5. How thick those forests must be
6. Are many of the people Indians
7. Visit this country in South America
8. Many people in Brazil need the Word of God

---

10. fragment, d
11. sentence
12. sentence
13. fragment, a
14. fragment, d

B. 1. <u>Algae</u> | <u>grows</u> in oceans, lakes, ponds, and streams.
2. <u>Microscopes</u> | <u>must be used</u> to see some of them.
3. Some <u>kinds</u> (of algae) | <u>are</u> large plants with many cells.
4. Most <u>algae</u> | <u>are classified</u> as plants.
5. <u>Seaweeds</u> | <u>are</u> large marine algae.
6. <u>You</u> | <u>have</u> never <u>eaten</u> algae?
7. The <u>Japanese</u> | <u>like</u> a food called nori.
8. <u>Nori</u> | <u>is made</u> from red algae.
9. <u>It</u> | <u>does taste</u> delicious.
10. Some <u>kinds</u> (of algae) | <u>form</u> slippery coatings on rocks.
11. A <u>turtle</u> | <u>may have</u> algae on its shell.
12. The <u>Lake of the Woods</u> | <u>was named</u> after the hills and forests around it.

C. 1. declarative   . (period)
2. interrogative **?** (question mark)
3. exclamatory **!** (exclamation point)
4. interrogative **?** (question mark)
5. exclamatory **!** (exclamation point)
6. interrogative **?** (question mark)
7. imperative   . (period)
8. declarative   . (period)

Chapter Two

Working With Sentences

Understanding Paragraphs

A
paragraph is a
group of sentences that all deal
with a single
topic.

𝔚hatsoever thy hand findeth to do, do it with thy might.

Ecclesiastes 9:10

10. Diagraming Sentence Skeletons

We often diagram a sentence to help us identify the different sentence parts. Diagraming also helps us to see clearly how the parts of the sentence work together.

The *skeleton* of a sentence is diagramed on a horizontal base line. The simple subject is put on the left half of the line, and the simple predicate is put on the right half. A vertical line separates the subject from the predicate.

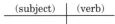

Study the diagrams of the following sentence skeletons.

Crisp yellow leaves fell to the ground.

God hears the prayers of His children.

If the simple subject is a noun phrase, be sure to write the whole phrase on the base line of the diagram. This is true whether or not the noun phrase is capitalized.

Sentences with noun phrases:

Guatemala City is the largest city in Guatemala.

The post office is in the center of town.

Nevin L. Nissley will conduct the devotional.

Lesson 10

Purpose: (1) To teach diagraming as a means of analyzing sentence parts. (2) To review working with sentences whose skeletons may be more difficult to find than those studied earlier (Lesson 5).

Oral Review:

1. Name the four sentence types. Give the correct end punctuation for each. (declarative, period; interrogative, question mark; imperative, period; exclamatory, exclamation point)
2. Which type of sentence
   a. states a fact? (declarative)
   b. gives a command or request? (imperative)
   c. asks a question? (interrogative)
   d. expresses strong feeling? (exclamatory)
3. The following verb phrases are interrupted by words that are not verbs. Identify the interrupting word in each phrase.

   a. will never know (never)
   b. could always be found (always)
   c. is still raining (still)
   d. will not be coming (not)
   e. has often been told (often)
   f. can hardly be (hardly)
4. What part of speech is a word like *not, never, always,* and *hardly*? (adverb)
5. How can you tell which words belong together in a proper noun phrase? (The words are usually capitalized.)

Lesson Introduction: When you are showing a friend how something is made or how it works, what can you do to make your explanation clearer? You can make a diagram. Many times a simple diagram, laid out on paper, helps to clarify something that would otherwise be difficult to comprehend.

The same thing is true for understanding how a sentence is constructed. A sentence diagram helps us to see the organization of a sentence. It helps us to see the relationships among words in a sentence. In this lesson we will see how to diagram sentence skeletons.

Lesson Outline:

1. Diagraming helps us see the parts of a sentence and how they work together.

2. The skeleton of a sentence is diagramed on a horizontal base line, with the simple subject on the left and the simple predicate (verb) on the right. They are separated by a vertical line.

(subject) | (verb)

If the simple predicate is a verb phrase, be sure to write the whole phrase on the base line of the diagram. Remember that the helping verbs you studied in Lesson 2 are always part of the verb phrase. Memorize them again if you have forgotten any.

When an adverb comes between parts of a verb phrase, do not write the adverb on the base line, since it is not part of the verb.

Sentences with verb phrases:

Karen <u>did</u> not <u>see</u> Nancy.

Karen	did see

Leon <u>has</u> almost <u>finished</u> his work.

Leon	has finished

The <u>students</u> <u>are</u> rapidly <u>improving</u>.

students	are improving

In many questions, part of the verb phrase comes before the simple subject and part of it comes after. Even though the verb phrase is split, the subject is placed on the left and the complete verb phrase on the right. It is helpful to reword the question as a statement before diagraming it.

Interrogative sentences:

<u>Have</u> <u>you</u> <u>seen</u> my brother?
 (you <u>Have seen</u> my brother)

you	Have seen

<u>Do</u> <u>you</u> <u>know</u> my father?
 (you <u>Do know</u> my father)

you	Do know

Remind the students to use the following steps for finding the skeleton of a sentence.
  a. Find the simple predicate (the verb).
  b. Ask *who* or *what* about the verb. The answer is the simple subject.
  c. Say the simple subject and simple predicate together to be sure they make sense.

Use the above steps to work through the following sentences. Diagram them on the chalkboard.

Some <u>plants</u> | <u>grow</u> under water.

plants	grow

Many <u>plants</u> | <u>are</u> very small.

plants	are

<u>We</u> | <u>see</u> plants every day.

We	see

3. If the simple subject is a noun phrase, write the whole phrase on the base line of the diagram. This is true whether or not the noun phrase is capitalized.

The <u>Potomac River</u> | <u>flows</u> between Maryland
    and Virginia.
<u>Chicken pox</u> | <u>is</u> generally a childhood illness.

Less common noun phrases, such as *potato beetle* and *buffalo bur,* are indicated as such in the pupil's text.

4. If the simple predicate is a verb phrase, write the whole phrase on the base line of the diagram. Use the following examples at the chalkboard. (If your students are weak on recognizing helping verbs, turn back to Lesson 2 and review them.)

The <u>potato beetle</u> | <u>did thrive</u> on buffalo burs.
Now <u>it</u> | <u>is living</u> on potato vines.
<u>They</u> | <u>had been found</u> mostly in the West.
By 1875 the <u>potato beetle</u> | <u>had spread</u> to the
    Atlantic.

5. When a verb phrase is split by an adverb, do not diagram the adverb as part of the verb phrase. Sixth grade students should be able to recognize adverbs most of the time. If they need some review, go over the following points.
  a. Adverbs tell *how, when, where,* and *to what degree.*

Is <u>Brother Luke</u> <u>coming</u>?
(Brother Luke <u>Is coming</u>)

Brother Luke	Is coming

Remember that *you* is understood in most commands. When diagraming such a command, write *you* in parentheses for the simple subject. If *you* is stated in the sentence, do not use parentheses.

Imperative sentences:
Rejoice evermore.

(you)	Rejoice

You start the song.

You	start

When a prepositional phrase comes between the simple subject and the simple predicate, be careful to choose the correct word for the subject. Remember, the subject of a sentence is never found in a prepositional phrase.

Sentences with prepositional phrases:
The milk in that jar is sour.

milk	is

The peaches from that tree are sweet.

peaches	are

Clever men of Gibeon deceived Joshua.

men	deceived

When you diagram sentences, be careful to keep the capital letters, but omit the punctuation marks.

b. Words like *not, never, ever,* and *always* are adverbs.
c. Many adverbs end with *-ly.*

Examples to use at the chalkboard.

<u>Farmers</u> | <u>do</u> not <u>like</u> potato beetles.
<u>They</u> | <u>must</u> often <u>spray</u> for the beetles.
The <u>beetles</u> | <u>have</u> swiftly <u>moved</u> east from one potato field to another.

6. *In many questions the verb phrase is split. Part of it comes before the simple subject, and part of it comes after.*

<u>Did</u> <u>you</u> <u>help</u> in the field?
<u>Did</u> the <u>beetle</u> <u>come</u> from Mexico?

7. *When diagraming an imperative sentence in which the subject* **you** *is understood, write* **you** *in parentheses for the simple subject.* Do not use parentheses if *you* is stated.

<u>Study</u> the helping verbs.

(you)	<u>Study</u>

<u>You</u> | <u>read</u> the story.

<u>You</u>	<u>read</u>

8. *When a prepositional phrase comes between the simple subject and the simple predicate, be careful to choose the right word for the subject.* Remember, the subject of a sentence is never found in a prepositional phrase.

See Lesson 5, where prepositional phrases were taught before. Use the following examples for practice in picking out prepositional phrases, especially phrases following the subject.

a. Large herds <u>of buffalo</u> once roamed <u>across the Great Plains</u> <u>of the United States.</u>
b. One group <u>of valuable food fishes</u> is the pompano.
c. Meat <u>from the pompano</u> has a rich flavor.
d. This kind <u>of fish</u> cannot be caught very well <u>with a hook</u> <u>on a line.</u>
e. The waters <u>along the Atlantic Coast</u> yield one kind <u>of pompano.</u>

★ **EXTRA PRACTICE**
Worksheet 7 *(Diagraming Sentence Skeletons)*

- The skeleton of a sentence is diagramed on a horizontal base line. The subject is placed on the left, the predicate is placed on the right, and a vertical line is placed between them.

- If the subject or the verb is a phrase, the entire phrase is placed on the diagram.

- When the subject of a sentence is *you* understood, *you* is written in parentheses.

- The subject of a sentence is never found in a prepositional phrase.

Class Practice

Give the skeleton of each sentence, and diagram it at the chalkboard.
1. David L. Stoner has left for Ontario.
2. Many of these apples have spots on them.
3. Oh, how I love Thy law!
4. Enoch walked with God.
5. What shall I bring unto the Lord?
6. The dog could not catch the rabbit.
7. Teach me Thy way, O Lord.
8. Can a leopard change his spots?
9. The man with the cane is my grandfather.
10. Each of the children said a verse by memory.

Written Exercises

Diagram the sentence skeletons.
1. Make a joyful noise unto the Lord.
2. The Lord is my strength.
3. O give thanks unto the Lord.
4. The boys have been working hard.
5. Can your little sister ride a bicycle?
6. Brother Martin drives a black van.
7. That wren always builds her nest here.
8. I did not hear you in time.
9. Pompeii was an ancient Italian city.

Lesson 10 Answers
Class Practice

1. David L. Stoner | has left
2. Many | have
3. I | love
4. Enoch | walked
5. I | shall bring
6. dog | could catch
7. (you) | Teach
8. leopard | Can change
9. man | is
10. Each | said

Written Exercises

1. (you) | Make
2. Lord | is
3. (you) | give
4. boys | have been working
5. sister | Can ride
6. Brother Martin | drives
7. wren | builds
8. I | did hear
9. Pompeii | was

10. It was completely demolished by a terrific eruption of Mount Vesuvius.
11. Mount Vesuvius erupted in A.D. 79.
12. The city was buried under heaps of ashes.
13. It was not excavated for almost 1,700 years.
14. When did the excavations begin?
15. A peasant discovered a buried wall in 1748.
16. Other men were soon digging.
17. Many of the ruins were preserved very well.
18. Houses in Pompeii had been rich and luxurious.
19. People can now visit the ruins of the city.
20. Imagine that!

10.   It | was demolished

11.   Mount Vesuvius | erupted

12.   city | was buried

13.   It | was excavated

14.   excavations | did begin

15.   peasant | discovered

16.   men | were digging

17.   Many | were preserved

18.   Houses | had been

19.   People | can visit

20.   (you) | Imagine

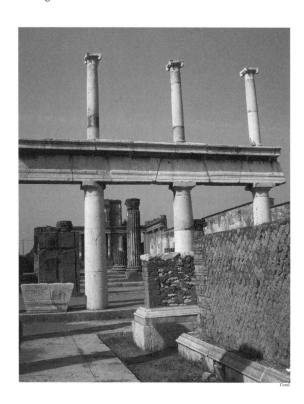

Corel

Review Exercises

Write a complete sentence to answer each question. [1–6]

1. What is a noun?
2. What is a verb?
3. What is a pronoun?
4. What is a sentence?
5. What is a clause?

---

11. Compound Subjects and Predicates

A sentence may have more than one subject. Sometimes two or more nouns or pronouns are joined by a conjunction to form a *compound subject*. In the following examples, the simple subjects are underlined and the conjunctions are in boldface.

> Boys **and** girls | enjoy learning.
> Paul **and** Barnabas | were traveling in Cyprus.
> You **or** I | will have to do it.

A conjunction is a word that joins other words together. You should remember that a conjunction is one of the eight parts of speech. The three most common conjunctions are *and, but,* and *or.*

A sentence may have more than one predicate. Two or more verbs may be joined by a conjunction to form a *compound predicate*. In the following examples, the simple predicates are underlined twice and the conjunctions are in boldface.

> The deer | snorted **and** ran away.
> The missionaries | preached **and** baptized among the Gentiles.
> The dog | chased the rabbit **but** soon lost its trail.

Study the following examples to see how compound subjects and predicates are diagramed. The compound part is put on a fork, and the conjunction is put on a dotted line inside the fork.

Lesson 11

Purpose: To identify and diagram compound subjects and predicates.

Oral Review:

1. What sentence parts form the skeleton of a sentence? (the simple subject and the simple predicate)
2. What steps should be followed to find the skeleton of a sentence? (Find the verb, and ask *who* or *what* about it. The answer is the simple subject. Say the subject and verb together to be sure they make sense.)
3. What should be done to most questions before they are diagramed? (Reword the question as a statement.)
4. What should you remember about diagraming commands? (In most commands, the subject *you* is understood. Write *you* in parentheses for the simple subject.)

Review Exercises

1. A noun is a word that names a person, place, thing, or idea.
2. A verb is a word that shows action or being.
3. A pronoun is a word that takes the place of a noun.
4. A sentence is a group of words that expresses a complete thought.
5. A clause is a group of words that has a skeleton (*or* a subject and a predicate).

---

5. What is a clause? (a group of words with a subject and a predicate)
6. What must a clause do in order to be a sentence? (express a complete thought)
7. What is missing in some clauses that are not sentences? (Some need additional words to make a complete thought. Some are missing a direct object. Some are missing a helping verb.)

Lesson Introduction: Discuss the meaning of *simple* and *compound*. *Simple* means "not complicated"; something simple often has a single, basic part. Something *compound* has more than one part. It means two or more parts joined together.

Read the following sentences to the students. Ask if they can improve the sentences.

> The ant bear is an anteater.
> The aardvark is an anteater.
> The anteater whips out its long tongue.
> The anteater sweeps termites into its mouth.

The sentences can be improved by combining the subjects and verbs.

> The ant bear and the aardvark are anteaters.
> The anteater whips out its long tongue and sweeps termites into its mouth.

Lesson Outline:

1. Two or more simple subjects may be joined by a conjunction to form a **compound subject.**

> Spring beauties **and** violets | are spring flowers.
> Johannes Kepler, Robert Boyle, **and** Michael Faraday | were famous scientists.
> Cake **or** cookies | will be served at lunch.

Compound subject:

Charles and I were reading.

Mary, Louise, and Ruby were singing together.

Compound predicate:

Jesus went into the temple and listened to the teachers.

In some sentences, the two parts of a compound predicate share the same helping verb. When this happens, the helping verb is placed on the base line before the fork. This shows that the helping verb goes with both main verbs.

It was snowing or raining for several days.

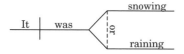

In the example above, the helping verb *was* goes with both main verbs: *snowing* and *raining.* Now notice the following sentence.

Barbara was running in the yard and fell.

2.   Two or more simple predicates may be joined by a conjunction to form a **compound predicate.**

Playing penguins | <u>run</u> around **and** <u>push</u> each other on the ice.

They | <u>float</u> away on moving ice floes **and** then <u>swim</u> back to their friends.

The polar bear cubs | <u>rolled</u> **or** <u>slid</u> down the snowbank.

***3.   A conjunction is a word that joins other words together. The three most common conjunctions are* and, but, *and* or.** A conjunction is one of the eight parts of speech. (*Teacher:* Conjunctions also join phrases and clauses, but that does not need to be mentioned here.)

4.   Compound subjects and predicates can be diagramed. The compound part is put on a fork, and the conjunction goes on a dotted line inside the fork.

a. Compound subject:

Martins and bluebirds nested in bird-houses on his property.

b. Compound predicate:

The pigs squealed and grunted all night.

c. Compound verbs that share the same helping verbs:

A flicker had been pecking and hammering at the old stump.

d. Compound verbs that do not share the same helping verbs:

He had been walking fast but now was out of breath.

e. Sentence with both a compound subject and a compound verb:

The parents and children talked and worked together.

★ **EXTRA PRACTICE**

Worksheet 8 (*Compound Subjects and Predicates*)

In this sentence, the helping verb goes only with the verb *running*, not with *fell*. "Barbara *was running*" is sensible, but "Barbara *was fell*" is not. Therefore, *was* is diagramed with *running*.

A sentence can have both a compound subject and a compound predicate.

Janice and her mother picked the beans and cooked them.

- Simple subjects joined by a conjunction form a compound subject.
- Simple predicates joined by a conjunction form a compound predicate.
- The three most common conjunctions are *and, but,* and *or.*

Class Practice

At the chalkboard, diagram the skeletons of these sentences.
1. King Agrippa talked to Paul and listened to his words.
2. The disciples fasted and prayed.
3. Rachel and Leah were sisters.
4. We have been thanking and praising God for His mercy to us.
5. Isaac and Rebekah had twin sons.
6. Paul and Barnabas were traveling and preaching.
7. The children were playing busily and forgot the time.
8. Did she draw or trace this picture?
9. She traced the outline but drew the details freehand.
10. The baby can crawl but cannot walk.
11. A robin or a wood thrush is sitting in that tree.
12. A chickadee and a junco are at the feeder.

Written Exercises

Diagram the skeletons of these sentences.
1. Ducks and geese were quacking and honking.
2. How many children came to school and studied diligently?

Written Exercises

3. Wheat, oats, and rice are used in breakfast cereals.
4. Mars or Venus is the nearest planet to Earth.
5. Genesis and Exodus were written by Moses.
6. Jesus appeared first to Mary and was seen later by the disciples.
7. The scribes and Pharisees feared and despised Jesus.
8. The family sings and prays together every morning.
9. We can bake the fish or fry it.
10. We had found the answer but did not write it on our papers.
11. James must eat better or rest more.
12. She will not ride or walk.
13. Oranges and strawberries contain vitamin C.
14. Harold or Milton climbed the tree and rescued the kitten.
15. The goose returned, built a nest, and is now brooding the eggs.
16. A male lion measures about nine feet in length and weighs about five hundred pounds.
17. Lions and tigers usually hunt at night and sleep during the day.
18. Africa and southern Asia have lions and tigers in their forests and grasslands.
19. The Middle East and northern Africa no longer have lions.
20. In the zoo we were watching the lions and heard their roars.

Review Exercises

A. Write *declarative, interrogative, imperative,* or *exclamatory.* Also write the correct end punctuation. [7]
   1. Come and look at this beautiful bird
   2. Does a cockatoo have a beautiful song as well
   3. It greets the day with an earsplitting shriek and screams all day long
   4. You should teach it some tricks
   5. What an interesting bird it must be

B. Diagram the skeletons of the following sentences. [10]
   1. What do cockatoos eat?
   2. Please get me one for a pet.
   3. Most cockatoos can actually say a few words.
   4. The shriek of a cockatoo is very loud!

Review Exercises

A. 1. imperative   . (period)
    or exclamatory ! (exclamation point)
  2. interrogative ? (question mark)
  3. declarative . (period)
  4. declarative . (period)
  5. exclamatory ! (exclamation point)

B. 1. cockatoos | do eat

  2. (you) | get

  3. cockatoos | can say

  4. shriek | is

3.

4.

5.

6.

7.

8.

9.

10.

11.

12.

13.

14.

(Numbers 15–20 are on page 67.)

12. Simple and Compound Sentences

So far this year, you have studied only simple sentences. A *simple sentence* is made of *one* clause, having only *one skeleton*.

Mary | <u>loved</u> Jesus.

Mary is the subject. *Loved* is the verb. There is only one skeleton, so this is a simple sentence.

Formulas can help you to recognize simple sentences. Use letters to stand for sentence parts and a plus sign for conjunctions.

S = subject   V = verb   + = conjunction

Following is the formula for the sentence above.

S | V   = simple sentence
Mary | <u>loved</u> Jesus.

A sentence may have a compound subject or a compound predicate, but it is still a simple sentence. Look at these examples.

S + S | V   = simple sentence
Mary and Martha | <u>loved</u> Jesus.

S | V + V   = simple sentence
Mary | <u>sat</u> and <u>listened</u> to Jesus' words.

Even if a sentence has both a compound subject and a compound predicate, the sentence is still a simple sentence.

S + S | V   + V = simple sentence
Mary and Martha | <u>invited</u> Jesus and <u>served</u> Him.

Look again at the formulas with the examples above. In each sentence, one or two subjects go with one or two verbs to form only one skeleton. This is the key to identifying a simple sentence: *one skeleton*.

A *compound sentence* is formed when *two* clauses are joined together. In a compound sentence you will always find *two skeletons*, one on each side of the conjunction. Notice the formula for a compound sentence.

S | V + S | V = compound sentence

Lesson 12

Purpose: To teach the difference between simple and compound sentences.

Oral Review:
1. What is a verb? (a word that shows action or being)
2. What is a noun? (a word that names a person, place, thing, or idea)
3. Name the part of speech described.
   a. It takes the place of a noun. (pronoun)
   b. It tells *how, when, where,* or *to what degree.* (adverb)
   c. It tells *which, whose, how many,* or *what kind of.* (adjective)
   d. It modifies a verb. (adverb)
   e. It modifies an adjective or adverb. (adverb)
   f. It modifies a noun or pronoun. (adjective)
4. Simple subjects or verbs joined by a conjunction are called what? (compound subjects or compound verbs)

5. What part of speech is used to join subjects? Give the three that are most common. (conjunction; and, but, or)
6. How is a compound part diagramed? (It is put on a fork.)
7. Can a sentence have both a compound subject and a compound predicate? (yes)

Written Quiz:
Diagram the skeletons of the following sentences.
1. Blue is a restful color.
2. The color of the sky blends perfectly with the greens of the plants.
3. The blue sky and red sunsets were made by God.
4. Even in the middle of the day, the sky looks black on the moon.
5. Study God's beautiful world and marvel at His creation.

Quiz Answers:
1. <u>blue | is</u>

2. <u>color | blends</u>

3.

4. <u>sky | looks</u>

5.

Lesson Introduction: Write the following sentence on the chalkboard, and ask students whether they think it is a simple sentence or a compound sentence.

> The beautiful sunset and the peaceful evening declared God's greatness and filled our souls with awe.

In spite of what they may think, and in spite of the fact that it is somewhat complex, this is indeed a simple sentence—simple at least by the definition of a simple sentence. It has only one skeleton, though both the subject and the predicate are compound. By the time you have taught this lesson, your students should be able to understand why this is a simple sentence.

Study these examples.

S | V   + S | V = compound sentence
The <u>boys</u> | <u>wanted</u> the dog, **but** <u>they</u> | <u>had</u> no money.

S | V   + S | V = compound sentence
<u>I</u> | <u>shall call</u> on the Lord, **and** <u>He</u> | <u>will hear</u> my prayer.

S | V   + S | V = compound sentence
The <u>Lord</u> | <u>is</u> high, **yet** <u>He</u> | <u>has</u> respect to the lowly.

Once again notice the formulas. Each compound sentence has two skeletons, one on each side of the conjunction.

Either of the clauses of a compound sentence could be written by itself as a simple sentence. But when they are combined into one sentence, they must be joined with both a comma and a conjunction. Some common conjunctions used to form compound sentences are *and, but, or, for, nor,* and *yet.* See how the following simple sentences are combined to make a compound sentence.

Two simple sentences:
<u>Harold</u> | <u>saw</u> the accident. <u>He</u> | <u>told</u> his father about it.

Compound sentence:
<u>Harold</u> | <u>saw</u> the accident, **and** <u>he</u> | <u>told</u> his father about it.

To diagram a compound sentence, diagram the two clauses side by side, with the conjunction on a dotted line between them. Here are the diagramed skeletons of the four compound sentences above.

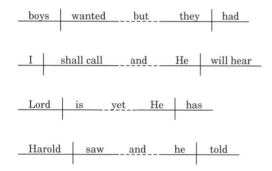

Lesson Outline:

1. A simple sentence *is made of* one *clause, having only* one skeleton. Many simple sentences are quite easy to identify.

<u>Apples</u> | <u>were sold</u> at the stand.
The younger <u>brother</u> | <u>bought</u> the birthright.

2. A simple sentence *may have* a compound subject *or* a compound predicate. It is still a simple sentence because it has only one skeleton.

Simple sentence with compound subject:
<u>Bananas</u> and <u>pineapples</u> | <u>were sold</u> at the market.

Simple sentences with compound predicates:
The <u>women</u> | <u>grind</u> the corn and <u>make</u> small cakes with the meal.
A thin <u>stream</u> of water | <u>splashed</u> and <u>sprayed</u> on its way down the cliff.

3. A simple sentence *may have* both a compound subject *and* a compound predicate. It is still a simple sentence because it has only one skeleton.

The <u>boys</u> and <u>girls</u> | <u>build</u> and <u>sell</u> handmade items.
<u>Robins</u> and <u>wrens</u> | <u>chirped</u> and <u>sang.</u>

4. A compound sentence *is made of* two clauses. It has two skeletons.

<u>Heaven</u> and <u>earth</u> | <u>shall pass</u> away, but My <u>words</u> | <u>shall</u> not <u>pass</u> away.
The <u>eyes</u> of the Lord | <u>are</u> upon the righteous, and His <u>ears</u> | <u>are</u> open unto their cry.

5. The two clauses of a compound sentence must be joined by a comma and a conjunction. Students will seldom miss the conjunction, but they may easily forget the comma. When the comma is missing, a run-on sentence results. This problem is treated further in Lesson 14, but for now be sure to emphasize the need for the comma.

Abraham prayed for his nephew<u>, and</u> God saved him.
The angels warned Lot<u>, yet</u> he lingered in Sodom.
The Lord rained brimstone on the wicked city<u>, but</u> Lot escaped with his family.

6. Some common conjunctions used to form compound sentences are and, but, or, for, nor, and yet.

7. Using formulas can help distinguish between simple sentences and compound sentences. Students can write S for the subject, V for the verb, and + for the conjunction. They can write the letters above the words in the sentence or elsewhere. They must realize that S | V makes a skeleton and that unless there is an S | V on each side of the conjunction, it is always a simple sentence.

S | V + V = simple sentence
Several <u>dolphins</u> | <u>swam</u> and <u>dived</u> beside the ship.

S + S | V = simple sentence
The <u>passengers</u> and <u>sailors</u> | <u>watch</u> them every day.

- A simple sentence has only one skeleton.

- A compound sentence has two skeletons.

- The two clauses of a compound sentence are joined by a comma and a conjunction.

- Some common conjunctions are *and, but, or, for, nor, and yet.*

- To diagram a compound sentence, diagram the two skeletons side by side, with the conjunction on a dotted line between them.

Class Practice

A. On the chalkboard, write the formula for each sentence. Tell where commas should be added.
  1. O give thanks unto the Lord for He is good.
  2. A wise man and a foolish man each built a house.
  3. Storms came and destroyed the house on the sand.
  4. Build your house on the solid rock and God will help you through all storms.

B. Diagram the skeletons of these compound sentences at the chalkboard.
  1. In Guatemala some people ride on buses, but many still walk great distances.
  2. The dirt roads are full of ruts, yet cars and trucks drive on them.
  3. The air is thin, and many visitors are not accustomed to it.
  4. You must speak Spanish, or you will need an interpreter.

C. Tell how to combine the following sentences to make compound sentences. Tell what conjunctions should be used and where commas should be placed.
  1. Frogs breathe with gills at first. They develop lungs later.
  2. Birds must eat much food. They have a high body temperature.
  3. Young amphibians live in water. Mature amphibians live on land.
  4. A bird may migrate many miles in the fall. It may stay in the same area all year.

Lesson 12 Answers
Class Practice
A. (If students have trouble with this part, copy the sentences on the chalkboard, underline the simple subjects once and the simple predicates twice, and draw a dividing line between the subject and the predicate of each clause.)
  1. S | V + S | V = compound sentence; comma after *Lord*
  2. S + S | V = simple sentence; no comma needed
  3. S | V + V = simple sentence; no comma needed
  4. S | V + S | V = compound sentence; comma after *rock*

B. 1. ___people___|___ride___--but--___many___|___walk___

  2.

  3. ___air___|___is___--and--___visitors___|___are accustomed___

  4. ___You___|___must speak___--or--___you___|___will need___

C. 1. Frogs breathe with gills at first, but (and) they develop lungs later.
  2. Birds must eat much food, for they have a high body temperature.
  3. Young amphibians live in water, but mature amphibians live on land.
  4. A bird may migrate many miles in the fall, or it may stay in the same area all year.

S + S | V + V = simple sentence
<u>Joan</u> and <u>Mary</u> | <u>watch</u> dolphins and <u>feed</u> sea gulls.

S | V + S | V = compound sentence
The <u>heavens</u> | <u>declare</u> the glory of God, **and** the <u>firmament</u> | <u>shows</u> His handiwork.

(*Teacher:* After the students are familiar with sentence formulas, you may wish to give them the following clue: One dividing line indicates a simple sentence; two dividing lines indicate a compound sentence.)

★ **EXTRA PRACTICE**
Worksheet 9 *(Compound Sentences)*

Written Exercises

A. Combine these simple sentences to make compound sentences. Use a comma and a suitable conjunction.
1. Herons eat frogs and little fish. Ducks eat various water plants.
2. Lizards have scales. Newts have soft, moist skin.
3. Keep the windows closed. The mosquitoes will come inside.
4. Karen was bitten by many mosquitoes. Now she is miserable.

B. Diagram the skeletons of these compound sentences.
1. The sky is growing darker, and it will surely rain.
2. Aunt Rachel visited us, and we had a pleasant time.
3. He had studied the chapter carefully, yet he could not say all the verses by memory.
4. The boys took the turtle to school, and afterward they released it.

C. Write the formula for each sentence, and write whether it is simple or compound. (All commas have been omitted.)
1. Herbert and his sisters attend Meadow Valley School.
2. We had enough money but we lost it.
3. The old man and his dog were tired and hungry.
4. Jesus asked a question but the lawyer had no answer.
5. The children raked the leaves and put them on the garden.
6. Peter was put into prison and the church was praying for him.
7. We finished our work and asked the teacher for more.
8. The snow continued all night and we could not get to school the next day.
9. Science and math are Frank's favorite subjects.
10. We must hurry or we shall surely be too late.

Review Exercises

List the following items.
1. Three noun phrases
2. All the helping verbs
3. Eight common prepositions
4. Five adverbs that sometimes interrupt verb phrases

Written Exercises

A. 1. Herons eat frogs and little fish, and (but) ducks eat various water plants.
2. Lizards have scales, but (and) newts have soft, moist skin.
3. Keep the windows closed, or the mosquitoes will come inside.
4. Karen was bitten by many mosquitoes, and now she is miserable.

B. 1. sky | is growing __and__ it | will rain

2. Aunt Rachel | visited __and__ we | had

3. He | had studied __yet__ he | could say

4. boys | took __and__ they | released

C. (If students have trouble with this, tell them to copy, underline, and divide as noted in Part A of Class Practice.)
1. S + S | V = simple sentence
2. S | V + S | V = compound sentence
3. S + S | V = simple sentence
4. S | V + S | V = compound sentence
5. S | V + V = simple sentence
6. S | V + S | V = compound sentence
7. S | V + V = simple sentence
8. S | V + S | V = compound sentence
9. S + S | V = simple sentence
10. S | V + S | V = compound sentence

Review Exercises

1. (Individual answers. Noun phrases may be common or proper.)
2. am, is, are, was, were, be, been, being
   have, has, had
   do, does, did
   may, might, must
   can—could, shall—should, will—would
3. (Sample answers.) of, by, in, on, at, to, for, from, near, with
4. (Sample answers.) not, never, ever, often, hardly, still, always, usually, seldom, sometimes, swiftly, rapidly

13. The Structure of a Paragraph

You have been learning about sentences. Now you will see how sentences are put together in a meaningful way. A group of sentences working together makes a paragraph.

You can easily identify a paragraph when you see one. Its first sentence is indented about half an inch from the left margin. The other sentences follow one after the other, filling up the lines. The left margin is kept straight, and the right margin is kept as straight as possible.

Why do we divide our writing into paragraphs? We make paragraphs to separate our ideas. All the sentences in one paragraph are about one main idea. When we change to another main idea, we begin another paragraph. That way the reader knows when we are moving from one thought to another. Thus, *a paragraph is a group of sentences that all deal with a single topic.*

Most paragraphs have one sentence, called the *topic sentence,* that tells what the paragraph is about. The topic sentence is usually the first sentence in the paragraph, and it clearly states what the topic is. All the other sentences develop the topic by saying more about it.

In the following paragraph, the topic sentence is underlined.

> <u>The migration of salmon is one of the marvels of God's creation.</u> Every spring, large schools of ocean salmon swim upstream to lay their eggs in fresh water. Instinct guides them to exactly the same place year after year. At a rate of about two to four miles per day, the salmon swim upstream, leaping over waterfalls and clearing most obstacles in their path. They have been known to jump as high as twelve feet out of the water. When the eggs are laid, the salmon die soon afterward.

Lesson 13

Purpose: To teach the form and structure of a paragraph.

Oral Review:
1. In writing directions, what order should you use? (the order things are to be done)
2. Why must written directions be especially clear? (because the reader cannot ask questions if he does not understand)
3. Every story deals with a problem. Why does this make the story interesting? (Readers want to know how the problem was solved.)
4. The first part of a story tells about a problem that someone had. What does the second part of the story do? (It tells how the problem was solved.)
5. What is a sentence? (a group of words that expresses a complete thought)
6. What is a clause? (a group of words with a subject and a predicate)
7. Is every clause a sentence? (no)
8. What must a clause do in order to be a sentence? (express a complete thought)

Lesson Introduction: Why do we divide our writing into paragraphs? We could get more on a page if we would write everything without indentations. How do we decide when to start a new paragraph? After writing about five or six lines? After writing about three or four sentences?

Paragraphs are very important in our writing. We must know how to make good paragraphs if we want to write effectively.

The topic of the paragraph is *the migration of salmon*. The first sentence expresses this main idea, and all the other sentences tell more about the migration of salmon.

Now look at the following paragraph. Actually, it should be two separate paragraphs because it is about two different topics. What are the two topics it develops? Where should the second paragraph begin?

Clouds are valuable to us because they protect us from the hot sun. On a very warm summer day, you have often been glad for the shade of a friendly cumulus cloud. Like a big umbrella, it gave you a few cool minutes while you were mowing the lawn or weeding the garden. Clouds also help to keep us warm. During the day, the earth soaks up heat from the sun. But at night the ground acts as a giant radiator. The heat rays leave the earth on their way to outer space. In this way the ground loses much of its heat and can become freezing cold. But if there are clouds in the night sky, they reflect the heat rays back down to the ground to heat it again.

—Adapted from *Nature Friend*

- A *paragraph* is a group of sentences that all deal with a single topic.

- The *topic sentence* of a paragraph tells what the paragraph is about.

- The first line of a paragraph is indented, and both margins are kept as straight as possible.

Class Practice

A. Answer these questions about the paragraph below.
   1. Which is the topic sentence?
   2. How many different types of houses does the writer tell you about?

People around the world live in different kinds of houses. In the tropical rain forest, they usually build their houses high up on poles to keep out snakes and animals. The roofs are thatched with leaves and grass. The walls are screens of palm fronds which allow cooling breezes to blow through. In the desert, many houses are made with thick mud walls and narrow windows. The walls absorb the heat of the sun and help to keep the house cool. At night, the thick walls gradually give up their heat and keep the house warm.

Lesson 13 Answers
Class Practice
A. 1. the first sentence (*People around the world live in different kinds of houses.*)
   2. two (houses in tropical rain forests and houses in deserts)

Lesson Outline:
  1. A paragraph has a definite form.
    a. The first sentence is indented about half an inch from the left margin.
    b. The other sentences follow one after the other, filling up the lines.
    c. The left margin is kept straight, and the right margin is kept as straight as possible. (*Teacher:* It is not mentioned in the lesson, but this would be a good time to emphasize to your pupils that they must divide words only between syllables.)

  2. A paragraph is a group of sentences that all deal with a single topic.
    a. All the sentences in one paragraph are about the same main idea.
    b. When we change to another main idea, we begin another paragraph.

  3. The topic sentence of a paragraph tells what the paragraph is about.
    a. The topic sentence is usually the first sentence in the paragraph. It clearly states what the topic is.
    b. All the other sentences develop the topic by saying more about it.

B. Read the three topic sentences and the rest of the paragraph below them. Decide which of the three would make the best topic sentence, and tell why the others are not suitable.
   a. The beaver has an interesting and useful tail.
   b. The tails of some animals are interesting and useful.
   c. The beaver uses his tail to steer when he swims.

   It is stiff and flat, and it looks like a paddle. It is about twelve inches long, six to seven inches wide, and three-fourths inch thick. A small part of the tail nearest the beaver's body has the same kind of fur as the body. The rest of the tail is covered with black, scaly skin and has only a few stiff hairs. The beaver uses his tail to steer when he swims. The tail is also used as a prop when the animal stands on his hind legs to eat or to cut down trees. When there is danger, a beaver slaps his tail on the water to make a loud noise and warn other beavers.

Written Exercises

A. Read the three topic sentences, and choose the best one for the rest of the paragraph below them.
   a. The orchard worker has many tasks to do in the spring.
   b. A farmer has many jobs to keep him busy.
   c. A fruit farmer has much work to do before he gets a harvest of fruit.

   In early spring he must prune his trees. He cuts out much healthy wood and any that is broken or diseased. After the trees are pruned, he must begin spraying them. Each year he sprays his trees at least four to six times. Once the fruit begins to grow, the orchard worker goes along and pulls some of the fruit from the tree. This thinning is necessary so that the remaining fruit will grow larger. Finally the worker picks the ripe fruit.

B. Use one of these topic sentences to begin a paragraph of your own. Complete the paragraph with sentences that tell more about the topic.
   1. A farmer's work may change from season to season, but he always has things to do.
   2. Pets often do strange and amusing things.
   3. Young people sometimes fail to appreciate the blessings of having an older brother or sister.

B. Best topic sentence: a
   Sentence *b* is too broad. It refers to "the tails of some animals," whereas the paragraph speaks only of the beaver's tail.
   Sentence *c* is too narrow. It refers to only one use of the beaver's tail, whereas the paragraph describes several uses.

Written Exercises

A. Best topic sentence: c

B. (Individual work.)

Lesson 11, Written Exercises *(continued)*

15.

16.

17.

18.

19.

20.

4. Earthworms, the smallest cultivators, are the farmer's friend.
5. St. Bernard dogs have helped man in important ways.
6. The habits of hummingbirds are interesting to study.

Review Exercises

Rewrite and improve the following directions. [8]

First, bore a hole in a maple tree. Hang a bucket on a spout to catch the sap. Before that, put a metal spout into the hole you made. After you have several gallons of sap, boil the sap down until you have maple syrup. Gather the sap every day for several days. Try your delicious treat on pancakes for breakfast. It may be best to boil the sap outdoors because of the great amount of moisture that is produced.

———————————

14. Avoiding Run-on Errors

When two or three vehicles run into each other on the highway, the results can be terrible. Cars are ruined, property is damaged, and people are hurt or killed. Running sentences into each other has less serious results, but it is still undesirable.

How do sentences run into each other? This happens when two or more sentences are written together as one sentence without the proper punctuation between them. The result is called a *run-on error*. Can you see the sentences that have been run together in the following examples?

> **Run-on errors:**
> A wise son maketh a glad father a foolish son is the heaviness of his mother.
> We have not seen her, she said she would come, is she here?

In the first example, no punctuation separates the two sentences. The second example has commas between the three sentences, but the sentences are still run together improperly.

There are three ways to correct a run-on error.

1. *End the first sentence with its proper punctuation* (period, question mark, or exclamation point), *and begin the second sentence with a capital letter.*

Review Exercises

(Sample paragraph.)

First, bore a hole in a maple tree. Put a metal spout into the hole, and hang a bucket on the spout. Gather the sap every day for several days. After you have several gallons of sap, put it into a large kettle and boil it down until you have maple syrup. It may be best to boil the sap outdoors because of the great amount of moisture that is produced. Try your delicious treat on pancakes for breakfast.

———————————

6. Name the four sentence types. Give the correct end punctuation for each. (declarative, period; interrogative, question mark; imperative, period; exclamatory, exclamation point)

Written Quiz:

Write the formula for each sentence. Write whether each sentence is simple or compound.

1. A marten looks somewhat like a weasel.
2. The pine marten is fairly common in the northern Rockies and lives in northern forests around the world.
3. The marten is about two feet long, and large males weigh about two pounds.
4. Martens and squirrels live in hollow trees.

Quiz Answers:

1. S | V = simple sentence
2. S | V + V = simple sentence
3. S | V + S | V = compound sentence
4. S + S | V = simple sentence

Lesson 14

Purpose: To identify and correct run-on errors. (In this English series, the terms *run-on error* and *run-on sentence* are used interchangeably. Both refer to the same error.)

Oral Review:

1. What is a simple sentence? (a sentence with only one skeleton)
2. Can a simple sentence have both a compound subject and a compound predicate? (yes)
3. What is a compound sentence? (a sentence with two clauses, either of which can stand by itself as a simple sentence)
4. Name some common conjunctions that can be used to form compound sentences. (and, but, or, for, nor, yet)
5. How are compound sentences diagramed? (Diagram the two clauses side by side, with the conjunction on a dotted line between them.)

A wise son maketh a glad father. A foolish son is the heaviness of his mother.

We have not seen her. She said she would come. Is she here?

2. *Use a comma and a conjunction between the sentences.* This forms a compound sentence, as you studied in Lesson 12.

A wise son maketh a glad father, but a foolish son is the heaviness of his mother.

3. *Use a semicolon between the sentences.* A semicolon looks like a comma with a dot above it (;). The semicolon takes the place of both the comma and the conjunction. The following sentences are properly joined by semicolons.

It rained several inches last night; the playground is very muddy.

Laura planted the tulip bulbs; her sister watered them.

Remember the common conjunctions used in compound sentences: *and, but, or, for, nor,* and *yet.* Be sure to use both a comma and a conjunction. Simply putting commas between run-on sentences does not correct them. A comma is not strong enough to join two sentences.

Incorrect:

A wise son maketh a glad father, a foolish son is the heaviness of his mother.

Joining sentences with only a conjunction does not correct the run-on error either. Be especially careful not to write several sentences in a row, all connected with *and*s and having no commas.

Incorrect:

A wise son maketh a glad father but a foolish son is the heaviness of his mother.

We were in a hurry and Charles failed to look carefully and he almost got hit by a car.

Lesson Introduction: Read the following paragraph to the students. Read it steadily, without pausing between thoughts.

Jesus was born in Bethlehem of Judea during the reign of King Herod wise men came to the king, asking, "Where is He that is born King of the Jews we have seen His star in the East and have come to worship Him."

This paragraph is made of one long run-on sentence. How does it make you feel to listen to it? Does it make sense?

What happens when vehicles run into each other? Usually there are serious results. Vehicles need space between them to avoid trouble.

When vehicles run into each other, there is pain and confusion. People do not arrive at their destinations on time, if at all. Something similar happens when sentences run into each other. There is mental pain and confusion, and the reader does not arrive at the right conclusion very soon, if ever! Today we want to learn how to recognize and correct run-on errors.

Lesson Outline:

1. When two or more sentences are written together as one sentence without the proper punctuation between them, the result is a **run-on error.**

The weather was poor we delayed the trip.

Keep the dog in the shed, he will annoy the steers.

2. There are three ways to correct a run-on error.

(1) *Use correct end punctuation and a capital letter.*

The weather was unfavorable. We delayed the trip.

Keep the dog in the shed. He will annoy the steers.

(2) *Use a comma and a conjunction.* Be sure to use the comma and the conjunction together.

The weather was unfavorable, and we delayed the trip.

Keep the dog in the shed, for he will annoy the steers.

(3) *Use a semicolon.* A semicolon is "stronger" than a comma. It can hold two clauses together without a conjunction.

The heavens declare the glory of God; the firmament shows His handiwork.

3. The words **and, but, or, for, nor,** *and* **yet** *are common conjunctions.* Be sure to use both a comma and a conjunction. Simply putting a comma

Correct:

A wise son maketh a glad father, but a foolish son is the heaviness of his mother.

We were in a hurry, and Charles failed to look carefully. He almost got hit by a car.

There is one exception to this rule. When clauses are *very short* and *closely related,* they may be joined by a conjunction alone. The following sentences are written correctly even though they have no commas with the conjunctions.

I helped him and he helped me.

Jane wrote it and I read it.

- A *run-on error* is two or more sentences written together incorrectly.

- There are three ways to correct a run-on error.
  1. Use correct end punctuation and a capital letter.
  2. Use a comma and a conjunction.
  3. Use a semicolon.

- The words *and, but, or, for, nor,* and *yet* are common conjunctions.

- When clauses are very short and closely related, they may be joined by a conjunction alone.

Class Practice

Tell which of the following sentences have run-on errors. Tell how each one can be corrected.

1. The venders peddled their wares in the streets, the tourists bought many things.
2. In the morning there was frost on the ground by noon the weather was as warm as a summer day.
3. The food was served and it was soon gone.
4. He was short of breath he had run all the way.
5. First we picked the tea later we washed the leaves.
6. Sarah put water on the stove, she waited for it to boil.
7. Soon the water boiled, and she put the tea leaves into the kettle.
8. There may be thousands of living creatures in a drop of water we cannot see them, they are extremely small.

or a conjunction between the clauses in a run-on sentence does not correct it.

Run-on: The earth will perish God will always remain.

Incorrect: The earth will perish, God will always remain.

Incorrect: The earth will perish but God will always remain.

Correct: The earth will perish, but God will always remain.

4. When clauses are very short and closely related, they may be joined by a conjunction alone.

Wrath is cruel and anger is outrageous.

We are weak but God is mighty.

★ **EXTRA PRACTICE**

Worksheet 10 *(Avoiding Run-on Errors)*

Lesson 14 Answers
Class Practice

(Sample answers. The three methods of correcting run-on errors are interchangeable in many cases.)

1. The venders peddled their wares in the streets, and the tourists bought many things.
2. In the morning there was frost on the ground, but by noon the weather was as warm as a summer day.
3. (correct)
4. He was short of breath, for he had run all the way.
5. First we picked the tea; later we washed the leaves.
6. Sarah put water on the stove, and she waited for it to boil.
7. (correct)
8. There may be thousands of living creatures in a drop of water. We cannot see them, for they are extremely small.

9. Have you ever used a microscope, you can see many tiny things in a drop of pond water you wouldn't want to drink it!

10. There are many things to learn, the world is full of the wonders of God, we should be amazed and delighted, how wise and good He is.

Written Exercises

A. Copy these sentences, and correct the run-on errors by using periods and capital letters.

1. God created the heavens and the earth He created them by His word He made them out of nothing.

2. The stars are very large and very far away, they produce enormous amounts of light and heat like the sun.

3. Toads and frogs are not reptiles but amphibians, they begin their lives in the water they are born with gills like those of fish.

4. All insects have three body parts and six legs spiders are not insects, spiders have eight legs and are different in other ways too.

5. Fish need oxygen like all animals, they have gills rather than lungs the gills allow them to breathe underwater.

B. Correct the run-on errors in these sentences by using a comma and a suitable conjunction. You do not need to copy sentences that are correct.

1. Birds are the only animals with feathers, they have no teeth.

2. The building was small and the students were few.

3. It looked like a moving haystack it was a man carrying a load of straw down the road.

4. The altitude of Guatemala City is about five thousand feet above sea level, the altitude of La Victoria is about nine thousand feet.

5. It is hot day and night on the coast of Guatemala in the mountains it is very cool at night.

6. We took the bus for the first part of our trip, we rode for several hours.

7. The clouds parted and the sun shone through.

8. Was that noise thunder was there an explosion?

9. Have you ever used a microscope? You can see many tiny things in a drop of pond water. You wouldn't want to drink it!

10. There are many things to learn. The world is full of the wonders of God, and we should be amazed and delighted. How wise and good He is!

Written Exercises

A. 1. God created the heavens and the earth. He created them by His word. He made them out of nothing.

2. The stars are very large and very far away. They produce enormous amounts of light and heat like the sun.

3. Toads and frogs are not reptiles but amphibians. They begin their lives in the water. They are born with gills like those of fish.

4. All insects have three body parts and six legs. Spiders are not insects. Spiders have eight legs and are different in other ways too.

5. Fish need oxygen like all animals. They have gills rather than lungs. The gills allow them to breathe underwater.

B. (Conjunctions may vary, but they must be sensible.)

1. Birds are the only animals with feathers, and they have no teeth.

2. (correct)

3. It looked like a moving haystack, but it was a man carrying a load of straw down the road.

4. The altitude of Guatemala City is about five thousand feet above sea level, and the altitude of La Victoria is about nine thousand feet.

5. It is hot day and night on the coast of Guatemala, but in the mountains it is very cool at night.

6. We took the bus for the first part of our trip, and we rode for several hours.

7. (correct)

8. Was that noise thunder, or was there an explosion?

C. Correct the run-on errors in these sentences by using a semicolon. Do not copy the sentences that are correct.
1. The sky was completely dark every star had disappeared.
2. Most storm clouds form high in the sky most rain starts as snow.
3. I didn't hear the telephone ring I must have been sleeping.
4. Arcturus is bright but Sirius is brighter.
5. Find the constellation Orion look for his sword and belt.
6. Learn to recognize the poison ivy plant its leaves grow in groups of three.
7. Grandfather saw a turtle in the water I saw a mud puppy by the pond.
8. Wilson A. Bentley spent over forty years examining and photographing snowflakes he never found two snowflakes that were exactly alike.

D. Correct this run-on error in all three ways taught in the lesson.

King Jehoiakim burned the roll he did not want to hear God's words.

Review Exercises

Write sentences according to the directions below.
1. Using a verb phrase containing three verbs
2. Using a form of *be*
3. Using a proper noun phrase that names a person
4. Using a proper noun phrase that names a place
5. A declarative sentence
6. An interrogative sentence
7. An imperative sentence

---

15. Word Order in Sentences

A good writer uses variety in the word order of his sentences. This makes his writing more interesting to read, and it is clearer as well.

In *normal word order,* the complete subject comes before the complete predicate.

C. 1. The sky was completely dark; every star had disappeared.
2. Most storm clouds form high in the sky; most rain starts as snow.
3. I didn't hear the telephone ring; I must have been sleeping.
4. (correct)
5. Find the constellation Orion; look for his sword and belt.
6. Learn to recognize the poison ivy plant; its leaves grow in groups of three.
7. Grandfather saw a turtle in the water; I saw a mud puppy by the pond.
8. Wilson A. Bentley spent over forty years examining and photographing snowflakes; he never found two snowflakes that were exactly alike.

D. (Order of answers may vary.)
1. King Jehoiakim burned the roll. He did not want to hear God's words.
2. King Jehoiakim burned the roll, for he did not want to hear God's words.
3. King Jehoiakim burned the roll; he did not want to hear God's words.

Review Exercises

(Individual sentences.)

Lesson 15

Purpose: To teach *various ways that words may be arranged in sentences. (*Previous experience:* Word order in questions called inverted order.)

Teacher: In earlier grades of this course, the term *inverted* was used in a more general way than in this lesson. Pupils were told that questions have "inverted" order and must be changed to normal order for diagraming. In this lesson, *inverted* takes on a more specific meaning. By the new definition, the word order of most questions is mixed rather than inverted.

Oral Review:

1. What is a run-on error? (the mistake of writing two or more sentences together without the proper punctuation between them)
2. How can a run-on error be corrected?
   (a. Use end punctuation and a capital letter.

b. Use a comma and a conjunction.
c. Use a semicolon.)
3. Can a run-on error be corrected by simply adding a comma? (no)
4. When may the comma be omitted in a compound sentence? (when the clauses are very short and closely related)
5. What is a sentence? (a group of words that expresses a complete thought)
6. What is a fragment? (a group of words that does not express a complete thought)
7. Name the sentence type.
   a. It states a fact. (declarative)
   b. It asks a question. (interrogative)
   c. It gives a command or request. (imperative)
   d. It expresses strong feeling. (exclamatory)

Sentence with normal word order:

<u>Billowy white clouds</u> <u>sailed across the blue sky</u>.

In *inverted word order*, the complete predicate comes before the complete subject.

Sentences with inverted word order:

<u>Across the blue sky sailed</u> <u>billowy white clouds</u>.

<u>Here come</u> <u>the geese</u>!

Before diagraming a sentence with inverted word order, put it in normal word order. This makes it easier to diagram.

Inverted word order:

<u>Here come</u> <u>the geese</u>!

Normal word order:

(the geese | come Here)

In *mixed word order*, part of the predicate comes before the subject and part of the predicate comes after. Most questions have mixed word order.

Sentences with mixed word order:

<u>Across the blue sky</u>, <u>billowy white clouds</u> <u>were sailing</u>.

<u>Then away</u> <u>he</u> <u>ran toward home</u>.

<u>Where can</u> <u>wisdom</u> <u>be found</u>?

In the first sentence above, the adverb phrase *Across the blue sky* is part of the predicate, but it comes before the subject. In the second sentence, the adverbs *Then* and *away* modify the verb, but they come before the subject. In the question, the adverb *Where* and the helping verb *can* come before the subject.

To tell quickly if a sentence has normal, inverted, or mixed word order, find the complete subject. Then see if the complete subject comes at the beginning, at the end, or in the middle.

Normal: <u>Two blind men</u> sat beside the road.
Inverted: Beside the road sat <u>two blind men</u>.
Mixed: Beside the road <u>two blind men</u> sat.

Lesson Introduction: How would you like it if everyone on your street had exactly the same kind of house? Suppose everyone's house was the same color, had the same shape, and was alike in almost every detail. You might say, "How boring that would be!"

Sentences can be the same way. If all the sentences in a paragraph or story are written in the same pattern, the writing will not be very appealing. Learn how to use variety in your writing by learning about different kinds of word order in sentences.

Lesson Outline:

1. In normal word order, *the complete subject comes before the complete predicate.*

<u>Chipmunks</u> <u>store seeds in their burrows for the winter</u>.

2. In inverted word order, *the complete predicate comes before the complete subject.*

<u>Away scampered</u> <u>the chipmunk</u>.

Before diagraming a sentence with inverted word order, put it in normal word order. This makes it easier to diagram.

(the chipmunk <u>scampered Away</u>)

<u>chipmunk | scampered</u>

3. In mixed word order, *part of the predicate comes before the subject and part of it comes after.* This is called mixed word order because it is partly normal (subject before predicate) and partly

Compare the following two paragraphs. They both give the same information, but the second paragraph is much more interesting because it has good sentence variety.

Without sentence variety:

Lightning is interesting to study. Lightning strikes somewhere on the earth about one hundred times per second. It strikes the Empire State Building many times each year, but it is conducted harmlessly to the ground by its steel structure. Lightning travels about twenty thousand miles per second. A bolt of lightning may be five times hotter than the surface of the sun. A single stroke of lightning may have fifteen million volts.

With sentence variety:

What do you know about lightning? Did you know that lightning strikes somewhere on earth about one hundred times every second? It strikes the Empire State Building many times each year, but it is conducted harmlessly to the ground by the steel structure. Down streaks the lightning, traveling about twenty thousand miles per second! A single bolt of lightning may be five times hotter than the surface of the sun, and it may have fifteen million volts.

- In a sentence with normal word order, the complete subject comes before the complete predicate.

- In a sentence with inverted word order, the complete predicate comes before the complete subject.

- In a sentence with mixed word order, part of the predicate comes before the subject and part of the predicate comes after. Most questions have mixed word order.

Class Practice

A. Tell whether the word order in these sentences is *inverted* or *mixed*. Read them in normal word order. Diagram the sentence skeletons at the chalkboard.
1. Across the stream the boys could see the excited steers.
2. Into the narrow crack slipped the startled beetles.
3. With his hammer, Father carefully pulled each nail.

inverted (predicate before subject). Most questions have mixed word order.

> In the tree a squirrel sat.
> Was Queen Esther a Jew?
> What hast thou done?

Discuss and give practice with the method for quickly determining the word order of a sentence. It is based on the fact that the complete subject is always a block of words uninterrupted by any words from the predicate. Underlining the complete subject is especially helpful for showing what the word order is. Also read the two sample paragraphs, and compare individual sentences to show the differences in word order.

★ **EXTRA PRACTICE**
Worksheet 11 *(Word Order in Sentences)*

Lesson 15 Answers
Class Practice

A. 1. mixed; The boys could see the excited steers across the stream.

  boys | could see

2. inverted; The startled beetles slipped into the narrow crack.

  beetles | slipped

3. mixed; Father carefully pulled each nail with his hammer.

  Father | pulled

4. In the window hung a small sign.
5. Can you see the highway from the roof?
6. Down poured the rain.
7. Kindly and tenderly Jesus spoke to the children.
8. Faithful and true are all His sayings.

B. Read the following sentences, changing them to mixed word order. Also change number 6 to inverted order.

> **Example:** The water rose rapidly after the storm.
> **Answer:**   After the storm, the water rose rapidly.

1. We will study mammals tomorrow.
2. A huge black cat was peering into the window.
3. We shall search again in the morning.
4. Jesus answered the man's question with authority and clarity.
5. The rich young ruler walked sadly away.
6. A bitter wind blew across the bare fields.

Written Exercises

A. Write *normal, inverted,* or *mixed* to tell in what order each sentence is written. Diagram the skeleton of each sentence.
1. Across the river we could see the blaze.
2. Here come the boys.
3. The turtle struggled clumsily up the steep bank.
4. Was the lion in that cave?
5. Around the high walls of Jericho the Israelites marched.
6. In his tent door sat Abraham.
7. Sarah made cakes on the hearth.
8. At the door stood some visitors.

B. Rewrite these sentences, changing their word order. Write *I* or *M* to tell whether your sentence has inverted or mixed word order.
1. The hikers found a tiny stone hut yesterday.
2. I cannot see without this flashlight.
3. The deer's tails went up.
4. They ran away then.
5. The wind blew with great force.
6. An ancient building stood near the top of the hill.
7. I will trust Thee forever.

B. 1. M; Yesterday the hikers found a tiny stone hut.
2. M; Without this flashlight I cannot see.
3. I; Up went the deer's tails.
4. M; Then away they ran.
   or M; Then they ran away.
   or M; Away they ran then.
5. M; With great force the wind blew.
6. M; Near the top of the hill an ancient building stood.
   or I; Near the top of the hill stood an ancient building.
7. M; Forever I will trust Thee.
   or M; Forever will I trust Thee.

4. inverted; A small sign hung in the window.

sign	hung

5. mixed; You can see the highway from the roof.

you	Can see

6. inverted; The rain poured down.

rain	poured

7. mixed; Jesus spoke kindly and tenderly to the children.

Jesus	spoke

8. inverted; All His sayings are faithful and true.

sayings	are

B. 1. Tomorrow we will study mammals.
2. Into the window a huge black cat was peering.
3. In the morning we shall search again.
4. With authority and clarity Jesus answered the man's question.
5. Sadly the rich young ruler walked away.
6. Across the bare fields a bitter wind blew.
   Across the bare fields blew a bitter wind.

Written Exercises

A. 1. mixed | we | could see |

2. inverted | boys | come |

3. normal | turtle | struggled |

4. mixed | lion | was |

5. ~~mixed~~ *inverted* | Israelites | marched |

6. inverted | Abraham | sat |

7. normal | Sarah | made |

8. inverted | visitors | stood |

C. All the sentences in this paragraph are in normal word order. Rewrite the paragraph, changing at least three sentences to inverted or mixed word order.

> Mother told Philip to bring some jars from the basement one day. He hurried to the steep, narrow stairs and started down. He found himself at the bottom about one second later. He had slid down the stairs on his back, banging his elbows on every step! Philip did not break any bones, but his elbows were very sore. He will not be in such a hurry after this.

Review Exercises

Read each group of words. If it is a complete sentence, write *declarative, interrogative, imperative,* or *exclamatory,* and write the correct end punctuation. If it is not a complete sentence, write *fragment.* [1, 7]

1. Did you ever wish you were as free as a bird
2. Do birds have chores to do
3. Yes, indeed, they do
4. They must build nests
5. Go and watch a pair of birds feeding their young
6. Cleaning, building, repairing, and many other jobs
7. What a blessing it is if children have regular chores to do
8. Prepared for a life of useful service

----

16. Unity and Coherence in a Paragraph

A paragraph is a group of sentences that develops a single topic. The topic sentence, usually the first sentence in the paragraph, gives a clear statement of what the topic is. All the other sentences support the topic sentence and say more about the topic.

When all the sentences in a paragraph tell about the same topic, the paragraph has *unity*. All the ideas fit together as one unit. But if a paragraph includes sentences that are about different topics, it no longer sticks to one main idea and its unity is broken. This makes the writing hard to understand. Imagine the reader's confusion if someone wrote a paragraph like this one.

Lesson 16

Purpose: (1) To teach unity in paragraphs. (2) To define *coherence in paragraphs, and to teach one way of achieving coherence. (*Previous experience:* Unity in paragraphs, and the order of time or importance without use of the term *coherence.*)

Oral Review:

1. What is a paragraph? (a group of sentences that all deal with a single topic)
2. What form does every paragraph have? (The first sentence is indented about half an inch from the left margin. The other sentences follow one after the other, filling up the lines. The left margin is kept straight, and the right margin is kept as straight as possible.)
3. What is a topic sentence? (the sentence that tells what a paragraph is about)

C. (Sample paragraph. Repositioned words and phrases are underlined.)

> <u>One day</u> Mother told Philip to bring some jars from the basement. He hurried to the steep, narrow stairs and started down. <u>About one second later</u> he found himself at the bottom. He had slid down the stairs on his back, banging his elbows on every step! Philip did not break any bones, but his elbows were very sore. <u>After this</u> he will not be in such a hurry.

Review Exercises

1. interrogative **?** (question mark)
2. interrogative **?** (question mark)
3. declarative . (period)
   or exclamatory **!** (exclamation point)
4. declarative . (period)
5. imperative . (period)
6. fragment
7. exclamatory **!** (exclamation point)
8. fragment

----

4. How can you vary your sentences to keep them interesting? (Vary their lengths and beginnings. Use the four different types of sentences. Use sentences with different kinds of word order: normal, inverted, and mixed.)
5. In writing directions, what order should you use? (the order that things are to be done)

Lesson Introduction: Discuss what it means when a group of people has unity. For example, at a barn raising, every worker has one purpose: to get a barn built. They all work together with that purpose in mind, and sometimes a whole barn is completed in one day! But suppose there were no unity. If some people would bring things to sell, and most of the others would simply want to visit with their friends, little or no building would get done in that case.

Our house is very large. It has fourteen rooms in all. Five of them are bedrooms. Three years ago we repaired our front porch. We have a large basement where we can play games and store our canned food. Even the attic has lots of room for storage. The kitchen is painted green and the family room is blue. This spring Father replaced several windows. We have a green bathroom. Even though our house is large, we like it because it is warm and cozy in the winter.

The topic sentence says, "Our house is very large." The next two sentences are about that topic, but the fourth sentence talks about repairing the front porch. That has nothing to do with having a large house! The next two sentences again show that the house is large because it has extra room in the attic and in the basement. But then the paragraph talks about a green kitchen, a blue family room, and replacing windows. If the writer wants to tell the reader about those other things, he may do so in other paragraphs. But he must not put these unrelated ideas into a paragraph about the size of his house.

Now find one sentence that should be taken out of the following paragraph because it spoils the unity.

The nest building of the friendly, fluttering barn swallow has excited stable boys for thousands of years. These swooping birds bring pellets of dark, wet mud and skillfully trowel them onto the lighter-colored masonry that has dried from the day before. Who taught these aerial acrobats to choose a beam high above the cats and cattle of the barn, and to plaster their mud-and-straw nest securely to it? Cats do prowl in barns, and they would think it a feast to eat barn swallows, young or old! The reinforced stucco dwelling is completed in less than a week. Then the birds cushion the nest with soft grass and feathers and lay their five perfect eggs in it. Soon it is the home of their noisy, demanding, ever-hungry babies.

—Adapted from *Nature Friend*

The sentence about cats prowling in barns does not belong in this paragraph. It does not tell about the nest building of barn swallows.

Coherence means "holding together." A coherent paragraph is one in which all the details fit together well so that the reader does not get lost or confused. There are at least three ways to make your paragraphs "hold together." You will study one way in this lesson and two more ways in the next lesson.

Introduce the term *coherence*. This is the idea of having logical connections between thoughts. Someone who is delirious may speak in a disconnected, incoherent way: "I got the handle now…try to pull harder… looks like we broke it…" A paragraph must have unity and coherence in order to convey a clear, meaningful message.

Lesson Outline:

1. A paragraph is a group of sentences that develops a single topic.

2. The topic sentence, usually the first sentence in the paragraph, gives a clear statement of what the topic is. All the other sentences support the topic sentence and say more about the topic.

3. When all the sentences in a paragraph tell about the topic given by the topic sentence, the paragraph has unity.

4. When all the details in a paragraph fit together well so that the reader does not get lost or confused, the paragraph has coherence. *Coherence* means "holding together."

5. One way to make a paragraph coherent is to give details in the order of time. In a story, tell things in the order they took place. In a set of directions, give things in the order they are to be done.

Give details in the order of time. Whenever you write about something that happened, tell things in the order they took place. If the order is mixed up, you might still know what you mean—but think of your poor reader! Make it easy for him. Show what was done *first*, what came *next*, what happened *after that*, and so on until everything is described.

The following two examples show how important it is to tell things in the order of time.

Paragraph with details in confusing order:

Jesus sent two disciples to bring a certain colt on which no man had ever sat. They found the colt, brought it to Jesus, and cast their garments on it. As the disciples untied it, the owners of the colt asked what they were doing. The disciples explained as Jesus had commanded them. They had found the colt tied by a door. The owners willingly let the disciples take it. So into Jerusalem went Jesus, riding on the colt.

Paragraph with details in correct order of time:

Jesus sent two disciples to bring a certain colt on which no man had ever sat. They found the colt tied by a door. As the disciples untied it, the owners of the colt asked what they were doing. The disciples explained as Jesus had commanded them. The owners willingly let the disciples take the colt. They brought it to Jesus and cast their garments on it. So into Jerusalem went Jesus, riding on the colt.

- A paragraph has unity when all the sentences tell about the topic given by the topic sentence.

- A paragraph has coherence when the sentences fit together in an orderly, sensible way.

- One way to make a paragraph coherent is to give details in the order of time.

Class Practice

A. Tell which sentences spoil the unity of this paragraph.

The Hittites were a nation in Asia Minor as early as 2000 B.C. But they disappeared from history, and in time even their name was forgotten. The Old Testament speaks of the Hittites in several different places. They are mentioned along with the Canaanites, Hivites, and Jebusites. Unbelievers laughed and said the Hittites had never existed. But in 1871 someone discovered a buried city which proved that there had indeed been a Hittite nation. People have also found an inscription that mentions Ahab, king of Israel. Later findings gave even more evidence of the ancient Hittites. These discoveries have helped to confirm that God's Word is perfectly true.

B. Tell which sentence below is the topic sentence. Tell in what order the other sentences should be written according to the order of time.
   1. So he asked to buy the cave of Machpelah, which belonged to Ephron.
   2. Abraham paid the price that Ephron quoted.
   3. Abraham had dealings with a Hittite named Ephron.
   4. At first Ephron offered to give the cave to Abraham, but later he said it was worth four hundred shekels of silver.
   5. Then a record was made, clearly stating that the cave, the field, and the trees in the field were now Abraham's property.
   6. When Sarah died, Abraham needed a burial place for her.

Written Exercises

A. Write the sentences that spoil the unity of this paragraph.

The Roman Empire helped to prepare the world for Christ's coming. Under the Romans, almost half of the known world at that time was united peacefully. America, of course, was unknown in those days. The Romans built many roads through the empire, which were a great help in spreading the Gospel. Most people in the Roman Empire understood Greek, so the first missionaries could preach in many different cities without having to learn new languages. The Greek language had been introduced by the Greeks, who ruled the world before the Romans. The Romans were no longer satisfied with their pagan gods, and this helped prepare them to hear the Gospel. Truly, God was directing the events of history according to His plan.

Lesson 16 Answers
Class Practice

A. *Sentences that do not belong:*
   They are mentioned along with the Canaanites, Hivites, and Jebusites.
   People have also found an inscription that mentions Ahab, king of Israel.

B. Topic sentence: number 3
   Correct order of other sentences: 6, 1, 4, 2, 5

Written Exercises

A. *Sentences that do not belong:*
   America, of course, was unknown in those days.
   The Greek language had been introduced by the Greeks, who ruled the world before the Romans.

B. Use these sentences to write a paragraph in the proper form. Find the topic sentence, and write it first. Then write the other sentences in the correct order.
1. Next, catch the dog!
2. Washing a dog is not hard if you do it right.
3. Then dry him with a clean, dry towel.
4. Let him shake himself and run free again.
5. Put him into the water, and hold him tightly as you soap and scrub him.
6. Then get your other supplies.
7. First, get a tub the right size and put warm water into it.

B.   Washing a dog is not hard if you do it right. First, get a tub the right size and put warm water into it. Then get your other supplies. Next, catch the dog! Put him into the water, and hold him tightly as you soap and scrub him. Then dry him with a clean, dry towel. Let him shake himself and run free again.

2, 7, 6, 1, 5, 3, 4

17. More About Coherence

You have learned that a paragraph has *unity* when all the sentences tell about a single topic. It has *coherence* when the sentences "hold together" in an orderly, sensible way. You know that one way to make paragraphs coherent is to give details in the order of time. Now you are ready to learn two more ways of gaining coherence in paragraphs.

Give details in the order of importance or interest. When details are arranged in this way, they are usually given from the least important or interesting to the most important or interesting. This allows the writer to put the strongest point last, where the reader will be most likely to remember it. The following paragraph is written in this kind of order.

Details arranged from least important to most important:

There are several good reasons for learning a language besides English. One reason is to learn how languages compare with each other, and to discover new and interesting ways of saying things. Every language has its own peculiar expressions, and they cannot always be translated into English. A second reason is so that you can communicate with people who do not know English. Above all, knowing a second language is important for sharing the Gospel with people who speak that language.

Lesson 17

Purpose: To teach two more ways of achieving coherence in paragraphs. (*Previous experience:* Order of time or importance, but no use of the term *transitional words.*)

Oral Review:
1. When does a paragraph have (*a*) unity? (*b*) coherence? (*a*. when all the sentences tell about the topic given by the topic sentence; *b*. when the sentences "hold together" in an orderly, sensible way)
2. What is one way to have coherence in a paragraph? (by writing details in the order of time)
3. Name and describe three different kinds of word order that sentences may have. (normal—complete subject before complete predicate; inverted—complete predicate before complete subject; mixed—part of predicate before subject and part of it after subject)
4. What is a run-on error? (the mistake of writing two or more sentences together with no punctuation or only a comma between them)
5. Give three ways to correct this sentence: *Yesterday it was raining today it is snowing.* (Use a period and a capital letter. Use a comma and the conjunction *but* or *and.* Use a semicolon.)

Lesson Introduction: Suppose your teacher told you that tomorrow your class will discuss Lesson 7 in history class. So you study Lesson 7 well, and you are prepared to discuss it in class. But when you get to class, you find that the teacher changed his mind and decided to give the chapter test instead. You fail miserably because you were not prepared for the test.

Or perhaps your friend invited you to go for a hike in the woods. When you arrive, you discover that he changed his mind and decided to take you visiting

A paragraph may also give details from the most important or interesting to the least important or interesting. But this is not as good, because it gives less emphasis to the strongest point. Compare the following paragraph with the previous sample.

Details arranged from most important to least important:
> There are several good reasons for learning a language besides English. Most important, knowing a second language makes it possible to share the Gospel with people who speak that language. A second reason is so that you can communicate with people who do not know English. It is also valuable to learn how languages compare with each other, and to discover new and interesting ways of saying things. Every language has its own peculiar expressions, and they cannot always be translated into English.

Use transitional words. These are words or phrases that show how sentences are related to each other. They act as signals to tell the reader what direction the next sentence will go. Various transitional words are used to show various kinds of relationships. Some of them are listed below.

Time: first, second, next, then, finally
> The potter dropped a lump of clay on the center of the wheel. <u>Then</u> he began molding it into the exact shape he wanted.

Addition: also, another, besides, again, further, moreover
> Saul had offered a sacrifice in violation of God's law. <u>Moreover</u>, he had not destroyed the Amalekites as God commanded, and he had sought advice from a witch.

Contrast: but, yet, however, still, nevertheless
> Ten spies said it was impossible to conquer Canaan. Two spies, <u>however</u>, declared that Israel was well able to take the land.

Example: for example, for instance, to illustrate
> Some mammals live in the ocean, but they still breathe air. The whale, <u>for example</u>, must come to the surface to breathe, or it will drown.

Result: therefore, thus, so, consequently, accordingly
> Christ has risen from the dead. <u>Therefore</u>, we have the hope that all Christians who die will rise to meet Him someday.

instead. How embarrassed you are to go visiting in hiking clothes! You think, "How much better it is to know what is coming so that I can be prepared!"

Of course, a Christian teacher or a true friend would never do such things. But sometimes a paragraph can do that. The topic sentence prepares your mind for what is coming next. If the sentences do not fulfill their purpose, the paragraph is hard to understand and you may be disappointed because you do not find out what you expected.

Lesson Outline:

1. A coherent paragraph is one in which all the details fit together in an orderly, sensible way. Coherent means "holding together."

2. One way to make a paragraph coherent is to give details in the order of time. This method was taught in the previous lesson.

3. A second way to make a paragraph coherent is to give details in the order of importance or interest. The details are usually arranged from the least important or interesting to the most important or interesting. This helps to build up to a climax. The strongest point is given last, where it is most likely to be remembered.

Details in a paragraph may also be arranged from the most important or interesting to the least important or interesting. But this arrangement is usually not as good, because it gives less emphasis to the strongest point. It can also produce an illogical anticlimax, as in "Hundreds of Anabaptists were killed, imprisoned, or fined."

Notice the transitional words in the following paragraph. They help you to understand how the sentences fit together.

> Rebekah had a plan to help Jacob receive the blessing instead of Esau. She had heard Isaac telling Esau to take his weapons and hunt venison. <u>Then</u> Esau had left with his quiver and bow. Rebekah quickly commanded Jacob to fetch two kids from the flock. <u>So</u> Jacob went to bring the kids. Rebekah prepared the meat, and Jacob took it in to Isaac. <u>But first</u> Isaac tried to make sure that this was really Esau. <u>Finally</u> he was convinced, and he gave Jacob the blessing. When he had just finished, <u>however,</u> Esau came in from hunting. He was bitterly disappointed that he had lost the blessing. Rebekah's scheme had worked.

- Paragraph coherence can be gained by arranging details in the order of importance or interest.

- Paragraph coherence can be gained by using transitional words.

Class Practice

A. Tell which words are transitional words in the following paragraph.

> One day in 1569, a thief catcher was pursuing an Anabaptist whose name was Dirk Willems. Dirk fled over some thin ice and got across at considerable danger. Then the thief catcher tried to follow him, but he broke through the ice. Dirk could easily have escaped to safety. He realized, however, that his enemy's life was in danger. So he turned back and helped the thief catcher to get out. For this reason the thief catcher wanted to let him go. Nevertheless, the town ruler insisted that he arrest Dirk as he had promised to do. In spite of Dirk's great kindness to his enemy, this noble man was burned at the stake because of the hatred of a wicked ruler.

Lesson 17 Answers
Class Practice

A. Then, however, So, For this reason, Nevertheless, In spite of

(*But* in the third sentence shows the relationship between clauses, not sentences. So it is a conjunction, not a transitional word.)

4. A third way to make a paragraph coherent is to use transitional words. Transitional words are words or phrases that show how sentences are related. They act as signals to tell the reader what direction the next sentence will go. Discuss the various categories of transitional words as shown in the lesson.

★ **EXTRA PRACTICE**
Worksheet 12 *(Unity and Coherence in a Paragraph)*

B. Tell whether the following sentences should be arranged in the *order
of time* or the *order of importance*. Then tell in what order they
should be written to make a coherent paragraph.

Topic sentence:

Always do your school homework in an orderly way, and you will
have little trouble being prepared for class.

1. If there is time, you may study outside information from reference books for extra interest.
2. Then, before your mind is too tired, study any lessons that take
extra concentration.
3. Last of all, clean up your work area, sharpen your pencils for the
next day, and arrange your books.
4. After that, you can do the less demanding studies, such as reading
and art.
5. First, make sure you have finished all the assignments that are
due the next morning.

B. order of importance
(Since the most important thing is done first
and the least important thing last, the sentences
would also be arranged in the order of time.)
Correct order: 5, 2, 4, 1, 3

Written Exercises

A. Write the four transitional words used in the following paragraph.

The *Martyrs Mirror* is a very worthwhile book. It contains many true stories of Christians who were tortured and killed for their faith. Another feature is the pictures of many who were martyred. The book also contains numerous letters written by suffering Christians in prison. Moreover, it has a list of all the Anabaptists who suffered persecution or martyrdom from 1525 to 1660. Finally, the *Martyrs Mirror* has several confessions of faith written by Christians of various times.

B. Use the following sentences to write a paragraph in proper form, with unity and coherence. Leave out the sentence that does not belong, and write the rest of the sentences in a logical order.
1. Put water into your pan, and light a candle.
2. Begin by folding a piece of paper in the shape of a small square pan.
3. Hold the pan in the flame.
4. Did you know that you can boil water in a paper pan?
5. Staple the corners so that water will not leak out of it.
6. The water will get hot enough to boil, but it will keep the paper from getting hot enough to burn.
7. A paper pan would not work very well for cooking food.
8. Then use string to make a handle for holding the pan over a flame.

Review Exercises

Write *normal, inverted,* or *mixed* to tell in what order each sentence is written. Diagram the skeleton of each sentence. [15]
1. That bird looks like a catbird.
2. The mockingbird is the best imitator of all birds.
3. On top of the pole the mockingbird danced and sang.
4. On a nest only a foot above the ground sat the mockingbird.
5. Some mockingbirds have imitated up to thirty bird songs in ten minutes.
6. In the nest were six eggs.
7. During the day and often at night he sings.
8. He can imitate the bark of a dog, the meow of a cat, the squeak of a dry wheel, or the whistle of a policeman!

Written Exercises

A. Another, also, Moreover, Finally

B. (Sentence 7 should be omitted.)

Did you know that you can boil water in a paper pan? Begin by folding a piece of paper in the shape of a small square pan. Staple the corners so that water will not leak out of it. Then use string to make a handle for holding the pan over a flame. Put water into your pan, and light a candle. Hold the pan in the flame. The water will get hot enough to boil, but it will keep the paper from getting hot enough to burn.

Review Exercises

1. normal   bird | looks

2. normal   mockingbird | is

3. mixed   danced
   mockingbird | and sang

4. inverted   mockingbird | sat

5. normal   mockingbirds | have imitated

6. inverted   eggs | were

7. mixed   he | sings

8. normal   He | can imitate

Challenge Exercises

Write a paragraph of your own, using a variety of sentence types: declarative, interrogative, imperative, and exclamatory. Vary the word order of your sentences: normal word order, inverted word order, and mixed word order. You may get ideas from the following topics.

1. A bird built a nest in the wren house I made.
2. In winter, you can attract a wide variety of birds to a feeder if you follow these simple steps.
3. I learned many things from my pet raccoon (or another pet) last summer.
4. There are many things to be thankful for on a rainy day.
5. The camel is an interesting creature.

---

18. Chapter 2 Review

Class Practice

A. Give six common conjunctions.

B. Diagram the sentence skeletons at the chalkboard.
1. Did you hear the crickets?
2. Crickets rub one wing over the other.
3. Listen to the beautiful night chorus.
4. How cheerful is a cricket's song!
5. Most kinds of crickets can hear.
6. Rose and Joan had swept and mopped the kitchen floor.
7. Martha was washing the dishes, broke a glass, and cut her finger.
8. Lightly and gracefully fluttered the butterfly.

C. Tell how to combine the following sentences to make compound sentences. Tell what conjunctions should be used and where commas should be placed.
1. I wanted the book. I did not have enough money.
2. The rain was pouring down. We got soaking wet.
3. Janet was reading. Carol was sewing.
4. Father went with us. We were too young to go alone.
5. They had to work. They would have no food.

Lesson 18

Purpose: To review what was taught in Chapter 2.

Challenge Exercises
(Individual paragraphs.)

Lesson 18 Answers
Class Practice

A. and, but, or, for, nor, yet

B.
1. you | Did hear
2. Crickets | rub
3. (you) | Listen
4. song | is
5. kinds | can hear
6. Rose / Joan and | had | swept / mopped and
7. Martha | was washing / broke / cut and
8. butterfly | fluttered

C. (Allow reasonable variation. No comma is needed if clauses are very short and closely related.)
1. I wanted the book, but I did not have enough money.
2. The rain was pouring down, and we got soaking wet.
3. Janet was reading and Carol was sewing.
4. Father went with us, for we were too young to go alone.
5. They had to work, or they would have no food.

D. On the chalkboard, write the formula for each sentence. Tell whether each sentence is *simple* or *compound.* Tell where commas should be added.
   1. The snapping turtle dug a hole in the bank and laid thirty eggs.
   2. A common snapping turtle may weigh twenty to thirty pounds but some giant snappers weigh sixty pounds.
   3. The common snapper and the Florida snapper closely resemble each other.
   4. An alligator snapper may weigh over two hundred pounds.
   5. A snapping turtle depends on its strong jaws for defense for it cannot retreat into its shell.

E. Tell whether each sentence is *correct* or has a *run-on error.* Tell how to correct each run-on error.
   1. We cut the sheep's wool, it was too thick for summer.
   2. Mothers give their children warm winter coats God gives the sheep warm fleece for the winter.
   3. The snowshoe rabbit has a brown coat in the summer, but in winter its fur becomes white.
   4. Some kinds of weasels change their colors they are dark in summer and white in winter a white weasel is called an ermine.

F. Tell whether each sentence has *normal, inverted,* or *mixed* word order. If a sentence has normal word order, change it to mixed order. If it has inverted or mixed word order, change it to normal order.
   1. Across the field a fox ran swiftly.
   2. In the den were seven fox pups.
   3. Through the woods rang the baying of the hounds.
   4. Carelessly the man walked in front of the den.
   5. The fox moved her pups away on the same day.
   6. She must hide her pups in a safer place.
   7. All through the season, the fox must hunt food for the pups.
   8. Many forest animals do their hunting at night.

G. Read the following paragraph, and decide which of the three suggestions would make the best topic sentence. Tell what is wrong with the other two.
   a. Before 1850, women used plants from the gardens and woods to make dye for cloth.

D. 1. S | V + V = simple sentence
   2. S | V + S | V = compound sentence; comma after *pounds*
   3. S + S | V = simple sentence
   4. S | V = simple sentence
   5. S | V + S | V = compound sentence; comma after *defense*

E. (Sample answers.)
   1. run-on error; We cut the sheep's wool, for it was too thick for summer.
   2. run-on error; Mothers give their children warm winter coats, but (and) God gives the sheep warm fleece for the winter.
   3. correct
   4. run-on error; Some kinds of weasels change their colors; they are dark in summer and white in winter. A white weasel is called an ermine.

F. 1. mixed; A fox ran swiftly across the field.
   2. inverted; Seven fox pups were in the den.
   3. inverted; The baying of the hounds rang through the woods.
   4. mixed; The man walked carelessly in front of the den.
   5. normal; On the same day the fox moved her pups away.
   6. normal; In a safer place she must hide her pups.
   7. mixed; The fox must hunt food for the pups all through the season.
   8. normal; At night many forest animals do their hunting.

b. Before 1850, women used red sumac berries from the woods to make dye for cloth.

c. Before 1850, women used plants from the gardens and woods to do many household jobs.

Yellow goldenrod flowers were used to make yellow dye. Carrots also made a nice yellow. Spinach produced a green color, and beets worked fine for rose. Red sumac berries turned the cloth red, while the leaves made a fine black. If a woman needed purple cloth, she dug up the roots of dandelions. Dye was not available from stores in those days, so the people found ways to make it themselves.

H. Tell which sentences do not belong in the following paragraph.

The fruit of the apple tree gives us many delicious things. Imagine salad and some other foods without vinegar! Think of a cold drink of apple cider on a hot summer day! Try an apple in your lunch with peanut butter in the hole where you took out the core. Peanut butter icing on chocolate cake is good in your lunch too. Put apple butter on a piece of homemade bread. Doesn't the thought of apple pie and apple dumplings make your mouth water? And what would a baby do without applesauce! Of course, other kinds of baby food are also important. We know the apple is one more good thing God made for us to use right and enjoy.

I. Tell which sentence is the topic sentence. Tell in what order the other sentences should be written.

1. She hung the cloth out to dry, and finally her long, hard job was finished.
2. The next day she boiled the plant material slowly for one hour. Next, she strained the mixture to remove all the plant material.
3. Dyeing cloth in pioneer days was hard work.
4. Then she had to chop up the plant parts and soak them in water overnight.
5. First, the woman had to gather the leaves, berries, or roots that made the color of dye she wanted.
6. She added alum to prevent fading. Then she put some dampened fabric into the dye and simmered it slowly until the fabric was the shade she wanted.

G. Best topic sentence: a

Sentence *b* is too narrow. It mentions only sumac berries, whereas the paragraph speaks of several more kinds of plants.

Sentence *c* is too broad. It refers to many household jobs, whereas the paragraph speaks only of dyeing cloth.

H. Peanut butter icing on chocolate cake is good in your lunch too.

Of course, other kinds of baby food are also important.

I. Topic sentence: 3

Order of other sentences: 5, 4, 2, 6, 1

J. Choose the topic sentence. Then tell in what order the sentences should be written, according to order of interest or importance.
1. At other times, they take an accident victim to the hospital to be treated for shock, even though he is not seriously hurt.
2. Ambulances are used for various reasons to carry sick or injured people.
3. Then there are the helicopter ambulances, which rush a severely injured person to a hospital where specialists work on him immediately to save his life.
4. Sometimes they simply transport a sick person from one place to another.
5. An ambulance may rush a person to the hospital when he is critically ill, such as when he just had a heart attack.

K. Find the transitional words in this paragraph.

Parrots are popular as pets. They are easy to tame, and they can learn to talk. Parrots can also imitate other sounds. For example, they can whistle tunes, sing songs, laugh, and cry. They can even mimic the sound of a squeaky hinge! However, parrots may carry a disease that can affect humans. For this reason all parrots must be examined by a health official before being shipped to the United States.

Written Exercises

A. Diagram the sentence skeletons.
1. Some people in Asia keep crickets as pets.
2. Rich people keep their crickets in tiny gold cages and carry them around with them.
3. Their "ears" are located on their front legs.
4. Count the number of chirps in a minute.
5. Add forty to the number, divide by four, and then add fifty.
6. Now you can tell the temperature in degrees Fahrenheit.
7. Grant Marshall did have a pet cricket.
8. Bees, ants, and crickets are insects.
9. In the fall, crickets sometimes move into homes, hide somewhere, and sing cheerfully all night long.
10. The aardvark is an interesting animal.
11. Dutch settlers in Africa named it in the 1600s.
12. Does its name mean "earth pig"?
13. It has a snout like that of a pig, but it does not resemble a pig in other ways.

J. Topic sentence: 2
Order of other sentences: 4, 1, 5, 3

K. also, For example, even, However, For this reason

Written Exercises

A. 1. people | keep

2. people | keep / and \ carry

3. "ears" | are located

4. (you) | Count

5. (you) | Add / and / divide / add

6. you | can tell

7. Grant Marshall | did have

8. Bees, ants, crickets | and | are

9. crickets | move / and / hide / sing

10. aardvark | is

11. settlers | named

12. name | Does mean

13. It | has -- but -- it | does resemble

14. The aardvark is not fierce, but it can slash with its claws.
15. With its sharp claws, the aardvark slashes open ant and termite nests, and with its eighteen-inch sticky tongue, it licks them up.
16. Swiftly and silently flew the migrating birds.

B. Combine these simple sentences to make compound sentences by using a comma and a suitable conjunction.
 1. Most parrots build nests in the holes of trees. Some dig burrows in the ground.
 2. One of the largest parrots is the yellow-headed amazon. One of the smallest is the white-fronted amazon.
 3. The yellow-headed amazon is fifteen inches long. The white-fronted amazon is only ten inches long.
 4. I heard a boy whistle. Maybe it was the parrot.

C. Write the formula for each sentence, and write whether it is *simple* or *compound*. Also write the words that should have commas after them, and add the missing commas.
 1. The picky parrot tasted his food and then would not eat it.
 2. The chickadees and woodpeckers stopped at the suet and nibbled little pieces.
 3. Downy woodpeckers eat only the suet but the chickadees and nuthatches eat the suet and seeds.
 4. The lovely purple finches eat hungrily at the feeder.
 5. Mother put the seeds into the feeder and Brian watched the birds come.
 6. Cardinals, purple finches, and evening grosbeaks have heavy beaks and they can easily crack seeds with them.

D. Correct the run-on errors in the following sentences by using periods and capital letters.
 1. Michigan is the only state that touches four of the five Great Lakes Michigan has eleven thousand lakes it is the only state that is divided into two parts.
 2. Crater Lake in Oregon is the deepest lake in the United States it is 1,982 feet deep and is at the top of an inactive volcano.
 3. New York City is the largest city in the United States it is the largest, busiest port in the nation people come from all over the world to see it.

14. aardvark | is _ _but_ _ _ it | can slash
15. aardvark | slashes _and_ _ it | licks
16. birds | flew

B. (Some conjunctions may vary.)
 1. Most parrots build nests in the holes of trees, but some dig burrows in the ground.
 2. One of the largest parrots is the yellow-headed amazon, and one of the smallest is the white-fronted amazon.
 3. The yellow-headed amazon is fifteen inches long, but the white-fronted amazon is only ten inches long.
 4. I heard a boy whistle, or maybe it was the parrot.

C. 1. S | V + V = simple
 2. S + S | V + V = simple
 3. S | V + S + S | V = compound; suet,
 4. S | V = simple
 5. S | V + S | V = compound; feeder,
 6. S + S + S | V + S | V = compound; beaks,
 (The first + may be omitted.)

D. 1. Michigan is the only state that touches four of the five Great Lakes. Michigan has eleven thousand lakes. It is the only state that is divided into two parts.
 2. Crater Lake in Oregon is the deepest lake in the United States. It is 1,982 feet deep and is at the top of an inactive volcano.
 3. New York City is the largest city in the United States. It is the largest, busiest port in the nation. People come from all over the world to see it.

E. Correct the run-on errors in these sentences by using a comma and a suitable conjunction.
   1. New Jersey is the fifth smallest state in the United States it has the largest number of people per square mile.
   2. The Erie Canal was built from Lake Erie to the Hudson River it was opened in 1825.
   3. Mules pulled barges in the early days of canals today tugboats pull large ships.

F. Correct the run-on error in each sentence by using a semicolon.
   1. Maine is the farthest east of all the states people in Maine can see the sun rise before anyone else in the United States.
   2. The Pilgrims landed at Plymouth, Massachusetts, in 1620 they held their first Thanksgiving feast in 1621.
   3. John Adams was the second president of the United States his son John Quincy Adams was the sixth president of the United States.

G. Write *normal, inverted,* or *mixed* to tell in what order each sentence is written.
   1. Early settlers in the Midwest built their houses of sod.
   2. On the Great Plains grew much grass but few trees.
   3. Since that time, people have planted many trees there.
   4. Which trees grow best on the Great Plains?
   5. Today many aspens, pines, and oaks grow in the Midwest.

H. Write the sentences that do not belong in this paragraph.

   Big cities that grew up overnight in the West became small villages almost as quickly. One example is Virginia City in the dry state of Nevada. In 1859 someone discovered the Comstock Lode in Nevada, which had great amounts of gold and silver mixed together. Thousands of people rushed to Nevada, and Virginia City grew up overnight. There is also a state called Virginia. More than 300 million dollars' worth of gold and silver was taken out. But soon most of the treasure was gone, people drifted away, and Virginia City became a village. Gold had been found in nearby California about ten years earlier.

E. 1. New Jersey is the fifth smallest state in the United States, but it has the largest number of people per square mile.
   2. The Erie Canal was built from Lake Erie to the Hudson River, and it was opened in 1825.
   3. Mules pulled barges in the early days of canals, but today tugboats pull large ships.

F. 1. Maine is the farthest east of all the states; people in Maine can see the sun rise before anyone else in the United States.
   2. The Pilgrims landed at Plymouth, Massachusetts, in 1620; they held their first Thanksgiving feast in 1621.
   3. John Adams was the second president of the United States; his son John Quincy Adams was the sixth president of the United States.

G. 1. normal
   2. inverted
   3. mixed
   4. normal
   5. mixed

H. There is also a state called Virginia.
   Gold had been found in nearby California about ten years earlier.

I. Write the numbers of the following sentences in the correct order to make a good paragraph. Begin with the topic sentence, which lists farm products in the order of importance. Then put the other sentence numbers in that order.

1. Millions of beef cattle are raised on huge ranches in the West.
2. The wheat-growing region extends across the Great Plains.
3. The most important farm products of the United States, in order of value, are beef cattle, milk, corn, soybeans, hogs, wheat, and cotton.
4. Almost all the country's cotton is raised in the South, the Southwest, and the state of California.
5. The nation's corn, soybeans, and hogs are produced in the Midwestern states.
6. Most of the milk is produced in the dairy belt, which extends from Minnesota to New York.

J. Write these sentences in paragraph form. Put the sentences in the correct order, beginning with the topic sentence. Add the following transitional words at suitable places: *First, Then, Finally.*

1. Keep watering it once or twice a week for a while so that it continues to do well.
2. Find a good place for it and plant it there.
3. You may want to try planting a seedling where you can enjoy watching it grow.
4. Be sure to water your seedling so that it gets a good start.
5. Find a seedling you like in a flower bed, along a fence, or in some other place that doesn't get mowed.

I. 3, 1, 6, 5, 2, 4

J. (Sample paragraph.)

You may want to try planting a seedling where you can enjoy watching it grow. <u>First</u> find a seedling you like in a flower bed, along a fence, or in some other place that doesn't get mowed. <u>Then</u> find a good place for it and plant it there. Be sure to water your seedling so that it gets a good start. <u>Finally,</u> keep watering it once or twice a week for a while so that it continues to do well.

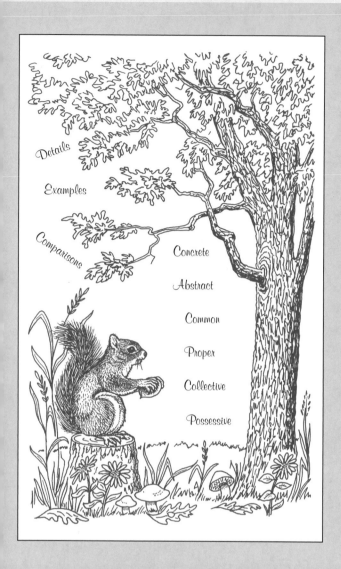

Details

Examples

Comparisons

Concrete

Abstract

Common

Proper

Collective

Possessive

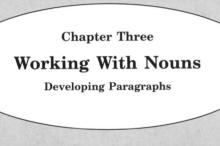

Chapter Three

Working With Nouns

Developing Paragraphs

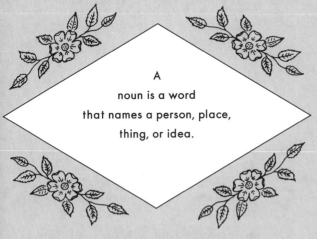

A
noun is a word
that names a person, place,
thing, or idea.

And whatsoever Adam called
every living creature, that was the name thereof.

Genesis 2:19

19. Recognizing Nouns

We call the things around us by their names. These names are *nouns*. *David, Chicago,* and *highway* are nouns that name a person, a place, and a thing. *Meditation, honesty,* and *illness* are nouns that name things we cannot see, but we know they exist.

A noun is a word that names a person, place, thing, or idea. The nouns in the following sentences are underlined.

> The <u>stranger</u> from the <u>city</u> bought <u>carrots</u> and <u>beans</u> from the <u>children</u> at the <u>booth</u>.
> The <u>harvest</u> of <u>soybeans</u> in <u>Indiana</u> and <u>Illinois</u> exceeded the <u>expectation</u> of the <u>farmers</u>.

Nouns may be concrete or abstract. A *concrete noun* is the name of something you can see or touch. It names a person, place, or thing. The names for all the objects in the world around you are concrete nouns.

Concrete nouns:

ship	hill	paper	tomato
tree	house	school	pupil

An *abstract noun* is the name of something you cannot see or touch. It names a quality, a condition, or an idea—a "thing" that has no substance. Most ideas are as real as something you can hold in your hand, even though you cannot see or touch them.

Abstract nouns:

love	memory	time	condition
concern	kindness	beauty	gravity

What are some helps for recognizing nouns? Most concrete nouns are easy to recognize because they name persons or objects. Many abstract nouns can be recognized by certain suffixes, like *-ness, -ion, -ity,* or *-ment.* In each of the following pairs, the second word is a noun made by adding one of these suffixes.

holy—holiness	pure—purity
promote—promotion	require—requirement

Lesson 19

Purpose: (1) To teach the recognition of nouns, including concrete and abstract nouns. (2) To introduce the *gender of nouns.

Oral Review:

1. What is a run-on error? (the mistake of writing two or more sentences together as one sentence)
2. Give three ways that a run-on error can be corrected.
   (a. Add correct end punctuation and a capital letter.
   b. Use a comma and a conjunction.
   c. Use a semicolon.)
3. What kind of clauses can be joined with a conjunction and no comma? (clauses that are very short and closely related)
4. Tell what kind of word order is described in each sentence.
   a. The complete predicate comes before the complete subject. (inverted)
   b. The complete subject comes before the complete predicate. (normal)
   c. Part of the predicate comes before the subject, and part of the predicate comes after. (mixed)

Lesson Introduction: Tell the pupils that the names of all the things around us are nouns. Help them to give some nouns by using the following clues. (Sample nouns are given.)

Concrete nouns:
> School supplies (books, paper, pencils, chalk)
> Furniture (chairs, tables, beds, desks)
> Farm animals (horses, cows, sheep, hogs)
> Vehicles for transportation (cars, trucks, trains, airplanes)
> Countries of the world (Japan, India, France, Canada)

Abstract nouns:
> What your mother showed by making breakfast this morning (love, kindness)
> Some other things your parents show to you (patience, godliness, concern, interest)
> Several parts of the fruit of the Spirit (love, joy, peace, gentleness, goodness, meekness)

Lesson Outline:

1. A noun is a word that names a person, place, thing, or idea.

You may want to point out that pronouns also refer to persons, places, and things, but that they take the place of nouns. Remind students that pronouns are not nouns. Give some examples of pronouns: *we, they, us, them, you, it, he, she, this, these.*

Spelling changes are sometimes made when noun suffixes are added. When *holy* is changed to *holiness,* the final *y* is changed to *i.* When *promote* is changed to *promotion,* the final *e* is dropped. Use a dictionary whenever you are not sure of the correct spelling.

Another help in recognizing nouns is to look for the words *a, an,* and *the.* These are called noun markers or articles. Noun markers are especially helpful in recognizing abstract nouns. In the following list, you can tell that the underlined words are nouns because it sounds right to use noun markers with them.

a <u>determination</u>   an <u>appointment</u>
the <u>friendliness</u>   the <u>dignity</u>

In the next list, the underlined words are not nouns, because they do not name objects or ideas. It does not sound right to use noun markers with them.

a <u>determine</u>   an <u>appoint</u>
the <u>friendly</u>   the <u>dignify</u>

The four *genders* of nouns are *masculine, feminine, neuter,* and *common.* Study the following definitions and examples.

Nouns of *masculine* gender refer to men and boys.

son   uncle   king   steward

Nouns of *feminine* gender refer to women and girls.

daughter   aunt   queen   stewardess

Nouns of *neuter* gender are neither masculine nor feminine.

house   chair   tree   strength

Nouns of *common* gender can be masculine, feminine, or both.

baby   child   friend   people

If you are not sure about the gender of a noun, think of a pronoun to replace it. *He* replaces masculine nouns, *she* replaces feminine nouns, and *it* replaces neuter nouns. If a noun could be replaced by either *he* or *she,* or if it names a mixed group of people, it is of common gender.

2. A concrete noun names something that can be seen or touched. An abstract noun names something that cannot be seen or touched. Abstract nouns name qualities, conditions, or ideas. Galatians 5:22, 23 lists the fruit of the Spirit—a good sampling of abstract nouns. See also 2 Peter 1:5–7.

3. Many abstract nouns have certain suffixes, like -ness, -ion, -ity, or -ment. These suffixes are used to change other parts of speech into nouns.

ill—illness   active—activity
vibrate—vibration   replace—replacement

4. Words that can be modified by the articles a, an, and the are nouns. The articles (noun markers) are especially helpful in finding abstract nouns.

<u>The requirement</u> sounds right, but <u>the require</u> does not.

Other examples:

<u>an application</u> versus <u>an apply</u>
<u>the belief</u> versus <u>the believe</u>

5. The four genders of nouns are masculine, feminine, neuter, and common.

Nouns of masculine gender refer to men and boys.
Nouns of feminine gender refer to women and girls.
Nouns of neuter gender are neither masculine nor feminine.
Nouns of common gender can be masculine, feminine, or both.

(*Teacher:* Gender in English does not have nearly the importance that it has in many other languages. In German, for instance, there are three definite articles: *der* [masculine], *die* [feminine], and *das* [neuter]. The gender of the article must agree with the gender of the noun that follows it. For example, the word *Hand* [for "hand"] is feminine in German. So the feminine article must be used with it [*die Hand*], any pronoun referring to *Hand* must be feminine, and any adjective describing *Hand* must have a feminine ending. When a person learns German, Spanish, Russian, or any other language in which gender has this significance, he must learn more than just the meaning of each noun. He must also learn its gender so that he can use the noun correctly in a sentence.

The only gender in English is natural gender. That is, if a word is masculine or feminine, it usually refers to a person or animal that is actually male or female. The only definite article is *the,* and it is used before nouns regardless of their gender. Thus, gender in a grammatical sense has almost no significance in modern English.)

★ **EXTRA PRACTICE**
Worksheet 13 (*Recognizing Nouns*)

- A noun is the name of a person, place, thing, or idea.

- A concrete noun names a person, place, or thing that can be seen or touched. An abstract noun names a quality, a condition, or an idea that has no substance.

- The four genders of nouns are masculine, feminine, neuter, and common.

Class Practice

A. Read each word, and tell whether it could be used as a noun.

1. cherry	7. ask	12. school
2. James	8. warm	13. December
3. for	9. early	14. am
4. hope	10. team	15. Thompson's Market
5. hatred	11. chose	16. and
6. Dr. Jones		

B. Change each word to a noun by adding the suffix *-ness, -ion, -ity,* or *-ment.* Write the new words on the chalkboard.

1. scarce	4. require	7. complete
2. polite	5. settle	8. great
3. real	6. agree	9. relate

C. Tell which words are nouns in the following paragraph. Give the gender of each noun you find.

Many of our favorite hymns were written by Fanny Crosby. Although blinded by improper treatment of her eyes at the age of six weeks, she was always a happy child. Her cheerfulness was an inspiration to many. This woman had such a remarkable memory that at a young age she memorized the first five books of the Old Testament and the first four books of the New Testament. Poetry came to her mind quickly, and it is said that she wrote "Safe in the Arms of Jesus" in thirty minutes. Truly our lives are richer because of the hymns she contributed to mankind.

D. Give nouns as described below.
1. Three different places. **Example:** park
2. Three parts of plants. **Example:** stem
3. Three organs of the human body. **Example:** heart

Lesson 19 Answers
Class Practice

A. (Notes in parentheses are suggestions for teacher comments.)
1. yes
2. yes
3. no (preposition)
4. yes (also a verb)
5. yes
6. yes
7. no (verb)
8. no (adjective or verb)
9. no (adjective or adverb)
10. yes (also a verb)
11. no (verb; *choice* would be a noun)
12. yes (also a verb)
13. yes
14. no (form of verb *be*)
15. yes
16. no (conjunction)

B.
1. scarcity *or* scarceness
2. politeness
3. reality *or* realness
4. requirement
5. settlement
6. agreement
7. completion *or* completeness
8. greatness
9. relation

C. (Nouns are underlined. Letters above nouns indicate gender.)

Many of our favorite <u>hymns</u> [N] were written by <u>Fanny Crosby</u> [F]. Although blinded by improper <u>treatment</u> [N] of her <u>eyes</u> [N] at the <u>age</u> [N] of six <u>weeks</u> [N], she was always a happy <u>child</u> [C]. Her <u>cheerfulness</u> [N] was an <u>inspiration</u> [N] to many. This <u>woman</u> [F] had such a remarkable <u>memory</u> [N] that at a young <u>age</u> [N] she memorized the first five <u>books</u> [N] of the <u>Old Testament</u> [N] and the first four <u>books</u> [N] of the <u>New Testament</u> [N]. <u>Poetry</u> [N] came to her <u>mind</u> [N] quickly, and it is said that she wrote "<u>Safe in the Arms of Jesus</u>" [N] in thirty <u>minutes</u> [N]. Truly our <u>lives</u> [N] are richer because of the <u>hymns</u> [N] she contributed to <u>mankind</u> [C].

D. (Individual answers.)

Written Exercises

A. Copy only the words that could be used as nouns.

1. oh	6. sing	11. trouble	16. bless
2. desk	7. load	12. after	17. cheer
3. bill	8. hear	13. fail	18. nurse
4. shook	9. love	14. church	19. later
5. tree	10. skillful	15. joy	20. Akron

B. Make a noun from each word by adding -ness, -ion, -ity, or -ment.

1. correct	4. create	7. awful
2. complex	5. final	8. excite
3. replace	6. develop	9. careful

C. Copy all the nouns. After each one, write M, F, N, or C to tell whether its gender is masculine, feminine, neuter, or common.
1. Cornelius was a centurion who lived at Caesarea.
2. He was a soldier in the army of Rome.
3. He was a devout man whose whole family feared God, and he gave much charity to his neighbors.
4. Cornelius was in prayer one day.
5. He saw a vision of an angel, who called his name.
6. The angel said, "Your prayers and your charity have ascended as a memorial before God."

D. Write your own groups of nouns as described below.
1. Four kinds of buildings. **Example:** store
2. Four kinds of workers. **Example:** carpenter
3. Four things that have to do with the weather. **Example:** snow
4. Four things that have to do with church life. **Example:** hymnal

E. Write sentences with nouns that name the following items. Underline all the nouns in your sentences.

1. A person	3. A thing
2. A place	4. An idea

Review Exercises

A. Correct the run-on errors in this paragraph by using periods and capital letters. [14]

A fawn weighs three to six pounds when it is born usually there are twins or triplets the mother gives her babies rich and creamy milk without it they could not stay healthy.

Written Exercises

A. 2. desk   9. love   18. nurse
   3. bill   11. trouble   20. Akron
   5. tree   14. church   17. cheer
   7. load   15. joy

B. 1. correction or correctness
   2. complexity or complexness (also complexion)
   3. replacement
   4. creation
   5. finality
   6. development
   7. awfulness
   8. excitement
   9. carefulness

C. 1. Cornelius—M; centurion—M; Caesarea—N
   2. soldier—M; army—C or N; Rome—N
   3. man—M; family—C; God—M; charity—N; neighbors—C
   4. Cornelius—M; prayer—N; day—N
   5. vision—N; angel—M; name—N
   6. angel—M; prayers—N; charity—N; memorial—N; God—M

D. (Individual work. Be sure students have original answers.)

E. (Individual work.)

Review Exercises

A. (Corrections are underlined.)

A fawn weighs three to six pounds when it is born. Usually there are twins or triplets. The mother gives her babies rich and creamy milk. Without it they could not stay healthy.

B. Correct the run-on errors in these sentences by using a comma and a suitable conjunction. [14]
1. God has given the fawn a protective coloration a fawn has no body scent for the first few days of its life.
2. You might find a fawn seemingly all alone the mother is usually watching from a hiding place nearby.

C. Correct the run-on errors in these sentences by using a semicolon. [14]
1. Newborn fawns usually stay in their hiding place they do not follow their mother until they can walk well enough.
2. Those week-old fawns are not too young to run they can go as fast as thirty-five miles per hour!
3. Deer usually run away from their enemies sometimes they stand motionless until the enemy leaves.

Challenge Exercises

Copy some Bible verses that contain abstract nouns. Underline all the abstract nouns.

---

20. Proper Nouns

All nouns can be placed in two general classes: common nouns and proper nouns. Everything about which we can speak has a common name. Many things have proper names also, but some do not.

A *common noun* is the *ordinary, general* name of a person, place, thing, or idea. For example, the noun *road* is the common name for a surface on which people drive cars.

Common nouns:
    boy   city   story   day   righteousness

A *proper noun* is the *specific, exact* name of a person, place, or thing. It distinguishes one particular thing from all others with the same common name. *Johnson Road* is a proper noun because it names one specific road and distinguishes it from all other surfaces called roads.

Proper nouns:
    James Shirk   Columbus   Lincoln   Hidden Treasure

B. (Corrections are underlined.)
1. God has given the fawn a protective coloration, and a fawn has no body scent for the first few days of its life.
2. You might find a fawn seemingly all alone, but the mother is usually watching from a hiding place nearby.

C. (Corrections are underlined.)
1. Newborn fawns usually stay in their hiding place; they do not follow their mother until they can walk well enough.
2. Those week-old fawns are not too young to run; they can go as fast as thirty-five miles per hour!
3. Deer usually run away from their enemies; sometimes they stand motionless until the enemy leaves.

Challenge Exercises

(Sample answers.)
Galatians 5:22, 23 describes the fruit of the Spirit.
Second Peter 1:5–7 lists Christian graces.
First Corinthians 13:13 mentions faith, hope, and charity.

Lesson 20

Purpose: (1) To teach the definition of common and proper nouns. (2) To teach the capitalization of proper nouns.

Oral Review:
1. Give the definition of a noun. (the name of a person, place, thing, or idea)
2. What is a concrete noun? (the name of something that can be seen or touched)
3. What is an abstract noun? (the name of a quality, condition, or idea that cannot be seen or touched)
4. What are two helps in recognizing abstract nouns? (Many abstract nouns have suffixes like -*ness*, -*ion*, -*ity*, and -*ment*. The articles *a*, *an*, and *the* can be used before nouns.)

Lesson Introduction: Ask the pupils what *common* means. (usual, ordinary, familiar) Ask them how *month* is common. (It is a name shared by twelve periods of time.) Tell them that the word *proper* has the old meaning "belonging to oneself." Thus, a proper noun is one's own specific name. Have the students give specific names for the following items.

    The largest state of the United States. (Alaska)
    The state that is made up of several islands. (Hawaii)
    The largest river system in the United States. (Mississippi)
    The largest ocean in the world. (Pacific)
    Your pet dog. (Sample answer: Rex)
    Your mother. (Sample answer: Miriam)

Each of these has its own name. The name belongs to it and no other. Learn more about proper nouns in today's lesson.

Proper nouns are written with capital letters. Words like *uncle, city, street, river,* and *mount* are also capitalized when they are part of a proper noun. Some kinds of proper nouns are listed in groups below.

1. *Names of particular persons, including initials and titles.*

Mark	Brother Daniel	Mr. L. W. Mason

2. *Names of towns, cities, states, counties, nations, and continents.*

Lowville	Maryland	Germany
Baltimore	Washington County	Europe

3. *Names of mountains, rivers, lakes, oceans, deserts, islands, and so forth.*

Mount Rushmore	Indian Ocean
Ohio River	Gobi Desert
Lake Tahoe	Ellesmere Island

4. *Titles of books, newspapers, magazines, poems, stories, chapters, articles, and so forth. An article (a, an, the), a conjunction (and, but, or), or a preposition of fewer than four letters is not capitalized unless it is the first or last word.*

Hold the Fort	A Faith Worth Dying For
The Ninety and Nine	Water From a Rock

5. *Names of organizations, schools, churches, and other groups.*

Charity Child Care Committee
Bethel Christian School
Providence Mennonite Church
Department of Commerce
Bethel Christian School Board
House of Representatives

6. *Names of parks, historic sites, historic events, documents, and so forth.*

Yellowstone National Park
French and Indian War
War of 1812
Constitution of the United States
Gettysburg Address
Bill of Rights

Lesson Outline:

1. A common noun is the general name of a person, place, thing, or idea. Common nouns are names shared by many things. There are many *rivers* and *oceans.* There are many *people* and *pets.*

2. A proper noun names a specific person, place, or thing. *Proper* means "belonging to one." There are many *rivers* but only one *Mackenzie River.* There are many *oceans* but only one *Atlantic Ocean.* There are many people; but when we use a proper noun for a person, we usually mean one particular person who has that name (*Alexander Brown, John K. L. Smith*). There are many different pets, but we usually mean one certain pet when we use a proper noun for a pet (*Lassie, Midnight, Pansy*).

3. Proper nouns are written with capital letters.

(1) *Names of particular persons, including initials and titles.*

(2) *Names of towns, cities, states, counties, nations, and continents.*

(3) *Names of mountains, rivers, lakes, oceans, deserts, islands, and so forth.*

(4) *Titles of books, newspapers, magazines, poems, stories, chapters, articles, and so forth. An article (a, an, the), a conjunction (and, but, or), or a preposition of fewer than four letters is not capitalized unless it is the first or last word.*

(5) *Names of organizations, schools, churches, and other groups.*

(6) *Names of parks, historic sites, historic events, documents, and so forth.*

7. *Calendar items such as months, holidays, and days of the week.* However, the names of seasons are not capitalized.

March	spring
Ascension Day	summer
Wednesday	fall (autumn)
	winter

8. *Names of particular ships, airplanes, trains, buildings, and monuments.*

S.S. *France*	Pentagon
Flyer	Washington Monument
Tom Thumb	Golden Gate Bridge

9. *Names of God and words referring to parts of the Bible.*

God	Pentateuch	Psalms
Jehovah	Old Testament	Ephesians
Christ	1 Kings	

10. *Brand names.* A common noun used with a brand name is not capitalized.

Post cereals	Dodge truck
Carnation milk	French's mustard

11. *Abbreviations and initials of proper nouns.*

Dept. of Education	John F. Kennedy

An adjective formed from a proper noun is a proper adjective. A proper adjective is capitalized.

India—Indian	England—English
Israel—Israelite	Bible—Biblical
America—American	

A common noun modified by a proper adjective is not capitalized.

Israelite woman	American invention

Some words can be used both as a proper noun and as a proper adjective. You must decide which it is by the way the word is used in the sentence. A proper adjective modifies another noun.

Their grandfather was an Indian. (proper noun)
Do you like this Indian food? (proper adjective)

---

(7) *Calendar items such as months, holidays, and days of the week.* But the names of seasons are common nouns.

(8) *Names of particular ships, airplanes, trains, buildings, and monuments.*

(9) *Names of God and words referring to parts of the Bible.*

(10) *Brand names.* But a common noun used with a brand name is not capitalized.

(11) *Abbreviations and initials of proper nouns.*

4. An adjective formed from a proper noun is capitalized. But a common noun modified by a proper adjective is not capitalized.

The <u>English</u> language was first spoken in <u>England.</u> *English* and *England* are capitalized, but *language* is not.

Some proper nouns can be used as proper adjectives. The only way to tell whether such a word is a noun or an adjective is by the way it is used in a sentence. Proper adjectives always modify nouns.

The <u>Bible</u> is the Word of God. (proper noun)
We learned five <u>Bible</u> verses this week. (proper adjective)

He speaks <u>English.</u> (proper noun)
He speaks the <u>English</u> language. (proper adjective)

★ **EXTRA PRACTICE**
Worksheet 14 *(Proper Nouns)*

> • A common noun is the general name of a person, place, thing, or idea. A proper noun is the name of one specific person, place, or thing.
>
> • Proper nouns are written with capital letters. These include the names, titles, and initials of specific persons; the names of cities, nations, mountains, oceans, and other geographical items; the titles of books, magazines, songs, and stories; calendar items such as months and holidays; and brand names.

Class Practice

A. Match the common nouns in the first column with the proper nouns in the second column. Write the words from the second column correctly on the chalkboard.

1. park
2. country
3. store
4. state
5. island
6. book

   a. simon's appliance and electric
   b. puerto rico
   c. glacier national park
   d. pilgrim's progress
   e. mexico
   f. south carolina

B. Tell which words below should be capitalized. Tell which words are proper adjectives.

1. The philippines is a country at the western edge of the pacific ocean.
2. A leading port is davao, but the busiest port and capital city is manila.
3. Chief islands of the philippines include bohol, cebu, leyte, luzon, negros, palawan, panay, and samar.
4. Have you ever read the book *streams of living water,* by martin carey?
5. Pizza and spaghetti are italian foods.
6. The indians attacked the jacob hochstetler family at the time of the french and indian war.
7. Father said that ascension day always comes on a thursday in the spring.

Lesson 20 Answers
Class Practice

A. 1. (c) Glacier National Park
  2. (e) Mexico
  3. (a) Simon's Appliance and Electric
  4. (f) South Carolina
  5. (b) Puerto Rico
  6. (d) Pilgrim's Progress

B. (Proper adjectives are underlined.)
  1. Philippines, Pacific Ocean
  2. Davao, Manila
  3. Philippines, Bohol, Cebu, Leyte, Luzon, Negros, Palawan, Panay, Samar
  4. *Streams (of) Living Water,* Martin Carey
  5. <u>Italian</u>
  6. Indians, <u>Jacob Hochstetler</u>, French (and) Indian War
  7. Ascension Day, Thursday

8. We like carnation powdered milk and cloister ice cream.
9. It is easier for spaniards to learn the portuguese language than it is for english people.
10. On sunday we sang the song "thine for service" from the *christian hymnal.*

Written Exercises

A. Write two proper nouns for each of these common nouns.
   1. book
   2. month
   3. city
   4. person
   5. dog
   6. country
   7. hymn
   8. state
   9. president
   10. lake

B. Copy and capitalize correctly.
   1. mrs. n. b. benz
   2. cambria, illinois
   3. brother elmer martin
   4. campbell's soup
   5. dr. ernest h. haulk
   6. friday, november 2
   7. the genesee river of new york
   8. independence day

C. Find each proper noun, and write it correctly.
   1. An official named ashpenaz, who served king nebuchadnezzar, gave these names to the four hebrews: belteshazzar, shadrach, meshach, and abednego.

8. Carnation, Cloister
9. Spaniards, <u>Portuguese</u>, <u>English</u>
10. Sunday, "Thine (for) Service," *Christian Hymnal*

Written Exercises

A. (Individual answers.)

B. 1. Mrs. N. B. Benz
   2. Cambria, Illinois
   3. Brother Elmer Martin
   4. Campbell's soup
   5. Dr. Ernest H. Haulk
   6. Friday, November 2
   7. the Genesee River of New York
   8. Independence Day

C. 1. Ashpenaz, King Nebuchadnezzar, Hebrews, Belteshazzar, Shadrach, Meshach, Abednego

2. Ancient palestine was divided into judea, samaria, and galilee.

3. We can read about king hezekiah in three books in the old testament: 2 kings, 2 chronicles, and isaiah.

4. The total area of the philippines is a little more than the area of wisconsin and michigan together.

5. On luzon, the largest of the islands, a volcano named mount mayon stands close to legaspi.

6. The philippine sea, the celebes sea, the sulu sea, and the south china sea surround the philippines.

7. Sauerkraut and frankfurters came from germany.

8. I liked the chapter "a glow in the dark" the best.

9. In exodus we read how the lord helped the israelites to cross the red sea on dry land.

10. A man named john deere invented the first riding plow.

11. Grades 5 and 6 of the hopeland christian school sang "mighty army of the young" by memory.

12. The golden gate bridge, one of the largest suspension bridges in the world, crosses the entrance of the san francisco bay.

13. The *tom thumb,* one of the first locomotives to pull a passenger train, was built by peter cooper.

D. Find each proper adjective, and write it correctly.

1. Do you like kellogg's cereals?

2. Apple pie and hamburgers are american foods.

3. We like lawry's salt on popcorn.

4. The roman citizens of paul's day used the greek language for everyday speech and the latin language for legal matters.

5. The jewish people used the hebrew language in religious matters.

Review Exercises

Write whether each sentence is *declarative, interrogative, imperative,* or *exclamatory.* (Only one sentence is exclamatory.) Also write the correct end punctuation. [7]

1. Which state of the United States has the highest population

2. California has more people than any other state in the United States

3. Tell me which country of the world has the greatest area

4. Isn't the United States one of the largest countries in the world

---

2. Palestine, Judea, Samaria, Galilee

3. King Hezekiah, Old Testament, 2 Kings, 2 Chronicles, Isaiah

4. Philippines, Wisconsin, Michigan

5. Luzon, Mount Mayon, Legaspi

6. Philippine Sea, Celebes Sea, Sulu Sea, South China Sea, Philippines

7. Germany

8. A Glow (in the) Dark

9. Exodus, Lord, Israelites, Red Sea

10. John Deere

11. Hopeland Christian School, "Mighty Army (of the) Young"

12. Golden Gate Bridge, San Francisco Bay

13. *Tom Thumb,* Peter Cooper

D. 1. Kellogg's

2. American

3. Lawry's

4. Roman, Paul's, Greek, Latin

5. Jewish, Hebrew

Review Exercises

1. interrogative   ?   (question mark)

2. declarative   .   (period)

3. imperative   .   (period)

4. interrogative   ?   (question mark)

5. Canada is larger than the United States
6. China, the most heavily populated country, has about one billion people.
7. What a crowded country that must be

5. declarative   .   (period)
6. declarative   .   (period)
7. exclamatory   !   (exclamation point)

21. Developing Paragraphs by Using Details

You have learned that a paragraph is a group of sentences that tells about one single topic. That single topic is expressed in the topic sentence. All the other sentences support the topic sentence and say more about it.

Once you have written a topic sentence, you need to show that it is true. Your goal is to convince the reader that you know what you are talking about, and that what you have said is true and worthwhile. This is what paragraph development is all about: writing things that will prove the truth of your topic sentence.

A paragraph is developed by putting details into it. Details are extremely important. They are so necessary that you cannot hope to convince anyone without them. Read the topic sentence of the following paragraph (underlined), and then read the sentences that follow. Can you tell what is wrong with the paragraph?

Hard work brings much satisfaction. I like to work hard. Most other people like it too if they really get at it. Hard work is much better than idleness. Being idle is not as satisfying as working hard. Few things bring as much satisfaction as hard work.

In the paragraph above, all the sentences after the topic sentence merely repeat and emphasize what the topic sentence says. None of them give any details to show that the topic sentence is true. How can the writer prove that hard work is so satisfying? Has he ever experienced it himself? What has he gained by working hard? What has he suffered through idleness? The paragraph does not accomplish much, because it gives no proof that the topic sentence is really true.

Lesson 21

Purpose: To teach how to develop paragraphs *by using details. (*Previous experience:* General practice with paragraph writing; developing paragraphs by giving examples.)

Oral Review:
1. When does a paragraph have unity? (when all the sentences tell about the topic given by the topic sentence)
2. When does a paragraph have coherence? (when the sentences "hold together" in an orderly, sensible way)
3. What things can you do to make a paragraph coherent? (Give details in the order of time or in the order of importance or interest. Use transitional words.)
4. Give some transitional words that help to make a paragraph coherent. (first, second, next, then, finally, soon, later, also, immediately, afterward, however, for example, therefore, for this reason)

5. In writing directions, what order should you use? (the order things are to be done)
6. In writing directions, what should you be careful to do? (Make sure the information is accurate. Write clearly so that the directions are simple to understand. Use transitional words like *first, second,* and *next.*)

Lesson Introduction: Ask students how they would feel if their family planned a picnic or a trip to the zoo one day, but when the day finally came, someone in the family got sick and they couldn't go after all. They would probably feel disappointed.

A paragraph can make you feel the same way. Its topic sentence may promise that an interesting paragraph will follow. But when you read the paragraph, you find that the other sentences do not tell about the topic sentence at all. How disappointing it can be!

The following paragraph is better. Notice how the details offer real proof that the topic sentence is true.

> <u>Hard work brings much satisfaction</u>. How good you feel when you look back over a job well done! You may also receive a compliment from your father or mother, and that is another reward. Money that you earn by working is worth more to you than money that someone gives you. A working man has a clear conscience because he has done something worthwhile and made good use of his time. He is satisfied and relaxed. Ecclesiastes 5:12 says, "The sleep of a labouring man is sweet."

When you write a paragraph, use solid facts to show that your topic sentence is true. You might also use facts to show what is wrong with an opposing idea. Be sure your statements are based on truth and not just on your opinions. The reader may challenge what you think, but it is hard to argue against solid facts. Compare the following sentences. Which set is more convincing?

> Honesty is the best way because it brings the best results. You will feel much better if you are honest than if you lie or cheat. (opinions)

> Honesty is the best way because God said it is right. The Bible pronounces a severe penalty on all liars and hypocrites. (facts)

As you learned before, the details in a paragraph must fit together well so that the reader does not get lost or confused. Remember that this is done by putting the details in some kind of logical order. They can be given in the order of time or in the order of importance or interest. Remember also to use sentence variety and good transitional words. All these things together will help to make your paragraphs meaningful, interesting, and convincing.

- A paragraph may be developed by using details. The details must show the reader that the topic sentence is true.

Today we want to study one way to develop paragraphs so that the sentences after the topic sentence will be interesting and meaningful.

Lesson Outline:

1. The sentences in a paragraph must develop the topic sentence. The sentences must all tell about the one topic introduced by the topic sentence.

2. The sentences of a properly developed paragraph must show that the topic sentence is true. The writer's goal should be to convince the reader. He must use details to prove that what he has said is true and worthwhile.

3. The details that develop a paragraph must be good, solid facts. Solid facts help to prove the topic sentence even though the topic sentence itself may be an opinion. Being able to find and sort out true and interesting details is a skill that the writer can develop.

4. Details must be arranged in such a way that the paragraph is clear and simple to understand. The details can be placed in the order of time or in the order of importance or interest. There should also be a variety of suitable transitional words. All these things together will help to make a paragraph interesting and effective.

★ **EXTRA PRACTICE**
Worksheet 15 *(Details in Paragraphs)*

Class Practice

A. Which paragraph is the better one? Tell why. In your own words, briefly give the details that support the topic sentence of the better paragraph.

1. My mother makes many sacrifices for our family. She uses much of her energy in preparing food, washing clothes, and cleaning the house. It also takes much of her energy to give us firm, loving discipline. She loses sleep to pray for us or to care for us when we are sick. It seems we cannot stop her from helping us; she seems to love doing all she can for our good. We can never show too much appreciation for the constant sacrifices of our mother.

2. Bird watching is a worthwhile hobby. You can put up a bird feeder outside a window. You can also hang a wren house in a tree. Scientists have learned much about birds by putting bands on their legs. Arctic terns fly the eleven thousand miles between the Arctic Circle and the Antarctic Circle twice each year!

B. Choose several of the topic sentences below, and briefly give some details that could be used to develop them.
1. Every boy should have a pet of some kind.
2. It takes much work to care for a pet rabbit.
3. We have an attractive classroom.
4. You can learn much from a good book.
5. There are many interesting things to see in Egypt.
6. Alaska is an interesting place to visit.

Written Exercises

A. List briefly the details that are used to develop the topic sentence of the following paragraph.

Animals have special ways to survive through freezing cold winters. An animal's body produces plenty of heat as long as it can find food. Mammals have thick fur that helps to keep in the body heat. Birds have warm downy feathers underneath their flight feathers. Some creatures keep warm by storing fat in their bodies and hibernating in dry caves or burrows. Foxes wrap their tails around their noses like scarves. And smaller animals such as field mice build warm tunnels under the snow. Certainly God designed the animals well to withstand cold weather.

6. a. in northern part, midnight sun can be seen in midsummer
   b. active volcanoes and high mountains, including Mount McKinley, highest mountain in the United States
   c. large trout and salmon in rivers
   d. coastal cities linked by ferries
   e. Eskimo villages along Arctic Coast
   f. totem poles at Ketchikan

Written Exercises

A. (Wording and main points may vary somewhat.)
1. body produces heat
2. heat kept in by thick fur
3. heat kept in by downy feathers
4. storing fat and hibernating
5. warm wrap-around tails
6. warm tunnels

Lesson 21 Answers
Class Practice

A. Paragraph 1 is the better paragraph. The details tell some of the sacrifices Mother makes.

The details in paragraph 2 do not support the topic sentence. They do not tell how or why bird watching is a worthwhile hobby.

Details to list on the chalkboard:
1. uses her energy in working for us
2. uses her energy to give us discipline
3. loses sleep to pray and care for us
4. hard to stop her from helping us
5. does all she can for our good

B. (Sample details.)
1. a. helps him to learn responsibility
   b. helps him to feel for the needs of another creature
   c. helps him to develop a regular routine for doing things
   d. teaches him many things about that animal
2. a. must be fed and watered regularly
   b. pen must be kept clean
   c. must be checked for disease
   d. must be protected from cold in winter
3. a. room is well lighted
   b. walls have been freshly painted
   c. desks are in straight rows
   d. bulletin board display is colorful and educational
   e. good maps and charts on walls
4. a. stories about families teach how to get along with others
   b. stories about adventures teach what other places in the world are like
   c. book on history teaches interesting things about the past
   d. book about crafts teaches how to do interesting projects
   e. reference book gives information for school assignments
5. a. Nile River, longest river in the world
   b. pyramids, some of which Joseph probably saw
   c. Great Sphinx at Giza
   d. old temples with picture writing on walls
   e. tall, pointed obelisks, built in honor of sun god
   f. tombs of rich pharaohs, and museums that display treasures from the tombs

B. Write a paragraph that is developed with meaningful details. You may begin with one of the topic sentences in Class Practice, Part B. You may also use a topic sentence of your own if it is approved by your teacher.

Review Exercises

Rewrite and improve the following directions. Put the steps in proper order, and leave out the sentence that does not belong. Use transitional words, such as *first, next,* and *also.* [16, 17]

A Good Way to Study for a Chapter Test

On index cards, copy some exercises that deal with the main points of the chapter, and write the answers on the back. First read through the whole chapter. Before you start reading, make sure you have a quiet place to study. We just studied a chapter about birds, and I enjoyed it very much. Read each card several times. See if you can say all the answers without looking. If you have trouble with any cards, keep studying them until you can give all the right answers promptly.

22. Nouns With Regular Plural Forms

Nouns do more than merely name things. The form of a noun shows whether it is a general name (common noun) or a specific name (proper noun). For most nouns, the form also shows whether it names one or more than one. For example, a word like *king* or *queen* refers to only one person, but words like *princes* and *servants* refer to more than one person.

A noun that names only one person, place, thing, or idea is a *singular noun.* A noun that names more than one is a *plural noun.*

Singular: boy, baby, town, home, potato
Plural: boys, babies, towns, homes, potatoes

The following rules tell how to form the plurals of regular nouns.
1. The plural forms of most nouns are made by adding -*s* to the singular forms.

animal—animals   purpose—purposes

Lesson 22

Purpose: To teach the concept and spelling of plural nouns.

Oral Review:
1. Name the sentence types described below.
   a. It simply states a fact. (declarative)
   b. It asks a question. (interrogative)
   c. It gives a command or request. (imperative)
   d. It expresses strong feeling. (exclamatory)
2. What is a common noun? (an ordinary, general name for a person, place, thing, or idea)
3. What is a proper noun? (the name of a specific person, place, or thing)
4. How must a proper noun be written? (with a capital letter)

B. (Individual work. Be sure to check topic sentences of the pupils' own choosing so that you can prevent the using of topics that are hard to develop. If you suspect that a student has chosen a difficult topic, ask him to share a few of the details he plans to use. If he cannot think of any good ones, he had better choose a different topic.)

Review Exercises
(Sample paragraph.)

A Good Way to Study for a Chapter Test
First make sure you have a quiet place to study. Next read through the whole chapter. On index cards, copy some exercises that deal with the main points of the chapter, and write the answers on the back. Then read each card several times. See if you can say all the answers without looking. If you have trouble with any cards, keep studying them until you can give all the right answers promptly.

Written Quiz:
1. Write the definition of a noun.
_____
_____
_____
2. Underline the four abstract nouns.
   house   kindness   field   air
   idea   joy   road   purity
3. Write a common noun for each of these proper nouns.
   a. Jericho _____   e. Matthew _____
   b. Pacific _____   f. Martha _____
   c. Bible _____   g. Texas _____
   d. Spain _____   h. August _____

Quiz Answers:
1. A noun is a word that names a person, place, thing, or idea.
2. kindness, idea, joy, purity
3. (Sample answers.)
   a. town, city   e. man, boy, brother, disciple
   b. ocean   f. woman, girl, sister
   c. book   g. state
   d. nation, country h. month

2. If a noun ends with *s, sh, ch, x,* or *z,* the plural form is made by adding *-es* so that it can be pronounced easily.

    bunch—bunches   box—boxes   quiz—quizzes

3. If a noun ends with *y* after a vowel, the plural form is made by adding *-s.* If a noun ends with *y* after a consonant, the *y* is changed to *i* and *-es* is added.

    monkey—monkeys   country—countries

4. For many nouns ending with *f* or *fe,* the *f* or *fe* is changed to *v* and *-es* is added. For others of these nouns, only *-s* is added. A few are spelled either way.

    shelf—shelves   belief—beliefs
    wife—wives   safe—safes
    scarf—scarfs *or* scarves

    Words like *belief* and *safe* have different meanings when the *f* or *fe* is changed to *v* and *-es* is added: *believes, saves. Believes* and *saves* are verbs, not nouns.

5. If a noun ends with *o* after a vowel, the plural form is made by adding *-s.* If a noun ends with *o* after a consonant, *-s* or *-es* is added. A few are spelled either way.

    patio—patios   tomato—tomatoes
    silo—silos   volcano—volcanoes *or* volcanos

    If a noun ending with *o* is a musical term, the plural form is generally made by adding *-s.*

    soprano—sopranos   alto—altos   piano—pianos

Some nouns have more than one plural form. Be sure to check the dictionary whenever you are in doubt. If the dictionary does not show any plural form, follow the rules in this lesson.

- A singular noun names only one. A plural noun names more than one.

- Check the dictionary when you need help with the spelling of a plural form.

Lesson Introduction: Ask the students what *singular* means. It refers to only one; its root word is *single. Plural* refers to more than one. It is related to the word *plus,* which has the idea of adding more.

Write the following words on the chalkboard. Ask students if they know what is wrong with them.

    foxs   bushs   patchs   berrys
    potatos   altoes   iglooes   rooves

Today we will study some rules for the plural forms of nouns.

Lesson Outline:

1. A singular noun names only one person, place, thing, or idea. The root word *single* means "only one."

Not a single <u>apple</u> is on this <u>tree.</u>

2. A plural noun names more than one. Plural refers to more than one. It is related to the word *plus,* which has the idea of adding more.

Many <u>apples</u> are on those <u>trees.</u>

3. Most plural forms are spelled according to certain rules.

(1) The plural forms of most nouns are made by adding *-s* to the singular forms.

    mineral—minerals   trap—traps
    message—messages   cabin—cabins

(2) If a noun ends with *s, sh, ch, x,* or *z,* the plural form is made by adding *-es* so that it can be pronounced easily.

    bus—buses   fox—foxes
    dish—dishes   quartz—quartzes
    match—matches

(3) If a noun ends with *y* after a vowel, the plural form is made by adding *-s.* If a noun ends with *y* after a consonant, the *y* is changed to *i* and *-es* is added.

    boy—boys
    ray—rays
    turkey—turkeys
    Monday—Mondays
    baby—babies
    city—cities
    ferry—ferries
    summary—summaries

(4) For many nouns ending with *f* or *fe,* the *f* or *fe* is changed to *v* and *-es* is added. For others of these nouns, only *-s* is added. A few are spelled either way.

    wolf—wolves   chief—chiefs
    sheaf—sheaves   roof—roofs
    life—lives   cliff—cliffs
    hoof—hooves *or* hoofs
    scarf—scarves *or* scarfs

    In words like *belief* and *safe,* the *f* or *fe* is not changed to *v,* because that changes the meaning of the word.

(5) If a noun ends with *o* after a vowel, the plural form is made by adding *-s.* If a noun ends with *o* after a consonant, *-s* or *-es* is added. A few are spelled either way.

    kangaroo—kangaroos
    ratio—ratios
    rodeo—rodeos
    trio—trios

Class Practice

A. On the chalkboard, write the correct plural form of each word. Give the number of the rule in the lesson that is followed in each case.

1. loaf
2. supply
3. solo
4. sandwich
5. grief
6. champion
7. studio
8. radish
9. tornado
10. chimney

B. In the following sentences, change all the nouns to plural forms. Make sure all the other words agree with the plural forms.
   1. A mosquito buzzed around the bush and the flower.
   2. The boy has a tomato in his lunch.
   3. The soprano and the alto sang well during music class.
   4. The child picked a beetle off the potato in this row.

Written Exercises

A. Write the plural form of each word. Check a dictionary if you are not sure of the correct spelling.

1. coin
2. sky
3. sheaf
4. trio
5. quilt
6. fly
7. box
8. echo
9. turkey
10. potato
11. thief
12. thrush
13. donkey
14. switch
15. tomato
16. cliff
17. chief
18. hero
19. guess
20. valley
21. strife
22. buzz
23. belief
24. volcano

B. Rewrite these sentences, changing each noun to its plural form. Also change other words to make them agree.
   1. The box contains a bicycle for the boy.
   2. Put the knife and the fork on the shelf with the spoon.
   3. The roof of the house is flat.
   4. The soprano and the alto will sing this note together.
   5. The mosquito thrives in swamp and marsh.

Lesson 22 Answers
Class Practice

A. 1. loaves, 4
    2. supplies, 3
    3. solos, 5
    4. sandwiches, 2
    5. griefs, 4
    6. champions, 1
    7. studios, 5
    8. radishes, 2
    9. tornadoes *or* tornados, 5
    10. chimneys, 3

B. 1. Mosquitoes buzzed around the bushes and the flowers.
    2. The boys have tomatoes in their lunches.
    3. The sopranos and the altos sang well during music classes.
    4. The children picked beetles off the potatoes in these rows.

Written Exercises

A. 1. coins
    2. skies
    3. sheaves
    4. trios
    5. quilts
    6. flies
    7. boxes
    8. echoes
    9. turkeys
    10. potatoes
    11. thieves
    12. thrushes
    13. donkeys
    14. switches
    15. tomatoes
    16. cliffs
    17. chiefs
    18. heroes
    19. guesses
    20. valleys
    21. strifes
    22. buzzes
    23. beliefs
    24. volcanoes *or* volcanos

B. 1. The boxes contain bicycles for the boys.
    2. Put the knives and the forks on the shelves with the spoons.
    3. The roofs of the houses are flat.
    4. The sopranos and the altos will sing these notes together.
    5. The mosquitoes (*or* mosquitos) thrive in swamps and marshes.

auto—autos
avocado—avocados
Filipino—Filipinos
photo—photos

echo—echoes
hero—heroes
potato—potatoes
Negro—Negroes

cargo—cargoes *or* cargos
mosquito—mosquitoes *or* mosquitos
zero—zeroes *or* zeros

For musical terms, the plural forms are generally made by adding -*s*.

altos   pianos   solos   sopranos

   4. Some nouns have more than one plural form. When in doubt, check the dictionary. This applies especially to nouns ending with *f* or *o*.

Review Exercises

A. Write whether the gender of each noun is *masculine, feminine, neuter,* or *common.* [19]

1. boy
2. teacher
3. town
4. friend
5. church
6. sister
7. song
8. book

B. Write a proper noun for each noun in Part A. [20]

---

23. Nouns With Irregular Plural Forms

A few nouns have plural forms that are made in irregular ways. Study the following groups of irregular plural forms.

1. The plural forms of seven nouns are made by changing the vowels.

foot—feet	louse—lice	man—men
goose—geese	mouse—mice	woman—women
tooth—teeth		

   Some of these nouns are used in compound words, such as *gentleman—gentlemen* and *dormouse—dormice.* But these seven nouns are the only root words whose plural forms are made by changing the vowels.

2. Three plural nouns end with *-en,* which is an old plural suffix.

   brother—brethren   child—children   ox—oxen

   Brethren is an old plural form. Today we usually use *brothers* instead.

3. Some nouns have the same form whether they are singular or plural. Most of them are names of animals.

deer—deer	swine—swine	salmon—salmon
sheep—sheep	fish—fish	trout—trout
moose—moose		

   Your <u>sheep</u> <u>are</u> all here, but my <u>sheep</u> <u>is</u> missing.

Lesson 23

Purpose: To teach the spelling of irregular plural forms of nouns.

Oral Review:

1. Tell which kind of word order is described in each sentence.
   a. The complete predicate comes before the complete subject. (inverted)
   b. The complete subject comes before the complete predicate. (normal)
   c. Part of the predicate comes before the subject, and part of the predicate comes after. (mixed)
2. What is a plural noun? (a word that names more than one person, place, thing, or idea)
3. Tell how to spell the following plural forms.
   a. Most plural nouns. (Add *-s.*)
   b. Nouns that end with *s, sh, ch, x,* or *z.* (Add *-es.*)

Review Exercises

A.
1. masculine
2. common
3. neuter
4. common
5. common *or* neuter
6. feminine
7. neuter
8. neuter

B. (Individual answers. Check for correct capitalization.)

---

   c. Nouns that end with *y* after a consonant. (Change the *y* to *i,* and add *-es.*)
   d. Nouns that end with *y* after a vowel. (Add *-s.*)
   e. Nouns that end with *f* or *fe.* (Add *-s,* or change the *f* or *fe* to *v* and add *-es.*)
   f. Nouns that end with *o* after a vowel. (Add *-s.*)
   g. Nouns that end with *o* after a consonant. (Add *-s* or *-es.*)
   h. Musical terms. (Add *-s.*)

Lesson Introduction: Write the following lists of words on the chalkboard, and ask the students whether they are singular or plural.

1. salmon, deer, sheep, trout
   These words can name one or more than one. They have the same form whether singular or plural.
2. measles, news, mathematics, mumps
   These words are singular even though they end with *s.*
3. trousers, scissors, pliers, tweezers
   These words are considered plural nouns, whether they name one thing or more than one.

Today we will study the rules for some irregular plural nouns.

Lesson Outline:

1. The plural forms of seven nouns are made by changing the vowels.

foot—feet	louse—lice	man—men
goose—geese	mouse—mice	woman—women
tooth—teeth		

4. A few nouns look like plural forms, but they are singular. There is no plural for these nouns. Because each of these nouns refers to just one thing, a singular verb is commonly used with them.

news	checkers (game)	mumps
statistics	measles	chicken pox
mathematics		

The <u>news</u> <u>is</u> encouraging. (not *are*)
<u>Measles</u> <u>is</u> a contagious disease. (not *are*)

5. Some nouns are usually considered plural whether they name one thing or more than one. Usually plural verbs are used with these nouns, and plural pronouns are used to replace them. Most nouns of this kind name something made of two main parts.

pliers	glasses (aid for eyesight)
scissors	tongs
trousers	tweezers

The <u>pliers</u> <u>have</u> been put where <u>they</u> belong.
    (*Have* and *they* are often used whether *pliers* means one tool or two.)
These <u>trousers</u> <u>are</u> dirty, but Mother will wash <u>them</u>.
    (*These, are,* and *them* are all plural.)

Remember to check a dictionary when you are not sure how to spell a plural form.

• Some nouns have irregular plural forms.

• Check the dictionary when you need help with the spelling of a plural form.

Class Practice

A. On the chalkboard, write the correct plural form of each word.

1. wife	5. calf	9. dairy
2. match	6. alley	10. tray
3. fox	7. army	11. buffalo
4. crutch	8. echo	12. woman

Lesson 23 Answers
Class Practice

A. 1. wives   7. armies
   2. matches   8. echoes
   3. foxes   9. dairies
   4. crutches   10. trays
   5. calves   11. buffaloes, buffalos, *or* buffalo
   6. alleys   12. women

Some of these nouns are used in compound words, such as in the following examples. But the number of "root nouns" is seven.

    forefoot—forefeet
    clubfoot—clubfeet
    dormouse—dormice
    titmouse—titmice
    chairman—chairmen
    gentleman—gentlemen
    policewoman—policewomen
    but mongoose—mongooses

2. Three plural nouns end with -en, which is an old plural suffix.

    brethren   children   oxen

Brethren is an old plural form. Today we usually use *brothers* instead. (Also compare *hosen* in Daniel 3:21.)

3. Some nouns have the same form whether they are singular or plural. Most of them are names of animals. It is not correct to say they have no plural form, because they have either singular or plural meanings.

| salmon | swine | fish |
| deer | sheep | trout |

(*Teacher:* The forms *deers* and *fishes* may be used in referring to different kinds or species. **Examples:** The largest deers of North America are moose and elk. Cod and mackerel are important food fishes.)

B. Tell whether each noun is *singular, plural,* or *either singular or plural.*
1. deer
2. news
3. tongs
4. salmon
5. trousers
6. molasses
7. scissors
8. mathematics
9. trout

C. Read the following sentences correctly.
1. The scissors is on the shelf.
2. Measles are uncomfortable and may be dangerous.
3. We caught twenty trouts in the cold, sparkling stream.

Written Exercises

A. For each noun, write *S, P,* or *E* to tell whether it is singular, plural, or either singular or plural.
1. swine
2. mumps
3. shears
4. measles
5. fish
6. pliers
7. mathematics
8. eyeglasses
9. headquarters

B. Copy each underlined word, and write *S* or *P* after it to tell whether it is singular or plural.
1. The grass is getting tall.
2. Grandfather has lost his spectacles.
3. White hair is a glory to old men.
4. Jesus healed leprosy and other diseases.
5. Polly has measles.
6. The boy's teeth were covered with sticky molasses.
7. Andrew has a pair of black trousers.
8. We saw a deer among the sheep.
9. Have you heard the news?
10. Mathematics is my favorite subject.

C. Write the better words.
1. Rabies (is, are) a dangerous disease.
2. Please hand me (that, those) tweezers.
3. Many (salmon, salmons) were swimming upstream.
4. The dull shears (was, were) almost useless.

Review Exercises

A. Write whether each sentence has *normal, inverted,* or *mixed* word order. Diagram the skeleton of each sentence. [15]
1. Down came the rain, sleet, and snow.

4. A few nouns look like plural forms, but they are singular. There is no plural for these nouns. Because each of these nouns refers to just one thing, a singular verb is commonly used with them.

measles   news
mathematics   mumps
chicken pox

Incorrect: Chicken pox are a disease.
Correct: Chicken pox is a disease.

5. Some nouns are usually considered plural whether they name one thing or more than one. Usually plural verbs are used with these nouns, and plural pronouns are used to replace them. Most nouns of this kind name something made of two main parts.

trousers   pliers   tweezers
scissors   tongs

B. 1. either singular or plural
2. singular
3. plural
4. either singular or plural
5. plural
6. singular
7. plural
8. singular
9. either singular or plural

C. (Corrections are underlined.)
1. The scissors are on the shelf.
2. Measles is uncomfortable and may be dangerous.
3. We caught twenty trout in the cold, sparkling stream.

Written Exercises

A. 1. E   4. S   7. S
2. S   5. E   8. P
3. P   6. P   9. E

B. 1. grass—S
2. spectacles—P
3. hair—S; men—P
4. leprosy—S; diseases—P
5. measles—S
6. teeth—P; molasses—S
7. trousers—P
8. deer—S; sheep—P
9. news—S
10. Mathematics—S

C. 1. is
2. those
3. salmon
4. were

Review Exercises

A. 1. inverted

2. The next day, a farmer's wife found a weak, tired fawn beside the chimney outside her cabin.
3. She fed him apples, oatmeal, and cornmeal.
4. How tame he became!
5. She had saved his life.

B. Rewrite these sentences, changing them to normal word order. [15]
1. Around and around buzzed the bee.
2. Nearby was some green grass.
3. For several weeks the fawn lived by the side of her house.
4. Happily he joined the herd again.

---

24. Developing Paragraphs by Using Examples and Illustrations

In Lesson 21 you learned that all the sentences in a paragraph must develop the topic sentence and that this is done by using details. You need to use suitable details to convince the reader that your topic sentence is true. Many different kinds of details can be used.

Examples and illustrations are specific kinds of details used to develop a paragraph. They form pictures in the reader's mind. They help to prove that the topic sentence is true by showing the reader what something is like. Notice the examples in the following paragraph.

Paragraph developed by several different examples:

My baby sister is sweet and lovable. She is a soft, roly-poly bundle. Often when I rock her, she just falls asleep in my arms. I like to talk to her because she usually smiles when I do. Once she laughed right out loud. She has a soft, quiet baby voice even when she cries. When she does cry, of course, I usually go and ask Mother if I may hold my dear baby sister again.

Will the reader be convinced that the writer's baby sister is sweet and lovable? He should be after he reads the examples. They tell how the baby feels to the touch, and what she looks and sounds like.

The paragraph above is developed by several different examples. A paragraph may also give just one example or illustration and go into detail about that one thing. This is called an extended example or

2. mixed   <u>wife | found</u>

3. normal   <u>She | fed</u>

4. mixed   <u>he | became</u>

5. normal   <u>She | had saved</u>

B. 1. The bee buzzed around and around.
2. Some green grass was nearby.
3. The fawn lived by the side of her house for several weeks.
4. He joined the herd again happily.

Lesson 24

Purpose: To teach how to develop paragraphs by using examples and illustrations. (*Previous experience:* Developing paragraphs by giving examples.)

Oral Review:
1. What does a paragraph need to develop its topic sentence? (details)
2. What should the details in a paragraph show about the topic sentence? (that the topic sentence is true and worthwhile)
3. In what order should details be given? (in an order that makes the paragraph simple to understand, such as the order of time or the order of importance or interest)
4. Name the kind of word order described in each sentence.
   a. The complete predicate comes before the complete subject. (inverted)
   b. The complete subject comes before the complete predicate. (normal)
   c. Part of the predicate comes before the subject, and part of the predicate comes after. (mixed)

Lesson Introduction: Ask students which kind of science lesson they prefer: a short one that teaches facts without using any illustrations, or a lesson that is longer because it has illustrations that help to teach the lesson. Most of us prefer the kind that uses illustrations, because they help us to understand the lesson better. Illustrations help us picture things in our mind.

Today's lesson is about developing paragraphs by using examples and illustrations.

illustration. The following paragraph uses the same topic sentence as the paragraph above, but it is developed by using just one incident.

Paragraph developed by one extended example:

My baby sister is sweet and lovable. The other day I was holding her and talking to her. She liked it best when I talked to her in baby words like *coo* and *goo*. Once while she was looking right at me, I tickled her chin and said, "Goo." All at once she laughed right out loud. It was the first time she ever did that! I would not trade my baby sister for anything in the world.

Examples and illustrations will help to make your paragraphs convincing. You may give a number of different illustrations, or you may use most of the paragraph to give just one extended illustration. If you use an actual happening or example, it will do much to prove that your topic sentence is true.

- Examples and illustrations are two kinds of details that can be used to develop a paragraph.

- A paragraph may be developed by several different examples or illustrations. It may also be developed by just one extended example or illustration.

Class Practice

A. Tell which paragraph is developed by using several examples or illustrations. Tell which paragraph is developed by using only one extended example or illustration.

1.   Weather patterns in Guatemala are different from weather patterns in Pennsylvania. The mountains of Guatemala have a fairly cold climate, but down at the coast—only a few hours' drive away—the climate is always warm. Guatemala does not have spring, summer, fall, and winter. Instead, it has a rainy season and a dry season. During the dry season, the mountains have frost at night but the days can get as warm as a summer day in Pennsylvania. Weather changes can be sudden and drastic, especially during the time between seasons.

Lesson Outline:

1. Examples and illustrations are specific kinds of details used to develop a paragraph. Such a paragraph usually begins with a topic sentence that makes a broad statement. It is followed by sentences that have the idea "For example,..." or "To illustrate,..." These words may not actually be used in the paragraph, but they help the writer to think of examples and illustrations that will form clear pictures in the reader's mind.

2. Examples and illustrations are used in two ways to develop paragraphs.

    a. *By giving several different examples or illustrations.* Each example or illustration is presented briefly.

    b. *By giving only one extended example or illustration.* This one example or illustration is described in considerable detail.

Lesson 24 Answers
Class Practice

A. Paragraph 1 uses several examples and illustrations. Paragraph 2 uses one extended illustration.

---

3. Illustrations make convincing paragraphs. They present actual happenings or examples that support the topic sentence with solid evidence.

★ **EXTRA PRACTICE**
    Worksheet 16 *(Examples and Illustrations in Paragraphs)*

2. Weather patterns in Guatemala are different from weather patterns in Pennsylvania. My sister and I found this out last November, when we visited some friends in Guatemala. One morning as we walked on a mountain road, the wind suddenly started blowing and a great mist rolled over us. Drops of rain began to fall. A few minutes later, the sky cleared and the sun shone brightly again. By afternoon it was as warm as a summer day, but that night we snuggled under several layers of warm blankets. The next morning there was frost on the ground!

B. What is the topic sentence in the paragraphs in Part A? In the paragraph that uses several examples, give briefly the examples that develop the topic sentence. In the other paragraph, tell what the extended illustration is.

Written Exercises

A. Write a paragraph that is developed by using several examples or illustrations. You may begin with one of the topic sentences shown below. You may also use a topic sentence of your own if it is approved by your teacher.
1. I have learned many interesting things this year.
2. I have made some careless mistakes.
3. A single act of disobedience can lead to terrible results.
4. Little brothers are very lovable.
5. We have had some interesting devotional periods this year.
6. Daniel faced a number of tests in Babylon.

B. Write another paragraph, but this time develop it by using only one extended example or illustration. Again choose one of the topics in Part A (or one that your teacher approves). You may write about the same topic as before or a different one.

Review Exercises

Write the correct words to fill in the blanks. You will not use all the words.

topic sentence	inverted	coherence	run-on
mixed	normal	unity	paragraph
compound			

1. When all the sentences in a paragraph develop one topic, the paragraph has ———.

B. **Topic sentence:**
Weather patterns in Guatemala are different from weather patterns in Pennsylvania.

Examples and illustrations in paragraph 1:
a. Great contrasts in climate just a short distance apart
b. Rainy season and dry season instead of spring, summer, fall, and winter
c. Sudden and drastic weather changes

Extended illustration in paragraph 2:
A day in the mountains of Guatemala

Written Exercises
A. (Individual work. Check for various examples and illustrations.)
B. (Individual work. Check for one extended example or illustration.)

Review Exercises
1. unity

2. In a paragraph with ———, the details fit together in such a way that the reader does not get lost or confused.

3. The ——— gives the main idea of a paragraph.

4. In a sentence with ——— word order, the complete predicate comes before the complete subject.

5. In a sentence with ——— word order, the complete subject comes before the complete predicate.

6. In a sentence with ——— word order, part of the predicate comes before the subject and part of the predicate comes after.

7. A ——— sentence has two clauses joined by a comma and a conjunction.

8. In a ——— error, two sentences are incorrectly written together as one sentence.

2. coherence
3. topic sentence
4. inverted
5. normal
6. mixed
7. compound
8. run-on

---

25. More Plural Nouns

Some nouns belong in special categories, and special care is needed to write their plural forms correctly. These include compound nouns, collective nouns, and nouns that have kept their foreign plural forms.

A *compound noun* is a noun made of two or more smaller words. There are three kinds of compound nouns.

Compound nouns:

1. Written as one word.

    airplane   newspaper   mailbox   gentleman

2. Written with a hyphen.

    sister-in-law   great-uncle   half-truth

3. Written as two words.

    high school   fountain pen   post office

In general, the plural form of a compound noun is made by changing the most important word (usually the last word) to its plural form.

airplanes	sisters-in-law	high schools
newspapers	great-uncles	fountain pens
mailboxes	half-truths	post offices
gentlemen		

Lesson 25

Purpose: (1) To teach the plurals of *compound and *collective nouns. (2) To teach some commonly used *foreign plural endings.

Oral Review:

1. Tell how to spell the following plural forms.
    a. Most plural nouns. (Add -*s.*)
    b. Nouns that end with *s, sh, ch, x,* or *z.* (Add -*es.*)
    c. Nouns that end with *y* after a consonant. (Change the *y* to *i* and add -*es.*)
    d. Nouns that end with *y* after a vowel. (Add -*s.*)
    e. Nouns that end with *f* or *fe.* (Add -*s,* or change the *f* or *fe* to *v* and add -*es.*)
    f. Nouns that end with *o* after a vowel. (Add -*s.*)
    g. Nouns that end with *o* after a consonant. (Add -*s* or -*es.*)
    h. Musical terms. (Add -*s.*)

2. a. Which three plural nouns end with -*en*? (brethren, children, oxen)
    b. Which seven plural nouns are made by changing vowels? (feet, geese, teeth, lice, mice, men, women)
    c. What are some plural nouns that are the same as the singular forms? (salmon, deer, swine, sheep, fish, trout, moose)
    d. What are some singular nouns that look like plural forms? (measles, news, mathematics, mumps, chicken pox)
    e. What are some nouns that name one thing but are usually considered plural? (trousers, scissors, pliers, tongs, tweezers)

3. Which is correct: *Measles is a disease* or *Measles are a disease?* (Measles is a disease.)

Lesson Introduction: Write the words *sandbox, newspaper, cupful,* and *brother-in-law* on the chalkboard. Ask students if they remember what special kind of nouns these are. (Compound nouns.) Ask if they know how to spell the plurals of these compound nouns. (*sandboxes, newspapers, cupfuls, brothers-in-law*)

Write *team, family,* and *school* on the chalkboard. Tell students that these are in another special class of nouns called *collective* nouns. Collective nouns name groups of persons or things. Ask the students which of the following is correct.

My family <u>is</u> coming to visit. (correct)
My family <u>are</u> coming to visit. (incorrect)

Write *larva, parenthesis,* and *radius* on the chalkboard. Ask students if they know how to spell their plurals. (*larvae* or *larvas, parentheses, radii* or *radiuses*)

Today we will study the plurals of compound and collective nouns and the rules for some commonly used foreign plural endings.

In a few cases, both words in a compound noun are changed to the plural form.

> manservant—menservants
> woman servant—women servants

If a noun ends with *-ful,* the plural form is made by adding *-s* to *-ful.*

> cupful—cupfuls   spoonful—spoonfuls

But be careful! When *full* is a separate word, *-s* is *not* added to *full.* Study the following sentences.

> Please bring three cups full of water.
> Inside the door stood two buckets full of milk.

A *collective noun* names a group of persons or things. Read the following examples.

Collective nouns:

team	school	family
assembly	class	flock

Even though a collective noun refers to more than one, it is singular because it names *one group.* For example, the noun *team* names several people working together. Even if the team has nine people, it is one unit trying to get one thing accomplished. So we say, "Our team *has* won the game." We do not say, "Our team *have* won the game." Here are a few more examples.

> Our <u>class</u> <u>is</u> studying the solar system. (not *are*)
> The <u>flock</u> of sheep <u>was</u> lying near the well. (not *were*)

Of course, a collective noun also has a plural form. If it refers to more than one *group,* it is a plural noun the same as other plural nouns.

> The two <u>classes</u> <u>are</u> studying the solar system together.
> Several <u>flocks</u> of sheep <u>were</u> lying near the well.

Many English nouns came from foreign languages. For some of these nouns, the plural forms are spelled according to the rules in foreign languages. They do not always end with *-s* as most English plurals do. Following are a few examples, along with the pronunciations of the plural forms.

> basis—bases (bā′·sēz′)
> fungus—fungi (fun′·jī)

Lesson Outline:

1. A compound noun is a noun made of two or more words. There are three kinds of compound nouns.

    (1) Written as one word.

> schoolbook   newsman   airplane

    (2) Written with a hyphen.

> brother-in-law   self-starter

    (3) Written as two words.

> mail carrier   fountain pen

2. In general, the plural form of a compound noun is made by changing the most important word to its plural form. This is usually the last word.

schoolbooks	brothers-in-law	mail carriers
newsmen	self-starters	fountain pens
airplanes		

In a few cases, both words in a compound noun are changed to the plural form.

> manservant—menservants

If a noun ends with *-ful,* the plural form is made by adding *-s* to *-ful.* This does not apply when a noun is followed by the word *full.*

> cupful—cupfuls, *but* two cups full of milk

The same spoon emptied twice is "two spoonfuls." But two separate spoons filled up are "two spoons full."

3. A collective noun names a group.

> team   assembly   class   congregation

Even though a collective noun refers to more than one, it is singular because it names *one group.* Therefore, a singular verb must be used with it. Singular verbs often end with *s.*

> My team <u>is</u> winning.
> Our family often <u>sings</u> together.
> Their class <u>goes</u> to a museum every year.

Of course, if more than one *group* is named, the plural form of the collective noun is used.

> The two families often <u>sing</u> together.

(*Teacher:* Only the singular usage of collective nouns is taught at this level. Constructions like "The class are having their pictures taken" are taught in grade 7.)

larva—larvae (lär′·vē)
radius—radii (rā′·dē·ī′)
parenthesis—parentheses (pə·ren′·thi·sēz′)

Some nouns with foreign plural forms also have regular plural forms. Always use your dictionary if you are not sure about the correct plural form.

radius—radii *or* radiuses
vertebra—vertebrae *or* vertebras

- The plural form of a compound noun is usually made by adding *-s* or *-es* to the most important word.

- A singular collective noun refers to a group, but it is still singular.

- Some plural forms have foreign spellings. Use the dictionary whenever you are not sure about a plural form.

Class Practice

A. Give the plural forms of the following nouns.
   1. father-in-law
   2. analysis
   3. great-aunt
   4. pupa
   5. armful
   6. crisis
   7. bacterium
   8. basketful
   9. manservant
   10. forefoot

B. Use a dictionary to find the two plural forms of each word. Write them on the chalkboard.
   1. antenna   2. index   3. spectrum

Written Exercises

A. Write the plural form of each noun. Use the dictionary if you need help.
   1. salmon
   2. keyhole
   3. century
   4. sheaf
   5. handful
   6. piano
   7. half
   8. panful
   9. eyetooth
   10. mother-in-law
   11. brother-in-law
   12. attorney at law

Lesson 25 Answers
Class Practice
A. 1. fathers-in-law
   2. analyses
   3. great-aunts
   4. pupae or pupas
   5. armfuls
   6. crises
   7. bacteria
   8. basketfuls
   9. menservants
   10. forefeet

B. 1. antennae, antennas
   2. indices, indexes
   3. spectra, spectrums

Written Exercises
A. 1. salmon
   2. keyholes
   3. centuries
   4. sheaves
   5. handfuls
   6. pianos
   7. halves
   8. panfuls
   9. eyeteeth
   10. mothers-in-law
   11. brothers-in-law
   12. attorneys at law

---

4. Some nouns have foreign plural endings. They do not end with *-s* as most English plural forms do. The spellings of these plural forms must simply be memorized. A dictionary will help you.

larva—larvae   parenthesis—parentheses

Some nouns with foreign plural forms also have regular plural forms. This usually happens when a technical term comes into general English usage.

amoeba—amoebae *or* amoebas
radius—radii *or* radiuses
nucleus—nuclei *or* nucleuses
medium—media *or* mediums

★ **EXTRA PRACTICE**
Worksheet 17 *(Plural Nouns)*

B. Write the two plural forms of each noun, using the dictionary for help.
1. cactus   3. formula   5. medium
2. aquarium   4. stratum   6. focus

C. Find each incorrect plural noun, and write it correctly.
1. The class is looking up facts, using various indexs.
2. The team has found several different kinds of fungee.
3. We saw the feetprints of many deer in the vallies.
4. The ovums developed into larvaa.
5. Draw three different radises in this circle.
6. The news was sent to the two sister-in-laws who lived in other countrys.
7. The nurse found two boxesful of books on how to deal with medical crisises.

Review Exercises

A. Write the plural form of each word. Check the dictionary if you are not sure. [22, 23]
1. wolf   6. moose   11. kangaroo
2. silo   7. lady   12. pliers
3. foot   8. trio   13. glass
4. shelf   9. mouse   14. reproof
5. potato   10. fox   15. tongs

B. For each underlined noun, write S or P to tell whether it is a singular or plural noun. [22–25]
1. The sad news is that many in our class have measles.
2. He broke the scissors and bent the tweezers while trying to fix the toy for the children.
3. The women asked the salesman the prices of the new trousers.
4. Charles kept up with his mathematics even though he had mumps.

Challenge Exercises

Write the plural form of each noun. Use the dictionary or encyclopedia for help.
1. commander in chief   3. stimulus   5. phenomenon
2. governor-general   4. axis   6. ellipsis

B. 1. cactuses, cacti   4. strata, stratums
2. aquariums, aquaria   5. media, mediums
3. formulas, formulae   6. focuses, foci

C. 1. indexes or indices
2. fungi or funguses
3. footprints, valleys
4. ova, larvae
5. radii or radiuses
6. sisters-in-law, countries
7. boxfuls or boxes full, crises

Review Exercises

A. 1. wolves   9. mice
2. silos   10. foxes
3. feet   11. kangaroos or kangaroo
4. shelves   12. pliers
5. potatoes   13. glasses
6. moose   14. reproofs
7. ladies   15. tongs
8. trios

B. 1. S, S, S
2. P, P, S, P
3. P, S, P, P
4. S, S

Challenge Exercises

1. commanders in chief
2. governors-general or governor-generals
3. stimuli
4. axes
5. phenomena or phenomenons
6. ellipses

26. Possessive Nouns

Read the following sentences. They both tell the same thing, but the second sentence uses fewer words. It is just as clear in meaning.

The boils of Job made him feel miserable.
Job's boils made him feel miserable.

The noun *Job's* makes the second sentence more clear and brief. It is a *possessive noun.* Possessive nouns show ownership or relationship. The apostrophe (') is used to form possessive nouns.

Is this <u>Martha's</u> book?
No, it is her <u>sister's</u> book.
The <u>visitor's</u> horse is eating <u>Mother's</u> flowers!

Most possessive nouns are used as adjectives to modify other nouns. Usually they tell *whose.*

Whose book is this? It is <u>Martha's</u> book.
Whose horse is that? It is the <u>visitor's</u> horse.

Study the following rules for making the possessive forms of nouns.
1. The possessive form of a singular noun is made by adding *'s.*

a bird<u>'s</u> feathers	Charles<u>'s</u> address
the baby<u>'s</u> fingers	our brother<u>'s</u> letter

2. The possessive form of a plural noun that ends with *-s* is made by adding an apostrophe after the *-s.*

our teacher<u>s'</u> names
the boy<u>s'</u> seats
a member<u>s'</u> meeting

3. If a plural noun does not end with *-s,* the possessive form is made by adding *'s.*

the children<u>'s</u> room
the mice<u>'s</u> nests
the deer<u>'s</u> trails

For a word like *Moses* or *Jesus,* only an apostrophe is added because the word ends with the *zus* sound. This is done to make the possessive forms easier to pronounce.

Moses<u>'</u> rod   Jesus<u>'</u> miracles

Lesson 26

Purpose: To teach the use and formation of possessive nouns.

Oral Review:
1. What is a compound noun? (a noun that is made of two or more words)
2. What is a collective noun? (a noun that names a group)
3. Give some examples of collective nouns. (team, assembly, class, family, flock)
4. Give the plural forms of the following nouns.
    a. schoolbook, airplane, mailbox, manservant, cupful (schoolbooks, airplanes, mailboxes, menservants, cupfuls)
    b. father-in-law, great-aunt, self-interest (fathers-in-law, great-aunts, self-interests)
    c. post office, full moon (post offices, full moons)

d. parenthesis, aquarium, larva, radius, index (parentheses, aquariums *or* aquaria, larvae *or* larvas, radii *or* radiuses, indexes *or* indices)

Written Quiz:
1. Write the definition of a noun. _____ _____
2. Write the plural form of each noun in the first blank. For b–d, also write proper nouns in the second blank. The first one is done for you.

	Plural Form	**Proper Noun**
a. pet	pets	Rex
b. man	_____	_____
c. country	_____	_____
d. child	_____	_____
e. wife	_____	
f. monkey	_____	
g. goose	_____	
h. trout	_____	

Quiz Answers:
1. A noun is a word that names a person, place, thing, or idea.
2. (Plural forms are given. Check for capitalization of proper nouns.)

b. men	f. monkeys
c. countries	g. geese
d. children	h. trout
e. wives	

Lesson Introduction: Read the following words to the class, and ask if they are correct.

moose's	man's	deer's
goose's	woman's	sheep's

Tell the pupils that these are proper English words. (If they are surprised, they are probably thinking of plural forms.) Write the words on the chalkboard. Tell the pupils that these are some examples of the possessive nouns that they will study today.

Write the following sentences on the chalkboard, and ask which one is most clear and brief.

Mr. Brown owns a white house.
The house of Mr. Brown is white.
Mr. Brown's house is white.

Possessive nouns are used to show ownership and to make sentences more clear and brief. In this lesson we will study rules for using possessive nouns.

Study the following chart, which shows the plural and possessive forms of several nouns.

Singular	Singular Possessive	Plural	Plural Possessive
worker	worker's	workers	workers'
man	man's	men	men's
monkey	monkey's	monkeys	monkeys'
enemy	enemy's	enemies	enemies'
life	life's	lives	lives'
Filipino	Filipino's	Filipinos	Filipinos'

Most possessive forms refer to people or animals. If a noun names an inanimate object (neither person nor animal), it is not usually written in the possessive form. For those nouns it is better to use a different expression, usually a phrase with *of* or some other preposition.

The house's roof was steep.
Better: The roof of the house was steep.

Father repaired the lawn mower's engine.
Better: Father repaired the engine of the lawn mower.

The trees' leaves are changing colors.
Better: The leaves on the trees are changing colors.

- A possessive noun shows ownership or relationship. It is often used as an adjective that tells *whose*.

- An apostrophe is used to make the possessive form of a noun.

- A possessive form is not generally used for a noun that names an inanimate object.

Class Practice

A. Rewrite these expressions on the chalkboard, using possessive nouns.
1. the work of my father
2. the letters of the parents
3. the interest of the children
4. the coat of the lady
5. the feathers of the geese

Lesson Outline:

1. A possessive noun is used to show ownership or relationship. It is usually an adjective that tells *whose* about another noun.

the pupil's book
the bird's feathers
Father's notes

2. Possessive forms are spelled according to certain rules.
(1) The possessive form of a singular noun is made by adding *'s.*

brother's   fox's   baby's   chief's

(2) The possessive form of a plural noun that ends with -s is made by adding an apostrophe after the s.

brothers'   wives'   babies'   foxes'

(3) If a plural noun does not end with -s, the possessive form is made by adding *'s.*

two mice's nests
five children's toys
three deer's tracks

For a word like *Moses* or *Jesus,* only an apostrophe is added because the word ends with the *zus* sound. No extra *uz* sound is added. The word is pronounced the same as without the apostrophe.

Moses'   Jesus'
(both pronounced in the usual way)

Lesson 26 Answers
Class Practice
A. 1. my father's work
2. the parents' letters
3. the children's interest
4. the lady's coat
5. the geese's feathers

B. Change each underlined phrase to the plural form, and write it on the chalkboard.
1. Our <u>sister's cake</u> is delicious.
2. The <u>man's idea</u> was excellent.
3. That <u>louse's bite</u> was irritating.
4. The <u>baby's face</u> is dirty.
5. The <u>ostrich's feather</u> was long.

C. Copy this chart on the chalkboard, and fill it in.

Singular	Singular Possessive	Plural	Plural Possessive
1. donkey	———	———	———
2. ox	———	———	———
3. brother	———	———	———
4. pupil	———	———	———
5. mouse	———	———	———
6. woman	———	———	———

D. Tell which of these expressions should be improved, and how.
1. the barn's walls
2. the man's gloves
3. the tractor's paint
4. the patch's color
5. the goat's horns

Written Exercises

A. Rewrite these expressions, using possessive forms.
1. the coats of the girls
2. the voice of the waiter
3. the address of Louise

B. Write the possessive form of each noun.

1. uncle		7. Alex	
2. soldier		8. prince	
3. babies		9. Irishman	
4. animals		10. chiefs	
5. rabbits		11. Doris	
6. waitress		12. wolf	

B. 1. sisters' cakes
2. men's ideas
3. lice's bites
4. babies' faces
5. ostriches' feathers

C. (Words in italics are given in the pupil's text.)
1. *donkey*   donkey's   donkeys   donkeys'
2. *ox*   ox's   oxen   oxen's
3. *brother*   brother's   brothers   brothers'
   or brethren   *or* brethren's
4. *pupil*   pupil's   pupils   pupils'
5. *mouse*   mouse's   mice   mice's
6. *woman*   woman's   women   women's

D. 1. the walls of the barn
2. (correct)
3. the paint of (on) the tractor
4. the color of the patch
5. (correct)

Written Exercises

A. 1. the girls' coats
2. the waiter's voice
3. Louise's address

B. 1. uncle's   5. rabbits'   9. Irishman's
2. soldier's   6. waitress's   10. chiefs'
3. babies'   7. Alex's   11. Doris's
4. animals'   8. prince's   12. wolf's

3. Possessive forms are not generally used for nouns that refer to inanimate objects. In referring to inanimate objects, it is usually better to use a prepositional phrase.

> **Examples:**
>   the store's windows, the road's lines
> **Better:**
>   the windows of the store, the lines on the road

(*Teacher:* Possessive forms are acceptable in certain expressions of value or distance, as *a month's wages* and *two days' journey.* Statements like "All the car's tires were flat" are becoming more acceptable today, but the approach in this English course is to discourage such expressions.)

★ **EXTRA PRACTICE**
Worksheet 18 *(Possessive Nouns)*

C. Copy and complete the chart.

Singular	Singular Possessive	Plural	Plural Possessive
1. minister	——	——	——
2. horseman	——	——	——
3. salmon	——	——	——
4. goose	——	——	——
5. fish	——	——	——
6. calf	——	——	——
7. larva	——	——	——
8. family	——	——	——

D. Improve these expressions.
1. the bed's posts
2. the stove's burners
3. the desk's drawers
4. the cabin's windows

Review Exercises

Diagram the skeletons. All but one are compound sentences. [12]
1. Snow falls in winter, and it also falls in summer.
2. Summer snow comes down as rain, for it melts on the way to the ground.
3. Snow forms directly from water vapor, but sleet forms from raindrops.
4. Sleet and hail begin as liquid rain but hit the ground as ice pellets.
5. Sometimes raindrops become colder than the freezing point, yet they do not freeze.
6. This rain freezes on contact, and it forms an icy glaze on roads, trees, and electric wires.
7. Then drivers must be very careful, or they may have serious accidents.

27. Developing Paragraphs by Comparison or Contrast

You have now studied several lessons on how to develop paragraphs. You know that all the sentences in a paragraph must develop the topic sentence and that details are important in developing a paragraph. You

---

C. (Words in italics are given in the pupil's text.)

1. *minister*	minister's	ministers	ministers'
2. *horseman*	horseman's	horsemen	horsemen's
3. *salmon*	salmon's	salmon	salmon's
4. *goose*	goose's	geese	geese's
5. *fish*	fish's	fish	fish's
		or fishes	*or* fishes'
6. *calf*	calf's	calves	calves'
7. *larva*	larva's	larvae	larvae's
8. *family*	family's	families	families'

D. 1. the posts of the bed
   2. the burners of (on) the stove
   3. the drawers of (in) the desk
   4. the windows of the cabin

Review Exercises

1. Snow | falls _and_ it | falls
2. snow | comes _for_ it | melts
3. Snow | forms _but_ sleet | forms
4. Sleet ... and ... but ... hail ... hit ... begin
5. raindrops | become _yet_ they | do freeze
6. rain | freezes _and_ it | forms
7. drivers | must be _or_ they | may have

Lesson 27

Purpose: To teach the development of paragraphs *by comparison or contrast.

Oral Review:
1. What is the purpose of examples and illustrations in a paragraph? (to give real proof that the topic sentence is true; to put clear pictures in the reader's mind)
2. Describe two ways to develop a paragraph by using examples or illustrations. (by giving several different examples or illustrations, or by giving one extended example or illustration)
3. When does a paragraph have unity? (when all the sentences tell about the topic given by the topic sentence)
4. When does a paragraph have coherence? (when all the sentences "hold together" in an orderly, sensible way)
5. What things can you do to make a paragraph coherent? (Give details in the order of time or in the order of importance or interest. Use transitional words.)
6. Give some transitional words that help to make a paragraph coherent. (first, second, next, then, soon, later, immediately, afterward, finally, for this reason, also, therefore, however, for example)

learned that using examples and illustrations is a good way to convince the reader that your topic sentence is true.

Giving comparisons or contrasts is another way of arranging details to develop a paragraph. When comparisons or contrasts are used, their purpose is to clarify or explain the topic so that the reader can understand it better.

Comparison is used in paragraphs to show similarities between two persons, places, things, or ideas. Such paragraphs are written to help the reader understand something by showing how it is like a common, familiar thing. When this is done, the paragraph usually tells about the more familiar thing first. See how this is done in the following paragraph.

Paragraph developed by comparison:

A hammer and the Bible are very different in size and shape, but they are alike in several ways. A hammer is a solid, unchanging tool. It can smash hard objects without being broken. When a carpenter builds a house, the hammer is one of his most valuable tools. The Bible is also solid and unchanging. Many men have tried to destroy or change it, yet it always stays the same. The Bible can break the hard hearts of sinful men. It is a valuable tool for building the church. Jeremiah surely spoke the truth when he said that God's Word is like a hammer.

This paragraph first describes a common, familiar object (the hammer) and tells about its uses. Then it shows how the Bible is similar in various ways.

Contrast is used to show differences between two persons, places, things, or ideas. When a paragraph is developed by contrast, it gives details about the ways in which two things are different. The following paragraph contrasts the personalities of two boys.

Paragraph developed by contrast:

My twin brothers, James and John, have always been as different as day and night. James was always a quiet, contented baby, but John never was! When Father took James to church, it seemed that the way he set him down was the way he stayed until Father picked him up again. But I can't tell you how many times Father had to take wiggly, squirmy John out of services for a lesson! Now that the twins are grown, what do you think they like to do? James sits patiently hour after hour working on lessons for Sunday

Lesson Introduction: Do you know what a gnu looks like? Perhaps it will help if I compare it to another animal. The gnu looks something like a zebra. It has stripes on its shoulders and neck as a zebra does. It is about the size of a zebra. It even has a tail like a zebra's. It may also help if I tell you how a gnu is different from a zebra. A zebra does not have horns, but a gnu has long horns that extend outward and curve upward. The zebra has a pleasant-looking face, but the gnu has a long, sad-looking face. Now do you have a picture in your mind of what a gnu looks like?

Comparisons and contrasts help us to learn. We grasp new ideas better if we compare them with what we already know. Today we want to learn how to develop paragraphs by using comparisons and contrasts.

Lesson Outline:

1. Comparisons or contrasts use details to clarify or explain the topic of the paragraph. Their purpose is to clarify or explain the topic so that the reader can understand it better. (Ultimately, comparisons or contrasts also help to prove that the topic sentence is true.)

2. Comparison is used to show similarities between two persons, places, things, or ideas. Here are some examples of comparisons.

God's people are like sheep.
Jesus is like a shepherd.
God's Word is like a shepherd's rod.

school books. But John can run three or four different construction projects at one time without getting flustered. The twins are certainly different, but they both live useful lives for God.

There are two ways to list comparisons or contrasts. One way is to give all the points about the first thing and then all the points about the second thing. The other way is to give the comparisons or contrasts by turns, point by point. These two ways are illustrated in the paragraphs above. Compare the following lists of the points they present.

First paragraph:
1. A hammer is an unchanging tool.
2. It can smash hard objects.
3. It is valuable for building houses.
4. The Bible is an unchanging Book.
5. It can break the hard hearts of sinful men.
6. It is valuable for building the church.

Second paragraph:
1. James was a quiet, contented baby.
2. John was a restless baby.
3. Now James works on lessons for Sunday school books.
4. John can run three or four different construction projects at one time.

A paragraph must be more than just a list of comparisons or contrasts. It must also include enough details to make the comparisons or contrasts meaningful. The following paragraph is not very meaningful or interesting, because it has no details to explain the comparisons.

> The Bible is like a mirror. When people look into a mirror, they can see what they look like; and when people read the Bible, they can see what their lives look like. People must look into a mirror before it can help them, and people must look into the Bible before it can help them. People don't always like what a mirror shows them, and people don't always like what the Bible shows them. So the Bible really is very much like a mirror.

In the paragraph above, every sentence that shows a comparison has two clauses that are almost the same. Sentences like these are tiresome to read. They need specific details, such as what people might see when they look into a mirror (dirty face or uncombed hair) and what they might see in their lives when they look into the Bible (pride

3. Contrast is used to show differences between two persons, places, things, or ideas. Here are some examples of contrasts.

> Sheep cannot choose between right and wrong, but people can.
> A shepherd cannot meet every need of every sheep, but Jesus can meet every need of every person. He even knows what each person is thinking!
> A rod has no life or power of its own, but God's Word is living and powerful.

4. There are two ways to list comparisons or contrasts in a paragraph.

a. *Give all the points about the first thing and then all the points about the second thing.* Refer to the sample paragraph about the Bible and the hammer.

b. *Give the comparisons or contrasts by turns, point by point.* Refer to the sample paragraph about the twins.

5. When a paragraph is developed by comparisons or contrasts, it must also include enough details to make the comparisons or contrasts meaningful. It is tiresome to read that Item A has a certain quality and Item B also has that quality, that Item A has a certain other quality and Item B also has that other quality, and so on. Specific details must be given about each quality so that the comparisons or contrasts are meaningful and effective. (Refer to the sample paragraph about the Bible and a mirror.)

or selfishness). Exactly how does a mirror or the Bible help a person who looks into it? What might a mirror or the Bible show people that they do not like?

Many paragraphs are developed by the use of several methods together. For example, comparison and contrast can be used in the same paragraph. In the paragraph about the hammer and the Bible, do you see the clause that shows a contrast? It is in the first sentence: "A hammer and the Bible are very different in size and shape." Whatever method you use, remember that all the sentences must develop the topic sentence and that they must be in a sensible order.

When you use comparison or contrast, end your paragraph with a concluding sentence that refers again to the comparison or contrast you have been making. Notice how this is done in each of the example paragraphs in this lesson.

- A paragraph can be developed by using comparison or contrast.

- Comparison shows similarities between things. Contrast shows differences between things.

- One way of showing comparison or contrast is to give all the points about the first thing and then all the points about the second thing. Another way is to give the comparisons or contrasts by turns, point by point.

Class Practice

A. Read the paragraph below, and do these exercises.
 1. Is this paragraph developed by comparison or by contrast?
 2. Give the comparisons or contrasts that it uses.
 3. Which method is used in this paragraph? Choose *a* or *b*.
   a. All the points about the first thing are given, and then all the points about the second thing.
   b. The comparisons or contrasts are given by turns, point by point.
 4. Read the concluding sentence, which refers again to the comparison made in the paragraph.
 5. This paragraph is about the same topic as the last sample paragraph in the lesson. Why is this paragraph better?

Lesson 27 Answers
Class Practice

A. 1. by comparison
   2. A mirror shows a person what he looks like.
       The Bible shows a person what his life looks like to God.
       Some people do not like to look into a mirror because they do not like what it shows them.
       Some people do not read the Bible because they do not like what it shows them about their lives.
       A mirror helps us to keep ourselves clean and neat.
       The Bible helps us to keep our lives pure in God's sight.
   3. b
   4. Both a mirror and the Bible are so beneficial that we should look into them every day.
   5. This paragraph has interesting and meaningful details that make the comparisons clear.

The Bible is like a mirror. When a person looks into a mirror, it shows him what he looks like. He can see right away if his hair is neat. When a person reads the Bible, it shows him what his life looks like to God. He can see if he is doing what God wants. Some people do not like to look into a mirror because they do not like what it shows them. They do not want to wash their faces or comb their hair. In the same way, some people do not read the Bible because they do not like what it shows about their lives. They do not want to change. A mirror helps us to keep ourselves clean and neat. The Bible helps us by showing how we can keep our lives pure in God's sight. Both a mirror and the Bible are so beneficial that we should look into them every day.

B. Choose one of these topic sentences. On the chalkboard, list some points that could be used to develop the paragraph by comparison or contrast.
  1. True Christians are like sheep.
  2. Joseph is an Old Testament type of Christ.
  3. The Christian is like salt (or light) in the world.
  4. Washing dishes is more enjoyable than weeding a garden.
  5. The Bible is like a sword (or fire, rock, map, or light).
  6. Butterflies are different from moths in several ways.
  7. Life in New Mexico (or any state or province) is different from life in Pennsylvania (or your home state or province).
  8. Dresses made from cotton fabric are better than (or not as good as) dresses made from knitted fabric.

B. (For number 1, see points 2 and 3 of the Lesson Outline. Suggested points are given here for numbers 6 and 8.)
  6. Most butterflies have thin bodies.
    Most butterflies rest with their wings raised.
    Butterflies have knobs at the tips of their antennae.
    Most butterflies are active during the day.
    Most moths have plump bodies.
    Most moths rest with their wings spread flat.
    Moths have hairlike or plume-shaped antennae that come to a point.
    Most moths are active at night.
  8. Cotton dresses are cooler in summer than knitted dresses.
    Cotton dresses are more absorbent than knitted dresses.
    Knitted dresses do not need ironing.
    Knitted dresses often cost less than cotton dresses.
    Knitted dresses do not fade as cotton dresses do.
    Knitted fabric is wider by the yard than cotton fabric.

Written Exercises

Choose one of the topic sentences in Class Practice, Part B, and write a paragraph using comparison or contrast (or both). You may choose a topic of your own if it is approved by your teacher. Do not choose a topic that is used in the lesson.

Review Exercises

Choose words from the list to answer the following questions. You will not use all the words. [16, 17]

topic sentence	finally	soon
coherence	time	first
transitional	later	unity
importance	next	form
transactional	interest	also

1. What does a paragraph have when all the sentences tell about the same topic?
2. What does a paragraph have when all the sentences fit together in an orderly, sensible way?
3. In what three kinds of order may the details of a paragraph be given?
4. What kind of words help to provide coherence in a paragraph?
5. What are six words that can be used as transitional words?

---

28. Chapter 3 Review

Class Practice

A. Tell which words in this list could be used as nouns.

1. labor
2. forth
3. singer
4. reports
5. pray
6. action
7. often
8. flight
9. quietness
10. remember
11. affection
12. different

B. Tell how to change these words to nouns by adding *-ness*, *-ion*, *-ity*, or *-ment*. Check the dictionary if you are not sure of the spelling.

1. late
2. adjust
3. active
4. tranquil
5. enlarge

Written Exercises

(Individual work.)

Review Exercises

1. unity
2. coherence
3. importance, time, interest
4. transitional
5. finally, later, next, soon, first, also

Lesson 28 Answers
Class Practice

A.
1. labor	8. flight
3. singer	9. quietness
4. reports	11. affection
6. action	

B.
1. lateness
2. adjustment
3. activeness, activity
4. tranquilness, tranquility
5. enlargement

Lesson 28

Purpose: To review the concepts taught in Chapter 3.

C. Tell which words are nouns in the following paragraph.

    A bat is a strange-looking mammal with unusual habits and abilities. It looks somewhat like a mouse with wings. Bats sleep during the day and hunt insects at night. They hang upside down in caves or barns to sleep. Some people have a fear of bats, but bats do not usually come near people. A bat uses a special kind of sonar to keep from bumping into things. It can find its way even in the dark. Bats can see with their eyes as well as with their ears. Truly God has made the bat a most fascinating animal.

D. Give a proper noun for each of these common nouns.
1. state   3. mountain   5. friend
2. ocean   4. dog

E. On the chalkboard, rewrite these expressions, using possessive forms.
1. the hat of the man   4. the dolls of the girls
2. the hats of the men   5. the work of the waitress
3. the doll of the girl   6. the work of the waitresses

F. Which of these expressions should be improved? How should they be changed?
1. the chair's legs   4. the squirrel's nuts
2. the frog's tongue   5. the desks' tops
3. the barn's windows   6. the lantern's glow

G. Tell which of these paragraphs is better, and why. Briefly give the details that support the topic sentence of the better paragraph.

1.   "A word fitly spoken is like apples of gold in pictures of silver" (Proverbs 25:11). Apples are a valuable food. They provide important vitamins and minerals. Gold and silver are two of the most valuable metals. Iron and copper are valuable too, but not as valuable as gold and silver. Good words are really more valuable than apples, gold, and silver.

2.   "A word fitly spoken is like apples of gold in pictures of silver" (Proverbs 25:11). There are several kinds of fitly spoken words. A kind word can cheer a lonely or burdened heart. A good word of advice or instruction can prevent a costly mistake. A word of encouragement can inspire a worker to do his task with joy. Truly a word spoken in the right way at the right time is beautiful, and it is more valuable than gold or silver.

C. (Nouns are underlined.)

    A <u>bat</u> is a strange-looking <u>mammal</u> with unusual <u>habits</u> and <u>abilities</u>. It looks somewhat like a <u>mouse</u> with <u>wings</u>. <u>Bats</u> sleep during the <u>day</u> and hunt <u>insects</u> at <u>night</u>. They hang upside down in <u>caves</u> or <u>barns</u> to sleep. Some <u>people</u> have a <u>fear</u> of <u>bats</u>, but <u>bats</u> do not usually come near <u>people</u>. A <u>bat</u> uses a special <u>kind</u> of <u>sonar</u> to keep from bumping into <u>things.</u> It can find its <u>way</u> even in the <u>dark</u>. <u>Bats</u> can see with their <u>eyes</u> as well as with their <u>ears</u>. Truly <u>God</u> has made the <u>bat</u> a most fascinating <u>animal</u>.

D. (Sample answers.)
1. New Jersey
2. Atlantic Ocean
3. Mount Hermon
4. Rover
5. Linda Martin

E. 1. the man's hat   4. the girls' dolls
   2. the men's hats   5. the waitress's work
   3. the girl's doll   6. the waitresses' work

F. 1. the legs of the chair
   2. (correct)
   3. the windows of the barn
   4. (correct)
   5. the tops of the desks
   6. the glow of the lantern

G. Paragraph 2 is better. The details support the topic sentence by giving examples to show that it is true.

Details or examples used:
1. A kind word brings cheer.
2. A word of advice can prevent a mistake.
3. A word of encouragement can inspire a worker.

(Note also how the last sentence restates and clarifies the topic sentence.)

H. Read the paragraph below, and answer these questions.
1. Is this paragraph developed by comparison or by contrast?
2. Which method is used in this paragraph? Choose *a* or *b*.
   a. All the points about the first thing are given, and then all the points about the second thing.
   b. The comparisons or contrasts are given by turns, point by point.
3. Which sentence ties the end of the paragraph to the beginning?

Our Little Kubota

Our little Kubota is almost the color of a horse, and it works like a horse. As you know, a horse pulls with all four legs. Well, our Kubota pulls with all four wheels. The traction is amazing. A little feed at the beginning of the day takes a horse a long way. Fill our Kubota's tank with fuel, and it is all set to work for hours. A hardworking horse makes little noise. You hear only a creaking harness, plodding footsteps, and deep breathing. Our Kubota, even when working hard, makes little more than a pleasant purr. Yes, our little Kubota is a real workhorse.

Written Exercises

A. List nouns as described below.
1. Names of four animals. **Example:** bear
2. Names of four kinds of vehicles. **Example:** train
3. Names of four periods of time. **Example:** day
4. Names of four things a farmer might use. **Example:** harrow
5. Four nouns to illustrate the four genders.

B. Find each proper noun, and write it correctly.
1. When brother daniel lived in ontario, he was the principal at the shady grove christian school.
2. Our teacher showed us an article on the atacama desert in the magazine called *nature friend.*
3. On the first wednesday in april, the students from the london mennonite school took a test on events during the french and indian war.
4. The first truly successful steam locomotive was the *rocket,* which was built in 1829 by two english inventors named george and robert stephenson.
5. Behold, god is my salvation; I will trust and not be afraid: for the lord jehovah is my strength and my song.

H. 1. by comparison
2. b
3. Yes, our little Kubota is a real workhorse.

Written Exercises

A. (Sample answers.)
1. dog, cow, sheep, deer, raccoon, squirrel
2. car, bus, ship, airplane, bicycle, carriage
3. hour, night, week, month, year, century
4. pitchfork, shovel, tractor, plow, disk, cultivator
5. boy, girl, person, book

B. 1. Brother Daniel, Ontario, Shady Grove Christian School
2. Atacama Desert, *Nature Friend*
3. Wednesday, April, London Mennonite School, French (and) Indian War
4. *Rocket,* English, George (and) Robert Stephenson
5. God, Lord Jehovah

C. Find each proper adjective, and write it correctly.
1. Aspirin, the drug in bayer tablets, was first made by a french chemist.
2. It is different from the drug in tylenol tablets.
3. A newer kind of pain reliever is used in advil tablets.
4. Penicillin was developed by english scientists of scottish, german, and australian backgrounds.

D. Write the plural form of each word.

1. purpose	7. memory	13. manservant
2. ox	8. belief	14. potato
3. trio	9. alto	15. mosquito
4. tooth	10. deer	16. cupful
5. loaf	11. pliers	17. fungus
6. glass	12. key	18. mailbox

E. Rewrite each sentence, changing all the nouns to plural forms. Include the nouns that show possession. (You will need to change some other words too.)
1. The adventurous boy emptied his pocket.
2. Out came a goose's feather, a deer's tooth, a paper airplane, and a card from a post office!
3. My brother-in-law told me this story.

F. Copy and complete this chart.

Singular	Singular Possessive	Plural	Plural Possessive
1. cow	——	——	——
2. pupil	——	——	——
3. trout	——	——	——
4. man	——	——	——
5. fox	——	——	——
6. calf	——	——	——
7. city	——	——	——
8. moose	——	——	——

G. Briefly list the comparisons or contrasts from the paragraph about the Kubota tractor in Class Practice, Part H.

———————————

C. 1. Bayer, French
2. Tylenol
3. Advil
4. English, Scottish, German, Australian

D. 1. purposes   10. deer
2. oxen   11. pliers
3. trios   12. keys
4. teeth   13. menservants
5. loaves   14. potatoes
6. glasses   15. mosquitoes, mosquitos
7. memories   16. cupfuls
8. beliefs   17. fungi, funguses
9. altos   18. mailboxes

E. (Wording may vary somewhat.)
1. The adventurous boys emptied their pockets.
2. Out came geese's feathers, deer's teeth, paper airplanes, and cards from post offices!
3. My brothers-in-law told me these stories.

F. (Words in italics are given in the pupil's text.)

1. *cow*	cow's	cows	cows'
2. *pupil*	pupil's	pupils	pupils'
3. *trout*	trout's	trout	trout's
4. *man*	man's	men	men's
5. *fox*	fox's	foxes	foxes'
6. *calf*	calf's	calves	calves'
7. *city*	city's	cities	cities'
8. *moose*	moose's	moose	moose's

G. (Allow reasonable variation.)
1. It is almost the color of a horse.
2. It works like a horse.
3. A horse pulls with all four legs, and the tractor pulls with all four wheels.
4. A horse eats little but works hard and long, and the tractor uses little fuel to work a long time.
5. A horse makes little noise, and the tractor makes only a pleasant purr.

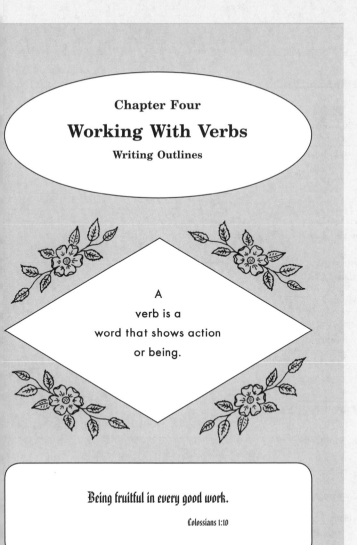

Chapter Four

Working With Verbs

Writing Outlines

A
verb is a
word that shows action
or being.

Being fruitful in every good work.

Colossians 1:10

29. Verbs

Every sentence must have a verb. The verb tells you what is happening. It tells what the subject does or is.

A verb is a word that shows *action* or *being*. These are the two main classes of verbs.

1. *Action verbs express any action that can be performed,* such as *speak, fly, walk,* and *remember.* There are so many action verbs that we could not list them all.

    Some verbs show physical action, and others show mental action.

    Physical action: jump, run, swing, slide, work
    Mental action: think, study, believe, memorize

    Have, has, and *had* are action verbs that show possession. They show that the subject of the sentence *owns* or *did own* something.

2. *The forms of* be *express being rather than action.* They give meaning to a sentence by showing that something exists or has existed. The forms of *be* are *am, is, are, was, were, be, been,* and *being.*

Sometimes two or more verbs are used together in a *verb phrase.* A verb phrase has a *main verb* and one or more *helping verbs.* The main verb is always the last word in a verb phrase. In the following sentences, the verb phrases are underlined twice.

Job | <u>was sitting</u> among the ashes.
Satan | <u>had smitten</u> him with sore boils.

Being familiar with the helping verbs will help you to recognize them quickly. You should remember these from Lesson 2.

Forms of *be*:   am, is, are, was, were, be, been, being
Forms of *have*:   have, has, had
Forms of *do*:   do, does, did
Forms of *may*:   may, might, must
Other helping verbs: can—could, shall—should, will—would

Verb phrases may be interrupted by words that are not verbs. The following words are never verbs: *not, never, hardly, always, ever,* and *surely.* These are adverbs that modify verbs.

Lesson 29

Purpose: To teach the basic facts about verbs.

Oral Review:

1. What is a possessive noun? (a noun that shows ownership or relationship)
2. A possessive noun is often used as what part of speech? (adjective)
3. Tell how these expressions should be improved: *the house's roof, the car's engine.* (the roof of the house, the engine of the car)
4. How should the possessive forms of *Moses* and *Jesus* be written? (Add only an apostrophe because these names already end with a *zus* sound.)

Lesson Introduction: Ask students to give the definition of a verb. (A verb is a word that shows action or being.) Ask them to give some examples of action verbs. (Sample answers: *jump, sing, dig, write, memorize*) Ask

someone to list the forms of *be.* (*am, is, are, was, were, be, been, being*) What do the following verbs make you think of?

leap	float	warble	dart
soar	spring	speed	whistle
bound	wave	hum	scatter

Descriptive verbs help make our language interesting. Today we want to study some basic facts about verbs.

Lesson Outline:

1. A verb is a word that shows **action or being.** (Be sure every student has memorized this definition.) Every sentence must have a verb.

2. There are two main classes of verbs.

(1) *Action verbs express action.* The action may be physical or mental. *Have, has,* and *had* are action verbs that show possession.

Physical action:
fly, drive, hop, sweep
Mental action:
learn, ponder, memorize, repeat

But Job | <u>did</u> not <u>sin</u> with his lips.
His faithfulness | <u>has</u> surely <u>inspired</u> many people.

Two verbs joined by *and, but,* or *or* are compound verbs.

She <u>jumped</u> or <u>skipped</u> the whole way.
She <u>smiled</u> and <u>told</u> her teacher.

• A verb is a word that shows action or being.

• A verb phrase includes a main verb and one or more helping verbs. The helping verbs are as follows:

Forms of *be*:	am, is, are, was, were, be, been, being
Forms of *have*:	have, has, had
Forms of *do*:	do, does, did
Forms of *may*:	may, might, must
Other helping verbs:	can—could, shall—should, will—would

Class Practice

Give the verbs and verb phrases in these sentences.
1. The heavens declare the glory of God.
2. The firmament is showing His handiwork.
3. We can see God's glory in the starry skies.
4. The stars do not speak; they have no voice.
5. But they are always telling about their Creator.
6. The sun is like a strong man in a race.
7. We must observe God's creation and praise Him.
8. We can discover His law and practice it diligently.
9. God has created many interesting creatures.
10. Monstrous blue whales leap from the surface of the sea.
11. Bald eagles can soar effortlessly over the countryside.
12. Little brown squirrels fly from branch to branch.
13. In the black of night, the keen-eyed owl clearly calls, *Who-who?*
14. Silvery fish dart here and there in clear pools.

Lesson 29 Answers
Class Practice

1. declare	9. has created
2. is showing	10. leap
3. can see	11. can soar
4. do speak, have	12. fly
5. are telling	13. calls
6. is	14. dart
7. must observe (and) praise	
8. can discover (and) practice	

(2) *The forms of* be *express being rather than action.* They give meaning to a sentence by showing that something exists or has existed. The forms of *be* are as follows:

am, is, are, was, were, be, been, being

3. Sometimes two or more verbs are used together in a verb phrase. A verb phrase has a main verb and one or more helping verbs. The main verb is always the last word in a verb phrase.

Review the list of helping verbs. Be sure all the students know them by memory.

Forms of *be*:	am, is, are, was, were, be, been, being
Forms of *have*:	have, has, had
Forms of *do*:	do, does, did
Forms of *may*:	may, might, must
Other helping verbs:	
	can—could, shall—should, will—would

4. Verb phrases may be interrupted by words that are not verbs. The following words are not verbs, but adverbs: *not, never, hardly, always, ever, surely.*

5. Two verbs joined by and, but, *or* **or are compound verbs.**

★ **EXTRA PRACTICE**
Worksheet 19 *(Verbs)*

Written Exercises

A. Write whether each word is *always* a verb or *never* a verb.

1. some
2. bury
3. announce
4. attic
5. allow
6. provide
7. almost
8. gradual
9. lose
10. certain
11. remind
12. agree
13. subtract
14. action
15. discuss
16. artist

B. Copy all the verbs and verb phrases in the following sentences.

1. The swallows, robins, and wrens have returned for the summer.
2. God has given the birds various instincts.
3. Birds establish their territories and mark their boundaries.
4. Birds do not drive fence posts or hang up signs.
5. They sing at the edges of their territories instead.
6. They are warning other birds of their boundaries.
7. They must find enough food for their babies.
8. We should always speak kindly and cheerfully.
9. Sister Irene has never seen a real turtle.
10. The huge pumpkin fell onto the road and burst apart.
11. Can the boys lift the rock off the road?
12. Please erase your errors completely.

C. Use the following verbs in sentences of your own. Use each pair in the same sentence.

1. pay, take
2. remember, write

Review Exercises

Diagram the sentence skeletons. [10, 11]

1. The United States bought Alaska from Russia in 1867.
2. William H. Seward was the secretary of state, and he paid about two cents an acre for it.
3. Some people did not approve the purchase, and they called Alaska "Seward's Icebox."
4. Alaska has many valuable natural resources.
5. Huge oil reserves have been found at Prudhoe Bay along the Arctic Coast.
6. The value of Alaska's natural resources has repaid its purchase price hundreds of times over.
7. In the largest state live the fewest people.

Written Exercises

A.
1. never
2. always
3. always
4. never
5. always
6. always
7. never
8. never
9. always
10. never
11. always
12. always
13. always
14. never
15. always
16. never

B.
1. have returned
2. has given
3. establish (and) mark
4. do drive (or) hang
5. sing
6. are warning
7. must find
8. should speak
9. has seen
10. fell (and) burst
11. Can lift
12. erase

C. (Individual sentences.)

Review Exercises

1. United States | bought

2. William H. Seward | was _and_ he | paid

3. people | did approve _and_ they | called

4. Alaska | has

5. reserves | have been found

   (*Oil reserves* may be diagrammed as the simple subject.)

6. value | has repaid

7. people | live

8. In such wild country, men do not build many roads.
9. Eskimos still hunt and fish in Alaska.
10. Towering mountains and beautiful scenery attract people to Alaska.
11. Find Mount McKinley, the highest peak in the United States.
12. Great endurance is a necessity in the cold wilderness.

---

30. Principal Parts of Regular Verbs

Verbs have three main forms called *principal parts*. The principal parts are used to express different meanings. For example, if we want to tell about something that is happening now, we use one form, or principal part, of the verb. If we want to tell about something that happened yesterday or last week, we must use a different principal part. The names of the three principal parts are as follows:

First principal part: *present* form
Second principal part: *past* form
Third principal part: *past participle*

You can easily remember the three principal parts of verbs by using them in sentences like the ones below.

Present: Today I <u>write</u>.
Past: Yesterday I <u>wrote</u>.
Past participle: Every day I <u>have written</u>.

As these sentences show, the first principal part of a verb (present form) is used to speak of an action happening at the present time. The second principal part (past form) is used to speak of an action happening in the past. The third principal part (past participle) also refers to an action in the past. But the past participle must be used with the helping verb *have, has,* or *had.*

In regular verbs, the past form and the past participle are exactly the same. They are made by adding *-ed* to the present form. Be sure to spell these forms with *-ed* correctly. Study the following rules and examples.

8. ___men___ | ___do build___

9. Eskimos — hunt and fish

10. mountains and scenery — attract

11. ___(you)___ | ___Find___

12. ___endurance___ | ___is___

Lesson 30

Purpose: To teach the three principal parts of regular verbs.

Oral Review:
1. Give the definition of a verb. (a word that shows action or being)
2. True or false: A complete sentence must have a verb. (true)
3. What are the two main classes of verbs? (action verbs and forms of *be*)
4. What are the forms of *be*? (am, is, are, was, were, be, been, being)
5. Name the two classes of action verbs, and give some examples in each class. (physical action: jump, fly, drive, sing; mental action: think, remember, enjoy, respect)
6. What is a possessive noun? (a noun that shows ownership or relationship)
7. A possessive noun is often used as what part of speech? (adjective)

Written Quiz:
1. Write the definition of a verb. _____
_____
2. Write the forms of *be*. _____ _____ _____
_____ _____ _____ _____ _____
3. Write the other helping verbs in groups.
_____ _____ _____
_____ _____ _____
_____ _____ _____
_____—_____; _____—_____; _____—_____

Quiz Answers:
1. A verb is a word that shows action or being.
2. am, is, are, was, were, be, been, being
3. have, has, had
   do, does, did
   may, might, must
   can—could, shall—should, will—would

1. If a verb ends with *e,* drop the *e* before adding *-ed.*

Present:	Today I <u>rake</u> the leaves.
Past:	Yesterday I <u>raked</u> the leaves.
Past participle:	Every day I <u>have raked</u> the leaves.

2. If a verb ends with *y* after a consonant, change the *y* to *i* and add *-ed.*

Present:	Today I <u>carry</u> the baskets.
Past:	Yesterday I <u>carried</u> the baskets.
Past participle:	Every day I <u>have carried</u> the baskets.

3. If a verb ends with *y* after a vowel, simply add *-ed.*

Present:	Today we <u>stay</u> here.
Past:	Yesterday we <u>stayed</u> here.
Past participle:	Every day we <u>have stayed</u> here.

4. If a one-syllable verb ends with a single consonant after a short vowel, double the final consonant and add *-ed.*

Present:	Today the boys <u>skip</u> this part.
Past:	Yesterday the boys <u>skipped</u> this part.
Past participle:	Every day the boys <u>have skipped</u> this part.

- Verbs have three principal parts:
  1. The first principal part (present form)
  2. The second principal part (past form)
  3. The third principal part (past participle)

- The second and third principal parts of regular verbs are made by adding *-ed* to the present form.

- The past participle must be used with the helping verb *have, has,* or *had.*

Lesson Introduction: Read the following sentences to the students. Ask if anything is wrong with them. Have pupils tell how to correct each one that is incorrect.

   Today I <u>carry</u> the groceries for Grandmother. (correct)

   Yesterday Jolene <u>carry</u> the bags for Mother. (carried)

   Little Gerald has never <u>carry</u> the big bags. (carried)

   If I <u>tag</u> you, you will be out. (correct)

   Yesterday I <u>tag</u> three people before the bell rang. (tagged)

   I have <u>tag</u> you three times now. (tagged)

Today we will study the three main forms of regular verbs, called the three principal parts.

Lesson Outline:

1. Verbs have three principal parts.

2. The first principal part is the **present form.** This is the basic form of the verb. It is used to express action or existence right now.

   tag   climb

3. The second principal part is the **past form.** Sometimes it is called the simple past form. This form expresses action or existence in the past.

   tagged   climbed

4. The third principal part is the **past participle.** It also expresses past action or existence, but it must be used with the helping verb *have, has,* or *had.*

   (have) tagged   (have) climbed

(*Teacher:* The lesson states that the past participle must be used with a form of *have.* This emphasis is given because of the common misuse of the past participle in expressions like "I seen" and "He done." But this rule applies only when a past participle is the main verb in the active voice. In Chapter 5 the pupils will learn that the passive voice of a verb is formed by using a past participle with a form of *be.* And in grade 7 they will learn that a past participle may be used alone to modify a noun, as in the phrase "a fallen tree.")

5. The second and third principal parts of regular verbs are made by adding **-ed** *to the first principal part.* These two parts are spelled the same, but the third principal part must be used with the helping verb *have, has,* or *had.*

Class Practice

A. Say and spell the missing principal parts. Use *have* with the past participle. The first one is done for you.

First (Present)	Second (Past)	Third (Past Participle)
1. remember	remembered	(have) remembered
2. bloom	——	——
3. thrive	——	——
4. move	——	——
5. rely	——	——
6. obey	——	——
7. tag	——	——
8. fill	——	——

B. Say each verb or verb phrase. Tell whether the verb is the *present* form, the *past* form, or the *past participle*.

1. Form a line along the wall.
2. He patched the leak with some rubber.
3. I have pressed his suit.
4. The impact dented the side of the car.
5. We treat him every year on his birthday.
6. I have hemmed the new dresses.
7. Have you identified the stranger yet?
8. We forced the door open and entered the empty room.
9. Trace the pattern, and pass it to me.
10. The horses dragged the logs out of the woods.

Lesson 30 Answers
Class Practice

A. (Words in italics are given in the pupil's text.)

1. *remember*	remembered	(have) remembered
2. *bloom*	bloomed	(have) bloomed
3. *thrive*	thrived	(have) thrived
4. *move*	moved	(have) moved
5. *rely*	relied	(have) relied
6. *obey*	obeyed	(have) obeyed
7. *tag*	tagged	(have) tagged
8. *fill*	filled	(have) filled

B.
1. Form, present
2. patched, past
3. have pressed, past participle
4. dented, past
5. treat, present
6. have hemmed, past participle
7. Have identified, past participle
8. forced, past; entered, past
9. Trace, present; pass, present
10. dragged, past

6. **Past forms with -ed *must be spelled correctly.***

(1) If a verb ends with *e*, drop the *e* before adding *-ed.*

hike—hiked   care—cared

(2) If a verb ends with *y* after a consonant, change the *y* to *i* and add *-ed.*

try—tried   carry—carried

(3) If a verb ends with *y* after a vowel, simply add *-ed.*

play—played   destroy—destroyed

(4) If a one-syllable verb ends with a single consonant after a short vowel, double the final consonant and add *-ed.*

rub—rubbed   step—stepped

Written Exercises

A. Copy the chart, and add the missing words. Include the helping verb *have* with each past participle. The first one is done for you.

First (Present)	Second (Past)	Third (Past Participle)
1. operate	operated	(have) operated
2. count	———	———
3. change	———	———
4. vary	———	———
5. destroy	———	———
6. stop	———	———
7. journey	———	———
8. stretch	———	———

B. Copy each verb or verb phrase. Write whether the verb is the *present* form, the *past* form, or the *past participle*.

Example: We finished all our work for today.
Answer: finished, past

1. Karen petted the poor little pup.
2. The kitten has played with the yarn a long time.
3. Have you copied all the exercises?
4. The workers stack the planks neatly.
5. This medicine has cured him of his fever.
6. The company has stored merchandise in this warehouse for several years.
7. The wise men rejoiced with exceeding great joy.
8. They had followed the star to Jesus.
9. The wise men opened their treasures.
10. They presented gold, frankincense, and myrrh to Jesus.
11. The wise men worshiped Jesus.
12. Today we also worship Jesus.
13. We hurried down that street toward the post office.
14. He has delivered your order.
15. All the sets seem complete.

Written Exercises

A. (Words in italics are given in the pupil's text.)

1. *operate*   *operated*   *(have) operated*
2. *count*   counted   (have) counted
3. *change*   changed   (have) changed
4. *vary*   varied   (have) varied
5. *destroy*   destroyed   (have) destroyed
6. *stop*   stopped   (have) stopped
7. *journey*   journeyed   (have) journeyed
8. *stretch*   stretched   (have) stretched

B. 1. petted, past
2. has played, past participle
3. Have copied, past participle
4. stack, present
5. has cured, past participle
6. has stored, past participle
7. rejoiced, past
8. had followed, past participle
9. opened, past
10. presented, past
11. worshiped, past
12. worship, present
13. hurried, past
14. has delivered, past participle
15. seem, present

Review Exercises

A. Copy the chart, and add the missing words. [22–26]

Singular	Singular Possessive	Plural	Plural Possessive
1. boy	———	———	———
2. hero	———	———	———
3. waitress	———	———	———
4. enemy	———	———	———
5. deer	———	———	———
6. baby	———	———	———
7. chief	———	———	———
8. wife	———	———	———

B. Change each underlined noun to the plural form. [22–26]

> **Example:** The <u>animal's cage</u> had to be cleaned that day.
> **Answer:** animals' cages

1. My <u>sister's dress</u> was lost in the baggage.
2. The <u>fox's den</u> was discovered.
3. The <u>girl's room</u> was in good order.
4. The <u>man's hat</u> blew off.

C. Rewrite each expression, using a possessive form. [26]
1. the voices of the children
2. the dogs of the boys
3. the miracles of Jesus
4. the meeting of the members
5. the horses of the man
6. the nests of the mice

———————————

Review Exercises

A. (Words in italics are given in the pupil's text.)

1. *boy*	boy's	boys	boys'
2. *hero*	hero's	heroes	heroes'
3. *waitress*	waitress's	waitresses	waitresses'
4. *enemy*	enemy's	enemies	enemies'
5. *deer*	deer's	deer	deer's
6. *baby*	baby's	babies	babies'
7. *chief*	chief's	chiefs	chiefs'
8. *wife*	wife's	wives	wives'

B. 1. sisters' dresses
   2. foxes' dens
   3. girls' rooms
   4. men's hats

C. 1. the children's voices
   2. the boys' dogs
   3. Jesus' miracles
   4. the members' meeting
   5. the man's horses
   6. the mice's nests

Principal Parts of Common Verbs

(Some verbs on this chart have alternate forms.)

First	Second	Third	First	Second	Third
(Present)	*(Past)*	*(Past Participle)*	*(Present)*	*(Past)*	*(Past Participle)*
be (is)	was	(have) been	*lie	lay	(have) lain
begin	began	(have) begun	pay	paid	(have) paid
blow	blew	(have) blown	put	put	(have) put
break	broke	(have) broken	*raise	raised	(have) raised
bring	brought	(have) brought	read	read	(have) read
*burst	burst	(have) burst	ride	rode	(have) ridden
buy	bought	(have) bought	ring	rang	(have) rung
catch	caught	(have) caught	*rise	rose	(have) risen
choose	chose	(have) chosen	run	ran	(have) run
*come	came	(have) come	*see	saw	(have) seen
cost	cost	(have) cost	send	sent	(have) sent
cut	cut	(have) cut	*set	set	(have) set
dig	dug	(have) dug	shine	shone	(have) shone
*do	did	(have) done	shoot	shot	(have) shot
*drag	dragged	(have) dragged	shut	shut	(have) shut
draw	drew	(have) drawn	sing	sang	(have) sung
drink	drank	(have) drunk	sink	sank	(have) sunk
*drown	drowned	(have) drowned	*sit	sat	(have) sat
eat	ate	(have) eaten	sleep	slept	(have) slept
fight	fought	(have) fought	speak	spoke	(have) spoken
find	found	(have) found	steal	stole	(have) stolen
fly	flew	(have) flown	*swim	swam	(have) swum
forget	forgot	(have) forgotten	*swing	swung	(have) swung
freeze	froze	(have) frozen	*tag	tagged	(have) tagged
give	gave	(have) given	take	took	(have) taken
*go	went	(have) gone	teach	taught	(have) taught
hold	held	(have) held	tear	tore	(have) torn
hurt	hurt	(have) hurt	tell	told	(have) told
keep	kept	(have) kept	think	thought	(have) thought
know	knew	(have) known	wear	wore	(have) worn
*lay	laid	(have) laid	weep	wept	(have) wept
*leave	left	(have) left	win	won	(have) won
*let	let	(have) let	write	wrote	(have) written

*These troublesome verbs are often used incorrectly.

31. Principal Parts of Irregular Verbs

You have studied the three main forms of verbs, which are called their three principal parts. In the last lesson you studied the principal parts of regular verbs. In this lesson you will study the principal parts of irregular verbs.

Remember the three sentences that help you to recall the principal parts of a verb.

Present:	Today I <u>talk</u>.
Past:	Yesterday I <u>talked</u>.
Past participle:	Every day I <u>have talked</u>.

For irregular verbs, the second principal part (past form) and the third principal part (past participle) are not formed by adding *-ed* as for regular verbs. Rather, they are formed in a number of different ways. Their principal parts have irregular spellings. *Ring* and *go* are two examples of irregular verbs.

Present:	Today I <u>ring</u> the bell.
Past:	Yesterday I <u>rang</u> the bell.
Past participle:	Every day I <u>have rung</u> the bell.

Present:	Today I <u>go</u>.
Past:	Yesterday I <u>went</u>.
Past participle:	Every day I <u>have gone</u>.

There is no rule to tell you how to form the second and third principal parts of irregular verbs. These forms must simply be memorized.

Many irregular verbs have three different forms, one for the first principal part, another for the second principal part, and still another for the third principal part. Study the following examples.

First (Present)	Second (Past)	Third (Past Participle)
ring	rang	(have) rung
go	went	(have) gone
break	broke	(have) broken
drink	drank	(have) drunk
fly	flew	(have) flown
know	knew	(have) known

Lesson 31

Purpose: To teach the principal parts of irregular verbs.

Oral Review:
1. In which class of verbs does *have* belong? (action verbs; also, helping verbs)
2. What is a verb phrase? (a main verb and one or more helping verbs used together)
3. List the helping verbs in groups. (am, is, are, was, were, be, been, being; have, has, had; do, does, did; may, might, must; can—could, shall—should, will—would)
4. What are the three main forms of verbs? Give two names for each. (first principal part—present form; second principal part—past form; third principal part—past participle)
5. Say and spell the other two principal parts of the following verbs.

   a. drag (dragged, [have] dragged)
   b. carry (carried, [have] carried)
   c. believe (believed, [have] believed)
   d. spray (sprayed, [have] sprayed)

Lesson Introduction: Read the following sentences to the students. Ask if they can correct the mistakes.

Today my sisters bring the cookies. (correct)
Yesterday Aunt Lucy bringed some. (brought)
They have bringed some every year. (have brought)

Yesterday I see two cardinals. (saw)
I had seed a blue jay on Monday. (had seen)
I often see crows flying above the trees. (correct)

The principal parts of many verbs are formed in irregular ways. Today we will study the principal parts of irregular verbs.

Some irregular verbs have the same spelling for the second and third principal parts. With a few, all three forms are spelled the same. See the following examples.

First (Present)	Second (Past)	Third (Past Participle)
bring	brought	(have) brought
buy	bought	(have) bought
dig	dug	(have) dug
put	put	(have) put
set	set	(have) set

The chart before this lesson shows the principal parts of many irregular verbs. Use the chart or a dictionary whenever you do not know the correct form of a verb. If no principal parts are shown, the past and the past participle are formed in the regular way, by adding *-ed*. If only one principal part is shown, the past and the past participle are the same.

Memorize the three forms of irregular verbs. Remember that the past participle must always be used with the helping verb *have, has,* or *had.* The past participle is never used alone as the main verb.

- The second principal part and the third principal part of irregular verbs are formed in a number of different ways. Memorize the principal parts of irregular verbs, and always use them correctly.

Class Practice

A. Say the three principal parts for each verb in this chart. Be sure to include *have* with the third principal part.

First (Present)	Second (Past)	Third (Past Participle)
1. come	———	———
2. sing	———	———
3. give	———	———
4. see	———	———
5. know	———	———
6. go	———	———
7. bring	———	———
8. drink	———	———

Lesson 31 Answers
Class Practice

A. (Words in italics are given in the pupil's text.)

1. *come*	came	(have) come
2. *sing*	sang	(have) sung
3. *give*	gave	(have) given
4. *see*	saw	(have) seen
5. *know*	knew	(have) known
6. *go*	went	(have) gone
7. *bring*	brought	(have) brought
8. *drink*	drank	(have) drunk

Lesson Outline:

1. For irregular verbs, the second principal part (past form) and the third principal part (past participle) are not formed by adding **-ed.** They are formed in a number of different ways.

2. Many irregular verbs have three different forms.

go	went	(have) gone
ride	rode	(have) ridden

3. Some irregular verbs have the same spelling for the second and third principal parts. With a few, all three forms are spelled the same.

fight	fought	(have) fought
swing	swung	(have) swung
shut	shut	(have) shut

4. Irregular verb forms must be memorized. There is no rule to tell you how to form the second and third principal parts. Always memorize the third principal part with the helping verb *have.* This will remind you that it is never used alone.

★ **EXTRA PRACTICE**
Worksheet 20 *(Principal Parts of Verbs)*
Worksheet 21 *(More Principal Parts)*

B. Give the correct form of each verb in parentheses. If there is no helping verb in the sentence, say the second principal part. If there is a helping verb, say the helping verb and the third principal part.
1. Father has (go) to the hardware store.
2. The wise men (see) the star and followed it.
3. Herod had not (know) about the new king.
4. Micah had (write) that Jesus would be born in Bethlehem.
5. You have (sing) my favorite hymn.
6. We (begin) early this morning.
7. Mother (give) the children some fresh cookies and milk.
8. We (do) all our work early.

Written Exercises

A. Copy each verb or verb phrase. Write whether the verb is the *present* form, the *past* form, or the *past participle*.

Example: Mother has bought some oranges.
Answer: has bought, past participle

1. Ronald has not come yet.
2. You write worthwhile letters.
3. They did their work well.
4. We know the answer.
5. My sister has gone to this school.
6. We sing this hymn often.
7. I had given them some books from this shelf.
8. They saw a moose along the road.
9. He had flown to Alaska several times.
10. They spoke about it sometimes.
11. The bells ring clearly.
12. The puppy has torn the book.
13. The boys drank all the lemonade.
14. Have you worn this dress lately?
15. Naomi and her husband had left the land of Israel.
16. Ruth spoke to Naomi with determination.
17. Orpah had gone back to her people.
18. Ruth and Naomi found rest with the people of God.

B. 1. has gone
2. saw
3. had known
4. had written
5. have sung
6. began
7. gave
8. did

Written Exercises
A. 1. has come—past participle
2. write—present
3. did—past
4. know—present
5. has gone—past participle
6. sing—present
7. had given—past participle
8. saw—past
9. had flown—past participle
10. spoke—past
11. ring—present
12. has torn—past participle
13. drank—past
14. Have worn—past participle
15. had left—past participle
16. spoke—past
17. had gone—past participle
18. found—past

B. Write the correct form of each verb in parentheses, using the second or third principal part. Use the third principal part only when there is a helping verb, and include the helping verb in your answer.

Example: Mother has (buy) some oranges.
Answer: has bought

1. The teachers have (speak) about the school trip.
2. Has he (fly) to Alaska?
3. Gary (ring) the fire alarm when he saw the smoke.
4. The puppy (tear) the book that was left on the porch.
5. The boys have (drink) the lemonade.
6. Had the children (see) the birds at the feeder?
7. Mother has (sing) our new song.
8. She has (wear) that sweater often.
9. David had (know) the memory verses from Psalm 119.
10. God has (give) many wonderful gifts.
11. The Lord (speak) to Moses on Mount Sinai.
12. He (write) on the tables of stone with His finger.
13. Ruth (go) and gleaned in the fields.
14. Boaz had (come) from Bethlehem.
15. He (speak) kind words to his workers.
16. Boaz (give) his workers a godly blessing.

C. Use the following verbs as indicated in sentences of your own.
1. the second principal part of *shake*
2. the third principal part of *know*
3. the first principal part of *taught*

Review Exercises

Write whether each sentence has *normal, inverted,* or *mixed* word order. If it has inverted or mixed order, write it in normal word order. [15]
1. At one time, cougars lived in most parts of North America.
2. With the increase of human population came the decrease of cougar territory.
3. Today most cougars are found in the western mountains.
4. Some cougars still live in the swamps of Florida.
5. In one mighty leap, a cougar can cover more than twenty feet.
6. A cougar's hind legs are longer than its front legs.
7. Because of this a cougar always appears to be walking downhill.

B. 1. have spoken
    2. Has flown
    3. rang
    4. tore
    5. have drunk
    6. Had seen
    7. has sung
    8. has worn
    9. had known
    10. has given
    11. spoke
    12. wrote
    13. went
    14. had come
    15. spoke
    16. gave

C. (Individual sentences.)

Review Exercises
1. mixed; Cougars lived in most parts of North America at one time.
2. inverted; The decrease of cougar territory came with the increase of human population.
3. mixed; Most cougars are found in the western mountains today.
4. normal
5. mixed; A cougar can cover more than twenty feet in one mighty leap.
6. normal
7. mixed; A cougar always appears to be walking downhill because of this.

32. Simple Verb Tenses

Tense means "time." The tense of a verb shows whether the action has already taken place, is now taking place, or will take place at some future time. There are three simple verb tenses: the *present tense,* the *past tense,* and the *future tense.*

Be careful not to confuse the tenses of verbs with the principal parts of verbs. The *tenses* are the different *times* that verbs tell about. The *principal parts* are the different *forms* used to show the different tenses.

Verbs in the *present tense* refer to action or existence now, in the present. The *first principal part* (present form) is used for the present tense. The verb ends with *-s* if the subject is a singular noun but is not *I* or *you.*

Verbs in the present tense:

The women <u>bake</u> cookies.	They <u>see</u> George.
The woman <u>bakes</u> cookies.	She <u>sees</u> George.

Verbs in the *past tense* refer to action or existence in the past. The *second principal part* (past form) is used for the past tense. A regular verb in the past tense ends with *-ed.* For an irregular verb, the form for the past tense is spelled in various ways.

Verbs in the past tense:

Regular verbs: They <u>arrived</u> yesterday.
The children <u>learned</u> the lessons.

Irregular verbs: We <u>found</u> several kinds of wild flowers.
They <u>were</u> small and colorful.
Last summer I <u>slept</u> here.

Verbs in the *future tense* refer to action or existence that will take place in the future. The future tense is expressed by using the *first principal part* (present form) with the helping verb *shall* or *will.* In formal writing, *shall* is used with the subjects *I* and *we. Will* is used in other kinds of writing and with all other subjects.

Verbs in the future tense:

I <u>shall write</u> to her.	Rain <u>will fall</u> soon.
We <u>shall plant</u> petunias.	He <u>will bring</u> the books.
	You <u>will be</u> late unless you hurry.

Lesson 32

Purpose: To teach the concept of tense, and the formation of the three simple tenses.

Oral Review:

1. What part of speech is a word like *not, never, always,* and *surely?* (adverb)
2. What is an irregular verb? (a verb whose second and third principal parts are not formed by adding *-ed*)
3. Give the principal parts of the following verbs.
   a. sing (sing, sang, [have] sung)
   b. go (go, went, [have] gone)
   c. know (know, knew, [have] known)
   d. do (do, did, [have] done)
   e. swim (swim, swam, [have] swum)
4. What is a verb? (a word that shows action or being)
5. What is a noun? (a word that names a person, place, thing, or idea)

6. Name the part of speech described.
   a. It takes the place of a noun. (pronoun)
   b. It tells *how, when,* or *where.* (adverb)
   c. It tells *which, whose, how many,* or *what kind of.* (adjective)
   d. It modifies a verb. (adverb)
   e. It modifies a noun or pronoun. (adjective)

Written Quiz:

Write the missing principal parts. Use *have* with the past participle.

Present	**Past**	**Past Participle**
1. drag		
2. study		
3. come		
4. forget		
5. bring		
6. find		
7. buy		
8. know		

Quiz Answers:

1.	dragged	(have) dragged
2.	studied	(have) studied
3.	came	(have) come
4.	forgot	(have) forgotten
5.	brought	(have) brought
6.	found	(have) found
7.	bought	(have) bought
8.	knew	(have) known

Lesson Introduction: We are creatures of time. The Bible tells us about many things that happened in the past. It tells us how we should live presently. Best of all, it tells us what our future home in heaven will be like.

Different forms of verbs are used to talk about time. Today we want to study these forms.

Lesson Outline:

1. **Tense** *means "time."*

2. ***There are three simple verb tenses: the* present tense, *the* past tense, *and the* future tense.** Discuss the difference between the principal parts and the tenses of verbs. The *tenses* are the different *times* that verbs tell about. The *principal parts* are the different *forms* used to show the different tenses.

3. ***Verbs in the* present tense *refer to action or existence now, in the present.*** The *first principal part* (present form) is used for the present tense.

The stars <u>speak</u> of God's glory. They <u>are</u> very bright.

The following chart shows the present, past, and future tenses of two regular verbs and two irregular verbs.

Present	Past	Future
stay	stayed	will stay
journey	journeyed	will journey
freeze	froze	will freeze
bring	brought	will bring

- *Tense* means "time."

- Verbs have three simple tenses.
  1. The present tense refers to action or existence in the present. The first principal part (present form) is used for the present tense.
  2. The past tense refers to action or existence in the past. The second principal part (past form) is used for the past tense.
  3. The future tense refers to action or existence that will take place in the future. The future tense is expressed by using the first principal part (present form) with the helping verb *shall* or *will*.

Class Practice

A. Give all three tenses for each verb. The first one is done for you.

	Present	Past	Future
1.	arrive	arrived	will arrive
2.	learn	———	———
3.	stay	———	———
4.	sleep	———	———
5.	have	———	———
6.	bring	———	———

B. Give each verb or verb phrase, and tell what tense it is.
1. The doctor examines the cut on Marie's finger.
2. It will not need stitches.
3. Solomon asked the Lord for wisdom.
4. The Lord gave him riches and wisdom.
5. The Lord will give wisdom to all seekers of truth.
6. Ask God for wisdom.

Lesson 32 Answers
Class Practice
A. (Words in italics are given in the pupil's text.)

1. *arrive*	arrived	*will arrive*
2. *learn*	learned	will learn
3. *stay*	stayed	will stay
4. *sleep*	slept	will sleep
5. *have*	had	will have
6. *bring*	brought	will bring

B. 1. examines—present
   2. will need—future
   3. asked—past
   4. gave—past
   5. will give—future
   6. Ask—present

If the subject is a singular noun (but is not *I* or *you*), the verb ends with *-s*.

Ella <u>draws</u> nicely.
Eldon <u>has</u> new boots.
He <u>is</u> a good worker.
I <u>am</u> glad to see you.
I <u>have</u> a letter for you.
You <u>are</u> old enough to help.

(*Teacher:* The verb *be* is different from other verbs in that it has more than one form for some of the principal parts. These forms are shown below.

First (Present)	Second (Past)	Third (Past Participle)
am, is, are	was, were	been

Be is the infinitive form of *be,* and *being* is the present participle.)

4. Verbs in the past tense refer to action or existence in the past. The *second principal part* (past form) is used for the past tense. A regular verb in the past tense ends with *-ed.* For an irregular verb, the form for the past tense is spelled in various ways.

Leonard <u>counted</u> his change twice. (regular verb)
Leslie <u>left</u> this morning. (irregular verb)

5. Verbs in the future tense refer to action or existence that will take place in the future. The future tense is expressed by using the *first principal part* (present form) with the helping verb *shall* or *will.* In formal writing, *shall* is used with the subjects *I* and *we. Will* is used in other kinds of writing and with all other subjects.

The beetles <u>will destroy</u> the crop.
We <u>shall spray</u> them.

C. Read each sentence as it is written. Next read it in the past tense, beginning with *yesterday*. Then read it in the future tense, beginning with *tomorrow*.
1. Doris does the ironing.
2. We plant our melons.
3. Snow falls.
4. I write several letters.
5. He knows the answer.
6. I go in the morning.

Written Exercises

A. Copy the chart, and fill in all the tenses for each verb.

Present	Past	Future
1. clean	———	———
2. hike	———	———
3. carry	———	———
4. draw	———	———
5. fly	———	———
6. ride	———	———
7. move	———	———
8. obey	———	———

B. Copy the verb in each sentence. After it, write the past tense and the future tense of that verb.

Example: He sings well.
Answer: sings, sang, will sing

1. My little brother sleeps soundly.
2. We have plenty of food.
3. Martha and Betty sew.
4. He brings the books with him.
5. I find nails and screws.
6. You sit near the fire.
7. We wait for him.
8. The ice floats over the dam.

C. Copy each verb or verb phrase, and write whether it is in the *present* tense, *past* tense, or *future* tense.
1. Doris copied all her exercises already.
2. A good rest will cure you.

Use the future tense to further clarify the difference between tenses and principal parts. The *future tense* is expressed by using the *present form* with the helping verb *shall* or *will*.

C. 1. Doris does the ironing.
     Yesterday Doris did the ironing.
     Tomorrow Doris will do the ironing.
2. We plant our melons.
     Yesterday we planted our melons.
     Tomorrow we shall (will) plant our melons.
3. Snow falls.
     Yesterday snow fell.
     Tomorrow snow will fall.
4. I write several letters.
     Yesterday I wrote several letters.
     Tomorrow I shall (will) write several letters.
5. He knows the answer.
     Yesterday he knew the answer.
     Tomorrow he will know the answer.
6. I go in the morning.
     Yesterday I went in the morning.
     Tomorrow I shall (will) go in the morning.

Written Exercises

A. (Words in italics are given in the pupil's text.)

1. *clean*	cleaned	will clean
2. *hike*	hiked	will hike
3. *carry*	carried	will carry
4. *draw*	drew	will draw
5. *fly*	flew	will fly
6. *ride*	rode	will ride
7. *move*	moved	will move
8. *obey*	obeyed	will obey

B. 1. sleeps, slept, will sleep
2. have, had, will have
3. sew, sewed, will sew
4. brings, brought, will bring
5. find, found, will find
6. sit, sat, will sit
7. wait, waited, will wait
8. floats, floated, will float

C. 1. copied—past
2. will cure—future

3. Fit the pieces of the puzzle together this way.
4. Gerald burned all the trash from that room.
5. Tonight the pond will freeze over.
6. Grandmother will send the book.
7. James likes to read.
8. The Amalekites captured the wives and children of David and his men.
9. David asked God for help.
10. God answered David's prayer.
11. God will listen to the prayers of His people.
12. God always hears His children.

D. Use all three tenses of the verbs *go* and *come* in sentences of your own.

Review Exercises

A. List the eight parts of speech.

B. Name each part of speech described below. Use some names more than once.
    1. It tells *which, whose, how many,* or *what kind of.*
    2. It joins words or groups of words.
    3. It expresses strong feeling and is not related to the rest of the sentence.
    4. It names a person, place, thing, or idea.
    5. It modifies a noun or pronoun.
    6. It modifies a verb, an adjective, or an adverb.
    7. It takes the place of a noun.
    8. It tells *how, when, where,* or *to what degree.*
    9. It is a connecting word that begins a phrase.
    10. It shows action or being.

3. Fit—present
4. burned—past
5. will freeze—future
6. will send—future
7. likes—present
8. captured—past
9. asked—past
10. answered—past
11. will listen—future
12. hears—present

D. (Individual sentences.)

Review Exercises

A. noun, pronoun, verb, adjective, adverb, preposition, conjunction, interjection

B. 1. adjective
    2. conjunction
    3. interjection
    4. noun
    5. adjective
    6. adverb
    7. pronoun
    8. adverb
    9. preposition
    10. verb

33. The Pattern of an Outline

An outline is an orderly arrangement of topics, subtopics, and details. Writers and speakers prepare outlines to organize their material. Readers and listeners make outlines as a help in remembering what they read or hear. An outline gives a brief summary of a composition. It

Lesson 33

Purpose: To teach the basic pattern of an outline.

IMPORTANT NOTE: Tell your pupils to choose a book, get it approved, and read it in preparation for giving a book report. (See Lesson 45.)

Oral Review:
1. What is a topic sentence? (a sentence that tells what a paragraph is about)
2. List several ways of developing a paragraph. (by using details, by using examples and illustrations, by using comparison or contrast)
3. What is needed to develop a good topic sentence? (details)
4. What should the details of a paragraph do? (show that the topic sentence is true)

5. In what order should details be given? (in an order that makes the paragraph simple to understand, such as the order of time or importance)

Lesson Introduction: Ask students, "How would you like to make something in a workshop that is not organized? What if the tools were not in their places, but were scattered here and there? The hammer would be in the nail box and the saw among the wood scraps. You would have to hunt for every tool you needed. How much easier it is when things are organized!"

An outline is a way to organize important ideas. Outlines make it easier for writers and speakers to prepare their material. Outlines help readers and listeners to remember what they read or hear. Today we want to study the basic pattern of an outline.

shows the contents and organization of the material.

Outlines need to follow a definite pattern, as shown below.

Title of Composition
I. Topic
   A. Subtopic
   B. Subtopic
      1. Point
         a. Subpoint
         b. Subpoint
      2. Point
II. Topic
   A. Subtopic
   B. Subtopic

Study the following outline about olive growing. Notice how the topics, subtopics, and points are arranged in a logical order.

Growing Olives in Palestine
I. Characteristics of olive trees
   A. Thrive in rocky soil
   B. Live and bear fruit for centuries
      1. Bear olives only after seven years' growth
      2. Bear a full crop every other year
II. Harvest of olives
   A. Occurs in October
   B. Done by beating with sticks
   C. Mentioned in Scriptures
      1. Deuteronomy 24:20
      2. Isaiah 17:6
III. Uses of olives
   A. Pickled for eating
   B. Squeezed for oil
      1. For cooking
      2. For anointing
      3. For light

Notice how the example above follows these rules for an outline.
1. Every outline must have a title.
2. An outline is divided into topics, subtopics, points, and subpoints.
3. Topics are marked with Roman numerals.

Lesson Outline:

  1. An outline is an orderly arrangement of topics, subtopics, and details.

  2. An outline must follow a definite pattern.
    (1) Every outline must have a title.
    (2) An outline is divided into topics, subtopics, points, and subpoints.
    (3) Topics are marked with Roman numerals.
    (4) Subtopics are marked with capital letters.
    (5) Points are marked with Arabic numerals (*1, 2,* and so on).
    (6) Subpoints are marked with small (lowercase) letters (*a, b,* and so on).
    (7) Each level of the outline has at least two parts. If there is an *A,* there is also a *B.* If there is a *1,* there is also a *2.* The reason is that each level indicates a division, and nothing can be divided into just one part.

  (*Note:* When there is only one point to give under a subhead, it is included after the subhead and set off by a dash, a colon, or parentheses. See how this is done for the Book of Acts in Written Exercises, Part A.)
    (8) Each level of the outline is indented.
    (9) The numeral or letter that marks each level is followed by a period.
    (10) Each topic, subtopic, and detail begins with a capital letter.
    (11) The topics, subtopics, and details are not stated as complete sentences. Therefore, no periods are used after any of them.

4. Subtopics are marked with capital letters.

5. Points are marked with Arabic numerals (*1, 2,* and so on).

6. Subpoints are marked with small letters (*a, b,* and so on).

7. Each level of the outline has at least two parts. If there is an *A,* there is also a *B.* If there is a *1,* there is also a *2.* The reason is that each level indicates a division, and nothing can be divided into just one part.

8. Each level of the outline is indented.

9. The numeral or letter that marks each level is followed by a period.

10. Each topic, subtopic, and detail begins with a capital letter.

11. The topics, subtopics, and details are not stated as complete sentences. Therefore, no periods are used after any of them.

• An outline is an orderly arrangement of topics, subtopics, and details. An outline always follows a definite pattern.

Class Practice

A. Tell where these subpoints belong on the following outline.

Oranges   Plums   Tangerines
Cherries   Grapefruits   Apples

Fruits We Eat

I. Citrus fruits
   A. _____
   B. _____
   C. _____
II. Other fruits
   A. _____
   B. _____
   C. _____

Lesson 33 Answers
Class Practice

A.   **Fruits We Eat**
   I. Citrus fruits
      A. Oranges
      B. Grapefruits
      C. Tangerines
   II. Other fruits
      A. Cherries
      B. Plums
      C. Apples

B. Tell what mistakes you see in this outline.

Some States and Provinces of North America

I. States of the United States
   A. Middle Atlantic
      1. Pennsylvania
      2. New Jersey
      3. New York
   B Southern
      1. Florida
      2. Georgia
      3. Texas
   C. North Central
    1. Wisconsin
      2. North Dakota
      3. Kansas
       4. Missouri
   D. western
      1. California
      2. Utah
      3. Nevada
II. Provinces of Canada
   A. Atlantic Provinces.
      1. Newfoundland
      2. Nova Scotia
      3. Prince Edward Island
   B Prairie Provinces
      1. Manitoba
      2. Saskatchewan
      3. Alberta
   C. Pacific Province
      1. British Columbia

B. 1. The letter *B* (under both topics) should have a period after it.
   2. The numbers under I(C) are not indented properly.
   3. *Western* in I(D) should be capitalized.
   4. *Atlantic Provinces* in II(A) should not have a period after it.
   5. There is only one item under II(C).

Written Exercises

A. Copy this outline correctly. Write the following words in their correct places. See the illustration if you are not sure where each book belongs.

Job	Micah	Mark	Major Prophets
Psalms	Nahum	Luke	Galatians
Romans	Matthew	John	Ephesians
Genesis	Joshua	Ezra	Colossians
Exodus	Judges		

Books of the Bible

I. Old Testament Books
  A. Books of Moses
    1. _____
    2. _____
  B. History
    1. _____
    2. _____
    3. _____
  C. Poetry
    1. _____
    2. _____
  D. _____
    1. Isaiah
    2. Jeremiah
  E. Minor Prophets
    1. Jonah
    2. _____
    3. _____

II. New Testament Books
  A. The Gospels
    1. _____
    2. _____
    3. _____
    4. _____
  B. History—Acts
  C. Epistles
    1. _____
    2. _____
    3. _____
    4. _____

Written Exercises

A.   **Books of the Bible**

I. Old Testament books
  A. Books of Moses
    1. Genesis
    2. Exodus
  B. History
    1. Joshua
    2. Judges
    3. Ezra
  C. Poetry
    1. Job
    2. Psalms
  D. Major Prophets
    1. Isaiah
    2. Jeremiah
  E. Minor Prophets
    1. Jonah
    2. Micah
    3. Nahum

II. New Testament books
  A. The Gospels
    1. Matthew
    2. Mark
    3. Luke
    4. John
  B. History—Acts
  C. Epistles
    1. Romans
    2. Galatians
    3. Ephesians
    4. Colossians

B. Copy the outline below, and complete it with the following words. (You will need to provide the title.) Be sure to follow the rules in the lesson.

torch	ripsaw	hammer	sewing machine
plane	needle	pipe wrench	pipe cutter
saws	scissors	crosscut saw	

I. Tailor's tools
  A. _____
  B. _____
  C. _____
II. Plumber's tools
  A. _____
  B. _____
  C. _____
III. Carpenter's tools
  A. _____
    1. _____
    2. _____
  B. _____
  C. _____

Review Exercises

Write *true* or *false* for each sentence.
1. A paragraph is a group of sentences that tells about a single topic.
2. A paragraph has unity when all the sentences develop the topic sentence.
3. The topic sentence of a paragraph usually comes at the end.
4. In a coherent paragraph, all the details fit together well so that the reader does not get lost or confused.
5. A coherent paragraph may give details in the order of time, importance, or interest.
6. The purpose of transitional words is to produce unity in a paragraph.
7. Details in a paragraph make the topic seem less important to the reader.
8. A paragraph can be developed by using convincing details, examples and illustrations, or comparison or contrast.

B.
Tools
I. Tailor's tools
  A. Needle
  B. Scissors
  C. Sewing machine
II. Plumber's tools
  A. Torch
  B. Pipe wrench
  C. Pipe cutter
III. Carpenter's tools
  A. Saws
    1. Ripsaw
    2. Crosscut saw
  B. Plane
  C. Hammer

Review Exercises
1. true
2. true
3. false
4. true
5. true
6. false (*Unity* should be *coherence.*)
7. false
8. true

Challenge Exercises

A. Make an outline like the one in Written Exercises, Part A, including all the books of the Bible.

B. Make an outline like the one in Class Practice, Part B, including all the states and provinces of North America.

---

34. Present Perfect Tense

You have learned that verbs have three main forms, called their principal parts. The following sentences are helpful for remembering the three principal parts.

Present: Today I <u>look</u>.
Past: Yesterday I <u>looked</u>.
Past participle: Every day I <u>have looked</u>.

You have also learned that verbs have three simple tenses. The *present* verb form is used for the *present tense;* the *past* form is used for the *past tense;* and the *present* form is used with *shall* or *will* for the *future tense.*

Verbs in the simple tenses:
Present tense: The girls <u>look</u> at Orion.
Past tense: The girls <u>looked</u> at Orion.
Future tense: The girls <u>will look</u> at Orion.

The tenses shown above are the *simple tenses.* They are formed by using the first and second principal parts. Another set of tenses is the *perfect tenses.* They are formed by using the third principal part (past participle). The perfect tenses are shown below.

Verbs in the perfect tenses:
Present perfect tense: The girls <u>have looked</u> at Orion.
Past perfect tense: The girls <u>had looked</u> at Orion.
Future perfect tense: The girls <u>will have looked</u> at Orion.

Lesson 34

Purpose: (1) To introduce *the perfect tenses. (2) To teach the formation and concept of *the present perfect tense.

Oral Review:
1. What does *tense* mean? (time)
2. Name the three simple tenses. (present tense, past tense, future tense)
3. When should the helping verb *shall* be used? (with *I* or *we* in formal writing)
4. Give the present, past, and future tenses of the following verbs.
   a. bring (bring, brought, will bring)
   b. count (count, counted, will count)
   c. ask (ask, asked, will ask)
5. Name the three principal parts of verbs. (present, past, past participle)

Challenge Exercises
(Individual work.)

6. Using the verb *see,* give three sentences that can help you to remember the three principal parts of a verb. (Today I *see.* Yesterday I *saw.* Every day I *have seen.*)
7. Give the three principal parts of the following verbs.
   a. bring (bring, brought, [have] brought)
   b. go (go, went, [have] gone)
   c. tag (tag, tagged, [have] tagged)
   d. do (do, did, [have] done)
   e. drink (drink, drank, [have] drunk)
   f. hike (hike, hiked, [have] hiked)

Lesson Introduction: Whether you are washing the car, weeding the garden, or sweeping the floor, no job is perfect until it is completed. This is the sense of the word *perfect* when it is used of verb tenses. Perfect tenses always refer to *completed action.* The three perfect tenses show three different times the action is finished: in the present (present perfect), in the past (past perfect), and in the future (future perfect). **Remember:** In English grammar, *perfect* means "completed."

Notice that there is a perfect tense for each of the simple tenses. In this lesson you will study only the *present perfect tense*. This tense is made by using *have* with plural subjects and *has* with singular subjects except *I* or *you*.

> The children <u>have done</u> the work. (plural subject)
> Amos <u>has signed</u> the papers. (singular subject)
> Where <u>have</u> you <u>been</u>? (subject <u>you</u>)

You can recognize perfect tenses by remembering this fact: *Every verb phrase in a perfect tense includes* have, has, *or* had *as a helping verb*. You know that the helping verb *shall* or *will* always means the future tense. In the same way, the helping verb *have, has,* or *had* always means a perfect tense. If the helping verb is *have* or *has,* it is a sure sign of the present perfect tense.

Verbs in the present perfect tense:
> I <u>have eaten</u> my sandwich.
> Ann <u>has written</u> a letter.

What is "perfect" about the perfect tenses? In English grammar, *perfect* means "completed." A perfect tense speaks of completed action. Thus, a verb in the present perfect tense tells about an action that is "perfect in the present." The action is completed as of now.

I have eaten my sandwich.
> **Meaning:** My action of eating is completed as of now.

Ann has written a letter.
> **Meaning:** Ann's action of writing is completed as of now.

- The perfect tenses are made by using a form of *have* as a helping verb with the past participle of a main verb.

- The present perfect tense is formed by using the helping verb *have* or *has* with the past participle of a main verb.

- The perfect tenses refer to completed action. The present perfect tense refers to an action completed as of the present time.

Lesson Outline:

1. Verbs have three principal parts and three simple tenses. Only the first and second principal parts are used for the simple tenses.

2. Verbs have a perfect tense for each of the simple tenses. In the perfect tenses, the helping verbs *have, has,* and *had* are always used with the third principal part of the verb.

Simple tenses	Perfect tenses
He sees.	He has seen.
He saw.	He had seen.
He will see.	He will have seen.

3. The present perfect tense is formed by using have *or* has *with the third principal part of a main verb. Use* have *with a plural subject and* has *with a singular subject except* I *or* you. **Remember:** Whenever *have* or *has* is used as a helping verb, it is a sure sign of the present perfect tense.

> They <u>have gone</u> to church.
> Joel <u>has read</u> that book before.
> I <u>have seen</u> it.

4. The present perfect tense refers to an action that is completed as of the present time. The action is "perfect in the present." (This point should be introduced and briefly discussed, but the main emphasis in this lesson should be on the *formation* of the present perfect tense.)

Class Practice

A. For each sentence, say *yes* or *no* to tell whether the verb is in the present perfect tense. If it is, give the helping verb that proves it.
1. The Gospel writers have recorded many things about Jesus.
2. Jesus opened the eyes of the blind.
3. Jesus has risen from the dead.
4. Jesus ascended to heaven.
5. He has been there ever since.
6. Jesus intercedes for us.
7. All good things have come from God.
8. God created the heaven and the earth in six days.
9. He has made everything beautiful.
10. We have many reasons for praising Him.

B. Give the verb or verb phrase of each sentence in Part A. Tell whether each one is in the *present tense, past tense,* or *present perfect tense.*

C. Give the verb in each sentence. Then give its past tense and its present perfect tense.

    Example: Amos signs the papers.
    Answer: signs, signed, has signed

1. You neglect your work.
2. The girls carry the baskets.
3. I ask this question.
4. He pushes the wagon.
5. Carl lifts the stone.
6. They print various stories.
7. We walk along the brook.
8. I do my work.

Written Exercises

A. Copy the verb or verb phrase in each sentence. Write whether each one is in the *present* tense, *past* tense, or *present perfect* tense.
1. All the students studied their lessons.
2. I have studied my lesson.
3. The sun has risen every morning.
4. It shows God's faithfulness to us.
5. Abraham lived many years ago.
6. He was a godly man.

Lesson 34 Answers
Class Practice
A. 1. yes, have
   2. no
   3. yes, has
   4. no
   5. yes, has
   6. no
   7. yes, have
   8. no
   9. yes, has
   10. no (*Have* is the main verb.)

B. 1. have recorded—present perfect tense
   2. opened—past tense
   3. has risen—present perfect tense
   4. ascended—past tense
   5. has been—present perfect tense
   6. intercedes—present tense
   7. have come—present perfect tense
   8. created—past tense
   9. has made—present perfect tense
   10. have—present tense

C. 1. neglect, neglected, have neglected
   2. carry, carried, have carried
   3. ask, asked, have asked
   4. pushes, pushed, has pushed
   5. lifts, lifted, has lifted
   6. print, printed, have printed
   7. walk, walked, have walked
   8. do, did, have done

Written Exercises
A. 1. studied—past
   2. have studied—present perfect
   3. has risen—present perfect
   4. shows—present
   5. lived—past
   6. was—past

7. James has forgotten his gloves.

8. Now he has cold hands.

9. Julie has been there a long time.

10. I have written her a long letter.

B. Write the present perfect tense of each verb in parentheses. Be sure to include the correct helping verb.

1. Mother (be) in the garden all morning.

2. We (help) her for two hours.

3. Gold and silver (be) valuable metals for many centuries.

4. Stanley (see) the Grand Canyon.

5. The geese (eat) three sacks of corn already.

6. They (grow) rapidly.

7. Luke (call) us every week.

8. The neighbors (bring) us some buns.

9. Our tomatoes (drown) because of all the rain.

10. Jesus (rise), and now He is alive forevermore.

11. Maurice (raise) rabbits for several years.

12. Finally the old dress (wear) out.

13. The operator (trace) the telephone call.

14. They (change) their number.

15. I (pay) the bill on time each month.

C. Write six sentences with the verbs *help* and *speak*. Use each word in the present tense, past tense, and present perfect tense.

Review Exercises

Copy the chart, and add the missing principal parts. Use *have* with the past participle. [30, 31]

First (Present)	Second (Past)	Third (Past Participle)
1. teach	——	——
2. destroy	——	——
3. stop	——	——
4. swim	——	——
5. shut	——	——
6. see	——	——
7. ring	——	——
8. drink	——	——

7. has forgotten—present perfect

8. has—present

9. has been—present perfect

10. have written—present perfect

B. 1. has been

2. have helped

3. have been

4. has seen

5. have eaten

6. have grown

7. has called

8. have brought

9. have drowned

10. has risen

11. has raised

12. has worn

13. has traced

14. have changed

15. have paid

C. (Individual sentences.)

Review Exercises

(Words in italics are given in the pupil's text.)

1. *teach*	taught	(have) taught
2. *destroy*	destroyed	(have) destroyed
3. *stop*	stopped	(have) stopped
4. *swim*	swam	(have) swum
5. *shut*	shut	(have) shut
6. *see*	saw	(have) seen
7. *ring*	rang	(have) rung
8. *drink*	drank	(have) drunk

35. Past Perfect Tense

The three principal parts of verbs are used for different verb tenses. All the simple tenses are formed by using the first and second principal parts.

> **Present tense:** The birds <u>fly</u>. (first principal part)
> **Past tense:**   The birds <u>flew</u>. (second principal part)
> **Future tense:** The birds <u>will fly</u>. (first principal part)

All the perfect tenses are formed by using the third principal part. You learned about the present perfect tense in the last lesson.

> **Present perfect tense:** The birds <u>have flown</u>.

In this lesson you will study the *past perfect tense*. This tense is formed by using the helping verb *had* with the third principal part of a verb.

> **Verbs in the past perfect tense:**
> Brother David <u>had rung</u> the bell.
> Elizabeth <u>had sung</u> the song correctly.
> I <u>had heard</u> the news before you told me.

You can recognize the past perfect tense by remembering this fact: *The helping verb* had *is always used in the past perfect tense.* In the present perfect tense, either *have* or *has* may be used. But only *had* is used in the past perfect tense.

You can easily tell the difference between the simple past tense and the past perfect tense. No helping verb is used in the simple past tense. The helping verb *had* is always used in the past perfect tense.

> **Simple past tense:**
> Esau wanted the blessing, but Jacob <u>received</u> it.
> **Past perfect tense:**
> Esau wanted the blessing, but Jacob <u>had received</u> it.

Remember that the perfect tenses refer to completed action. The past perfect tense tells about an action that was "perfect in the past." The action was completed by a certain past time, which is often stated in the sentence.

> Before Father arrived, we <u>had done</u> our work.
> **Meaning:**   Our action of doing was completed by the time
>   Father arrived.

Lesson 35

Purpose: To teach the formation and concept of *the past perfect tense.

Oral Review:
1. What helping verbs are always used in the perfect tenses? (have, has, had)
2. What helping verb is always used in the present perfect tense? (have *or* has)
3. Give the present perfect tense of the following verbs.
   a. carry (have [*or* has] carried)
   b. lift (have [*or* has] lifted)
   c. go (have [*or* has] gone)
   d. write (have [*or* has] written)
   e. grow (have [*or* has] grown)
4. What is a possessive noun? (a noun that shows ownership or relationship)
5. A possessive noun is often used as what part of speech? (adjective)

6. How is the possessive form of a word such as *Moses* and *Jesus* formed? (Add only an apostrophe because the last syllable ends with the *zus* sound.)

Lesson Introduction: Read the following sentences. Ask the students if the two sentences mean the same thing.

> Father opened the door, but the visitor left.
> Father opened the door, but the visitor had left.

The first sentence tells you only that two things happened. It could mean that the visitor left after Father opened the door. But the second sentence makes it clear that the visitor *completed* his action of leaving by the time Father opened the door. This is a characteristic of the past perfect tense, as of all the perfect tenses. It shows completed action. Today we will study the formation and meaning of the past perfect tense.

They found a flashlight, but the fox <u>had escaped</u>.
Meaning: The fox's action of escaping was completed by the time they found a flashlight.

- The past perfect tense is formed by using the helping verb *had* with the past participle of a main verb.

- The past perfect tense refers to an action that was completed by a certain time in the past.

Class Practice

A. Give the verbs and verb phrases in these sentences. Tell whether each one is in the *past tense,* the *past perfect tense,* or the *present perfect tense.*
1. David and his brother did the chores.
2. Before we arrived, they had milked three cows.
3. The twins have fed the calves.
4. Saul came home after his father had found the lost donkeys.
5. Before Saul met Samuel, God had told Samuel about him.
6. Samuel anointed Saul to be king.
7. Saul prophesied and praised the Lord.
8. Have you read that story recently?

B. Give the past perfect tense of each verb in parentheses. Be sure to use the correct verb form and the correct helping verb.

Example: The mechanic (fix) the engine before lunch.
Answer: had fixed

1. Harvey (go) out the door before the telephone rang.
2. By the next morning the ship (sink).
3. Achan (steal) some things from Jericho.
4. The cow was dirty because she (lie) in the mud.
5. We (have) six inches of snow before last week.
6. Elisha (be) a farmer before he became a prophet.

Lesson 35 Answers
Class Practice
A. 1. did—past tense
   2. arrived—past tense; had milked—past perfect tense
   3. have fed—present perfect tense
   4. came—past tense; had found—past perfect tense
   5. met—past tense; had told—past perfect tense
   6. anointed—past tense
   7. prophesied—past tense; praised—past tense
   8. Have read—present perfect tense

B. 1. had gone
   2. had sunk
   3. had stolen
   4. had lain
   5. had had
   6. had been

Lesson Outline:
*1. The past perfect tense is formed by using **had** with the third principal part of a main verb.* Whenever *had* is used as a helping verb, it is a sure sign of the past perfect tense.

We <u>had planted</u> four trees before the storm came.
Alice <u>had mailed</u> six cards by last Friday.

2. The past perfect tense can easily be distinguished from the simple past tense. In the simple past tense, the *past* form of a verb is always used *without* a helping verb. In the past perfect tense, the *past participle* of a verb is always used with the helping verb *had.*

Simple past:
Bertha <u>looked</u> for flowers in the woods.
She <u>gathered</u> many different kinds.

Past perfect:
We <u>had sat</u> for ten minutes before the bus started.
No one answered until I <u>had called</u> four times.

3. The past perfect tense refers to an action that was completed by a certain time in the past. The action was "perfect in the past." Again, introduce this point and discuss it briefly, but place the main emphasis on the formation of the past perfect tense.

Written Exercises

A. Copy the verbs and verb phrases in these sentences. Write whether the tense of each one is *past, past perfect,* or *present perfect.* (Most sentences have more than one verb or verb phrase.)
1. We assembled again after we had eaten our lunches.
2. Timothy had seen the accident, and he told us about it.
3. The boys finished before the girls had started.
4. Jane has made a small motto for Mother.
5. Saul had been a humble man before he disobeyed.
6. One thief had repented while he hung on the cross.
7. After we had sung, Brother James read a Scripture passage.
8. Long icicles have formed on the eaves.

B. Write the past perfect tense of each verb in parentheses. Be sure to use the correct verb form and the correct helping verb.

Example: The wild geese (fly) south before the cold weather came.
Answer: had flown

1. The hailstorm (destroy) many crops.
2. We (travel) through a tunnel before we stopped for lunch.
3. I (feed) the chickens before breakfast.
4. After the children (sing) three songs, the visitors left.
5. By midnight the water (rise) almost to the bridge.
6. I (know) that, but I forgot about it.
7. My older brother (wear) that coat the year before.
8. A few animals (get) sick during the cold weather.

Review Exercises

A. Change each verb in parentheses to the tense shown in italics. Be sure to use the correct helping verbs when they are needed. [32–35]
1. The girls (take) two umbrellas. *present perfect*
2. Shirley and Juanita (go) to Guatemala. *future*
3. Father (know) this man long before I met him. *past perfect*
4. This jacket (wear) out. *present perfect*
5. The girls (see) the deer. *past*
6. I could not use my tape measure because someone (break) it. *past perfect*
7. The baby (have) blue eyes. *present*
8. After I (write) the letter, I cleaned my room. *past perfect*
9. Spring (be) late that year. *past perfect*
10. I (mow) the hay after I cultivate the corn. *future*

Written Exercises

A. 1. assembled—past; had eaten—past perfect
2. had seen—past perfect; told—past
3. finished—past; had started—past perfect
4. has made—present perfect
5. had been—past perfect; disobeyed—past
6. had repented—past perfect; hung—past
7. had sung—past perfect; read—past
8. have formed—present perfect

B. 1. had destroyed
2. had traveled
3. had fed
4. had sung
5. had risen
6. had known
7. had worn
8. had gotten

Review Exercises

A. 1. have taken
2. will go
3. had known
4. has worn
5. saw
6. had broken
7. has
8. had written
9. had been
10. shall (will) mow

B. Copy each word, and add the missing words. [26]

Singular	Singular Possessive	Plural	Plural Possessive
1. wolf	——	——	——
2. city	——	——	——
3. child	——	——	——
4. donkey	——	——	——
5. girl	——	——	——

C. Rewrite these expressions, using possessive forms. [26]
1. the jobs of the waitresses
2. the table of the waitress
3. the baseball bat of a boy
4. the baseballs of the boys
5. the shoes of the men

B. (Words in italics are given in the pupil's text.)

1. *wolf*	wolf's	wolves	wolves'
2. *city*	city's	cities	cities'
3. *child*	child's	children	children's
4. *donkey*	donkey's	donkeys	donkeys'
5. *girl*	girl's	girls	girls'

C. 1. the waitresses' jobs
2. the waitress's table
3. a boy's baseball bat
4. the boys' baseballs
5. the men's shoes

---

36. Future Perfect Tense

You have learned that the helping verbs *have, has,* and *had* are always used with the *past participle* to form the perfect tenses of verbs. In the present perfect tense, the helping verb is *have* or *has.* In the past perfect tense, the helping verb is *had.*

Present perfect tense:
He <u>has written</u>.
They <u>have gone</u>.

Past perfect tense:
He <u>had written</u>.
They <u>had gone</u>.

Another perfect tense is the *future perfect tense.* This tense is formed with the helping verbs *shall have* or *will have* and the past participle of the verb.

Verbs in the future perfect tense:
We <u>shall have finished</u> our work by noon tomorrow.
Sam <u>will have left</u> before you get here.

Whenever the helping verbs *shall have* or *will have* are used, you can

Lesson 36

Purpose: To teach the formation and concept of *the future perfect tense.

Oral Review:
1. How is the past perfect tense formed? (by using the helping verb *had* with the past participle of a main verb)
2. Give the past perfect tense of the following verbs.
   a. sleep (had slept)
   b. go (had gone)
   c. sit (had sat)
3. How is the present perfect tense formed? (by using the helping verb *have* or *has* with the past participle of a main verb)
4. Give the present perfect and the past perfect tenses of the following verbs.
   a. keep (have kept, had kept)
   b. throw (have thrown, had thrown)
   c. sit (have sat, had sat)

Lesson Introduction: Suppose the teacher says you must memorize a certain poem before two o'clock tomorrow. Which of the following would you say to assure him that you will know the poem by then?

I will memorize the poem.
At two o'clock tomorrow, I will memorize the poem.
At two o'clock tomorrow, I will have memorized the poem.

The first sentence does not tell when you will memorize the poem. Your teacher may be afraid you will not start until next month. The second sentence could mean that you will only start learning it at two o'clock tomorrow. But the third sentence means that you will have *completed* learning the poem by two o'clock tomorrow. Today we will study the formation and meaning of the future perfect tense.

be sure the verb is in the future perfect tense. Be careful not to confuse this tense with the simple future tense, in which only the helping verb *shall* or *will* is used. The helping verb *have* is not used in the simple future tense. Also, the *present* form of the main verb is used in the simple future tense, but the *past participle* is used in the future perfect tense.

Simple future tense:
> I <u>shall study</u> my lesson.
> They <u>will work</u> six hours.

Future perfect tense:
> I <u>shall have studied</u> my lesson by noon.
> They <u>will have worked</u> six hours by evening.

Remember that the perfect tenses refer to completed action. The future perfect tense tells about an action that will be "perfect in the future." The action will be completed by a future time that is usually stated in the sentence.

> I <u>shall have made</u> my decision before five o'clock.
> **Meaning:**   My action of making a decision will be completed by five o'clock.

> The ministers <u>will have arrived</u> in Nigeria by noon tomorrow.
> **Meaning:**   Their action of arriving will be completed by noon tomorrow.

- The future perfect tense is formed by using the helping verbs *shall have* or *will have* with the past participle of a main verb.

- The future perfect tense refers to an action that will be completed by a certain time in the future.

Class Practice

A. Tell whether the underlined verb phrases are in the *future tense* or the *future perfect tense*.
  1. Father <u>will have decided</u> before we arrive.
  2. I hope that someday this calf <u>will become</u> a cow.

Lesson 36 Answers
Class Practice
A. 1. future perfect tense
   2. future tense

Lesson Outline:

1. The future perfect tense is formed by using **shall have** *or* **will have** *with the third principal part of a main verb.* The helping verbs *shall have* or *will have* are a sure sign of the future perfect tense.

> We <u>shall have traveled</u> hundreds of miles before the day is over.
> Alice <u>will have mailed</u> five cards by next Wednesday.

2. The future perfect tense can easily be distinguished from the simple future tense. In the simple future tense, the *present* form of a verb is used with only *shall* or *will*. In the future perfect tense, the *past participle* of a verb is used with *shall have* or *will have*. **Remember:** All perfect tenses are made with forms of *have*.

Simple future:
> I <u>shall sleep</u> for eight hours.
> The men <u>will finish</u> the house.

Future perfect:
> By morning I <u>shall have slept</u> for eight hours.
> By Friday the men <u>will have finished</u> the house.

3. The future perfect tense refers to an action that will be completed by a future time that is usually stated in the sentence. The action will be "perfect in the future." As before, stress the formation of the future perfect tense more than the meaning.

★ **EXTRA PRACTICE**
Worksheet 22 *(Verb Tenses)*

3. I <u>shall have called</u> you before tomorrow evening.
4. By the time I leave, they <u>will have planted</u> four trees.
5. The glass <u>will break</u> if you drop it.

B. Give the future perfect tense of each verb in parentheses. Be sure to use the correct verb form and the correct helping verbs.

Example: We hope that we (be) at the store by Thursday.
Answer: shall have been

1. By tomorrow evening I (study) my lesson for Tuesday.
2. You (write) five letters when you have finished.
3. By Saturday, the Martins (make) six hundred cupcakes to sell.
4. Before his trip is over, Wayne (ride) on six different buses.
5. Joel (read) the three books by Saturday.
6. Before the end of the week, Sarah (bring) ten different children to Bible school.

C. Change the verb in each sentence to the future and future perfect tenses.

Example: They drive six hundred miles.
Answer: will drive, will have driven

1. They shake all the rugs.
2. The ice freezes sufficiently.
3. We sing five songs.
4. The baby drinks six bottles of formula.

Written Exercises

A. Copy each verb or verb phrase, and write whether it is in the *future* tense or the *future perfect* tense.
1. The baby will have slept two hours by four o'clock.
2. Surely Philip will have found the cows before dark.
3. By 3:00 we shall have sat in school for six hours.
4. Sheldon will feed these calves.
5. The geese will have left by next week.
6. Katie will glue the pictures onto the page.
7. A full moon will occur on Tuesday.
8. By noon tomorrow we shall have dug twenty ditches.

3. future perfect tense
4. future perfect tense
5. future tense

B. 1. shall (will) have studied
   2. will have written
   3. will have made
   4. will have ridden
   5. will have read
   6. will have brought

C. 1. will shake, will have shaken
   2. will freeze, will have frozen
   3. shall (will) sing, shall (will) have sung
   4. will drink, will have drunk

Written Exercises

A. 1. will have slept—future perfect
   2. will have found—future perfect
   3. shall have sat—future perfect
   4. will feed—future
   5. will have left—future perfect
   6. will glue—future
   7. will occur—future
   8. shall have dug—future perfect

B. Write the future perfect tense of each verb in parentheses. Be sure to use the correct verb form and the correct helping verbs.

Example: After the next load, the boys (tag) all the sheep.
Answer: will have tagged

1. If Mark gets one more mushroom, he (find) ten altogether.
2. Soon Dolores (cut) out ten dresses.
3. Laurel (draw) twenty pictures when this one is finished.
4. I (write) six poems about nature when this one is done.
5. Phyllis (give) away several bouquets by Friday.
6. By tomorrow this time, I (eat) my lunch.
7. At the end of this year, Brother John (teach) ten years.
8. We (study) three countries by the time we finish this chapter.

C. Copy the verb in each sentence, and write its future and future perfect tenses.
1. Grandmother visits all her children.
2. School begins in September.
3. Brother Joseph speaks three times at the meetings.
4. The children sleep ten hours.

Review Exercises

Copy the verb or verb phrase in each sentence. Write which tense it is: *present, past, future, present perfect, past perfect,* or *future perfect.* [32–36]

1. My cousins go to that school.
2. Dwight had thrown the ball to me.
3. Nathan's family will have left by then.
4. Marilyn forgot the price.
5. Gladys has kept the secret.
6. Robert will plant petunias.
7. The girls had sung the song well.
8. Father went to the market.
9. They have lived there for a year.
10. Nancy knows Sandra.
11. Mark will write a poem.
12. By autumn the corn will have grown tall.

B. 1. will have found
   2. will have cut
   3. will have drawn
   4. shall (will) have written
   5. will have given
   6. shall (will) have eaten
   7. will have taught
   8. shall (will) have studied

C. 1. visits, will visit, will have visited
   2. begins, will begin, will have begun
   3. speaks, will speak, will have spoken
   4. sleep, will sleep, will have slept

Review Exercises

1. go—present
2. had thrown—past perfect
3. will have left—future perfect
4. forgot—past
5. has kept—present perfect
6. will plant—future
7. had sung—past perfect
8. went—past
9. have lived—present perfect
10. knows—present
11. will write—future
12. will have grown—future perfect

37. Sentence and Topical Outlines

Outlines can be written in different forms. On a *topical outline,* each point is given as only a word or phrase. This is the kind of outline that you studied in Lesson 33. A topical outline does not have complete sentences.

On a *sentence outline,* each point is given as a complete sentence. Every sentence ends with the correct punctuation.

A writer must decide whether he will use a topical outline or a sentence outline. If some points on his outline are complete sentences, all the points should be complete sentences. Phrases should not be mixed with sentences on the same outline.

Also remember that every outline must have a title. The title gives the main idea of the outline.

Sentence outline:

Butterflies, Moths, and Skippers

I. Butterflies have special characteristics.
   A. The abdomen is narrow and straight-sided.
   B. The tips of the antennae have knobs.
   C. The head is easy to see.
   D. They sit with their wings together over their backs.
II. Moths have special characteristics.
   A. The abdomen is broad and puffy.
   B. The antennae have many different shapes.
   C. The head is usually not easy to see.
   D. They sit differently from butterflies.
      1. They sit with wings outspread like an airplane.
      2. Some sit with wings like a tent or upside-down V.
III. Skippers have special characteristics.
   A. The abdomen is much like a moth's.
   B. The antennae are far apart on the head.
   C. The wings are short and small.
   D. They are named for their fast, darting flight.
   E. They sit with their front wings together and back wings spread out.

Lesson 37

Purpose: To teach *the difference between topical outlines and sentence outlines.

Oral Review:

1. Every outline must begin with what? (a title)
2. Why do writers and speakers use outlines? (to organize their material)
3. Why do readers and listeners use outlines? (to help them remember what they read or hear)
4. What does an outline show? (a brief summary of a composition; the contents and organization of the material)
5. Give some helps for writing good directions. (Make sure the information is accurate. Write clearly so that the directions are simple to understand. Use transitional words like *first, second,* and *next.*)
6. In writing directions, what order should you use? (the order things are to be done; the order of time)

Lesson Introduction: Ask the students, "How would you like to have the same thing in your lunch every day? Suppose you always had a sandwich of luncheon meat and lettuce, a piece of chocolate cake, and some peaches. How long would you enjoy your school lunches?" Variety makes life interesting. It helps us in other ways too.

There are various ways to make good outlines. Today we want to study two different kinds of outlines and some rules for writing them.

Lesson Outline:

1. Two kinds of outlines are the topical outline and the sentence outline. A topical outline has only words or phrases for each point. A sentence outline has complete sentences.

This same outline can be shortened to a topical outline, as shown below.

Topical outline:

Butterflies, Moths, and Skippers
I. Characteristics of butterflies
   A. Narrow, straight-sided abdomen
   B. Knobbed antennae
   C. Head distinct from body
   D. Wings held together over back
II. Characteristics of moths
   A. Broad, puffy abdomen
   B. Antennae in many different shapes
   C. Head not distinct from body
   D. Wings held differently from butterfly's
      1. Outspread like airplane
      2. Held in an upside-down V
III. Characteristics of skippers
   A. Abdomen similar to moth's
   B. Antennae far apart on head
   C. Small, short wings
   D. Fast, darting flight
   E. Position of wings
      1. Front wings together
      2. Hind wings spread out

On a good outline, the points are parallel. This means each topic has a similar form. All the points in a set should start with nouns, verbs, or adjectives, or they should be alike in some other way. Sometimes all the points in a set begin with the same letter.

Suppose the main points from the outline above were written as in the following example. Can you see that the topics are not parallel?

I. Characteristics of butterflies
II. Moth characteristics
III. Skippers and their characteristics

Of course the points cannot always be perfectly parallel. But they should be made as nearly parallel as possible.

2. All the points on an outline should be complete sentences, or none should be complete sentences. Complete and incomplete sentences should not be mixed on the same outline.

3. Every outline must have a title, whether it is a topical outline or a sentence outline. The title gives the main idea of the outline.

4. On a good outline, the points are as nearly parallel as possible. Each point should have a similar form. All the points in a set should start with nouns, verbs, or adjectives, or they should be alike in some other way. Sometimes all the points in a set begin with the same letter.

- A sentence outline has complete sentences for each point. A topical outline has only words or phrases.
- The points on a topical outline should be as nearly parallel as possible.

Class Practice

A. Reword some of the following points to make the outline parallel.

How Homes Are Heated
I. With furnaces
   A. Wood-burning furnaces
   B. Furnaces that burn coal
   C. Some furnaces use oil.
II. Electricity
   A. Baseboard
   B. In the ceiling
   C. Some heat and circulate water.
III. Using energy from the sun or the earth
   A. Active solar heating
   B. Using passive solar heating
   C. Obtaining geothermal heat

B. On the chalkboard, change the outline in Part A to a sentence outline.

Written Exercises

A. Change this sentence outline into a topical outline.

Important Rivers of the World
I. Europe has several rivers that are important for transportation.
   A. The Rhine River is the most important inland waterway of Europe.
   B. The Volga River is the longest river in Europe.
   C. The Danube River is the second longest river in Europe.
II. Africa has some large, famous rivers.
   A. The Nile River is the longest river in the world.
   B. The Congo River is the second largest river in the world.

Lesson 37 Answers
Class Practice

A.   **How Homes Are Heated**
I. With furnaces
   A. Wood-burning furnaces
   B. Coal-burning furnaces
   C. Oil-burning furnaces
II. With electricity
   A. Heaters along the baseboard
   B. Heaters in the ceiling
   C. Systems that heat and circulate water
III. With energy from the sun or the earth
   A. Active solar heating
   B. Passive solar heating
   C. Geothermal heating

B.   **How Homes Are Heated**
I. Some homes are heated with furnaces.
   A. Some furnaces burn firewood.
   B. Some furnaces burn coal.
   C. Some furnaces burn fuel oil.
II. Some homes are heated with electricity.
   A. Heaters may be placed along the baseboard.
   B. Heating coils may be placed in the ceiling.
   C. Some systems heat and circulate water.
III. Some homes are heated with energy from the sun or the earth.
   A. In active solar heating, the house is warmed by special devices that collect and distribute heat from the sun.
   B. In passive solar heating, the house is warmed by sunlight shining through large insulated windows on the south side.
   C. Geothermal heating systems use heat from underground.

Written Exercises

A. (Sample outline. Underlined items are optional.)

Important Rivers of the World
I. Rivers of Europe
   A. Rhine River—<u>most important inland waterway of Europe</u>
   B. Volga River—<u>longest river in Europe</u>
   C. Danube River—<u>second longest river in Europe</u>
II. Rivers of Africa
   A. Nile River—<u>longest river in the world</u>
   B. Congo River—<u>second largest river in the world</u>

III. Civilizations of Asia were built around several important rivers.
  A. China has two outstanding rivers.
    1. The Yangtze River is the third longest river in the world.
    2. The Huang He River was a center of ancient Chinese civilization.
  B. Early civilizations of Mesopotamia were built around two large rivers.
    1. The Tigris River runs a fairly straight course.
    2. The Euphrates River is more winding.
  C. The Indus River was the center of an ancient civilization in India.
IV. The Mississippi and the Amazon are rivers of America.
  A. The Mississippi is the largest river system in North America.
  B. The Amazon River, of South America, is the largest river in the world.

B. Rewrite the following outline, making all the points parallel to the first one.

Important Lands of Europe

I. Germany: Land of the Reformation
II. Switzerland: Land where the Alps are
III. The Netherlands: Dikes and polders are found there.
IV. Scandinavia: where the Vikings lived
V. Spain and Portugal: Many explorers came from this land.

Review Exercises

Copy the correct answers in parentheses.

1. Every good story tells about (a personal experience, an exciting event, a problem that was solved).
2. In a set of directions, the steps should be given (in the order they are to be done, in the order of interest, as briefly as possible).
3. Writing a good story includes all the following except (organizing notes, writing clearly, sticking to the main idea, adding all the details that come to mind).
4. Writing a good set of directions includes all the following except (making sure the information is accurate, making sure you enjoy doing what you explain, writing in complete sentences, using a variety of sentences).

III. Rivers of Asia
  A. Rivers of China
    1. Yangtze River—third longest river in the world
    2. Huang He River—center of ancient Chinese civilization
  B. Rivers of Mesopotamia
    1. Tigris River
    2. Euphrates River
  C. River of India—the Indus River
IV. Rivers of America
  A. Mississippi River—largest river system in North America
  B. Amazon River—largest river in the world

B. (Allow reasonable variation.)

Important Lands of Europe

I. Germany: Land of the Reformation
II. Switzerland: Land of the Alps
III. The Netherlands: Land of dikes and polders
IV. Scandinavia: Land of the Vikings
V. Spain and Portugal: Land of explorers

Review Exercises

1. a problem that was solved
2. in the order they are to be done
3. adding all the details that come to mind
4. making sure you enjoy doing what you explain

5. Paragraph development can be improved in all the following ways except (using details, using examples, using a comparison, using better handwriting, using a contrast).

6. Good transitional words include all the following except (first, second, finally, then, forward, soon, next).

7. Every outline should have all the following except (a title, complete sentences, an orderly pattern, points as nearly parallel as possible).

---

38. Transitive Verbs and Direct Objects

You have learned that verbs show action or being. One kind of verb that shows action is a *transitive* verb. A transitive verb passes its action to a noun or pronoun, which is the receiver of the action. The thought of a transitive verb is not complete without a receiver of the action.

Read the following sentences. They do not seem complete, because the transitive verb has no receiver for its action. We wonder, "What did Sheila bring?" and "What did Julie throw?"

Sheila brought.   Julie threw.

A *direct object* is a noun or pronoun that receives the action of a transitive verb. A direct object usually comes after the verb and answers the question *whom* or *what*. To find a direct object, say the subject and verb together and ask *whom* or *what*. The noun or pronoun that answers the question is the direct object.

Verbs with direct objects:
Esau sold his birthright to his brother Jacob.
(Esau sold *what*? The direct object is *birthright*.)

During the storm, an angel comforted Paul.
(Angel comforted *whom*? The direct object is *Paul*.)

Paul encouraged them with the reassuring message.
(Paul encouraged *whom*? The direct object is *them*.)

A direct object is diagramed on the base line after the subject and verb, with a vertical line between the verb and the direct object. This line does not go through the base line but rests upon it.

5. using better handwriting
6. forward
7. complete sentences

Lesson 38

Purpose: To teach the recognition of *transitive verbs and direct objects. (*Previous experience:* Verbs with direct objects, without using the term *transitive*.)

Oral Review:

1. How is the present perfect tense formed? (by using *have* or *has* with the past participle of a main verb)

2. How is the past perfect tense formed? (by using *had* with the past participle of a main verb)

3. How is the future perfect tense formed? (by using *shall have* or *will have* with the past participle of a main verb)

4. For each of the following verbs, give the present perfect tense, the past perfect tense, and the future perfect tense.
   a. take (have taken, had taken, will have taken)
   b. read (have read, had read, will have read)
   c. put (have put, had put, will have put)
   d. freeze (have frozen, had frozen, will have frozen)

5. What is a plural noun? (a word that names more than one person, place, thing, or idea)

6. Tell which word is better.
   a. Measles (is, are) a disease. (is)
   b. The scissors (is, are) sharp. (are)
   c. The news (was, were) good. (was)

7. Spell the plural forms of the following words.
   a. loaf (loaves)   d. child (children)
   b. potato (potatoes)   e. goose (geese)
   c. alto (altos)   f. belief (beliefs)

Written Quiz:
Write the missing tenses.

Simple Present	Simple Past	Simple Future	Present Perfect	Past Perfect	Future Perfect
1. buy					
2. freeze					
3. go					
4. swim					
5. come					
6. think					

Quiz Answers:

	Simple Present	Simple Past	Simple Future	Present Perfect	Past Perfect	Future Perfect
1.	bought	will buy	have bought	had bought	will have bought
2.	froze	will freeze	have frozen	had frozen	will have frozen
3.	went	will go	have gone	had gone	will have gone
4.	swam	will swim	have swum	had swum	will have swum
5.	came	will come	have come	had come	will have come
6.	thought	will think	have thought	had thought	will have thought

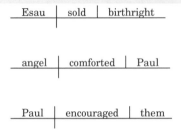

A compound direct object is diagramed on a fork after the vertical line that rests on the base line.

Jane knitted a scarf and some mittens.

If sentences have compound verbs with direct objects, they are diagramed as shown below.

We washed the dishes and folded the clothes.

We washed and dried the dishes.

Lesson Introduction: What does the prefix *trans-* mean? (over *or* across) Some words that begin with this prefix are *transportation, transaction,* and *translate.* Transportation is that which moves people or things across an area. A transaction is an action between two parties. To translate is to change over from one language to another. Today we will study *transitive* verbs. They are verbs that pass their action over, or across, to another word in the sentence.

Lesson Outline:

   1. A transitive verb passes action to a receiver. A transitive verb needs a noun or pronoun to receive its action. The thought of the sentence may not be complete without a receiver of the action.

      The little black dog chased the big white cat.
      Compare: The little black dog chased. (incomplete thought)

   2. A direct object is a noun or pronoun that receives the action of a transitive verb. A direct object usually comes after the verb and answers the question *whom or what.*

      The ball <u>shattered</u> the <u>window.</u>
      Jehu <u>drove</u> his <u>chariot</u> furiously.

   Be sure that the students are able to define a direct object and that they associate a direct object with *receiving action.*

   3. To find a direct object, say the subject and verb together and ask whom *or* what. Insist on this procedure, and drill it thoroughly.

      Brother Henry faced the congregation solemnly.
      (Brother Henry faced *whom*? The direct object is *congregation.*)

> • A transitive verb passes action to another word in the sentence.
>
> • A direct object receives the action of a transitive verb.
>
> • A direct object is always a noun or a pronoun.

Class Practice

A. Give the transitive verbs and their direct objects. Be sure to get all the words in a verb phrase.
1. The Lord will bless His faithful people.
2. The Holy Spirit moved the prophets to speak for God.
3. God had kept Daniel safe from the lions.
4. Father passed the slow-moving vehicles.
5. Susan has written many stories and poems.

B. At the chalkboard, diagram the skeletons and direct objects of these sentences.
1. Someday Jesus will take His bride to heaven.
2. A soft answer turneth away wrath.
3. Jane read a very interesting book.
4. May we bake a white cake and some chocolate cookies?
5. Donald took the clock apart and lost the screws.

Written Exercises

A. Write the transitive verbs and their direct objects. Be sure to get all the words in a verb phrase.
1. Peter and John entered the temple.
2. Jesus healed the ten lepers.
3. God provides many good things for us.
4. We shall soon learn the answers.
5. Anna swept and mopped the floor.
6. Jesus loves you and me.
7. David was helping the neighbors for several hours.
8. The wild geese ate the corn.
9. Marcia showed the interesting picture to her friends.
10. Eldon could not find Mark and him.

Lesson 38 Answers
Class Practice
A. 1. will bless, people
2. moved, prophets
3. had kept, Daniel
4. passed, vehicles
5. has written, stories (and) poems

B. 1. Jesus | will take | bride

2. answer | turneth | wrath

3. Jane | read | book

4.

5.
we | May bake | cake and cookies

Donald took clock and lost screws

Written Exercises
A. 1. entered, temple
2. healed, lepers
3. provides, things
4. shall learn, answers
5. swept (and) mopped, floor
6. loves, you, me
7. was helping, neighbors
8. ate, corn
9. showed, picture
10. could find, Mark (and) him

4. A direct object is diagramed on the base line after the subject and verb, with a vertical line between the verb and the direct object. This line does not go through the base line but rests upon it. Illustrate with the following sentences at the chalkboard.

Mother made a new coat.

Mother | made | coat

Some young boys helped the farmer.

boys | helped | farmer

5. A compound direct object is diagramed on a fork after the vertical line that rests on the base line. Diagram examples on the chalkboard.

Lisa swept the porch and the steps.

Lisa | swept | porch and steps

Loren raked the leaves and hauled them away.

Loren raked | leaves and hauled | them

Larry scraped and painted the trim.
(*Note:* If two verbs have the same direct object, the following pattern is used.)

Larry scraped and painted | trim

B. Diagram the skeletons and direct objects of these sentences.
1. Did Ray find the keys?
2. Take this book with you.
3. Soon all the children removed their coats.
4. Please feed the calves and water the chickens.
5. The sheep and goats also need feed and water.
6. Paul and Silas came to Philippi and taught the people.

Review Exercises

Write the plural form of each noun. If a noun is always singular or is usually considered plural, simply copy it. [22, 23]

1. donkey
2. chief
3. city
4. goose
5. potato
6. roof
7. pliers
8. mouse
9. fox
10. scissors
11. news
12. woman
13. baby
14. measles
15. child
16. ox

39. Action Verbs That Are Not Transitive

You have learned that a transitive verb passes action to a receiver. A direct object is a noun or pronoun that receives the action of a transitive verb.

> Harry whistled a merry tune.
>> Harry whistled *what*? *Tune* is the direct object. *Whistled* is a transitive verb in this sentence because it passes action to the noun *tune*.

Not all action verbs pass action to a direct object. Sometimes an action verb is followed by an adverb instead of a direct object.

> Harry whistled cheerfully.
>> Harry whistled *what*? There is no word to answer this question. *Cheerfully* is an adverb that tells *how*. There is no direct object, and *whistled* is not a transitive verb in this sentence.

Review Exercises
1. donkeys
2. chiefs
3. cities
4. geese
5. potatoes
6. roofs
7. pliers
8. mice
9. foxes
10. scissors
11. news
12. women
13. babies
14. measles
15. children
16. oxen

Lesson 39

Purpose: To teach that *some action verbs are transitive and some are not, and how to tell the difference. (The expression *not transitive* is used instead of the term *intransitive,* to rivet the meaning of *transitive.*)

Oral Review:
1. What is a transitive verb? (a verb that passes action to a receiver)
2. What is a direct object? (a noun or pronoun that receives the action of a transitive verb)
3. Tell how to find a direct object. (Say the subject and verb together, and ask *whom* or *what*.)
4. What is a proper noun? (the name of a specific person, place, or thing)
5. How must proper nouns be written? (with capital letters)

Lesson Introduction: Write the following sentences on the chalkboard. Ask students if they can pick out the subjects, verbs, and direct objects.

> Father drove carefully up the narrow mountain road.
> We ate at the table in the living room.
> The girls stopped at the end of the lane.

These sentences have no direct objects. (Father did not drive the mountain, we did not eat the table or the living room, and the girls did not stop the end or the lane.) Not all action verbs are transitive. Today's lesson is about action verbs that do not pass action to a receiver.

Sometimes an action verb is followed by a noun or pronoun in a prepositional phrase. But that noun or pronoun cannot be the direct object, for a direct object is never in a prepositional phrase.

> Harry whistled with enthusiasm.
>> Harry whistled *what*? There is no word to answer this question. *With enthusiasm* is a prepositional phrase that tells *how*. There is no direct object, and *whistled* is not a transitive verb in this sentence.

Study the following sentences and their diagrams. In each sentence with a direct object, the direct object tells *whom* or *what*. In each sentence without a direct object, there is no word to tell *whom* or *what*.

> Father called me.

Father	called	me

> Father called loudly.

Father	called	(*Loudly* tells *how*.)

> We often sing that song.

We	sing	song

> We often sing at school.

We	sing	(*At school* tells *where*.)

It is not hard to tell the difference between an action verb that is transitive and one that is not transitive. If a verb is transitive, it always passes action to a receiver.

Lesson Outline:

1. Not all action verbs pass action to a direct object.

2. Sometimes an action verb is followed by an adverb instead of a direct object.

> My two brothers ran swiftly.
>> The adverb *swiftly* tells *how*.

> The butterfly hatched soon.
>> The adverb *soon* tells *when*.

3. Sometimes an action verb is followed by a prepositional phrase, which contains a noun or pronoun. That noun or pronoun cannot be the direct object, for a direct object is never in a prepositional phrase.

> The butterfly struggled out of the cocoon.
> We must hurry to the station.
> Joel and I raced to the end of the yard.

- Not all action verbs pass action to a direct object.

- An action verb may be followed by an adverb or a prepositional phrase instead of a direct object.

Class Practice

A. Give the verb in each sentence, and tell whether it is *transitive* or *not transitive*. If it is transitive, also give the direct object.
1. My cat catches mice.
2. Sister Norma read the papers.
3. The children were watching the birds.
4. Joel is still standing in line.
5. Please close the door.
6. A small bird fell from the tree.
7. A mouse scurried across the bare floor.
8. We ordered a new sofa for the living room.
9. The squirrels chattered noisily at the cat.
10. Grace saw the little foxes in front of their den.

B. At the chalkboard, diagram the sentence skeletons and direct objects of the sentences in Part A.

Written Exercises

A. Number your paper from 1 to 16. Write only the verbs or verb phrases that are not transitive.
1. My sisters are picking apples.
2. Miriam can draw quite well.
3. Everyone should sing heartily.
4. Joshua and the Israelites conquered Jericho.
5. Ananias could not deceive Peter.
6. The class talked about the accident.
7. Shirley carefully lifted the cover.
8. Gerald and I soon smelled the smoke.
9. The soup simmered on the burner for one hour.
10. The cook simmered the soup for one hour.
11. Arthur organized his desk at recess.
12. The bird was soaring high in the blue sky.

Lesson 39 Answers
Class Practice
A.
1. catches—transitive; mice
2. read—transitive; papers
3. were watching—transitive; birds
4. is standing—not transitive
5. close—transitive; door
6. fell—not transitive
7. scurried—not transitive
8. ordered—transitive; sofa
9. chattered—not transitive
10. saw—transitive; foxes

B.
1. cat | catches | mice
2. Sister Norma | read | papers
3. children | were watching | birds
4. Joel | is standing
5. (you) | close | door
6. bird | fell
7. mouse | scurried
8. We | ordered | sofa
9. squirrels | chattered
10. Grace | saw | foxes

Written Exercises
A.
1.
2. can draw
3. should sing
4.
5.
6. talked
7.
8.
9. simmered
10.
11.
12. was soaring

13. The teacher assigned the next lesson.
14. Some children learn easily.
15. We traded our papers.
16. Janice traded with me.

B. Diagram the sentence skeletons and direct objects of numbers 1–10 in Part A.

C. Use each verb in two sentences, first as a verb that is transitive and then as a verb that is not transitive.
  1. eat   2. read   3. play

Review Exercises

A. Copy the verb or verb phrase in each sentence. Write the present perfect, past perfect, and future perfect tenses of each verb. [34–36]

  Examples: a. Peter digs worms.
  b. They will see many new birds.

  Answers: a. digs, has dug, had dug, will have dug
  b. will see, has seen, had seen, will have seen

1. Timothy tells what happened.
2. She waits for us.
3. Richard will study diligently.
4. We begin early.

B. Copy correctly each word that needs a capital letter. [20]
  1. Have you ever seen the grand canyon of arizona?
  2. Long ago, produce was floated down the mississippi river in flatboats and was sold in new orleans.
  3. Did the minersville christian school open this fall?
  4. Do you prefer american food or italian food?
  5. Are kellogg's cereals better than post cereals?
  6. On friday, mrs. elizabeth d. fulton and miss barbara gauss went to see dr. fred l. frey, who is an english doctor.
  7. Yesterday mr. martin w. allen and mr. ludwig m. hooke talked with brother ira d. martin.
  8. dr. j. k. lee sees patients at the memphis general hospital.
  9. The lord will hear when i call on him.
  10. O lord, my god, in thee do i put my trust.

13.
14. learn
15.
16. traded

B. 1. sisters | are picking | apples

  2. Miriam | can draw

  3. Everyone | should sing

  4. Joshua
      Israelites } (and) conquered | Jericho

  5. Ananias | could deceive | Peter

  6. class | talked

  7. Shirley | lifted | cover

  8. Gerald
      I } (and) smelled | smoke

  9. soup | simmered

  10. cook | simmered | soup

C. (Individual sentences.)

Review Exercises

A. 1. tells, has told, had told, will have told
  2. waits, has waited, had waited, will have waited
  3. will study, has studied, had studied, will have studied
  4. begin, have begun, had begun, shall (will) have begun

B. 1. Grand Canyon, Arizona
  2. Mississippi River, New Orleans
  3. Minersville Christian School
  4. American, Italian
  5. Kellogg's, Post
  6. Friday, Mrs. Elizabeth D. Fulton, Miss Barbara Gauss, Dr. Fred L. Frey, English
  7. Mr. Martin W. Allen, Mr. Ludwig M. Hooke, Brother Ira D. Martin
  8. Dr. J. K. Lee, Memphis General Hospital
  9. Lord, I, Him
  10. Lord, God, Thee, I

40. Transitive Verbs and Indirect Objects

You have learned that a transitive verb passes its action to a receiver, and that a direct object receives the action of a transitive verb. A direct object answers the question *whom* or *what* after the skeleton.

> Moses viewed Canaan from the mountaintop.
> (Moses viewed *what*? The direct object is *Canaan.*)

A transitive verb may also have an *indirect object.* An indirect object is a noun or pronoun that tells *to whom or what* or *for whom or what* the action of the verb is done. An indirect object always comes between a verb and a direct object.

> subject   verb   indirect object   direct object
> ↓   ↓   ↓   ↓
> Marilyn   wrote   her   cousin   a   letter.

To find an indirect object, first say the subject, the verb, and the direct object together. Then ask *to whom or what* or *for whom or what.* The answer will be the indirect object.

> **Sentences with indirect objects:**
> Sister Gladys showed the class some pictures.
>> Sister Gladys showed *what*? The direct object is *pictures.*
>> Sister Gladys showed pictures *to whom*? The indirect object is *class.*
>
> Father bought us a good book.
>> Father bought *what*? The direct object is *book.* Father bought book *for whom*? The indirect object is *us.*

Be careful not to confuse an indirect object with a direct object.

> My sister baked me a pie.
>> Sister baked *what*? The direct object is *pie.*
>> Sister baked pie *for whom*? The indirect object is *me.*
>> My sister baked a *pie;* she did not bake *me*!

Also be careful not to confuse an indirect object with the object of a preposition. An indirect object is never found in a prepositional phrase. It never comes after a word like *to* or *for.* Compare these two sentences.

Lesson 40

Purpose: To show the use of *indirect objects with transitive verbs.

Oral Review:
1. What is a transitive verb? (a verb that passes action to a receiver)
2. Are all action verbs transitive? (no)
3. Name the three principal parts of verbs. Give two names for each. (first principal part—present form; second principal part—past form; third principal part—past participle)
4. Say and spell the second and third principal parts of the following verbs.
   a. wear (wore, [have] worn)
   b. carry (carried, [have] carried)
   c. teach (taught, [have] taught)
   d. ride (rode, [have] ridden)

Lesson Introduction: Read each of the following sentences to the students. Ask if they can think of another way to say the same thing. (You may need to help them.)

> You may give the flowers to Grandmother.
> We told the story to Judy.
> We will make some soup for Gerald.

We can say the same thing by using an indirect object. This is also a correct way of speaking.

> You may give Grandmother the flowers.
> We told Judy the story.
> We will make Gerald some soup.

Today we will study indirect objects.

Lesson Outline:
1. Every transitive verb must have a receiver of the action. A direct object receives action and answers the question *whom* or *what* after the skeleton.

2. A transitive verb with a direct object may also have an indirect object. *An indirect object tells* to whom or what *or* for whom or what *the action of the verb is done.* Be sure students master the definition of an indirect object.

3. An indirect object always comes between a verb and a direct object. There cannot be an indirect object unless there is a direct object.

4. To find an indirect object, first say the subject, the verb, and the direct object together. Then ask to whom or what *or* for whom or what. *The answer will be the indirect object.* Drill this procedure in class.

> Kind friends offered the homeless family their help.
> Our grandfather can tell us many old stories.

My sister baked <u>me</u> a pie. (indirect object)
My sister baked a pie for <u>me</u>. (object of preposition)

Both sentences have exactly the same meaning. But *me* cannot be an indirect object in the second sentence for two reasons.
   (1) *Me* does not come between the verb and the direct object.
   (2) *Me* comes after the preposition *for*.

Any sentence with an indirect object can be changed to a sentence with a prepositional phrase. Some sentences with prepositional phrases can also be changed to sentences with indirect objects. But an indirect object and the object of a preposition are never the same.

Indirect object:
   The girls sent <u>Grandmother</u> some cards.
Object of preposition:
   The girls sent some cards to <u>Grandmother</u>.

Indirect object:
   Susan sold the <u>customer</u> from town some eggs.
Object of preposition:
   Susan sold some eggs to the <u>customer</u> from town.

An indirect object is diagramed on a horizontal line beneath the base line, with a slanted line connecting the indirect object to the verb.

Diane told the children a story.

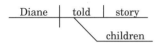

Father made the boys a rabbit pen.

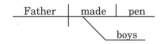

5. An indirect object must not be confused with other kinds of objects.
   a. *A direct object.* A direct object *directly* receives the action of a verb. It is sensible to say the subject, the verb, and the direct object together.

   Mother cut me a slice of bread.
      ("Mother cut me" is not sensible, but "Mother cut slice" is sensible.)

   b. *The object of a preposition.* An indirect object is never found in a prepositional phrase.

   Verna showed <u>each</u> of her visitors the greenhouse.
   She showed <u>me</u> the kittens in the barn.

6. Any sentence with an indirect object can be changed to a sentence with a prepositional phrase.
Since an indirect object tells *to whom or what* or *for whom or what,* the indirect object can be changed to the object of the preposition *to* or *for.*

   Mother bought me a coat.
   Mother bought a coat for me.

   The salesman sold him a new freezer.
   The salesman sold a new freezer to him.

(*Teacher:* Because the indirect object is readily changed to the object of a preposition, some consider it as an elliptical form of a prepositional phrase, with the preposition understood. That is a misconception. The indirect object is actually a carryover from Old English, in which this word order was used [subject-verb-indirect object], and the indirect object was in the dative case. The dative case was eventually absorbed by the objective case, but the indirect object remained.)

An indirect object can be compound. Study the following example.

Mother bought Karen and me a new storybook.

- An indirect object tells *to whom or what* or *for whom or what* the action of the verb is done.

- An indirect object is always found between the verb and the direct object in a sentence.

Class Practice

A. Tell whether each sentence has an indirect object. If it does, tell what it is.
   1. Dennis and I will build Fido a house.
   2. The noise must have been thunder.
   3. Jesus taught His disciples many things.
   4. We found the lost book in the barrel.
   5. A housefly can move its wings very fast.
   6. Someone has sent my brother these books.
   7. He will bring the little ones a surprise.
   8. The deer stood in the water near to the shore.

B. Diagram the skeletons, direct objects, and indirect objects at the chalkboard.
   1. My brother carved me a whistle.
   2. The Lord gave Moses the Ten Commandments.
   3. Brother Lester found the visitor a seat.
   4. Evelyn brought me a chocolate bar.

7. An indirect object is diagramed on a horizontal line beneath the base line. A slanted line connects the indirect object to the verb. A compound indirect object is diagramed on a fork.

The girls are taking the sick children some hot soup.

I sent Grandmother and Grandfather a letter.

Lesson 40 Answers
Class Practice
A. 1. yes; Fido
   2. no
   3. yes; disciples
   4. no
   5. no
   6. yes; brother
   7. yes; ones
   8. no

B. 1.   brother │ carved │ whistle
                          ＼ me

   2.   Lord │ gave │ Ten Commandments
                       ＼ Moses

   3.   Brother Lester │ found │ seat
                                 ＼ visitor

   4.   Evelyn │ bought │ bar
                          ＼ me

★ **EXTRA PRACTICE**
Worksheet 23 *(Diagraming Direct and Indirect Objects)*

5. Father gave each of the workers a check.
6. We shall send the sick girl and boy a card.

C. Read each sentence in Part B, changing the indirect object to the object of a preposition.

D. Read the following sentences, changing the object of the preposition to an indirect object.
   1. I will give some water to the flowers.
   2. The farmer fed some hay to his steers.

Written Exercises

A. Diagram the skeletons, direct objects, and indirect objects.
   1. Aunt Sarah has baked our family a fresh blueberry pie.
   2. We are making a chart for science class.
   3. We can sell the driver some fresh vegetables.
   4. The old wagon was sinking rapidly into the mud.
   5. Brother Sensenig has given the school these lovely rosebushes.
   6. I must write the man a bill for the various repairs.
   7. Adam gave each animal a name.
   8. Marla often writes her sister a letter.
   9. This rug feels very soft.
   10. Sandra felt the soft rug too.

B. Rewrite each sentence so that the indirect object becomes the object of a preposition at the end of the sentence.
   1. Jesse fed the calves some grain.
   2. Jeffrey sent his sick cousin a card.
   3. Mother sewed Nathan a jacket.
   4. The farmer gave his cows some alfalfa hay.

C. Rewrite each sentence so that the object of the preposition becomes an indirect object.
   1. Arlene read a story to the children.
   2. We bought more feed for the chickens.
   3. The boys made a bookcase for Mother.
   4. Curtis brought the mail to Father.

B. 1. Jesse fed some grain to the calves.
   2. Jeffrey sent a card to his sick cousin.
   3. Mother sewed a jacket for Nathan.
   4. The farmer gave some alfalfa hay to his cows.

C. 1. Arlene read the children a story.
   2. We bought the chickens more feed.
   3. The boys made Mother a bookcase.
   4. Curtis brought Father the mail.

5.

6.

C. 1. My brother carved a whistle for me.
   2. The Lord gave the Ten Commandments to Moses.
   3. Brother Lester found a seat for the visitor.
   4. Evelyn brought a chocolate bar to (for) me.
   5. Father gave a check to each of the workers.
   6. We shall send a card to the sick girl and boy.

D. 1. I will give the flowers some water.
   2. The farmer fed his steers some hay.

Written Exercises

A. 1.

   2. We | are making | chart

   3. We | can sell | vegetables
                          driver

   4. wagon | was sinking

   5. Brother Sensenig | has given | rosebushes
                                       school

   6. I | must write | bill
                        man

   7. Adam | gave | name
                     animal

   8. Marla | writes | letter
                        sister

   9. rug | feels

   10. Sandra | felt | rug

Review Exercises

A. Copy each verb, and add the missing principal parts. [30, 31]

First (Present)	Second (Past)	Third (Past Participle)
1. blow	———	———
2. burst	———	———
3. hold	———	———
4. swing	———	———
5. tag	———	———
6. refuse	———	———
7. worry	———	———
8. knit	———	———

B. Copy each verb or verb phrase, and write what tense it is: *present, past, future, present perfect, past perfect,* or *future perfect.* [32–36]

1. Mother bought two watermelons at the supermarket.
2. I have fought a good fight.
3. The apostle Paul had kept the faith.
4. Jesus wept at Lazarus's grave.
5. Jonathan has cut his finger.
6. This costs too much.
7. By then Laura will have drawn three horses.
8. Will you read the new book?

Review Exercises

A. (Words in italics are given in the pupil's text.)

1. *blow*	blew	(have) blown
2. *burst*	burst	(have) burst
3. *hold*	held	(have) held
4. *swing*	swung	(have) swung
5. *tag*	tagged	(have) tagged
6. *refuse*	refused	(have) refused
7. *worry*	worried	(have) worried
8. *knit*	knit	(have) knit
	or knitted	*or* (have) knitted

B. 1. bought—past
2. have fought—present perfect
3. had kept—past perfect
4. wept—past
5. has cut—present perfect
6. costs—present
7. will have drawn—future perfect
8. Will read—future

41. Forming an Outline From a Composition

An outline is an orderly arrangement of main ideas and less important ideas. It is like a map, guiding you as you study. An outline shows how the ideas in a composition are organized. This makes it easy to see how the ideas are related to each other.

To make an outline from a composition, write in order the main idea of each paragraph. You know that the main idea of a paragraph is found in the topic sentence. The main idea of each paragraph becomes a main topic on the outline.

Lesson 41

Purpose: To teach how to form an outline from written material.

Oral Review:

1. Every outline must begin with what? (a title)
2. Why do writers and speakers use outlines? (to organize their material)
3. Why do readers and listeners use outlines? (to help them remember what they read or hear)
4. What does an outline show? (a brief summary of a composition; the contents and organization of the material)
5. How is a sentence outline different from a topical outline? (A sentence outline has complete sentences, but a topical outline has only words or phrases.)
6. If the various points on an outline have a similar form, we say that they are———. (parallel)

Lesson Introduction: Ask students, "How would you like to be lost in a large city without a map? You wouldn't know where in the city you are. You wouldn't know whether you should travel north or south, east or west, to reach the place where you want to go. A map of the city with street names on it would be very helpful to you."

In your studies, an outline can help you in a similar way. It shows how the various ideas are arranged and how they are related to each other. It can give you a sense of direction as you study.

Today we want to learn how to write an outline from a composition.

Study the following composition and the outline that follows it. The topic sentences are underlined.

Living in Tents in Bible Times

<u>Many people lived in tents in Bible times.</u> Genesis 4 says that Jabal was the father of those who dwelt in tents. He must have been the first tent dweller. The patriarchs lived in tents. Genesis 12 tells how Abraham pitched his tent near Bethel. In Genesis 26 we read that Isaac pitched his tent in the valley of Gerar, and in Genesis 33 we see that Jacob pitched his tent before a city of Shechem. The children of Israel lived in tents during the forty years in the wilderness. Some of them also lived in tents after they reached Canaan.

<u>How was a tent made?</u> A tent was usually made of black goats' hair. It was often in an oblong shape. Many tents had only two or three rooms. The rooms were separated by goats'-hair curtains.

<u>A tent had various furnishings.</u> Rugs were often used for floor coverings. The beds were mats that could be rolled up during the day. A piece of leather was spread out on the ground for a table. The seats were the floor. For an oven, a hollow was made in the ground and several stones were placed in it. Skin bags and leather buckets were used to carry water and other liquids.

Living in Tents in Bible Times
  I. Who lived in tents
 II. How tents were made
III. How tents were furnished

This simple outline does not include nearly all the details in the composition. We can go through the composition again, pick out the details that were used to develop the paragraphs, and add them to the outline. These details will be subtopics and points on the outline. Study the following outline with this added information.

Living in Tents in Bible Times
  I. Who lived in tents
    A. Jabal
    B. The patriarchs
      1. Abraham
      2. Isaac
      3. Jacob

Lesson Outline:

1. An outline is an orderly arrangement of main ideas and less important ideas. The degree of importance is indicated by Roman numerals, capital letters, and so forth.

2. To make an outline from a composition, write in order the main idea of each paragraph. The main idea of each paragraph becomes a main topic on the outline.

3. The details used to develop the paragraphs become the subtopics and points on the outline.

4. Making an outline from a composition helps you to see the main ideas of the composition and the way they are related to each other. Outlining will help you in your studies.

★ EXTRA PRACTICE
Worksheet 24 *(Outlining)*

C. The Israelites
    1. In the wilderness
    2. In Canaan
II. How tents were made
  A. With black goats' hair
  B. In an oblong shape
  C. With two or three rooms
III. How tents were furnished
  A. Rugs for floor coverings
  B. Mats for beds
  C. Piece of leather for table
  D. Floor for seats
  E. Hollow in ground for oven
  F. Skin bags and leather buckets for liquids

Making an outline from a composition helps you to see the main ideas of the composition. It also helps you to see how the different ideas are related to each other. Organizing the material in this way will help you to remember it better. It will help you in your studies.

- When an outline is formed from a composition, the main idea of each paragraph becomes a main topic on the outline.

- The details used to develop the paragraphs become subtopics and points on the outline.

Class Practice

Form a sentence outline and a topical outline from the first paragraph of the composition "Mining Coal" in Written Exercises. Do this together as a class activity.

Written Exercises

Write a topical outline from the following composition. Use a Roman numeral for the main topic of each paragraph.

Mining Coal

When was coal first used? The Chinese used it already in the 300s to heat buildings and smelt metals. By the year 1000, coal was an important fuel in China. Commercial coal mining began in Europe during

Lesson 41 Answers
Class Practice

Mining Coal

I. When was coal first used?
  A. The Chinese used it already in the 300s.
  B. Europeans began using it in the 1200s and especially in the 1600s.
  C. American Indians used it long before white men came.

Mining Coal

I. First use of coal
  A. By Chinese in the 300s
  B. By Europeans in the 1200s and 1600s
  C. By American Indians before white men came

the 1200s, but coal was not an important fuel there until a severe shortage of wood developed in the 1600s. Then many Europeans began using coal. In North America, the Indians dug coal out of hillsides long before white men came. Some Indians used coal for baking pottery.

What kinds of mines are used to dig coal? Surface mines were used first. Indians and white pioneers simply dug coal out of hillside mines where coal was easy to get. Surface mines today are strip mines, where layers of rock and soil are stripped away to uncover the coal beneath. Underground mines came into use as coal deposits became harder to reach. In a drift mine, a tunnel is dug straight into the side of a hill to follow a coal seam. A mine with a sloping tunnel is called a slope mine. To reach coal far below the surface, a shaft mine is used. Such a mine has a tunnel going straight down into the ground, with side tunnels extending into the seams of coal.

What are some dangers of coal mining? One danger in underground mines is cave-ins. Walls and ceilings must be carefully braced so that they do not collapse. A second danger is gases such as carbon dioxide, carbon monoxide, and methane, which can cause miners to suffocate. Instruments are used to check for the accumulation of these gases, and powerful fans blow fresh air into an underground mine. When miners hit an underground river, they often face a third danger—flooding. Large pumps must be used to direct the water safely outside. A fourth danger is fire, which is sometimes caused when explosives are used in the presence of certain gases. Coal mining still has some dangers, but they are not nearly as great today as they were long ago.

Review Exercises

Read these two sets of directions, and write the title of the set that is better. Then write two reasons why it is better. [8]

How to Make a Model Volcano

It is best to do this project outside. First make a mountain of sand inside a box. Bury a small soup can up to its top in the mountain, keeping the top open. Then put two tablespoons baking soda into the can. Add several drops of red food coloring. Pour three-fourths cup vinegar over the soda in the can. Your volcano will erupt instantly!

Written Exercises

(Allow reasonable variation. After checking students' outlines, you may want to give them each a copy of these answers.)

Mining Coal

I. First use of coal
   A. By Chinese in the 300s
   B. By Europeans in the 1200s and 1600s
   C. By American Indians before white men came
II. Kinds of coal mines
   A. Surface mines
      1. Hillside mines
      2. Strip mines
   B. Underground mines
      1. Drift mines
      2. Slope mines
      3. Shaft mines
III. Dangers of coal mining
   A. Cave-ins
   B. Underground gases
   C. Floods
   D. Fires

Review Exercises

How to Make a Model Volcano
(Sample reasons.)
1. The directions are given more accurately.
2. The directions are given in the correct order.
3. Transitional words are used.

A Model Volcano

Make a mountain of sand. Bury a can inside the mountain. Put some baking soda into the can. Pour almost a full cup of vinegar over the soda in the can. It is best to do this project outside. Put food coloring into the can. The mountain of sand should be inside the box.

Challenge Exercises

Outline the chapter you are presently studying in science or history.

---

42. The Linking Verb *Be* and Predicate Nominatives

Most verbs are words of action. But the verb *be* expresses being rather than action. *Be* is never transitive; it cannot pass action to a direct object because it does not express action. The forms of *be* are *am, is, are, was, were, be, been,* and *being.*

If an action verb is followed by a noun, the noun is usually a direct object. A form of *be* may also be followed by a noun (or a pronoun), but it is not a direct object. Look at the following sentences.

> This book is an old <u>hymnal</u>.
> My teacher was <u>she</u>.

In the sentences above, *hymnal* and *she* cannot be direct objects, because they follow forms of *be*. They are *predicate nominatives* (also called predicate nouns or pronouns). A predicate nominative is a noun or pronoun in the predicate that renames the subject.

The verbs in the sentences above are *linking verbs* rather than action verbs. A linking verb joins a word in the predicate to the subject. All the forms of *be* can be used as linking verbs.

A linking verb is like an equal sign in arithmetic. When it is followed by a predicate nominative, it shows that a noun or pronoun in the predicate is equal to the subject.

> This <u>book</u> is an old <u>hymnal</u>. (book = hymnal)
> My <u>teacher</u> was <u>she</u>. (teacher = she)

Lesson 42

Purpose: To teach linking verbs followed by predicate nominatives.

Oral Review:
1. What is a transitive verb? (a verb that passes action to a receiver)
2. What is a direct object? (a noun or pronoun that receives the action of a transitive verb)
3. What is an indirect object? (a noun or pronoun that tells *to whom or what* or *for whom or what* the action of the verb is done)
4. Can a sentence have an indirect object if it has no direct object? (no)
5. Tell how to find a direct object. (Say the subject and verb together, and ask *whom* or *what.*)
6. Tell how to find an indirect object. (Say the subject, the verb, and the direct object together. Then ask *to whom or what* or *for whom or what.*)

Challenge Exercises
(Individual work.)

---

7. What does *tense* mean? (time)
8. Name the three simple tenses. (present tense, past tense, future tense)
9. What helping verbs are used in the perfect tenses? (have, has, had)

Written Quiz:
1. Write the definition of a verb.
2. What does *tense* mean?
3. What kind of action verb passes its action to a receiver?
4. What do we call a noun that follows an action verb and receives its action?
5. What do we call a noun that follows an action verb and tells *to whom or what* or *for whom or what* the action of the verb is done?
6. If a sentence has an indirect object, what other kind of object must it have?
7. Choose the correct words.
   a. An indirect object is (sometimes, never) found in a prepositional phrase.
   b. A sentence with an indirect object can (sometimes, always) be rewritten as a sentence with a prepositional phrase.

Quiz Answers:
1. A verb is a word that shows action or being.
2. time
3. transitive verb
4. direct object
5. indirect object
6. direct object
7. a. never
   b. always

Since the subject and the predicate nominative are equal, they can usually be exchanged and the sentence still has the same meaning. Subjects and direct objects cannot be exchanged in this way.

> Saul was Israel's first <u>king</u>. Israel's first <u>king</u> was <u>Saul</u>.
>   (Sentences have predicate nominatives; meaning is the same.)
> <u>Saul</u> defeated the <u>Philistines</u>. The <u>Philistines</u> defeated <u>Saul</u>.
>   (Sentences have direct objects; meanings are different.)

A form of *be* is a linking verb only when it is the main verb. When it is used with an action verb, it is a helping verb.

> Henry <u>was chopping</u> the wood. (*Was* is a helping verb.)
> They <u>are</u> my brothers. (*Are* is a linking verb.)
> Brother Harry <u>has been</u> my teacher. (*Been* is a linking verb.)

A predicate nominative is diagramed on the base line after the skeleton, with a slanted line between the verb and the predicate nominative. The slanted line leans toward the subject to show that the predicate nominative renames the subject.

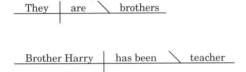

A predicate nominative may also be compound.

> The visitors were she and they.

> - A predicate nominative is a noun or pronoun that follows a linking verb and renames the subject.
> - The forms of *be* are often used as linking verbs.

Lesson Introduction: Write the following sentence on the chalkboard. Ask students to point out the subject and verb of the sentence.

> John is a carpenter.

Is *carpenter* a direct object? Why not? The verb is not an action verb. It is a form of *be* that is used to link *John* and *carpenter.* How are the two nouns related? *John* names a person and acts as the subject. *Carpenter* names the same person again and acts as a predicate nominative.

Today we will study linking verbs and predicate nominatives.

Lesson Outline:

***1. A noun or pronoun that follows a linking verb and renames the subject is a* predicate nominative.** These may also be called predicate nouns or pronouns. Be sure students master the definition of a predicate nominative.

This machine is a <u>combine.</u>
My cousins are <u>they.</u>

A linking verb is usually a form of the verb *be.* All the forms of *be* can be used as linking verbs.

2. A linking verb is like an equal sign in arithmetic. When it is followed by a predicate nominative, it shows that a noun or pronoun in the predicate is equal to the subject.

That <u>building</u> was a <u>school.</u> (building = school)

Since the subject and the predicate nominative are equal, they can usually be exchanged and the sentence still means the same. Subjects and direct objects cannot be exchanged in this way.

My <u>cousins</u> are <u>they.</u> <u>They</u> are my <u>cousins.</u>
  (same meaning)
<u>James</u> helped <u>Andrew</u>. <u>Andrew</u> helped <u>James</u>.
  (different meanings)

3. A form of* be *is a linking verb only when it is the main verb. When it is used with an action verb, it is a helping verb.

My cousins <u>are</u> they. (linking verb)
My cousins <u>are coming</u>. (helping verb)

4. A predicate nominative is diagramed on the base line after the skeleton, with a slanted line between the verb and the predicate nominative. The slanted line leans toward the subject to show that the predicate nominative renames the subject. Place the following diagrams on the chalkboard, and stress the meaning of the slanted line.

Candles are dim lights.

| Candles | are \ lights |

The drivers were they.

| drivers | were \ they |

A compound predicate nominative is diagramed on a fork.

The teachers are he and she.

Class Practice

A. Tell whether each sentence has an *action verb* or a *linking verb*, and whether the verb is followed by a *direct object* or a *predicate nominative*.

1. Those tall trees are Douglas firs.
2. The men were planting Douglas firs.
3. Sister Eunice knows our teacher.
4. Sister Eunice will be our teacher.
5. Uncle Amos hired a good worker.
6. Uncle Amos has been a good worker.
7. Robert is the new African pupil.
8. Robert visited the new African pupil.
9. The learners will be you and I.
10. The fastest workers were he and she.

B. On the chalkboard, diagram the skeleton and the predicate nominative of each sentence in Part A that has a linking verb.

Written Exercises

A. Diagram the skeleton and predicate nominative of each sentence.
1. I am the Bread of Life.
2. Ye are the light of the world.
3. Ye shall be My people.
4. The Lord is my rock.
5. The Good Shepherd is He.
6. The Bible is the best Book.

B. Copy each verb, and write A for action or L for linking after it. Also copy each direct object or predicate nominative, and write DO or PN to tell which it is.

Examples: a. The teachers will be he and she.
                 b. The teachers will help us.

Answers: a. will be—L; he—PN; she—PN
               b. will help—A; us—DO

1. The children made Mother a flower garden.
2. These little animals must be moles and shrews.
3. The first Americans were Indians.
4. Muddy water was flooding the road.
5. The nurses were she and they.

Lesson 42 Answers
Class Practice

A. 1. linking verb, predicate nominative
    2. action verb, direct object
    3. action verb, direct object
    4. linking verb, predicate nominative
    5. action verb, direct object
    6. linking verb, predicate nominative
    7. linking verb, predicate nominative
    8. action verb, direct object
    9. linking verb, predicate nominative
    10. linking verb, predicate nominative

B. 1.   trees | are \ Douglas firs

    (Omitting *Douglas* may be considered correct.)

    4.   Sister Eunice | will be \ teacher

    6.   Uncle Amos | has been \ worker

    7.   Robert | is \ pupil

    9.

    10.
    workers | were \ and [he / she]

Written Exercises

A. 1.   I | am \ Bread of Life

   2.   Ye | are \ light

   3.   Ye | shall be \ people

   4.   Lord | is \ rock

   5.   Good Shepherd | is \ He

   6.   Bible | is \ book

B. 1. made—A; garden—DO
    2. must be—L; moles—PN; shrews—PN
    3. were—L; Indians—PN
    4. was flooding—A; road—DO
    5. were—L; she—PN; they—PN

6. My little sister's favorite dessert is sherbet.
7. I shall always remember that strange man.
8. Charles is selling those people some strawberries.
9. One day this book will be a valued possession.
10. The visitors were officers and soldiers from a nearby camp.
11. They asked the minister a difficult question.
12. Every good student must be a hard worker.
13. I am he.
14. My father showed the boys the solution.

C. Four sentences in Part B have indirect objects. Write the numbers of those sentences, and write the indirect objects.

Review Exercises

A. Write all six tenses of each verb. [32–36]

Example: go
Answer: go, went, will go, have gone, had gone, will have gone

1. help
2. bring
3. sleep
4. forget

B. For each verb in parentheses, write the tense shown in italics. [32–36]
1. When I throw the ball, my dog (catch) it in his mouth. *simple present*
2. Father (dig) the ditch for the water pipes. *present perfect*
3. Be careful, or you (break) the shovel handle. *simple future*
4. The water (freeze) during the night. *past perfect*
5. I (put) it into the freezer. *present perfect*
6. Leon (ride) with us to church. *simple past*
7. The fox (run) away by the time we got there. *past perfect*
8. By Monday morning, James (go) home. *future perfect*
9. I (write) the letter by tomorrow evening. *future perfect*
10. Yesterday the swallows (come) back. *past tense*

C. Diagram the skeleton of each sentence that has a transitive verb. Include any direct object or indirect object on your diagram. [38–40]
1. John found his friend a book.
2. We hurried past the strange dog.
3. The other boys gathered wood for the fire.
4. This house was once a church building.

---

6. is—L; sherbet—PN
7. shall remember—A; man—DO
8. is selling—A; strawberries—DO
9. will be—L; possession—PN
10. were—L; officers—PN; soldiers—PN
11. asked—A; question—DO
12. must be—L; worker—PN
13. am—L; he—PN
14. showed—A; solution—DO

C. 1. Mother
    8. people
   11. minister
   14. boys

Review Exercises

A. 1. help, helped, will help, have helped, had helped, will have helped
   2. bring, brought, will bring, have brought, had brought, will have brought
   3. sleep, slept, will sleep, have slept, had slept, will have slept
   4. forget, forgot, will forget, have forgotten, had forgotten, will have forgotten

B. 1. catches
    2. has dug
    3. will break
    4. had frozen
    5. have put
    6. rode
    7. had run
    8. will have gone
    9. shall (will) have written
   10. came

C. 1.   John | found | book
                        \ friend

   3.   boys | gathered | wood

43. Linking Verbs and Predicate Adjectives

You have learned that a linking verb links the subject to a word in the predicate. All the forms of *be* can be used as linking verbs. The word that is linked to the subject may be a noun or pronoun that renames the subject. If so, it is a predicate nominative.

Sentences with predicate nominatives:
> That star is <u>Sirius</u>.
> My cousin is <u>she</u>.

A linking verb may also link the subject to an *adjective* in the predicate. Such an adjective is called a *predicate adjective*. A predicate adjective follows a linking verb and modifies the subject.

Sentences with predicate adjectives:
> The road is <u>rough</u>.
>> The linking verb *is* links *road* and *rough*. We know that *rough* modifies *road* because it is sensible to say *rough road*.
> You should always be <u>kind</u>.
>> The linking verb *should be* links *You* and *kind*. We do not usually say *kind you*, but *kind* does modify *You*. It tells what kind of person you should be.

There are other verbs besides the forms of *be* that can be linking verbs. In grade 5 you studied the linking verbs in the first line below. They may be called verbs of *sense* because they refer to the five senses of the body. The second line shows some more words that may be linking verbs. You should memorize all these linking verbs.

Verbs of sense: taste, feel, smell, sound, look, appear
Other linking verbs: grow, seem, stay, become, remain

> The news <u>sounds</u> good.
>> **Compare:** The news *is* good.
> The child <u>seemed</u> ill.
>> **Compare:** The child *was* ill.

Predicate adjectives are diagrammed like predicate nominatives. The line before the predicate adjective leans toward the subject to show that the adjective describes the subject.

Lesson 43

Purpose: To teach linking verbs followed by predicate adjectives.

Oral Review:
1. Give the forms of *be*. (am, is, are, was, were, be, been, being)
2. Are the forms of *be* ever used (*a*) as transitive verbs? (*b*) as linking verbs? (*a.* no; *b.* yes)
3. What is a predicate nominative? (a noun or pronoun that follows a linking verb and renames the subject)
4. What is a transitive verb? (a verb that passes action to a receiver)
5. What is a direct object? (a noun or pronoun that receives the action of a transitive verb)
6. What is an indirect object? (a noun or pronoun that tells *to whom or what* or *for whom or what* the action of the verb is done)
7. Can a sentence have an indirect object if it has no direct object? (no)

Lesson Introduction: Call attention to the work of a link in a chain. What does it do? It usually connects two other links, one on each side of it. But not all links have the same function. Sometimes a link is connected to something else, like a hook.

The same is true of linking verbs. A linking verb may join a subject to a noun or pronoun that renames the subject. But it may also link the subject to an adjective. In this lesson we will study linking verbs and predicate adjectives.

Lesson Outline:

1. Sometimes a linking verb is followed by an adjective that modifies the subject. Such an adjective is called a predicate adjective.

> The melon was <u>sweet.</u>
> Uncle William is <u>tall.</u>

2. A predicate adjective is an adjective that follows a linking verb and modifies the subject. Be sure students master this definition.

3. A number of different verbs can be used as linking verbs. They include verbs in the following groups. Students should memorize these linking verbs.

Forms of *be*:
> am, is, are, was, were, be, been, being
Verbs of sense:
> taste, feel, smell, sound, look, appear
Other linking verbs:
> grow, seem, stay, become, remain

In a sentence like "The news sounds good," we know that *sounds* is a linking verb because it can be replaced by *is*. This point is taught further in the next lesson.

4. Predicate adjectives are diagrammed like predicate nominatives. The line before the predicate adjective leans toward the subject to show that the adjective describes the subject.

The weather feels pleasant.

The predicate adjective may be compound.

The baby was hungry and tired.

> • A predicate adjective follows a linking verb and modifies the subject of the sentence.
>
> • Linking verbs include the forms of *be* and verbs such as the following:
>   taste, feel, smell, sound, look, appear
>   grow, seem, stay, become, remain

Class Practice

A. Find the linking verbs and predicate adjectives in these sentences.
   1. These ripe apples are sweet.
   2. Our garden is hard and dry.
   3. Their work usually seemed easy.
   4. The sky quickly grew dark.
   5. The bigger cat looked annoyed.

B. Give the linking verb in each sentence. Also give the predicate nominative or predicate adjective, and tell which one it is.
   1. My little brother is a good worker.
   2. This work may be too difficult for him.
   3. These old nuts taste strange.
   4. The trash can in the kitchen has become full.
   5. Those five cattle are Father's steers.
   6. The steers are becoming restless and noisy.

C. On the chalkboard, diagram the skeletons, predicate nominatives, and predicate adjectives in Part B.

The owl sounds lonely.

Miriam was being helpful.

Miriam | was being \ helpful

A compound predicate adjective is diagramed on a fork.

The grass has grown quite lush and tall.

Lesson 43 Answers
Class Practice

A. 1. are, sweet
   2. is, hard (and) dry
   3. seemed, easy
   4. grew, dark
   5. looked, annoyed

B. 1. is, worker—predicate nominative
   2. may be, difficult—predicate adjective
   3. taste, strange—predicate adjective
   4. has become, full—predicate adjective
   5. are, steers—predicate nominative
   6. are becoming, restless (and) noisy—predicate adjective

C. 1. brother | is \ worker

   2. work | may be \ difficult

   3. nuts | taste \ strange

   4. trash can | has become \ full
   (*Trash* may be omitted.)

   5. cattle | are \ steers

   6.
                                      restless
       steers | are becoming \ and
                                      noisy

★ **EXTRA PRACTICE**
   Worksheet 25 (*Diagraming Predicate Nominatives and Predicate Adjectives*)

Written Exercises

A. Write the linking verbs and predicate adjectives in these sentences. Be sure to get all the words in the verb phrases.
1. Goliath was extremely tall.
2. The birds in the trees sounded happy.
3. The answer will soon be clear.
4. Some of the flowers became droopy.
5. A warm sweater would feel comfortable.
6. His younger brother was growing nervous.

B. Diagram the skeletons, predicate nominatives, and predicate adjectives of these sentences. Above each predicate nominative or predicate adjective on your diagrams, write *PN* or *PA* to tell which one it is.
1. The fresh fruit tasted delicious.
2. Our old dog looks weary.
3. Their early flowers are pansies.
4. That second boy must be he.
5. The Weavers have always been friendly.
6. The next arrivals will be they.
7. Soon the thick ice becomes soft.
8. Those men were sailors.
9. Can those people be we?
10. He will probably be late today.
11. The first day seemed very long.
12. The other tall girl was she.

C. Write sentences of your own, using these verbs with predicate adjectives.
1. am   3. seem   5. look
2. was   4. sound

Review Exercises

Diagram the skeletons of only the sentences with transitive verbs. Include the direct and indirect objects on your diagrams. [38–40]
1. Alma and Betty have written their brother a note.
2. Our leader has shown us a good example.
3. Lush green plants were growing along the canal.
4. The eastern sky was growing bright.
5. That old man had been a teamster.
6. The children gathered leaves for a science project.

Written Exercises

A. 1. was, tall
2. sounded, happy
3. will be, clear
4. became, droopy
5. would feel, comfortable
6. was growing, nervous

B.
1.
   fruit | tasted \ delicious (PA)

2. dog | looks \ weary (PA)

3. flowers | are \ pansies (PN)

4. boy | must be \ he (PN)

5. Weavers | have been \ friendly (PA)

6. arrivals | will be \ they (PN)

7. ice | becomes \ soft (PA)

8. men | were \ sailors (PN)

9. people | Can be \ we (PN)

10. He | will be \ late (PA)

11. day | seemed \ long (PA)

12. girl | was \ she (PN)

C. (Individual sentences.)

Review Exercises

1.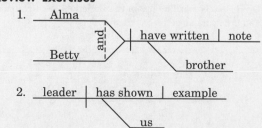
   Alma / Betty (and) have written | note
   brother

2. leader | has shown | example
   us

6. children | gathered | leaves

7. Many anxious people gathered before the doorway.
8. Our brother made the kittens a box.
9. Finally the ground became warm.
10. Jesus told His listeners many parables.
11. God shows the honest seeker the truth.
12. God's children are kind and patient.

Challenge Exercises

Follow the directions.
1. Write a sentence with a direct object and an indirect object. Diagram your sentence.
2. Write a sentence with a compound indirect object. Diagram your sentence.
3. Write a sentence with a compound predicate nominative. Diagram your sentence.
4. Write a sentence with a predicate adjective. Do not use any of the forms of *be*. Diagram your sentence.

---

44. Linking Verbs or Action Verbs?

You have learned that verbs other than forms of *be* may be linking verbs. Here are the other linking verbs you have met.

Verbs of sense: taste, feel, smell, sound, look, appear
Other linking verbs: grow, seem, stay, become, remain

The verbs shown above are not always linking verbs. Sometimes they are action verbs. They may or may not be used as transitive verbs, passing action to a direct object. Look at the following sentences.

The alarm sounded harsh.
Wesley sounded the alarm.
The alarm sounded harshly in the morning.

In the first sentence, *harsh* is a predicate adjective describing the subject *alarm*. We know that *sounded* is a linking verb because it can be replaced by a form of *be:* The alarm *was* harsh.

In the second sentence, *sounded* is not a linking verb, because it cannot be replaced by a form of *be.* It is not sensible to say, "Wesley was

Lesson 44

Purpose: To teach about verbs that are sometimes linking verbs and sometimes action verbs.

Oral Review:
1. What is a predicate adjective? (an adjective that follows a linking verb and modifies the subject)
2. Give the verbs that can be used as linking verbs.
   (**Forms of *be:***
      am, is, are, was, were, be, been, being
   Verbs of sense:
      taste, feel, smell, sound, look, appear
   Other linking verbs:
      grow, seem, stay, become, remain)
3. What is a run-on error? (the mistake of writing two or more sentences together without the proper punctuation between them)
4. How can a run-on error be corrected? (by using end punctuation and a capital letter; by using a comma

8. <u>brother | made | box</u>
               \ kittens

10. <u>Jesus | told | parables</u>
              \ listeners

11. <u>God | shows | truth</u>
              \ seeker

Challenge Exercises
(Individual work.)

---

and a conjunction; by using a semicolon)
5. Why can you not correct a run-on error by simply using a comma? (a comma alone is not strong enough to join two sentences)

Written Quiz:
Underline the correct answers.
1. A direct object follows a (transitive, linking) verb.
2. A predicate adjective follows a (transitive, linking) verb.
3. A (predicate nominative, predicate adjective) follows a linking verb and renames the subject of the sentence.
4. (A direct object, An indirect object) tells *to whom or what* or *for whom or what* the action of the verb is done.
5. (Action verbs, Forms of *be*) are never transitive.
6. If a sentence has an indirect object, it must also have a (direct object, predicate nominative).
7. A (direct object, predicate nominative) receives the action of a verb.
8. (A predicate nominative, An indirect object) comes between an action verb and a direct object.
9. A (transitive, linking) verb passes action to a receiver.
10. *Taste, feel, smell, sound, look, appear, grow, seem, stay, become,* and *remain* are (always, sometimes) linking verbs.

Quiz Answers:
1. transitive
2. linking

the alarm." *Sounded* expresses action, and *alarm* is the receiver of the action. So *alarm* is the direct object, and *sounded* is a transitive verb.

Now look at the third sentence. The verb *sounded* is not a linking verb, because it is not sensible to say, "The alarm was harshly." (*Harshly* is an adverb that tells *how*.) *Sounded* is not followed by a predicate nominative or a predicate adjective. Neither is it followed by a direct object. (*Morning* is in a prepositional phrase.) Therefore, *sounded* is simply an action verb; it does not pass the action to any word in the sentence.

So be careful. Verbs like *sound, feel, grow,* and *remain* are not always linking verbs. Sometimes they are used in these two other ways—as transitive verbs with direct objects or as action verbs that are not transitive.

Remember the test for linking verbs. If the verb can be replaced by a form of *be* without changing the meaning of the sentence, it is a linking verb.

> He <u>looked</u> sick.
>> **Think:** He *was* sick. *Looked* is a linking verb because the meaning is about the same.
> He <u>looked</u> outside.
>> **Think:** He *was* outside. *Looked* is not a linking verb, because the meaning is different.

Another test is to see whether the subject is doing the action expressed by the verb. If so, the verb cannot be a linking verb. Linking verbs do not express action; they simply link the subject to a predicate nominative or predicate adjective. Compare the following sentences.

> The trees grew swiftly.
> The trees grew old.

In the first sentence, the trees did the action of growing. *Swiftly* is an adverb that tells how the trees grew. There is no predicate nominative or predicate adjective. So *grew* is an action verb, not a linking verb.

The second sentence does not emphasize the action of growing. It simply says that the trees grew (became) old. The sentence could be changed to "The trees were old," and it would mean about the same. Also, the predicate adjective *old* describes the subject *trees*. So *grew* is a linking verb.

3. predicate nominative
4. An indirect object
5. Forms of be
6. direct object
7. direct object
8. An indirect object
9. transitive
10. sometimes

Lesson Introduction: Ask the students if *taste* is a linking verb. Of course it is. We just studied that in the last lesson. Then write the following sentence on the chalkboard.

> Aunt Flora tasted the soup.

If *taste* is a linking verb, what word does it link to the subject? Is *soup* a predicate nominative? No, because *soup* does not rename Aunt Flora. Does the sentence have a predicate adjective? No, because *soup* is a noun, not an adjective.

Then *taste* is not a linking verb after all—at least not in this sentence. What kind of verb is it? We shall find out in this lesson.

Lesson Outline:

1. The verbs taste, feel, smell, sound, look, appear, *and* grow, seem, stay, become, remain *are not always linking verbs.* Sometimes they are used in two other ways—as transitive verbs with direct objects or as action verbs that are not transitive.

2. Three tests will help you tell whether a verb is a linking verb or an action verb.

> a. *If the verb can be replaced by a form of* be, *without changing the meaning of the sentence, it is a linking verb.* If a form of *be* does not fit, the verb is an action verb.
>
>> The sun <u>appeared</u> bright.
>> **Compare:** The sun was bright.
>>> *Appeared* is a linking verb because the meaning is about the same.
>>
>> The sun <u>appeared</u> this morning.
>> **Compare:** The sun was this morning.
>>> *Appeared* is not a linking verb, because the meaning is different.
>
> b. *See whether there is any word in the predicate that could be linked to the subject.* Either a predicate nominative or a predicate adjective must follow a linking verb. A predicate nominative or a predicate adjective is never found in a prepositional phrase.
>
>> He will <u>remain</u> the manager for next year. (linking verb followed by predicate nominative)
>>
>> Please <u>remain</u> in the house. (action verb followed by prepositional phrase)
>>
>> The weather might <u>stay</u> cold awhile. (linking verb followed by predicate adjective)
>>
>> We might <u>stay</u> here tonight. (action verb followed by adverbs)
>
> c. *If the subject is doing the action expressed by the verb, the verb must be an action verb.* It is not a linking verb.

Students may need plenty of class practice in order to master this lesson.

★ **EXTRA PRACTICE**
Worksheet 26 (*Diagraming Review*)

You cannot tell whether a verb is a linking verb or an action verb just by looking at the verb itself. You must also look at other words in the sentence. If there is a predicate nominative or a predicate adjective, the verb must be a linking verb. If the verb expresses action—and especially if a direct object receives the action—it must be an action verb.

- Verbs of sense (*taste, feel, smell, sound, look, appear*) and other linking verbs (*grow, seem, stay, become, remain*) are not always used as linking verbs. Sometimes they are transitive verbs with direct objects, and sometimes they are action verbs that are not transitive.

Class Practice

A. Tell whether the verb in each sentence is a *linking verb* or an *action verb*. Read each sentence that has a linking verb, replacing that verb with a form of *be*.
1. This watermelon tastes sweet.
2. We tasted the different kinds of cakes.
3. The girls felt the soft, silky cloth.
4. The cloth felt soft and silky.
5. The twins have grown rapidly.
6. They grew tomatoes in their garden plot.
7. The tomatoes looked red and juicy.
8. The floor becomes wet and slippery.
9. The teacher sounded the bell.
10. The bell sounded quite musical.

B. Tell whether each verb is a *linking verb,* an *action verb that is transitive,* or an *action verb that is not transitive.*
1. John felt sick in the morning.
2. John felt a pebble in his shoe.
3. The new baby appeared quite healthy.
4. Soon Jason appeared around the corner.
5. Jonathan became David's friend.
6. Jonathan helped his friend.
7. Audrey looked up quickly.
8. Loren looked cheerful.

Lesson 44 Answers
Class Practice

A. 1. linking verb; This watermelon is sweet.
2. action verb
3. action verb
4. linking verb; The cloth was soft and silky.
5. action verb
6. action verb
7. linking verb; The tomatoes were red and juicy.
8. linking verb; The floor is wet and slippery.
9. action verb
10. linking verb; The bell was quite musical.

B. 1. linking verb
2. action verb that is transitive
3. linking verb
4. action verb that is not transitive
5. linking verb
6. action verb that is transitive
7. action verb that is not transitive
8. linking verb

C. On the chalkboard, diagram the skeletons, direct objects, predicate nominatives, and predicate adjectives in Part A. Label the verbs *A* for action verb or *L* for linking verb. Use *DO, PN,* or *PA* to label the direct objects, predicate nominatives, and predicate adjectives.

Written Exercises

A. Copy the verb or verb phrase in each sentence, and write *A* for action or *L* for linking after it. If it is a linking verb, also copy the predicate nominative or predicate adjective and label it *PN* or *PA*.

Examples: a. Ben tasted the cookies.
  b. The new potatoes tasted delicious.

Answers: a. tasted—A
  b. tasted—L; delicious—PA

1. The teacher looked into his desk.
2. Your idea sounds good to me.
3. The room looks clean.
4. The fireman sounded the alarm.
5. The pie smells delicious.
6. Your room has become a tidy place.
7. Suddenly a deer appeared on the road.
8. In a few minutes the audience grew silent.
9. Sharon remained quiet for a while.
10. I have grown many pansies.
11. Hugo has become a carpenter.
12. The work seems hard.
13. The dessert was a thick pudding.
14. Stay here by the suitcases.
15. The bananas stayed green for days.
16. Gerald appeared fearful after his experience.
17. The students remain in their seats.
18. The homemade bread tasted good.

B. Diagram the skeletons, direct objects, predicate nominatives, and predicate adjectives of these sentences.
1. Soon tiny plants appeared above the surface.
2. The plants appeared healthy.
3. The pigs grow fatter every day.
4. The farmer grows much corn for them.
5. The children looked strong and healthy.

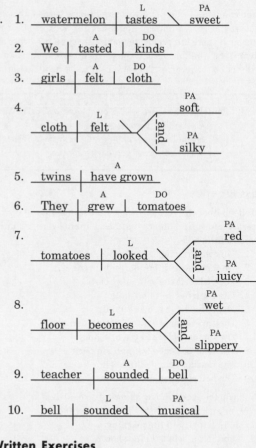

Written Exercises

A. 1. looked—A
   2. sounds—L; good—PA
   3. looks—L; clean—PA
   4. sounded—A
   5. smells—L; delicious—PA
   6. has become—L; place—PN
   7. appeared—A
   8. grew—L; silent—PA
   9. remained—L; quiet—PA
   10. have grown—A
   11. has become—L; carpenter—PN
   12. seems—L; hard—PA
   13. was—L; pudding—PN
   14. Stay—A
   15. stayed—L; green—PA
   16. appeared—L; fearful—PA
   17. remain—A
   18. tastes—L; good—PA

B. 1. plants | appeared
   2. plants | appeared \ healthy
   3. pigs | grow \ fatter
   4. farmer | grows | corn

6. Look at the beautiful sunset.
7. I will taste the soup for you.
8. It tastes rich and spicy.
9. Sick children should remain inside the house.
10. The boy remains ill.
11. I shall soon become an artist.
12. The boys look happy most of the time.
13. Feel the sticky stem of this plant.
14. She feels quite well again.

Review Exercises

Correct the run-on errors as indicated. [14]
1. Use periods and capital letters.
   a. The earth spins on its axis like a fast-moving top a person standing at the equator moves over 1,000 miles an hour most jets don't even fly that fast.
   b. The earth is also revolving around the sun it takes the earth one year to make a complete revolution the earth travels 65,600 miles per hour not even a rocket can fly that fast.
2. Use commas and suitable conjunctions.
   a. We are traveling very fast we do not get dizzy.
   b. The earth moves smoothly it never stops or makes sudden changes in speed.
3. Use semicolons.
   a. The earth is constantly moving it never stops.
   b. The sun appears to travel around the earth actually the earth is traveling around the sun.

---

45. Giving an Oral Book Report

A book report can give much valuable information. It tells what a book is about, and it also reveals how well you have read the book. If a book report is well done, it can help other people decide to read a certain book.

To give an oral book report, first choose a book that is approved by your teacher or parents. Read the whole book before you begin preparing for your report.

(Numbers 6–11 are on page 196.)

12. boys | look \ happy

13. (you) | Feel | stem

14. She | feels \ well

Review Exercises

1. a. The earth spins on its axis like a fast-moving top. A person standing at the equator moves over 1,000 miles an hour. Most jets do not even fly that fast.
   b. The earth is also revolving around the sun. It takes the earth one year to make a complete revolution. The earth travels 65,600 miles per hour. Not even a rocket can fly that fast.
2. a. We are traveling very fast, yet (but) we do not get dizzy.
   b. The earth moves smoothly, for (and) it never stops or makes sudden changes in speed.
3. a. The earth is constantly moving; it never stops.
   b. The sun appears to travel around the earth; actually the earth is traveling around the sun.

Lesson 45

Purpose: To teach how to give an oral book report. (*Previous experience:* Oral and written book reports.)

Oral Review:

1. What does an outline show? (a brief summary of a composition; the contents and organization of the material)
2. How is a sentence outline different from a topical outline? (A sentence outline has complete sentences, but a topical outline does not.)
3. How can you make an outline from a written composition? (Use the main idea of each paragraph as a main topic on the outline. Use the details that develop the paragraphs as subtopics and points under the main topics.)

4. When does a paragraph have unity? (when all the sentences tell about the topic given by the topic sentence)
5. When does a paragraph have coherence? (when the sentences "hold together" in an orderly, sensible way)
6. What are some things that help to make a paragraph coherent? (giving details in the order of time; giving details in the order of importance or interest; using transitional words)

Lesson Introduction: We can learn many good things from the experiences of others. When others read good books and tell us about them, it helps us to learn more good things. It may help us to want to read the same good books. Learn to give good book reports. They will be helpful to you and to others.

Make a list of points that you will cover when you give your report. Your points should include the following four kinds of information.

1. The title of the book, the name of the author, the copyright date of the book, and a place where the book can be found.
2. The setting and main characters of the book.
3. The main events in the book.
4. Your opinion of the book.

The setting is the place and time of the story. In what country, city, or state did it happen? Did it happen in recent times, in the pioneer days of America, or when? The main characters are the most important people in the story. You should give a brief description of them, and you may also include what you think of each character.

The main events of a book are the main problems that the characters faced and the way they dealt with the problems. Briefly tell what happened, but do not give the outcome. A good way to do this is to ask questions about things that happened in the book. Leave your listeners in suspense so that they will want to read the book too.

When you give your opinion of the book, tell what you enjoyed most about the story. Tell what lesson the story teaches, or give some other reason why you think others should read the book.

Write your notes briefly. Do not write every word you plan to say, but prepare to *tell* your report. It would be good to practice giving the report to someone at home.

Sample notes for an oral book report:
1. *Evangelists in Chains,* by Elizabeth Wagler
   Copyright date, 1983
   Available from Rod and Staff Publishers
2. *Setting:* Mountain valley of northern Austria during the 1500s
   Main characters: Peter Hans, a nineteen-year-old boy
                        People from his family and church
3. *Main events:* Imprisonment of Peter, his father, and others
                   Crushed dreams and hopes
                   Traveling evangelists even in chains
4. *Opinion:* A challenge to your faith and obedience
               A challenge to share the truth with others

When you give your report, remember to stand up straight, wear a pleasant expression, and speak loudly and clearly enough so that everyone can understand you easily. You should have your notes handy

Lesson Outline:

1. A book report can give valuable information. It tells what a book is about. It shows how well you have read a book. And it may help others decide to read a certain book.

2. A book report gives only basic information about a book. It does not mention everything that happened, and it does not give the outcome. Notes for an oral book report should include the following four kinds of information.

    (1) *Basic facts.* These include the title of the book, the name of the author, the copyright date of the book, and a place where the book can be found.

    (2) *The setting and main characters.* The setting is the place and time of the story. The main characters are the most important people in the story.

    (3) *The main events.* These are the main problems that the characters faced and the way they dealt with the problems.

    (4) *An opinion of the book.* The person reporting should tell what he enjoyed about the book and why others should read it.

3. To give an oral book report, remember the rules for speaking to a group. Stand up straight and wear a pleasant expression. Speak loudly and clearly enough so that everyone can understand you easily. Look at your listeners, and talk directly to them. Have your notes handy, and glance at them only when you need them. Do not have your eyes glued to your notes, to the floor, or to the back wall.

so that you can glance at them when you need them. But you should not have your eyes glued to your notes, to the floor, or to the back wall. Look at your listeners, and talk to *them*.

The following paragraphs show what a person might say when he gives an oral report on the book *Evangelists in Chains*.

Evangelists in Chains was written by Elizabeth Wagler. It was copyrighted in 1983 and is available from Rod and Staff Publishers.

This story took place in a mountain valley of northern Austria during the 1500s. The main character is a nineteen-year-old boy named Peter Hans. Other main characters are people from Peter's family and his church. His father especially was an encouragement to him as they suffered together. Peter's mother influenced him by her godly life and prayers. His sister was a Christian, and she encouraged Peter by her letters. The ministers of his church gave him hope and encouragement through their sermons in prison.

Peter and his father, with some other men from their church, were captured by soldiers and put into prison for their faith. The men suffered from cold and hunger. They were no longer free to work or to be with their families. Some of the men died from the hardships of prison life. Peter's faith was tested, but it grew stronger as he faced many temptations there. His dreams and hopes seemed crushed, yet some surprises awaited him. The men became traveling evangelists even in their chains as they shared the Gospel wherever they went. What would happen to the men? Would they ever be free again? Peter learned to trust in the Lord whatever the outcome.

You should read this book. It will challenge your faith. It will help you to trust the Lord as He leads in your life. It will challenge you to obey the Bible no matter what difficulties you may face. It will challenge you to share the truth with others.

- A book report gives basic information about a book. It does not tell the whole story.

- A book report may help others decide to read a certain book.

Class Practice

Answer the following questions about book reports.

1. How do book reports help other people?
2. How much of a book should you read before you give a report on it?
3. What should you do to prepare for an oral book report?
4. What four kinds of information should you give in a book report?
5. What is the setting?
6. What parts of the story should you tell? What part should you not tell?

Written Exercises

Prepare to give an oral report on a book you have read recently. Follow the directions given in the lesson.

Review Exercises

Tell whether each paragraph is developed by examples and illustrations or by comparison or contrast. [24, 27]

Paragraph A:

Mealtime Customs

Tent dwellers in Bible times had mealtime customs that were quite different from ours. We usually sit in chairs around a table, but they sat around a cloth on the ground. We eat with knives, forks, and spoons, but they washed their hands carefully before each meal and ate with their fingers. Instead of dipping soup into each person's plate, everyone ate from a large central dish with soup, sauce, or gravy in it. Our bread is in slices cut from a loaf, but theirs was paper-thin. Each person would tear off a piece of bread, dip it into the dish, and eat it. As a special sign of friendship, they would place a choice morsel of food on a little piece of bread and give it to a friend.

Paragraph B:

Early Rising

In Bible times, people in Palestine usually got up very early in the morning. Genesis 22 tells us that Abraham rose early in the morning to take Isaac to the land of Moriah. Exodus 34 says that Moses rose early to go up on Mount Sinai. Job rose early in the

Lesson 45 Answers
Class Practice

1. If a book report is given well, it may help other people decide to read that book.
2. You should read the whole book.
3. Write a list of the main points to be covered. It is also good to practice giving the report to someone at home.
4. a. The title of the book, the name of the author, the copyright date of the book, and a place where the book can be found.
   b. The setting and main characters of the book.
   c. The main events in the book.
   d. Your opinion of the book.
5. The setting is the place and time of the story.
6. Describe the main problems of the story. Do not give the outcome.

Written Exercises

(Book reports are individual work. Give each pupil a date when his report is due. Collect the notes for final checking afterward.)

Review Exercises

Paragraph A: comparison or contrast
Paragraph B: examples and illustrations

morning to offer sacrifices for his children. Mark wrote that Jesus rose a great while before day to pray. This habit of rising early is due partly to the climate in Palestine. For most of the year, it is cool for only a few hours after sunrise. Then the heat becomes so great that heavy work is difficult.

---

46. Chapter 4 Review

Class Practice

A. Answer the following questions.
1. What is a verb?
2. What is a transitive verb?
3. What is a direct object?
4. What is an indirect object?
5. If a sentence has an indirect object, what else must it have?
6. What kind of notes should you write to prepare for an oral book report?
7. What four kinds of information should you include in a book report?
8. What is the setting of a story?
9. Every outline must begin with a what?
10. What word describes the points on an outline if they have a similar form?

B. Say the three principal parts of each verb. Use *have* with the past participle.

First (Present)	Second (Past)	Third (Past Participle)
1. like	——	——
2. grow	——	——
3. wear	——	——
4. burst	——	——
5. bring	——	——
6. come	——	——
7. reach	——	——

Lesson 46

Purpose: To review the concepts taught in Chapter 4.

Lesson 46 Answers
Class Practice

A. 1. a word that shows action or being
2. a verb that passes action to a receiver
3. a noun or pronoun that receives the action of a transitive verb
4. a noun or pronoun that tells *to whom or what* or *for whom or what* the action of the verb is done
5. a direct object
6. a list of the main points
7. (a) the title of the book, the name of the author, the copyright date of the book, and a place where the book can be found
(b) the setting and main characters of the book
(c) the main events in the book
(d) your opinion of the book
8. the place and time of the story
9. a title
10. parallel

B. (Words in italics are given in the pupil's text.)

1. *like*	liked	(have) liked
2. *grow*	grew	(have) grown
3. *wear*	wore	(have) worn
4. *burst*	burst	(have) burst
5. *bring*	brought	(have) brought
6. *come*	came	(have) come
7. *reach*	reached	(have) reached

C. Give the six tenses of each verb: present, past, future, present perfect, past perfect, and future perfect.
1. begin   3. cost   5. sleep
2. choose   4. know   6. buy

D. Give the tense of each underlined verb.
1. The ice has frozen solid.
2. Sharon writes letters every Sunday.
3. Father had dug the ditch before it rained.
4. Susan will receive the recipe tomorrow.
5. Mother has prepared a meal for the visitors.
6. Lorene had done all her work beforehand.
7. By the time they leave, I shall have listed all their names.
8. Gerald kept all the notes from his classes.

E. Read each sentence, changing the indirect object to the object of a preposition at the end of the sentence.
1. My brother made his teacher a bookstand.
2. We shall take our grandmother a cake.

F. Tell how to finish the outline below with the following words. Tell how to improve the main topics so that they are parallel.

Tornadoes	Cumulus	Rain
Nimbus	Hail	Thunderstorms
Hurricanes	Blizzards	Sleet
Snow	Cirrus	Stratus

Elements of the Weather
   I. Kinds of clouds
  II. Precipitation and its forms
 III. Storm types

Written Exercises

A. Copy all the verbs and verb phrases from the following sentences.
1. Lorraine has remembered the buns, but she forgot the butter.
2. The bread smells good, and the buns taste delicious!
3. By the time we finish, we shall have made six kinds of dough.
4. Lou Ann mixed the cakes and kneaded the bread dough.
5. Janelle had never made these cookies before.
6. We do often make them for Grandmother.
7. Erma has surely learned how by this time.
8. Ida has not been making these very long.

C. 1. begin, began, will begin, have begun, had begun, will have begun
2. choose, chose, will choose, have chosen, had chosen, will have chosen
3. cost, cost, will cost, have cost, had cost, will have cost
4. know, knew, will know, have known, had known, will have known
5. sleep, slept, will sleep, have slept, had slept, will have slept
6. buy, bought, will buy, have bought, had bought, will have bought

D. 1. present perfect
2. present
3. past perfect
4. future
5. present perfect
6. past perfect
7. future perfect
8. past

E. 1. My brother made a bookstand for his teacher.
2. We shall take a cake to our grandmother.

F. **Elements of the Weather**
   I. Clouds
     A. Nimbus
     B. Cumulus
     C. Cirrus
     D. Stratus
  II. Precipitation
     A. Snow
     B. Hail
     C. Rain
     D. Sleet
 III. Storms
     A. Tornadoes
     B. Hurricanes
     C. Blizzards
     D. Thunderstorms

Written Exercises

A. 1. has remembered, forgot
2. smells, taste
3. finish, shall have made
4. mixed, kneaded
5. had made
6. do make
7. has learned
8. has been making

B. For each verb in parentheses, write the tense indicated in italics. Be sure to use the correct helping verbs.
1. The strong wind (blow) this tree down. *past*
2. Melinda (give) the package to Melody. *present perfect*
3. Merle (cut) his finger on these knives before the shield was on. *past perfect*
4. Father and the boys (dig) this ditch before the plumbers come. *future perfect*
5. Do not drop that dish, or it (break). *future*
6. By the end of the month, the price (rise). *future perfect*
7. Leah (tear) her dress before we went hiking. *past perfect*
8. The Martin family (go) to Canada. *present perfect*

C. Diagram the skeletons of the following sentences. Also diagram the direct objects, indirect objects, predicate nominatives, and predicate adjectives.
1. The children gathered leaves for an art project.
2. My brother made the rabbits a cage.
3. Aunt Mary's pumpkin pies always taste delicious.
4. Each of us tasted a piece.
5. Anna and Barbara have written their cousin a letter.
6. Finally the ground became warm.
7. The eastern sky was growing bright.
8. Many anxious people gathered before the doorway.
9. His uncle is a preacher.
10. Jesus taught the people many truths.
11. God showed Peter a vision.
12. God's children are kind and patient.

D. Here is a topical outline of the composition that follows. Copy and complete parts III and IV, choosing points from the list given.

Pictures of Jesus in the Gospels
I. Gospel of Matthew
  A. Was apparently written to Jews
    1. Has sixty references to Jewish prophecies
    2. Has forty quotations from the Old Testament
  B. Shows Jesus as a king
    1. Wise men's search for the King of the Jews
    2. Prophecy about Jesus' triumphal entry as a king

B. 1. blew
2. has given
3. had cut
4. will have dug
5. will break
6. will have risen
7. had torn
8. has gone

C. 1. 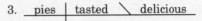 children | gathered | leaves

2. brother | made | cage
   \ rabbits

3. pies | tasted \ delicious

4. Each | tasted | piece

5. Anna and Barbara | have written | letter
   \ cousin

6. 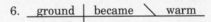 ground | became \ warm

7. 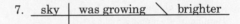 sky | was growing \ brighter

8. people | gathered

9. uncle | is \ preacher

10. Jesus | taught | truths
    \ people

11. God | showed | vision
    \ Peter

12. children | are \ kind and patient

II. Gospel of Mark
  A. Was written for Gentiles
    1. Has few references to Old Testament prophecy
    2. Explains Jewish words and customs
  B. Shows Jesus as a servant
    1. Had no time to eat
    2. Had no time to rest
III. Gospel of Luke
  A. Written for Theophilus
    1.
    2.
  B. Shows Jesus as the Son of man
    1.
    2.
    3.
IV. Gospel of John
  A. Records miracles showing Jesus as the Son of God
    1.
    2.
  B. Records words of Jesus showing His divinity
    1.
    2.

Points for parts III and IV
  "I am's" of Jesus
  Probably a Greek
  Raising of Lazarus
  Possibly a nobleman
  Healing of the man born blind
  Records His saying, "Blessed are the poor"
  Shows that Jesus helped publicans and sinners
  Times when Jesus said He was sent from God
  Shows His healing the sick and cleansing the lepers

D. III. Gospel of Luke
  A. Written for Theophilus
    1. Probably a Greek
    2. Possibly a nobleman
  B. Shows Jesus as the Son of man
    1. Shows that Jesus helped publicans and sinners
    2. Records His saying, "Blessed are the poor"
    3. Shows His healing the sick and cleansing the lepers
IV. Gospel of John
  A. Records miracles showing Jesus as the Son of God
    1. Healing of the man born blind
    2. Raising of Lazarus
  B. Records words of Jesus showing His divinity
    1. "I am's" of Jesus
    2. Times when Jesus said He was sent from God

Pictures of Jesus in the Gospels

The Gospel of Matthew shows Jesus as the King of the Jews. This Gospel was apparently written to the Jews. It has sixty references to Jewish prophecies. It also has forty direct quotations from the Old Testament. Many references show Jesus as a king. When the wise men sought Jesus, they asked, "Where is He that is born King of the Jews?" In describing Jesus' triumphal entry into Jerusalem, Matthew quoted the prophecy that says, "Behold, thy king cometh unto thee."

The Gospel of Mark shows Jesus as a servant. Its style shows that the book was written mainly for Gentiles. It contains few references to Old Testament prophecy. It carefully explains Jewish words and customs so that the reader is sure to understand them. Many passages show Jesus as a servant. Chapter 3 tells how Jesus was so busy with the multitudes that He did not have time to eat. Chapter 6 says that Jesus and His disciples had no time to rest.

The Gospel of Luke shows Jesus as the Son of man. Luke wrote this book for Theophilus, a person who is unknown today. Theophilus was probably a Greek. He may have been a nobleman because he is addressed as "most excellent Theophilus." Luke gave many examples to show Jesus' concern for needy mankind. He showed that Jesus came to help publicans and sinners. He wrote how Jesus said to His disciples, "Blessed are the poor." He showed how Jesus healed the sick and cleansed the lepers.

The Gospel of John shows Jesus as the Son of God. John recorded miracles by which Jesus' power as the Son of God is clearly seen. One such miracle is the healing of the man who was born blind. Another is the raising of Lazarus after he was dead four days. John wrote words of Jesus which show that He is divine. He recorded many "I am's" of Jesus. John also wrote about many times when Jesus said He was sent from God.

Chapter Five

Using Verbs Correctly

Writing Reports

Some
verbs are very
much alike, yet they have
different meanings.

How forcible are right words!

Job 6:25

47. Using *Lay* and *Lie*

Some verbs are very much alike, yet they have different meanings. The verbs *lay* and *lie* are often confused. Do you know how to use them correctly? Which sentence in each of the following pairs is correct?

The queen bee <u>lay</u> two thousand eggs in one day.
or The queen bee <u>laid</u> two thousand eggs in one day.

This drone <u>has laid</u> in the hive all day.
or This drone <u>has lain</u> in the hive all day.

The larvae are <u>laying</u> in their cells, waiting to be fed.
or The larvae are <u>lying</u> in their cells, waiting to be fed.

The verb *lay* means "to put or place (something)." *Lay* is a transitive verb. Its principal parts are shown below.

Present	Past	Past Participle
lay	laid	(have) laid

The principal parts of *lay* are used correctly in these sentences.

The masons <u>lay</u> the blocks carefully. (present form)
(The masons *put or place* the blocks.)

Howard <u>laid</u> his pencil down. (past form)
(Howard *put or placed* his pencil.)

Susan has <u>laid</u> the spoons on the table. (past participle)
(Susan has *put or placed* the spoons.)

The verb *lie* means "to rest or recline." *Lie* is not transitive. It has three principal parts.

Present	Past	Past Participle
lie	lay	(have) lain

The principal parts of *lie* are used correctly in these sentences.

Snow <u>lies</u> on the lawn. (present form)
(Snow *rests* on the lawn.)

The dog <u>lay</u> on Mother's flowers. (past form)
(The dog *rested or reclined* on the flowers.)

She <u>has lain</u> in bed all morning. (past participle)
(She has *rested or reclined* in bed.)

Lesson 47

Purpose: To teach the correct usage of the problem verbs *lay* and *lie*.

Oral Review:

1. Tell whether each sentence has an action verb or a linking verb.
   a. That arrangement seems odd. (linking)
   b. Mr. Herman tasted the apple pie. (action)
   c. He is looking out the window. (action)
2. What is a verb? (a word that shows action or being)
3. What two parts does every sentence have? (subject, predicate)
4. What does the subject of a sentence tell? (*who* or *what* the sentence is about)
5. What does the predicate of a sentence tell? (what the subject does or is)
6. What part of speech is the simple predicate? (verb)

Lesson Introduction: Does your dog obey you when you command, "Lay down, Rover"? No? Well, what is he supposed to lay down? His head? His bone? Maybe if you use correct English, your dog will obey you. What is the correct way to tell your dog to rest on the ground? (Lie down, Rover.) Do you know how to use *lay* and *lie* correctly?

Lesson Outline:

1. The verb lay *means "to put or place (something)." Its principal parts are* lay, laid, (have) laid.

2. Lay *is a transitive verb.* It always passes its action to another word in the sentence, usually the direct object.

(*Teacher:* In the passive voice, the subject receives the action of *lay* and there is usually no direct object. [**Example:** These eggs were laid today.] However, the passive voice is not included in the exercises so

Both *lay* and *lie* have *-ing* forms. Usually a form of *be* is used with these forms.

> The men **were** <u>laying</u> a new carpet.
> His old coat **was** <u>lying</u> on the lawn.

Whenever you must choose between a form of *lay* and a form of *lie,* you can use two tests to help you.

Test 1: *Which definition fits the sentence?* Try this test on the following sentences. Which verb is correct?

> Mother <u>lays</u> on the couch.
> *or* Mother <u>lies</u> on the couch.

Mother *rests or reclines* on the couch. She does not *put or place* anything on the couch. So the correct verb is *lies.*

> The carpenters have <u>laid</u> the floor tile.
> *or* The carpenters have <u>lain</u> the floor tile.

The carpenters have *put or placed* the floor tile. They have not *rested or reclined* the floor tile. So the correct verb is *laid.*

Test 2: *Does the sentence have a direct object?* If it does, the verb is transitive and must be a form of *lay.* If it does not, the verb is not transitive and must be a form of *lie.* Consider these sentences again.

> Mother <u>lays</u> on the couch.
> *or* Mother <u>lies</u> on the couch.

Mother lays *whom* or *what*? There is nothing to receive the action of the verb, so the verb is not transitive. The correct choice is *lies.*

> The carpenters have <u>laid</u> the floor tile.
> *or* The carpenters have <u>lain</u> the floor tile.

The carpenters have laid *what*? They have laid the *floor tile.* There is a direct object, so the verb is transitive. The correct choice is *laid.*

Notice that *lay* is the present form of *lay* (meaning "to put or place [something]"). *Lay* is also the past form of *lie* (meaning "to rest or recline"). You must be especially careful not to confuse these two different meanings of *lay.*

> You may <u>lay</u> (put) the books down.
> Yesterday Martha <u>lay</u> (rested) in bed with chicken pox.

that students can accurately test whether to use *lay* or *lie* by checking for a direct object.)

3. The verb lie **means "to rest or recline." Its principal parts are** lie, lay, (have) lain.

4. Lie **is not transitive.** It never has a direct object.

5. Both lay **and** lie **have -ing forms:** laying, lying. Usually a form of *be* is used with these forms. (*Teacher:* Grade 6 is the first level where the *-ing* forms of these verbs are taught.)

6. Two tests can be used to decide whether lay **or** lie **is correct in a sentence.**

Test 1: *Which definition fits the sentence?* If you want a verb that means "to put or place," use a form of *lay.* If you want the meaning "to rest or recline," use a form of *lie.*

Test 2: *Does the sentence have a direct object?* If it does, use a form of the transitive verb *lay.* If it does not, use a form of *lie,* which is not transitive.

For more help in distinguishing *lay* and *lie,* use memory aids such as the following:

a. *Laid* ends with *d. Direct object* begins with a *d. Laid* needs a direct object.

b. *Lain* and *lane* can be associated by the following sentence.

> The paper <u>has lain</u> in the <u>lane</u> all day.

c. *Laid* and *lain* can be distinguished in the following manner.

> Chickens should not lay eggs in the lane.
> **Think:** "The hen <u>has laid</u> an egg,"
> not "<u>has lain</u> an egg."

Make attractive posters with captions to illustrate the above memory aids.

- The verb *lay* means "to put or place (something)." *Lay* is transitive and usually passes its action to a direct object. Its principal parts are *lay, laid, (have) laid.*

- The verb *lie* means "to rest or recline." *Lie* is not transitive and never has a direct object. Its principal parts are *lie, lay, (have) lain.*

Class Practice

Tell whether the following sentences are correct. Read each sentence correctly.

1. A queen bee lays up to two thousand eggs per day.
2. The bee larvae are laying in their cells, waiting to be fed.
3. God has stretched out the heavens like a curtain and has lain the beams of His chambers in the waters.
4. The wolf also shall dwell with the lamb, and the leopard shall lay down with the kid.
5. The Lord lays up sound wisdom for the righteous.
6. Those who serve the Lord are laying up treasures in heaven.
7. The sheep laid contentedly on the green grass.
8. The flock has laid there several hours.
9. The shepherd lay the injured sheep gently on the ground.
10. Then he laid down his rod and staff.
11. A shepherd laid in the doorway of the sheepfold at night.
12. The Good Shepherd lays down His life for the sheep.

Written Exercises

A. Write the correct words in parentheses. If you write a form of *lay,* also write the direct object.
1. Snow has (laid, lain) on Mount Hood all summer.
2. The girls were (laying, lying) old newspapers between the rows of beans.
3. Gwen (laid, lay) down to rest.
4. (Lay, Lie) down, Fido.
5. The boy (laid, lay) his pack on the table while he ate.
6. My pet raccoon has (laid, lain) here on the seat to sleep.
7. The little kittens (laid, lay) in the clothes basket sleeping.

Lesson 47 Answers
Class Practice

(Corrections are underlined.)
1. correct
2. The bee larvae are <u>lying</u> in their cells, waiting to be fed.
3. God has stretched out the heavens like a curtain and has <u>laid</u> the beams of His chambers in the waters.
4. The wolf also shall dwell with the lamb, and the leopard shall <u>lie</u> down with the kid.
5. correct
6. correct
7. The sheep <u>lay</u> contentedly on the green grass.
8. The flock has <u>lain</u> there several hours.
9. The shepherd <u>laid</u> the injured sheep gently on the ground.
10. correct
11. A shepherd <u>lay</u> in the doorway of the sheepfold at night.
12. correct

Written Exercises

A. 1. lain
2. laying, newspapers
3. lay
4. Lie
5. laid, pack
6. lain
7. lay

8. The mother cat had (laid, lay) them there.
9. Yesterday we (laid, lay) the carpet in the new house.
10. The contented cow (laid, lay) in the pasture, chewing her cud.
11. She has (laid, lain) there for several hours.
12. Mother (laid, lay) the sleeping baby on the bed.

B. For each blank, write the correct form of *lay* or *lie.*
1. —— quietly while I rub your back.
2. Baby Joan is —— in her crib.
3. Wesley has —— his coat on this chair.
4. Please —— this hat on the shelf.
5. The opossum —— still until we left, pretending to be dead.
6. Grandfather has —— many bricks in his lifetime.
7. The papers were —— on his desk.
8. The snow did not —— on the ground very long.

C. Write the principal parts of *lay,* and use each form in a sentence of your own.

D. Write the principal parts of *lie,* and use each form in a sentence of your own.

Review Exercises

Diagram the skeletons of these sentences. Include the direct and indirect objects, predicate nominatives, and predicate adjectives. [38–43]
1. Faith makes all things possible, and love makes them easy.
2. Mount Waialeale is the wettest place in the world.
3. Where is Mount Waialeale found?
4. This Hawaiian mountain receives about 460 inches of rainfall each year.
5. What a large amount of rainfall that is!
6. Stand up and read us your report on volcanoes.
7. By Monday I shall have read this book twice.
8. I do not always read this fast.
9. Nancy's report about constellations was excellent.
10. Beautiful mountains and valleys are found in Oregon.

8. laid, them
9. laid, carpet
10. lay
11. lain
12. laid, baby

B. 1. Lie
2. lying
3. laid
4. lay
5. lay
6. laid
7. lying
8. lie

C. lay, laid, (have) laid
(Individual sentences.)

D. lie, lay, (have) lain
(Individual sentences.)

Review Exercises

1. Faith | makes | things _and_ love | makes | them
2. Mount Waialeale | is \ place
3. Mount Waialeale | is found
4. mountain | receives | inches
5. that | is \ amount
6. (you) | Stand _and_ read | report \ us
7. I | shall have read | book
8. I | do read
9. report | was \ excellent
10. mountains _and_ valleys | are found

48. Using *Raise* and *Rise*

The verbs *raise* and *rise* are similar in sound but different in meaning. You should not find it difficult to use them correctly.

The verb *raise* means "to cause (something) to go up or grow up." It is a regular transitive verb. Study its principal parts and the example sentences that follow.

Present	**Past**	**Past Participle**
raise	raised	(have) raised

Alma <u>raises</u> hamsters. (causes hamsters to grow up)
We <u>raised</u> the stone. (caused the stone to go up)
Father has <u>raised</u> the window. (has caused the window to go up)

The verb *rise* means "to get up or go up." *Rise* is an irregular verb and is not transitive. Study its principal parts and the example sentences that follow.

Present	**Past**	**Past Participle**
rise	rose	(have) risen

The moon <u>rises</u> early. (goes up)
Smoke <u>rose</u> above the fire. (went up)
The children <u>have risen</u>. (have gotten up)

Both *raise* and *rise* have -*ing* forms. Usually a form of *be* is used with these forms.

The men **were** <u>raising</u> a new barn after the fire.
The moon **is** <u>rising</u> in the night sky.

Since *raise* is transitive and *rise* is not transitive, you can again use two tests to help you decide whether a form of *raise* or a form of *rise* fits in a sentence.

Test 1: *Which definition fits the sentence?* Consider the following examples.

The bread in the pan <u>raised</u> slowly.
or The bread in the pan <u>rose</u> slowly.

Did the bread *go up,* or did it *cause (something) to go up?* The bread *went up,* so the correct verb is *rose.*

Lesson 48

Purpose: To teach the correct usage of the problem verbs *raise* and *rise.*

Oral Review:
1. Which verb means "to put or place (something)," *lay* or *lie?* (lay)
2. What does the verb *lie* mean? (to rest or recline)
3. Which verb is followed by a direct object, *lay* or *lie?* (lay)
4. What are the principal parts of *lay?* (lay, laid, [have] laid)
5. What are the principal parts of *lie?* (lie, lay, [have] lain)
6. What is a possessive noun? (a noun that shows possession or ownership)
7. A possessive noun is often used as what part of speech? (adjective)

Written Quiz:
1. Write the definition of a verb.

   _____

   _____

2. Write the term for a word in the predicate that receives the action of the verb. _____
3. Underline the correct word or words.

   If a verb passes action to a receiver, it is (transitive, not transitive).

4. Write four linking verbs in each set.
   Forms of *be:*   _____, _____, _____, _____
   Verbs of sense: _____, _____, _____, _____
   Other linking verbs:_____, _____, _____, _____

Quiz Answers:
1. A verb is a word that shows action or being.
2. direct object
3. transitive
4. (Any four in each set.)
   am, is, are, was, were, be, been, being
   taste, feel, smell, sound, look, appear
   grow, seem, stay, become, remain

Test 2: *Does the sentence have a direct object?* Here are two more sentences to try.

> We <u>raise</u> our hearts in praise to God.
> *or* We <u>rise</u> our hearts in praise to God.

We raise *what*? We raise our *hearts*. The sentence has a direct object. The correct choice is the transitive verb *raise*.

- The verb *raise* means "to cause (something) to go up or grow up." *Raise* is transitive and usually passes its action to a direct object. Its principal parts are *raise, raised, (have) raised*.

- The verb *rise* means "to get up or go up." *Rise* is not transitive and never has a direct object. Its principal parts are *rise, rose, (have) risen*.

Class Practice

Tell whether the following sentences are correct. Read each sentence correctly.

1. Please raise your hand before you speak.
2. My uncle was raising turkeys for market.
3. The smoke raised above the roofs.
4. The water level is raising an inch a day.
5. The sun rose at five o'clock.
6. At what time will the sun raise tomorrow?
7. The speaker had rose to his feet.
8. Please raise your voice so that we can hear you.
9. The price of meat has raised.
10. The chicken raised its wings to fly.
11. The temperature has raised since three o'clock.
12. The bread is raising.
13. We have risen pigs and chickens.
14. We rose a little money for a colt.
15. Rise the bed while I put this caster under the leg.
16. The river has raised three inches since the rain.

Lesson Introduction: Read the following sentences, and ask if the students can correct them.

> The kite raised above the treetops. (<u>rose</u>)
> He has risen an interesting question. (has <u>raised</u>)
> The students have risen their hands. (have <u>raised</u>)
> The bread dough is raising slowly. (is <u>rising</u>)

The verbs *raise* and *rise* are similar in sound and meaning. In this lesson you will study their correct usage.

Lesson Outline:

1. The verb **raise** *means "to cause (something) to go up or grow up." Its principal parts are* **raise, raised, (have) raised.**

2. **Raise** *is a transitive verb.* It usually has a direct object.

Lesson 48 Answers
Class Practice

(Corrections are marked.)

1. correct
2. correct
3. The smoke <u>rose</u> above the roofs.
4. The water level is <u>rising</u> an inch a day.
5. correct
6. At what time will the sun <u>rise</u> tomorrow?
7. The speaker had <u>risen</u> to his feet.
   or The speaker ~~had~~ rose to his feet.
8. correct
9. The price of meat has <u>risen.</u>
10. correct
11. The temperature has <u>risen</u> since three o'clock.
12. The bread is <u>rising.</u>
13. We have <u>raised</u> pigs and chickens.
14. We <u>raised</u> a little money for a colt.
15. <u>Raise</u> the bed while I put this caster under the leg.
16. The river has <u>risen</u> three inches since the rain.

---

3. The verb **rise** *means "to get up or go up." Its principal parts are* **rise, rose, (have) risen.**

4. **Rise** *is not transitive.* It never has a direct object.

5. **Both** raise *and* **rise** *have* **-ing** *forms:* **raising, rising.** Usually a form of *be* is used with these forms.

6. Two tests can be used to decide whether a form of **raise** *or a form of* **rise** *is correct in a sentence.*

> **Test 1:** *Which definition fits the sentence?*
> **Test 2:** *Does the sentence have a direct object?*

Written Exercises

A. Write the correct words in parentheses. If you write a form of *raise,* also write the direct object.
1. Jesus healed sick folks and (raised, rose) dead people to life.
2. God (raised, rose) Jesus from the dead and set Him at His own right hand.
3. God has (raised, risen) the believers and has made them sit together in heavenly places.
4. The service was over, and the people had (raised, risen) to pray.
5. Jesus (raised, rose) from the grave on the third day.
6. We will (raise, rise) hymns of praise to our Creator in the days of our youth.
7. In old age, a person often sleeps poorly and (raises, rises) at the singing of the birds.
8. At midnight I will (raise, rise) to give thanks into Thee.

B. For each blank, write the correct form of *raise* or *rise.*
1. The bubbles ——— to the top of the liquid.
2. As the jellyfish searched for food, it ——— in the water and then sank again.
3. Does the moon ——— in the east?
4. Have you ——— your English score yet?
5. Harold's scores have ——— during this marking period.
6. Hard work ——— his scores higher than they had been.
7. Have the farmers ——— the price of beef?
8. Up ——— the sun like a bright orange ball.

C. Write the principal parts of *raise,* and use each form in a sentence of your own.

D. Write the principal parts of *rise,* and use each form in a sentence of your own.

Review Exercises

A. Write the correct form of *lay* or *lie* for each blank. [47]
1. Freshwater eels ——— their eggs in the Sargasso Sea.
2. Fishermen catch eels in nets and ——— them in their boats.
3. Some eels are ——— in the mud when they are caught.
4. Some fishermen ——— out bait for the eels.
5. The eels cannot resist worms that are ——— in the water.
6. Yesterday several eels ——— in this fisherman's net.

Written Exercises

A. 1. raised, people
2. raised, Jesus
3. raised, believers
4. risen
5. rose
6. raise, hymns
7. rises
8. rise

B. 1. rise *or* rose
2. rose
3. rise
4. raised
5. risen
6. raised
7. raised
8. rose *or* rises

C. raise, raised, (have) raised
(Individual sentences.)

D. rise, rose, (have) risen
(Individual sentences.)

Review Exercises

A. 1. lay
2. lay
3. lying
4. lay
5. lying
6. lay

7. When the fishermen come, it seems that some fish ——— very still at the bottom of the river.
8. The old fisherman has ——— down to rest.
9. A young fisherman had ——— his coat here.
10. Mother ——— the good eel meat in the pan to fry.

B. Rewrite these expressions, using possessive forms. [26]

Example: the net of the fisherman
Answer: the fisherman's net

1. the recipe of Mary
2. the kite of the boy
3. the bicycles of the boys
4. the tools of the men
5. the meeting of the workers

Challenge Exercises

Write a Bible story in your own words, using *lay* and *lie* or *raise* and *rise* correctly. For ideas, see Matthew 9:18–26; Mark 1:29–31; Mark 2:1–5; and John 11:1–44.

---

49. Using *Set* and *Sit*

The verbs *set* and *sit* are often confused. Are the peach baskets *setting* or *sitting* on the lawn? Did Homer *set* them there, or did he *sit* them there? Learn to use the forms of *set* and *sit* correctly.

The verb *set* means "to put or place (something)," and it is transitive. Notice its irregular principal parts—they do not change at all!

Present	**Past**	**Past Participle**
set	set	(have) set

Study these sentences, which use the three principal parts of *set*.

James <u>sets</u> up the chairs for the services.
   (*puts or places* the chairs)

Alice <u>set</u> the glasses on the table.
   (*put or placed* the glasses)

They <u>have set</u> their packages on the shelf.
   (*have put or placed* their packages)

---

7. lie
8. lain
9. laid
10. laid

B. 1. Mary's recipe
2. the boy's kite
3. the boys' bicycles
4. the men's tools
5. the workers' meeting

Challenge Exercises
(Individual work.)

Lesson 49

Purpose: To teach the correct usage of the problem verbs *set* and *sit*.

Oral Review:
1. Which verb means "to cause (something) to go up or grow up," *raise* or *rise*? (raise)
2. What does *rise* mean? (to get up or go up)
3. Which verb is followed by a direct object, *raise* or *rise*? (raise)
4. Which verb means "to put or place (something)," *lay* or *lie*? (lay)
5. What does *lie* mean? (to rest or recline)
6. Which verb is followed by a direct object, *lay* or *lie*? (lay)
7. What is a predicate nominative? (a noun or pronoun that follows a linking verb and renames the subject)
8. What is a predicate adjective? (an adjective that follows a linking verb and modifies the subject)

Lesson Introduction: Suppose your family is driving down the road to town. Suddenly the car engine sputters and coughs a few times, then dies out. Your father pulls to the side of the road as your car coasts to a stop. A glance at the fuel gauge tells the story: your car is out of gas. Now what will you do? You will have to flag down another motorist or else walk for gas.

You know what you must do, but do you know what has happened? Has your car let you *set,* or has it let you *sit*? (Your car has let you *sit;* that is, it has allowed you to have a seat—by the side of the road!) Can you use these words properly in other situations?

Lesson Outline:
1. The verb set *means "to put or place (something)." Its principal parts are* set, set, (have) set. (All three forms are the same.)

The verb *sit* means "to rest or be seated." *Sit* is an irregular verb and is never transitive. Study its principal parts and their use in the sentences below.

Present	Past	Past Participle
sit	sat	(have) sat

The boys <u>sit</u> quietly during devotions. (are seated)
They <u>sat</u> beside their mother. (were seated)
The box <u>has sat</u> on the shelf for a week. (has rested)

Usually a form of *be* is used with the *-ing* forms of these verbs.

Why <u>are</u> you <u>setting</u> the peanuts on the counter?
The congregation <u>was sitting</u> quietly during the sermon.

To decide which of these verbs is correct in a sentence, use the same tests that you learned earlier.

Test 1: *Which definition fits the sentence?* Use this test to choose the correct verb in each of the following sentences.

The baby is (setting, sitting) in a mud puddle!
    (The baby is *resting,* so *sitting* is correct.)

Frank (set, sat) his books on the kitchen table.
    (Frank *put* his books, so *set* is correct.)

Our Bibles should not just (set, sit) and collect dust.
    (Our Bibles should not just *rest,* so *sit* is correct.)

Test 2: *Does the sentence have a direct object?* In the three sentences above, only the second one has a direct object. (Frank set *what?* Frank set *books.*) Therefore, the second sentence is the only one that should use a form of *set.* Each of the other two must use a form of *sit.*

- The verb *set* means "to put or place (something)." *Set* is transitive and usually passes its action to a direct object. Its principal parts are *set, set, (have) set.*

- The verb *sit* means "to rest or be seated." *Sit* is not transitive and never has a direct object. Its principal parts are *sit, sat, (have) sat.*

---

2. Set *is a transitive verb.* It usually requires a direct object.

3. *The verb* sit *means "to rest or be seated." Its principal parts are* sit, sat, (have) sat.

4. Sit *is not transitive.* It never has a direct object.

5. *The* -ing *forms of* set *and* sit *are* setting *and* sitting. Usually a form of *be* is used with these forms.

6. *Two tests can be used to decide whether a form of* set *or a form of* sit *is correct in a sentence.*

Test 1: *Which definition fits the sentence?*
Test 2: *Does the sentence have a direct object?*

★ **EXTRA PRACTICE**
Worksheet 27 *(Lay and Lie, Raise and Rise, Set and
                        Sit)*

Class Practice

Tell whether the following sentences are correct. Read each sentence correctly.

1. Please sit the dishes on the table for me.
2. We set the pretty geranium in the window.
3. We all set on our blankets.
4. Everyone set down to eat.
5. The vase sat on that shelf for many years.
6. The kittens have often set on the edge of the porch.
7. We set the candles on the shelf.
8. We were setting in our chairs for three hours.
9. Set down and tell us the news.
10. We have set near the fire.
11. We had sat down to eat.
12. Sit down while I comb your hair.
13. We have sat the dishes on the table.
14. Set the butter on the table too.

Written Exercises

A. Write the correct words in parentheses. If you write a form of *set,* also write the direct object.

1. James accidentally (set, sat) on a freshly painted bench.
2. They have (set, sat) their packages on the table.
3. We have not (set, sat) here very long yet.
4. The village (sets, sits) in a deep valley.
5. We have been (setting, sitting) the table against the wall.
6. Ruth was (setting, sitting) next to me.
7. You may (set, sit) on the bench.
8. (Set, Sit) the box of chalk on the floor.
9. Where have you (set, sat) the chairs?
10. There is a box (setting, sitting) in the driveway.
11. He has (set, sat) in the vacant seat by me.
12. Now you may (set, sit) the basket on the desk.

B. Write the correct form of *set* or *sit* for each blank.

1. The four lepers outside Samaria said, "Why should we ——— here till we die?"
2. When the lepers came to the Syrian camp, the tents, provisions, and everything else were ——— just as the Syrians had left them.

Lesson 49 Answers
Class Practice

(Corrections are underlined.)

1. Please <u>set</u> the dishes on the table for me.
2. correct
3. We all <u>sat</u> on our blankets.
4. Everyone <u>sat</u> down to eat.
5. correct
6. The kittens have often <u>sat</u> on the edge of the porch.
7. correct
8. We were <u>sitting</u> in our chairs for three hours.
9. <u>Sit</u> down and tell us the news.
10. We have <u>sat</u> near the fire.
11. correct
12. correct
13. We have <u>set</u> the dishes on the table.
14. correct

Written Exercises

A. 1. sat
    2. set, packages
    3. sat
    4. sits
    5. setting, table
    6. sitting
    7. sit
    8. Set, box
    9. set, chairs
    10. sitting
    11. sat
    12. set, basket

B. 1. sit
    2. sitting

3. Soon the lepers had eaten and drunk, had gotten silver, gold, and raiment, and had ———— them in a hiding place.

4. The lepers decided that they should not have ———— there selfishly enjoying themselves, but they should have shared the good news.

5. Jesus healed the blind man who ———— by the wayside begging.

6. I will ———— no wicked thing before mine eyes.

7. ———— a watch, O Lord, before my mouth; keep the door of my lips.

8. God has ———— the sun, moon, and stars in the heavens.

C. Write the principal parts of *set,* and use each form in a sentence of your own.

D. Write the principal parts of *sit,* and use each form in a sentence of your own.

Review Exercises

A. Write the correct words in parentheses. [47, 48]

1. All turtles (lay, lie) their eggs on land.
2. After the mother turtle has (laid, lain) her eggs and covered them, she leaves them.
3. The eggs (lay, lie) under the ground and are warmed by the sun.
4. Some sea turtles have (laid, lain) up to two hundred eggs.
5. The African pancake tortoise (lays, lies) only one egg at a time.
6. A baby desert tortoise hatches after (laying, lying) inside its shell for about one hundred days.
7. We watched the sun as it (raised, rose) over the sea.
8. Father (raised, rose) his hand when it was time for us to come back.
9. The sun was (raising, rising) higher and higher.
10. By noon the sun had (raised, risen) to its zenith.

B. Diagram the skeletons, predicate nominatives, and predicate adjectives. Label the predicate nominatives *PN* and the predicate adjectives *PA.* (The words in italics are noun phrases.) [42, 43]

1. That huge creature is a *grizzly bear.*
2. Mark's pet was a playful crow.

---

3. set
4. sat
5. sat
6. set
7. Set
8. set

C. set, set, (have) set
(Individual sentences.)

D. sit, sat, (have) sat
(Individual sentences.)

Review Exercises

A. 1. lay
2. laid
3. lie
4. laid
5. lays
6. lying
7. rose
8. raised
9. rising
10. risen

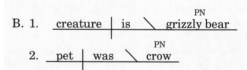

B. 1. creature | is \ grizzly bear (PN)

2. pet | was \ crow (PN)

3. The *great horned owl* is dangerous to small animals like the skunk.
4. A favorite food of raccoons is frogs.
5. The *blue jay* in her painting looks lifelike.

————————————

3.
$$\text{great horned owl} \mid \text{is} \setminus \overset{\text{PA}}{\text{dangerous}}$$

4.
$$\text{food} \mid \text{is} \setminus \overset{\text{PN}}{\text{frogs}}$$

5.
$$\text{blue jay} \mid \text{looks} \setminus \overset{\text{PA}}{\text{lifelike}}$$

50. Taking Notes for a Report

To be a good writer, you must learn how to take notes well. In Chapter 4 you learned about outlines. Now you are ready to take notes and make an outline from them.

First choose a topic that is interesting to you. (Your teacher can help you with this.) Then find information on your topic, using textbooks, encyclopedias, and other books from your library at school or at home. Using more than one reference source helps to make your report more informative and interesting. It is also easier to write in your own words when you must combine facts from two or more sources of information.

As you read, take notes only on information that fits your topic. For example, suppose you plan to write a report about training a dog. In your reading you find some interesting facts about feeding dogs. Should you write them down? No, because they are not related to your topic of training a dog.

The notes you write will be points that you may want to use in your report. Write down only main ideas and key words, using short phrases instead of whole sentences or paragraphs. As much as possible, write notes in your own words rather than copying someone else's writing. Write plenty of notes; it is easier to discard some than to go back through the reference books looking for more information.

Suppose you are planning to write a report called "The Habits of Alligators." In the library you find the following article—just what you are looking for! As you read it, you take notes on any ideas that you may want to include in your report. But remember, you must not take notes on facts other than those about alligators' habits—even if they are quite interesting.

The paragraphs have been numbered for easy reference. After the article is a set of notes that you might write from it.

Lesson 50

Purpose: To teach how to take notes for a report.

Teacher: This lesson is quite involved, and it is the basis for several later lessons. You will need a thorough understanding of the material yourself so that you can teach it to your students. Therefore, be sure to prepare carefully for this lesson and for the other composition lessons in this chapter.

Oral Review:

1. What information should a book report contain? (the title of the book, the name of the author, the copyright date, a place where the book can be found, the setting, a description of the main characters, the main events in the book, and the reporter's opinion of the book)
2. What is the setting of a story? (the place and time of the story)
3. What parts of the story should you tell in a book report? What parts should you not tell? (Describe briefly the main problems in the story, but do not give the outcome.)
4. When does a paragraph have unity? (when all the sentences tell about the topic given by the topic sentence)
5. What is a coherent paragraph? (a paragraph in which all the sentences "hold together" in an orderly, sensible way)
6. What are some things you can do to make a paragraph coherent? (Give details in the order of time, importance, or interest. Use transitional words.)

Reference Source 1:

Learning About Alligators

1   Alligators are reptiles. They have backbones, they breathe with lungs, and they have dry, scaly skin. They thrive best where the atmosphere is hot and steamy. They live in or near freshwater swamps and lakes. In the United States, alligators live along the Gulf of Mexico and the southern Atlantic coast.

2   The jaws and teeth of an alligator are two fearsome weapons. Its teeth are heavy and sharp, and its jaw muscles are powerful enough to crush cattle bones. Surprisingly though, once an alligator's jaws are closed, a man can easily hold them shut with his hands.

3   An alligator's eyes have three eyelids. The upper and lower lids are opaque. The third lid is transparent and keeps out water when the alligator is swimming or diving.

4   Even though an alligator's ears are hidden under flaps behind the eyes, alligators can hear very well. Alligators have been trained to respond when called by name. Experienced hunters can attract alligators by making the right sounds.

5   The alligator's long, low body is shaped somewhat like a lizard's except that the alligator's body and tail are larger and thicker. A newly hatched alligator is about nine inches long. His body grows about one foot longer each year. A male alligator may grow to a length of twelve feet and a weight of five hundred pounds. In deep water an alligator tucks his legs against his body; and with mighty sweeps of his powerful tail, he swims at amazing speeds.

Lesson Introduction: It can be fascinating and informative to hear or read a report that someone has made on something he is interested in. But how can we give an interesting report? How can we get information from a reference source without copying from it? How can we write reports in our own words? How can we organize our notes so that the report is given in a logical order? In this lesson you will begin to explore some of the answers to these questions.

Lesson Outline:

1. To prepare for a report, choose a topic that is interesting to you. This may be half the job. Choosing a topic that is interesting to you will help you to give an interesting report.

At this point, students may not be able to choose topics that they can cover well in a few paragraphs. The topic for Written Exercises has been chosen for them.

2. Using more than one reference source helps to make your report more informative and interesting.

3. As you read, take notes on points that will be good to use in your report.

    a. Write only main ideas and key words, using your own words as much as possible. Do not copy whole sentences or paragraphs.

    b. Write plenty of notes. It is easier to discard some information than to go back through the reference books looking for more.

    c. Take notes only on information that fits your topic.

    d. Mark paragraph divisions in your notes. Use blank spaces or indentation to show where each set of notes begins. This will help you find the main ideas more easily when you organize your notes.

6   The alligator's legs and feet help him more on land than in water. The legs are short, yet he can use them to lift his body clear of the ground with just the tip of his tail touching. On land an alligator is clumsy and slow. He can move with surprising speed for a short distance, but he tires easily. His webbed hind feet are a help in paddling through shallow water.

7   An alligator spends much of his time on the banks of a stream, basking in the sun. Being cold-blooded, he needs the heat of the sun to keep warm. On extremely warm days, however, he may hide under the water, under bushes, or in a burrow or den.

8   An alligator usually digs a burrow or den in the bank of a river. He pushes into the mud with his long snout while swishing his tail back and forth to wash away the mud. He may dig a hole forty feet long, with bends as needed to avoid rocks and tree roots. At the far end, he makes a room large enough so that he can turn around.

9   In winter the alligator may hibernate in his burrow. Sometimes an alligator digs a basin in the deepest part of a pond or swamp. Such a "gator hole" contains water even in a dry season when other parts of the pond or swamp are dry. By this God-given instinct, the alligator saves himself and other animals that would otherwise die.

10   Alligators eat mostly fish. Newly hatched alligators eat small water animals such as water insects. Older alligators may attack larger animals along the shore, such as muskrats or raccoons. Rarely does an alligator attack an animal as large as a bear.

11   Alligators like marshmallows and bits of sandwiches, but it can be dangerous to feed them. When an alligator gets used to being fed, he seems to think that anything thrown at him is food. Alligators swallow many hard objects. Young alligators swallow twigs and pebbles, and older ones swallow bigger rocks and chunks of wood. In zoos they swallow things like coins or bottles. The most likely reason they swallow hard objects is to help them grind the food in their stomachs. Alligators swallow their food whole; they cannot chew.

12   Alligators do most of their feeding at night. Often they lie quietly in the water, waiting for something to catch. An alligator may use his tail to catch his food. When a school of fish passes nearby, he swirls his body into an almost complete circle. Then he uses

his tail to knock the food toward his jaws. Once a chicken came too near to an alligator's tail, perhaps thinking it was a log. The alligator knocked the chicken high into the air and caught it in his jaws before it fell to the ground.

13   Alligators do not usually attack people, but a mother alligator guarding her nest can be dangerous. She remains nearby, nearly hidden in the water or bushes, guarding her nest hour after hour. But raccoons or skunks rarely get a chance to eat the eggs because not even a hungry bear wants to fight a mother alligator! When an enemy approaches her nest, she hisses a warning. If he comes closer, she will lunge forward, her mouth wide open. Once a man came too close to a nest, and he spent most of an afternoon in a tree while a mother alligator hissed at him from below.

14   God made interesting creatures when He made alligators. They are interesting to watch and study, and they are also helpful to man. But as we learn about them, we must heed their God-given instincts and keep a safe distance.

Sample notes:

The Habits of Alligators

(Paragraphs 1–6 give no information about alligators' habits.)

Paragraph 7

   Spend much time basking in sun

   Hide under water, under bushes, or in burrow or den when too
      warm

Paragraph 8
    Dig burrow or den with long snout
    Wash away mud by waving tail back and forth
    Make burrow up to 40 feet long
    Make large room at end

Paragraph 9
    May hibernate in den in winter
    Sometimes dig holes in deepest part of pond or swamp
    These "gator holes" save alligators and other animals in dry
        weather

Paragraph 10
    Eat mostly fish
    Young ones eat small animals like water insects
    Older ones eat animals like muskrats and raccoons

Paragraph 11
    Like to eat marshmallows and sandwiches
    Swallow hard objects like rocks and pieces of wood, perhaps to
        grind their food
    Swallow food whole because they cannot chew

Paragraph 12
    Catch food mostly at night
    Lie quietly in water waiting for prey
    Use tail to knock food toward mouth

Paragraph 13
    Seldom attack people
    Mother alligator fierce when guarding nest
    Remains hidden nearby
    Hisses a warning
    Lunges forward with mouth open

Did you notice that some of the paragraphs have no notes taken from them? This is because those paragraphs have no information on the *habits of alligators*. Also notice that no whole sentences are copied. The notes are brief, yet there are plenty of them. The notes are separated according to paragraphs because that makes it easier to write an outline from them later.

- Notes for a report should include only the information that fits a chosen topic. They should consist of main ideas and key words that are written in phrases rather than complete sentences.

- Using more than one reference source helps to make a report more informative and interesting.

Class Practice

A. Read the second reference source about alligators. Find more information on "The Habits of Alligators." Tell your teacher what notes to write on the chalkboard.

Reference Source 2:

The Alligator

1   The American alligator lives in swamps, lakes, and marshes. It does not often leave fresh water. Alligators have webbed toes. When swimming, they fold their legs along their sides. Their long, strong tails send them swiftly through the water. They have a long, flat head, shaped so that the eyes, ears, and nose are the highest points on the head. They lie hidden in the water, breathing easily and looking like a log. Only the eyes, the ears, and the tip of the nose show. Black bony plates cover their bodies.

2   Flaps of skin keep water out of the alligator's ears. Clear eyelids cover the animal's eyes while it looks around underwater. Even the alligator's throat has a little stopper made of skin that keeps out water while its mouth is open underwater. When the mouth is closed, there is no large tooth showing as is true of the crocodile.

3   An alligator's skin is so tough that before modern rifles were invented, bullets could not penetrate it. The skin is watertight and has no sweat glands to keep his body from drying out. The color of the skin is a dull olive gray. Young alligators have yellow marks across their bodies, which fade away as they grow older. Alligator skin was once popular for making durable leather articles, such as handbags and ladies' shoes.

4   Alligators hunt food mostly at night. About three-fourths of the alligator's food is little creatures such as insects, shrimps, crabs, and crayfish. Larger animals like water birds, turtles, fish, muskrats, and snakes are eaten when the alligator is grown. In rare cases,

Lesson 50 Answers
Class Practice

A. (If time is limited, do only several paragraphs in class. These notes are also printed in the pupil's book in Lesson 53. You can refer the students to them for some of the paragraphs. Be sure their books are not open to Lesson 53 when you ask them to give their own ideas for notes.)

(Sample notes from Reference Source 2.)

The Habits of Alligators
Paragraph 4
   Hunt food mostly at night
   Usually eat smaller animals
   Seldom attack people

alligators have eaten bears. They seldom attack people.

5   Alligators are five or six years old before they have young ones of their own. In the spring the female alligator pulls together a big pile of leaves, grass, cattails, decaying vegetation, and mud. This pile may be four to seven feet wide and two to three feet high. She may work three days and nights building her nest. She digs a hole in the top of the nest pile with her back feet. There she lays her twenty-five to sixty eggs about the size of a large goose egg and then covers them over with more nesting material.

6   The eggs are incubated by heat from the sun and from decaying vegetation. God has given alligators the ability to keep the temperature of the nest just right. The female alligator stays around the nest to keep the eggs from harm because some animals, such as raccoons and skunks, would eat them. The eggs hatch in about eight weeks.

7   Mother alligators help their young alligators in several ways. Often newly hatched alligators have trouble getting from the nest pile. When they peep for help, the female alligator comes and rakes away the leaves and mud to set them free. Because many predators like to eat young alligators, the mother sometimes helps them reach the nearest water by carrying them there in her mouth or on her head.

8   Alligators know how to swim as soon as they are hatched. The young may stay in the same water hole with their mother for a year or two. Sometimes they climb on her back or the back of another alligator to sun themselves. They may eat food their mother or another alligator has caught. A large alligator that has killed a pig or some other animal swims about with big chunks hanging out of its mouth. The mother and other alligators allow the babies to come and nibble at the food hanging from their mouths.

9   Mother alligators call their young by grunting like a pig. Baby alligators cry with a moaning grunt that sounds like *umph-umph-umph* at a high pitch. After the age of four, young alligators' voices change and they begin to bellow. The sound is a little uncertain at first, but with practice the voice gets deeper and louder. An adult alligator has a throaty, bellowing roar that can be heard over a mile away.

Paragraph 5
    Female builds nest in spring
    Uses leaves, grass, cattails, decaying vegetation, and mud
    Up to 7 feet wide and 3 feet high
    Lays 25–60 eggs size of a large goose egg
    Covers eggs with nesting material

Paragraph 6
    Allows eggs to be warmed by the sun and decaying vegetation
    Stays near nest to guard eggs

Paragraph 7
    Newly hatched alligators peep for help
    Mother sets them free from nest
    Mother may carry them to nearest water in mouth or on head

Paragraph 8
    Young can swim as soon as they are hatched
    Mothers let young ones nibble food hanging from mouth

Paragraph 9
    Mothers call young by grunting like a pig
    Babies make high-pitched cries
    At four years old, voice changes; they begin bellowing
    Bellowing roar of adult can be heard over a mile away

Written Exercises, Part B *(Continued)*

Paragraph 2
    Flaps of skin keep water out of ears
    Eyes have clear eyelids for underwater
    Little skin stopper in throat to keep out water
    When mouth is closed, no large tooth shows as that of crocodile

Paragraph 3
    Skin is tough
    Bullets could not penetrate before use of modern rifles
    Watertight skin
    No sweat glands—to prevent drying out
    Skin is dull olive gray
    Yellow marks on young alligator fade away in older ones
    Once popular for making attractive handbags

10   When an alligator bellows, he raises his head slightly but keeps his mouth shut. He blows out his breath in a series of long, rumbling roars. An alligator's roar has been described as sounding like thunder, the voices of a thousand bullfrogs, or the rumble of a passing train. In a swamp, the bellow of an alligator can actually send tremors through the ground that can be felt.

B. Now go back to the first reference source in the lesson text. Pick out information from the first several paragraphs for a report on "The Body of an Alligator." Tell your teacher what notes you would write.

Written Exercises

A. From the first reference source, write a set of notes on "The Body of an Alligator."

B. From the second reference source, write a second set of notes on "The Body of an Alligator."

NOTE: Save your notes from this lesson. You will need them in Lessons 53 and 56.

Review Exercises

A. Write the sentence that spoils the unity of this paragraph. [16]

The skunk is helpful to man. A farmer might not think so when a skunk raids his chicken house and steals the eggs. A farmer boy might not think so when the skunk sprays his pet dog. Dogs should be taught to stay away from skunks, but some never learn. But the skunk finds and digs up turtle eggs, and this helps to keep down the turtle population. Since the turtle destroys young ducks and fish, the skunk is really helping man when he eats their eggs.

B. Write the numbers of the rules that you should follow for coherence in a paragraph. [16, 17]
1. Give details in the order of time.
2. Give details in the order of importance or interest.
3. Join a number of sentences with *and then.*
4. Use transitional words such as *first, second, finally, next,* and *then.*
5. Be sure all the sentences tell about the same topic.
6. Use transitional words such as *also, therefore, however, for this reason,* and *in spite of.*

B. (Sample notes from Reference Source 2.)

The Body of an Alligator

Paragraph 1
    Webbed toes
    Long, strong tail
    Long, flat head with eyes, ears, and nose as highest points
    Only eyes, ears, and tip of nose show when under water
    Black bony plates cover body

(Notes for paragraphs 2 and 3 are on page 225.)

Review Exercises

A. Dogs should be taught to stay away from skunks, but some never learn.

B. 1, 2, 4, 6

Paragraph 10
    Bellow made by blowing out breath while keeping mouth shut
    Sounds like thunder, many bullfrogs, or passing train
    Makes ground tremble

B. (See notes in Written Exercises, Part A.)

Written Exercises

(Be sure these notes are saved; the students will need them for the next two lessons on reports. It is recommended that the teacher collect the students' notes so that none are lost.)
A. (Sample notes from Reference Source 1.)

The Body of an Alligator

Paragraph 1
    Alligators are reptiles
    Have backbones
    Breathe with lungs
    Have dry, scaly skin
Paragraph 2
    Have heavy, sharp teeth
    Powerful jaws can crush bones of large animals
    Man can hold jaws shut with his hands after jaws are closed
Paragraph 3
    Has upper and lower opaque eyelids
    Has third transparent lid to keep out water
Paragraph 4
    Ears hidden under flaps behind eyes
    Have good hearing
Paragraph 5
    Have long, low body
    Have thick body and tail
    Tail used for swimming
    Newly hatched—about nine inches long
    Grow about one foot a year
    Male up to 12 feet long and up to 500 pounds
Paragraph 6
    Legs short, yet lift body off ground
    Clumsy and slow on land
    Can move swiftly for short distance, but tires easily
    Uses webbed hind feet to paddle through shallow water
Paragraph 7
    Cold-blooded, therefore basks in sun to keep warm
    Hides under water, under bushes, or in dens to keep cool
Paragraph 8
    Has long snout

51. Using *Let* and *Leave*

Which is correct? "Please *let* me have it" or "Please *leave* me have it"? Should you say "I *let* my books at school" or "I *left* my books at school"? Learn the meanings and correct usage of *let* and *leave*.

The verb *let* means "to allow or permit." It is an irregular verb because all three of its principal parts are the same.

Present	**Past**	**Past Participle**
let	let	(have) let

The principal parts of *let* are used correctly in these sentences.

Father <u>lets</u> us raise goats. (allows or permits)
Araunah <u>let</u> David buy his threshing floor. (allowed)
The boys <u>have let</u> the wagon roll into the pond. (allowed)

The verb *let* is always followed by another verb form. Notice the two verb forms in each of the example sentences.

Father <u>lets</u> us <u>raise</u> goats.
Araunah <u>let</u> David <u>buy</u> his threshing floor.
The boys <u>have let</u> the wagon <u>roll</u> into the pond.

The verb *leave* means "to depart, go away from, or allow to remain." Study its principal parts and the sentences illustrating their use.

Present	**Past**	**Past Participle**
leave	left	(have) left

Please <u>leave</u> as soon as possible. (depart)
We <u>left</u> the room and played outside. (went away from)
Mrs. Miller <u>has left</u> her purse here. (allowed to remain)

The *-ing* forms of *let* and *leave* are *letting* and *leaving*.

When you must choose between a form of *let* and a form of *leave*, two tests can help you decide.

Test 1: *Which definition fits the sentence?* Since both definitions include the idea of allowing, this may be hard to tell. One verb means "to allow" and the other means "to allow to remain." But if you think carefully, you should be able to choose the right one. Which of the following sentences is correct?

       Please <u>let</u> the butter on the table.
or Please <u>leave</u> the butter on the table.

Lesson 51

Purpose: To teach the correct usage of the problem verbs *let* and *leave*.

Oral Review:

1. Which verb means "to put or place (something)," *set* or *sit*? (set)
2. What is the definition of *sit*? (to rest or be seated)
3. Which verb is followed by a direct object, *set* or *sit*? (set)
4. What does *tense* mean? (time)
5. Name the six tenses of verbs. (present tense, past tense, future tense, present perfect tense, past perfect tense, future perfect tense)
6. What helping verbs do perfect tense verbs always use? (have, has, had)
7. What helping verb is used in the past perfect tense? (had)

Lesson Introduction: Write the following sentence on the chalkboard, and ask the pupils what it means.

      Elisha wanted to go with Elijah, and Elijah left him.

This sentence does not mean that Elijah allowed Elisha to go with him, but that Elijah departed from Elisha! We must be careful to use *let* and *leave* correctly, or we may say something completely different from what we mean.

Lesson Outline:

1. The verb let *means "to allow or permit." Its principal parts are the same:* let, let, (have) let.

2. The verb leave *means "to depart, go away from, or allow to remain." Its principal parts are* leave, left, (have) left.

Shall we "allow the butter on the table" or "allow the butter to remain on the table"? The second meaning fits, so the correct verb is *leave*.

> Father <u>let</u> the children sleep late.
> *or* Father <u>left</u> the children sleep late.

You may think that *left* sounds right, but Father simply *allowed* the children to sleep late. So *let* is the correct verb.

Test 2: *Is the verb followed by another verb form? Let* is always used with another verb form, but *leave* is never used in that way. This test makes it simple to choose the right verb in the examples in Test 1.

> Please (let, leave) the butter on the table.

The sentence has only one verb form. Therefore, *leave* is correct.

> Father (let, left) the children sleep late.

This sentence has a second verb form—*sleep.* So the correct verb is *let.*
Be careful with this second test though, for sometimes the second verb form is understood.

> Father <u>lets</u> us <u>raise</u> goats.
> He will not <u>let</u> us next year.
> **Meaning:** He will not <u>let</u> us <u>raise</u> goats next year.

- *Let* means "to allow or permit." Its principal parts are *let, let, (have) let. Let* is always followed by another verb form, either expressed or understood.

- *Leave* means "to depart, go away from, or allow to remain." Its principal parts are *leave, left, (have) left.*

Class Practice

Tell whether the following sentences are correct. Read each sentence correctly.
1. Will you leave me go if I finish my work first?
2. We left her choose the material she wanted for a dress.
3. By leaving the door open, you let the cat come in.
4. Will you be leaving the children go along tomorrow?
5. Be sure to let the keys in the car.
6. The visitors left early this morning.

3. Let *is always followed by another verb form.*
Leave is never used in this way. (*Teacher:* The verb form that follows *let* is an infinitive with *to* omitted. Compare "Let me go" with "Allow me to go.")

4. The -ing *forms of* let *and* leave *are* letting *and* leaving.

5. Two tests can be used to decide whether a form of let *or a form of* leave *is correct in a sentence.*

> **Test 1:** *Which definition fits the sentence?* Since both definitions include the idea of allowing, this may be hard to tell. *Let* means "to allow," and *leave* means "to allow to remain."

> **Test 2:** *Is the verb followed by another verb form?* Sometimes the second verb form is understood.

Lesson 51 Answers
Class Practice
(Corrections are underlined.)
1. Will you <u>let</u> me go if I finish my work first?
2. We <u>let</u> her choose the material she wanted for a dress.
3. correct
4. Will you be <u>letting</u> the children go along tomorrow?
5. Be sure to <u>leave</u> the keys in the car.
6. correct

Note that the second test is different from the second test in previous lessons. Here, we are not looking for a direct object. That is because *let* and *leave* can both be transitive, and *leave* is not always transitive.

★ **EXTRA PRACTICE**
Worksheet 28 *(Let and Leave)*

7. When you go, do not let your purse behind.
8. He left me use his eraser.
9. I have left the visitors come in.
10. They let Roger alone.
11. Have they left him stay alone?
12. What time shall we leave in the morning?

Written Exercises

A. Write the correct words in parentheses. If you write *let,* also write the other verb form.
1. Who (let, left) the door wide open?
2. The teacher has not (let, left) us whisper in school.
3. He (let, left) his books at school when he went home.
4. (Let, Leave) the people of God be joyful.
5. (Let, Leave) us walk in the light of the Lord.
6. A child (let, left) to himself brings his mother to shame.
7. Who hath ears to hear, (let, leave) him hear.
8. The shepherd has (let, left) the ninety-nine and has gone into the mountains to seek the one that is lost.
9. If your brother has something against you, (let, leave) your gift before the altar and first be reconciled to him.
10. They have not (let, left) the most important things for last.
11. The soldiers did not (let, leave) one stone upon another when they destroyed the temple.
12. The Jewish rulers (let, left) the apostles go again.
13. Jesus said, "Peace I (let, leave) with you."
14. The disciples had (let, left) their nets behind to follow Jesus.
15. The woman was (letting, leaving) her waterpot at the well to tell others about Jesus.
16. She had (let, left) Jesus give her the words of life.

B. Write the principal parts of *let,* and use each form in a sentence of your own.

C. Write the principal parts of *leave,* and use each form in a sentence of your own.

Review Exercises

A. Write the correct words in parentheses. [47–49]
1. Under God's care we can (lay, lie) down and sleep in safety.

---

7. When you go, do not <u>leave</u> your purse behind.
8. He <u>let</u> me use his eraser.
9. I have <u>let</u> the visitors come in.
10. They <u>left</u> Roger alone. (The original sentence may also be considered correct, for it may mean "They let Roger [be] alone.")
11. Have they <u>let</u> him stay alone?
12. correct

Written Exercises

A. 1. left
2. let, whisper
3. left
4. Let, be
5. Let, walk
6. left
7. let, hear
8. left
9. leave
10. left
11. leave
12. let, go
13. leave
14. left
15. leaving
16. let, give

B. let, let, (have) let
(Individual sentences.)

C. leave, left, (have) left
(Individual sentences.)

Review Exercises

A. 1. lie

2. The Lord (raised, rose) a deliverer to help the Israelites when they cried to Him.
3. Mary was (setting, sitting) and learning at Jesus' feet.
4. Jesus had (raised, risen) Lazarus from the dead.
5. Jesus (raised, rose) from the grave on the third day.
6. Jesus ascended to heaven and (set, sat) down at the right hand of God.

B. Copy each verb or verb phrase, and write whether it is in the *present* tense, *past* tense, or *future* tense. [32]
1. We have a pet crow.
2. Joel taught him tricks.
3. He left us at the end of summer.
4. We miss him.
5. Maybe he will come back to us.

C. Copy each verb phrase, and write whether it is in the *present perfect* tense, *past perfect* tense, or *future perfect* tense. [34–36]
1. The crow had appeared one day just before summer vacation.
2. He has made himself perfectly at home.
3. Within a week he had learned many things.
4. He has often eaten from their hands.
5. By winter he will likely have learned many more tricks.

2. raised
3. sitting
4. raised
5. rose
6. sat

B. 1. have—present
2. taught—past
3. left—past
4. miss—present
5. will come—future

C. 1. had appeared—past perfect
2. has made—present perfect
3. had learned—past perfect
4. has eaten—present perfect
5. will have learned—future perfect

52. Other Troublesome Verbs

Read the following sentence. Do you know which verb is correct?

Myron (can, may) ride my bicycle.

You cannot choose the correct verb unless you know what the sentence means. Does it mean that Myron *is able to* ride my bicycle or that Myron *has permission to* ride my bicycle? Either verb is correct, depending on the meaning that is intended.

Yet people often use *can* when it is clear that they mean *may*. *Can* means "to be able to." *May* means "to be permitted to." Develop the habit of using these verbs correctly.

I <u>can</u> understand the lesson.
(I *am able to* understand the lesson.)

3. What is a transitive verb? (a verb that passes action to a receiver)
4. What is a direct object? (a noun or pronoun that receives the action of a transitive verb)
5. What is an indirect object? (a noun or pronoun that tells *to whom or what* or *for whom or what* the action of the verb is done)
6. What is a predicate nominative? (a noun or pronoun that follows a linking verb and renames the subject)
7. What is a predicate adjective? (an adjective that follows a linking verb and modifies the subject)

Lesson 52

Purpose: (1) To teach the correct usage of *can, may, teach,* and *learn.* (2) To teach the correct past forms of *tag, drag, drown, attack,* and *burst.* (3) To teach that *could have, should have,* and *would have* should be used rather than *could of, should of,* and *would of.*

Oral Review:
1. Answer these questions about *raise* and *rise.*
   a. Which verb means "to cause (something) to go up or grow up"? (raise)
   b. What does *rise* mean? (to get up or go up)
   c. Which verb is followed by a direct object? (raise)
2. Answer these questions about *lay* and *lie.*
   a. Which verb means "to put or place (something)"? (lay)
   b. What does *lie* mean? (to rest or recline)
   c. Which verb is followed by a direct object? (lay)

Written Quiz:
A. Match these verbs to the meanings and descriptions below. You will use some letters more than once.

a. lay   e. set
b. lie   f. sit
c. raise   g. let
d. rise   h. leave

_____ 1. To get up or go up
_____ 2. To allow or permit
_____ 3. To rest or be seated
_____ 4. To rest or recline
_____ 5. To depart or go away from
_____ 6. To cause (something) to go up or grow up
_____ 7. To put or place (something) (2 answers)
_____ 8. Verbs that can have a direct object (3 answers)

Mabel <u>may</u> open the window if she <u>can</u>.
(Mabel *has permission to* open the window if she *is able to*.)

Teach and *learn* are two more verbs that are sometimes used wrong. *Teach* means "to give knowledge or instruction." *Learn* means "to gain knowledge." Your parents can *teach* you many things, but they cannot *learn* you anything. You must do the learning.

Incorrect: Father will <u>learn</u> me how to do it.
Correct: Father will <u>teach</u> me how to do it.
Correct: I will <u>learn</u> the right way.

Past forms can also cause trouble. Do you know which forms are correct in the following sentences?

The dog (dragged, drug) the boots off the porch.
I am out because Carol (tagged, tug) me.
The balloon sailed into the briers and (burst, bursted, busted).

In each sentence above, the correct past form is the first one shown. Learn the correct past forms of the following verbs.

Present	Past
tag	tagged (<u>not</u> tug)
drag	dragged (<u>not</u> drug)
drown	drowned (<u>not</u> drownded)
attack	attacked (<u>not</u> attackted)
burst	burst (<u>not</u> bursted <u>or</u> busted)

Another mistake is to use *of* for *have,* as in the following example.

You should of told me, and I would of come. I could of.

Of is not a verb. It is not correct to use *could of, should of,* or *would of.* These phrases come from carelessly saying *could have, should have,* and *would have.*

Incorrect: He <u>would of</u> done it if he <u>could of</u>.
Correct: He <u>would have</u> done it if he <u>could have</u>.

If you use incorrect forms, other people will know that either you cannot speak English very well or you are careless in your use of English. Learn and use the correct forms so that you can communicate clearly and effectively.

_____ 9. Verb that is always followed by another verb form

B. Choose the correct verb for each sentence, and write it in the correct form for that sentence.

_____ 1. Yesterday morning the sun (raise, rise) at six o'clock.
_____ 2. The workers were mixing mortar and (lay, lie) bricks.
_____ 3. Hannah (raise, rise) her son to serve the Lord.
_____ 4. That old car has (set, sit) there for years.
_____ 5. Father (let, leave) me drill the holes.
_____ 6. Joshua had (set, sit) an ambush behind the city.
_____ 7. Mother (let, leave) and forgot her purse.
_____ 8. The alligator (lay, lie) in the sun and warmed itself.

Quiz Answers:

A. 1. d	6. c
2. g	7. a, e
3. f	8. a, c, e (*also* g, h)
4. b	9. g
5. h	

B. 1. rose	5. let *or* lets
2. laying	6. set
3. raised	7. left
4. sat	8. lay

Lesson Introduction: What should a teacher say to a student who asks, "Can I get a drink?" Maybe the teacher should say, "You know better than I do. Do you feel strong enough to walk to the water fountain?" Usually the person will correct himself and ask, "May I get a drink?" He really means "Am I allowed to get a drink?" and not "Am I able to get a drink?"

Ask the students if they remember the proper usage of these verbs. If they don't, do they want you to *teach* them or *learn* them the proper usage? Do they know which of the following sentences are incorrect?

My sister learned me how to make this candy. (incorrect)
Joel learned Spanish when he was four years old. (correct)
Our third grade teacher learned us how to divide fractions. (incorrect)

Today we will study the correct usage of several more verbs.

Lesson Outline:

1. **Can** *means "to be able to."* **May** *means "to be permitted to."*

2. **Teach** *means "to give knowledge or instruction."* **Learn** *means "to gain knowledge."* One person cannot learn another person anything. One person teaches another.

- *Can* means "to be able to." *May* means "to be permitted to."

- *Teach* means "to give knowledge or instruction." *Learn* means "to gain knowledge."

- Use the correct past forms of the following verbs: *tag—tagged, drag—dragged, drown—drowned, attack—attacked, burst—burst.*

- Use *could have, should have,* and *would have* rather than *could of, should of,* and *would of.*

Class Practice

A. Tell which sentences are incorrect. Read each sentence correctly.
1. Mother said I can come after my work is finished.
2. Can your baby brother walk?
3. Can I take a jug of water to the workers?
4. You should of paid attention during class.
5. Can you make a whole meal by yourself?
6. I would of come if I could of found a way.
7. The molasses tank burst and made a terrible mess.
8. Father learned me how to change the oil in a car.
9. Two calves drownded in the flood.
10. The dog drug his house into the lane.
11. Indians attackted the Jacob Hochstetler family one night.
12. If you don't know how to play, we can soon learn you.
13. Maria tagged me, so I am caught.
14. He blew up the plastic bag and busted it.
15. A bulldozer drug the logs out of the woods.
16. Mother taught me how to cook spaghetti.
17. She has learned me many other things too.
18. I learn more quickly when I listen carefully.

B. Change the verbs to the simple past tense.
1. The pipes burst in the winter.
2. The bull attacks the noisy dog.
3. The flood drowns the muskrats.
4. Alma quickly tags Priscilla.
5. The chain drags on the road.

3. Be sure to use correct past forms. Many people use incorrect past forms for the following verbs.

> tag (tagged, *not* tug)
> drag (dragged, *not* drug)
> drown (drowned, *not* drownded)
> attack (attacked, *not* attackted)
> burst (burst, *not* bursted *or* busted)

4. Use could have, should have, *and* would have *rather than* could of, should of, *and* would of. *Of* is not a verb. These phrases come from the careless pronunciation of *could have, should have,* and *would have.*

★ **EXTRA PRACTICE**
Worksheet 29 *(Troublesome Verbs)*

Lesson 52 Answers
Class Practice
A. (Corrections are underlined.)
1. Mother said I <u>may</u> come after my work is finished.
2. (correct)
3. <u>May</u> I take a jug of water to the workers?
4. You should <u>have</u> paid attention during class.
5. (correct)
6. I would <u>have</u> come if I could <u>have</u> found a way.
7. (correct)
8. Father <u>taught</u> me how to change the oil in a car.
9. Two calves <u>drowned</u> in the flood.
10. The dog <u>dragged</u> his house into the lane.
11. Indians <u>attacked</u> the Jacob Hochstetler family one night.
12. If you don't know how to play, we can soon <u>teach</u> you.
13. (correct)
14. He blew up the plastic bag and <u>burst</u> it.
15. A bulldozer <u>dragged</u> the logs out of the woods.
16. (correct)
17. She has <u>taught</u> me many other things too.
18. (correct)

B. 1. burst
   2. attacked
   3. drowned
   4. tagged
   5. dragged

Written Exercises

Write the correct words.

1. (Can, May) you get all your work done tonight?
2. (Can, May) I see the pictures in your album?
3. (Can, May) I read the letter too?
4. (Can, May) you lift that heavy box?
5. I lifted it, but I (could have, could of) hurt my back.
6. I (should have, should of) asked someone to help me.
7. We boys (would have, would of) lifted it gladly.
8. You (should not have, should not of) tried to do it alone.
9. Mother (taught, learned) me to always close the door.
10. Our class has (taught, learned) arithmetic since first grade.
11. Last year the teacher (taught, learned) us Spanish.
12. Sister Rose and her class are (teaching, learning) a poem together.
13. I'm sure Brian (tagged, tug) you, so you're out of the game.
14. Your dirty shoes have (dragged, drug) mud into the house.
15. My pretty balloon has finally (burst, bursted).
16. Dorcas used too much water and (drowned, drownded) the plants.
17. The bag fell onto the concrete and (burst, busted) open.
18. The fever (attacked, attackted) almost everyone in the town.

Review Exercises

A. Write the correct verb for each sentence. [47–51]

1. My car (let, left) me (set, sit) this morning!
2. Please (let, leave) me help you change the tire.
3. You may (set, sit) the toolbox where I had (let, left) it.
4. Do you like to (lay, lie) on the cool grass?
5. You may (lay, lie) a rug on the grass and (lay, lie) on it.
6. The men have (laid, lain) new blacktop on the driveway.
7. Ben (laid, lain) the ball beside his bat.
8. The bird that hit the window (laid, lay) still awhile, but later it flew away.
9. The papers have (laid, lain) in that box for years.
10. Grandmother has (laid, lain) a paper there every week.
11. Gerald (laid, lay) down his pencil and took up his book.
12. A good mason can (lay, lie) many bricks in a day's time.
13. (Lay, Lie) your books aside and come for lunch.

Written Exercises

1. Can
2. May
3. May
4. Can
5. could have
6. should have
7. would have
8. should not have
9. taught
10. learned
11. taught
12. learning
13. tagged
14. dragged
15. burst
16. drowned
17. burst
18. attacked

Review Exercises

A. 1. let, sit
2. let
3. set, left
4. lie
5. lay, lie
6. laid
7. laid
8. lay
9. lain
10. laid
11. laid
12. lay
13. Lay

14. When the sun comes up, the temperature will (raise, rise).
15. Emily (raised, rose) her hand to ask a question.
16. Mother has (laid, lain) the wraps on the bed.
17. Scott (laid, lay) down for a nap.
18. Sharon (laid, lay) the baby into the cradle.

B. Diagram the skeletons of the following sentences. Include all the direct objects, indirect objects, predicate nominatives, and predicate adjectives. [38–43]
1. Have you ever seen a shark?
2. Some sharks have rows and rows of sharp teeth.
3. The hammerhead is a dangerous shark.
4. The *whale shark* is not dangerous, for it eats only fish and plants.
5. A *white shark* is a powerful swimmer.
6. My teacher told me a story about sharks.

14. rise
15. raised
16. laid
17. lay
18. laid

B. 1.

2.

3. hammerhead | is \ shark

4.
whale shark | is \ dangerous for it | eats fish and plants

5. white shark | is \ swimmer

6. teacher | told | story / me

53. Organizing Your Notes

After you have taken notes, you need to organize them before you try to write a report. Otherwise your report will simply give details in a haphazard way and will have little value or meaning.

How should you organize your notes? One of the best ways is to form an outline as you learned in Chapter 4. See how this is done with the notes from Lesson 50, which are shown below.

The Habits of Alligators

From Reference Source 1:
Paragraph 7
   Spend much time basking in sun
   Hide under water, under bushes, or in burrow or den when too warm
Paragraph 8
   Dig burrow or den with long snout
   Wash away mud by waving tail back and forth
   Make burrow up to 40 feet long
   Make large room at end

Lesson 53

Purpose: To teach how to organize notes into an outline.

Oral Review:
1. Why should you use more than one reference source when taking notes for a report? (It helps to make your report more informative and interesting.)
2. How should you take notes as you find information? (Write only main ideas and key words.)
3. Why should you write plenty of notes when finding information? (It is easier to discard some notes than to go back through the reference books looking for more information.)
4. Why do writers and speakers use outlines? (to organize their material)
5. What does an outline show? (a brief summary of a composition; the contents and organization of the material)

Lesson Introduction: Imagine that a new grocery store has just opened near your home, and your mother has taken you along to go shopping there. But when you arrive, you find that the grocer has not bothered to organize things on the shelves. Instead, everything is just where someone happened to put it! On the first shelf are several boxes of powdered milk. Beside them are a few bunches of bananas, followed by some boxes of cereal and several jars of mustard. Your mother pulls out her shopping list, and the two of you walk slowly along the shelves, looking for the items she needs. What a time you are going to have finding your groceries!

Today you are like that new grocer. Instead of a jumble of groceries on shelves, you have a disorganized list of facts—about alligators—in your notes. Just as a grocer needs to organize his products for his customers, so you must sort out your information and arrange it in order for your readers. Today's lesson

Paragraph 9
    May hibernate in den in winter
    Sometimes dig holes in deepest part of pond or swamp
    These "gator holes" save alligators and other animals in dry
        weather
Paragraph 10
    Eat mostly fish
    Young ones eat small animals like water insects
    Older ones eat animals like muskrats and raccoons
Paragraph 11
    Like to eat marshmallows and sandwiches
    Swallow hard objects like rocks and pieces of wood, perhaps to
        grind their food
    Swallow food whole because they cannot chew
Paragraph 12
    Catch food mostly at night
    Lie quietly in water waiting for prey
    Use tail to knock food toward mouth
Paragraph 13
    Seldom attack people
    Mother alligator fierce when guarding nest
    Remains hidden nearby
    Hisses a warning
    Lunges forward with mouth open

From Reference Source 2:
Paragraph 4
    Hunt food mostly at night
    Usually eat smaller animals
    Seldom attack people
Paragraph 5
    Female builds nest in spring
    Uses leaves, grass, cattails, decaying vegetation, and mud
    Up to 7 feet wide and 3 feet high
    Lays 25–60 eggs size of a large goose egg
    Covers eggs with nesting material
Paragraph 6
    Allows eggs to be warmed by the sun and decaying vegetation
    Stays near nest to guard eggs

will give you direction in accomplishing that task.

(*Teacher:* The above analogy could be extended to help students see that related items must be placed together and that one main idea should lead logically to the next.)

Lesson Outline:

1. Identify the main idea of the notes from each paragraph. You can get help by noticing the paragraph divisions in your notes. Then decide what the main ideas are that you want to include in your report.

2. Combine the main ideas from all the reference sources. All similar points belong together.

3. Arrange the main ideas in a logical order on an outline. Sometimes one point leads to another. There is room for variation, but the arrangement should be as sensible and orderly as possible.

4. Place the details in your notes under the main ideas where they fit. The outline should show the general plan and provide a sense of direction. The notes themselves can provide details as needed in the actual writing of the report.

Paragraph 7
> Newly hatched alligators peep for help
> Mother sets them free from nest
> Mother may carry them to nearest water in mouth or on head

Paragraph 8
> Young can swim as soon as they are hatched
> Mothers let young ones nibble food hanging from mouth

Paragraph 9
> Mothers call young by grunting like a pig
> Babies make high-pitched cry
> At four years old, voice changes; they begin bellowing
> Bellowing roar of adult can be heard over a mile away

Paragraph 10
> Bellow made by blowing out breath while keeping mouth shut
> Sounds like thunder, many bullfrogs, or passing train
> Makes ground tremble

So many notes! How will we ever organize them into something clear and meaningful? If you work one step at a time, the job will not be too difficult.

Step 1: *Identify the main idea of the notes from each paragraph.* Often you can identify the main idea in each set of notes by identifying the main idea of the paragraph from which you took the notes. If you took your notes correctly, you can easily see the original paragraph divisions. From those main ideas, decide what the main ideas are that you want to include in your report. Study the main ideas from each list of notes as shown below.

Main ideas from Reference Source 1:
1. Keeping warm or cool enough (paragraph 7)
2. Digging burrows, dens, and "gator holes" (paragraphs 8 and 9)
3. Eating habits (paragraphs 10, 11, and 12)
4. Guarding the nest (paragraph 13)

Main ideas from Reference Source 2:
1. Eating habits (paragraph 4)
2. Nesting habits (paragraphs 5 and 6)
3. Caring for young alligators (paragraphs 7 and 8)
4. Sounds made by alligators (paragraphs 9 and 10)

Step 2: *Combine the main ideas from all the reference sources.* Decide which main ideas fit together. In the sample notes, "Guarding the nest" and "Nesting habits" go together. "Eating habits" is in both sets, so those main ideas belong together.

Step 3: *Arrange the main ideas in a logical order on an outline.* The main ideas must follow one another in a sensible way. For instance, your report might say that since alligators sometimes get too warm when they are in the sun, they dig burrows in which to cool off. So a sensible point to put after keeping warm would be one on digging burrows. Or after you mention nesting habits, it would be sensible to describe next how mothers care for their young.

There is room for some variation in the order. For instance, what should come after "Digging burrows"? It might be "Eating habits," "Building nests," or some other main idea. Whatever order you choose, be sure to arrange the main ideas in a way that is logical and meaningful.

Study the following outline, which shows only main ideas. It was made by combining main ideas as described in Step 2.

The Habits of Alligators

I.   Keeping warm or cool enough
II. Digging burrows, dens, and "gator holes"
III. Eating habits
IV. Nesting habits
V.   Caring for young alligators
VI. Sounds made by alligators

Step 4: *Place the details in your notes under the main ideas where they fit.* Subtopics must be placed under the topics that they match. For instance, in the above outline you would not put the point about hibernation under "Eating habits" or "Caring for young alligators." Hibernation has to do with how alligators use their burrows, so it goes under "Digging burrows, dens, and 'gator holes.'"

Your outline does not need to include all the details that are in your notes. Keep your notes so that you can refer to them when you write your report. Your outline will give you a sense of direction when you write your report, and your notes will help you to add meaningful details.

Arranging notes in outline form is an important skill that you will find very useful in life. After you have mastered this skill, you may use it so often that it becomes a habit.

Written Exercises

(Be sure these outlines are saved for later use. Again, it would be wise for the teacher to collect the students' papers.)

(Sample outline.)

The Body of an Alligator

I.   Head
   A. Shape
      1. Is long and flat
      2. Has eyes, ears, nose at highest points
      3. Has long snout
   B. Jaws
      1. Have heavy, sharp teeth
      2. Are powerful
      3. Are weak when closed
   C. Throat—has a flap that closes under water
   D. Eyes
      1. Have three eyelids
      2. Have transparent lids that close under water
   E. Ears
      1. Are hidden under flaps
      2. Can hear well
II. Main Body
   A. Shape—long and low
   B. Tail—powerful
   C. Legs and feet
      1. Short legs
      2. Webbed hind feet
   D. Rate of growth
      1. Are about 9 inches long when hatched
      2. Grow about 1 foot each year
      3. Grow up to 12 feet long
      4. Weigh up to 500 pounds
III. Skin
   A. Tough scales
   B. No sweat glands—to prevent drying out
   C. Attractive appearance
   D. Color
      1. Dull olive gray
      2. Yellow marks when young

- To organize notes for a report, use the following steps.
    1. Identify the main idea of the notes from each paragraph.
    2. Combine the main ideas from all the reference sources.
    3. Arrange the main ideas in a logical order on an outline.
    4. Place the details in your notes under the main ideas where they fit.

Class Practice

Work together as a class to complete the outline "The Habits of Alligators" at the chalkboard. Write details from the notes as subpoints under the main topics where they belong.

Written Exercises

Following the steps given in the lesson, organize the notes you took on "The Body of an Alligator" to make an outline of your own. Do not throw away your notes. You will need them later when you write a report.

Review Exercises

Write *true* or *false*. [33]
1. Every outline must have a title.
2. The main topics of an outline are marked with Roman numerals.
3. A main topic begins with a capital letter, but a subtopic begins with a small letter.
4. All the points at each level of an outline are indented the same amount.
5. A period is placed after each numeral or capital letter that marks a point on the outline.
6. A period is also placed at the end of each point.

Lesson 53 Answers
Class Practice

The Habits of Alligators
I. Keeping warm or cool enough
   A. Basking in the sun
   B. Hiding in burrows
II. Digging burrows, dens, and "gator holes"
   A. Size and shape
   B. Usefulness
      1. Hibernation
      2. Help to other animals
III. Eating habits
   A. What they eat
      1. Mostly fish
      2. Different foods according to size
      3. Special treats
      4. Unusual objects
   B. How they catch food
      1. At night
      2. Under water
      3. With help of tail
IV. Nesting habits
   A. Construction of nest
   B. Description of eggs
   C. Fierce guarding by female
V. Caring for young alligators
   A. Setting young free
   B. Feeding the young
VI. Sounds made by alligators
   A. Mother alligators' calls
   B. Baby alligators' cries
   C. Young alligators' bellows
   D. Adult alligators' roars

(Written Exercises are on Page 237.)

Review Exercises
1. true
2. true
3. false
4. true
5. true
6. false

54. Agreement of Subjects and Verbs

The verb in a sentence must *agree,* or work together, with the subject. If the subject is singular, the verb must be singular; and if the subject is plural, the verb must be plural.

Singular: He walks several miles to church.
Plural: We walk quietly to our Sunday school class.

There is one main exception to this rule. A plural verb must be used when the subject is *I* or *you.*

Subject *I*:   I usually <u>walk</u> home from school.
Subject *you*: You often <u>walk</u> with me.

Usually you choose the correct verb form without even thinking about it. You learned that when you learned to talk! However, there are several cases when you must use special care to make sure the verb agrees with the subject.

1. *Use a plural verb with any two subjects joined by* and. A plural verb is used because the subject includes more than one.

   Incorrect: <u>Lois</u> and <u>Linda</u> <u>is</u> in the same grade.
   Correct: <u>Lois</u> and <u>Linda</u> <u>are</u> in the same grade.
   Correct: <u>Lois</u> and the <u>twins</u> <u>are</u> in the same grade.

2. *Use a singular verb with two singular subjects joined by* or. *The verb is singular because only one of the subjects is performing the action.*

   Incorrect: <u>Father</u> or <u>Mother</u> <u>bring</u> us to school every day.
   Correct: <u>Father</u> or <u>Mother</u> <u>brings</u> us to school every day.

3. *Be sure the verb agrees with the subject when a sentence begins with* there *or* here. *There* or *here* is not the subject, even though it begins the sentence.

   There <u>are</u> some baby <u>birds</u> in that nest.
   Here <u>is</u> a baby <u>bird</u> in this nest.

   Sometimes a sentence that begins with *there* or *here* has a compound subject. Be sure to use the correct verb form in such a

Lesson 54

Purpose: To teach rules for subject–verb agreement.

Oral Review:
1. What does *learn* mean? (to gain knowledge)
2. What does *teach* mean? (to give knowledge or instruction)
3. Name the three principal parts of verbs. Give two names for each. (first principal part—present form; second principal part—past form; third principal part—past participle)
4. Give the principal parts of the following verbs.
   a. tag (tagged, [have] tagged; *not* tug)
   b. drag (dragged, [have] dragged; *not* drug)
   c. drown (drowned, [have] drowned; *not* drownded)
   d. attack (attacked, [have] attacked; *not* attackted)
   e. burst (burst, [have] burst; *not* bursted *or* busted)
   f. lay (laid, [have] laid)
   g. lie (lay, [have] lain)

Written Quiz:
A. Match these verbs to the meanings and descriptions below. You will use some letters more than once.

a. lay   f. sit
b. lie   g. can
c. raise   h. may
d. rise   i. teach
e. set   j. learn

_____ 1. To give knowledge or instruction
_____ 2. To rest or be seated
_____ 3. To rest or recline
_____ 4. To get up or go up
_____ 5. To gain knowledge
_____ 6. To be able to
_____ 7. To cause (something) to go up or grow up
_____ 8. To be permitted to
_____ 9. To put or place (something) (2 answers)
_____ 10. Verbs that can have a direct object (3 answers)

sentence. Two singular subjects joined by *and* take a plural verb. Two singular subjects joined by *or* take a singular verb.

> Here <u>are</u> a <u>knife</u> and a <u>fork</u> for you. (not <u>is</u>)
> There <u>is</u> an <u>apple</u> or an <u>orange</u> in the bag. (not <u>are</u>)

Remember that the contraction *there's* stands for *there is* and is singular. Likewise, *here's* means *here is* and is singular.

> There'<u>s</u> a new <u>kind</u> of bird in our woods.
> There <u>are</u> many <u>kinds</u> of birds in our woods.

4. *Use* does *and* doesn't *with singular subjects. Use* do *and* don't *with plural subjects, compound subjects, and the pronouns* I *and* you. The most common problem with these words is the contraction *don't*. If you are not sure whether to use *don't* or *doesn't*, try *do not* or *does not* first.

> **Incorrect:** He <u>don't</u> visit us very often.
> > **Compare:** He do not visit us very often.
> **Correct:** He <u>doesn't</u> visit us very often.
> > **Compare:** He does not visit us very often.
> **Correct:** We <u>don't</u> remember what was said.
> > Marie and Karen <u>don't</u> have pencils
> > I <u>don't</u> know the answer.
> > You <u>don't</u> want a goat.

5. *Be sure the subject and verb agree when a prepositional phrase comes between them.* The verb must agree with the subject, not with the object of the preposition.

> subject   object
> ↓   ↓
> The <u>books</u> on this shelf <u>are</u> history books.

The verb agrees with the plural subject *books*, not with *shelf*. Here are two more examples.

> One <u>jar</u> of peaches <u>was</u> spoiled. (not <u>were</u>)
> Several <u>cans</u> of paint <u>were</u> sold. (not <u>was</u>)

B. Cross out each wrong word, and write the correct word.

_____ 1. Please learn me the song you were singing.
_____ 2. The boys were attackted by a swarm of hornets.
_____ 3. Who drug the hose out of the garage?
_____ 4. All the Egyptian soldiers drownded in the sea.
_____ 5. I wish you would of been here yesterday.
_____ 6. Little Anthony tug along behind the rest.
_____ 7. Suddenly a deer bursted into sight.
_____ 8. We should of been walking more quietly.

Quiz Answers:

A. 1. i   6. g
2. f   7. c
3. b   8. h
4. d   9. a, e
5. j   10. a, c, e (*also* i, j)

B. 1. ~~learn~~ teach
2. ~~attackted~~ attacked
3. ~~drug~~ dragged
4. ~~drownded~~ drowned
5. ~~of~~ have
6. ~~tug~~ tagged
7. ~~bursted~~ burst
8. ~~of~~ have

Lesson Introduction: In Acts 15 we read that Paul and Barnabas wanted to go on a second missionary journey together. But they could not agree about taking John Mark along, so they went on separate journeys. Subjects and verbs must also agree in order to work well together. Ask the students what is wrong with the following sentences. (Subjects and verbs do not agree.)

> He don't remember how to do that.
> Jane and Janet is twins.
> There's several blue jays in the maple tree.
> A bushel of apples weigh forty-two pounds.

Today we will see how subjects and verbs should work together.

- Use a singular verb with a singular subject, and a plural verb with a plural subject.

- Use a plural verb with two singular subjects joined by *and.*

- Use a singular verb with two singular subjects joined by *or.*

- Be sure the verb agrees with the subject when a sentence begins with *there* or *here.*

- Use *does* and *doesn't* with singular subjects. Use *do* and *don't* with plural subjects, compound subjects, and the pronouns *I* and *you.*

- Be sure the subject and verb agree when a prepositional phrase comes between them.

Class Practice

Tell which verbs are correct. Check by saying the subjects and verbs together to see if they agree.

1. There (is, are) some fish that can live out of water.
2. The mudskipper and the lungfish (do, does) not spend all their time in water.
3. The African lungfish (live, lives) in water, but it can live out of the water and breathe air for years.
4. (There's, There are) years when rivers dry up, but the lungfish (don't, doesn't) dry out, because it (roll, rolls) itself into a tight ball.
5. It (dig, digs) itself into the mud and (leave, leaves) an air hole, and then it (sleep, sleeps) till the rains come.
6. Here (is, are) some air holes.
7. One of the scientists (dig, digs) up lungfish and (send, sends) them to special aquariums and zoos.
8. A scientist or a zoo keeper carefully (unroll, unrolls) the lungfish.
9. Howard (don't, doesn't) want to lose that interesting fish.
10. One of the men (make, makes) sure the dried lungfish ball does not break.
11. After the lungfish is in water, it (don't, doesn't) waste time waking up; neither (do, does) it stay curled up.

Lesson 54 Answers
Class Practice

1. are
2. do
3. lives
4. There are, doesn't, rolls
5. digs, leaves, sleeps
6. are
7. digs, sends
8. unrolls
9. doesn't
10. makes
11. doesn't, does

Lesson Outline:

1. The verb in a sentence must agree with the subject of the sentence. If the subject is singular, the verb must be singular; and if the subject is plural, the verb must be plural.

2. Sometimes you need to use special care to make sure the verb agrees with the subject.

(1) *Use a plural verb with any two subjects joined by* and.

James and John <u>are</u> brothers. (not *is*)

(2) *Use a singular verb with two singular subjects joined by* or. The verb is singular because only one of the subjects is performing the action.

James or John <u>is planning</u> to go. (not *are planning*)

(3) *Be sure the verb agrees with the subject when a sentence begins with* there *or* here. *There* or *here* is not the subject, even though it begins the sentence. Be careful not to use *there is, there's,* or *there was* with a plural subject or with two singular subjects joined by *and.*

(4) *Use* does *and* doesn't *with singular subjects. Use* do *and* don't *with plural subjects, compound subjects, and the pronouns* I *and* you. If you are not sure whether to use *don't* or *doesn't,* try *do not* or *does not.*

(5) *Be sure the subject and verb agree when a prepositional phrase comes between them.* The verb must agree with the subject, not with the object of the preposition.

★ **EXTRA PRACTICE**
Worksheet 30 *(Subject and Verb Agreement)*

12. It (eat, eats) much food because it (need, needs) to regain the weight it lost in the dry season.

13. A fish with brilliant colors (is, are) swimming below our ship.

14. God (have, has) made all things beautiful, and nature (help, helps) us to see His greatness.

Written Exercises

Write the simple subjects, and then write the correct words in parentheses.

1. (There's, There are) another fish that spends some time out of water.

2. This fish (don't, doesn't) even act like a fish.

3. A mudskipper (climb, climbs) trees, and it (walk, walks), (skip, skips), and (jump, jumps) around on mud flats.

4. It (don't, doesn't) have feet, but its front fins (is, are) almost like legs.

5. Here (is, are) a fish that skips so fast that a person (isn't, aren't) able to keep up.

6. A fly or a beetle (make, makes) a tasty bite for a mudskipper.

7. (Do, Does) you think that a mudskipper and a lungfish really (do, does) act like fish?

8. (There's, There are) an insect that can jump one hundred times its height.

9. Each one of the fleas (have, has) a special joint in its legs, and this joint (help, helps) it to jump.

10. The man with glasses (teach, teaches) fleas to do tricks.

11. Some of his fleas (jump, jumps) through hoops, and others (pull, pulls) little carts around.

12. Most people (don't, doesn't) like fleas, because they (is, are) hard to get rid of.

13. Fleas (have, has) hard, smooth outside skeletons, and they (slip, slips) easily through fur and fingers.

14. A dip in suds (help, helps) to get rid of fleas because they (don't, doesn't) like soap and water.

15. There (is, are) many things that men (don't, doesn't) understand.

16. Even a tiny plant or animal sometimes (present, presents) puzzling questions.

17. The God of all the earth (keep, keeps) us safe in His care.

18. The God of the heavens (love, loves) us and (care, cares) for us.

---

12. eats, needs
13. is
14. has, helps

Written Exercises

(Simple subjects are underlined for clarity.)

1. <u>fish</u>, There's
2. <u>fish</u>, doesn't
3. <u>mudskipper</u>, climbs; <u>it</u>, walks, skips, jumps
4. <u>It</u>, doesn't; <u>fins</u>, are
5. <u>fish</u>, is; <u>person</u>, isn't
6. <u>fly</u> (or) <u>beetle</u>, makes
7. <u>you</u>, Do; <u>mudskipper</u> (and) <u>lungfish</u>, do
8. <u>insect</u>, There's
9. <u>one</u>, has; <u>joint</u>, helps
10. <u>man</u>, teaches
11. <u>Some</u>, jump; <u>others</u>, pull
12. <u>people</u>, don't; <u>they</u>, are
13. <u>Fleas</u>, have; <u>they</u>, slip
14. <u>dip</u>, helps; <u>they</u>, don't
15. <u>things</u>, are; <u>men</u>, don't
16. <u>plant</u> (or) <u>animal</u>, presents
17. <u>God</u>, keeps
18. <u>God</u>, loves, cares

Review Exercises

A. Write all three principal parts of each verb. Use *have* with the past participle. [30, 31]

1. find
2. puff
3. slip
4. leave
5. raise
6. lie
7. lay
8. let

B. Write the correct past form of each verb in parentheses. If the helping verb *have, has,* or *had* is used in the sentence, write the helping verb and the past participle. [31]

    Example: I have never (fly) in an airplane.
    Answer: have flown

1. Irma has (find) the answer.
2. We (leave) some books there for you.
3. Floyd (raise) his hand.
4. My cat (lie) in the sun all morning.
5. The men have (lay) the carpet already.
6. Our visitors had (ring) the doorbell several times.
7. The mothers (bring) the children to school.
8. My dog has (dig) another hole in Mother's garden.
9. I have (tag) you, and now you are caught.
10. Mary Beth had never (wear) that dress before.
11. I (send) the letter yesterday.
12. My aunt has often (let) me help her with the baking.

Review Exercises

A.
1. find, found, (have) found
2. puff, puffed, (have) puffed
3. slip, slipped, (have) slipped
4. leave, left, (have) left
5. raise, raised, (have) raised
6. lie, lay, (have) lain
7. lay, laid, (have) laid
8. let, let, (have) let

B.
1. has found
2. left
3. raised
4. lay
5. have laid
6. had rung
7. brought
8. has dug
9. have tagged
10. had worn
11. sent
12. has let

55. Active and Passive Voice

You have learned that a transitive verb is an action verb that passes its action to another word in the sentence. The word that receives the action is usually the direct object.

> Lot chose the best land.
>
> Lot chose what? *Land* receives the action of the verb *chose.*

However, transitive verbs do not always pass their action to a direct object. Notice that the sentence below means exactly the same thing as the one above. But *land,* which had been the direct object, is now the subject.

> The best land was chosen by Lot.

Who or what receives the action of *chosen*? The receiver is still *land.* But in this sentence, the transitive verb passes its action back to the *subject.*

You can now see that a transitive verb may pass its action to either of two receivers: the *direct object* or the *subject.* This difference in receivers is what determines the *voice* of the verb.

When a transitive verb passes its action to a direct object, the verb is in the *active voice.* The subject in such a sentence is *active;* it *performs* the action of the verb. In each of the following sentences, the subject is underlined. Notice how the subject performs the action, and the direct object receives the action.

Active voice:
> A huge <u>giant</u> challenged the Israelites.

giant	challenged	Israelites

> <u>David</u> chose five smooth stones.

David	chose	stones

> The humble shepherd <u>boy</u> killed Goliath.

boy	killed	Goliath

Lesson 55

Purpose: (1) To introduce the concept of *voice for transitive verbs. (2) To show *the difference between active and passive voice.

Oral Review:
1. What do we mean when we say that the subject and verb of a sentence must agree? (If the subject is singular, the verb must be singular. If the subject is plural, the verb must be plural.)
2. Give the meaning of *singular* and *plural.* (A singular word refers to only one, and a plural word refers to more than one.)
3. Is *don't* singular or plural? (plural)
4. (*a*) If a sentence has a compound subject, when should the verb be singular? (*b*) When should it be plural? (*a.* when singular subjects are joined by *or;* *b.* when any two subjects are joined by *and*)

Lesson Introduction: Some children are very *active.* They always seem to be running, jumping, shouting, and playing. Others are *passive.* They are more quiet, and they allow others to perform the action while they watch. Instead of making things happen, they let things happen to them.

Sentences are much like children in this respect. Sometimes the subject of a sentence is active, and sometimes it is passive. For this reason we have *active voice* and *passive voice,* as we will study in this lesson.

When a transitive verb passes its action back to the subject, the verb is in the *passive voice.* The subject in such a sentence is not active. It is *passive;* it *receives* the action of the verb. In each of the following sentences, the subject is underlined. Notice how the subject receives the action of the verb rather than doing it. Also notice that the sentences do not have direct objects.

Passive voice:
The Israelites were challenged by a huge giant.

Israelites	were challenged

Five smooth stones were chosen by David.

stones	were chosen

Goliath was killed by the humble shepherd boy.

Goliath	was killed

When a simple predicate is in the passive voice, it is always a verb phrase. The helping verb is a form of *be,* and the main verb is a past participle. If any of these is missing, you can be sure that a verb is not in the passive voice. Look at the following sentences. Can you tell which one is in the passive voice?

The Philistines fled in great fear.
The Israelites were destroying their enemies.
David was praised by the women.

The first sentence does not contain a verb phrase, so it cannot be passive. The second sentence contains a verb phrase with a form of *be,* but the main verb is not a past participle. It cannot be passive either. The third sentence contains a verb phrase in which the helping verb is a form of *be* and the main verb is a past participle. So the third sentence is in the passive voice. Another proof is the fact that *David* receives the action of *praised.*

Lesson Outline:

1. A transitive verb can pass its action to either of two receivers: the **direct** *object or the* **subject.**

2. When a transitive verb passes its action to a direct object, the verb is in the **active voice.** The subject in such a sentence is *active;* it performs the action of the verb.

3. When a transitive verb passes its action back to the subject, the verb is in the **passive voice.** The subject in such a sentence is not active but passive. It receives the action instead of performing the action.

4. A simple predicate in the passive voice is always a verb phrase. The helping verb is a form of be, and the main verb is a past participle.

- A transitive verb may be in the *active voice* or the *passive voice*.

- When a transitive verb is in the active voice, the subject performs the action and the direct object receives the action.

- When a transitive verb is in the passive voice, the subject receives the action and there is no direct object.

- A simple predicate in the passive voice is always a verb phrase. The helping verb is a form of *be*, and the main verb is a past participle.

Class Practice

A. In each sentence, tell which word is the receiver of the action and whether that word is the *subject* or the *direct object*. Then tell whether the verb is in the *active* or the *passive* voice.
   1. A large, colorful poster was drawn by him.
   2. The steers are breaking the gate.
   3. We found a turtle under the bridge.
   4. Letters were sent by the parents.
   5. Many bugs are eaten by bluebirds and swallows.
   6. The children ate the doughnuts.
   7. My uncle Amos lays concrete blocks.
   8. The four melons were taken by the second customer.
   9. I know the answer.
   10. We were greeted by the new teacher.

B. In Part A, pick out the form of *be* and the past participle that is used in each sentence with a passive verb.

Written Exercises

A. For each sentence, copy the word that receives the action. Write whether it is the *subject* or the *direct object,* and whether the verb is in the *active* or the *passive* voice.
   1. At the brook Cherith, Elijah was fed by ravens.
   2. Ravens brought bread and meat to Elijah.
   3. Later, a widow made cakes for Elijah.
   4. The meal and oil were supplied by the Lord.
   5. A sudden illness took the son's life.

Lesson 55 Answers
Class Practice
A. 1. poster—subject—passive
    2. gate—direct object—active
    3. turtle—direct object—active
    4. Letters—subject—passive
    5. bugs—subject—passive
    6. doughnuts—direct object—active
    7. blocks—direct object—active
    8. melons—subject—passive
    9. answer—direct object—active
    10. We—subject—passive

B. (In each verb phrase, the first word is the form of *be* and the second is the past participle.)
    1. was drawn
    4. were sent
    5. are eaten
    8. were taken
    10. were greeted

Written Exercises
A. 1. Elijah—subject—passive
    2. bread (and) meat—direct object—active
    3. cakes—direct object—active
    4. meal (and) oil—subject—passive
    5. life—direct object—active

6. He was restored to life by Elijah.
7. The child was carried back to his mother.
8. After this, the woman believed Elijah's words.

B. Copy the subject of each sentence, and write whether it is the *doer* or the *receiver* of the action. Then write whether the voice of the verb is *active* or *passive*.
  1. James tears the cloth into strips.
  2. The papers were gathered by us.
  3. We had gathered the papers for them.
  4. Someone inside raised the window.
  5. Carpets are woven by Indians and Iranians.
  6. Indians and Iranians have woven beautiful carpets.
  7. The bus is driven by Brother Wilson.
  8. The flowers were picked by them.
  9. They did pick these flowers.
 10. The bushes were covered by fresh white snow.

C. Copy only the verb phrases that are in the passive voice. Draw one line under the form of *be* and two lines under the past participle (the main verb).
  1. The fresh white snow covered even the bushes.
  2. Some money was found by my little sister.
  3. My little sister found some money.
  4. The class is beginning the test eagerly.
  5. Moles and shrews are hunted by this cat.
  6. The wrong instructions were given.
  7. Mrs. Porter speaks Spanish.
  8. The tree was shaken by the boys.

Review Exercises

Diagram the skeleton of each sentence. Include any direct or indirect objects, predicate nominatives, and predicate adjectives. [38–43]
  1. Silkworm farms in Japan raise silkworms by the billions and mulberry trees by the millions.
  2. Do silkworms eat mulberry leaves?
  3. After several weeks the silkworm spins itself a cocoon.
  4. Farmers send the cocoons to a factory, and big machines unwind the thin threads off each cocoon.

---

6. He—subject—passive
7. child—subject—passive
8. words—direct object—active

B. 1. James—doer—active
  2. papers—receiver—passive
  3. We—doer—active
  4. Someone—doer—active
  5. Carpets—receiver—passive
  6. Indians (and) Iranians—doer—active
  7. bus—receiver—passive
  8. flowers—receiver—passive
  9. They—doer—active
 10. bushes—receiver—passive

C. 2. <u>was</u> <u><u>found</u></u>
  5. <u>are</u> <u><u>hunted</u></u>
  6. <u>were</u> <u><u>given</u></u>
  8. <u>was</u> <u><u>shaken</u></u>

Review Exercises

1.

2. silkworms | Do eat | leaves

3.

4. Farmers | send | cocoons and machines | unwind | threads

5. First they must unwind the thread of twenty thousand cocoons, and then they can make one pound of silk.
6. Farmers do not send all their cocoons to the factory.
7. Moths come out of some cocoons and lay hundreds of eggs.
8. Soon the eggs hatch, and more worms are spinning silk.
9. Silk is a beautiful cloth, but it is quite expensive.

---

56. Writing a Report: First Draft

You have learned how to take notes from several reference sources and use them to make an outline. Now you are ready to write a report by using the notes you took and the outline you made.

Here is a sample outline on "The Habits of Alligators." It was made by using notes taken on the two reference sources in Lesson 50.

The Habits of Alligators

I. Keeping warm or cool enough
  A. Basking in the sun
  B. Hiding in burrows
II. Digging burrows, dens, and "gator holes"
  A. Size and shape
  B. Usefulness
    1. Hibernation
    2. Help to other animals
III. Eating habits
  A. What they eat
    1. Mostly fish
    2. Different foods according to size
    3. Special treats
    4. Unusual objects
  B. How they catch food
    1. At night
    2. Under water
    3. With help of tail

5. they | must unwind | thread _and_ they | can make | poun
6. Farmers | do send | cocoons
7. Moths |< come _and_ lay | hundreds
8. eggs | hatch _and_ worms | are spinning | silk
9. silk | is \ cloth _but_ it | is \ expensive

Lesson 56

Purpose: To teach how to write the first draft of a report by using notes that have been organized into an outline.

Oral Review:
1. Why should the notes for a report be organized? (so that the report will be orderly and meaningful)
2. In what order should the main ideas of a report be arranged? (in a sensible order; in such a way that one idea logically follows another)
3. Why should you keep your notes after you have made an outline? (You may need to refer to them to add meaningful details to your report.)
4. In writing directions, what order should you use? (the order of time; the order things are to be done)
5. What points should you remember when you write directions? (Make sure the information is accurate. Write clearly so that the directions can be understood easily. Use transitional words to make the directions more coherent.)

Lesson Introduction: When you take a trip, one of the first steps is to map out the route you will travel. You are not ready to start driving until you know where you will drive! After the route has been planned, you can travel easily to your destination by simply following your directions.

When you write a report, you must also plan before you begin. You have already done that planning in two previous lessons. Now you are ready to follow the route you have mapped out with your outline, and to begin your "journey."

Lesson Outline:
1. Decide what to put into each paragraph.
  a. Plan one paragraph for each topic or sub-topic on the outline.

IV. Nesting habits
    A. Construction of nest
    B. Description of eggs
    C. Fierce guarding by female
V. Caring for young alligators
    A. Setting young free
    B. Feeding the young
VI. Sounds made by alligators
    A. Mother alligators' calls
    B. Baby alligators' cries
    C. Young alligators' bellows
    D. Adult alligators' roars

How can we write a report from this outline? Reports are usually written in two drafts. The first draft is the rough, unpolished form of the report, and the second draft is the report in its finished form. This lesson deals with writing the first draft, which includes two steps.

Step 1: *Decide what to put into each paragraph.* This can be done by planning one paragraph for each topic or subtopic on the outline. So the first paragraph in the sample report will tell how alligators keep warm or cool enough.

The first sentence in a report introduces the whole report as well as the first paragraph. So the topic sentence of the first paragraph should be written in such a way that it does both. And the last sentence of the last paragraph should be written in such a way that it gives a finishing touch to your report.

Step 2: *Write your first draft.* After you write each topic sentence, develop the paragraph for each by using the information on your outline. Include interesting details from the notes you took; they are like spice in your report.

Write in complete sentences, leaving every other line blank so that you can mark changes later. In your first draft, do not worry about getting everything perfect. Concentrate on following your outline and getting the information into your report. Keep writing even if you are not satisfied with some of your sentences. The next lesson will show you how to improve your report before you write the second draft. The following sample shows the first three paragraphs of a report based on the outline.

    b. The first sentence in a report should introduce the whole report as well as the first paragraph.
    c. The last sentence of the last paragraph should give a finishing touch to the report.

2. Write your first draft.
    a. For each paragraph, write a topic sentence that tells what the rest of the paragraph is about.
    b. Develop each paragraph by using the information on your outline. Check your notes for interesting details. These details help to make your report interesting and meaningful.
    c. Write in complete sentences.
    d. Write on every other line so that you have room to mark changes later.

The Habits of Alligators

If you ever see an alligator during the day, he will probably be basking in the sunshine. This creature spends much time warming himself in the sun because he is a cold-blooded animal. But sometimes an alligator gets too warm and needs to find a cool place. Then he may hide under water, under bushes, or in a burrow or den.

An alligator digs out a burrow or den by using his long snout. He washes away the mud by waving his long tail back and forth. The burrow may be as much as forty feet long and may have a large room at the end. In winter the alligator may hibernate in his burrow. He may also dig a hole in the deepest part of a swamp or pond and stay there over winter. This "gator hole" helps to save other animals when the rest of the swamp or pond dries up.

Most of the alligator's food is fish. Baby alligators eat small things like water insects, and adult alligators may eat raccoons or muskrats. Alligators in zoos or parks like to eat marshmallows and sandwiches. If anything is thrown at them, they seem to think it is food! Alligators also swallow hard objects such as rocks and pieces of wood. They do not use their teeth to chew their food, but they swallow it whole. The hard objects may help to grind the food in their stomachs.

• To begin writing a report from an outline, use the following steps.
  1. Decide what to put into each paragraph.
  2. Write your first draft.

Class Practice

A. Study the following paragraphs, which are based on the fourth main topic of the outline. Which is the better paragraph? Tell what is wrong with the other one.

1. Alligators build nests. I read once that they use mostly cattails. They probably push them together with their feet. The size of the nest is really big. She lays many eggs, too, and they are quite large. Alligators stay nearby to guard their eggs. One time I saw a picture of one with her chin right on the nest, but maybe it was a crocodile. Alligators and crocodiles do look alike in many ways.

Lesson 56 Answers
Class Practice

A. Paragraph 2 is better.

Paragraph 1 includes too many details from the imagination. It uses uncertain terms such as *probably* and *maybe*. It uses vague descriptions like *really big* and *quite large*. Some ideas are not taken from the notes, and the last sentence does not even fit the topic of the paragraph.

2.   The female builds a nest by scooping together leaves, grass, cattails, mud, and decaying vegetation. Her nest may be a mound as much as seven feet wide and three feet high. In it she lays twenty-five to sixty eggs the size of a large goose egg. Then she covers the eggs with nesting material and stays nearby to guard them from predators. They are warmed by the sun and by decaying vegetation until they hatch.

B. Study the following paragraphs, which are based on the sixth main topic of the outline. Which is the better paragraph? Tell what is wrong with the other one.

1.   Alligators make a variety of sounds. Mothers call their young with a sound that sounds like a pig grunting. A baby makes a high-pitched cry until he is four years old. Then his voice changes, and he begins practicing to bellow. His bellows gradually become stronger, and finally he can roar so loudly that the ground trembles and he can be heard over a mile away! God certainly made an interesting animal when He made the alligator.

2.   Alligators make interesting sounds. Mother alligators call their babies. Baby alligators cry. Young alligators bellow. Adult alligators roar.

Written Exercises

Begin writing a report from your outline on "The Body of an Alligator." Follow the steps given in the lesson.

Review Exercises

Copy each verb or verb phrase, and write whether it is an *action* or a *linking* verb. If it is a linking verb, write the word in the predicate that is linked to the subject. [44]
1. We looked out the window.
2. The sky looked dark.
3. On Friday the sky had been cloudy all day.
4. This tastes homemade.
5. Mother tasted the soup.
6. It tasted salty.

B. Paragraph 1 is better.

Paragraph 2 has only the bare facts of the outline. It does not describe the different sounds or give any other interesting details.

Written Exercises

(Individual work. You need not take grades on this lesson, since pupils are simply writing the first draft of their reports.)

Review Exercises

1. looked—action
2. looked—linking, dark
3. had been—linking, cloudy
4. tastes—linking, homemade
5. tasted—action
6. tasted—linking, salty

57. Writing a Report: Second Draft

You should usually not try to write the first and second draft of a composition all at one time. It is better to lay aside the first draft at least until the next day and then come back to it. In this way, you will have a fresh view of your work and you will be better able to see what improvements are needed.

In Lesson 56 you studied the two steps for writing the first draft of a report. They are shown here.

Step 1: *Decide what to put into each paragraph.*

Step 2: *Write your first draft.*

To write the second draft of your report, follow steps 3 and 4.

Step 3: *Proofread the first draft.* This means you should look for ways to improve it. Check for mistakes in spelling, punctuation, and grammar. Reword sentences that do not read smoothly and clearly. Improve your sentence variety by making some longer sentences and some shorter sentences. Use different types of sentences and different kinds of word order. All these changes can be marked in the blank spaces that you left when you wrote your first draft. Notice the following examples.

Original:

An alligator sometimes gets too warm. He needs to find a cool place. He may hide in a burrow or den.
(choppy sentences without variety)

Revised:

An alligator sometimes gets too warm and needs to find a cool place. He may hide in a burrow or den.
(two sentences joined with compound predicate)

Revised:

Sometimes an alligator gets too warm and needs to find a cool place. Then he may hide in a burrow or den.
(sentences with varied beginnings)

Original:

They seem to think that anything thrown at them is food.
(declarative sentence with common word order)

Revised:

If anything is thrown at them, they seem to think it is food!
(exclamatory sentence with more interesting word order)

Lesson 57

Purpose: To teach how to write the second draft of a report by revising and rewriting the first draft.

Oral Review:

1. The notes for a report should be organized into an ————. (outline)
2. True or false: An outline should include all the details that you plan to put into your report. (false)
3. What are the two steps in writing the first draft of a report? (Step 1: Decide what to put into each paragraph. Step 2: Write your first draft.)
4. (*a*) What is the first draft of a report? (*b*) What is the second draft? (*a*. the report in its rough, unpolished form; *b*. the report in its finished form)

Lesson Introduction: Continue the comparison between taking a trip and writing a report. Ask, "Have you ever watched a driver's hands on the steering wheel as you were riding down the road?" His hands are never motionless very long. Even though the driver knows exactly where he is going, he must still make constant, small "course corrections" to keep the car on the road. He cannot set the steering wheel at one point and expect to arrive at his destination—even if the road is perfectly straight.

The same is true when you write a report. No matter how well you plan it, you must make many small corrections along the way in order to arrive at your destination—an interesting, well-written report.

Lesson Outline:

(*Teacher:* Points 1 and 2 are a review of Lesson 56.)

1. Decide what to put into each paragraph.

2. Write your first draft.

3. Proofread the first draft. Mark changes in the blank spaces that you left when you wrote your first draft.

   a. Check for mistakes in spelling, punctuation, and grammar.

   b. Try to improve the sentence variety. Use some longer sentences and some shorter sentences. Use different types of sentences and different kinds of word order.

4. Write your second draft. Rewrite the report, making the corrections you have marked.

Do not be afraid to make changes. Cross out words, rewrite sentences, add ideas, and remove anything you do not like. Even the best writers mark their first drafts with many changes!

Step 4: *Write your second draft.* Rewrite the report, making the corrections you have marked. Follow the points below to give a neat, attractive appearance to your report.

1. Use composition paper rather than tablet paper.
2. If you write with ink, use either blue or black.
3. Use neat handwriting, and write on only one side of each page.
4. Center the title on the top line.
5. Leave a blank line between the title and the report.
6. Leave margins along both edges of the paper, and keep them as straight as you can.
7. Leave a margin at the bottom of each page. Do not write on the last two or three lines.
8. Follow any other directions that your teacher gives.

- To write a report from an outline, use the following steps.
  1. Decide what to put into each paragraph.
  2. Write your first draft.
  3. Proofread the first draft.
  4. Write your second draft.

Class Practice

Improve these sentences as indicated in parentheses.
1. Alligators are reptiles. Crocodiles are reptiles too. (Join into one sentence with a compound subject.)
2. A mother alligator will not leave you come near her nest. (Correct the grammar.)
3. Baby alligators eat small things like water insects, adult alligators may eat raccoons or muskrats. (Correct the run-on error.)
4. A big man put a big box on a big shelf. (Avoid repetition by using other words for *big*.)
5. The shelf and everything on it came down. (Change to an exclamatory sentence beginning with *down.*)

Lesson 57 Answers
Class Practice
1. Alligators and crocodiles are reptiles.
2. A mother alligator will not <u>let</u> you come near her nest.
3. Baby alligators eat small things like water insects, <u>and</u> adult alligators may eat raccoons or muskrats.
4. A <u>tall</u> man put a <u>heavy</u> box on a <u>wide</u> shelf.
5. Down came the shelf and everything on it!

Written Exercises, Part B *(continued)*
The Body of an Alligator

The alligator is a large reptile with a long, flat head. His eyes, ears, and nose are the highest points on his head so that he can hide under water with only those parts showing. He has a long snout, and his mouth is filled with heavy, sharp teeth. An alligator's jaws are so powerful that they can crush the bones of large animals. But when his jaws are shut, a man can hold them closed with his bare hands. His throat has a little flap that closes to keep water out. He also has a set of transparent eyelids that let him see under water. Though his ears are hidden under flaps, he can hear very well.

An alligator has a long, low body. He uses his powerful tail to swim and sometimes to knock fish toward his mouth. His legs are short, and he uses his webbed hind feet to paddle in shallow water. On land he is usually slow and clumsy, and he tires easily. A newly hatched alligator is only about nine inches long, but he grows about one foot every year! The largest alligators are about twelve feet long and weigh about five hundred pounds.

The scales of an alligator's skin are like black bony plates, and they are so tough that long ago not even bullets could penetrate them. The alligator has no sweat glands, and this helps to keep his body from drying out. The color of his skin is an attractive dull olive gray. Young alligators have yellow markings on the skin, but these fade away later. Truly the alligator was fearfully and wonderfully made by our wise Creator.

6. Jesus told a story about a woman. She had ten coins. (Change *she* to *who,* and join into one sentence.)
7. You can imagine how the woman felt when she lost one coin. (Change to an imperative sentence.)
8. She wondered where it could be. (Change to an interrogative sentence.)
9. The women lighted a lamp swept her house and searched carefuly for the coin. (Correct two spelling errors, and add the missing commas.)
10. She was very glad when she found the coin. (Change to an exclamatory sentence beginning with *how.*)

Written Exercises

A. Proofread the first draft of your report "The Body of an Alligator." Mark the changes that should be made. Keep your corrected first draft for your teacher to see.

B. Rewrite your report, making the changes you marked.

---

58. More About Active and Passive Voice

In Chapter 4 you studied the three simple verb tenses: present tense, past tense, and future tense. You changed from one tense to another by using a different principal part. Here is the verb *find* in all three tenses, in the active voice.

Active voice:
Present tense: He <u>finds</u> his lost eraser. (present form)
Past tense: He <u>found</u> his lost eraser. (past form)
Future tense: He <u>will find</u> his lost eraser.
                             (present form with *will*)

Passive verbs also have these three tenses. But you cannot change from one tense to another by using a different principal part, for the main verb is always a past participle. Instead, you must use a different form of the helping verb *be.* See how these changes are made in the following sentences.

6. Jesus told a story about a woman who had ten coins.
7. Imagine how the woman felt when she lost one coin.
8. Where could it be?
9. The <u>woman</u> lighted a lamp, swept her house, and searched <u>carefully</u> for the coin.
10. How glad she was when she found the coin!

Written Exercises

A. (Individual work. It is suggested that you look at each pupil's corrected first draft and make helpful suggestions before he writes the second draft.)

B. (Individual work. Check pupils' reports specifically for the points mentioned in Step 3: *Proofread the first draft.* Those points are summarized here.
   1. Correct spelling, punctuation, and grammar.
   2. Smoothness and clarity of expression.
   3. Variety in sentence lengths, sentence types, and word order in sentences.)

(Sample report is on page 253.)

Lesson 58

Purpose: To further develop the concepts of active and passive voice.

Oral Review:

1. What two kinds of voice do verbs have? (active, passive)
2. True or false: A verb has voice only if it is transitive. (true)
3. What is the voice of the verb when the subject performs the action? (active)
4. What is the voice of the verb when the subject receives the action? (passive)
5. Describe the simple predicate when a verb is in the passive voice. (It is a verb phrase in which a form of *be* is used with a past participle.)
6. What do we mean when we say that the subject and verb of a sentence must agree? (If the subject is singular, the verb must be singular. If the subject is plural, the verb must be plural.)
7. Give the meaning of *singular* and *plural.* (A singular word refers to only one, and a plural word refers to more than one.)
8. (*a*) If a sentence has a compound subject, when should the verb be singular? (*b*) When should it be plural? (*a.* when singular subjects are joined by *or; b.* when singular or plural subjects are joined by *and*)

Written Quiz:

Underline the correct words in parentheses.
   1. A (direct object, predicate nominative) is a noun or pronoun that receives the action of a verb.
   2. A (linking, transitive) verb passes action to a receiver.

Passive voice:
   Present tense: His lost eraser <u>is found</u>. (present form of *be*)
   Past tense: His lost eraser <u>was found</u>. (past form of *be*)
   Future tense: His lost eraser <u>will be found</u>.
                 (present form of *be* with *will*)

Sentences can easily be changed from active voice to passive voice. To do this, reword the sentence so that the direct object becomes the subject. Change the simple predicate to a verb phrase in which the helping verb is a form of *be* and the main verb is a past participle. See how this is done in the following sentences.

direct object

Active voice: Brother Charles introduced the <u>visitors</u>.

subject

Passive voice: The <u>visitors</u> were introduced by Brother Charles.

Sentences can also be changed from passive voice to active voice. This is done by changing the subject to the direct object. Study this change in the following sentences.

subject

Passive voice: The <u>barn</u> was rebuilt by members of the church.

direct object

Active voice: Members of the church rebuilt the <u>barn</u>.

In most writing, the active voice is better because it is more direct and forceful than the passive voice. Compare the following sentences. Which one states the fact more effectively?

   A good sermon was preached by Brother Noah.
   Brother Noah preached a good sermon.

However, there are two cases when you may want to use the passive voice in writing. First, you can use it sometimes for the sake of variety. Second, you can use it when the doer of an action is not known or is not important in a sentence. Here are two examples.

   The train was delayed for three hours.
      (We do not know what delayed the train.)

3. A (predicate adjective, predicate nominative) follows a linking verb and modifies the subject.
4. A (predicate adjective, predicate nominative) follows a linking verb and renames the subject.
5. (A direct object, An indirect object) tells *to whom or what* or *for whom or what* the action of the verb is done.
6. (Singular, Plural) words refer to only one.
7. The contraction *don't* is (singular, plural).
8. If a sentence has two subjects joined by *and,* the verb should be (singular, plural).
9. When the subject receives the action, the verb is in the (active, passive) voice.
10. When the subject performs the action, the verb is in the (active, passive) voice.

Quiz Answers:
   1. direct object
   2. transitive
   3. predicate adjective
   4. predicate nominative
   5. An indirect object
   6. Singular
   7. plural
   8. plural
   9. passive
   10. active

Lesson Introduction: Read the following paragraph to your students and see if they like it.

> Yesterday at recess softball was played. When it was my turn to hit, the bat was swung by me with all my might. But the ball was hit to Michael and was caught. Next a home run was hit. After that, two more outs were made and the field was taken by us. Two fly balls were caught, and the third batter was put out at first. Then the bell was rung, and our game was over.

Can they tell why it sounds so clumsy and roundabout? Every sentence is in the passive voice. Passive voice is important and useful, but we must know how to use it properly. Compare the following paragraph.

> Yesterday at recess we played softball. When it was my turn to hit, I swung the bat with all my might. But I hit the ball to Michael, and he caught it. Next Jason hit a home run. After that, our team made two more outs and we took the field. Robert caught two fly balls, and Jason put the third batter out at first. Then the teacher rang the bell, and our game was over.

The Panama Canal was finished in 1914.
(The doer of the action is not important in the sentence.)

- To change a sentence from active voice to passive voice, change the direct object to the subject. Change the simple predicate to a verb phrase in which a form of *be* is used with the past participle of the main verb.

- To change a sentence from passive voice to active voice, change the subject to the direct object.

- In most writing, the active voice is better because it is more direct and forceful than the passive voice.

Class Practice

A. Change each verb to the past tense and the future tense, but keep them in the passive voice.
1. Twelve barrels of water are poured onto Elijah's altar.
2. The sacrifice, the water, and the wood are burned up.
3. A great rain is sent from God.

B. Change these sentences to the active voice.
1. The songbooks were distributed by Nelson.
2. The morning message was brought by Brother John.
3. The students were taken to the museum by the parents.
4. A two-hour traffic jam was caused by the accident.

C. Change these sentences to the passive voice.
1. God answered Elijah's prayer.
2. The fire licked up even the water in the ditch.
3. The rainstorm drenched Ahab.

Written Exercises

A. Rewrite each sentence in the past tense and the future tense, but keep the passive voice.
1. Elijah is given strength for forty days.
2. God's voice is heard in the cave.
3. Rocks are crumbled by a strong wind.
4. The ground is shaken by an earthquake.
5. Many trees are burned by the fire.

Lesson Outline:

1. Both active and passive verbs have different tenses. In the active voice, tenses are changed by using a different principal part of the main verb. In the passive voice, tenses are changed by using a different form of the helping verb *be.*

2. To change a sentence from active voice to passive voice, change the direct object to the subject. Also change the simple predicate to a verb phrase in which the helping verb is a form of *be* and the main verb is a past participle.

3. To change a sentence from passive voice to active voice, change the subject to the direct object.

Lesson 58 Answers
Class Practice

A. 1. Twelve barrels of water were poured onto Elijah's altar.
Twelve barrels of water will be poured onto Elijah's altar.
2. The sacrifice, the water, and the wood were burned up.
The sacrifice, the water, and the wood will be burned up.
3. A great rain was sent from God.
A great rain will be sent from God.

B. 1. Nelson distributed the songbooks.
2. Brother John brought the morning message.
3. The parents took the students to the museum.
4. The accident caused a two-hour traffic jam.

C. 1. Elijah's prayer was answered by God.
2. Even the water in the ditch was licked up by the fire.
3. Ahab was drenched by the rainstorm.

Written Exercises

A. 1. Elijah was given strength for forty days.
Elijah will be given strength for forty days.
2. God's voice was heard in the cave.
God's voice will be heard in the cave.
3. Rocks were crumbled by a strong wind.
Rocks will be crumbled by a strong wind.
4. The ground was shaken by an earthquake.
The ground will be shaken by an earthquake.
5. Many trees were burned by the fire.
Many trees will be burned by the fire.

---

4. Usually, the active voice is better because it is more direct and forceful than the passive voice.
a. The passive voice can be used for variety.
b. The passive voice can be used when the doer of an action is not known or is not important in a sentence.

> A question was raised about the homework assignment.
> The service was prolonged for fifteen more minutes.

★ **EXTRA PRACTICE**
Worksheet 31 *(Active and Passive Voice)*

B. Change these sentences to the passive voice.
1. God called Elijah to serve Him.
2. God protected Elijah.
3. Elijah taught the people.

C. Change these sentences to the active voice.
1. A still, small voice was heard by Elijah.
2. God was still worshiped by seven thousand people.
3. Elisha was anointed by Elijah.
4. Elijah was followed by Elisha.

D. In three of the passive sentences below, the doer of the action is named in a prepositional phrase. Such sentences would be more forceful in the active voice. In the other three sentences, the doer is not named because it is unknown or unimportant. The passive voice is better in those sentences.

Find each sentence in which the doer is named in a prepositional phrase, and rewrite it in the active voice.
1. The corn was bought by Mrs. Brown.
2. A message was sent to me.
3. My bicycle was stolen last night.
4. This package was sent from Grandmother.
5. The windows were cleaned by Sarah.
6. Dessert will be served soon.

Review Exercises

Write the correct verbs. [54]
1. Gerald always (do, does) the charts.
2. He (don't, doesn't) often forget.
3. There (is, are) several right ways to do it.
4. (There's, There are) a bluebird and a junco in that tree.
5. A sparrow or a starling (have, has) built this nest.
6. Mary and Martha (was, were) special friends of Jesus.

Challenge Exercises

Improve this paragraph by using the active voice in more of the sentences.

Jesus was followed by great crowds of people. A leper came and fell on his face before Jesus. Jesus was worshiped by the leper. "You can heal me if You are willing," he said. Jesus was moved with compassion and said, "I am willing." The leper was touched by Jesus and

B. 1. Elijah was called by God to serve Him.
2. Elijah was protected by God.
3. The people were taught by Elijah.

C. 1. Elijah heard a still, small voice.
2. Seven thousand people still worshiped God.
3. Elijah anointed Elisha.
4. Elisha followed Elijah.

D. 1. Mrs. Brown bought the corn.
4. Grandmother sent this package.
5. Sarah cleaned the windows.

Review Exercises

1. does
2. doesn't
3. are
4. There are
5. has
6. were

Challenge Exercises

(Sample paragraph.)

Great crowds of people followed Jesus. A leper came, fell on his face before Jesus, and worshiped Him. "You can heal me if You are willing," he said. Jesus was moved with compassion and said, "I am willing." Jesus touched the leper and healed him immediately. Jesus told the leper to show himself to the priest and to tell no one else. But the leper spread abroad the news of Jesus' kind deed.

was healed immediately. The leper was told by Jesus to show himself to the priest and to tell no one else. But the news of Jesus' kind deed was spread abroad by the leper.

———————————

59. Chapter 5 Review

Class Practice

A. Give the principal parts of each verb.

Present	Past	Past Participle
1. leave	——	——
2. drag	——	——
3. tag	——	——
4. burst	——	——
5. drown	——	——
6. attack	——	——
7. teach	——	——

B. Give the correct verbs from the following list.

lay	set	can
lie	sit	may
raise	let	teach
rise	leave	learn

1. Which verbs have these meanings?
   a. To get up or go up
   b. To rest or be seated
   c. To be able to
   d. To be permitted to
   e. To cause (something) to go up or grow up
   f. To give knowledge or instruction
   g. To depart or go away from
   h. To rest or recline
   i. To allow or permit
   j. To gain knowledge

Lesson 59 Answers
Class Practice

A. (Words in italics are given in the pupil's text.)

1. *leave*	left	(have) left
2. *drag*	dragged	(have) dragged
3. *tag*	tagged	(have) tagged
4. *burst*	burst	(have) burst
5. *drown*	drowned	(have) drowned
6. *attack*	attacked	(have) attacked
7. *teach*	taught	(have) taught

B. 1.
   a. rise   f. teach
   b. sit   g. leave
   c. can   h. lie
   d. may   i. let
   e. raise   j. learn

Lesson 59

Purpose: To review the concepts taught in Chapter 5.

2. Which two verbs mean "to put or place (something)"?
3. Which verb is the present form of *left*?
4. Which verbs may be followed by direct objects?
5. Which verb is always followed by another verb form, expressed or understood?

C. Tell which words receive the action of the verbs. Tell whether each receiver is a *subject* or a *direct object*. Also tell whether the verb is in the *active* or the *passive* voice.
   1. Rebekah covered Jacob's hands and neck with goats' skins.
   2. Jacob's hands and neck were covered with goats' skins.
   3. Isaac blessed Jacob.
   4. Jacob was blessed by Isaac.

D. Give the correct words.
   1. When you prepare to write a report, you should take ——— on the information you find in reference sources.
   2. You should get information from (only one, more than one) reference source.
   3. You (may, must not) copy whole sentences and paragraphs.
   4. You should take notes on (all the points, every point that fits your chosen topic).
   5. You should organize your notes into an ———.
   6. All the points in your notes (need, do not need) to be included on your outline.
   7. As you write your report, you should refer to your ——— and your ———.
   8. You should ——— your first draft by looking for ways to improve the report.

Written Exercises

A. Write all the principal parts.

Present	Past	Past Participle
1. lay	———	———
2. lie	———	———
3. raise	———	———
4. rise	———	———
5. set	———	———
6. sit	———	———
7. let	———	———

2. lay, set
3. leave
4. lay, raise, set (Also accept *let, leave, teach,* and *learn,* but do not emphasize these.)
5. let

C. 1. hands (and) neck, direct object, active
   2. hands (and) neck, subject, passive
   3. Jacob, direct object, active
   4. Jacob, subject, passive

D. 1. notes
   2. more than one
   3. must not
   4. every point that fits your chosen topic
   5. outline
   6. do not need
   7. outline, notes
   8. proofread

Written Exercises

A. (Words in italics are given in the pupil's text.)

1. *lay*	laid	(have) laid
2. *lie*	lay	(have) lain
3. *raise*	raised	(have) raised
4. *rise*	rose	(have) risen
5. *set*	set	(have) set
6. *sit*	sat	(have) sat
7. *let*	let	(have) let

B. Write the correct words in parentheses.
1. Abraham (raised, rose) up early to go to the land of Moriah.
2. After two days he (raised, rose) his eyes and saw Mount Moriah in the distance.
3. Abraham built an altar and (laid, lay) the wood on it.
4. Abraham (let, left) the servants behind with the donkey.
5. He (let, left) Isaac carry the wood.
6. The angel said, "(Lay, Lie) not your hand upon the lad."
7. God could (of, have) (raised, risen) Isaac from the dead, but He provided a ram instead.
8. (Can, May) you remember the rest of the story?
9. (Can, May) I tell you more about Abraham tomorrow?
10. The teacher (taught, learned) the students about Abraham's prompt obedience.
11. The Bible story book is (setting, sitting) on the teacher's desk.
12. The elephants (dragged, drug) the large logs out of the jungle.
13. One baby elephant (tagged, tug) along behind its mother.
14. She would have (attacked, attackted) any person or animal that tried to hurt her baby.
15. The little elephant would not have (drowned, drownded) in the pool, for elephants are excellent swimmers.
16. An angry elephant (burst, bursted) through the forest and temporarily scattered the herd.

C. Write the subjects of the following sentences. Then write the correct words in parentheses that must agree with the subjects.
1. (There's, There are) a few stories in the Bible about twins.
2. Jacob and Esau (was, were) twin brothers.
3. There (was, were) another set of twins named Pharez and Zarah.
4. Isaac (don't, doesn't) know that the twin before him is not Esau.
5. Jacob and Rebekah (don't, doesn't) know that someday God will let Jacob be deceived by Laban.
6. (Here's, Here are) a lesson: "Be sure your sin will find you out."
7. A set of twins (is, are) mentioned in Genesis 38.
8. One of the boys (was, were) named Zarah, which means "rising" or "shining."
9. Several of the books on this shelf (tell, tells) the story.
10. The teacher of the younger grades (teach, teaches) Bible stories in reading class.

B. 1. rose
2. raised
3. laid
4. left
5. let
6. Lay
7. have, raised
8. Can
9. May
10. taught
11. sitting
12. dragged
13. tagged
14. attacked
15. drowned
16. burst

C. 1. stories, There are
2. Jacob (and) Esau, were
3. set, was
4. Isaac, doesn't
5. Jacob (and) Rebekah, don't
6. lesson, Here's
7. set, is
8. One, was
9. Several, tell
10. teacher, teaches

D. Copy the subject of each sentence, and write whether it is the *doer* or the *receiver* of the action. Then write whether the voice of the verb is *active* or *passive*.
1. Isaac sent Jacob to Laban's house.
2. Jacob was sent to his uncle Laban's home.
3. Laban gave Leah to Jacob for a wife.
4. Flocks were given to Jacob by Laban.

E. Rewrite each sentence in the past tense and the future tense, keeping the passive voice.
1. The sheep are led by their shepherds.
2. The trough is filled by the shepherdess.
3. The stone is removed by the strong men.

F. Change these sentences to the passive voice.
1. Esau met Jacob peacefully.
2. Jacob sent messengers to Esau.
3. Jacob protected Rachel and Joseph.

G. Change these sentences to the active voice.
1. Jacob was kissed by Esau.
2. His wives and children were presented to Esau by Jacob.
3. Jacob's gifts were accepted by Esau.

H. Write *true* or *false*.
1. You should choose a certain topic and take notes only on ideas related to that topic.
2. You should write down main ideas and key words when you take notes.
3. You should copy a few whole sentences and paragraphs when you take notes.
4. Your report will be confusing if you use more than two sources of information.
5. You should write as few notes as necessary; it is easier to find more information than to discard some notes.
6. You should carefully organize your notes before writing your report.

D. 1. Isaac, doer, active
2. Jacob, receiver, passive
3. Laban, doer, active
4. Flocks, receiver, passive

E. 1. The sheep were led by their shepherds.
The sheep will be led by their shepherds.
2. The trough was filled by the shepherdess.
The trough will be filled by the shepherdess.
3. The stone was removed by the strong men.
The stone will be removed by the strong men.

F. 1. Jacob was met peacefully by Esau.
2. Messengers were sent by Jacob to Esau.
3. Rachel and Joseph were protected by Jacob.

G. 1. Esau kissed Jacob.
2. Jacob presented his wives and children to Esau.
3. Esau accepted Jacob's gifts.

H. 1. true
2. true
3. false
4. false
5. false
6. true

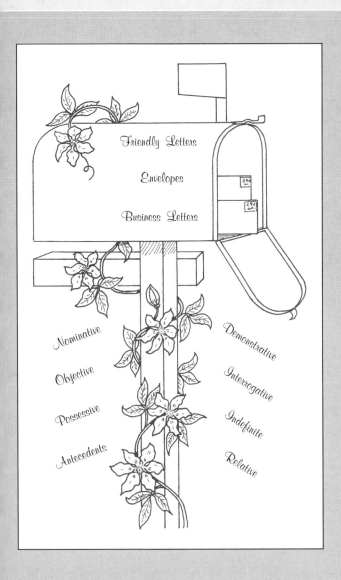

Friendly Letters

Envelopes

Business Letters

Nominative

Objective

Possessive

Antecedents

Demonstrative

Interrogative

Indefinite

Relative

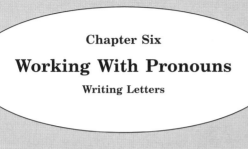

Chapter Six

Working With Pronouns

Writing Letters

A
pronoun is
a word that takes the place
of a noun.

For precept must be upon precept,
precept upon precept; line upon line, line upon line;
here a little, and there a little.

Isaiah 28:10

Personal Pronouns
Nominative Case

	Singular	Plural
First person:	I	we
Second person:	you (thou)	you (ye)
Third person:	he, she, it	they

Objective Case

	Singular	Plural
First person:	me	us
Second person:	you (thee)	you
Third person:	him, her, it	them

Possessive Case

	Singular	Plural
First person:	my, mine	our, ours
Second person:	your, yours (thy, thine)	your, yours
Third person:	his, her, hers, its	their, theirs

(Archaic pronouns are in parentheses.)

60. Personal Pronouns

A pronoun is another of the eight parts of speech. A pronoun is a word that takes the place of a noun. We use pronouns freely, for they help to make our sentences flow smoothly. Notice how the nouns in the first sentence below are replaced by pronouns in the second sentence.

Margie saw the man drop the box.
She   saw   him drop   it.

Lesson 60

Purpose: To teach personal pronouns, including their antecedents and their *person, number, case, and *gender.

Teacher: Lesson 67 of this chapter is on business letters. It would be good to prepare for that lesson ahead of time by obtaining addresses of suitable places to which the students can write.

Oral Review:

1. What is a transitive verb? (a verb that passes action to a receiver)
2. What two kinds of voice do verbs have? (active, passive)
3. What is the voice of the verb when the subject performs the action? (active)
4. What is the voice of the verb when the subject receives the action? (passive)

5. What kind of verb phrase is used for the passive voice? (a form of *be* with a past participle)
6. Which should be used most in writing, active voice or passive voice? (active voice)
7. When is it desirable to use the passive voice? (The passive voice may be used for variety. It may also be used when the doer of an action is not known or is not important in a sentence.)

Lesson Introduction: Read the following story to the students. Ask them what is wrong with it.

Phoebe Brown was a famous American hymn writer. One of Phoebe Brown's most popular hymns is called "I Love to Steal Awhile Away." Phoebe Brown wrote the hymn to answer a question that a neighbor lady had asked Phoebe Brown.

Phoebe Brown was living in a small house at the time, with four small children and a sick sister. Phoebe Brown had no place in her house to pray alone. So for a while every evening, Phoebe Brown went into the neighbor's garden to pray.

One night the neighbor lady came and rudely interrupted Phoebe Brown. The neighbor lady said, "Mrs. Brown, why does Mrs. Brown come up at evening so near this neighbor lady's house and then go back without coming in? If Mrs. Brown wants something, why doesn't Mrs. Brown come in and ask for something?"

Phoebe Brown went home in tears and wrote the hymn "I Love to Steal Awhile Away" as an apology to Phoebe Brown's neighbor lady.

Personal pronouns refer mainly to *persons*. You can see this when you consider the list of personal pronouns on page 264. However, some of these pronouns may refer to animals or to nonliving objects.

Personal pronouns have different forms to indicate *person, number, case,* and *gender*. These differences are explained in this lesson.

Person

Personal pronouns show three different persons: first, second, and third. *First person pronouns* refer to the person speaking (*I, we*). *Second person pronouns* refer to the person spoken to (*you*). *Third person pronouns* refer to the person or thing spoken about (*he, she, it, they*).

> I read John 3 this morning.
> (I—first person; refers to person speaking)

> What did you read today?
> (you—second person; refers to person spoken to)

> Father gave him a Bible.
> (him—third person; refers to person spoken about)

Personal pronouns have different forms according to their person. By contrast, nouns are nearly always third person. The reason is that when you speak, you use *I* or *me* instead of your own name, and *you* instead of the name of the person to whom you are speaking. If you use a noun, it usually names a person or thing that you are speaking about.

Number

Number refers to whether a pronoun is singular or plural. A word naming only one person or thing is singular; a word naming two or more persons or things is plural. You can tell by the meaning of a pronoun whether it is singular or plural.

> **Singular pronouns:** I, me, he, him, she, her, it
> **Plural pronouns:**   we, us, they, them

The pronoun *you* is different from the rest because it may be singular or plural. You must know what *you* refers to before you can tell its number.

> **Singular:** Henry, you surely do neat work. (refers to *Henry*)
> **Plural:**   Boys, where did you put my hammer? (refers to *boys*)

This story would sound better if it used more personal pronouns. It gets tiresome to hear the same nouns over and over. In this lesson we will study personal pronouns.

Lesson Outline:

1. A pronoun is a word that takes the place of a noun. A pronoun is another of the eight parts of speech.

2. Personal pronouns *refer mainly to* persons. See the list of personal pronouns at the beginning of this chapter in the pupil's book.

3. Personal pronouns have person, number, case, and gender. Discuss these points only briefly. Refer the students to the chart at the beginning of the chapter.

a. *Person* is either first, second, or third.

> *First person pronouns* refer to the person speaking (*I, we*).
> *Second person pronouns* refer to the person spoken to (*you*).
> *Third person pronouns* refer to the person or thing spoken about (*he, she, it, they*).

b. *Number* is either singular or plural.

> **Singular pronouns:**
> I, me, he, him, she, her, it

> **Plural pronouns:**
> we, us, they, them
> The pronoun *you* may be singular or plural.

c. *Case* is either nominative, objective, or possessive.

d. *Gender* is either masculine, feminine, neuter, or common.

> Pronouns of *masculine* gender refer to men and boys.

> he, him, his

> Pronouns of *feminine* gender refer to women and girls.

> she, her, hers

> Pronouns of *neuter* gender are neither masculine nor feminine.

> it, its

Case

The three cases of pronouns are *nominative, objective,* and *possessive.* The chart on page 264 shows the forms for each case. You will learn about pronoun cases in the next several lessons.

Gender

Pronouns show gender. They are *masculine, feminine, neuter,* or *common.*

Pronouns of *masculine* gender refer to men and boys.

    he   him   his

Jacob needed to leave home. He went to Laban's house.

Pronouns of *feminine* gender refer to women and girls.

    she   her   hers

Rachel was the daughter of Laban. She became Jacob's wife.

Pronouns of *neuter* gender are neither masculine nor feminine.

    it   its

Jacob returned to Canaan. It was his homeland.

Pronouns of *common* gender can be masculine or feminine. If they are plural, these pronouns may stand for nouns of all three genders: masculine, feminine, neuter, or any combination of these.

I	you	we	they
me	your	us	them
my	yours	our	their
mine		ours	theirs

Jacob had twelve sons and one daughter. They were his children.

Since a pronoun takes the place of a noun, every pronoun has an *antecedent.* The antecedent is the noun for which the pronoun stands.

Lester wrote about the eclipse.
He watched it through a very dark glass.
    Lester is the antecedent of *He. Eclipse* is the antecedent of *it.*

Pronouns of *common* gender can be masculine or feminine. If they are plural, these pronouns may stand for nouns of all three genders: masculine, feminine, neuter, or any combination of these.

    I, me, my, mine, you, your, yours, we, us, our, ours, they, them, their, theirs

(*Teacher:* In a sentence like "The girls wore their sweaters," the gender of *their* is common, even though its antecedent in this case is feminine. Pronouns like *I, you, we,* and *they* have common gender regardless of the gender of their antecedents.

Technically speaking, nouns also have case and gender. But the case of nouns has little grammatical significance, the same as the gender of nouns (see note in Lesson 19). The only nouns whose form shows a specific case are possessive nouns (boy's, boys'), and the only nouns whose form shows a specific gender are a few nouns with feminine endings (hostess, heroine). Thus, hardly any words except pronouns have forms that show case and gender.)

4. An antecedent *is the noun for which a pronoun stands.* In writing, antecedents must be kept clear. The antecedent is usually found somewhere near and before the pronoun that takes its place.

    O magnify the Lord with me, and let us exalt
        His Name together.
        What is the antecedent of *His*? Exalt whose
           Name? The Lord's Name. The antecedent is *Lord.*

- A pronoun is a word that takes the place of a noun.
- *Personal pronouns* refer mainly to *persons*.
- Personal pronouns have different forms to indicate *person, number, case,* and *gender*.
- An *antecedent* is the noun for which a pronoun stands.

Class Practice

A. Replace the underlined words with personal pronouns.
   1. The storekeeper told Father and me the price of the drill.
   2. Charity and I picked the tomatoes.
   3. The drivers were ready to leave soon.

B. Tell which words are personal pronouns. Give the antecedent of each one.
   1. Jesus said to the parents of the little maid, "Weep not; she is not dead, but sleepeth."
   2. He took her by the hand and called, saying, "Maid, arise."
   3. And her spirit came again, and she arose straightway: and He commanded to give her some food.

C. Find each personal pronoun, and give its person, number, and gender.
   1. Ruth and Orpah left their native land to go with Naomi.
   2. Ruth and Orpah both wished to stay with her.
   3. After much discussion, Orpah decided that she would return to her homeland.
   4. Were many tears shed at their parting?
   5. But Ruth said, "Do not intreat me to leave you."
   6. They arrived in Bethlehem during barley harvest.
   7. Boaz showed great kindness to them.
   8. He let her glean in his fields.

Written Exercises

A. Replace the underlined words with personal pronouns.
   1. James and Doris are with Frank and Judy.
   2. The boys fed the dogs.
   3. Those children are our visitors.

Lesson 60 Answers
Class Practice
A. 1. He, us, it
   2. We, them
   3. They

B. 1. she—maid
   2. He—Jesus; her—maid
   3. her—maid; she—maid; He—Jesus; her—maid

C. 1. their—third person, plural, common
   2. her—third person, singular, feminine
   3. she—third person, singular, feminine
      her—third person, singular, feminine
   4. their—third person, plural, common
   5. me—first person, singular, common
      you—second person, singular, common
   6. They—third person, plural, common
   7. them—third person, plural, common
   8. He—third person, singular, masculine
      her—third person, singular, feminine
      his—third person, singular, masculine

Written Exercises
A. 1. He, she, him, her
   2. They, them
   3. They

4. Bruce and I can see the men.
5. This one is Anna's.
6. Robert's is on the table.
7. Vernon called Grandfather and me.
8. The girls helped Mother with Mother's work.

B. Copy the personal pronouns in these sentences, and write the person, number, and gender of each.

> **Example:**   We saw him with you.
> **Answer:**   We—first person, plural, common
>   him—third person, singular, masculine
>   you—second person, singular *or* plural, common

1. She and I met them.
2. Are these cards yours?
3. No, I believe they are his.
4. Where are ours?
5. They took them for her.
6. Who are they?
7. Is it she?
8. No, it is they.
9. Trust in the Lord with all your heart.
10. In all your ways acknowledge Him.

C. Copy each personal pronoun, and write its antecedent.
1. Father said he wanted to start early.
2. Did the Martins say when they will arrive?
3. Jesus asked, "Who touched My clothes?"
4. The woman was healed of her disease.
5. Jesus said to the woman, "Your faith has saved you; go in peace."
6. Jesus said to Simon, "I have something to tell you."
7. Jesus asked, "What is a man profited if he shall gain the whole world and lose his own soul?"
8. Jesus said to the disciples, "Cast your net on the right side of the ship."

4. We, them
5. hers
6. His
7. He, us
8. They, her

B. 1. She—third person, singular, feminine
       I—first person, singular, common
       them—third person, plural, common
    2. yours—second person, singular *or* plural, common
    3. I—first person, singular, common
       they—third person, plural, common
       his—third person, singular, masculine
    4. ours—first person, plural, common
    5. They—third person, plural, common
       them—third person, plural, common
       her—third person, singular, feminine
    6. they—third person, plural, common
    7. it—third person, singular, neuter *or* common
       she—third person, singular, feminine
    8. it—third person, singular, neuter *or* common
       they—third person, plural, common
    9. your—second person, singular *or* plural, common
   10. your—second person, singular *or* plural, common
       Him—third person, singular, masculine

C. 1. he—Father
   2. they—Martins
   3. My—Jesus
   4. her—woman
   5. Your—woman; you—woman
   6. I—Jesus; you—Simon
   7. he—man; his—man
   8. your—disciples

Review Exercises

Copy each verb or verb phrase. After it, write the word that receives its action, and write whether the verb is in the *active* or *passive* voice. [55]

1. Twenty-two thousand men were dismissed by Gideon.
2. The Midianites were feared greatly.
3. Only three hundred vigilant soldiers helped Gideon.
4. Gideon and his men blew the trumpets and broke the pitchers.
5. The Midianites were defeated.

---

61. Pronouns in the Nominative Case

Personal pronouns have three *cases:* nominative, objective, and possessive. You may remember studying subject pronouns, object pronouns, and possessive pronouns in earlier grades. The subject pronouns are in the nominative case.

Here are the nominative case pronouns as shown on page 264. *Thou* and *ye* are in parentheses because they are the archaic forms used in the King James Bible instead of *you.* Memorize the pronouns on this chart.

Nominative Case

	Singular	*Plural*
First person:	I	we
Second person:	you (thou)	you (ye)
Third person:	he, she, it	they

When pronouns are used in sentences, there are two places where they must always be in the nominative case. Learn them well so that you can avoid mistakes.

1. *The* subject *of a sentence must always be in the nominative case.* Usually you have no problem choosing the correct pronoun as the subject of a sentence. Which one is correct in this sentence?

   (He, Him) offered to help us.

Lesson 61

Purpose: To teach the use of nominative case pronouns.

Oral Review:

1. Give the definition of a pronoun. (a word that takes the place of a noun)
2. What is an antecedent? (the noun for which a pronoun stands)
3. Name the six tenses of verbs. (present tense, past tense, future tense, present perfect tense, past perfect tense, future perfect tense)
4. What helping verbs are always used in the perfect tenses? (have, has, had)
5. What do we mean when we say that the subject and verb in a sentence must agree? (If the subject is singular, the verb must be singular. If the subject is plural, the verb must be plural.)

Review Exercises

1. were dismissed, men, passive
2. were feared, Midianites, passive
3. helped, Gideon, active
4. blew, trumpets, active
   broke, pitchers, active
5. were defeated, Midianites, passive

Lesson Introduction: The word *case* has several different meanings. In language it has to do with the form of a word for the way it is used in a sentence. Pronouns have three cases: the nominative case, the objective case, and the possessive case. The correct case must be chosen for the way a pronoun is used in a sentence.

Ask the students if they know what pronouns should be corrected in the following story. (Pronouns in the wrong case are underlined.)

Philip P. Bliss was once in a children's meeting. While <u>him</u> was helping to sing the song "Oh, How I Love Jesus," <u>him</u> thought about how poor his own love to God seemed in comparison to God's love for man. So <u>him</u> wrote a song that tells about God's love for us. It is the familiar hymn that begins with these words: "I am so glad that our Father in heaven / Tells of His love in the book He has given."

You know which word is correct without even thinking. But be sure you also understand the *reason* it is correct. The nominative form *he* is used because the pronoun is the subject of the sentence.

Also look at these sentences, which use the archaic forms of *you*. In each one, *thou* or *ye* is properly used because it is the subject of the sentence.

> <u>Thou</u> art my hiding place.
> <u>Ye</u> are the light of the world.

2. A predicate nominative *must always be in the nominative case.* A predicate nominative is a noun or pronoun that follows a linking verb (a form of *be*) and renames the subject of the sentence. Many people use incorrect forms for predicate nominatives, so you cannot always choose the correct word by what sounds right. Which pronouns are correct in the following sentences?

> My teacher is (he, him).
> Is your mother (she, her)?
> Our guests are (they, them).

In each sentence, the pronoun renames the subject. It is a predicate nominative, so the nominative form must be used. Remember that a subject and a predicate nominative can be exchanged and the sentence will mean the same.

> My teacher is <u>he</u>.
> **Compare:** He is my teacher.

> Is your mother <u>she</u>?
> **Compare:** Is she your mother?

> Our guests are <u>they</u>.
> **Compare:** They are our guests.

A predicate nominative is diagramed on the base line after the verb, whether it is a noun or a pronoun. A slanted line that leans toward the subject is placed before the predicate nominative to show that it refers to the subject.

Today we will study nominative case pronouns and their correct use.

Lesson Outline:

1. Personal pronouns have three cases: nominative, objective, and possessive.

2. The nominative case pronouns are I, you, he, she, it, we, *and* they. *The archaic forms of* you *are* thou *and* ye.

3. Nominative case pronouns are used in two places.

(1) The *subject* of a sentence must always be in the nominative case.

(2) A *predicate nominative* must always be in the nominative case.

4. A predicate nominative is diagramed on the base line after the verb. A slanted line that leans toward the subject is placed before the predicate nominative to show that it refers to the subject.

She is my friend.

She	is \ friend

My friend is she.

friend	is \ she

- The nominative case pronouns are *I, you, he, she, it, we,* and *they.* The archaic forms of *you* are *thou* and *ye.*

- When a pronoun is a subject or a predicate nominative, it must be in the nominative case.

Class Practice

A. Choose the correct pronouns. Tell whether each pronoun is used as a *subject* or a *predicate nominative.* Practice reading each sentence correctly.
1. Rhoda swept the floors, and (I, me) dusted the furniture.
2. Who is there? Is it (she, her)?
3. Father did the hardest parts, and (they, them) worked with us.
4. The teacher might be (she, her).
5. My cousins are (they, them).
6. Joan came soon, and (she, her) finished early.
7. The winner is (he, him).
8. The workers are (they, them).
9. James will bring the wagon, and (I, me) will help you.
10. (Thou, Thee) openest Thine hand and satisfiest the desire of every living thing.
11. O Lord, (Thou, Thee) art my refuge and my portion in the land of the living.
12. If (thou, thee) faint in the day of adversity, thy strength is small.

B. On the chalkboard, diagram the sentence skeletons, predicate nominatives, and direct objects of sentences 3–9 in Part A. Include the correct pronouns on your diagrams.

Written Exercises

A. Write the correct pronouns. After each one, write whether it is a *subject* or a *predicate nominative.*
1. (He, Him) saw the fishermen.
2. The fishermen were (they, them).
3. Jesus called them, and (they, them) left their nets.
4. (They, Them) followed Jesus immediately.

Lesson 61 Answers
Class Practice

A. 1. I—subject
    2. she—predicate nominative
    3. they—subject
    4. she—predicate nominative
    5. they—predicate nominative
    6. she—subject
    7. he—predicate nominative
    8. they—predicate nominative
    9. I—subject
    10. Thou—subject
    11. Thou—subject
    12. thou—subject

B. 3. Father | did | parts _and_ they | worked
    4. teacher | might be \ she
    5. cousins | are \ they
    6. Joan | came _and_ she | finished
    7. winner | is \ he
    8. workers | are \ they
    9. James | will bring | wagon _and_ I | will help | you

Written Exercises

A. 1. He—subject
    2. they—predicate nominative
    3. they—subject
    4. They—subject

5. (They, Them) were the sons of Zebedee.
6. The writer of the Book of Revelation was (he, him).
7. The beloved disciple was (he, him).
8. It was (he, him).
9. The brothers are (they, them).
10. The fastest worker was (he, him).
11. (She, Her) was here early in the afternoon.
12. (They, Them) are polite children.
13. I saw the visitors, but who were (they, them)?
14. (He, Him) came and showed them how to do it.
15. Jason wrote the story, and (she, her) drew the pictures.
16. (They, Them) planned the schedule and called the workers.
17. Who art (thou, thee)?
18. (Thou, Thee) hast established the earth, and it abideth.
19. "The tree that thou sawest . . . is (thou, thee), O king," said Daniel.
20. Lord, (Thou, Thee) hast been our dwelling place in all generations.

B. Diagram the sentence skeletons and predicate nominatives.
1. They came on the train.
2. Was it he at the back door?
3. He is the oldest boy.
4. Mother's helper was she.

Review Exercises

A. Write each verb or verb phrase, and give the tense. [32–36]
1. Will the Lord help Gideon?
2. How were Gideon and his men encouraged in the Lord?
3. A Midianite told about his dream.
4. A cake of barley bread had upset one of the tents.
5. You have dreamed about Gideon.
6. Surely he will defeat all the Midianites.
7. God is with Gideon.
8. Before midnight, Israel will have defeated Midian.

B. Write the correct verbs in parentheses. [54]
1. There (was, were) only three hundred men in Gideon's army.
2. (There's, There are) so many Midianites that they cannot be numbered.

5. They—subject
6. he—predicate nominative
7. he—predicate nominative
8. he—predicate nominative
9. they—predicate nominative
10. he—predicate nominative
11. She—subject
12. They—subject
13. they—predicate nominative
14. He—subject
15. she—subject
16. They—subject
17. thou—predicate nominative
18. Thou—subject
19. thou—predicate nominative
20. Thou—subject

B. 1. They | came

2. it | Was \ he

3. He | is \ boy

4. helper | was \ she

Review Exercises

A. 1. Will help—future
2. were encouraged—past
3. told—past
4. had upset—past perfect
5. have dreamed—present perfect
6. will defeat—future
7. is—present
8. will have defeated—future perfect

B. 1. were
2. There are

3. Here (is, are) several verses about Gideon.

4. (Here's, Here are) the Sunday school books you wanted.

5. Brother Gerald (don't, doesn't) teach my class every Sunday.

3. are

4. Here are

5. doesn't

---

62. Pronouns in the Objective Case

Pronouns have three cases: nominative, objective, and possessive. Here are the objective case pronouns as listed on page 264. Memorize the pronouns on this chart.

Objective Case

	Singular	Plural
First person:	me	us
Second person:	you (thee)	you
Third person:	him, her, it	them

The pronouns *you* and *it* are the same in the objective case as in the nominative case. The archaic *thee* used in the King James Bible is the singular form of *you.*

When pronouns are used in sentences, there are three places where they must always be in the objective case. It will help you to remember what these three places are if you remember that all three are objects.

1. *A direct object must always be in the objective case.*

God will bless (they, them) abundantly.

The sentence skeleton is *God will bless.* God will bless *whom*? The objective form *them* must be used because the pronoun is a direct object.

In the following sentence, the archaic form *thee* is used as a direct object.

The Lord bless <u>thee</u>.

Remember that a direct object is diagramed after the verb, with a vertical line between.

subject	action verb	direct object

Lesson 62

Purpose: To teach the use of objective case pronouns.

Oral Review:

1. Give the nominative case pronouns. (I, you, he, she, it, we, they; *archaic:* thou, ye)

2. Nominative case pronouns can be used as what two sentence parts? (subject, predicate nominative)

3. What is a predicate nominative? (a noun or pronoun that follows a linking verb and renames the subject of a sentence)

4. Spell the plural form of each noun.
   a. child (children)   d. goose (geese)
   b. ox (oxen)   e. deer (deer)
   c. foot (feet)   f. trout (trout)

5. Name the eight parts of speech. (noun, pronoun, verb, adjective, adverb, preposition, conjunction, interjection)

Lesson Introduction: It is important to use the right tool for the job you want to do. A knife does not make a good screwdriver. A wrench should not be used for a hammer. Many things have been damaged because the tool did not match the job for which it was used.

In the same way, the case of a pronoun must match the way it is used in a sentence. Today we will study objective case pronouns and learn how to use them correctly.

Lesson Outline:

1. The objective case pronouns are me, you, him, her, it, us, *and* them. *The archaic form of* you *is* thee. The pronouns *you* and *it* are the same in the objective case as in the nominative case.

2. Objective case pronouns are used in three places.

   (1) A *direct object* must always be in the objective case.

   (2) An *indirect object* must always be in the objective case.

   (3) The *object of a preposition* must always be in the objective case.

2. *An* indirect object *must always be in the objective case.* An indirect object comes between an action verb and a direct object, and it tells *to whom or what* or *for whom or what.*

He gave (we, us) the message.

He gave the message *to whom?* The objective form *us* must be used because the pronoun is an indirect object.

Note the use of the archaic form *thee* as an indirect object.

The Lord will give <u>thee</u> peace.

Remember that an indirect object is diagramed on a horizontal line beneath the base line, with a slanted line connecting the indirect object to the verb.

3. *The* object of a preposition *must always be in the objective case.*

The Lord has been gracious to (I, me.)

The preposition is *to.* To *whom?* The objective form *me* must be used because the pronoun is the object of a preposition.

The following sentence uses the archaic form *thee* as the object of a preposition.

The Lord make His face shine upon <u>thee</u>.

The object of a preposition is diagramed on a horizontal line beneath the base line. A slanted line connects it to the word modified by the prepositional phrase. That word may be a noun or a verb.

- The objective case pronouns are *me, you, him, her, it, us,* and *them.* The archaic form of *you* is *thee.*

- When a pronoun is a direct object, an indirect object, or the object of a preposition, it must be in the objective case.

Class Practice

A. Choose the correct pronouns. Tell whether each one is a *direct object,* an *indirect object,* or the *object of a preposition.* Practice reading each sentence correctly.
1. Charles worked with (I, me).
2. We will help (he, him).
3. Give (she, her) the flowers.
4. Did you give (he, him) the apples?
5. It is a gift from (he, him).
6. Aunt Helen wrote a letter to (she, her).
7. The children sang three songs for (she, her).
8. The carpenter showed (they, them) the new house.
9. He crowneth (thou, thee) with lovingkindness and tender mercies.
10. Unto (Thou, Thee), O Lord, do I lift up my soul.

B. On the chalkboard, diagram the sentence skeletons of sentences 1–8 in Part A. Include the direct objects, indirect objects, and prepositional phrases.

Written Exercises

A. Write the correct pronouns. After each one, write *DO, IO,* or *OP* to tell whether it is the direct object, indirect object, or object of a preposition.
1. Ruby called (we, us) on the telephone.
2. The experience taught (she, her) a lesson.
3. I should pay (he, him) three dollars.
4. Did someone warn (they, them)?
5. Phyllis took (we, us) to the store.
6. Give this paper to (he, him).
7. Did you find (she, her)?
8. Bring (I, me) the mail, please.
9. Mother bought pretzels for (we, us).

Lesson 62 Answers
Class Practice
A. 1. me—object of a preposition
    2. him—direct object
    3. her—indirect object
    4. him—indirect object
    5. him—object of a preposition
    6. her—object of a preposition
    7. her—object of a preposition
    8. them—indirect object
    9. thee—direct object
    10. Thee—object of a preposition

B. 1.

    2.

    3.

    4.

    5.

    6.

    7.

    8.

Written Exercises
A. 1. us—DO
    2. her—IO
    3. him—IO
    4. them—DO
    5. us—DO
    6. him—OP
    7. her—DO
    8. me—IO
    9. us—OP

10. A kind man gave (we, us) directions.
11. Did the medicine help (they, them)?
12. I asked (he, him) for directions.
13. Let another man praise (thou, thee), and not thine own mouth.
14. My son, keep my words, and lay up my commandments with (thou, thee).

B. Diagram the sentence skeletons, direct objects, indirect objects, and prepositional phrases.
1. Grandmother helped us with the peaches.
2. He told Sarah the story.
3. Please bring them with you.
4. Mother gave her some cookies.

Review Exercises

A. Copy each personal pronoun in Part B of Written Exercises. After each one, write its person, number, case, and gender. [60–62]

   Sample answer: she—third, singular, nominative, feminine

B. Write the plural form of each noun. [22–25]

1. sky	5. roof	9. ox
2. echo	6. goose	10. fish
3. box	7. gentleman	11. moose
4. thrush	8. mouse	12. foot

---

63. Writing a Friendly Letter

How can you share news with someone you probably will not see for a long time? How can you give help or encouragement to someone who is not with you? How can you give or accept an invitation or thank someone for a favor shown when he lives far away from you? One way is to write letters. Letters written for these reasons are called friendly letters.

A friendly letter has five parts: the *heading, greeting, body, closing,* and *signature.* The heading gives the address from which you are writing, and it also gives the date. The greeting is just that—a greeting to your friend. The body of the letter is the main part, in which you write

10. us—IO
11. them—DO
12. him—DO
13. thee—DO
14. thee—OP

B. 1.

2.

3.

4.

Review Exercises

A. 1. us—first, plural, objective, common
2. He—third, singular, nominative, masculine
3. them—third, plural, objective, common
   you—second, singular *or* plural, objective, common
4. her—third, singular, objective, feminine

B. 1. skies	5. roofs	9. oxen
2. echoes	6. geese	10. fish
3. boxes	7. gentlemen	11. moose
4. thrushes	8. mice	12. feet

Lesson 63

Purpose: To teach the rules for writing a friendly letter and for addressing an envelope.

Oral Review:

1. Briefly give the main steps in writing a report. (Take notes from several reference sources. Organize your notes into an outline. Write the first draft of the report. Mark improvements that should be made. Write the second draft of the report.)
2. List several ways of developing a paragraph. (by using details, by using examples and illustrations, by using comparison or contrast)
3. Some paragraphs are developed by showing similarities between two people, places, things, or ideas. What is this method called? (comparison)
4. Some paragraphs are developed by showing differences between two people, places, things, or ideas. What is this method called? (contrast)

Written Quiz:

1. Write the definition of a pronoun. _____
   _____

2. List the nominative case pronouns. (Include one archaic pronoun.) _____
   _____

3. List the objective case pronouns. (Include one archaic pronoun.) _____
   _____

4. Name the two sentence parts for which the nominative case must be used. _____
   _____

the things you have to say. The closing is your parting word or words (a sort of good-bye), and the signature is your name, showing whom the letter is from.

Greetings and closings usually follow a standard pattern. Here are some examples.

Greetings: Dear friend, Dear Cousin Mary, Dear Frank,
Closings: Yours truly, Your cousin, Sincerely,

The five letter parts are shown in the following letter.

Heading

Route 2, Box 2160
Clinton, IA 52732
April 14, 20--

Greeting

Dear Uncle Luke,

"The Lord by wisdom hath founded the earth; by understanding hath he established the heavens. By his knowledge the depths are broken up, and the clouds drop down the dew" (Proverbs 3:19, 20).

Body

I am happy to write and tell you that Father agrees to let me visit you this summer. I shall be coming to Pennsylvania in early June. (It's too soon to give an exact date.) I expect to fly to Philadelphia, and I hope you can meet me there.

I am very pleased and excited about this opportunity, and I want to thank you in advance.

Closing

Your loving nephew,

Signature

Vernon

Quiz Answers:
1. A pronoun is a word that takes the place of a noun.
2. I, you, he, she, it, we, they (thou, ye)
3. me, you, him, her, it, us, them (thee)
4. subject, predicate nominative

Lesson Introduction: Did you ever go to the mailbox and find it empty? Were you disappointed? Were you hoping to get an interesting letter? The Bible says, "As ye would that men should do to you, do ye also to them likewise." Most people enjoy receiving letters, so you should learn to write good letters.

What kind of letters should you write? Today you will see what friendly letters are, why they are written, and how they are written.

Lesson Outline:

1. Friendly letters are written for several reasons.
   a. To share news with someone whom you may not see for a long time.
   b. To give help or encouragement to someone who is not with you.
   c. To give or accept an invitation.
   d. To thank someone for a favor shown when he lives far away.

2. A friendly letter has five parts: the heading, greeting, body, closing, and signature.

3. Use correct capitalization when you write a friendly letter.
   a. The first word in the greeting of a letter and the first word in the closing must be capitalized.
   b. Capital letters are used for all proper nouns, such as the names of streets, cities, states, and months.
   c. The abbreviations *Mr.* and *Mrs.* are always capitalized.
   d. Titles of respect, such as *doctor* and *uncle,* are capitalized when they are used with names: *Doctor Ferlyn, Dr. Long, Uncle John.*
   e. For state names, the postal service has developed a list of two-letter abbreviations to be used with Zip Codes. These are completely capitalized and have no end punctuation. (See the list at the end of the lesson.)

Use correct capitalization when you write a friendly letter. The first word in the greeting of a letter and the first word in the closing must be capitalized. Capital letters are used for all proper nouns, such as the names of streets, cities, states, and months. The abbreviations *Mr.* and *Mrs.* are always capitalized. Titles of respect, such as *doctor* and *uncle,* are capitalized when they are used with names: *Doctor Merle, Dr. Merle, Uncle David.* For state names, the postal service has developed a list of two-letter abbreviations to be used with Zip Codes. These are completely capitalized and have no end punctuation. See the list at the end of this lesson.

PA 17519	MD 21719	NY 14218

Use correct punctuation in a friendly letter. In the heading, place a comma between a route number and a box number, between the name of the city and the state, and between the number of the day and the year. Do not place a comma between a house number and a street name, or between the state abbreviation and the Zip Code. Put a comma after the greeting and after the closing.

Incorrect:	**Correct:**
1133, Maple Street	1133 Maple Street
Bethel, PA, 19507	Bethel, PA 19507
November 8 20—	November 8, 20—

Notice where the heading, closing, and signature are written. The heading is close to the right margin. The left edge of the heading, closing, and signature are in line with each other.

The body of the letter should be written neatly and courteously. Use complete sentences, and develop your paragraphs with interesting details. Keep the left margin straight and the right margin as straight as possible.

When you write an address on an envelope, be sure to write neatly and correctly so that the letter reaches its destination. In the United States, the postal service wants the receiver's address to be printed with all capital letters and with no punctuation. Mail addressed in this way can be sorted more efficiently.

The receiver's address should be written in about the center of the envelope. It usually contains three lines. The person's name is written in the first line, the street address (or route and box number) in the second line, and the city, state, and Zip Code in the third line. If the title *Mr., Mrs.,* or *Miss* is used, it should be written before the person's name.

Teacher: In the time since this book was originally published, the value of all capital letters and no punctuation in mailing addresses has diminished. Shift the emphasis to neatness and to printing each part precisely as the official source gave the address. This contributes the most toward efficient mailing service.

4. ***Use correct punctuation in a friendly letter.***
   a. Several commas are needed in the heading.
      1) Between a route number and a box number
      2) Between the name of the city and the state
      3) Between the number of the day and the year
   b. Commas are *not* needed in some places in a heading.
      1) No comma between a house number and a street name
      2) No comma between the state abbreviation and the Zip Code
   c. Put a comma after the greeting and after the closing.

5. ***Place the parts of a letter correctly.***
   a. The heading is close to the right margin.
   b. The left edge of the heading, closing, and signature are in line with each other.

6. ***Address the envelope neatly and correctly.***
   a. The receiver's address should be written in about the center of the envelope, usually in three lines. In the United States, the postal service wants the receiver's address to be printed with all capital letters and with no punctuation.
      1) The person's name is written in the first line. If the title *Mr., Mrs.,* or *Miss* is used, it is written before the person's name.
      2) The street address (or route and box number) is put in the second line.
      3) The city, state, and Zip Code are put in the third line.
   b. The sender's address should be written in the upper left corner. This is the return address, and it has the same form as the receiver's address.

The sender's address should be written in the upper left corner. This is the return address, and it is arranged in the same way as the receiver's address. The following illustration shows an envelope properly addressed for mailing.

Vernon Martin
Route 2. Box 2160
Clinton, IA 52732

MR LUKE MARTIN
361 MAPLE DRIVE
NARVON PA 17555

- Friendly letters are written to share news, to give encouragement, to give or accept an invitation, or to thank someone for a favor shown.

- The five parts of a friendly letter are the heading, greeting, body, closing, and signature.

- A clear, courteous friendly letter is written with correct capitalization and punctuation.

Class Practice

Give the answers.
1. What are the parts of a friendly letter? Name them in the order that they appear.
2. What are three purposes for writing friendly letters?
3. Why is it important to address an envelope in clear handwriting and in good form?

★ EXTRA PRACTICE
Worksheet 38 (Friendly Letter)

Lesson 63 Answers
Class Practice
1. heading, greeting, body, closing, signature
2. (Sample answers.) to share news with others, to encourage someone, to give or accept an invitation, to thank someone for a favor shown
3. so that the letter will reach its destination

4. Name the places where capitalization is always used in a friendly letter.
5. Name four places where commas are always used in a friendly letter.
6. Name two places where commas are used in addressing envelopes.
7. Where should Zip Codes be written on an envelope?

Written Exercises

A. Write each letter part correctly.

1. rachel mast
   125 pine road
   caney ky 41407
2. dear esther
3. dear aunt susan
4. loren miller
5. mr jay owens

6. miss esther martin
   route 1 box 17
   bearsville ny 12409
7. your loving friend
8. yours truly
9. your cousin
10. sincerely yours

B. Write a friendly letter to a family member or good friend who lives in another community. Prepare an envelope to go with the letter. Be clear, courteous, and neat. Here are some suggestions.
1. Invite him to your house.
2. Encourage him because he is ill.
3. Tell something interesting that has happened to you.
4. Tell him that you left something at his home during a recent visit (or that he left something at your home).
5. Thank him for something he or his family has done for you.

Review Exercises

Write *true* or *false* for each sentence.
1. A paragraph is a group of sentences that develops a single topic.
2. A paragraph has unity when all the sentences tell about one main topic.
3. You can produce unity in a paragraph by giving details in the order of time or importance, or by using transitional words.
4. A coherent paragraph is one in which all the details fit together well so that the reader does not get lost or confused.
5. Paragraphs can be developed by the use of convincing details, examples and illustrations, and comparison or contrast.

4. the words *Route* and *Box,* the names of the street, city, state, and month; the first word in the greeting and in the closing; the signature
5. between the name of the city and the state abbreviation, between the day and the year, after the greeting, after the closing
6. between the route number and the box number in the sender's address, between the name of the city and the state abbreviation in the sender's address
7. after the state abbreviation in both the receiver's address and the return address

Written Exercises

A. 1. Rachel Mast
   125 Pine Road
   Caney, KY 41407
2. Dear Esther,
3. Dear Aunt Susan,
4. Loren Miller
5. Mr. Jay Owens

6. Miss Esther Martin
   Route 1, Box 17
   Bearsville, NY 12409
7. Your loving friend,
8. Yours truly,
9. Your cousin,
10. Sincerely yours,

B. (Individual work.)

Review Exercises

1. true
2. true
3. false (Coherence is produced in these ways.)
4. true
5. true

◄Challenge Exercises

Memorize the two-letter abbreviation for each state.

AL	Alabama	LA	Louisiana	OH	Ohio
AK	Alaska	ME	Maine	OK	Oklahoma
AZ	Arizona	MD	Maryland	OR	Oregon
AR	Arkansas	MA	Massachusetts	PA	Pennsylvania
CA	California	MI	Michigan	RI	Rhode Island
CO	Colorado	MN	Minnesota	SC	South Carolina
CT	Connecticut	MS	Mississippi	SD	South Dakota
DE	Delaware	MO	Missouri	TN	Tennessee
FL	Florida	MT	Montana	TX	Texas
GA	Georgia	NE	Nebraska	UT	Utah
HI	Hawaii	NV	Nevada	VT	Vermont
ID	Idaho	NH	New Hampshire	VA	Virginia
IL	Illinois	NJ	New Jersey	WA	Washington
IN	Indiana	NM	New Mexico	WV	West Virginia
IA	Iowa	NY	New York	WI	Wisconsin
KS	Kansas	NC	North Carolina	WY	Wyoming
KY	Kentucky	ND	North Dakota		

Challenge Exercises
(Individual work.)

---

64. Using Pronouns Correctly

You have studied the uses of nominative case pronouns and objective case pronouns. You have learned to choose the correct word by seeing how it is used in a sentence. Usually you will have no difficulty, but there are some trouble spots, which this lesson points out to you. Form right language habits by recognizing the use of pronouns and practicing the correct forms.

One trouble spot is compound constructions. When a sentence has a compound part, you must be especially careful to use the correct pronoun. Do this by deciding what part of the sentence the pronoun is. Then you can decide whether the nominative case or the objective case should be used. Can you choose the correct pronoun for each of the following examples without reading the explanations?

Lesson 64

Purpose: To focus on areas of difficulty in using pronouns.

Oral Review:
1. Name the nominative case pronouns. (I, you, he, she, it, we, they; *archaic:* thou, ye)
2. Nominative case pronouns can be used as what two sentence parts? (subject, predicate nominative)
3. Name the objective case pronouns. (me, you, him, her, it, us, them; *archaic:* thee)
4. Objective case pronouns can be used as what three sentence parts? (direct object, indirect object, object of a preposition)
5. Name the four sentence types. Give the correct end punctuation and the function of each. (declarative, period, states a fact; interrogative, question mark, asks a question; imperative, period, gives a command or request; exclamatory, exclamation point, expresses strong feeling)
6. a. Which verb means "to be able to," *can* or *may*? (can)
   b. What is the meaning of *may*? (to be permitted to)
   c. Which verb means "to rest or recline," *lay* or *lie*? (lie)
   d. Which verbs mean "to put or place (something)"? (lay, set)
   e. Which verb is usually followed by a direct object, *lay* or *lie*? (lay)
   f. Which verb means "to get up or go up," *raise* or *rise*? (rise)
   g. Which verb means "to cause (something) to go up or grow up"? (raise)
   h. Which verb means "to gain knowledge"? (learn)

Ralph and (she, her) saw them.
(Subject; use nominative *she.*)

It was Joann and (they, them).
(Predicate nominative; use nominative *they.*)

The dog bit Cheryl and (he, him).
(Direct object; use objective *him.*)

We gave Julie and (she, her) the papers.
(Indirect object; use objective *her.*)

This package is for Jerry and (they, them).
(Object of preposition; use objective *them.*)

Another help for choosing the correct word is to use the pronoun alone, without the other part of the compound construction. Study the following examples.

Ralph and (she, her) saw them.
Think: *She saw them* or *Her saw them?*
She is correct, so *Ralph and she* is correct.

The dog bit Cheryl and (he, him).
Think: The dog bit *he* or The dog bit *him?*
Him is correct, so *Cheryl and him* is correct.

A diagram can help you decide which pronoun to use. If a pronoun is diagramed as a subject or a predicate nominative, it must be in the nominative case. And if a pronoun is diagramed as a direct object, an indirect object, or the object of a preposition, it must be in the objective case.

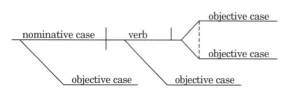

i. Which verb means "to give knowledge or instruction"? (teach)
j. Give the correct past forms of the following verbs.
  (1) tag (tagged, *not* tug)
  (2) drag (dragged, *not* drug)
  (3) drown (drowned, *not* drownded)
  (4) attack (attacked, *not* attackted)
  (5) burst (burst, *not* bursted *or* busted)

Lesson Introduction: In the disorder called amnesia (am·nē·zhə), a person suffers the partial or total loss of his memory. Let us imagine an office worker with amnesia. He may put his glasses in his calculator *case,* his calculator in the typewriter *case,* and the typewriter in the book*case.* Can you imagine his problems later when he tries to find things?

There is a lesson in this story. Always use the correct *case!*

Lesson Outline:
  1. The correct pronoun must be used when a sentence has a compound part. Often it is helpful to use the pronoun alone when deciding which is the correct pronoun.
  a. Use nominative case pronouns for compound subjects.
  b. Use nominative case pronouns for compound predicate nominatives.
  c. Use objective case pronouns for compound direct objects.
  d. Use objective case pronouns for compound indirect objects.
  e. Use objective case pronouns for compound objects of prepositions.

  2. A diagram can be helpful in deciding which case to use.

A second trouble spot is a pronoun that is followed by an appositive. An appositive is a noun that is used directly after another word to clarify it. Do you know which pronoun is correct in the following sentence?

(We, Us) girls will help Mother.

In this sentence, the pronoun is the subject and *girls* is an appositive. So the nominative case must be used: *We* girls will help.

When a pronoun is followed by an appositive, first decide what sentence part the pronoun is filling; then choose the correct pronoun. Try these examples.

(We, Us) boys are going to play baseball.
    (Subject; use nominative *We.*)

Grandmother's visitors were (we, us) girls.
    (Predicate nominative; use nominative *we.*)

They will not hear (we, us) boys.
    (Direct object; use objective *us.*)

Charlotte gave (we, us) girls some cookies.
    (Indirect object; use objective *us.*)

It will be easy for (we, us) girls.
    (Object of preposition; use objective *us.*)

Saying the pronoun without the appositive is helpful in deciding which pronoun is correct.

(We, Us) boys are going to play baseball.
    Think: *We are going* or *Us are going*?
             We is correct, so *We boys* is correct.

It will be easy for (we, us) girls.
    Think: *easy for we* or *easy for us*?
             Us is correct, so *us girls* is correct.

- When a pronoun is in a compound part or is followed by an appositive, first decide how the pronoun is used in the sentence. Then choose the correct case for that use.

---

3. The correct pronoun case must be used when a pronoun is followed by an appositive. An appositive is a noun that is used directly after another word to clarify it.

    a. When a pronoun is a subject or predicate nominative followed by an appositive, use the nominative case.

    b. When a pronoun is an object followed by an appositive, use the objective case. Such a pronoun may be a direct object, an indirect object, or the object of a preposition.

4. Saying the pronoun without the appositive is helpful in deciding which pronoun is correct.

★ EXTRA PRACTICE
Worksheet 33 *(Using Pronouns Correctly)*
Worksheet 34 *(More Practice With Pronoun Usage)*

Class Practice

A. Tell how each pronoun is used, and then say the correct pronoun. Practice reading each sentence correctly.
  1. (We, Us) children rode along.
  2. Joan and (I, me) drew that picture.
  3. It was (we, us) children.
  4. Grandmother gave (we, us) children each an apple.
  5. The speakers were Brother Amos and (he, him).
  6. Grandmother helped Sara and (I, me).
  7. We showed the teacher and (she, her) the butterflies.
  8. Give these flowers to Sister Ellen and (she, her).
  9. The letters were for (we, us) boys.
  10. Uncle Jerry will teach (we, us) boys.

B. On the chalkboard, diagram the skeletons, predicate nominatives, direct and indirect objects, and prepositional phrases in the sentences from Part A.

C. Read each sentence correctly.
  1. We brought Alice and she extra blankets.
  2. The children went with Father and she.
  3. Us boys need to start early.
  4. It must be James and them.
  5. The day was long for Mother and they.
  6. The teacher and her had a long talk.
  7. The fish in the tank could not see we visitors.
  8. He got a note from Marie and I.
  9. My brother and him were catching catfish.
  10. I am sure it was them.

Written Exercises

A. Write the correct pronouns. After each one, write *S, PN, DO, IO,* or *OP* to tell whether it is a subject, predicate nominative, direct object, indirect object, or object of a preposition.
  1. (We, Us) friends write letters often.
  2. It was (we, us) boys who helped Father.
  3. The children and (we, us) enjoy singing together.
  4. This note is for your teacher and (he, him).
  5. We told Carrie and (she, her).
  6. I gave Mother and (she, her) the message.

C. (Corrections are underlined.)
  1. We brought Alice and <u>her</u> extra blankets.
  2. The children went with Father and <u>her.</u>
  3. <u>We</u> boys need to start early.
  4. It must be James and <u>they.</u>
  5. The day was long for Mother and <u>them.</u>
  6. The teacher and <u>she</u> had a long talk.
  7. The fish in the tank could not see <u>us</u> visitors.
  8. He got a note from Marie and <u>me.</u>
  9. My brother and <u>he</u> were catching catfish.
  10. I am sure it was <u>they.</u>

Written Exercises

A. 1. We—S
  2. we—PN
  3. we—S
  4. him—OP
  5. her—DO
  6. her—IO

Lesson 64 Answers
Class Practice

A. 1. subject, We
  2. subject, I
  3. predicate nominative, we
  4. indirect object, us
  5. predicate nominative, he
  6. direct object, me
  7. indirect object, her
  8. object of a preposition, her
  9. object of a preposition, us
  10. direct object, us

B. 1.

We | rode

2.

3.

It | was \ we

4.

5.

6.

7.

8.

9.

letters | were
for
us

10.

Uncle Jerry | will teach | us

7. Aunt Susan read to (we, us) children.

8. Uncle Joseph told (we, us) boys some stories.

9. The boys pulled the little girls and (he, him) up the hill on the wagon.

10. Uncle James pushed (he, him) and (I, me) high on the swing.

11. Uncle David gave this to (he, him) and (I, me).

12. Brother John and (he, him) led the singing.

13. It was (we, us) boys who raked the yard.

14. It was (they, them) who were here singing last night.

15. I gave Mary and (she, her) the song sheets.

16. He told (we, us) boys the way to his house.

B. Diagram the skeletons, predicate nominatives, direct and indirect objects, and prepositional phrases. Include the correct pronouns on your diagrams.

1. (We, Us) children helped Mother all morning.

2. It was (we, us) girls.

3. Naomi and (she, her) came back.

4. Naomi told Ruth and (she, her) the truth.

5. Boaz showed kindness to Ruth and (she, her).

6. Father told (we, us) boys.

7. Mother gave (we, us) girls instructions.

8. Grandfather handed the tools to (we, us) boys.

Review Exercises

A. Write whether each sentence is *declarative, interrogative, imperative,* or *exclamatory.* (There is one of each kind.) Also write the correct end punctuation. [7]

1. Did you know that there are about two thousand different kinds of frogs known in the world

2. Come and look at this wood frog on a log

3. The West African goliath frog grows to be almost one foot long

4. What a large frog that is

B. Write the correct verbs in parentheses. [47–51]

1. The opossum (laid, lay) motionless.

2. It has not (laid, lain) there long.

3. The dog soon (let, left) the opossum because it looked dead.

4. After the dog was gone, the opossum (raised, rose) its head.

7. us—OP

8. us—IO

9. him—DO

10. him—DO; me—DO

11. him—OP; me—OP

12. he—S

13. we—PN

14. they—PN

15. her—IO

16. us—IO

B. 1. We | helped | Mother

2. It | was \ we

3.

4.

5.

6. Father | told | us

7. Mother | gave | instructions
        \ us

8. Grandfather | handed | tools
           \ to
              \ us

Review Exercises

A. 1. interrogative **?** (question mark)

2. imperative   . (period)

3. declarative   . (period)

4. exclamatory **!** (exclamation point)

B. 1. lay

2. lain

3. left

4. raised

5. Several edible gourds were (setting, sitting) on the table.
6. Grandmother and Grandfather had (set, sat) them there.
7. They (let, left) us keep them.
8. Nancy (laid, lay) some gourds aside.

5. sitting
6. set
7. let
8. laid

---

65. Possessive Pronouns and Demonstrative Pronouns

You have studied personal pronouns in the *nominative case* and in the *objective case*. You are now ready to learn about *possessive case* pronouns.

Possessive Pronouns

Pronouns in the possessive case show possession or ownership. Here they are as on the chart on page 264. The words in parentheses are the archaic forms. (*Thy* is used before a consonant sound, and *thine* is used before a vowel sound.)

Possessive Case

	Singular	*Plural*
First person:	my, mine	our, ours
Second person:	your, yours (thy, thine)	your, yours
Third person:	his, her, hers, its	their, theirs

You are not likely to confuse possessive pronouns with pronouns in the other cases. But you must be careful in several other areas.

1. *Do not use an apostrophe to form a possessive personal pronoun.* Apostrophes are used to make the possessive forms of nouns, but never of personal pronouns.

   Correct: Jane's lunch, Leon's glove, book that had been Mother's

   Correct: her lunch, his glove, book that had been hers

   Incorrect: her' lunch, his' glove, book that had been her's

2. *Do not confuse possessive pronouns with contractions.* An apostrophe is used with some personal pronouns to form contractions.

Lesson 65

Purpose: (1) To identify possessive and demonstrative pronouns. (2) To teach their correct use.

Oral Review:
1. Give the correct pronoun: *Nancy and (she, her) each wrote a poem.* (she)
2. What is a predicate nominative? (a noun or pronoun that follows a linking verb and renames the subject)
3. What is a direct object? (a noun or pronoun that receives the action of a transitive verb)
4. What questions does an indirect object answer? (*to whom or what* or *for whom or what*)
5. Give the correct pronoun: *Send it to Larry and (he, him).* (him)
6. What is an appositive? (a noun that is used directly after another word to clarify it)

7. What is a predicate adjective? (an adjective that follows a linking verb and modifies the subject)

Lesson Introduction: What difference can the students see between the possessive pronouns in the chart of this lesson and the possessive nouns that they studied in Chapter 3? No apostrophes are used with personal pronouns. The probable reason is that the plural forms of personal pronouns (*we, us, they, them*) are not made by adding *-s*. So the possessive forms that end with *s* can be written without an apostrophe.

Demonstrative pronouns may be introduced in the following manner. Suppose someone is *demonstrating* how to use an electric typewriter. Imagine some of the things he would probably say. "*This* is the switch that turns on the machine. *That* is the carriage return key. *These* are the levers used to put in paper and to adjust the line spacing. *Those*

Be sure to remember that they are contractions and not possessive forms. You must distinguish between the two.

Possessive Forms	Contractions
its	it's (it is)
your	you're (you are)
their	they're (they are)

Whenever you see an apostrophe used with a personal pronoun, think of the words that the contraction comes from. These sentences use the different forms correctly.

<u>It's</u> turning on <u>its</u> side.
    It's side would mean "it is side."
<u>You're</u> dropping some of <u>your</u> papers.
    You're papers would mean "you are papers."
<u>They're</u> painting <u>their</u> house a different color.
    They're house would mean "they are house."

3. *When a possessive pronoun modifies a noun, it is used as an adjective. When a possessive pronoun stands alone, it is a pronoun.*

<u>My</u> coat was given to Gerald.
    My is used as an adjective modifying *coat.*

The coat is now <u>his</u>.
    His is a pronoun standing alone.

Please give me <u>her</u> number.
    Her is used as an adjective modifying *number.*

I think this is <u>hers</u>.
    Hers is a pronoun standing alone.

Demonstrative Pronouns

Possessive pronouns are personal pronouns in the possessive case. But the *demonstrative pronouns* are in a different class altogether. They are not personal pronouns.

A demonstrative pronoun is used to point out something. The four demonstrative pronouns are *this, that, these,* and *those.*

<u>This</u> is my coat; <u>that</u> is yours.
<u>These</u> are my gloves; <u>those</u> are yours.

are the keys for automatic underlining and automatic centering."

The words *this, that, these,* and *those* are used to demonstrate. So it is logical that they are known as demonstrative pronouns.

Lesson Outline:

1. The possessive case pronouns show possession or ownership.

***2. The possessive case pronouns are* my, mine, your, yours, his, her, hers, its, our, ours, their, *and* theirs. *The archaic forms of* your *and* yours *are* thy *and* thine. *Thy* is used before a consonant sound, and *thine* is used before a vowel sound.

3. Be careful to use possessive pronouns correctly.

  (1) *Do not use an apostrophe to form a possessive personal pronoun.*

  (2) *Do not confuse possessive pronouns with contractions.* The only time an apostrophe is used with a personal pronoun is to form a contraction.

    <u>It's</u> means "it is."
    <u>You're</u> means "you are."
    <u>They're</u> means "they are."

  (3) *When a possessive pronoun modifies a noun, it is used as an adjective. When a possessive pronoun stands alone, it is a pronoun.*

***4. The demonstrative pronouns are* this, that, these, *and* those.** A demonstrative pronoun is used to point out something.

  a. *This* and *that* are singular.
  b. *These* and *those* are plural.
  c. *This* and *these* are used to point out things nearby.

This and *that* are singular. *These* and *those* are plural. *This* and *these* are used to point out things nearby. *That* and *those* are used to point out things farther away.

This, that, these, and *those* are adjectives when they tell *which* about a noun. They are pronouns when they stand alone.

> <u>This</u> paper is mine. (adjective that tells which paper)
> <u>This</u> is my paper. (pronoun that means *this paper*)

> <u>That</u> book is yours. (adjective that tells which book)
> <u>That</u> is your book. (pronoun that means *that book*)

Be sure to use demonstrative pronouns correctly. Here are two rules.

1. *Do not use* here *or* there *with demonstrative pronouns.* Do not say "this here" or "that there."

> **Incorrect:** <u>This here</u> is a little fox with soft, red fur.
> **Correct:**   <u>This</u> is a little fox with soft, red fur.

> **Incorrect:** <u>That there</u> squirrel is a fox squirrel.
> **Correct:**   <u>That</u> squirrel is a fox squirrel.

2. *Do not use* them *as a demonstrative pronoun or as an adjective.*

> **Incorrect:** <u>Them</u> raccoons surely are curious.
> **Correct:**   <u>Those</u> raccoons surely are curious.

- The possessive case pronouns are *my, mine, your, yours, his, her, hers, its, our, ours, their,* and *theirs.* The archaic forms of *your* and *yours* are *thy* and *thine.*

- An apostrophe is never used to make the possessive form of a personal pronoun.

- The demonstrative pronouns are *this, that, these,* and *those.*

- *This, that, these,* and *those* are adjectives when they tell *which* about a noun. They are pronouns when they stand alone.

- Do not use *here* or *there* with demonstrative pronouns.

- Do not use *them* as a demonstrative pronoun or as an adjective.

> d. *That* and *those* are used to point out things farther away.
> e. *This, that, these,* and *those* are often used as adjectives to modify nouns.

5. *Be careful to use demonstrative pronouns correctly.*

> (1) *Do not use* here *or* there *with demonstrative pronouns.* Do not say "this here" or "that there."
> (2) *Do not use* them *as a demonstrative pronoun or as an adjective.* The correct word is usually *those.*

★ **EXTRA PRACTICE**
Worksheet 35 *(Practice With Pronouns)*

Class Practice

A. Find each possessive pronoun or demonstrative pronoun, and tell which kind it is.
1. This is my Father's world.
2. Our Father which art in heaven, hallowed be Thy name.
3. Give us this day our daily bread.
4. If ye forgive men their trespasses, your heavenly Father will also forgive you.
5. If thine enemy be hungry, give him bread to eat; . . . for thou shalt heap coals of fire on his head.
6. What is that to thee? Follow thou Me.

B. Read the following sentences correctly.
1. These here are fine apples; them are no good.
2. This here wire should not be used outside. Take that there roll.
3. Carol brought them there cookies, and I brought these here.

C. Choose the correct words in parentheses.
1. (Its, It's) time for (your, you're) test.
2. (Your, You're) taking the test in (their, they're) classroom.
3. (Its, It's) about five pages long, and (your, you're) looking at the first page.
4. The longest story is (hers, her's).

D. Tell whether each underlined word is a *pronoun* or an *adjective*. If it is an adjective, tell which word it modifies.
1. These were his words.
2. These books were written by him.
3. This book is mine to keep.
4. Those are ours.

Written Exercises

A. Copy all the possessive pronouns and demonstrative pronouns, including the ones used as adjectives. After each one, write *P* or *D* to tell whether it is possessive or demonstrative.
1. This sickness is not unto death, but it is for the glory of God.
2. Their brother Lazarus had died four days before Jesus came.
3. Lord, if Thou hadst been here, my brother had not died.
4. Thy brother shall rise again.
5. Believest thou this?
6. These friends are here to weep with Mary and Martha.

Lesson 65 Answers
Class Practice

A. 1. This—demonstrative; my—possessive
2. Our—possessive; Thy—possessive
3. this—demonstrative (used as an adjective); our—possessive
4. their—possessive; your—possessive
5. thine—possessive; his—possessive
6. that—demonstrative

B. (Corrections are marked.)
1. These ~~here~~ are fine apples; those are no good.
2. This ~~here~~ wire should not be used outside. Take that ~~there~~ roll.
3. Carol brought those ~~there~~ cookies, and I brought these ~~here.~~

C. 1. It's, your
2. You're, their
3. It's, you're
4. hers

D. 1. pronoun, adjective—words
2. adjective—books
3. adjective—book; pronoun
4. pronoun, pronoun

Written Exercises

A. 1. This—D
2. Their—P
3. my—P
4. Thy—P
5. this—D
6. These—D

7. Jesus, their Master, wept too.
8. Lazarus heard His voice and came forth.
9. Jesus told His friends to loosen the graveclothes around Lazarus.
10. These things were done to strengthen their faith.
11. Bow down thine ear, and hear the words of the wise, and apply thine heart unto my knowledge.
12. Let thine heart retain my words: keep my commandments, and live.

B. Write the correct words in parentheses.
1. (Your, You're) time is up; (its, it's) time for lunch.
2. (Your, You're) grades are passing; (your, you're) doing good work.
3. (Its, It's) doors are open, and (your, you're) things are ready.
4. (Their, They're) painting (their, they're) new house white.
5. (His, His') typewriter is old, but it works well.
6. (This, This here) key sticks sometimes.
7. (Them, Those) keys should be cleaned.
8. (That, That there) book is the one you should study.

C. Write *adj.* or *pron.* to tell how each underlined word is used. If the word is an adjective, write the word it modifies.
1. O Daniel, has <u>your</u> God saved you from the lions?
2. <u>My</u> God has sent His angel to shut <u>their</u> mouths.
3. He is the living God; the kingdom is <u>His</u>.
4. <u>His</u> kingdom will last forever.
5. I am <u>His</u>, and He is <u>mine</u>.
6. <u>This</u> is the true God of heaven.
7. <u>These</u> wicked men had plotted against Daniel.
8. The evil plan was <u>theirs</u>, and <u>that</u> was <u>their</u> punishment.
9. God rewarded <u>His</u> servant Daniel for <u>his</u> faithfulness.
10. I am <u>Thine</u>; save me, for I have sought <u>Thy</u> precepts.
11. Be not wise in <u>thine</u> own eyes: fear the Lord, and depart from evil.

D. Use the following words correctly in sentences of your own.
1. its   2. your   3. their   4. those

Review Exercises

Diagram the skeletons, direct and indirect objects, predicate nominatives, and predicate adjectives. [38–43]

7. their—P
8. His—P
9. His—P
10. These—D; their—P
11. thine—P; thine—P; my—P
12. thine—P; my—P; my—P

B. 1. Your, it's
2. Your, you're
3. Its, your
4. They're, their
5. His
6. This
7. Those
8. That

C. 1. adj.—God
2. adj.—God; adj.—mouths
3. pron.
4. adj.—kingdom
5. pron.; pron.
6. pron.
7. adj.—men
8. pron.; pron.; adj.—punishment
9. adj.—servant; adj.—faithfulness
10. pron.; adj.—precepts
11. adj.—eyes

D. (Individual answers.)

1. The only marsupial in America is the opossum.
2. Opossums eat many different vegetables.
3. The girls sent Grandmother some raisin bread.
4. The date palm is a very useful tree.
5. The climate is hot and dry.

Marlin Boll

Review Exercises

1. marsupial | is \ opossum

2. Opossums | eat | vegetables

3. girls | sent | bread
   (*Raisin bread* \ Grandmother
   may be diagramed as a noun phrase.)

4. date palm | is \ tree   (Students may omit *date*.)

5.
   climate | is \ and < hot / dry

---

66. Indefinite Pronouns

You have learned about personal and demonstrative pronouns. A third class of pronouns is the *indefinite pronouns.* Indefinite pronouns do not refer to definite persons, places, things, or ideas.

Three Kinds of Indefinite Pronouns

1. *Some indefinite pronouns are always singular.* Here is a list of the most common singular indefinite pronouns.

each	anybody	somebody
either	anyone	someone
neither	everybody	nobody
one	everyone	no one
another		

   (*No one* is a compound pronoun spelled as two words.)

Lesson 66

Purpose: (1) To identify indefinite pronouns. (2) To teach their correct use.

Oral Review:

1. Name some possessive pronouns. (my, mine, your, yours, his, her, hers, its, our, ours, their, theirs; *archaic:* thy, thine)
2. Give the correct spelling of each contraction or possessive pronoun.
   a. <u>It's</u> time to give the kitten <u>its</u> milk.
   b. Wear <u>your</u> coat if <u>you're</u> going outside.
   c. <u>They're</u> starting to water <u>their</u> flowers already.
3. Give the demonstrative pronouns. (this, that, these, those)

4. Tell how to correct the following sentences.
   a. This here paper is mine. (Omit *here*.)
   b. Let's buy that there desk. (Omit *there*.)
   c. Them chairs are beautifully made. (Change *them* to *those*.)
5. What is a possessive noun? (a noun that shows possession or ownership)
6. A possessive noun is often used as what part of speech? (adjective)
7. Spell the singular possessive, plural, and plural possessive forms of the following nouns.
   a. ox (ox's, oxen, oxen's)
   b. boy (boy's, boys, boys')

Since these pronouns are singular, they must be used with singular verb forms. (Present tense singular verbs often end with -*s*.) You will not likely use the wrong verb form in sentences like these.

<u>Everybody</u> <u>has</u> his lunch here.
<u>Nobody</u> <u>walks</u> to school.

You must be more careful in sentences where an indefinite pronoun is followed by a prepositional phrase. The verb in the sentence must agree with the *subject* of the sentence, not with the *object of the preposition*.

Incorrect: <u>Each</u> of the girls <u>are</u> bringing a recipe.
Correct: <u>Each</u> of the girls <u>is</u> bringing a recipe.
          The verb must agree with the subject *Each*, not with *girls*. *Each* is singular—it means *each one*. *Girls* is the object of the preposition *of*.

All other words that refer to the subject must also agree with it in number. In the following sentence, which words sound correct to you?

Everybody must take (his seat, their seats).

Everybody is singular—it means every *single* body! So any words referring to the subject must be singular as well. We must say *his* (not *their*), and we must say *seat* because every person has one seat.

<u>Everybody</u> must take <u>his</u> <u>seat</u>.

2. *Some indefinite pronouns are always plural.* The indefinite pronouns in the following list are always plural.

both   few   several   many

Since these pronouns are plural, they must always be used with plural verb forms. (Remember that most plural verbs do not end with -*s*.) Again, be sure the verb agrees with the subject and not with the object of the preposition.

<u>Both</u> <u>come</u> at once.

Written Quiz:
Match the letters of the terms to their descriptions. You will not use all the letters.

a. direct object   e. possessive
b. indirect object   f. nominative
c. appositive   g. objective
d. predicate nominative

_____ 1. It is a noun or pronoun that follows a linking verb and renames the subject.

_____ 2. It is a noun or pronoun that follows an action verb and receives its action.

_____ 3. It is a noun that directly follows another word to clarify it.

_____ 4. It is the correct case for a pronoun used as a subject or a predicate nominative.

_____ 5. It is the correct case for a pronoun used as a direct object, an indirect object, or the object of a preposition.

_____ 6. It answers the question *to whom or what* or *for whom or what* about the verb.

Quiz Answers:

1. d	4. f
2. a	5. g
3. c	6. b

Lesson Introduction: Indefinite pronouns are needed in our language because sometimes it is not definite who did something. But we should be careful to use definite words when we can so that we make ourselves clear. Read the following paragraph to see what can happen when too many indefinite pronouns are used.

This is a story about four people named Everybody, Somebody, Anybody, and Nobody. There was an important job to be done, and Everybody was asked to do it. Everybody was sure Somebody would do it. Anybody could have done it, but Nobody did it. Somebody got angry about that because it was Everybody's job. Everybody thought Anybody could do it, but Nobody realized that Everybody wouldn't do it. It ended up that Everybody blamed Somebody when Nobody did what Anybody could have done.

Such are the problems when we are too *indefinite*!

Several <u>are</u> here already.
Several of the children <u>walk</u> home from school.
<u>Many</u> of the leaves <u>have fallen</u> to the ground.

3. *Some indefinite pronouns may be singular or plural,* depending on how they are used in a sentence.

some   any   none   all   most

To decide whether a pronoun is singular or plural, you must consider the meaning of the sentence. Often your clue is in a prepositional phrase following the subject. Study the following examples.

None of the cake <u>was</u> eaten.
> *None* is singular because it refers to *cake,* which is singular. Use a singular verb.

None of the cookies <u>were</u> eaten.
> *None* is plural because it refers to *cookies,* which is plural. Use a plural verb.

Indefinite Pronouns Used as Adjectives

Many singular indefinite pronouns have a possessive form that ends with an apostrophe and *s* (*'s*). This is different from personal pronouns, which never have apostrophes in the possessive case.

<u>Somebody's</u> coat is lying on the grass.
<u>One's</u> troubles seem small compared to another's.
Do not mind <u>everyone's</u> business, just your own.

The possessive pronouns above are used as adjectives. Other indefinite pronouns are also used as adjectives when they come just before a noun and modify that noun. Study the following sentences.

<u>Many</u> people followed Jesus for the loaves and fishes. (adjective)
<u>Many</u> followed Jesus for the loaves and fishes. (pronoun)

<u>Some</u> papers are missing. (adjective)
<u>Some</u> of the papers are missing. (pronoun)

<u>Another's</u> burdens should cause us sorrow too. (adjective)

Lesson Outline:

1. Indefinite pronouns do not refer to definite persons, places, things, or ideas.

2. There are three kinds of indefinite pronouns.

  (1) *Some indefinite pronouns are always singular.* They include the following: *each, either, neither, one, another, anybody, anyone, everybody, everyone, somebody, someone, nobody, no one.* (Can pupils guess why the pronoun *no one* is spelled as two words?)

    a. These indefinite pronouns must be used with singular verb forms. (Present tense singular verbs usually end with *-s.*)

    b. When an indefinite pronoun is followed by a prepositional phrase, the verb must agree with the subject of the sentence, not with the object of the preposition.

<u>One</u> of the boys <u>is</u> giving a report on elephants. (not *are*)

    c. All other words that refer to the subject must also agree with it in number.

      Incorrect: Everyone is bringing their <u>lunches</u>.
      Correct: Everyone is bringing <u>his lunch</u>.

  (2) *Some indefinite pronouns are always plural.* They include the following: *both, few, several, many.* These pronouns must be used with plural verb forms. (Most plural verbs do not end in *-s.*)

<u>Many</u> <u>tell</u> a new story each time.
<u>Few</u> <u>report</u> on foreign countries.

  (3) *Some indefinite pronouns may be singular or plural,* depending on how they are used. They include the following: *some, any, none, all, most.*

    The meaning of the sentence can help you decide whether the verb should be singular or plural. Often a clue is found in a prepositional phrase after the pronoun. Study the following examples.

<u>Some</u> of the paint <u>is</u> spilled.
<u>Some</u> of the papers <u>are</u> lost.

> - An indefinite pronoun does not refer to a definite person, place, thing, or idea.
>
> - The following indefinite pronouns are always singular: *each, either, neither, one, another, anybody, anyone, everybody, everyone, somebody, someone, nobody, no one.*
>
> - The following indefinite pronouns are always plural: *both, few, several, many.*
>
> - The following indefinite pronouns may be singular or plural, depending on how they are used in a sentence: *some, any, none, all, most.*
>
> - An indefinite pronoun can be used as an adjective.

Class Practice

A. Say each indefinite pronoun, and tell whether it is *singular, plural,* or *either.*
1. Everyone thought somebody would do it.
2. Some needed several more.
3. A few brought some, but many didn't have any.
4. Someone left a baseball glove outside.
5. No one knew whose coat it was.

B. Some of the following sentences have mistakes. Read each sentence correctly, without changing the tense of the verb.
1. Each of the boys take a turn pitching the ball.
2. Both of the girls is a good seamstress.
3. Some of the boys can tie interesting knots.
4. None of the snow have melted yet.
5. Most of the ice cubes has been used up.
6. Everybody must bring their own lunch tomorrow.
7. Each student was sitting in their own seats.
8. Each of the students tell how to do something.

C. Tell whether each underlined word is used as a *pronoun* or an *adjective.* If it is an adjective, tell which word it modifies.
1. <u>Several</u> students memorized the Sermon on the Mount.
2. <u>Most</u> of the students can say Matthew 5:1–16.
3. <u>Many</u> students are able to recite it without error.
4. <u>None</u> have recited Psalm 119 yet.
5. <u>Someone's</u> books are on my desk.

3. Many singular indefinite pronouns have a possessive form that ends with an apostrophe and s ('s).

<u>Everybody's</u> business is <u>nobody's</u> business.
<u>Nobody's</u> work was completed before recess.

(*Teacher:* Since these possessive forms are made by using *'s,* some grammarians classify indefinite pronouns as nouns.)

4. Indefinite pronouns are frequently used as adjectives. This is true when they come just before a noun and modify it.

★ **EXTRA PRACTICE**
Worksheet 36 (*Possessive, Demonstrative, and Indefinite Pronouns*)

Lesson 66 Answers
Class Practice

A. 1. Everyone—singular; somebody—singular
2. Some—plural; several—plural
3. few—plural; some—either; many—plural; any—either
4. Someone—singular
5. No one—singular

B. (Corrections are marked.)
1. Each of the boys <u>takes</u> a turn pitching the ball.
2. Both of the girls <u>are</u> a good <u>seamstresses.</u>
3. Some of the boys can tie interesting knots. (correct)
4. None of the snow <u>has</u> melted yet.
5. Most of the ice cubes <u>have</u> been used up.
6. Everybody must bring <u>his</u> own lunch tomorrow.
7. Each student was sitting in <u>his</u> own <u>seat.</u>
8. Each of the students <u>tells</u> how to do something.

C. 1. adjective—students
2. pronoun
3. adjective—students
4. pronoun
5. adjective—books

Written Exercises

A. Write the subject of each sentence. Then write the correct verb to agree with the subject.
1. Each of the prisoners (was, were) troubled by his dream.
2. No one (was, were) able to interpret the dream.
3. Neither (was, were) able to comfort the other.
4. But someone (was, were) there who loved God.
5. Both (was, were) told the meaning of their dreams.
6. None of Joseph's words (fall, falls) to the ground.
7. All of them (come, comes) true.
8. None of the wise men (has, have) an interpretation for Pharaoh's dream.
9. No one in the group (has, have) the answer.
10. Nobody (is, are) able to interpret the dream.
11. Finally somebody (remember, remembers) Joseph.
12. Everyone (wait, waits) until Joseph is ready.
13. Both of the dreams (is, are) told.
14. All of the mystery (is, are) solved; God gave Joseph the answer.
15. None of the secrets (is, are) left uncovered.

B. Write *pron.* or *adj.* to tell whether each underlined word is a pronoun or an adjective. If it is an adjective, write the word it modifies.
1. Pharaoh said to Joseph, "God has showed you all this, and none are so wise and discreet as you are."
2. None of the people except Pharaoh were greater than Joseph.
3. When Joseph rode in the chariot, it was announced to many people, "Bow the knee."
4. No one escaped the famine that came after the seven plenteous years.
5. The famine was so severe that the people did not have any money left to buy food.
6. Each one brought his cattle to Joseph.
7. Soon all the cattle were sold.
8. So everyone sold all his land to Joseph.
9. Soon everyone's possessions were gone.
10. Now the king owned everything in Egypt.
11. All the people were saved from the terrible famine.
12. God used Joseph to save all of them from the famine.

Written Exercises

A.
1. Each, was
2. No one, was
3. Neither, was
4. someone, was
5. Both, were
6. None, fall
7. All, come
8. None, have
9. No one, has
10. Nobody, is
11. somebody, remembers
12. Everyone, waits
13. Both, are
14. All, is
15. None, are

B.
1. pron.
2. pron.
3. adj.—people
4. pron.
5. adj.—money
6. adj.—one
7. adj.—cattle
8. pron.; adj.—land
9. adj.—possessions
10. pron.
11. adj.—people
12. pron.

Review Exercises

A. Write the correct words in parentheses. [61–65]
1. Jacob and (he, him) were brothers.
2. Isaac blessed Jacob and (he, him).
3. "I am (he, him)," said Jacob.
4. Isaac gave (he, him) the birthright because he thought it was Esau.
5. "(Them, Those) wells are ours," said the herdsmen of Gerar.
6. "No, (we, us) servants dug this well, and it is (ours, our's)!" argued Isaac's servants.
7. "(Its, It's) not (your, you're) well," they said.
8. (Its, It's) the third well they had dug.
9. "(This, This here) well shall be called Rehoboth, for now the Lord has made room for us," said Isaac.
10. God has protected (we, us) children.

B. Copy the possessive nouns. After each one, write *S* or *P* to tell whether it is singular or plural. [26]
1. The shepherd's flock follows when he calls.
2. Each of the shepherds' flocks followed its own shepherd.
3. The lambs' wool is pure white.
4. The little black lamb's wool is soft.

Review Exercises

A. 1. he
    2. him
    3. he
    4. him
    5. Those
    6. we, ours
    7. It's, your
    8. It's
    9. This
    10. us

B. 1. shepherd's—S
   2. shepherds'—P
   3. lambs'—P
   4. lamb's—S

---

67. Writing a Business Letter

Sometimes you may want to write a letter to purchase something by mail, to inquire about a purchase, or to seek information. What kind of letter should you write? A friendly letter does not serve this purpose, so a *business letter* is used.

A business letter has the same five parts as a friendly letter: *heading, greeting, body, closing,* and *signature.* In addition, a business letter also has an *inside address.* An inside address is the address of the person or company to whom you are writing.

The same rules of capitalization and punctuation are used for business letters as for friendly letters, with one exception. In a business letter, a colon rather than a comma is used after the greeting.

A business letter has a more formal greeting and closing than a

Lesson 67

Purpose: To teach the form and mechanics of *a business letter.

Oral Review:
1. What are some reasons for writing friendly letters? (to share with someone you may not see for a long time; to give help or encouragement to someone who is not with you; to give or accept an invitation; to thank someone for a favor shown)
2. Name the five parts of a friendly letter. (heading, greeting, body, closing, signature)
3. Why should you use more than one reference source when taking notes? (It helps to make your report more informative and interesting.)
4. How should you take notes as you find information for a report? (Write only main ideas and key words.)
5. Why should you write plenty of notes when finding information? (It is easier to discard some notes than to go back through the reference books looking for more information.)

Lesson Introduction: When you write a friendly letter, you may use plain white paper or colorful stationery. You may write in black ink or in blue, green, pink, or some other color. You may write briefly about a number of different things, or you may write many details about just a few things.

A business letter is different. You should always use plain white paper and blue or black ink. You should write briefly and clearly, without including extra details that may be annoying to the person who reads the letter. Your letter may be written in a warm and friendly way, but it must follow the proper form of a business letter.

friendly letter does. Here are some standard greetings used for business letters.

Dear Sir: Gentlemen: Dear Mr. Martin: Dear Madam:

Use *Dear Sir* when you do not know the person's name. Use *Gentlemen* when you are writing to a company. Some standard closings for business letters are shown below.

Yours truly,   Very truly yours,   Sincerely yours,

The body of the letter should be written neatly and courteously, using complete sentences. Keep the left margin straight and the right margin as straight as possible. Often it is good to begin the body of a business letter with these words: *I would appreciate information on . . .* or *I wish to order . . .* or *Please send me . . . .* Make the body brief and clear, and say exactly what you want. Remember that the person who reads the letter may have many letters to read each day.

Notice that the heading, closing, and signature are written in the same positions as in a friendly letter. The heading is close to the right margin. The left edge of the heading, closing, and signature are in line with each other. The left edge of the inside address is at the left margin. A blank space should be left between each letter part and the next. Such a space is especially important between the inside address and the greeting.

Heading

123 Best Road
Lehman, PA 18627
November 9, 20—

Inside Address

Pennsylvania Power and Light Company
Two North Main Street
Allentown, PA 18104

Greeting   Dear Sirs:

Body

Please send me a copy of the pamphlet *Heating the Home in Winter Weather,* which you offered with last month's billing. I would also appreciate receiving any material about home heating that you may have, which would be suitable for display on the wall of our classroom.

Closing

Sincerely,

Signature

Nancy Mellinger

Lesson Outline:

1. A business letter is written to purchase something by mail, to inquire about a purchase, or to seek information.

2. The six parts of a business letter are the heading, inside address, greeting, body, closing, and signature.

    a. The heading, closing, and signature are written in the same positions as in a friendly letter.

    b. The heading is close to the right margin.

    c. The left edge of the heading, closing, and signature are in line with each other.

    d. The left edge of the inside address is at the left margin.

3. A business letter is punctuated in the same way as a friendly letter except that a colon is placed after the greeting.

4. The greeting and the closing in a business letter are more formal than in a friendly letter.

Common greetings:
    Dear Sir: Gentlemen:
    Dear Mr. Martin: Dear Madam:

Common closings:
    Yours truly,
    Very truly yours,
    Sincerely yours,

5. The body of a business letter should be brief and clear.

    a. Write neatly and courteously, using complete sentences.

    b. Keep the left margin straight and the right margin as straight as possible.

    c. Use good beginnings.

        I would appreciate information on...
        I wish to order...
        Please send me...

★ **EXTRA PRACTICE**
Worksheet 37 *(Business Letters)*

A business letter is usually sent in a long business envelope rather than the smaller size commonly used for friendly letters. The receiver's address and the return address are written in the same positions as for a friendly letter. Remember that the United States Postal Service wants the receiver's address printed with all capital letters and with no punctuation, as in the following illustration.

Nancy Mellinger
123 Best Road
Lehman, PA 18627

PENNSYLVANIA POWER AND LIGHT COMPANY

TWO NORTH MAIN STREET

ALLENTOWN PA 18104

- A business letter is written to purchase something by mail, to inquire about a purchase, or to seek information.

- The six parts of a business letter are the heading, inside address, greeting, body, closing, and signature.

- In a business letter, a colon is used after the greeting. The greeting and the closing are more formal than in a friendly letter.

- The body of a business letter should be brief and clear.

Class Practice

Point out the errors in the following letter, and suggest how the body could be improved.

262, hickory view ave
new holland PA, 17557
February 2 20—

Delaware State Travel Service
630, State College road
dover de, 19901
dear Friends,

I am from sixth grade at New Holland Christian School. I would like information on your state. We are studying your state in our class. I like studying your state.

Thank you
Janice Martin

Written Exercises

A. Rewrite the business letter in Class Practice, making the needed improvements.

B. Write a business letter of your own, using one of the following suggestions. (Your teacher may need to help you find addresses.) After your work is checked, you may actually send your letter if your teacher approves.
   1. Write for information about the state parks and other points of interest in a certain state. (To get an address, find an encyclopedia article on that state and look under a heading such as "Places to Visit." Often you can obtain free seals, brochures, and other interesting items.)
   2. Write to the closest zoo for information on the zoo and its history.
   3. Write to a local business place for information on its products and its history. Perhaps you can write to a brother in the church who has a business.
   4. Write to a local place of interest, perhaps the place your class plans to visit on your school trip this year. Ask about their visiting hours, special tours, and other information that would help to make your visit enjoyable.

C. Correctly address an envelope for the business letter you wrote in Part B.

Lesson 67 Answers
Class Practice
(See the sample letter in Part A of Written Exercises; note the added space after the inside address and after the closing. Also note that the greeting and the closing are more appropriate, that the request is more specific, and that the unnecessary details have been removed.)

Written Exercises
A. (Sample letter, with corrections marked.)

262, Hickory View Ave.
New Holland, PA, 17557
February 2, 20—

Delaware State Travel Service
630, State College Road
Dover, DE, 19901

Gentlemen:

I would appreciate receiving information on your state parks and forests. Also please send me any material that would be suitable for wall display in our classroom.

Very truly yours,

Janice Martin

B–C. (Provide suitable addresses, or help the students to find them. If the letters are actually sent, be sure to check the incoming material before the students have access to it.)

Review Exercises

Decide which of the following is *not* one of the steps in writing a report. Write the remaining steps in the correct order, and number them from 1 to 7. [50–57]

Take plenty of notes on key words and main ideas.
Write the first draft of the report.
Find several sources of information.
Decide what information may be copied word for word.
Choose a topic that is interesting to you.
Write the second draft of the report.
Write an outline based on your notes.
Proofread the first draft, and mark changes that are needed.

Challenge Exercises

Write a report on one of the following topics. Follow the rules you learned for writing reports.

1. Report on interesting things to see in a certain state of the United States.
2. Report on the behavior of a certain zoo animal of your choice (but not the alligator).
3. Report on a certain product manufactured in your area.
4. Report on a local place of interest and its history.
5. Did you send the business letter that you wrote for this lesson? If so, plan to write a report based on the information you receive.

---

68. Interrogative Pronouns

You know that an interrogative sentence asks a question. Can you guess the meaning of *interrogate* (in·ter′·ə·gāt′)? It means "to question." A judge may *interrogate* a person who had an accident. He may ask the following questions.

<u>What</u> is your name?   <u>Who</u> was the other driver?
<u>What</u> is your address?   <u>Whose</u> is the car you were driving?

Review Exercises

(The following sentence should be omitted: *Decide what information may be copied word for word.*)

1. Choose a topic that is interesting to you.
2. Find several sources of information.
3. Take plenty of notes on key words and main ideas.
4. Write an outline based on your notes.
5. Write the first draft of the report.
6. Proofread the first draft, and mark changes that are needed.
7. Write the second draft of the report.

Challenge Exercises

(Individual work.)

Lesson 68

Purpose: To teach interrogative pronouns.

Oral Review:

1. Tell whether the following indefinite pronouns are singular or plural.
   - a. each (singular)
   - b. both (plural)
   - c. nobody (singular)
   - d. few (plural)
   - e. anyone (singular)
   - f. several (plural)
   - g. many (plural)
   - h. either (singular)

2. Name five indefinite pronouns that can be singular or plural, depending on the meaning of the sentence. (some, any, none, all, most)

3. Do verbs that end with *-s* agree with singular subjects or plural subjects? (singular subjects)

4. Should an indefinite pronoun ever be written with an apostrophe? (yes, when it shows possession)

5. Give a sentence with an indefinite pronoun used as an adjective. (*Sample answer:* God has given us *many* friends.)

6. Give the correct verb: *One of these plants (is, are) a rose.* (is)

Lesson Introduction: Do any of your students have little brothers or sisters? Then surely they know how many questions little children can ask.

<u>What</u> is this?
<u>Who</u> is that man?
<u>Whose</u> house are we going to?
<u>Which</u> potato shall I eat?

Notice the words that begin many of these questions. No wonder they are called *interrogative* pronouns. Though they are used freely by little children, sixth graders still have a few things to learn about these words.

The word *interrogative* comes from *interrogate*. An *interrogative pronoun* asks a question. *Who, whom, whose, which,* and *what* are interrogative pronouns when they introduce questions.

> <u>Who</u> can tell us the answer?
> <u>What</u> did you see in the cave?
> <u>Whose</u> is that cap on the ground?

Remember that pronouns take the place of nouns. The answer to the question introduced by an interrogative pronoun will contain the noun (or pronoun) that the interrogative pronoun stands for. In the first sentence above, *the teacher* can answer the question *who.* In the second question, *a shaggy bear* can answer the question *what. Teacher* and *bear* are the antecedents of the interrogative pronouns in these sentences.

An interrogative pronoun can also be used as an adjective. It is an adjective when it modifies another noun or pronoun.

> <u>Which</u> **picture** shall I buy?
> *Which* modifies *picture.*

> <u>Which</u> shall I buy?
> *Which* is a pronoun standing alone.

Learn to use the interrogative pronouns *who* and *whom* correctly. *Who* is in the nominative case and must be used as a *subject* or a *predicate nominative. Whom* is in the objective case and must be used for a *direct object,* an *indirect object,* or the *object of a preposition.*

> <u>Who</u> are the visitors? (subject)
> The man at the door was <u>who</u>? (predicate nominative)
> You told <u>whom</u>? (direct object)
> You sent <u>whom</u> the book? (indirect object)
> The package was sent to <u>whom</u>? (object of a preposition)

Lesson Outline:

1. An interrogative pronoun is used to ask a question.

2. The pronouns who, whom, whose, which, and what are interrogative pronouns when they are used to introduce questions. The answer to the question contains the antecedent of the interrogative pronoun.

3. An interrogative pronoun can be used as an adjective. It is an adjective when it modifies a noun or pronoun.

4. The interrogative pronoun who is in the nominative case. It must be used as a subject or a predicate nominative.

5. The interrogative pronoun whom is in the objective case. It must be used as an object—a direct object, an indirect object, or the object of a preposition.

(*Teacher:* According to the rule, an indirect object always comes between the verb and the direct object. A sentence like "Whom shall I give this?" is an exception because it is not in normal word order.)

6. There are some helps for deciding which is the correct pronoun to use.

   a. In deciding whether to use *who* or *whom* in a sentence, try substituting *he* for *who,* and *him* for *whom.*

   b. If the sentence is written in inverted order, changing it to normal word order is helpful in deciding whether *who* or *whom* is correct.

   c. Do not confuse the interrogative pronoun *whose* with the contraction *who's. Whose* is a possessive form. *Who's* means "who is."

★ **EXTRA PRACTICE**
Worksheet 38 *(Possessive, Demonstrative, Indefinite, and Interrogative Pronouns)*

If you are not sure whether to use *who* or *whom* in a sentence, there is a check you can use. Try substituting *he* for *who,* and *him* for *whom.*

> You helped (*who* or *whom*?)?
> **Think:**   You helped <u>him</u>.
> **Therefore:** You helped <u>whom</u>?

> (*Who* or *Whom*?) is helping?
> **Think:**   <u>He</u> is helping.
> **Therefore:** <u>Who</u> is helping?

In many sentences with interrogative pronouns, the word order is inverted. Changing these sentences to normal word order is helpful in deciding whether *who* or *whom* is correct.

> (*Who* or *Whom*?) did you call?
> **Think:**   You did call <u>whom</u>? (direct object)
> **Therefore:** <u>Whom</u> did you call?

Do not confuse the interrogative pronoun *whose* with the contraction *who's*. *Whose* is a possessive form; no apostrophe is used with it. *Who's* means "who is."

> **Incorrect:** <u>Who's</u> purse is this? (means "Who is purse is this?")
> **Correct:**   <u>Whose</u> purse is this?
>   <u>Who's</u> at the door?

- The interrogative pronouns are *who, whom, whose, which,* and *what.*

- *Who* is a nominative case pronoun and is used as a subject or a predicate nominative.

- *Whom* is an objective case pronoun and is used as a direct object, an indirect object, or the object of a preposition.

- Do not confuse the interrogative pronoun *whose* with the contraction *who's*.

Class Practice

A. Find the interrogative pronouns. Tell whether each one is used as a *pronoun* or an *adjective*.
   1. Who will go for us?
   2. This is whose?
   3. Whom shall I ask to help me?
   4. You chose which little puppy?
   5. Which did you bring?
   6. Whose handwriting is this?
   7. What did you say?
   8. What number shall I use?

B. Find the interrogative pronouns, and tell whether each one is used as a *subject, predicate nominative, direct object,* or *indirect object.* (Some sentences should first be changed to normal order.)
   1. Who is your teacher?
   2. Your friend is who?
   3. Whom did you meet?
   4. This is whose?
   5. Which is which?
   6. Whom shall I give this?

C. On the chalkboard, diagram the skeletons, direct objects, indirect objects, predicate nominatives, and predicate adjectives of the sentences in Part B.

D. In each sentence, tell which pronoun in parentheses is correct, and tell how it is used. Practice reading the sentences correctly.
   1. (Who, Whom) did you invite?
   2. (Who, Whom) is she?
   3. The book is for (who, whom)?
   4. (Whose, Who's) reading now?
   5. (Whose, Who's) voice do I hear?

Written Exercises

A. Copy the interrogative pronouns in these sentences. Write *adj.* after each one that is used as an adjective.
   1. Who is your teacher?
   2. Which book will you study?
   3. Whom did you see at church yesterday?
   4. What subjects do you have in the morning?

Lesson 68 Answers
Class Practice

A. 1. Who—pronoun
   2. whose—pronoun
   3. Whom—pronoun
   4. which—adjective
   5. Which—pronoun
   6. Whose—adjective
   7. What—pronoun
   8. What—adjective

B. (*Teacher:* If a sentence like "Who are they?" is reworded for analysis, *who* may be considered the predicate nominative (*they are who*). So it would not be wrong to call *who* the predicate nominative in a sentence like number 1. But since few students will do this, the answer key gives only the most likely answer for such sentences.)
   1. Who—subject
   2. who—predicate nominative
   3. Whom—direct object
   4. whose—predicate nominative
   5. Which—subject; which—predicate nominative
   6. Whom—indirect object

C. 1. Who | is \ teacher

   2. friend | is \ who

   3. you | did meet | Whom

   4. This | is \ whose

   5. Which | is \ which

   6. I | shall give | this
            \ Whom

D. 1. Whom—direct object
   2. Who—subject
   3. whom—object of a preposition
   4. Who's—contraction for *who is*
   5. Whose—adjective (possessive form)

Written Exercises

A. 1. Who
   2. Which—adj.
   3. Whom
   4. What—adj.

5. Which is yours?
6. This pocketknife is whose?
7. What is the date today?
8. Which of the boys finished first?

B. Diagram the skeletons, direct objects, indirect objects, and predicate nominatives. Also include the interrogative pronouns used as adjectives.
   1. Who was Abner's father?
   2. Whom did Elisha anoint?
   3. What lesson was Jesus teaching?
   4. Whom did you tell the story?
   5. Whose cross did Simon carry?
   6. What is a scepter?
   7. Which would you do?
   8. Which book do you want?

C. Write the correct words. Be ready to tell in class why you chose the ones you did.
   1. (Who, Whom) was the author of the wise words in Proverbs 30?
   2. (Who, Whom) did God call from a burning bush?
   3. Aaron assisted (who, whom) in his work?
   4. (Who, Whom) was the first king of Israel?
   5. The last king of Israel was (who, whom)?
   6. The Epistle to the Ephesians was written by (who, whom)?
   7. A donkey asked (who, whom) some questions?
   8. (Whose, Who's) standing in the path?
   9. (Whose, Who's) life was in danger?
   10. (Who, Whom) did Balaam finally obey?

D. Use three interrogative pronouns in sentences of your own. Use *whom* correctly in one of them.

Review Exercises

A. Write the subject of each sentence. Then write the word or words in parentheses that agree with the subject. [54, 66]
   1. (There's, There are) about twenty-eight thousand kinds of beetles in the United States and Canada.
   2. None of the beetles from the United States or Canada (is, are) as large as the beetles found in the tropics.
   3. Several of the kinds from jungles (is, are) six or more inches long!

5. Which
6. whose (may be labeled *adj.*)
7. What
8. Which

B. 1. Who | was \ father

2. Elisha | did anoint | Whom

3. Jesus | was teaching | lesson
   \ What

4. you | did tell | story
   \ Whom

5. Simon | did carry | cross
   \ Whose

6. What | is \ scepter

7. you | would do | Which

8. you | do want | book
   \ Which

C. (Reasons in parentheses are to be given in class.)
   1. Who (subject)
   2. Whom (direct object)
   3. whom (direct object)
   4. Who (subject)
   5. who (predicate nominative)
   6. whom (object of a preposition)
   7. whom (indirect object)
   8. Who's (contraction for *who is*)
   9. Whose (possessive form)
   10. Whom (direct object)

D. (Individual answers.)

Review Exercises

A. 1. kinds, There are
   2. None, are
   3. Several, are

4. Some of the natives from Cuba and Puerto Rico (tie, ties) large fire-flies on their feet to light their way on mountain trails at night.

5. (Don't, Doesn't) anybody know about the bombardier beetles that can spray a foaming, bad-smelling chemical on their enemies?

6. One of the beetles (is, are) able to pull ninety times (its, their) own weight.

3. Copy the two personal pronouns in each sentence. After each pronoun, write its person, number, case, and gender. [60–65]

1. Alice told me about them.
2. Is it Carol's coat or yours?
3. He brought Father and her some flowers.

---

69. Relative Pronouns and Relative Clauses

You have learned that the pronouns *who, whom, whose, which,* and *what* are *interrogative pronouns* when they are used to introduce questions. Now consider the following sentence.

The boy <u>who</u> discovered the fire ran for an extinguisher.

Is *who* an interrogative pronoun in this sentence? No, because the sentence does not ask a question. *Who* is a *relative pronoun.* Look at the sentence again, and notice two things about the relative pronoun.

1. A relative *pronoun* relates *directly to another word in the sentence.*

The boy <u>who</u> discovered the fire ran for an extinguisher.

What is the antecedent of the pronoun *who? Who* discovered the fire? The boy. So *who* relates to *boy,* its antecedent. A relative pronoun comes directly after its antecedent. Here are several more examples.

Brother Brian is a man <u>whom</u> you can trust.
    Whom relates to its antecedent *man.*

Grandpa, <u>whose</u> children are grown, loves his grandchildren.
    Whose relates to its antecedent *Grandpa.*

---

4. Some, tie
5. anybody, Doesn't
6. One, is, its

B. 1. me—first, singular, objective, common
    them—third, plural, objective, common

2. it—third, singular, nominative, neuter
    yours—second, singular, possessive, common

3. He—third, singular, nominative, masculine
    her—third, singular, objective, feminine

Lesson 69

Purpose: To introduce *relative pronouns and *relative clauses.

Oral Review:

1. When the pronouns *who, whom, whose, which,* and *what* are used to introduce questions, what kind of pronouns are they? (interrogative pronouns)

2. When is an interrogative pronoun used as an adjective? (when it modifies a noun or pronoun)

3. How should the pronoun *who* be used? (as a subject or a predicate nominative)

4. How should the pronoun *whom* be used? (as a direct object, an indirect object, or the object of a preposition)

5. What is the meaning of *who's?* (who is)

6. What two kinds of voice do verbs have? (active, passive)

7. What is the voice of the verb when the subject performs the action? (active)

8. What is the voice of the verb when the subject receives the action? (passive)

Lesson Introduction: Who is your relative? It is someone connected to you because he has the same ancestors, or he may be connected through someone's marriage.

What is a *relative* pronoun? It is a pronoun that is connected to another word in the same sentence. It is different from other pronouns, however, because it also connects other words to its antecedent. In this lesson we will learn about these words that *relate* strongly to other words.

The young donkey, <u>which</u> had never been ridden before, was brought to Jesus. (*Which* relates to its antecedent *donkey.*)

2. *A relative pronoun introduces a* relative clause, *which modifies the antecedent of the relative pronoun.* Again consider the first example sentence. Notice that the pronoun *who* introduces a clause (a group of words with a subject and a verb).

subject | verb
The boy (<u>who</u> | <u>discovered</u> the fire) ran for an extinguisher.
The clause *who discovered the fire* modifies *boy,* telling *which* boy. Since the entire clause relates to the boy, it is a *relative clause.*

The other interrogative pronouns can also function as relative pronouns. Study the following examples; the relative clauses are in parentheses.

Interrogative:	**Relative:**
<u>Who</u> can do this job?	The man (<u>who</u> can do this job) will be paid well.
<u>Whom</u> should we pay?	Stephen is the man (<u>whom</u> we should pay).
<u>Whose</u> is this book?	The girl (<u>whose</u> book this is) left yesterday.
<u>Which</u> do we need?	The tool (<u>which</u> we need) is broken.
<u>What</u> did you see?	The bear (<u>that</u> I saw) was asleep.

In the last pair of sentences, notice that the interrogative pronoun *What* is replaced by the relative pronoun *that.* This is the only difference between the relative pronouns and the interrogative pronouns.

Relative pronouns: who, whom, whose, which, that

What happens if a relative clause is removed from a sentence? Since it is a separate clause, the rest of the sentence still makes sense. Study the following example.

The birds (<u>that</u> the children are feeding) are called juncos.
The birds are called juncos.

A relative clause provides more details, but the sentence is complete without it. This fact can help you to recognize relative clauses in sentences. If a clause begins with a relative pronoun and is not needed to make the sentence complete, it is a relative clause.

Lesson Outline:

1. The relative pronouns are **who, whom, whose, which,** *and* **that.** They are the same as the interrogative pronouns except that *what* is replaced by *that.* Relative pronouns are not used to introduce questions, as interrogative pronouns are.

2. A relative pronoun is different from an interrogative pronoun.

(1) *A* relative *pronoun* relates *directly to another word in the sentence.*

(2) *A relative pronoun introduces a* relative clause, *which modifies the antecedent of the relative pronoun.* The clause follows a noun or pronoun and modifies it by telling *which.* The noun or pronoun modified is the antecedent of the relative pronoun. (*Teacher:* Relative clauses are adjective clauses, and they are taught as such in Chapter 8.)

3. A relative clause provides additional details, but the sentence is complete without it. This makes it easy to pick out a relative clause from the rest of the sentence.

★ **EXTRA PRACTICE**
Worksheet 39 *(Relative Pronouns)*

- The relative pronouns are *who, whom, whose, which,* and *that.*

- A relative pronoun relates directly to another word in the sentence, which is its antecedent.

- A relative pronoun introduces a relative clause, which modifies the antecedent of the relative pronoun. The relative clause can be removed from a sentence, and the sentence will still be complete.

Class Practice

A. Tell whether each underlined word is an *interrogative* pronoun or a *relative* pronoun.
  1. Everyone <u>who</u> was there saw him.
  2. <u>Whom</u> did Father meet in the city?
  3. This is the man <u>whom</u> you met yesterday.
  4. Continue in the things <u>that</u> you have learned.
  5. <u>What</u> is always the first name in the Bible list of apostles?
  6. <u>Which</u> of the roads leads to your house?
  7. The road <u>that</u> leads to our house is closed.
  8. <u>Who</u> helped the children <u>whose</u> wagon was broken down?

B. Tell which words are relative pronouns, and give their antecedents.
  1. Dorcas was a woman who was full of good deeds.
  2. The book that we read had been borrowed.
  3. You are blessed of the Lord, who made heaven and earth.
  4. A city that is set on a hill cannot be hidden.

C. Read only the relative clauses in the following sentences. Then read each sentence without the relative clause.
  1. The girl whom you saw is my niece.
  2. The book that I just read is about pioneer life.
  3. Here is a man who wants to speak with you.
  4. George will find a red cherry, which is ripe.

Written Exercises

A. Write *interrogative* or *relative* to identify each underlined pronoun.
  1. <u>Whom</u> did you meet there?
  2. The boy <u>whom</u> you met was Herbert.
  3. <u>Which</u> of the apples will you take?

Lesson 69 Answers
Class Practice
A. 1. relative
   2. interrogative
   3. relative
   4. relative
   5. interrogative
   6. interrogative
   7. relative
   8. interrogative, relative

B. 1. who—woman
   2. that—book
   3. who—Lord
   4. that—city

C. 1. whom you saw; The girl is my niece.
   2. that I just read; The book is about pioneer life.
   3. who wants to speak with you; Here is a man.
   4. which is ripe; George will find a red cherry.

Written Exercises
A. 1. interrogative
    2. relative
    3. interrogative

4. This apple, <u>which</u> is a Winesap, is the one I want.
5. We saw a sign <u>that</u> showed us the way.
6. <u>What</u> did you ask me?
7. He <u>who</u> follows Christ shall not walk in darkness.
8. <u>Who</u> climbed into a sycamore tree to see Jesus?
9. Dorcas, <u>whom</u> Peter raised from the dead, had done many kind deeds.
10. <u>What</u> is the name of the man <u>whose</u> daughter Jesus raised to life?

B. Write each relative pronoun and its antecedent.
   1. People who love the Lord obey Him.
   2. This is the day that the Lord has made.
   3. We know the people whom we love.
   4. Those that fed the swine fled to the city.
   5. The man whom Jesus healed wanted to follow Him.
   6. He lived in a strange land, which was far from his home.

C. Copy only the relative clauses in these sentences.
   1. Father repaired the roof, which the storm had damaged.
   2. The visitor whom I met lives in Missouri.
   3. Peace that passes understanding shall keep your hearts.
   4. Haman was a man whose pride brought him low.
   5. He has an old Bible, which is quite worn.
   6. His mother, who taught him about God, was Eunice.

D. Use these relative clauses in original sentences.
   1. that Sister Alice read to us
   2. whom the dog bit yesterday
   3. who brought the frog to school

Review Exercises

Write the word that receives the action of each verb, and label it *S* for subject or *DO* for direct object. Then write whether the sentence is in the *active* or the *passive* voice. [55]
   1. Daryl has rung the bell.
   2. The bell has been rung.
   3. The leaves have been blown away.
   4. June wrote several letters yesterday.
   5. Father is planting peas.
   6. The book was placed on the shelf.

---

4. relative
5. relative
6. interrogative
7. relative
8. interrogative
9. relative
10. interrogative, relative

B. 1. who—People
   2. that—day
   3. whom—people
   4. that—Those
   5. whom—man
   6. which—land

C. 1. which the storm had damaged
   2. whom I met
   3. that passes understanding
   4. whose pride brought him low
   5. which is quite worn
   6. who taught him about God

D. (Individual work.)

Review Exercises

   1. bell—DO, active
   2. bell—S, passive
   3. leaves—S, passive
   4. letters—DO, active
   5. peas—DO, active
   6. book—S, passive

70. Using Relative Pronouns Correctly

You have learned that a relative pronoun always introduces a relative clause. It is a clause because it has a subject and a verb. In many sentences, the relative pronoun is the subject of the relative clause.

> The prophet (<u>who</u> warned Jeroboam) refused his dinner invitation.
> <u>Who</u> <u>warned</u>. *Who* is the subject.

> He started for his home, (<u>which</u> was in Judah).
> <u>Which</u> <u>was</u>. *Which* is the subject.

The relative pronoun is not always the subject. It may also fill some other place in the relative clause. The relative pronoun may be a predicate nominative, a direct object, an indirect object, the object of a preposition, or a modifier. Study the following examples. The relative clauses are in parentheses.

> An old man went down the road (<u>that</u> the prophet had taken).
> <u>Prophet</u> <u>had taken</u> that. *That* is the direct object.

> The old man (with <u>whom</u> the prophet returned) had lied to him.
> <u>Prophet</u> <u>returned</u> with whom. *Whom* is the object of a preposition.

> The prophet (<u>whom</u> the old man had served a meal) was killed by a lion.
> <u>Man</u> <u>had served</u> whom meal. *Whom* is the indirect object.

> This is an example of a man (<u>whose</u> disobedience cost his life).
> *Whose* modifies <u>disobedience</u>. *Whose* is an adjective.

As you can see in the examples above, the word order in a relative clause may be inverted. Changing the clause to normal word order is helpful in deciding what sentence part the relative pronoun is.

> The sycamore tree, (<u>which</u> Zacchaeus climbed), stood along the road.
> **Normal word order:** Zacchaeus climbed which.
> *Which* is a direct object.
> Zacchaeus was changed from the cheater (<u>that</u> he had been).
> **Normal word order:** He had been that.
> *That* is a predicate nominative.

How do we know when to use the words *who, whom,* or *whose* in relative clauses? The answer is found by knowing what part of the clause the word fills. If the relative pronoun is a subject or a predicate

No— see next page

5. a. What is a predicate nominative? (a noun or pronoun that follows a linking verb and renames the subject)
   b. Choose the correct pronoun: *It was (they, them).* (they)
6. a. What is a direct object? (a noun or pronoun that receives the action of a transitive verb)
   b. Choose the correct pronoun: *We saw Mary and (he, him).* (him)
7. What questions does an indirect object answer? (*to whom or what* or *for whom or what*)
8. Which is correct? *We gave Nathan and (he, him) an apple.* (him)

Written Quiz:

A. Answer this question.
   What is the antecedent of a pronoun?

_____

B. Before each group of pronouns, write the letter of the kind that it is.

   a. personal—nominative case   e. demonstrative
   b. personal—objective case   f. indefinite
   c. personal—possessive case   g. interrogative
   d. personal—archaic   h. relative

   _____ 1. me, you, him, her, it, us, them
   _____ 2. who, whom, whose, which, that
   _____ 3. my, mine, your, yours, his, her, hers, its, our, ours, their, theirs
   _____ 4. some, any, none, all, most, each, either, one, nobody, anyone, anybody, both, few, several, many
   _____ 5. this, that, these, those
   _____ 6. I, you, he, she, it, we, they
   _____ 7. who, whom, whose, which, what
   _____ 8. thou, thee, thy, thine, ye

Lesson 70

Purpose: To teach *how to use relative pronouns correctly. (*Previous experience:* Correct use of *who* and *whom* as interrogative pronouns.)

Oral Review:

1. In what class are the pronouns *who, whom, whose, which,* and *that*? (relative pronouns; They can also be interrogative pronouns with one exception—*what* replaces *that.*)
2. A relative pronoun introduces what kind of clause? (a relative clause)
3. A relative pronoun relates what two things? (It relates a relative clause to a noun or pronoun—the antecedent of the relative pronoun—in the main part of the sentence.)
4. Choose the correct pronoun, and give the reason for your choice: *Joanna and (she, her) told us.* (she, because the subject must be nominative)

nominative, you must use the nominative case *who*. If the relative pronoun is an object, you must use the objective case *whom*. If it shows possession, you must use the possessive form *whose*.

The man (<u>who</u> fell out the window) was Eutychus.
<u>Who</u> <u>fell</u>. Nominative case *who* is used for a subject.

One man (<u>whom</u> Paul healed) was Publius.
Paul <u>healed</u> whom. Objective case *whom* is used for a direct object.

The people (to <u>whom</u> Paul preached) listened attentively.
Paul <u>preached</u> to whom. Objective case *whom* is used for the object of a preposition.

There is another rule for using relative pronouns correctly. Use *who* or *whom* in referring to people, and *which* in referring to animals or objects. *That* and *whose* may refer to people, animals, or objects.

It was Jennifer <u>who</u> helped us yesterday. (not *which*)
The lambs <u>which</u> we sold were all black. (not *whom*)
The boy <u>that</u> cleaned the floor used a broom <u>that</u> was black.
The people <u>whose</u> language was confounded had planned a tower <u>whose</u> top would reach to heaven.

- A relative pronoun can be used as several different parts of a dependent clause.

- Use the nominative case *who* when a relative pronoun is the subject or the predicate nominative in a relative clause.

- Use the objective case *whom* when the relative pronoun is the object in a relative clause.

- Use the possessive case *whose* when the relative pronoun is a modifier in a relative clause.

- Use *who* or *whom* in referring to people, and *which* in referring to animals or objects. *That* and *whose* may refer to people, animals, or objects.

C. Read each set of pronouns. Write *singular* if those pronouns are always singular, *plural* if they are always plural, and *either* if they may be singular or plural.

_____ 1. both, few, several, many
_____ 2. each, either, neither, one, another, anybody, anyone, everybody, everyone, somebody, someone, nobody, no one
_____ 3. some, any, none, all, most

Quiz Answers:

A. the noun for which the pronoun stands

B. 1. b   5. e
   2. h   6. a
   3. c   7. g
   4. f   8. d

C. 1. plural
   2. singular
   3. either

Lesson Introduction: Since this is another lesson on relative pronouns, let us consider one of your relatives—say a cousin. We will imagine that you have a cousin named Thomas. Now Thomas is a *cousin* to you. But he is not only a cousin. Thomas's parents would say he is their *son*. His sisters would declare he is their *brother*. At least four people could claim him as their *grandson,* and your parents would call him a *nephew*. Thomas is related to a number of people in various ways.

Relative pronouns are also related in various ways to the other words in a sentence.

Class Practice

A. Tell whether the pronoun in parentheses is used as a *subject,* a *direct object,* or the *object of a preposition.* Tell which pronoun in parentheses should be used. Then read each sentence correctly.
1. Daniel, (who, whom) prayed to God three times a day, was thrown into the lions' den.
2. King Darius, (who, whom) had not slept all night, hurried to the den early in the morning.
3. Is thy God, (who, whom) thou servest continually, able to deliver thee from the lions?
4. The God to (who, whom) Daniel prayed did save him from the lions.

B. For each sentence, decide which pronoun in parentheses is correct. Then read the sentence correctly.
1. An angel shut the mouths of the lions (who, which) were in the den.
2. The prayers (whom, which) Daniel offered faithfully were answered.
3. Our church helped the family (whose, which) house burned.
4. We enjoyed visiting with the people (whom, which) we had invited.
5. The farm was sold to the man (who, that) offered the most money.

Written Exercises

A. Write the correct pronouns in parentheses. After each one, write *S, DO,* or *OP* to tell whether it is a subject, a direct object, or the object of a preposition.
1. Eli the priest, to (who, whom) Samuel went, had not called.
2. Dorcas, (who, whom) Peter raised to life, helped the poor.
3. The Ethiopian (who, whom) was reading the Scriptures was puzzled.
4. Philip, (who, whom) knew Jesus, explained the passage to him.
5. Jesus, about (who, whom) Isaiah wrote, was the Lamb (who, whom) gave His life for all men.
6. The Ethiopian to (who, whom) Philip preached asked to be baptized.
7. Philip, (who, whom) was a deacon, baptized the Ethiopian.
8. Then the Ethiopian (who, whom) was baptized saw Philip no more.

Lesson Outline:

1. A relative pronoun can be used in several different ways in a relative clause. The relative pronoun may be a subject, a predicate nominative, a direct object, an indirect object, the object of a preposition, or a modifier. Since the word order in a relative clause may be inverted, changing the clause to normal word order is helpful in deciding what sentence part the relative pronoun is.

(*Teacher:* A relative clause is an adjective clause, but that term is not used until these clauses are studied again in Chapter 8.)

2. The correct case of a relative pronoun must be used, according to the place it fills in the relative clause.

    a. Use the nominative case *who* for a subject or a predicate nominative.

Lesson 70 Answers
Class Practice

A. 1. subject, who
   2. subject, who
   3. direct object, whom
   4. object of a preposition, whom

B. 1. which
   2. which
   3. whose
   4. whom
   5. who *or* that

Written Exercises

A. 1. whom—OP
   2. whom—DO
   3. who—S
   4. who—S
   5. whom—OP; who—S
   6. whom—OP
   7. who—S
   8. who—S

    b. Use the objective case *whom* for an object (direct object, indirect object, or object of a preposition).
    c. Use the possessive case *whose* for an adjective that shows possession.

3. Use **who** *or* **whom** *in referring to people, and* **which** *in referring to animals or objects. That and whose may refer to people, animals, or objects.*

★ **EXTRA PRACTICE**
Worksheet 40 *(Using Relative Pronouns)*

B. Write the correct pronouns in parentheses. Write whether each pronoun refers to a *person,* an *animal,* or an *object.*
1. The animals (who, that) built this dam are beavers.
2. The Lord, (who, which) made them, taught them to work together.
3. A beaver's ax is the teeth (who, which) are in his mouth.
4. Some of the ditches (whom, that) beavers dig are thirty inches deep and eighteen inches wide.
5. These sluices, (who, which) is what the ditches are called, are made for dragging logs to the water.
6. Beavers (who, that) are younger help the older ones.
7. People (that, which) have studied beavers are amazed at their abilities.
8. My friend Jonathan, (whose, which) family traveled to the western states, has seen the beavers' large dams.
9. His brother, (who, which) writes interesting articles about beavers, has spent many hours watching them and reading about them.
10. The students, (whose, which) teacher told stories and drew pictures on the board, were also enthusiastic.

C. Use these relative clauses in original sentences. Underline the clause, and circle the word it modifies.
1. who will teach at Brownsville
2. whose money was returned
3. whom we met at church
4. which Father wanted to buy
5. that we planted in front of the house

Review Exercises

Write the correct words in parentheses. [62–68]
1. Evelyn and (she, her) wrote the stories.
2. We helped Bertha and (he, him).
3. Lois read Grandmother and (he, him) a story.
4. We translated (that, that there) story for Maria and (she, her).
5. (We, Us) girls read some stories to (they, them).
6. (Who, Whom) wrote the book?
7. For (who, whom) was the book written?
8. Some of the teachers helped (we, us) girls with our project.
9. Brother Martin showed (we, us) boys his old books.

B.
1. that—animal
2. who—person
3. which—object
4. that—object
5. which—object
6. that—animal
7. that—person
8. whose—person
9. who—person
10. whose—person

C. (Individual work.)

Review Exercises

1. she
2. him
3. him
4. that, her
5. We, them
6. Who
7. whom
8. us
9. us

10. Some of (them, those) books were very old.

11. Each of the girls (bring, brings) one songbook.

12. (Its, It's) cover is old and torn.

Challenge Exercises

Diagram the relative clauses from the sentences in Written Exercises, Part A. The examples given here are from the last two in Class Practice, Part A.

3. thou | servest | whom
   continually

4. Daniel | prayed
   to whom

71. Courtesy and Clarity on the Telephone

The Bible says, "Let your speech be alway with grace, seasoned with salt, that ye may know how ye ought to answer every man" (Colossians 4:6). Speaking courteously and respectfully on the telephone is one way to obey this verse.

Read this telephone conversation, and study the paragraphs that follow it.

Ring! Ring!

Voice: Hello; Elam Martin's.

Sister Anna: Hello; this is Anna Yoder. May I speak with Sister Gloria?

Voice: Mother can't come to the phone just now. This is Beverly. Shall I ask her to call back, or may I take a message?

Lesson 71

Purpose: To teach effective and courteous use of the telephone.

Oral Review:

1. A business letter has what part in addition to the five parts of a friendly letter? (inside address)

2. How is the greeting of a business letter punctuated differently from the greeting of a friendly letter? (The greeting of a business letter is followed by a colon rather than a comma.)

3. What information should the beginning of a book report contain? (the title of the book, the name of the author, the copyright date, a place where the book can be found)

4. What other information should a book report contain? (a description of the main characters, the setting, the plot, and the reporter's opinion of the book)

10. those

11. brings

12. Its

Challenge Exercises

1. Samuel | went
   to whom

2. Peter | raised | whom
   to life

3. who | was reading | Scriptures
   the

4. who | knew | Jesus

5. Isaiah | wrote
   about whom

   who | gave | life
   for men His
   all

6. Philip | preached
   to whom

7. who | was \ deacon
   a

8. who | was baptized

5. (a) What parts of the story should you tell in a book report? (b) What part should you not tell? (a. the main problems; b. the outcome)

Lesson Introduction: Have you ever tried to call someone, and a very young child answered the telephone? How did you feel when the child could not answer your questions properly? Or did you ever make a call that was answered rudely by a person who seemed to wish you hadn't bothered him? No doubt you have also called a person who spoke politely and made you feel glad you called him.

How do you respond to people on the telephone? It is easier to find fault in others than in ourselves. We may be doing the very things that we do not like others to do. We should cultivate speech that is "with grace, seasoned with salt," as the Bible says it should be. In this lesson we will study some common rules of courtesy in using the telephone.

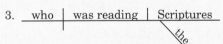

Sister Anna:	Will you please take a message? At the sewing circle on Friday, we will need all the sewing machines that are available. She should bring hers along if she can.
Beverly:	Okay, I'll write that down. You want Mother to bring her sewing machine along to the sewing circle on Friday.
Sister Anna:	Yes, Beverly, that's correct. Thank you! Good-bye.
Beverly:	Good-bye, Sister Anna.

The persons in this telephone conversation followed some important rules for using the telephone. Both parties identified themselves promptly. Beverly offered to take a message or have her mother return the call. Sister Anna said exactly what she wanted, and Beverly repeated the message and wrote it down. Sister Anna was the one who made the call, so she was the one who said "good-bye" first. Both speakers used courtesy and clear English.

When you make a telephone call, be sure you dial the right number. If you do not know a number, find it in the telephone directory or ask someone to help you find it. If you reach the wrong party, be sure to apologize. Even if the person says "That's all right," you know you have disturbed him unnecessarily.

When you are calling and no one answers right away, let the telephone ring about seven times. It is usually not necessary to let it ring much longer, unless you know that the person needs extra time to get to the telephone.

As soon as someone answers, tell who you are. You may ask a polite question such as "How are you?" but do not wait long to state the reason for your call.

When you answer the telephone, tell the caller what place he has reached and who you are. If the caller wants to speak to someone who is not available, offer to take a message. Be sure you understand the message accurately, and write it down.

Be courteous and respectful when using the telephone. In order to speak clearly, keep the mouthpiece about an inch from your mouth, and hold the earpiece lightly against your ear. Speak loudly enough so that your listener can hear you easily, but do not shout.

Do not make calls that are pointless or unnecessarily long. Be respectful of the other person's time.

If someone calls you, let him say "Good-by" first unless you must end the call for some reason. Otherwise, you may cut off the conversation before the caller has finished his business.

1) In a home, give the family name.
2) At a business place, give the name of the business.
b. *If the caller wants to speak to someone who is not available, offer to take a message.*
1) Be sure you understand the message accurately.
2) Write it down so that you do not forget it.
3) Pass the message on to the intended person as promptly as you can.

3. *Be courteous and respectful when using the telephone.*

a. *In order to speak clearly, keep the mouthpiece about an inch from your mouth, and hold the earpiece lightly against your ear.* Speak loudly enough so that your listener can hear you easily, but do not shout.
b. *Do not make calls that are pointless or unnecessarily long.* Be respectful of the other person's time. You may ask a polite question like "How are you?" but do not wait long to state the reason for your call.
c. *Let the person who made the call end the conversation.* Otherwise, you may cut off the conversation before the caller has finished his business. Unless you must end the call for some reason, let the person who called say "Good-bye" first.

Lesson Outline:

1. *Follow the correct procedure when you make a telephone call.*

a. *Be sure to dial the right number.* If you do not know a number, find it in the telephone directory or ask someone to help you find it. If you reach the wrong party, be sure to apologize.
b. *If no one answers right away, let the telephone ring about seven times.* It is usually not necessary to let it ring much longer, unless you know that the person needs extra time to get to the telephone.
c. *As soon as someone answers, tell who you are and why you called.*

2. *Follow the correct procedure when you answer the telephone.*

a. *Tell the caller what place he has reached and who you are.*

• Be courteous and respectful when using the telephone.

Class Practice

A. Eunice Weaver calls Jeanne Martin to get the math assignment for the next day. Show how the call should go, by having one student say the things Eunice should say and another student the things Jeanne should say.

B. Brother Carl Miller is calling your father to tell him the school board meeting this evening has been canceled. He also wants your father to relay the message to Brother Jacob Anderson. Your father is not at home, so you answer the telephone. You then call Brother Jacob and give him the message. Show how each telephone call should go by having different students say what each person should say.

Written Exercises

In your own words, write out a courteous and proper telephone conversation for Part A in Class Practice.

Review Exercises

Choose and write the one best answer for each question. [45]
1. What is the first thing you should do in preparing for a book report?
   a. Write an outline.
   b. Read the book.
   c. Take notes.
2. Which information should you *not* give in a book report?
   a. The title of the book.
   b. The name of the author and the copyright date.
   c. A description of the setting and main characters.
   d. The plot of the story.
   e. The outcome of the story.
   f. Your opinion of the book.

Lesson 71 Answers
Class Practice

A. (Sample answer.)

Jeanne: Hello; Martins' residence, Jeanne speaking.

Eunice: Hello; this is Eunice Weaver. Could you please give me the math assignment for tomorrow, Jeanne?

Jeanne: Oh, certainly, Eunice. I have my math book along home. Here it is, Lesson 100, pages 216–217.

Eunice: Thank you, Jeanne. Have a good evening. Good-bye.

Jeanne: Same to you, Eunice. Good-bye.

B. (Sample answer.)

Randy: Hello; Martins' residence, Randy speaking.

Carl Miller: Hello, Randy, this is Carl Miller. Is your father home?

Randy: No, I'm sorry, he's not. May I take a message?

Carl Miller: Yes, thank you. Tell your father that the school board meeting has been canceled for this evening. Can you also call Brother Jacob Anderson and give him the message?

Randy: The school board meeting has been canceled for this evening. Yes, I can call Brother Jacob.

Carl Miller: Thank you, Randy. Have a good evening. Good-bye.

Randy: Same to you. Good-bye.

*   *   *   *   *

Jacob Anderson: Hello; Jacob Anderson speaking.

Randy: Hello; this is Randy Martin calling. Brother Carl Miller asked me to give you the message that the school board meeting has been canceled for this evening.

Jacob Anderson: Oh, thank you, Randy.

Randy: You're welcome. Have a good evening. Good-bye.

Jacob Anderson: Same to you. Good-bye.

Written Exercises

(See sample answer for Class Practice, Part A.)

Review Exercises

1. b. Read the book.
2. e. The outcome of the story.

72. Chapter 6 Review

Class Practice

A. Name the kind of pronouns in each set. Choose from this list.

demonstrative	personal—nominative case
indefinite	personal—objective case
interrogative	personal—possessive case
relative	

1. this, that, these, those
2. I, you, he, she, it, we, they
3. my, mine, your, yours, his, her, hers, its, our, ours, their, theirs
4. some, any, none, all, most, each, either, one, nobody, anyone, anybody, both, few, several, many
5. who, whom, whose, which, what
6. me, you, him, her, it, us, them
7. who, whom, whose, which, that

B. Tell whether the pronouns in each list are *always singular, always plural,* or *either singular or plural.*
1. both, few, several, many
2. each, either, neither, one, another, anybody, anyone, everybody, everyone, somebody, someone, nobody, no one
3. some, any, none, all, most

C. Read each sentence, exchanging the subject and the predicate nominative.
1. He is the fastest runner.
2. The caller at the door was he.
3. They are the cooks.
4. The seamstress was she.

D. Tell whether the underlined pronouns are *interrogative* or *relative.* Give the antecedent of each relative pronoun, and read the clause that it introduces.
1. Who is bringing the fruit?
2. The girl who is bringing the fruit will be late.
3. Which rabbit is yours?
4. The rabbit which is yours has escaped from his pen.

Lesson 72 Answers
Class Practice
A. 1. demonstrative
   2. personal—nominative case
   3. personal—possessive case
   4. indefinite
   5. interrogative
   6. personal—objective case
   7. relative

B. 1. always plural
   2. always singular
   3. either singular or plural

C. 1. The fastest runner is he.
   2. He was the caller at the door.
   3. The cooks are they.
   4. She was the seamstress.

D. 1. interrogative
   2. relative, girl, who is bringing the fruit
   3. interrogative
   4. relative, rabbit, which is yours

Lesson 72

Purpose: To review the concepts taught in Chapter 6.

C. Read the following sentences correctly.
1. The rabbit who had escaped is in the window well.
2. The girl which brought the young turkey also brought a guinea hen.
3. Them chicks belong to Mary.
4. These here are John's.

F. Give the answers.
1. Name the parts of a friendly letter in the order in which they appear.
2. What part does a business letter have that a friendly letter does not have?
3. Name three reasons for writing friendly letters.
4. Why is it important to address an envelope in clear handwriting and in good form?
5. Look at the letter in Written Exercises, Part H. Is it a friendly letter or a business letter?

G. Tell how the following telephone conversation should be improved.

Ring! Ring!
"Hello," said Hilda Keppel.
"Hello. Is this the Keppels'?" asked Mrs. Brown.
"Yes."
"To whom am I speaking?"
"Hilda."
"May I speak to your mother?" asked Mrs. Brown.
"No," replied Hilda.
"Can you give her a message?" Mrs. Brown asked.
"Uh-huh," replied Hilda.
"Tell her I would like to place an order for two loaves of her home-made bread next week," said Mrs. Brown.
"All right. Good-bye," said Hilda.

Written Exercises

A. Copy the personal pronouns. After each one, write its person, number, case, and gender.
1. He showed her where to find them.
2. My letter was sent to you girls and to him.
3. Our house is older than theirs.
4. "Cast thy bread upon the waters: for thou shalt find it after many days" (Ecclesiastes 11:1).

E. (Corrections are marked.)
1. The rabbit <u>that</u> had escaped is in the window well.
2. The girl <u>who</u> brought the young turkey also brought a guinea hen.
3. <u>Those</u> chicks belong to Mary.
4. These <s>here</s> are John's.

F. 1. heading, greeting, body, closing, signature
2. inside address
3. (Any three.) to share news, to give help or encouragement, to give or accept an invitation, to thank someone for a favor shown
4. to be courteous; so that the letter reaches its destination
5. a business letter

G. Hilda should have given her name promptly.
She should have answered more courteously when Mrs. Brown asked to speak to her mother.
She should have offered to take a message (instead of waiting until Mrs. Brown asked and then saying "uh-huh").
She should have repeated the message and written it down.
She should have let Mrs. Brown say "Good-bye" first.

Written Exercises

A. 1. He—third, singular, nominative, masculine
her—third, singular, objective, feminine
them—third, plural, objective, common
2. My—first, singular, possessive, common
you—second, plural, objective, common
him—third, singular, objective, masculine
3. Our—first, plural, possessive, common
theirs—third, plural, possessive, common
4. thy—second, singular, possessive, common
thou—second, singular, nominative, common
it—third, singular, objective, neuter

B. Copy each personal pronoun, and write its antecedent.
1. Father wrote his name on the paper, put it into an envelope, and sealed it.
2. Jesus said to Peter, "What is that to thee? Follow thou Me."

C. Write the correct pronouns. After each one, write *S, PN, DO, IO,* or *OP* to tell whether it is a subject, predicate nominative, direct object, indirect object, or object of a preposition.
1. The people and (he, him) followed Jesus.
2. (Who, Whom) was Bartimaeus calling?
3. To (who, whom) was Jesus speaking?
4. The man (who, whom) had been blind was (he, him).
5. Jesus healed Bartimaeus and (he, him).
6. Jesus had compassion on the people and (he, him).
7. (We, Us) girls sang a new song together.
8. Brother John taught (we, us) boys the song too.
9. They sang it to (we, us) older women.
10. Mary brought Mother and (I, me) those flowers.
11. The students (who, whom) had a bird in their classroom made a report.
12. The teacher to (who, whom) I spoke did not know his name.
13. The person (who, whom) we told was glad to know.
14. The person (who, whom) lost the parakeet identified the bird.

D. Write the correct words in parentheses.
1. (Its, It's) time to go to (their, they're) house.
2. (Your, You're) drawing of a squirrel is good except that (its, it's) tail is too long.
3. As for (its, it's) ears, (their, they're) not even (there, they're).

E. Write *adj.* or *pron.* to tell how each underlined word is used. If the word is an adjective, write the word it modifies.
1. <u>That</u> snail climbed right up the side of the glass.
2. <u>This</u> is not a poisonous kind.
3. <u>Some</u> ocean-dwelling snails are poisonous, but <u>most</u> of them are harmless.
4. A <u>few</u> are as small as a pinhead.
5. <u>Each</u> carries his little house with him.
6. <u>His</u> is in <u>her</u> aquarium.
7. <u>Which</u> kind of snail is two feet long?
8. <u>Who</u> wrote that there are over eighty thousand varieties of snails?

B. 1. his—Father; it—paper; it—envelope
   2. thee—Peter; thou—Peter; Me—Jesus

C. 1. he—S
   2. Whom—DO
   3. whom—OP
   4. who—S; he—PN
   5. him—DO
   6. him—OP
   7. We—S
   8. us—IO
   9. us—OP
   10. me—IO
   11. who—S
   12. whom—OP
   13. whom—DO
   14. who—S

D. 1. It's, their
   2. Your, its
   3. its, they're, there

E. 1. adj.—snail
   2. pron.
   3. adj.—snails; pron.
   4. pron.
   5. pron.
   6. pron.; adj.—aquarium
   7. adj.—kind
   8. pron.

F. Write the correct words in parentheses. When you write a verb, also write the subject that it agrees with.
1. One of the students (is, are) not here.
2. Few (has, have) brought (his, their) lunches.
3. Each of the girls (is, are) bringing (her, their) own.
4. None of the boys (is, are) ready yet.
5. None of the glue (was, were) spilled.
6. Both of us (has, have) a new pen.

G. Write whether each underlined pronoun is *interrogative* or *relative*. Write the antecedent of each relative pronoun.
1. <u>Who</u> saw the strange bird first?
2. The boy <u>who</u> saw the strange bird first told the teacher.
3. <u>Whose</u> is it?
4. The girl <u>whose</u> parrot came along to school may come to my desk.
5. The bird <u>which</u> has a yellow head is a cockatiel.

H. Rewrite the following letter, correcting the errors and improving the body.

> 361 mobile drive
> Montgomery Al 36108
> january 1 20—
>
> public inquiries
> national park service
> washington, DC 20013
>
> gentlemen;
>
> My name is melinda neville. My class will soon be studying the state of Alaska. We studied Alabama last week. I like studying geography a lot. I would appreciate information on the state parks of Alaska that would help us in our study.
>
> sincerely
>
> melinda neville

———————————————

F. 1. One is
2. Few have, their
3. Each is, her
4. None are
5. None was
6. Both have

G. 1. interrogative
2. relative—boy
3. interrogative
4. relative—girl
5. relative—bird

H. (Corrections are marked; note also the proper alignment of the closing and signature. Wording of the body may vary.)

> 361 Mobile Drive
> Montgomery, AL 36108
> January 1, 20—
>
> Public Inquiries
> National Park Service
> Washington, DC 20013
>
> Gentlemen:
>
> ~~My name is melinda neville.~~ My class will soon be studying the state of Alaska. ~~We studied Alabama last week. I like studying geography a lot.~~ I would appreciate receiving information on the state parks of Alaska that would help us in our study.
>
> Sincerely,
>
> Melinda Neville

Chapter Seven

Using Correct Capitalization and Punctuation

Writing Stories

Capital
letters and punctuation
marks help us to better read
what others have
written.

One jot or one tittle shall in no wise pass . . . till all be fulfilled.

Matthew 5:18

73. Using Capital Letters

You already know the main rules for capitalizing words and abbreviations. They are listed below.

1. *Capitalize the first word of every sentence.* This includes the first word in a direct quotation.

2. *Capitalize the first word in every line of poetry.*

Diligence

<u>D</u>o each task with diligence,
<u>W</u>hether large or small;
<u>W</u>hat seems insignificant
<u>M</u>ay be best of all.

—Ada L. Wine

3. *Capitalize every personal name.* Also capitalize initials used with the names of persons.

   A. W. Tozer   C. B. White   Alice M. Long

4. *Capitalize a title that is part of a name.*

   Aunt Martha   Grandpa Weaver
   Uncle Alvin   Brother John

   When a noun is used as a title *before* a name, it is usually capitalized because it is considered part of the name. If the same noun comes *after* a name, it is not capitalized because it is not part of the name.

   Will <u>Governor Smith</u> reduce taxes?
   Will <u>Nolan Smith</u>, the new <u>governor</u>, reduce taxes?

   We all admire the wisdom of <u>King Solomon</u>.
   <u>Solomon</u> was the wisest <u>king</u> of Israel.

5. *Capitalize a title when it is used alone as a name.* One common example is the use of a title such as *father, mother,* or *uncle* in direct address. But when these titles are used after articles, possessive pronouns, or other limiting adjectives, they are not usually capitalized.

   When can I leave the hospital, <u>Doctor</u>?
   (used in direct address)
   He asked the <u>doctor</u> an important question.
   (used after an article)

Lesson 73

Purpose: To teach some basic rules of capitalization.

Oral Review:

1. Does a relative pronoun introduce a phrase or a clause? (a clause)
2. A relative pronoun can be used as what parts of a relative clause? (subject, predicate nominative, direct object, indirect object, object of a preposition, modifier)
3. The pronoun *who* can be used as what sentence parts? (subject, predicate nominative)
4. Which relative pronoun shows possession? (whose)
5. Which relative pronoun does *not* refer to people? (which)
6. Give two examples of pronouns in each of the following categories.
   a. personal—nominative case (I, you, he, she, it, we, they)
   b. personal—objective case (me, you, him, her, it, us, them)
   c. personal—possessive case (my, mine, your, yours, his, her, hers, its, our, ours, their, theirs)
   d. personal—archaic (thou, thee, thy, thine, ye)
   e. demonstrative (this, that, these, those)
   f. interrogative (who, whom, whose, which, what)
   g. indefinite (anyone, somebody, all, many, some, any, none, few, most, everyone, nobody)
   h. relative (who, whom, whose, which, that)

Lesson Introduction: How would you like it if writing were done in all small letters or all capital letters? It might be easy to write like that, but what about reading it? Long ago, there were no capitalization rules; in fact, much writing was done in all capital letters and with no spaces between words. Illustrate by writing the following saying on the board.

Charles asked <u>Mother</u> where his lunch was. (used as a name)
His <u>mother</u> visited school yesterday.
 (used after a possessive pronoun)

When you are not sure whether to capitalize a title, try substituting a name for the title. You should capitalize the title only if you can replace it with a personal name.

My (Mother, mother) helped me with the work.
 Think: My <u>Sara</u> helped me with the work.
    (incorrect; use *mother*)

I believe (Mother, mother) can do it for me.
 Think: I believe <u>Sara</u> can do it for me.
    (correct; use *Mother*)

6. *Capitalize* I *and* O *when they are used as words.*

 Forever will <u>I</u> praise Thee, <u>O</u> my Lord!

7. *Use proper capitalization in the heading, the greeting, the closing, and the signature of a letter.* In the heading, this includes all proper nouns, such as the name of the street, the city, the state, and the month. In the greeting and the closing, you must capitalize the first word. The signature is your name, which of course must be capitalized.

 115 Maple Street
 Altoona, PA 16601
 April 19, 20—

 Dear Amy,   Sincerely yours,
 My dear sister,   Yours truly,

- Capitalize the first word of every sentence, the first word in a direct quotation, and the first word in every line of poetry.

- Capitalize every personal name and any initial or title.

- Capitalize a title used as a name.

- Capitalize *I* and *O* when they are written as words.

- Use proper capitalization in the address, the date, the greeting, the closing, and the signature of a letter.

AJOYTHATISSHAREDISAJOYMADEDOUBLE
(A joy that is shared is a joy made double.)

If you learn the rules of capitalization well, it will help your readers to understand what you write.

Lesson Outline:

1. Capitalize the first word of every sentence and the first word in a direct quotation.

2. Capitalize the first word in every line of poetry.

3. Capitalize every personal name and any initial used with the name.

4. Capitalize a title that is part of a name. When a noun is used as a title *before* a name, it is usually capitalized because it is considered part of the name. If the same noun comes *after* a name, it is not capitalized because it is not part of the name.

 <u>King</u> George, <u>but</u> George, <u>king</u> of England

5. Capitalize a title when it is used alone as a name. When a title such as *father, mother,* or *uncle* is used after an article, possessive pronoun, or other limiting adjective, it is not usually capitalized.

 I saw <u>Grandfather</u>. *but* I saw my <u>grandfather</u>.

When you are not sure whether to capitalize a title, try substituting a name for the title. You should capitalize the title only if you can replace it with a personal name.

6. Capitalize I *and* O *when they are used as words.*

7. Use proper capitalization in the heading, the greeting, the closing, and the signature of a letter.

★ **EXTRA PRACTICE**
Worksheet 41 *(Using Capital Letters)*

Class Practice

Tell which words need to be capitalized.

1. a horse can't pull while kicking;
    this fact i merely mention;
    and he can't kick while pulling—
    which is my chief contention.

2. "but thou, o Lord, art a shield for me; my glory, and the lifter up of mine head" (Psalm 3:3).

3. aunt martha read an interesting poem to us, written by h. w. longfellow.

4. thomas jefferson, a former president, once wrote to john adams, "i cannot live without books."

5. my mother read the verse from job that says, "with the ancient is wisdom; and in length of days is understanding."

6. do you know when queen elizabeth I ruled in england?

7.

54 birch road
alma, ne 68920
july 17, 20—

dear sister rose,

thank you for being my teacher this past year. i appreciate all you have done for me. i hope you have a refreshing summer vacation.

with warm regards,
jean

Written Exercises

Copy the following sentences, stanza, and letter parts, using correct capitalization. Underline all the letters you capitalize.

1. hear me when i call, o God of my righteousness.
2. j. g. saxe wrote a poem about six blind men and an elephant.
3. my brother repeated the words that jesus said: "ask, and it shall be given you; seek, and ye shall find; knock, and it shall be opened unto you."
4. I think grandma martin has gone to see a. b. smith, her doctor.
5. tell me, father, where I can find the hammer.
6. we read that king solomon received much cedar wood from hiram, king of tyre.

7.   **being kind**
try to practice being kind;
then most surely you will find
someone who is very near
needing comfort, help, or cheer.
—Ada L. Wine

8.   117 main street
                                             holland, mi 49424
                                             may 4, 20—

dear gerald,
      in 1 Peter 5:7 we read, "he careth for you."
      we had an interesting school trip on may 1. you should have
been along, gerald! The teachers, sister phoebe martin and brother
ivan lapp, took us to a historic coal mine. it was cold in the mine,
and water dripped on our heads from time to time. we saw where
miners used to dig coal out of the ground, and how different tunnels branched off the main tunnel. at one place the mine had even
caved in, but the part we were in is checked daily for safety. When
our guide, mr. n. snowden, turned all the lights off, we could see
how pitch-dark it really is under the ground!
      come and see us sometime soon.

                                             your friend,
                                             mervin l. white

Review Exercises

For each group of pronouns, write the letter of the kind that it is.
[61–69]

a. personal—nominative case	e. demonstrative
b. personal—objective case	f. indefinite
c. personal—possessive case	g. interrogative
d. personal—archaic	h. relative

1. thou, thee, thy, thine
2. me, you, him, her, it, us, them
3. this, that, these, those
4. anyone, somebody, few, all, many
5. I, you, he, she, it, we, they
6. who, whom, whose, which, that
7. my, your, his, her, ours, theirs
8. who, whom, whose, which, what

7.   **Being Kind**
Try to practice being kind,
Then most surely you will find
Someone who is very near
Needing comfort, help, or cheer.

8.   117 Main Street
                                             Holland, MI 49424
                                             May 4, 20—

Dear Gerald,
      In 1 Peter 5:7 we read, "He careth for you."
      We had an interesting school trip on May 1.
You should have been along, Gerald! The teachers, Sister Phoebe Martin and Brother Ivan Lapp,
took us to a historic coal mine. It was cold in the
mine, and water dripped on our heads from time
to time. We saw where miners used to dig coal
out of the ground, and how different tunnels
branched off the main tunnel. At one place the
mine had even caved in, but the part we were
in is checked daily for safety. When our guide,
Mr. N. Snowden, turned all the lights off, we
could see how pitch-dark it really is under the
ground!
      Come and see us sometime soon.

                                             Your friend,
                                             Mervin L. White

Review Exercises

1. d		5. a
2. b		6. h
3. e		7. c
4. f		8. g

74. Capitalizing Proper Nouns and Proper Adjectives

Every proper noun must be capitalized. A proper noun names a particular person, place, or thing. Review the following rules of capitalization.

1. *Capitalize a noun or pronoun that refers to God.*

> In the beginning was the <u>Word</u>.
> The <u>Father</u>, the <u>Son</u>, and the <u>Holy Spirit</u> are all present in Luke 3:22.
> When <u>He</u> calls me, I will answer <u>Him</u>.

When the King James Bible was written, there were no rules for capitalizing pronouns referring to God. So when we copy directly from the Bible, we usually write pronouns for God in small letters. (Verses quoted from the Bible are in quotation marks and usually have the reference added.) In all other writing, we capitalize the pronouns that refer to God.

Bible verse:
> "Casting all your care upon him; for he careth for you" (1 Peter 5:7).

Other writing:
> We should cast our cares on Him because He cares for us.

2. *Capitalize the names of the days of the week and the months of the year. Do not capitalize the names of the seasons.*

Sunday	January	spring
Monday	February	summer
Thursday	June	fall (autumn)
Saturday	October	winter

> The second <u>Wednesday</u> of <u>August</u> was the warmest day of the <u>summer</u>.
> On <u>Friday</u>, <u>September</u> 23, <u>autumn</u> arrived.

3. *Capitalize the first and last words and all important words in the title of a book, newspaper, magazine, song, story, or poem.* Do not capitalize the articles *a, an,* and *the;* the conjunctions *and, but,* and *or;* or a preposition with fewer than four letters, unless it is the first or last word in the title.

Lesson 74

Purpose: To review the capitalization of proper nouns and proper adjectives.

Oral Review:

1. List the capitalization rules you have studied so far.
   (a. Capitalize the first word of every sentence, every direct quotation, and every line of poetry.
   b. Capitalize every personal name, with any initial or title.
   c. Capitalize a title when it is used alone as a name.
   d. Capitalize *I* and *O* when they are used as words.
   e. Use proper capitalization in the heading, the greeting, the closing, and the signature of a letter.)
2. Choose the correct verbs.
   a. (Lay, Lie) in present tense means "to rest or recline." (Lie)
   b. (Set, Sit) means "to put or place (something)." (Set)
   c. (Raise, Rise) means "to cause (something) to go up or grow up." (Raise)
   d. (Let, Leave) means "to depart or go away from." (Leave)
   e. (Set, Sit) means "to rest or be seated." (Sit)
   f. (Let, Leave) is always followed by another verb form. (Let)
   g. (Lay, Lie) means "to put or place (something)." (Lay)
   h. (Raise, Rise) means "to get up or go up." (Rise)
3. Give the correct past tense forms of the following verbs.
   a. tag (tagged)
   b. drag (dragged)
   c. attack (attacked)
4. What is a run-on error? (the mistake of writing two or more sentences together without the proper punctuation between them)

Title of a book:
Home Fires at the Foot of the Rockies

Title of a magazine:
Nature Friend

Title of a song:
"Dare to Be a Daniel"
(*Be* has only two letters, but it is a verb.)

Title of a story:
"The Family Across the Road"
(*Across* is a preposition, but it has six letters.)

Title of a poem:
"The Blind Men and the Elephant"

4. *Capitalize a common noun that is part of a proper noun.* Many place names include words like *street, river, lake,* and *mountain.* These words are part of the name and should be capitalized.

Pennsylvania Avenue	Little Bighorn River
Empire State Building	Black Horse Road
Allegheny Mountain	Grant Christian School

Words like *school, hill, street, creek, lake,* and *mountain* are not capitalized when they are not part of a name.

We visited <u>Little Mountain School</u> beside the <u>Red River</u>.
The <u>school</u> is on a little <u>mountain</u> beside a <u>river</u>.

5. *Capitalize an abbreviation made from a proper noun or used with a proper noun.* Use a dictionary if you are not sure whether an abbreviation should be capitalized.

<u>Ill.</u> (for Illinois)	<u>Dr.</u> Richard Calhoun
<u>Mrs.</u> Smith	Adam Martin, <u>Jr.</u>

6. *Capitalize a proper adjective, which is formed from a proper noun.*

Proper Noun	Proper Adjective
America	American
Rome	Roman
France	French
Poland	Polish
China	Chinese
Texas	Texan
Canada	Canadian

5. How can a run-on error be corrected? (Punctuate correctly between the sentences by using end punctuation and a capital letter, a comma and a conjunction, or a semicolon.)

Lesson Introduction: The word *proper* has the archaic meaning of belonging particularly to oneself. How does this word fit with proper nouns? Many animals may be dogs, but the name *Rex* belongs to only one particular dog. Even though other dogs may have the name *Rex,* still *Rex* is the particular name belonging to this one dog.

Proper adjectives are formed from proper nouns. Learn the rules for capitalizing proper nouns and proper adjectives.

Lesson Outline:

1. Capitalize a noun or pronoun that refers to God. When the King James Bible was written, there were no rules for capitalizing pronouns referring to God. It is correct to write pronouns for God in small letters when copying directly from the Bible. In all other writing, capitalize pronouns that refer to God.

2. Capitalize the names of the days of the week and the months of the year. Do not capitalize the names of the seasons.

3. Capitalize the first and last words and all important words in the title of a book, newspaper, magazine, song, story, and poem. Do not capitalize the articles *a, an,* and *the;* the conjunctions *and, but,* and *or;* or a preposition with fewer than four letters, unless it is the first or last word in the title.

4. Capitalize a common noun that is part of a proper noun. Words like *school, street, lake,* and *mountain* are not capitalized when they are not part of a name.

Skippack Mennonite School   Schuylkill River

5. Capitalize an abbreviation made from a proper noun or used with a proper noun. Check a dictionary when you are not sure whether an abbreviation should be capitalized.

Md. (for Maryland)
Mr. Sherman
Dr. Short

When a proper adjective comes just before a common noun, the common noun is usually *not* capitalized.

French toast   Roman soldier
Canadian friend   American car

- Capitalize a noun or pronoun that refers to God.

- Capitalize the names of the days of the week and the months of the year, but not the names of the seasons.

- Capitalize the first and last words and all important words in the title of a book, newspaper, magazine, song, story, or poem.

- Capitalize a common noun that is part of a proper noun.

- Capitalize an abbreviation made from a proper noun or used with a proper noun.

- Capitalize a proper adjective, which is formed from a proper noun.

Class Practice

Tell which words need capital letters.

1. if jesus came to your house
      to spend a day or two,
   if he came unexpectedly,
      i wonder what you'd do.

   i know you'd give your nicest room
      to such an honored Guest,
   and all the food you'd serve to him
      would be the very best.
                          —Author unknown

2. the snow is like a blanket that
      god spreads across the land
   where wheat and oats and barley sleep,
      awaiting spring's command.

3. in australia, winter begins in may and ends in october.
4. the summer months in australia are from november to april.

Lesson 74 Answers
Class Practice
(Corrections are underlined.)

1. If Jesus came to your house
      To spend a day or two,
   If He came unexpectedly,
      I wonder what you'd do.

   I know you'd give your nicest room
      To such an honored Guest,
   And all the food you'd serve to Him
      Would be the very best.

2. The snow is like a blanket that
      God spreads across the land
   Where wheat and oats and barley sleep,
      Awaiting spring's command.

3. In Australia, winter begins in May and ends in October.

4. The summer months in Australia are from November to April.

---

6. Capitalize a proper adjective, which is formed from a proper noun.

Russia—Russian
Bible—Biblical
Mexico—Mexican

When a proper adjective comes just before a common noun, the common noun is usually *not* capitalized.

Mexican dinner   Chinese man

★ **EXTRA PRACTICE**
Worksheet 42 *(More Capital Letters)*
Worksheet 43 *(Capital Letters in Proper Nouns and Proper Adjectives)*

5. in a book about australia called *the land down under,* i read about the red desert.

6. the first day of the week is always sunday, and the second day is monday.

7. the antarctic peninsula points toward the tip of south america.

8. the great dividing range is the largest mountain range of australia.

9. mr. richard byrd flew over antarctica and made many maps of it.

10. captain james cook claimed australia for great britain.

11. roald amundsen was a norwegian who led a group of explorers to the South Pole.

12. an english explorer named robert f. scott went to antarctica at the same time.

13. the chinese were probably the first to use coal for heating.

14. david went the second mile for a roman soldier.

Written Exercises

A. Copy the following stanzas and titles, using correct capitalization. Underline each letter that you capitalize.

1.   sometimes i walk in the shadow,
    sometimes in the sunlight clear;
but whether in gloom or brightness,
    the lord is very near.
                —Anonymous

2.   **god's care**
the grasses are clothed
and the ravens are fed
    from his store;
but you, who are loved
and guarded and led,
    how much more

will he clothe and feed you and give you his care?
then leave it with him; he has everywhere
    ample store.
                —Anonymous

5. In a book about A̲ustralia called *T̲he L̲and D̲own U̲nder,* I̲ read about the R̲ed D̲esert.

6. T̲he first day of the week is always S̲unday, and the second day is M̲onday.

7. T̲he A̲ntarctic P̲eninsula points toward the tip of S̲outh A̲merica.

8. T̲he G̲reat D̲ividing R̲ange is the largest mountain range of A̲ustralia.

9. M̲r. R̲ichard B̲yrd flew over A̲ntarctica and made many maps of it.

10. C̲aptain J̲ames C̲ook claimed A̲ustralia for G̲reat B̲ritain.

11. R̲oald A̲mundsen was a N̲orwegian who led a group of explorers to the South Pole.

12. A̲n E̲nglish explorer named R̲obert F̲. S̲cott went to A̲ntarctica at the same time.

13. T̲he C̲hinese were probably the first to use coal for heating.

14. D̲avid went the second mile for a R̲oman soldier.

Written Exercises

A. 1. S̲ometimes I̲ walk in the shadow,
    S̲ometimes in the sunlight clear;
B̲ut whether in gloom or brightness,
    T̲he L̲ord is very near.

2.   **G̲od's C̲are**
T̲he grasses are clothed
A̲nd the ravens are fed
    F̲rom H̲is store;
B̲ut you, who are loved
A̲nd guarded and led,
    H̲ow much more
W̲ill H̲e clothe and feed you and give you H̲is care?
T̲hen leave it with H̲im; H̲e has everywhere
    A̲mple store.

B. Write correctly each word that should be capitalized but is not.
1. in antarctica the sun drops a little lower in the sky every autumn day.
2. finally, in winter, the sun does not shine at all.
3. during summer the sun never sets, but shines day and night.
4. from november to april, the warmest temperature in summer is about 32 degrees Fahrenheit.
5. mr. andrew uses the english language at home, the spanish language at work, and the french language with his mother.
6. mr. and mrs. martin took jonathan and adam, jr., to see the empire state building.
7. black horse road runs along the black creek for several miles.
8. our italian friend, dr. savant, lives on cherry avenue in the city of baltimore.
9. point barrow is the northernmost point of alaska and the united states.
10. the mont blanc tunnel runs under mont blanc, the highest mountain in the alps, for almost eight miles.

C. Write a proper adjective for each proper noun. Use a dictionary if you need help.
1. England   3. Germany   5. France
2. Italy   4. Poland   6. Switzerland

D. Write each of the following in abbreviated form.
1. Wednesday   3. February   5. California
2. Sunday   4. Doctor Brown 6. Allan, Junior

Review Exercises

Write the correct verbs. [48–52]
1. The little ants (drug, dragged) crumbs of food several times their size to their nest.
2. One ant almost (drownded, drowned) when it fell into a puddle of water.
3. The red ants (attacked, attackted) the intruding black ants.
4. The huge soap bubbles (raised, rose) high into the air before they (busted, burst).
5. (May, Can) I (set, sit) this vase on your windowsill?

B. 1. In, Antarctica
2. Finally
3. During
4. From, November, April
5. Mr. Andrew, English, Spanish, French
6. Mr. (and) Mrs. Martin, Jonathan, Adam, Jr., Empire State Building
7. Black Horse Road, Black Creek
8. Our, Italian, Dr. Savant, Cherry Avenue, Baltimore
9. Point Barrow, Alaska, United States
10. The, Mont Blanc Tunnel, Mont Blanc, Alps

C. 1. English   4. Polish
2. Italian   5. French
3. German   6. Swiss

D. 1. Wed.   4. Dr. Brown
2. Sun.   5. CA, Cal., or Calif.
3. Feb.   6. Allan, Jr.

Review Exercises

1. dragged
2. drowned
3. attacked
4. rose, burst
5. May, set

75. The Three Parts of a Story

In Chapter 1 you learned that every story tells about a problem to be solved. That problem is the *conflict* in the story. In this chapter you will learn more about writing an effective story.

A story can be divided into three main parts: the *beginning,* the *middle,* and the *ending.* Each of these parts must be well written to make a good story.

The Beginning

The beginning of a story should arouse the reader's interest. It should make him want to find out what the rest of the story is about. The beginning must tell who, when, where, what, and why in order to keep the reader's interest.

You tell *who* by introducing the characters of your story. The first character you mention should be the *main character*—the one on whom the story centers. If any other character is mentioned, the story should show how he is related to the main character.

When and *where* a story takes place is known as the *setting.* Do not give details that are not important to the story. For instance, do not give an exact time or date unless it is significant to the story. But give enough details so that the reader can understand when and where the story took place. Study the following examples of statements that help to show the settings of different stories.

When:
> By 10:00 that morning, the ground was covered with snow.
> The hazy clouds could not keep the August sun from pouring its heat upon us.

Where:
> The playground at Shady Glen School was too quiet for comfort.
> The Millers' back yard, with its grape arbor, orchard trees, and woodpile, was the perfect place for hide-and-seek.

The problem or conflict in a story tells *what* the story is about. This problem is not fully explained in the beginning of the story. But the beginning should give a hint of the conflict so that the reader will want to find out more.

Finally, the *why* of a story is the author's reason for writing it. The author does not usually tell directly what lesson he wants to teach.

Lesson 75

Purpose: To teach the three main parts of a good story.

Teacher: This lesson is fairly long and involved. Be sure to allow enough time to teach it thoroughly.

Oral Review:

1. What is the most important rule to remember when speaking on the telephone? (Always speak courteously and respectfully.)
2. What are some other rules for using the telephone?
   (a. Be sure to dial the right number.
   b. Keep the mouthpiece about an inch from your mouth, and hold the earpiece lightly against your ear.
   c. Identify yourself promptly.
   d. If the caller wants to speak to someone who is not available, offer to take a message.
   e. Do not make calls that are pointless or unnecessarily long.
   f. Let the person who made the call end the conversation.)
3. Name the five parts of a friendly letter. (heading, greeting, body, closing, signature)
4. Name the extra part that a business letter has. (inside address)
5. State two reasons for writing friendly letters. (to share news, to give help or encouragement, to give or accept an invitation, to thank someone for a favor shown)

Lesson Introduction: Did you know that your life is like a story? Our lives should be living stories that illustrate the truth according to God's commands. For example, God has commanded us to be kind, so our lives should illustrate to others what true kindness is.

Rather, he uses the story to *show* the lesson. The beginning of the story often gives a hint of what the lesson will be.

The beginning of a story gives only the information that is needed to understand the story. In the short stories that you will write, this will generally be only one or two paragraphs.

Read the following two story beginnings. How many ways can you see that the first one is better than the second?

> Linford donned his coat quickly and hurried outside for recess. "Oh, I forgot to sharpen my pencils!" exclaimed Linford. "I'd better go in right away, or I won't have any pencils to use." As Linford stepped into the classroom, he saw Daniel standing beside the teacher's desk, looking at a book. Surely it could not be . . . but yes, it was the sixth grade math teacher's manual.
>
> "P-please, Linford," Daniel stammered, "don't tell Brother James."
>
> Linford was surprised. "Why, I never thought Daniel would do something like this." His mind was whirling as he sharpened his pencils.
>
> * * * * *
>
> Daniel glanced at the clock. It was 9:50 A.M. on Wednesday morning one winter day. "Oh, no," he thought, "only ten minutes left. I'll never finish this math on time."
>
> When Brother James dismissed them, all the boys except Daniel hurried out for recess.
>
> "Oh, I forgot to sharpen my pencils!" exclaimed Linford. "I'd better go in right away, or I won't have any pencils to use." His grandmother had just given him some new pencils.
>
> "Hurry back out!" called Mark. "We'll need your help." Daniel and Linford were good players, and Mark hated to lose two good players off his team.
>
> As Linford stepped inside, he saw Daniel looking at the sixth grade math teacher's manual.
>
> Linford was surprised. "Why, I never thought Daniel would do something like this."

The first story begins with Linford, the main character. But the second story introduces two other characters before it gets to Linford. The first story gives the setting in a natural way; the second one gives too many details that are not important to the story. The first story gives better hints to the conflict and purpose of the story.

No two people are alike; they have a variety of experiences. And if two people have similar experiences, they do not respond in exactly the same way. All of us have experiences that others would enjoy hearing about.

In this chapter you will learn how to write stories about some of the interesting happenings in your life. You will learn how to write in a way that will be helpful to those who read your stories.

Lesson Outline:

1. A good story has three main parts: the beginning, the middle, and the ending.

2. The beginning of a story should arouse the reader's interest. In a short story, the beginning should be only one or two paragraphs long.

The beginning should introduce the main character by mentioning him first. If other characters are mentioned, their relationship to the main character should be clear. The beginning should give the setting by telling when and where. It should include enough details to be interesting, but no unrelated details. The beginning should hint at the conflict and purpose of the story.

3. The middle of a story should describe the conflict in the story. The conflict is the problem to be solved. There are three kinds of conflict.

(1) The main character may be in conflict with another person.

(2) The main character may be in conflict with his circumstances.

(3) The main character may be in conflict with his own conscience.

The conflict does not need to be something great or unusual. Simple, everyday happenings have conflict in them too.

The Middle

The middle of a story is its main part. Here we live with the main character as he deals with his conflict, and we read on anxiously to discover how he will overcome his problem. Every story must show conflict in order to hold the reader's attention.

Just as you face different kinds of problems in real life, stories show different kinds of conflict. The three main kinds of conflict are described below.

1. *The main character may be in conflict with another person.* The story of Joseph being sold by his brothers has this kind of conflict. In a story about a disobedient child, the child is in conflict with his parents.

2. *The main character may be in conflict with his circumstances.* A child faces this kind of conflict when his plans for a hike are spoiled because of rain. So does a child who suffers from sickness or an accident.

3. *The main character may be in conflict with his own conscience.* For example, a person may be tempted to lie or cheat. Whenever a person knows what is right but finds it hard to do right, he is facing this kind of conflict.

The conflict in a story does not need to be something great or unusual. Simple, everyday happenings have conflict in them too. Do not think you must write about a boy being chased by wolves or a girl being tempted to steal hundreds of dollars. Something as simple as a child trying to overcome a bad habit can result in a great struggle. You have likely discovered that yourself.

Near the end of the story, the conflict rises to its highest point of intensity. The main character comes face to face with his problem, and he either overcomes it in victory or goes down in defeat. This is called the *climax* of the story.

The Ending

The ending of a story tells what happened after the climax. Since the conflict is over, the reader is satisfied and there is not much action left to write about. So the ending should be short and to the point.

Do not end a story by stating the lesson that you intend to teach. The lesson should be clear from the story itself. If it is not clear, you will not impress anyone by tacking the lesson onto the end!

4. The conflict should come to a climax near the end of the story. In the climax, the conflict rises to its highest point of intensity and the conflict is settled.

5. The ending of a story tells what happened after the climax. With the climax reached, the conflict is over and the action quickly ends. Therefore, the ending should be short and to the point.

6. Every story should have a definite purpose. The writer should want to teach a lesson through his story. But he does not need to state that lesson at the end of the story. The lesson should be clear from the story itself.

Read the following sets of paragraphs. Both show the climax and ending of a story. Which one is better?

When Linford went back out to play, all the enjoyment seemed to have gone out of the game. "Should I tell Brother James?" he thought. "What if Daniel doesn't like me anymore?"

Finally Linford decided to ask Father what to do.

When Linford related to Father what had taken place, he said, "And I just don't know if I should tell Brother James."

His father told him to tell the teacher.

Linford told the teacher early the next morning. The teacher thanked Linford for telling.

We should always ask our parents for advice. We should be honest and tell the teacher even though it means telling on a close friend. The teacher can take measures to correct it. Also we will have a lighter heart when we do what we know is right.

    *   *   *   *   *

Linford did not know what to do. Should he tell, or shouldn't he? Finally Linford decided to talk with his father about it. After Linford related the story, he said, "And I just don't know if I should tell Brother James. Would I be a tattletale then?"

"No, you would not be a tattletale, Linford," Father said thoughtfully. "It's very important that you tell Brother James something like this so that he can take care of the problem."

Linford told the teacher early the next morning when Brother James was alone in the classroom.

"Thank you for telling me," Brother James said. "I appreciate your honesty in this, even though Daniel is your close friend."

Linford left the room with a lighter heart, satisfied that he had done right.

The second set is better because it *shows* rather than tells the lesson of the story. Father and the teacher give the lesson in conversation with Linford. The second story also has a better conclusion. Linford leaves with a happy heart because he knows he has done what is right.

- A good story has three main parts: the beginning, the middle, and the ending.

- The beginning of a story should arouse the reader's interest by introducing the main character or characters, by describing the setting briefly, and by hinting at the conflict and purpose of the story.

- The middle of a story should describe the conflict and lead to a climax.

- The ending of a story should conclude the story. It should be short and to the point.

Class Practice

A. Tell which story beginning is better, and why.

1.   "Be careful!" Mother called as Gerald stumbled sleepily. "Help me get the little children to bed," she said.

    Marie unlocked the door and snapped on the light. "Gerald, come back! You're making muddy tracks all over the floor!" she wailed.

    "Oh, we must clear out this smoke!" Mother hurried to open the windows. Soon it was very cold in the house.

    In the basement, little wisps of smoke curled from every joint of the stovepipe and seeped out around the edges of the stove door.

2.   "Marie, help me get the little children to bed," said Mother as Father braked to a stop in front of the house late one cold winter night.

    Marie unlocked the door and snapped on the kitchen light. "Whew, it's smoky in here!" she exclaimed.

    "Oh, we must clear out this smoke!" Mother hurried to open the windows. She opened the basement door and coughed as smoke swirled around her.

    Downstairs Mother found Father leaning over the woodstove. Little wisps of smoke curled from every joint of the stovepipe and seeped out around the edges of the stove door.

Lesson 75 Answers
Class Practice

A. Beginning 2 is better for the following reasons.
   (1) It begins with the main character, Marie (instead of Mother and Gerald).
   (2) It gives the setting by showing that the family was entering their own house on a winter night. (This is not clear in the other beginning.)
   (3) It clearly suggests that the conflict of the story has to do with a house full of smoke (rather than a sleepy boy, getting children to bed, muddy tracks, or a cold house).

B. Identify which of the three kinds of conflict is shown in each of these.

1. When Linford went back out to play, all the enjoyment seemed to have gone out of the game. "Should I tell Brother James?" he thought. "What if Daniel doesn't like me anymore?"

2. "What shall we do?" Marie coughed. Her eyes watered, and she was shivering. Tears threatened to spill over.

   "It looks like everything is covered with smoke," Mother said helplessly.

   "This is going to be more of a job than we can handle ourselves," Father decided. "We'll all go to bed, as best we can, and in the morning we'll get some help."

   The next morning Father called Brother Elvin, the deacon of their church. "You'll need help," Brother Elvin agreed. "I'll take care of it."

   The first carload of helpers arrived before they had finished breakfast.

C. Tell which ending is better, and why.

1. Mrs. Ruftin, a neighbor, wanted to hear the whole story. "It must be nice to have friends who will pitch in and help you like this," she said.

   The house hummed with activity. Mother met Father in the hallway. "I hardly know what to do," she said, throwing up her hands. "They're doing it all!"

2. Mrs. Ruftin, a neighbor, wanted to hear the whole story. "It must be nice to have friends who will pitch in and help you like this," she said.

   Mother agreed heartily. "It's a real blessing to have Christian friends who help bear our burdens."

   Marie was no longer tempted to feel frustrated and discouraged. In her heart she thanked the Lord for helping them in this time of need.

Written Exercises

Choose an idea for a story to write in a later lesson. Write brief notes to answer the following questions. Be sure to save your notes for use in Lesson 82.

1. Who is the main character of your story?

B. 1. Conflict with another person, and conflict with the main character's own conscience. (If Linford told on Daniel, Daniel might not be his friend anymore. If Linford did not tell, he would be guilty of helping his friend to hide his wrongdoing.)

2. Conflict with circumstances. (Marie was tempted to be discouraged because of the smoke-filled house.)

C. Ending 2 is better. It shows that the conflict is settled and that the writer's purpose is to encourage the reader to trust in God. (The other ending does not come to a clear conclusion. According to the last sentence, Mother is perhaps still frustrated, even though help has come.)

Written Exercises

(Individual work. It is suggested that you collect the pupils' notes so that none are lost.)

2. Are there any other characters? If so, write who they are and how they are related to the main character.
3. When and where does your story take place?
4. What is the conflict in your story—the main problem to be solved?
5. What lesson will your story teach?

Review Exercises

Write the answers. [63, 67]

1. Name the five parts of a friendly letter.
2. Name the extra part in a business letter.
3. Give two reasons for writing friendly letters.

---

76. End Punctuation

Punctuation marks help us to read what others have written. How would you like to get a letter from a friend written this way?

> DEAR FRIEND HOW ARE YOU TODAY TRULY THE MERCIES OF THE LORD ARE NEW EVERY MORNING ARE THEY NOT WE PLAN TO COME THROUGH YOUR TOWN THE FIRST TUESDAY OF NEXT MONTH MAY WE LODGE AT YOUR HOUSE THAT EVENING PLEASE LET US KNOW SINCERELY HANS

Long ago, writing was harder to read because there were no special rules for punctuation. Writers used whatever marks they chose, and printers used whatever marks they had in their typecases. The ancient Greeks used semicolons for question marks.

In the 1400s and 1500s, people began to follow rules for punctuation so that writing could be understood more easily. Learn the rules of correct punctuation well so that your writing is simple to read.

1. *Use a period after a declarative or an imperative sentence.*

    Ships have been built for hundreds of years.
    Come and see the pictures of ships in these books.

2. *Use a question mark after an interrogative sentence.*

    Which Indians used the birch bark canoe?
    Who first used sails on their ships?

Review Exercises

1. heading, greeting, body, closing, signature
2. inside address
3. (Any two.) to share news, to give help or encouragement, to give or accept an invitation, to thank someone for a favor shown

---

Lesson 76

Purpose: To teach the use of periods, question marks, and exclamation points.

Oral Review:

1. List the capitalization rules you have studied so far.
   (a. Capitalize the first word of every sentence, every direct quotation, and every line of poetry.
   b. Capitalize every personal name, with its initials and titles.
   c. Capitalize a title when it is used as a name.
   d. Capitalize *I* and *O* when they are used as words.
   e. Use proper capitalization in the heading, the greeting, the closing, and the signature of a letter.
   f. Capitalize a noun or pronoun that refers to God.
   g. Capitalize the names of days and months, but not seasons.
   h. Capitalize the first and last words and all important words in the title of a book, newspaper, magazine, song, story, or poem.
   i. Capitalize a common noun that is part of a proper noun.
   j. Capitalize an abbreviation made from a proper noun or used with a proper noun.
   k. Capitalize a proper adjective.)
2. What is a proper noun? (the name of a specific person, place, or thing)

Lesson Introduction: Have one of the students read the following paragraph orally.

> I CLEANED MY ROOM ON TUESDAY IN A DRAWER I FOUND MY LOST BOOKS IN THE CRACKS AROUND THE WINDOW I CLEANED AWAY SOME SPIDERS I WASHED AND WAXED THE FLOOR WITH A MOP I DUSTED THE FURNITURE

3. *Use an exclamation point after an exclamatory sentence or a strong interjection.*

> Oh! What a large ship that is!
> What! Do you mean sailors could not tell where they were?

4. *Use a period after each initial that is part of a name.*

> Mrs. L. A. Johnson   Dr. Ronald M. Towers

5. *Use periods after most abbreviations.* An abbreviation is a short form that stands for one or more longer words.

a. Many names of measures can be abbreviated.

inch—in.	teaspoon—tsp.	second—sec.
foot—ft.	tablespoon—tbsp.	minute—min.
yard—yd.	cup—c.	hour—hr.
mile—mi.	pint—pt.	week—wk.
peck—pk.	quart—qt.	month—mo.
bushel—bu.	gallon—gal.	year—yr.
dozen—doz.		

b. The names of the months of the year and the days of the week can be abbreviated.

January—Jan.	September—Sept.
April—Apr.	October—Oct.
August—Aug.	November—Nov.

Sunday—Sun.	Tuesday—Tues.
Monday—Mon.	Wednesday—Wed.

c. Some abbreviations come from foreign words.

> A.M. from Latin *ante meridiem* (before midday)
> P.M. from Latin *post meridiem* (after midday)
> A.D. from Latin *anno Domini* (in the year of the Lord; that is, after Christ's birth)
> (B.C. stands for the English phrase "before Christ.")
> etc. from Latin *et cetera* (and the rest)
> lb. from Latin *libra* (pound)
> oz. from Italian *onza* (ounce)

WITH A KNIFE I SCRAPED OFF SOME OLD LOOSE PAINT WITH A BRUSH AND SOME WHITE PAINT I PAINTED THE WOODWORK.

(I cleaned my room on Tuesday. In a drawer I found my lost books. In the cracks around the window I cleaned away some spiders. I washed and waxed the floor with a mop. I dusted the furniture. With a knife I scraped off some old loose paint. With a brush and some white paint I painted the woodwork.)

Isn't it much easier to read when punctuation marks are used? Learn well the rules for correct end punctuation.

Lesson Outline:

1. Use a period after a declarative or an imperative sentence.

2. Use a question mark after an interrogative sentence.

3. Use an exclamation point after an exclamatory sentence or a strong interjection.

4. Use a period after each initial that is part of a name.

> Mrs. J. M. Howard   Dr. Mark L. Marshall

5. Use periods after most abbreviations.

6. Use no periods with some abbreviations for well-known phrases or for the names of certain organizations.

7. For state names in addresses, use the two-letter abbreviations developed by the postal service to be used with Zip Codes.

6. *Use no periods with some abbreviations for well-known phrases or for the names of certain organizations.*

> KJV—King James Version
> WW II—World War II
> UN—United Nations
> POW—prisoner of war
> TVA—Tennessee Valley Authority
> UPS—United Parcel Service
> IRS—Internal Revenue Service
> FBI—Federal Bureau of Investigation

7. *For state names in addresses, use the two-letter abbreviations developed by the postal service to be used with Zip Codes.* These are printed with all capital letters and no end punctuation. See the list at the end of Lesson 63. (Remember that the mailing address on an envelope should be printed in all capital letters.)

> BETHLEHEM PA 18016   NORFOLK NE 68701

8. *Most abbreviations should not be used in general writing, such as letters, stories, and reports.* But they may be used in note-taking, or in school lessons, such as English and math.
   A few standard abbreviations may be used in all writing.
   a. Abbreviations used with proper nouns. (Note that the title *Miss* is not an abbreviation. Also note that if an abbreviation comes at the end of a sentence, only one period is needed.)

> Mr.—Mister   Sr.—Senior
> Mrs.—Mistress   Jr.—Junior
> Dr.—Doctor
>
> The visitor was Clarence Miller, Jr.

   b. Abbreviations used in writing a time or date.

> A.M.   P.M.   B.C.   A.D.

Use your dictionary for reference. Check it when you are not sure about the form of an abbreviation.

8.   Most abbreviations should not be used in general writing, such as letters, stories, and reports. Abbreviations used with proper nouns or in writing a time or date may be used in all writing. Check a dictionary when you are not sure about the form of an abbreviation.

★ **EXTRA PRACTICE**
Worksheet 44 *(End Punctuation)*

- Use a period after a declarative or an imperative sentence, a question mark after an interrogative sentence, and an exclamation point after an exclamatory sentence or a strong interjection.

- Use a period after each initial that is part of a name.

- Use a period after most abbreviations.

- Use no period with some abbreviations for well-known phrases or for the names of certain organizations.

- For state names in addresses, use the two-letter abbreviations developed by the postal service to be used with Zip Codes.

- Most abbreviations should not be used in general writing, such as letters, stories, and reports.

Class Practice

A. Tell how to divide each group of words into sentences with proper capitalization and end punctuation.
1. Do you hear that robin how cheerfully he sings we should sing too
2. What an enormous tree that is what kind is it find it in the field guide

B. Give the meaning of each abbreviation.
1. in.   4. mi.   7. KJV
2. pk.   5. mo.   8. NY
3. yd.   6. Wed.   9. A.M.

C. Tell whether each abbreviation may be used in general writing.
1. A.M.   4. lb.   7. Jr.
2. Mrs.   5. KJV   8. Aug.
3. oz.   6. B.C.

Written Exercises

A. Divide each group of words into sentences with proper capitalization and end punctuation.
1. See how fast he runs is something chasing him well what a dog
2. Was that thunder hurry and get the clothes in here comes the rain
3. I can hear the breakers can you hear them roar what a tremendous noise they make the ocean is four miles away

Lesson 76 Answers
Class Practice
A. (Corrections are underlined.)
1. Do you hear that robin? How cheerfully he sings! We should sing too.
2. What an enormous tree that is! What kind is it? Find it in the field guide.

B. 1. inch   6. Wednesday
   2. peck   7. King James Version
   3. yard   8. New York
   4. mile   9. before midday
   5. month

C. 1. yes   5. no
   2. yes   6. yes
   3. no   7. yes
   4. no   8. no

Written Exercises
A. (Corrections are underlined. In some places, commas or periods may be used instead of exclamation points.)
1. See how fast he runs! Is something chasing him? Well! What a dog!
2. Was that thunder? Hurry and get the clothes in. Here comes the rain!
3. I can hear the breakers. Can you hear them roar? What a tremendous noise they make! The ocean is four miles away!

B. Copy these sentences, and add the missing periods, question marks, and exclamation points.
1. Weren't the Jews taken captive to Babylon about 500 BC
2. The Roman Empire fell about AD 500
3. Be here by 1:00 PM to meet Mr and Mrs Homer
4. How seriously wrong I was

C. Write the postal service abbreviations for the following states.
1. Virginia   3. Pennsylvania   5. Maryland
2. Illinois   4. Ohio   6. Texas

D. Write the correct abbreviations for these words.
1. teaspoon   5. second   9. before midday
2. cup   6. bushel   10. in the year of the Lord
3. inch   7. month   11. pound
4. peck   8. September   12. World War I

E. Write one of each of the four types of sentences, using the correct end punctuation. Include one strong interjection in one of your sentences.

Review Exercises

Correct the run-on errors as indicated. [14]
1. Use end punctuation and capital letters.

butterflies' scales come in many colors yellow, brown, black, and red colors are made by pigments in the scales shimmering colors like gold, silver, and shiny green or blue are made by light reflecting off the surface of the scales

2. Use commas and suitable conjunctions.
a. My brother caught a little catfish he gave it to me.
b. I had waited a long time I had caught no fish.
c. I will put this little fish on my hook then I can pretend I caught a fish.
3. Use semicolons.
a. Suddenly my pole gave a tremendous jerk my brother had to help me hold it.
b. On my line was the biggest catfish we had ever seen it had swallowed the little one!

B. (Corrections are underlined.)
1. Weren't the Jews taken captive to Babylon about 500 B.C.?
2. The Roman Empire fell about A.D. 500.
3. Be here by 1:00 P.M. to meet Mr. and Mrs. Homer.
4. How seriously wrong I was!

C. 1. VA   4. OH
   2. IL   5. MD
   3. PA   6. TX

D. 1. tsp.   7. mo.
   2. c.   8. Sept.
   3. in.   9. A.M.
   4. pk.   10. A.D.
   5. sec.   11. lb.
   6. bu.   12. WW I

E. (Individual sentences.)

Review Exercises

1. Butterflies' scales come in many colors. Yellow, brown, black, and red colors are made by pigments in the scales. Shimmering colors like gold, silver, and shiny green or blue are made by light reflecting off the surface of the scales.
2. a. My brother caught a little catfish, and he gave it to me.
   b. I had waited a long time, but I had caught no fish.
   c. I will put this little fish on my hook, and then I can pretend I caught a fish.
3. a. Suddenly my pole gave a tremendous jerk; my brother had to help me hold it.
   b. On my line was the biggest catfish we had ever seen; it had swallowed the little one!

77. Direct Quotations

Sometimes in writing we want to repeat the exact words of a speaker or writer. The exact words of a speaker or writer are a *direct quotation*. The other words in the sentence are called *explanatory words*. In the following sentence, the explanatory words are underlined.

"Where do you live?" <u>Eunice inquired</u>.

Direct quotations can be written in different ways. The quoted words may come first in a sentence, or they may come last. Direct quotations are put at different places in sentences for variety.

<u>"Oh, look at this!"</u> called Robert. (quotation first)
Robert called, <u>"Oh, look at this!"</u> (quotation last)

Use the following rules to write a sentence in which the direct quotation comes first.

1. *Place quotation marks around the quoted words.*
2. *Begin the quotation with a capital letter.*

    "<u>W</u>e haven't started yet," Andy admitted.

3. *Place the correct punctuation at the end of the quoted words.* Use a comma after a statement or command, a question mark after a question, and an exclamation point after an exclamation. The mark at the end of the quoted words comes *before* the ending quotation marks.

    "My father works here<u>,</u>" said Nathan. (statement)
    "Bake a cake<u>,</u>" Mother directed. (command)
    "Will you help us<u>?</u>" they asked. (question)
    "That was a mountain lion<u>!</u>" shouted Darvin. (exclamation)

4. *Put a period after the explanatory words at the end of the sentence.* This is done because the whole sentence is usually a statement, even though the direct quotation may be a question or an exclamation.

    "Could we wait on your porch?" asked the children<u>.</u>
    "I never saw a mountain lion around here before!" exclaimed Allen<u>.</u>

Use the following rules to write a sentence in which the direct quotation comes last.

Lesson 77

Purpose: To teach how to punctuate direct quotations.

Oral Review:
1. Name the four sentence types and their correct end punctuation. (declarative—period; interrogative—question mark; imperative—period; exclamatory—exclamation point)
2. What part of speech standing alone is sometimes followed by an exclamation point? (a strong interjection)
3. Name some items besides sentences that end with periods. (abbreviations, initials)
4. Name the kind of pronouns in each group.
    a. this, that, these, those (demonstrative)
    b. who, whom, whose, which, that (relative)
    c. anybody, anyone, each, either, few, many, several, most (indefinite)
    d. who, whom, whose, which, what (interrogative)
    e. I, you, he, she, it, we, they (personal—nominative case)
    f. me, you, him, her, it, us, them (personal—objective case)

Lesson Introduction: Call the students' attention to the following sentences in Mark 6:14, 15.

And [Herod] said, That John the Baptist was risen from the dead....
Others said, That it is Elias.
And others said, That it is a prophet, or as one of the prophets.

These sentences repeat the exact words of several speakers. But the direct quotations seem strange to us because they begin with *that*. They are worded this way because in Greek, the word for *that* was used to introduce direct quotations. Today we use quotation marks when we write the exact words of a speaker.

Lesson Outline:
1. The exact words of a speaker or writer are a **direct quotation.** *The other words in the sentence are called* **explanatory words.**

2. Direct quotations are put at different places in sentences for variety. Sometimes the quotation comes first, and sometimes it comes last.

1. *Place quotation marks around the quoted words.*
2. *Begin the first word with a capital letter,* since it is the beginning of the sentence. *Also begin the direct quotation with a capital letter.* This is done because the speaker's words are a sentence within a longer sentence.

> <u>I</u>n his report Andrew said, "<u>A</u> jackrabbit can leap over ten times its body length in one jump."

3. *Place a comma at the end of the explanatory words.* Be sure to place this comma *before* the beginning quotation marks.

> He added<u>,</u> "A person who is good at jumping can jump only about five times his own length."

4. *At the end of the quotation, place a period, a question mark, or an exclamation point, depending on whether the quotation tells, asks, or exclaims.* The mark at the end of the quoted words comes *before* the ending quotation marks.

> Andrew continued, "A flea, by comparison, can jump 350 times its body length<u>!</u>"
> He also said, "An elephant can't jump at all<u>.</u>"
> Then he added, "But why would an elephant need to jump<u>?</u>"

- A direct quotation is enclosed in quotation marks, and a comma usually separates it from the explanatory words.
- A direct quotation begins with a capital letter because the speaker's words are a sentence within a longer sentence.
- Other punctuation marks usually come before quotation marks.

Class Practice

Each sentence below has two mistakes. Tell how to correct the mistakes.

1. Karen said, "oh, look, this book says some ants can lift about fifty times their own weight.
2. Samuel exclaimed, "that's about like a person lifting four tons"!
3. "it also says an ant can carry the weight a long way, Karen continued.

3. To write a sentence in which the direct quotation comes first, use the following rules.

(1) *Place quotation marks around the quoted words.*
(2) *Begin the quotation with a capital letter.*
(3) *Place the correct punctuation at the end of the quoted words.* Use a comma after a statement or command, a question mark after a question, and an exclamation point after an exclamation. The mark at the end of the quoted words comes *before* the ending quotation marks.
(4) *Put a period after the explanatory words at the end of the sentence.* A period is used because the whole sentence is usually a statement, even though the direct quotation may be a question or an exclamation.

Lesson 77 Answers
Class Practice
(Corrections are marked.)

1. Karen said, "<u>O</u>h, look, this book says some ants can lift about fifty times their own weight.<u>"</u>
2. Samuel exclaimed, "<u>T</u>hat's about like a person lifting four tons<u>!</u>"
3. "<u>I</u>t also says an ant can carry the weight a long way<u>,</u>" Karen continued.

4. To write a sentence in which the direct quotation comes last, use the following rules.

(1) *Place quotation marks around the quoted words.*
(2) *Begin the first word of the sentence and the first word of the direct quotation with capital letters.* The second capital letter is used because the speaker's words are a sentence within a longer sentence.
(3) *Place a comma at the end of the explanatory words.* This comma is placed *before* the beginning quotation marks.
(4) *At the end of the quotation, place a period, a question mark, or an exclamation point, depending on whether the quotation tells, asks, or exclaims.* The mark at the end of the quoted words comes *before* the ending quotation marks.

4. "How much weight can one person lift," Roy asked?

5. "A person can lift as much as his own weight," but even that is difficult for many men", Kevin answered.

Written Exercises

Copy each sentence, and add the correct punctuation and capital letters.

1. rise up and walk said Peter
2. Jesus said I am the Good Shepherd
3. if I go away, I will come again He told them
4. Lord, how can we know the way asked Thomas
5. he asked them have ye any meat
6. the teacher asked how many know the answer
7. help the little ones Mother told us
8. my home is far away said the stranger
9. Ray asked is it true that the fastest animal is the cheetah
10. Jay answered yes, a cheetah can run seventy miles per hour
11. a cheetah can go from standing still to forty-five miles per hour in only two seconds said Joshua
12. he added but a cheetah cannot keep up his speed for a long distance
13. Ronald said an antelope or a gazelle doesn't tire nearly as quickly
14. the pronghorn antelope can maintain a speed of sixty miles per hour he continued
15. Brother Martin said God gave these animals the special abilities of speed and endurance to outrun the cheetah
16. he continued God also gave the cheetah the ability of extra speed so that he can catch his food
17. so if an antelope or a gazelle sees the cheetah in time, he can escape Ray concluded
18. Brother Martin said that is right

Review Exercises

A. Copy the underlined pronouns. Identify each one by writing *P* for personal, *D* for demonstrative, *ID* for indefinite, *IR* for interrogative, or *R* for relative. [61–69]

1. Was it they who called us?
2. My sister gave that to me.
3. Everyone seems to like it.
4. Who brought him the papers?

---

4. "How much weight can one person lift?" Roy asked.

5. "A person can lift as much as his own weight," but even that is difficult for many men," Kevin answered.

Written Exercises

(Corrections are underlined.)

1. "Rise up and walk," said Peter.
2. Jesus said, "I am the Good Shepherd."
3. "If I go away, I will come again." He told them.
4. "Lord, how can we know the way?" asked Thomas.
5. He asked them, "Have ye any meat?"
6. The teacher asked, "How many know the answer?"
7. "Help the little ones," Mother told us.
8. "My home is far away," said the stranger.
9. Ray asked, "Is it true that the fastest animal is the cheetah?"
10. Jay answered, "Yes, a cheetah can run seventy miles per hour."
11. "A cheetah can go from standing still to forty-five miles per hour in only two seconds," said Joshua.
12. He added, "But a cheetah cannot keep up his speed for a long distance."
13. Ronald said, "An antelope or a gazelle doesn't tire nearly as quickly."
14. "The pronghorn antelope can maintain a speed of sixty miles per hour," he continued.
15. Brother Martin said, "God gave these animals the special abilities of speed and endurance to outrun the cheetah."
16. He continued, "God also gave the cheetah the ability of extra speed so that he can catch his food."
17. "So if an antelope or a gazelle sees the cheetah in time, he can escape." Ray concluded.
18. Brother Martin said, "That is right."

Review Exercises

A. 1. they—P; who—R; us—P
   2. My—P; that—D; me—P
   3. Everyone—ID; it—P
   4. Who—IR; him—P

B. Write correctly each word that is not capitalized but should be. [20, 73, 74]

1. christian miller arrived in philadelphia in 1737, having sailed from rotterdam in the netherlands to america for religious freedom.

2. (a) the lord is my Shepherd, i shall not want;

(b) he maketh me down to lie

(c) in pastures green, he leadeth me

(d) the quiet waters by.

(e) his yoke is easy, his burden is light,

(f) i've found it so, i've found it so;

(g) he leadeth me by day and by night,

(h) where living waters flow.

—Author unknown

---

78. Direct and Indirect Quotations

When we tell what a speaker has said or a writer has written, we are using a *quotation*. It may be a *direct quotation* or an *indirect quotation*.

A direct quotation repeats the exact words of a speaker or writer.

> Jesus said, "Blessed are the pure in heart: for they shall see God."
> Solomon wrote, "A wise man will hear, and will increase learning."

An indirect quotation tells what a person said, without repeating his exact words.

> Jesus said that the pure in heart are blessed, for they shall see God.
> Solomon wrote that a wise man will hear and will increase learning.

Here are the four main differences between direct and indirect quotations.

1. Quotation marks are used with a direct quotation, but not with an indirect quotation.

> "The fence needs to be painted," said Father. (direct quotation)
> Father said that the fence needs to be painted. (indirect quotation)

B. 1. Christian Miller, Philadelphia, Rotterdam, Netherlands, America

2. a. The, Lord, I   e. His, His
   b. He   f. I've, I've
   c. In, He   g. He
   d. The   h. Where

Lesson 78

Purpose: To compare direct and indirect quotations.

Oral Review:

1. What is a direct quotation? (the exact words of the speaker)

2. In the following sentence, tell which words are the direct quotation and which words are the explanatory words. *"Look, it is raining!" exclaimed Justin.* (direct quotation—*Look, it is raining;* explanatory words—*exclaimed Justin*)

3. What is a transitive verb? (a verb that passes action to a receiver)

4. What sentence parts can follow a transitive verb? (direct object, indirect object)

5. What sentence parts can follow a linking verb? (predicate nominative, predicate adjective)

Lesson Introduction: Do the students know what is meant by a paraphrase? When we paraphrase what someone said, we express the same ideas in different words. Here are two common sayings, along with paraphrases.

> Cleanliness is next to godliness.
> **Paraphrase:**
> Cleanliness and godliness go hand in hand.
> Strike while the iron is hot.
> **Paraphrase:**
> Act while you have the opportunity.

An indirect quotation is a sort of paraphrase. It tells what a speaker said, but it does not repeat his exact words. In this lesson we will compare direct and indirect quotations.

Lesson Outline:

1. A direct quotation repeats the exact words of a speaker or writer. Quotation marks are used with a direct quotation.

2. The word *that* often comes before an indirect quotation.

> Doris said to us, "My mother is coming to school today."
> Doris told us <u>that</u> her mother is coming to school today.

3. Some pronouns may be different in an indirect quotation.

> The boys suggested, "<u>We</u> can do the work for <u>you</u>."
> The boys suggested that <u>they</u> could do the work for <u>us</u>.

4. Some verb forms may be different in an indirect quotation.

> "<u>Are</u> the birds cold in wet weather?" asked Timothy.
> Timothy asked if the birds <u>were</u> cold in wet weather.
> "We <u>will</u> soon be there!" exclaimed Doris.
> Doris exclaimed that they <u>would</u> soon be there.

- A direct quotation repeats the exact words of a speaker or writer. An indirect quotation tells what a speaker said, without repeating his exact words.

- When a direct quotation is changed to an indirect quotation, the quotation marks are removed, the word *that* may be added, and some pronouns and verb forms may change.

Class Practice

A. Tell whether each sentence has a *direct quotation,* an *indirect quotation,* or *no quotation* at all. (All quotation marks have been omitted.)
1. I have filled all the boxes, Amos announced.
2. Amos announced that he had filled all the boxes.
3. Amos carried the boxes to the van.
4. At breakfast Donna said that today is the shortest day of the year.
5. Barbara said that the thermometer showed 20°.
6. The thermometer shows 20°, said Barbara.

B. Read each direct quotation as an indirect quotation.
1. Jonathan said, "It is twelve o'clock already!"
2. "I should make pies today," said Rosene.
3. Mother said to Aunt Mary, "I haven't seen you for a long time!"

Lesson 78 Answers
Class Practice

A. 1. direct quotation
   2. indirect quotation
   3. no quotation
   4. indirect quotation
   5. indirect quotation
   6. direct quotation

B. (Verb forms may vary.)
   1. Jonathan said that it was twelve o'clock already.
   2. Rosene said that she should make pies today.
   3. Mother told Aunt Mary that she had not seen her for a long time.

---

2. An indirect quotation tells what a person said, without repeating his exact words. It is different from a direct quotation in the following ways.
   (1) No quotation marks are used with an indirect quotation.
   (2) The word *that* often comes before an indirect quotation.
   (3) Some pronouns may be different in an indirect quotation.
   (4) Some verb forms may be different in an indirect quotation.

> **Direct:** Sidney said, "<u>I</u> <u>will</u> help <u>you</u>."
> **Indirect:** Sidney said that <u>he</u> <u>would</u> help <u>them.</u>

★ EXTRA PRACTICE
Worksheet 45 *(Direct and Indirect Quotations)*

C. Read each indirect quotation as a direct quotation.
1. Lloyd said that he was sure it would be very useful.
2. Mervin asked them if they could stay for supper.
3. Mark exclaimed that he had never before seen such a playful goat.

Written Exercises

A. Write *direct* or *indirect* to tell what kind of quotation is found in each sentence. (All quotation marks have been omitted.)
1. Come quickly, Donald, called Peter.
2. I'll be right there, Donald answered.
3. Donald said that he would be right there.
4. Daniel said that the cows were out.
5. Mark said, Let's chase them all back in.
6. Daniel said that they should tie the gate shut the next time.
7. Janelle said that she would like to go skating.
8. No, you shouldn't, because the ice is too thin, Father said.

B. Write each sentence, changing the indirect quotation to a direct quotation.
1. Charlotte said that she found this sweater lying in the lane.
2. Harold told us that we may sit here awhile.

C. Write each sentence, changing the direct quotation to an indirect quotation.
1. My sister said, "I saw the new lambs in the pasture."
2. "You must water the strawberries," Henry told us.

Review Exercises

A. Copy the verb or verb phrase in each sentence. If there is a word that receives the action, also copy that word. [55]
1. The recipe for this apple pie was invented in the 1800s.
2. My aunt wrote the recipe for us.
3. Jonathan had come in the morning.
4. The bell has already rung.
5. The trumpets were blown before each assembly.
6. The priests always blew the trumpets.

B. After each answer in Part A, write *transitive* or *not transitive* to label the verb. [55]

C. (Verb forms may vary.)
1. Lloyd said, "I am sure it will be very useful."
2. Mervin asked, "Can you stay for supper?"
3. Mark exclaimed, "I have never before seen such a playful goat!"

Written Exercises
A. 1. direct
2. direct
3. indirect
4. indirect
5. direct
6. indirect
7. indirect
8. direct

B. (Verb forms may vary.)
1. Charlotte said, "I found this sweater lying in the lane."
2. Harold told us, "You may sit here awhile."

C. (Verb forms may vary.)
1. My sister said that she saw the new lambs in the pasture.
2. Henry told us that we must water the strawberries.

Review Exercises
A–B.
1. was invented, recipe—transitive
2. wrote, recipe—transitive
3. had come—not transitive
4. has rung—not transitive
5. were blown, trumpets—transitive
6. blew, trumpets—transitive

79. Dialogue in a Story

Dialogue in a story is written conversation. Dialogue helps to make a story more interesting. It helps the reader to "see" the action, and it makes the characters seem more real. Compare the two story beginnings below. Which one makes the characters seem more real?

> Kathy couldn't wait to tell her friend Brenda the news she had just gotten from her cousin. She told Brenda that Smithville School had lice. Brenda was so surprised that her mouth dropped open.
>
> *   *   *   *   *
>
> "Oh, Brenda," Kathy burst out the moment the two of them got together at school. "I got a letter from my cousin yesterday. Guess what they have at Smithville School?"
>
> "Is it a gerbil?" Brenda guessed.
>
> "Oh, no, nothing like that," Kathy groaned. "Lice," she hissed. Brenda's mouth dropped open, and she was speechless.

The second beginning is better because it *shows* the action by using dialogue instead of just telling what happened. As we hear the characters talking to each other, the story and the characters seem to come alive.

In dialogue, be careful to put quotation marks only where they belong. If a speaker says several sentences together, do not put quotation marks around every sentence. Put them only at the beginning and end of the whole quotation. The words that simply tell the story should not be inside quotation marks. In the example below, the direct quotation is in italics.

> <u>"I'm glad I don't go to that school,"</u> Kathy declared. <u>"Just thinking about lice is enough to get me scratching. It would be absolutely horrifying to have lice, with the treatments and all!"</u>
>
> The door opened, and more students arrived.

Begin a new paragraph in your story each time you begin a new topic. (See the last sentence in the example above.) Also begin a new paragraph each time a different person begins to speak. Notice how this second rule is observed in the following paragraphs.

> "Good morning, Elsie," Brenda greeted her classmate.
>
> "Good morning," Elsie returned, and then she broke into a wide yawn.
>
> "Did you get to bed late?" Kathy teased.

Lesson 79

Purpose: (1) To teach the rules for writing dialogue. (2) To show how to use dialogue to make a story interesting.

Oral Review:

1. What are the three main parts of a story? (the beginning, the middle, and the ending)
2. What should each part of a story do? (The beginning should arouse the reader's interest. The middle should describe the conflict and lead to a climax. The ending should conclude the story.)
3. What should the ending of a story not do? (It should not tell what lesson the story teaches.)
4. When does a paragraph have unity? (when all the sentences tell about the topic given by the topic sentence)
5. When does a paragraph have coherence? (when all the sentences "hold together" in an orderly, sensible way)
6. What are some ways to give coherence to a paragraph? (Give details in the order of time. Give details in the order of importance or interest. Use transitional words.)
7. List some transitional words that help to make a paragraph coherent. (first, second, next, then, finally, soon, later, also, immediately, afterward, however, for example, therefore, for this reason)

Lesson Introduction: Which of the following stories seems more interesting?

> Gary was riding his grandfather's horse. His father had told him not to make the horse gallop. But Gary wanted to find out how it felt, so he made the horse go faster. Just then a rabbit leaped out of some weeds, and Gary fell off the horse. He ended up in the hospital. There he

"Yes, we did," Elsie replied with a smile. "My father just started a week of revival meetings at Smithville."

Do not use only the word *said* in the explanatory words. There are other words that give more meaning to the story. The previous conversation would be less interesting if it used only *said*.

"Good morning, Elsie," Brenda <u>said</u> to her classmate.

"Good morning," <u>said</u> Elsie, and then she broke into a wide yawn.

"Did you get to bed late?" Kathy <u>said</u>.

"Yes, we did," Elsie <u>said</u> with a smile. "My father just started a week of revival meetings at Smithville."

You cannot use a different explanatory word in every sentence. *Said* is often the best word to use. But you should use other words when they add meaning. Try to use some of the following when they fit well in your stories.

asked	whispered	declared	continued
called	exclaimed	asserted	suggested
added	shouted	demanded	countered
stated	complained	insisted	admonished

Keep the dialogue natural. That is, write conversation in the way people actually talk. Two things especially will help to make your conversations sound natural. One is *contractions,* and the other is *incomplete sentences.* It is true that neither of these should be used in formal writing, such as a report. But in the dialogue of a story, these are fully acceptable because this is the way people actually speak. Notice how the contractions and incomplete sentences make the following dialogue sound true to life.

"Oh, Mother, Kathy <u>doesn't</u> seem to like me anymore," Elsie shared that evening as they were doing the dishes.

"Why, what makes you think that?" asked Mother.

"<u>The look on her face.</u> Several times today I noticed her looking at me as grimly as if <u>she'd</u> lost her last friend," Elsie began. "When I smiled at her, she <u>didn't</u> smile back."

"<u>Didn't she</u>? Well, maybe she was having an especially hard time with her lessons," Mother suggested helpfully.

"<u>Maybe,</u>" Elsie said doubtfully. "But Kathy has never treated me like this before."

told his father that he was sorry. His father forgave him and said that he hoped Gary had learned his lesson of obedience.

*　　*　　*　　*　　*

"I'd like the horse to gallop," thought Gary. "Father said we shouldn't go fast, but maybe he won't care if I make the horse gallop just a little."

The horse began galloping as the meadow came into sight. But just then a rabbit leaped out of the weeds and frightened the horse. He bucked, and Gary went flying through the air.

When Gary opened his eyes, he was in a hospital bed. "Father," he whispered, "I made the horse run. If I had not been galloping, I don't think this would have happened. I'm sorry, Father."

"I forgive you," Father assured Gary. "I hope this proves to be a valuable lesson for you."

The second story is more interesting because it uses conversation instead of just telling the story. Today we want to study the use of conversation in stories.

Lesson Outline:

Dialogue in a story is written conversation.
The rules for writing dialogue are as follows:

    a. Put quotation marks at the beginning and end of each quotation. Do not put quotation marks around every sentence.

    b. Begin a new paragraph each time a different person begins to speak.

    c. Use variety in dialogue.

        1) Do not always use *said* in the explanatory words.

        2) Use some longer quotations and some shorter ones.

"Make sure you do your part to be friendly, but <u>don't</u> be over-bearing in it," Mother advised.

When you use dialogue, the sentences should vary in length. Natural conversation has some long sentences and some short ones. Do not write quotations that are too long, because they do not sound natural.

Another way to have variety in dialogue is to use different kinds of quotations. Begin some sentences with explanatory words and some with direct quotations.

Finally, have the characters in your story speak according to their age level. Their language should sound natural for themselves, but they should not use slang, poor grammar, or other unsuitable expressions.

- Use dialogue in a story to make the story more interesting.

- Begin a new paragraph every time a different person begins to speak.

- Keep conversation natural.

Class Practice

A. Tell where the quotation marks and paragraph divisions should be.

Do I have to go to school this morning? Kathy pleaded with her mother. I have a headache. Just a headache doesn't seem like a good-enough reason to stay at home, Kathy's mother answered. Take a Tylenol tablet, and see if you feel better soon. Tylenol probably won't help it, Kathy grumbled while she braided her hair. Is something else the matter? Mother eyed her daughter closely. It's those lice! Kathy burst into tears. I'm just sure Elsie got them at Smithville on Sunday. Next thing I'll have them too!

B. Tell how to improve the following dialogue so that it sounds more natural and has better variety.

"Kathy, Kathy, I had no idea you were so upset about this. Getting head lice would not be the worst thing that could happen," Mother said.

"What could be worse!" said Kathy.

"Losing Elsie as a friend would be worse. In Proverbs it says that a brother offended is harder to be won than a strong city," Mother said to Kathy. "I am sure Elsie's family will do what they can to avoid

3) Write some sentences with the quotation first and some with the quotation last.

d. Keep the dialogue natural.

1) Use contractions and sentence fragments as in natural conversation.

2) Have the characters speak according to their age level, but do not use slang, poor grammar, or other unsuitable expressions.

★ **EXTRA PRACTICE**
Worksheet 46 *(Using Dialogue in Stories)*

Lesson 79 Answers
Class Practice

A. (Quotation marks are underlined.)

<u>"</u>Do I have to go to school this morning?<u>"</u> Kathy pleaded with her mother. <u>"</u>I have a headache.<u>"</u>

<u>"</u>Just a headache doesn't seem like a good-enough reason to stay at home,<u>"</u> Kathy's mother answered. <u>"</u>Take a Tylenol tablet, and see if you feel better soon.<u>"</u>

<u>"</u>Tylenol probably won't help it,<u>"</u> Kathy grumbled while she braided her hair.

<u>"</u>Is something else the matter?<u>"</u> Mother eyed her daughter closely.

<u>"</u>It's those lice!<u>"</u> Kathy burst into tears. <u>"</u>I'm just sure Elsie got them at Smithville on Sunday. Next thing I'll have them too!<u>"</u>

B. (Sample answer. Changes are underlined.)

"Kathy, Kathy," <u>Mother chided.</u> "I had no idea you were so upset about this. Getting head lice <u>wouldn't</u> be the worst thing that could happen."

"What could be worse!" <u>cried</u> Kathy.

"<u>Losing Elsie as a friend.</u> In Proverbs it says that a brother offended is harder to be won than a strong city," Mother <u>reminded</u> Kathy. "<u>I'm</u> sure Elsie's family will do what they can to avoid getting lice. But it will take more than head lice to keep Elsie's father from doing his duty as a minister at Smithville. I <u>wouldn't</u> be surprised if Elsie has detected your attitude."

getting lice. But it will take more than head lice to keep Elsie's father from doing his duty as a minister at Smithville. I would not be surprised if Elsie has detected your attitude," Mother said.

Several moments passed in silence. "She probably has detected it. I will have to apologize to Elsie for the way I have been acting," Kathy said.

"That sounds better. We are not wishing for lice, but if we get them, we can be treated for them just as others have been," Mother said with a smile.

Written Exercises

A. Rewrite this dialogue, using correct punctuation and paragraph division.

Juanita said Since school started, I hardly have time to read my book anymore. I know agreed Noreen. I wish there'd be some way of getting more time to read. Don't you think we could read a little bit right now before we go to sleep? asked Juanita. So a few evenings passed, and each night the girls read a little longer. I'm afraid Mother will see that the light is on in here Juanita worried one evening. Maybe we shouldn't be reading. But we don't need to go to bed so early reasoned Noreen. We deserve a little time to read. I guess you're right Juanita agreed slowly. All at once a floorboard creaked in the hall. The books closed instantly, and the light switch snapped off. We're caught Noreen whispered. It's ten o'clock! breathed Juanita. The door opened, and Mother appeared. What's going on in here? she wondered. The next morning Father called Noreen and Juanita to his study. You were being disobedient as well as acting a lie he said. After the punishment each girl said I'm sorry. I won't do it again. I'm sure you won't Father told them. We're expecting you to do better after this.

B. Rewrite this dialogue, making it more natural and using more variety.

"How was school today?" asked Mother.

"Oh, school wasn't too bad today," said Beth. "You see, it's this way. It seems the girls do not care to be with me anymore. I cannot understand it."

Mother asked, "Are you remembering to follow the verse which says that a man who has friends must show himself friendly? I think you should try being more friendly to the girls."

Several moments passed in silence. "She prob-ably has," Kathy finally admitted. "I'll have to apol-ogize to Elsie for the way I've been acting."

"That sounds better," Mother encouraged. "We aren't wishing for lice, but if we get them, we can be treated for them just as others have been."

Written Exercises

A. (Corrections are underlined. Allow some variation in paragraph divisions, except at places where a new speaker begins.)

Juanita said, "Since school started, I hardly have time to read my book anymore."

"I know," agreed Noreen. "I wish there'd be some way of getting more time to read."

"Don't you think we could read a little bit right now before we go to sleep?" asked Juanita. So a few evenings passed, and each night the girls read a little longer.

"I'm afraid Mother will see that the light is on in here," Juanita worried one evening. "Maybe we shouldn't be reading."

"But we don't need to go to bed so early," rea-soned Noreen. "We deserve a little time to read."

"I guess you're right," Juanita agreed slowly.

All at once a floorboard creaked in the hall. The books closed instantly, and the light switch snapped off.

"We're caught," Noreen whispered.

"It's ten o'clock!" breathed Juanita.

The door opened and Mother appeared. "What's going on in here?" she wondered.

The next morning Father called Noreen and Juanita to his study. "You were being disobedient as well as acting a lie," he said.

After the punishment each girl said, "I'm sorry. I won't do it again."

"I'm sure you won't," Father told them. "We're expecting you to do better after this."

B. (Sample dialogue.)

"How was school today?" asked Mother.

"Oh, not too bad," replied Beth. "You see, it's this way. It seems the girls don't care to be with me anymore. I can't understand it."

"Are you remembering to follow the verse which says that a man who has friends must show him-self friendly?" asked Mother. "I think you should try being more friendly to the girls."

"I guess you are right, Mother. I need to try harder to be friendly," said Beth.

"Oh, Mother, it worked!" said Beth the next day. "I had a much better time with my friends today. I am so glad for the advice you gave me."

Review Exercises

A. Write the number of the paragraph below that has better *unity*. [16]

1.   The aardvark is a strange creature. *Aardvark* comes from the Dutch expression for "earth pig." Many Dutch settlers moved to South Africa long ago, taking their language with them. The aardvark is more like an anteater than a pig. It eats ants like an anteater. The giant anteater lives in damp tropical forests and grassy plains of Central and South America. With its claws, the aardvark rips open the nests of ants and termites. Anteaters also tear open ant nests and eat the insects.

2.   The aardvark is a strange creature. It is about the size of a hog, and it has thick, gray-brown hair. It has long ears like a rabbit's and sharp claws like a raccoon's. The word *aardvark* means "earth pig." Dutch settlers in Africa gave it that name because it has a snout like a pig's and it digs burrows in the earth. But the aardvark is more like an anteater than a pig. With its claws, it rips open the nests of ants and termites. Then it uses its long, sticky tongue to catch and eat the insects.

B. Write the number of the paragraph that has better *coherence*. [16, 17]

1.   The Panama Canal is the only canal in the world that connects two oceans. In 1882 a French company began digging the canal, but they ran into such great problems that they gave up. One of the problems was diseases spread by mosquitoes. Because of malaria and yellow fever, twenty thousand workers died. Then a man named William C. Gorgas took measures to control the mosquitoes that carried these diseases. Working with several other people, he greatly reduced the number of deaths caused by malaria and yellow fever. Finally in 1907, President Roosevelt appointed a company to continue digging the canal. The Panama Canal was finished in 1914.

"I guess you're right, Mother," Beth answered. "I'll try harder."

The next day Beth exclaimed, "Oh, Mother, it worked! I had a much better time with my friends today. I'm so glad for the advice you gave me."

Review Exercises

A. paragraph 2

B. paragraph 1

2.   The Panama Canal is the only canal in the world that connects two oceans. In 1907 President Roosevelt appointed a company to dig the canal. A French company had begun digging the canal in 1882, but they ran into problems. Many workers became sick with malaria and yellow fever. A man named William C. Gorgas worked to wipe out the mosquitoes that carried the diseases. He greatly reduced the number of deaths caused by these diseases. But twenty thousand French workers had died. This caused the French to give up. The Panama Canal was finished in 1914.

80. Divided Quotations

Some direct quotations are divided. The explanatory words separate the quotation into two parts.

> "Did you know," <u>asked Martin,</u> "that birds have been used to send messages?"

> "Long ago," <u>he continued,</u> "the Chinese used homing pigeons to carry mail."

Some divided quotations are made of only one sentence. Others are made of two sentences.

One sentence:
> "This was also done more recently," said Martin, "when the French in Paris used pigeons in the 1870s."

Two sentences:
> "This was also done more recently," said Martin. "The French in Paris used pigeons in the 1870s."

Use the following steps to punctuate and capitalize divided quotations.
1. *Find the quoted words, and put quotation marks around them.* In the following sentence, the quoted words are underlined.

> "<u>An army surrounded Paris,</u>" said Martin, "<u>and the people could not travel in or out.</u>"

Lesson 80

Purpose: To teach how to punctuate divided quotations.

Oral Review:

1. What are some differences between direct quotations and indirect quotations?
   (a. A direct quotation repeats the exact words of a speaker, but an indirect quotation does not.
   b. Quotation marks are used with a direct quotation, but not with an indirect quotation.
   c. The word *that* often comes before an indirect quotation.
   d. Some pronouns may be different in an indirect quotation.
   e. Some verb forms may be different in an indirect quotation.)

2. When is a verb in the active voice? (when a direct object receives the action of the verb)

3. When is a verb in the passive voice? (when the subject receives the action of the verb)

Lesson Introduction: Sentences with direct quotations are written in several ways for the sake of variety. The pupils have studied two of these ways; read the following examples to illustrate. (*Emu* is pronounced ē·mū.)

Quotations first:
> "Emus are the second largest birds in the world," said Martin.
> "Are ostriches bigger?" asked Edwin.
> "Yes, ostriches are the only birds that are bigger," said Martin.

Quotations last:
> Martin said, "The male emu sits on the eggs for about eight weeks to keep them warm."
> Edwin asked, "Do you mean the male does it instead of the female?"
> Martin replied, "Yes, and the male also baby-sits for six months after they are hatched!"

Is there another way to write direct quotations? Yes, there is. Listen to the following sentences.

> "These emus are one year old," said Martin. "They are as big as adults."
> "Adult emus," said Martin, "have colorful neck patches that the young do not have."

The last two sentences contain *divided quotations.* Today we will learn how to capitalize and punctuate divided quotations.

Lesson Outline:

1. In a divided quotation, the explanatory words separate the quotation into two parts. The quotation may be one sentence or two sentences.

> "The visitors have arrived," <u>said Martha,</u> "just in time for supper."
> "Come in," <u>said Mervin.</u> "Can you stay for supper?"

2. *Use a capital letter at the beginning of the direct quotation.* In a divided quotation, the beginning of the direct quotation is at the same place as the beginning of the sentence that contains it.

> "The Frenchmen outside Paris used homing pigeons," continued Martin, "to send letters into the city."

3. *Decide whether the quoted words make one or two sentences.* If the words on either side of the explanatory words cannot stand alone, the quotation is made of only one sentence. If each set of quoted words can stand alone, the quotation is made of two sentences.

One sentence:
> "Messages were put into small canisters," said Martin, "and were attached to the pigeons." (The underlined words cannot stand alone as a sentence.)

Two sentences:
> "Messages were put into small canisters," said Martin. "They were attached to the pigeons." (Each set of quoted words can stand alone as a sentence.)

4. *If the divided quotation is made of only one sentence, continue with the following steps.*
   a. Use commas to separate the explanatory words from the quotation. Remember that commas come *before* quotation marks.

   > "Thirty thousand letters could be placed in each canister," explained Martin, "because the Frenchmen first reduced the letters by photography."

   b. Add the needed end punctuation. Remember that end marks come *before* quotation marks.

   > "The Frenchmen were determined," said Martin, "to get the messages through."

   c. Begin the second part of the divided quotation with a small letter, unless of course the first word is capitalized for some other reason.

   > "The same letters were sent with thirty-five different pigeons," said Martin, "so that each message would be sure to get through."

2. Use the following steps to punctuate and capitalize divided quotations correctly.

(1) *Find the quoted words, and put quotation marks around them.*

> "I should make pies today" Rosene planned aloud "and also carrot salad"
> "First I should do the cooking" Rosene thought "later I must do the cleaning"

(2) *Use a capital letter at the beginning of the direct quotation.* In a divided quotation, the beginning of the direct quotation is at the same place as the beginning of the sentence that contains it.

> "We just found out," said Henry, "that our silo is nearly empty!"
> "It seems that you just filled it," said David. "How could it be empty already?"

(3) *Decide whether the quoted words make one or two sentences.* If the words on either side of the explanatory words cannot stand alone, the quotation is made of only one sentence. If each set of quoted words can stand alone, the quotation is made of two sentences.

One sentence:
> "We must cook noodles," said Mother, "because we are out of potatoes."

Two sentences:
> "We must cook noodles," said Mother. "We are out of potatoes."

(4) *If the divided quotation is made of only one sentence, continue with the following steps.*

a) Use commas to separate the explanatory words from the quotation. Remember that commas come *before* quotation marks.

> "Dale," little David begged, "will you help me play a game?"

b) Add the needed end punctuation. Remember that end marks come *before* quotation marks.

> "This pen," said the salesman, "should last a long time."

"If the pigeons get through," thought a French boy, "I might get a letter today."

5. *If the divided quotation is made of two sentences, continue with the following steps.*
   a. Include the explanatory words with the first sentence.

   "The print of the letters was too tiny to read," <u>said Galen</u>. "The postmen of Paris had to project the letters on screens and copy them by hand."

   b. Place a period after the explanatory words. (The first sentence is punctuated like a sentence with the direct quotation coming first.)

   "In this way, mail was delivered to homes in the city," said Arlen<u>.</u> "It was called the pigeon post!"

   c. Begin the second sentence with a capital letter, and use the correct punctuation at the end.

   "In this way, mail was delivered to homes in the city," said Arlen. "<u>It</u> was called the pigeon post<u>!</u>"

- In a sentence with a divided quotation, each part of the quotation is enclosed in quotation marks.
- The second part of a divided quotation usually does not begin with a capital letter unless it begins a new sentence or is capitalized for another reason.

Class Practice

Tell how to correct the mistakes in the following sentences.
1. "As soon as you arrive," Mother instructed, "Call and tell us."
2. "Why do we see so many bees?" asked Sharon, "when we eat outside."
3. "The insects you see, replied Robert, are probably yellow jackets."
4. "Yellow jackets like sweet foods" continued Robert "like you probably have on your picnics."
5. "That is not a bee" exclaimed Mark. "it's a hummingbird."
6. "Several years ago we put up a feeder," said Mother, "the hummingbirds have come back each summer."

c) Begin the second part of the divided quotation with a small letter, unless the first word is capitalized for some other reason.

"It is wonderful," said Darrel, "<u>t</u>hat God gives us helpful friends."
"After I finish this job," Dale decided, "<u>I</u> will play with David."

(5) *If the divided quotation is made of two sentences, continue with the following steps.*
a) Include the explanatory words with the first sentence.

"The roses have sold well," <u>said Mary.</u> "There are hardly any left."

Lesson 80 Answers
Class Practice

(Corrections are underlined.)
1. "As soon as you arrive," Mother instructed, "<u>c</u>all and tell us."
2. "Why do we see so many bees," asked Sharon, "when we eat outside<u>?</u>"
3. "The insects you see<u>,</u>" replied Robert, "<u>a</u>re probably yellow jackets."
4. "Yellow jackets like sweet foods<u>,</u>" continued Robert<u>,</u> "like you probably have on your picnics."
5. "That is not a bee<u>!</u>" exclaimed Mark. "<u>I</u>t's a hummingbird."
6. "Several years ago we put up a feeder," said Mother<u>.</u> "<u>T</u>he hummingbirds have come back each summer."

---

b) Place a period after the explanatory words. (The first sentence is punctuated like a sentence with the direct quotation coming first.)

"These are good pens," said the salesman<u>.</u> "I sell many of them."

c) Begin the second sentence with a capital letter, and use the correct punctuation at the end.

"I hope we go to see the old bridge," thought Carol. "<u>I</u>t would be nice to walk down there<u>.</u>"

★ **EXTRA PRACTICE**
Worksheet 47 *(More Practice With Direct Quotations)*

Written Exercises

Copy these sentences, and add the correct capitalization and punctuation.

1. did you know asked John that Jupiter is about thirteen hundred times as large as the earth
2. if you could drive to the sun Galen wondered how long would it take to get there in a car
3. at fifty-five miles per hour said Robert it would take about 190 years to reach the sun
4. after all Robert added the sun is 93 million miles away
5. it's good that the sun is so far away said Galen if it were too close, we would burn up
6. I'm glad the sun is not too far away either added Robert everything would freeze then
7. because God knows exactly what we need Brother Joel added the distance is just right
8. on Saturn said Thomas winds blow about four times faster than the fastest winds ever clocked on earth
9. on that huge planet said Brother Joel winds blow up to eleven hundred miles per hour
10. did you say asked Grace that the Milky Way is a galaxy
11. do you mean Grace wondered that the white band of light is really a galaxy of millions of stars
12. do you know how the Milky Way got its name asked Brother Joel people long ago thought the white light from the thousands of stars looked like a stream of spilled milk
13. our word *galaxy* comes from the Greek word for milk said Robert isn't that interesting
14. God has created all these wonders said Brother Joel what a mighty God He is

Review Exercises

In these sentences, the main verbs are underlined twice and the receivers of their action are underlined once. Write whether each receiver is a *subject* or a *direct object,* and whether the verb is in the *active* or the *passive* voice. [55]

1. Why do dogs bury bones?
2. God taught them to save leftover food.
3. Often, however, buried bones are forgotten by well-fed dogs.

Written Exercises

(Corrections are underlined.)

1. "Did you know," asked John, "that Jupiter is about thirteen hundred times as large as the earth?"
2. "If you could drive to the sun," Galen wondered, "how long would it take to get there in a car?"
3. "At fifty-five miles per hour," said Robert, "it would take about 190 years to reach the sun."
4. "After all," Robert added, "the sun is 93 million miles away."
5. "It's good that the sun is so far away," said Galen. "If it were too close, we would burn up."
6. "I'm glad the sun is not too far away either," added Robert. "Everything would freeze then."
7. "Because God knows exactly what we need," Brother Joel added, "the distance is just right."
8. "On Saturn," said Thomas, "winds blow about four times faster than the fastest winds ever clocked on earth."
9. "On that huge planet," said Brother Joel, "winds blow up to eleven hundred miles per hour."
10. "Did you say," asked Grace, "that the Milky Way is a galaxy?"
11. "Do you mean," Grace wondered, "that the white band of light is really a galaxy of millions of stars?"
12. "Do you know how the Milky Way got its name?" asked Brother Joel. "People long ago thought the white light from the thousands of stars looked like a stream of spilled milk."
13. "Our word *galaxy* comes from the Greek word for milk," said Robert. "Isn't that interesting?"
14. "God has created all these wonders," said Brother Joel. "What a mighty God He is!"

Review Exercises

1. direct object—active
2. direct object—active
3. subject—passive

4. How much leftover <u>food</u> in your refrigerator is eventually <u>forgotten</u>?

5. When <u>cats</u> are <u>fed</u> too well, they may not <u>catch</u> many <u>mice</u>.

Challenge Exercises

Copy the following poem, and add the missing capitalization and punctuation. This poem contains many direct quotations that tell how people in some other countries greet each other.

how do you do?

how can you friend? the swedish say.
　　the dutch, how do you fare
how do you have yourself today
　　has quite a polish air.

in italy, how do you stand?
　　will greet you every hour;
in turkey, when one takes your hand
　　be under god's great power

how do you carry you is heard
　　when frenchmen so inquire,
while egypt's friendly greeting word
　　is how do you perspire?

thin may thy shadow never grow,
　　the persian wish is true;
his arab cousin, bowing low,
　　says praise god! how are you

but cutest of them all is when
　　two chinese meet, for thrice
they shake their own two hands and then
　　ask have you eaten rice
　　　　　　　　—H. Bedford Jones

A man that hath friends must shew himself friendly.

Proverbs 18:24

4. subject—passive

5. subject—passive; direct object—active

Challenge Exercises

(Corrections are underlined.)

How Do You Do?

"<u>H</u>ow can you<u>,</u> friend<u>?</u>" the <u>S</u>wedish say.
　　The <u>D</u>utch, "<u>H</u>ow do you fare<u>?</u>"
"<u>H</u>ow do you have yourself today<u>?</u>"
　　Has quite a <u>P</u>olish air.

In <u>I</u>taly, "<u>H</u>ow do you stand<u>?</u>"
　　<u>W</u>ill greet you every hour;
In <u>T</u>urkey, when one takes your hand,
　　"<u>B</u>e under <u>G</u>od's great power<u>.</u>"

"<u>H</u>ow do you carry you<u>?</u>" is heard
　　<u>W</u>hen Frenchmen so inquire,
While Egypt's friendly greeting word
　　Is<u>,</u> "<u>H</u>ow do you perspire<u>?</u>"

"<u>T</u>hin may thy shadows never grow<u>,</u>"
　　The <u>P</u>ersian wish is true;
His <u>A</u>rab cousin, bowing low,
　　Says, "<u>P</u>raise <u>G</u>od! <u>H</u>ow are you<u>?</u>"

But cutest of them all is when
　　<u>T</u>wo <u>C</u>hinese meet, for thrice
They shake their own two hands and then
　　Ask<u>,</u> "<u>H</u>ave you eaten rice<u>?</u>"

81. Commas in a Series

Commas are among the most commonly used punctuation marks. Do commas make a difference? Read the following sentences.

> What can you make with ice cream and milk?
> What can you make with ice, cream, and milk?

Commas do make a difference! They completely change the meaning of the sentences above. Learn the following rules for using commas.

1. *Words in a series are separated by commas.* (A series is a list of several items in a row.) Words in a series may be nouns, verbs, or some other part of speech.

   > The New England States are Maine, Vermont, New Hampshire, Massachusetts, Connecticut, and Rhode Island.
   > The girls washed, swept, dusted, and painted all day.

2. *Phrases in a series are separated by commas.*

   > There were books on the table, on the floor, and on the shelf.
   > During the Great Depression, many people ate beans and potatoes for breakfast, for dinner, and for supper.

3. *Two or more descriptive adjectives modifying the same noun are often separated by commas.* Notice the use of commas in the following examples. Observe that no comma is placed after the last adjective, just before the noun that is modified.

   > A dark, threatening sky developed as the day went on.
   > The apples were red, shiny, and expensive.
   > The roaring, tumbling, splashing water plunged over the falls.

But how can you tell when to use commas between the adjectives? First, remember that commas are used only after descriptive adjectives (those that tell *what kind of*). Articles (*a, an, the*) and adjectives that tell *which, whose,* and *how many* are limiting adjectives. These limiting adjectives are not followed by commas.

Correct:
> Gerald has a large, black, friendly dog.
> *Large, black,* and *friendly* are all descriptive adjectives.

Incorrect:
> John's, five, little puppies are growing rapidly.
> *John's* and *five* are limiting adjectives.

Lesson 81

Purpose: To teach several rules for using commas.

Oral Review:
1. What is a divided quotation? (a quotation that is separated into two parts by explanatory words)
2. When does the second part of a divided quotation begin with a capital letter? (when it begins a new sentence or is capitalized for another reason)
3. What kinds of abbreviations do not end with periods? (abbreviations for well-known phrases, abbreviations for names of certain organizations, and postal service abbreviations for state names)
4. What kinds of abbreviations may be used in all writing? (abbreviations used with proper nouns and in writing a time or date)

Lesson Introduction: Write the following sentence on the chalkboard. Tell students that all the punctuation marks are missing. Ask if they can tell how many items this person had for sale.

> Martha said that she had ice cream pie and strawberries to sell

If we simply add a period, the sentence means that two different items were for sale. But with commas added, it could refer to as many as four different items. Illustrate on the chalkboard.

> Martha said that she had ice cream, pie, and strawberries to sell.
> Martha said that she had ice, cream pie, and strawberries to sell.
> Martha said that she had ice, cream, pie, and strawberries to sell.

Learn how to use commas correctly so that your writing is clear.

Second, if the adjectives are descriptive adjectives, try placing the word *and* between them. If it sounds right to use *and,* separate the adjectives with a comma. If it sounds odd, do not use a comma. Use this test to decide whether the underlined adjectives in these sentences should be separated by commas.

> I nearly dropped the <u>big clumsy</u> package.
> > **Think:** *Big and clumsy package* sounds right. Use a comma.
> > **Write:** I nearly dropped the big, clumsy package.

> The <u>kind old</u> gentleman held the door open for my mother.
> > **Think:** *Kind and old gentleman* sounds odd. Do not use a comma.
> > **Write:** The kind old gentleman held the door open for my mother.

> Three <u>pleasant cheerful young</u> men were distributing Gospel tracts.
> > **Think:** *Pleasant and cheerful men* sounds right; use a comma. *Cheerful and young men* sounds odd; do not use a comma.
> > **Write:** Three pleasant, cheerful young men were distributing Gospel tracts.

Finally, remember that a comma indicates a pause. Do you pause between the adjectives as you read the sentence? If so, you should probably place a comma between them. Notice how this is true as you read the examples above.

It is not always easy to tell whether a comma is needed. But as you think carefully and gain practice, you will find that it becomes easier to decide.

- Words or phrases in a series are separated by commas.

- Two or more descriptive adjectives modifying the same noun are often separated by commas. A comma should be placed between two adjectives if they are descriptive adjectives, if it sounds right to use *and* between them, and if there is a pause between them in reading.

Lesson Outline:

1. Words in a series are separated by commas. The words may be nouns, verbs, or some other part of speech.

2. Phrases in a series are separated by commas.

3. Two or more descriptive adjectives modifying the same noun are often separated by commas. A limiting adjective is not followed by a comma.

> a. No comma is placed after the last adjective, just before the noun that is modified.
> b. A comma is placed between two adjectives if it sounds right to use *and* between them.
> c. A comma is placed between two adjectives if there is a pause between them in reading.

Class Practice

A. Read these sentences, saying *comma* at each place where a comma is needed. Try saying *and* for all the commas after adjectives.
1. Boots shoes slippers and sandals are all made of leather.
2. There were geese in the grass on the rocks and on the water of the lake.
3. Did you ever see such sparkling white snow?
4. Sarah uses this thick warm quilt in the wintertime.
5. We pumped water from an old hand pump.

B. Tell which commas are not needed in the following sentences.
1. Many, other, little boats were on the lake.
2. Bananas, oranges, and mangoes, are tropical fruits.
3. We bought a large, intelligent, German, shepherd dog.
4. Jesus entered the small, fishing boat, sat down, and began to teach.

Written Exercises

A. Copy each word that needs a comma after it, and add the missing comma. (Commas are not needed in all the sentences.)
1. The rabbit nibbled at the clover looked up and hopped away.
2. The boys were selling cabbage squash carrots and beans.
3. Our older boys dug raked trimmed and planted.
4. On the shelf you will find books tablets pencils and erasers.
5. The little boy observed listened and learned much.
6. They have a friendly Old English sheepdog.
7. The cinnamon graham crackers are tasty.
8. They passed out tracts in front of the store along the sidewalk and on the street corners.
9. Abraham Isaac and Jacob are called the patriarchs.
10. Peter James and John went up the mountain with Christ.
11. A poor unselfish widow cast her last two mites into the treasury.
12. Jesus visited Galilee Samaria Judea and Decapolis.
13. The small fragile boat was tossed on the angry stormy sea.
14. Jesus quickly changed the stormy raging sea to a calm peaceful place.

B. Write sentences of your own with the following kinds of series.
1. a series of nouns
2. a series of verbs
3. a series of phrases
4. a series of adjectives modifying the same noun

Lesson 81 Answers
Class Practice

A. (Corrections are underlined.)
1. Boots, shoes, slippers, and sandals are all made of leather.
2. There were geese in the grass, on the rocks, and on the water of the lake.
3. Did you ever see such sparkling white snow?
4. Sarah uses this thick, warm quilt in the wintertime.
5. We pumped water from an old hand pump.

B. (Corrections are marked.)
1. Many, other, little boats were on the lake.
2. Bananas, oranges, and mangoes, are tropical fruit.
3. We bought a large, intelligent, German, shepherd dog.
4. Jesus entered the small, fishing boat, sat down, and began to teach.

Written Exercises

A. 1. clover, up,
  2. cabbage, squash, carrots,
  3. dug, raked, trimmed,
  4. books, tablets, pencils,
  5. observed, listened,
  6. (correct)
  7. (correct)
  8. store, sidewalk,
  9. Abraham, Isaac,
 10. Peter, James,
 11. poor,
 12. Galilee, Samaria, Judea,
 13. small, angry,
 14. stormy, calm,

B. (Individual sentences.)

Review Exercises

Diagram the skeletons of the following sentences. Also diagram the direct objects, indirect objects, and predicate nominatives. [38–42]

1. Was it they in that car?
2. My brother told me in the morning.
3. Gerald gave John the book, and John passed it on to Nathan.
4. Here is an interesting story.

---

82. Writing a Story: First Draft

In order to write a good story, you must plan your story well. Use an orderly method, and proceed step by step from start to finish. The following points will help you.

Step 1: *Get the conflict clear in your mind.* What is the problem that must be solved? You will find it helpful to write a sentence or two briefly stating what the conflict will be.

Example:
> A boy hears about different accidents and wonders how people can make such foolish mistakes. Then he makes a foolish mistake himself and learns a lesson from it.

Step 2: *Decide who will be the main character.* What kind of person is he or she? What kind of people are the other characters in the story?

Example:
Main character: Daniel, who seems quite sure of himself
Other characters: Rhonda, Daniel's sister
Allen, a neighbor
Daniel's Christian father

Step 3: *Write a good beginning for the story.* You will need to introduce the main character and show the setting right at the beginning. (This is the *who, when,* and *where.*) You will also need to introduce the

---

Review Exercises

1. it | Was \ they
2. brother | told | me
3. Gerald | gave | book _and_ John | passed | it \ John
4. story | is

Lesson 82

Purpose: To teach the steps in writing the first draft of a story.

Oral Review:
1. What is dialogue? (written conversation in a story)
2. Where should you put quotation marks in dialogue? (only around direct quotations; only at the beginning and end of an entire quotation, not around every quoted sentence)
3. In dialogue, when should you begin a new paragraph? (when a different person begins to speak and when a new topic is introduced)
4. How can you have good sentence variety in dialogue? (Have some sentences with direct quotations first, some with direct quotations last, and some with divided quotations. Do not always use *said* in the explanatory words. Use some longer quotations and some shorter ones.)

Lesson Introduction: Ask students how many of them like to hear or read a good story. How many like to tell a story? How many like to *write* a story? But someone must write a story before we can read it!

Actually, writing a story yourself is even more interesting than studying how to write stories. Oh, no, it is not easier. It is much harder! But if you will put your best into writing a good story yourself, you will without question find this work more interesting than the last two lessons on how to write stories.

Lesson Outline:
The steps for writing the first draft of a story are as follows:
1. ***Get the conflict clear in your mind.***
   a. Decide what problem will need to be solved.
   b. It is helpful to write a sentence or two, briefly stating what the conflict will be.

conflict and give a hint of your purpose. (This is the *what* and *why*.) Notice how these things are done in the story beginning below.

> "Good-bye!" Daniel called to his friends, Evan and Mark, as he and his sister got off the school van.
>
> "Good-bye!" they returned as the van started on its way again.
>
> "Did you hear about Greg's accident?" Daniel asked Rhonda as they walked in the lane together.
>
> "Yes, I did," Rhonda answered. "It's too bad. It sounds as though he'll have to miss several weeks of school with his broken arm and leg. I feel sorry for him."
>
> "I don't really," Daniel said. "That was a dumb thing to do. I would have known better than to jump off that limb. Why, it must be ten feet off the ground, and there are rocks under the tree. He just got what he asked for."

Step 4: *Write the middle part of the story.* Show how the happenings build up and lead to the "highest point," or climax.

> That evening Father and Daniel were working in the shop when Allen, a neighbor, stopped in for a few minutes. "Did you hear about Leroy Fannin's accident?" he asked. "He was out last night on his bicycle. It got dark before he arrived home, and the lights on his bicycle weren't working. A car hit him from behind, and now Leroy is in the hospital with serious head injuries," Allen informed them.
>
> "Why are some people so careless?" Daniel asked Father when Allen had left. "Anyone should know better than to be out on the road after dark without lights."
>
> "We don't always know why, Daniel," Father answered. "It certainly is unwise to be out on the road on a bicycle after dark without lights. But maybe Leroy didn't realize that his lights weren't working until it got dark. He probably did need to get home."
>
> Daniel shrugged. "Maybe," he said, but he did not sound convinced.
>
> Several days later Daniel's family was butchering, and Daniel was using the meat grinder. "Something seems to be wrong here," he thought. "It must be plugged up." Without thinking, Daniel put his hand down into the grinder to try to unplug it.

2. ***Decide who will be the main character.*** Decide what kind of person he is and what kind of people the other characters are in the story.

3. ***Write a good beginning for the story.*** (As you write the first draft of the story, use only every other line so that it will be easy to mark changes.)

    a. Show the main character and the setting right at the beginning—the *who, when,* and *where.*

    b. Introduce the conflict, and give a hint of your purpose—the *what* and *why.*

4. ***Write the middle part of the story.*** Show how the happenings build up and lead to the climax.

5. ***Write a good ending for the story.*** Bring the story to a close quickly after the climax is reached.

6. ***Write an interesting title for the story.***

    a. A title should be short, rarely over five words.

    b. A title should be interesting and catchy.

    c. A title must not tell too much or give away the outcome of the story.

"Oh-h-h! Ou-ouch!" Daniel cried. He pulled his hand quickly out of the grinder, but it was too late. Blood flowed from deep gashes in two of his fingers and from several cuts in his other fingers.

Father acted quickly, getting cold, wet cloths to wrap around Daniel's hand. Soon they were on their way to the hospital. A sober Daniel entered the emergency room, where a doctor stitched his mangled fingers.

Step 5: *Write a good ending for the story.* Bring the story to a close quickly after the climax is reached. Be sure to *show* rather than *tell* the lesson of the story.

"The Lord may be using this to teach you a lesson," Father said kindly. "I have heard you several times lately exclaiming about other people's foolish mistakes and declaring that you would never do such a thing. Let's be careful not to judge others when they make mistakes. And let's realize that God can use even our mistakes for a good purpose if we have right attitudes about them."

Daniel nodded. "This is a painful lesson," he said, "and I'm sure my fingers will be a reminder for a long time not to judge others unkindly for the mistakes they make."

Step 6: *Write an interesting title for the story.* It is usually better to decide on a title after the story is written, although a good idea for a title may come to you sooner. A title should be short, rarely over five words. It should be interesting and catchy so that the reader will want to find out what the story is about. But a title should not tell too much, and it must never give away the outcome of the story.

Good: Just Foolish?
Poor: Daniel Makes a Foolish Mistake (tells too much)

Good: The Big Smoke
Poor: When the House Was Full of Smoke (too long; tells too much)

Good: Should I Tell?
Poor: Telling Was the Right Thing (gives away the outcome)

In Lessons 56 and 57, you learned that reports are usually written in two drafts. The same is true of stories. The first draft is the rough, unpolished form, and the second draft is the story in its final form.

When you write the first draft of a story, leave every other line blank so that you can mark changes later. Write in complete sentences, but do not lose too much time in trying to make everything exactly right. Concentrate rather on getting the basic story on paper. You can make improvements later as you revise your story and write the second draft.

- To write a story, use the following steps.
  1. Get the conflict clear in your mind.
  2. Decide who will be the main character.
  3. Write a good beginning for the story.
  4. Write the middle part of the story.
  5. Write a good ending for the story.
  6. Write an interesting title for the story.

Class Practice

Give the answers.

1. What is meant by conflict in a story? What is a good way of getting the conflict clear in your mind?
2. What five questions must you answer when you write a story?
3. What term refers to the "highest point" in a story?
4. What two things must you remember about the ending of a story?
5. Describe a good story title. What must a title *not* do?

Written Exercises

Use your story notes from Lesson 75 to write the first draft of a story. Follow the steps taught in this lesson.

Review Exercises

Write *true* or *false* for each sentence.

1. A paragraph has unity when all the sentences in the paragraph tell about the topic given in the topic sentence.
2. If a topic sentence is good, few details are needed to develop it.
3. The details should show that the topic sentence is true.
4. Giving convincing details, using examples and illustrations, and using comparison or contrast are some good ways to develop paragraphs.

Lesson 82 Answers
Class Practice

1. a problem that must be solved; by writing a sentence or two briefly stating what the conflict will be.
2. who, when, where, what, why
3. climax
4. The story should end quickly after the climax is reached. The story should *show* rather than *tell* the lesson that it teaches.
5. It should be interesting, catchy, and short (rarely over five words). It must not tell too much or give away the outcome of the story.

Written Exercises

(Individual work. You need not take grades on this lesson, since pupils are simply writing the first draft of their stories.)

Review Exercises

1. true
2. false
3. true
4. true

5. A paragraph that is developed by contrast shows differences between two persons, places, things, or ideas.
6. When using comparison or contrast, you must list all the points about one thing before you mention any points about the second thing.

5. true
6. false

---

83. Commas That Set Off Words

Commas help us when we read. They also help us to write clearly. In this lesson you will study several more ways that commas are used in sentences.

1. *Use commas to set off an appositive.* An appositive is a noun coming after another noun or a pronoun to explain it more fully. Sometimes the appositive includes modifiers. The appositives in these sentences are underlined.

> Our first president, <u>George Washington,</u> was from Virginia.
> The opossum, <u>a marsupial,</u> has a pouch in which to carry her young.
> The coyote, <u>an expert at surviving and adapting,</u> continues to spread its range into new territories.

2. *Use commas to set off a noun of direct address.* A noun of direct address names the person to whom one is speaking. Sometimes a noun of direct address includes modifiers.

> I want you to know, <u>Vernon,</u> that the job is still available.
> Your answer, <u>my friend,</u> has greatly encouraged me.

When a noun of direct address comes at the beginning or end of a sentence, only one comma is needed.

> Lynn, did you see that it is snowing?
> It probably won't snow very much, Mark.

3. *Use commas to set off a parenthetical element.* Parenthetical elements are words that interrupt the main thought of a sentence. You can easily pick out a parenthetical element. It stands out as an inserted thought, and it is not needed to make the sentence complete.

Lesson 83

Purpose: (1) To identify appositives, nouns of direct address, and parenthetical elements. (2) To teach that they are set off by commas.

Oral Review:
1. Give the rules for using commas that you have studied.
   (a. Use commas to set off direct quotations.
   b. Use commas to separate words or phrases in a series.
   c. Use commas to separate two or more descriptive adjectives that modify the same noun.)
2. What rules are helpful in knowing where to place commas after adjectives?
   (a. Place commas after descriptive adjectives but not after limiting adjectives.
   b. Do not place a comma after the last adjective, just before a noun.

   c. Place a comma between two descriptive adjectives only if it sounds right to say *and* between them and if there is a pause between them in reading.)
3. What is a limiting adjective? (one that tells *which, whose,* or *how many*)
4. Nominative case pronouns can be used as what two sentence parts? (subject, predicate nominative)
5. Objective case pronouns can be used as what sentence parts? (direct object, indirect object, object of a preposition)

Lesson Introduction: Write the following sentence with no punctuation on the chalkboard. Ask the students how many people will paint the barn.

> Dennis you and I will paint the barn

The sentence can have two meanings, depending on how it is punctuated.

> Dennis, you and I will paint the barn.
> Dennis, you, and I will paint the barn.

You have all learned, <u>I suppose,</u> that the building has been sold.

We shall try, <u>of course,</u> to find a new meeting place soon.

It is much easier, <u>you know,</u> to tear down than to build up.

This whole matter, <u>I am sure,</u> can easily be explained.

Appositives, nouns of direct address, and parenthetical elements are alike in that they are not needed for a sentence to make sense. These words and phrases are not needed to *prevent* confusion, but they can easily *cause* confusion if they are not set off with commas. The following sentences show that commas can indeed make a great difference.

Please help my friend because the need is great.
> *Friend* is a direct object.

Please help, my friend, because the need is great.
> *Friend* is a noun of direct address.

- Use commas to set off appositives, nouns of direct address, and parenthetical elements from the rest of a sentence.

Class Practice

A. Identify each item within commas as an *appositive,* a *noun of direct address,* or a *parenthetical element.*
1. The second man, Noah Weaver, has always been a good worker.
2. I shall not forget, Shirley, how kind you have been.
3. He will come, I expect, sometime after dark.
4. Other boys and girls, you must recognize, are much less fortunate.
5. I want to visit your farm, Uncle Reynold, as soon as I have time.
6. My kitten, a gift from our neighbor, has black-and-white fur.

B. Tell whether each sentence has an *appositive,* a *noun of direct address,* or *neither.*
1. Aunt Susan, our neighbor will be glad to help.
2. Aunt Susan, our neighbor, will be glad to help.
3. Please call Grandmother when you get home.
4. Please call, Grandmother, when you get home.

Lesson 83 Answers
Class Practice
A. 1. appositive
   2. noun of direct address
   3. parenthetical element
   4. parenthetical element
   5. noun of direct address
   6. appositive

B. 1. noun of direct address
   2. appositive
   3. neither (*Grandmother* is a direct object.)
   4. noun of direct address

This lesson has several more rules on using commas to make writing clear.

Lesson Outline:

1. Use commas to set off an appositive. An appositive is a noun coming after another noun or pronoun to explain it. Sometimes the appositive includes modifiers.

When an appositive comes in the middle of a sentence, commas must be placed before and after it. When it comes at the end of a sentence, only one comma is needed.

2. Use commas to set off a noun of direct address. A noun of direct address names the person to whom one is speaking. Sometimes a noun of direct address includes modifiers.

When a noun of direct address comes in the middle of a sentence, commas must be placed before and after it. When it comes at the beginning or end of a sentence, only one comma is needed.

3. Use commas to set off a parenthetical element. Parenthetical elements are words that interrupt the main thought of a sentence. They are called parenthetical elements because they could be enclosed in parentheses; the sentence would be complete without them.

★ **EXTRA PRACTICE**
Worksheet 48 *(Using Commas in Sentences)*

C. Read these sentences, saying *comma* at each place where a comma is needed.
1. During the summer of course the stream always dries up.
2. In six months my friend you will see a remarkable change.
3. Emil a native of Poland speaks several Slavic languages.
4. The large tree an old Norway maple completely blocked the front window.
5. Wait here Paul until the rain stops.
6. Flies and mosquitoes annoying pests to us are serious threats in many countries.

Written Exercises

A. Copy each word that should have a comma after it, and add the missing comma.
1. Lillian who invented pretzels?
2. They were given as treats to Italian children several hundred years ago Marlin.
3. In fact they were first called *pretiola,* which means "little rewards."
4. Soon of course the name changed to *pretzel.*
5. Howard my cousin works in a pretzel bakery.
6. Soft pretzels in fact were invented before hard ones.
7. Who invented hard pretzels Doreen?
8. The baker's helper a young German boy fell asleep while watching some pretzels bake.
9. The baker as you can guess was not very happy about that.
10. He was ready to throw out all those pretzels Maria.
11. Then he saw his helpers eating the pretzels even though they were hard as if they liked them.
12. The baker it is said passed them out to people in the street.
13. Hard pretzels surprisingly enough were well liked; and soon customers were asking for them.
14. The first commercial pretzel baker in America Julius Sturgis made and sold them in Lititz, Pennsylvania, in 1861.

B. Write whether each sentence has an *appositive,* a *noun of direct address,* or *neither.*
1. We tried to call, Father, but the line was busy each time.
2. We tried to call Father, but the line was busy each time.
3. Brother Charles, my teacher, would like to meet you.
4. Brother Charles, my teacher would like to meet you.

C. 1. During the summer (comma) of course (comma) the stream always dries up.
2. In six months (comma) my friend (comma) you will see a remarkable change.
3. Emil (comma) a native of Poland (comma) speaks several Slavic languages.
4. The large tree (comma) an old Norway maple (comma) completely blocked the front window.
5. Wait here (comma) Paul (comma) until the rain stops.
6. Flies and mosquitoes (comma) annoying pests to us (comma) are serious threats in many countries.

Written Exercises

A. 1. Lillian,
    2. ago,
    3. fact,
    4. Soon, course,
    5. Howard, *or* Howard, cousin,
    6. pretzels, fact,
    7. pretzels,
    8. helper, boy,
    9. baker, guess,
    10. pretzels,
    11. pretzels, hard,
    12. baker, said,
    13. pretzels, enough,
    14. America, Sturgis,

B. 1. noun of direct address
   2. neither (*Father* is a direct object.)
   3. appositive
   4. noun of direct address

C. Write sentences of your own as described below. Use commas correctly.

1. A sentence using *Brother Henry* as an appositive.
2. A sentence using *it is clear* as a parenthetical element.
3. A sentence using *neighbor* as a noun of direct address.
4. A sentence using *I'm sure* as a parenthetical element.

Review Exercises

Write the correct words. [62, 64]

1. The woman invited Elisha and (he, him).
2. (She, Her) and her husband built (he, him) a room.
3. Elisha and (he, him) went to visit the prophets at Gilgal.
4. Elisha's servant prepared food for the prophets and (they, them).
5. Poisonous gourds were found in the food; Elisha and (they, them) might die!
6. "Throw in some meal," Elisha said to (they, them).
7. (We, Us) prophets of Gilgal want you to go with (we, us) to Jordan.
8. Elisha, please go with (we, us) your servants to build a house for (we, us) prophets.

C. (Individual sentences.)

Review Exercises

1. him
2. She, him
3. he
4. them
5. they
6. them
7. We, us
8. us, us

---

84. More Practice With Commas

When we are speaking, the tone of our voice helps to explain what we mean. But in writing we cannot use our voice to make the meaning clear. We use punctuation marks for this purpose. A comma represents a slight pause and a change in voice pitch. In this lesson you will study some more rules for using commas.

1. *Use a comma before the conjunction in a compound sentence.*

He was in a hurry, but he did the work well.

Remember, a compound sentence has a skeleton on each side of the conjunction. A simple sentence may have a compound subject or a compound predicate, but it has only one skeleton. Do not place a comma between a subject and a verb. Do not place a comma before a conjunction if it joins only two subjects or two verbs.

Lesson 84

Purpose: (1) To review rules for using commas with a conjunction in compound sentences, and in letters. (2) To teach rules for using commas in items before the subject.

Oral Review:

1. Give the rules for using commas that you have studied so far.
   (a. Use commas to set off direct quotations.
   b. Use commas to separate words or phrases in a series.
   c. Use commas to separate two or more descriptive adjectives that modify the same noun, if it sounds right to say *and* between them.
   d. Use commas to set off appositives, nouns of direct address, and parenthetical elements.)
2. What is an appositive? (a noun that is used directly after another noun or pronoun to clarify it)
3. What is a noun of direct address? (a noun that names the person to whom one is speaking)
4. What is a parenthetical element? (a word or phrase that interrupts the main thought of a sentence)
5. Give the verbs that can be used as linking verbs.
   (**Forms of *be*:**
   am, is, are, was, were, be, been, being
   Verbs of sense:
   taste, feel, smell, sound, look, appear
   Other linking verbs:
   grow, seem, stay, become, remain)

Lesson Introduction: Imagine what it would be like if there were no road signs. Without warning signs about sharp curves, more cars would run off the road. With no stop signs, there would be more accidents at intersections. Drivers need road signs to tell them when to slow down or stop.

Incorrect:

The boys, found the den of a bear.
The bear dug it out, and hibernated.
Jacob, and Tim looked, and listened.

Correct:

The boys found the den of a bear.
The bear dug it out and hibernated.
Jacob and Tim looked and listened.

2. *Use commas correctly in letters and addresses.* In the heading of a letter, use a comma to separate the route number from the box number, the city from the state, and the day from the year. Use a comma after the greeting and after the closing. Do not place a comma between a house number and a street name or between a state name and a Zip Code.

Incorrect:

315, State Street
Zanesville OH, 43701

Correct:

315 State Street
Zanesville, OH 43701

Remember that on an envelope, the postal service wants the receiver's address printed with all capital letters and with no punctuation.

315 STATE STREET
ZANESVILLE OH 43701

3. *Use a comma after* yes *or* no *and after a mild interjection like* oh *or* well *when these words come at the beginning of a sentence.* Remember that interjections are words that show strong feeling and are not related to the rest of the sentence.

No, we have never heard such an explanation before.
Well, I suppose it could be possible.

Remember that a strong interjection is followed by an exclamation point and that the following words begin a new sentence.

Well! How could I have forgotten to add the salt?
Indeed! We never said such a thing!

Punctuation marks are like road signs. Commas tell the reader when to slow down, and periods tell him when to stop. If we use these "road signs," people can read our writing without getting confused. In this lesson we will study several more rules for using commas.

Lesson Outline:

1. Use a comma before the conjunction in a compound sentence. A compound sentence has a skeleton on each side of the conjunction. A simple sentence may have a compound subject or a compound predicate, but it has only one skeleton. Do not place a comma between a subject and a verb. Do not place a comma before a conjunction if it joins only two subjects or two verbs.

2. Use commas correctly in letters and addresses.

a. In the heading of a letter, use a comma to separate the route number from the box number, the city from the state, and the day from the year.

b. Use a comma after the greeting and after the closing.

c. Do not place a comma between a house number and a street name or between a state name and a Zip Code.

3. Use a comma after yes *or* no **and after a mild interjection like** oh *or* well **when these words come at the beginning of a sentence.**

4. *When an adverb phrase comes before the subject of a sentence, it is usually followed by a comma.*

> In the evening, the snow began falling fast.
> During the snowstorm, the villagers heard the wolves howling.

- A comma is used before the conjunction in a compound sentence.

- Commas are used in letters and addresses.

- A comma is used after *yes* or *no* and after a mild interjection like *oh* or *well* when these words come at the beginning of a sentence.

- When an adverb phrase comes before the subject of a sentence, it is usually followed by a comma.

Class Practice

Read these sentences and letter parts, saying *comma* at each place where a comma is needed.
1. Peas and carrots taste good and they are nutritious as well.
2. Yes I heard it too.
3. 234 Cartwright Road
   Sweet Valley PA 18656
   September 13 20—
4. Dear Marvin
5. Sincerely
   Richard
6. Late in the afternoon the men returned with their families.
7. Across the river we could see the deer.
8. Oh it was a lovely scene!

Written Exercises

A. Copy these letter parts, and add the missing commas.
1. 115 Vista Lane
   Collingdale PA 19023
   Sept. 4 20—

4. *When an adverb phrase comes before the subject of a sentence, it is usually followed by a comma.*

> Before noon, the sun was shining.

Note: The comma may be omitted if a short, simple introductory phrase is read without a pause—especially if the meaning is quite clear.

> At last they arrived.
> By then he had forgotten.

★ EXTRA PRACTICE
Worksheet 49 *(More Practice With Commas)*

Lesson 84 Answers
Class Practice
1. Peas and carrots taste good (comma) and they are nutritious as well.
2. Yes (comma) I heard it too.
3. 234 Cartwright Road
   Sweet Valley (comma) PA 18656
   September 13 (comma) 20—
4. Dear Marvin (comma)
5. Sincerely (comma)
   Richard
6. Late in the afternoon (comma) the men returned with their families.
7. Across the river (comma) we could see the deer.
8. Oh (comma) it was a lovely scene!

Written Exercises
A. (Commas are underlined.)
1. 115 Vista Lane
   Collingdale, PA 19023
   Sept. 4, 20—

2. Route 4 Box 250
   Fayette UT 84630
   June 3 20—

3. Dear Joan

4. Your friend
   Judith

B. Copy each word that should have a comma after it, and add the missing comma.
   1. Righteousness exalteth a nation but sin is a reproach to any people.
   2. For some animals' protection God has given them the ability to hibernate.
   3. Oh the boys think they heard a bear snoring out in the woods.
   4. Well why would a bear snore while it is hibernating?
   5. During hibernation bears are in a very deep sleep.
   6. Yes the warm weather could have roused it enough to snore.
   7. Deep inside the den they saw a whimpering cub.
   8. In April the mother bear left the den.

C. Write two compound sentences of your own, using commas correctly.

Review Exercises

A. Write whether the underlined verbs are *linking* verbs or *action* verbs. [44]
   1. A dog <u>is</u> more than a good pet.
   2. Some dogs <u>are trained</u> to find certain things.
   3. They <u>smell</u> nests of termites in old buildings.
   4. Some dogs <u>sniff</u> out illegal drugs that people try to smuggle into the United States.
   5. If a suitcase <u>smells</u> suspicious, the traveler must stop.
   6. The collie <u>has been used</u> for many years to herd sheep.
   7. Your collie <u>looks</u> handsome since you brushed his coat.
   8. This German shepherd and the night watchman <u>look</u> for trouble in the museum at night.

2. Route 4, Box 250
   Fayette, UT 84630
   June 3, 20—

3. Dear Joan,

4. Your friend,
   Judith

B. 1. nation,
   2. protection,
   3. Oh,
   4. Well,
   5. hibernation,
   6. Yes,
   7. den,
   8. April,

C. (Individual sentences.)

Review Exercises

A. 1. linking
   2. action
   3. action
   4. action
   5. linking
   6. action
   7. linking
   8. action

B. Copy each word that should be followed by a comma, and add the missing comma. [81, 83]
1. That dog a black Labrador retriever picks up things his handicapped owner has dropped.
2. Dogs work in homes in museums in airports in meadows in the woods on city streets and in many other places.
3. The dachshund in fact was used long ago in Germany to help chase badgers out of their burrows.
4. The Saint Bernard is a large friendly brown dog that helps to rescue lost people in the Alps.
5. Her pet likes to eat crispy brown graham crackers.

B. 1. dog, retriever,
2. homes, museums, airports, meadows, woods, streets,
3. dachshund, fact,
4. large, friendly,
5. crispy,

---

85. Writing a Story: Second Draft

You should usually not try to write the first and second drafts of a story all at one time. As with a report, it is better to lay aside the first draft at least until the next day and then come back to it. In this way you will have a fresh view of your work, and you will be better able to make improvements.

In Lesson 82 you studied the six steps for writing the first draft of a story. They are shown here.

Step 1: *Get the conflict clear in your mind.*
Step 2: *Decide who will be the main character.*
Step 3: *Write a good beginning for the story.*
Step 4: *Write the middle part of the story.*
Step 5: *Write a good ending for the story.*
Step 6: *Write an interesting title for the story.*

To write the second draft of your story, follow steps 7 and 8.

Step 7: *Proofread and improve the first draft of the story.* Use the following questions in checking the first draft of your story.

a. *Are the important facts introduced promptly?*

Poor: (setting and main character not clear)
"Good-bye!" called Ellen and Mark as they waved to their friends.

Lesson 85

Purpose: To teach the steps in writing the second draft of a story.

Oral Review:
1. What are the steps in writing the first draft of a story? (Get the conflict clear in your mind. Decide who will be the main character. Write a good beginning, middle part, and ending for the story. Write an interesting title for the story.)
2. What are some ways to make dialogue sound natural? (Use contractions and incomplete sentences. Have characters speak according to their age level. Have variety in the length of quotations.)
3. List several ways of developing a paragraph. (by using details, by using examples and illustrations, by using comparison or contrast)

4. What kind of development is used when a paragraph shows similarities between two persons, places, things, or ideas? (comparison)
5. What kind of development is used when a paragraph shows differences between two persons, places, things, or ideas? (contrast)

Lesson Introduction: Remind pupils of the similarity between revising a report and steering a car (Lesson 57). It takes careful steering to bring any vehicle to its destination; but a large, heavy truck is harder to steer than a car. In the same way, it usually takes more effort to revise a story than a report because a story carries a heavier "load" of imaginative thinking. But if we do our best, we can enjoy the satisfaction of producing an interesting, well-written story.

"Good-bye!" replied Rhonda and Daniel as they started walking in the lane.

"Did you hear about Greg's accident?" Rhonda asked Daniel.

Good:

"Good-bye!" Daniel called to his friends, Evan and Mark, as he and his sister got out of the school van.

"Good-bye!" they returned as the van started on its way again.

"Did you hear about Greg's accident?" Daniel asked Rhonda as they walked in the lane together.

b. *Is the conflict clear? Do events build up to a climax in a natural, logical way?*

Poor: (unrelated problem brought in)

That evening Father and Daniel were working together in the shop. Daniel was trying to put a roof on his birdhouse, but things were not going well for him. "Why can't I make these nails go in straight?" he asked.

Father came over for a look. "Your wood has quite a few knots," he observed. "It helps if you put a bit of soap on the tip of the nail. Then make sure you hit the nail squarely each time as you hammer it in."

Later Allen, a neighbor, stopped in for a few minutes. "Did you hear about Leroy Fannin's accident?" he asked. "He was out last night on his bicycle...."

Good:

That evening Father and Daniel were working in the shop when Allen, a neighbor, stopped in for a few minutes. "Did you hear about Leroy Fannin's accident?" he asked. "He was out last night on his bicycle. It got dark before he arrived home, and the lights on his bicycle weren't working. A car hit him from behind, and now Leroy is in the hospital with serious head injuries," Allen informed them.

"Why are some people so careless?" Daniel asked Father when Allen had left. "Anyone should know better than to be out on the road after dark without lights."

Lesson Outline:

(*Teacher:* Points 1–6 are a review of Lesson 82.)

1. *Get the conflict clear in your mind.*

2. *Decide who will be the main character.*

3. *Write a good beginning for the story.*

4. *Write the middle part of the story.*

5. *Write a good ending for the story.*

6. *Write an interesting title for the story.*

7. *Proofread and improve the first draft of the story.* Use the following questions.

   a. Are the important facts introduced promptly?

   b. Is the conflict clear? Do events build up to a climax in a natural, logical way?

   c. Is the dialogue natural?

   d. Does the story end promptly after the climax? Does the ending show the purpose of the story, rather than telling it?

   e. Did you use correct grammar, punctuation, and spelling?

Mark your corrections and improvements in the blank lines of the first draft. Change and reword sentences until you are satisfied that the story is as good as you can possibly make it.

8. *Write the story in its final form.*

   a. Include the improvements you marked.

   b. Do not leave blank lines.

   c. Use neat penmanship, and leave good margins.

   d. Keep the left margin straight and the right margin as straight as possible.

c. *Is the dialogue natural?*

Poor: (all complete sentences and no contractions)

"We do not always know why such things happen, Daniel," Father answered. "It certainly is unwise to be out on the road on a bicycle after dark without lights. But maybe Leroy did not realize that his lights were not working until it got dark. He probably did need to get home."

Daniel shrugged. "Maybe that is how it was," he said, but he did not sound convinced.

Good:

"We don't always know why, Daniel," Father answered. "It certainly is unwise to be out on the road on a bicycle after dark without lights. But maybe Leroy didn't realize that his lights weren't working until it got dark. He probably did need to get home."

Daniel shrugged. "Maybe," he said, but he did not sound convinced.

d. *Does the story end promptly after the climax? Does the ending show the purpose of the story, rather than telling it?*

Poor: (lesson told rather than shown)

The Lord used this experience to teach Daniel a lesson. He learned not to be critical of others when they make mistakes. He also learned that God can use even a mistake for a good purpose. It was a painful lesson; but for a long time afterward, Daniel's fingers were a good reminder that he must not judge others unkindly.

Good:

"The Lord may be using this to teach you a lesson," Father said kindly. "I have heard you several times lately exclaiming about other people's foolish mistakes, and declaring that you would never do such a thing. Let's be careful not to judge others when they make mistakes. And let's realize that God can use even our mistakes for a good purpose if we have right attitudes about them."

Daniel nodded. "This is a painful lesson," he said, "and I'm sure my fingers will be a reminder for a long time not to judge others unkindly for the mistakes they make."

e. *Did you use correct grammar, punctuation, and spelling?*

"Did you hear about Greg's accident," Daniel asked Rhonda

as they walk~~ed~~ in the lane together?

Soon they were on ~~there~~ *their* way to the hospital. A sober

Daniel entered the emer~~g~~jency room, where a doctor st~~i~~ched

his mangled fingers.

Mark your corrections and improvements in the blank lines you left between the lines of your story. Change and reword sentences until you are satisfied that the story is as good as you can possibly make it.

Step 8: *Write the story in its final form.* Include the improvements that you marked. Do not leave blank lines in this second draft. Use neat penmanship, and leave good margins. Keep the left margin straight and the right margin as straight as possible.

- To write a story, use the following steps.
  1. Get the conflict clear in your mind.
  2. Decide who will be the main character.
  3. Write a good beginning for the story.
  4. Write the middle part of the story.
  5. Write a good ending for the story.
  6. Write an interesting title for the story.
  7. Proofread and improve the story.
  8. Write the story in its final form.

Class Practice

Do the following exercises with the paragraphs.
1. Tell how to improve this story opening.

  "I don't know what is the matter with Mary Ann," Ruth thought. "She just ignores me. And today wasn't the first time!"

Lesson 85 Answers
Class Practice

(*Teacher:* You may wish to keep the class period fairly short so that the pupils have plenty of time to work on their stories. You could discuss most of the following items briefly and then read the improvements from the answer key.)

1. (Not enough information is given about the setting. The following paragraph should come first.)

  Ruth quietly looked out the van window. The other children were all chattering happily about their Sunday school lessons or about little tidbits of information that their friends had shared. But not Ruth.

Ruth saw Father watching her in the rearview mirror, and she quickly sat up straight. Father, she well knew, had little time for long faces and dismal hearts. Sooner or later he would find out what was wrong!

2. Find one error in grammar, two errors in punctuation, and four errors in spelling.

The next day Ruth came huffishly into the kitchen. "Mother, when I went past Mary Anns house, I seen her picking cherries and I called to her, but she totaly ignored me!" In fact, her skirt gave a little flounce as if she had purposely turned the other way. I can't believe anyone could be so unfreindly!"

"Maybe she didn't hear you," Mother consoled with a smile. "Give her the benifit of the doubt. Or maybe it was even someone else."

"I know it was Mary Ann, because I recogized her old school dress," Ruth said, "even though I couldn't see her very well in the branches."

3. Tell how to improve this dialogue.

Several days later Mother came into the kitchen with a bag of groceries. "Ruth," she said, "Mary Ann was still up in that cherry tree, and she did not wave at me either when I waved. At first I did not know what to think of that. But then I realized it was only a dress hanging in the tree, probably to scare the birds." Mother laughed heartily, and Ruth also joined in.

"Ruth," Mother said after a while, "I think probably most of your suspicions about Mary Ann are empty. They are probably about as weightless as that dress without any body in it!"

4. Tell how to improve this story ending.

"Oh, Mother," said Ruth after prayer meeting, "I told Mary Ann how we called and waved to her dress in the cherry tree, and how we couldn't understand why she didn't respond. We both had to laugh. She seemed like herself tonight. In fact, she had thought I was ignoring her, and she couldn't figure out why!"

Ruth was happy as she sat in the van. It always makes us happy when right attitudes are restored. We need to remember that wrong attitudes are often based on empty imaginations.

2. (Corrections are marked.)

The next day Ruth came huffishly into the kitchen. "Mother, when I went past Mary Ann's house, I saw her picking cherries and I called to her, but she totally ignored me!" In fact, her skirt gave a little flounce as if she had purposely turned the other way. I can't believe anyone could be so unfriendly!"

"Maybe she didn't hear you," Mother consoled with a smile. "Give her the benefit of the doubt. Or maybe it was even someone else."

"I know it was Mary Ann, because I recognized her old school dress," Ruth said, "even though I couldn't see her very well in the branches."

3. (Changes are marked.)

Several days later Mother came into the kitchen with a bag of groceries. "Ruth," she said, "Mary Ann was still up in that cherry tree, and she didn't wave at me either when I waved. At first I didn't know what to think of that. (Or: Think of that!) But then I realized it was only a dress hanging in the tree, probably to scare the birds." Mother laughed heartily, and Ruth also joined in.

"Ruth," Mother said after a while, "I think probably most of your suspicions about Mary Ann are empty. ~~They are probably~~ About as weightless as that dress without anybody in it!"

4. (Ending tells the lesson rather than showing it. The following paragraph is better.)

Ruth sat happily in her corner of the van. It felt so good to have right attitudes restored between herself and Mary Ann. She did not want to ever begin imagining things again!

Written Exercises

A. Proofread the first draft of the story that you began writing in Lesson 82. Mark the changes that should be made. Keep your corrected first draft for your teacher to see.

B. Write the second draft of your story, making the changes you marked.

---

86. Apostrophes

The apostrophe (') has two main uses. It is used in possessive forms and in contractions.

Possessive Forms

You have already learned much about possessive forms. Remember that a possessive noun or pronoun tells *whose*. A possessive form is used as an adjective when it comes before a noun.

1. The possessive case of most singular nouns is formed by adding *'s*. This includes most singular nouns that end with *s*.

Harold's book	the waitress's pencil
the cat's paws	Charles's brother
a day's wages	the octopus's arms

   For a singular noun ending with a *zus* sound, the possessive form would be awkward to pronounce if *'s* were added. Therefore, the possessive form is made by adding only an apostrophe.

Moses' sister	Jesus' words

2. If a plural noun ends with *-s,* the possessive case is formed by adding only an apostrophe. If a plural noun does not end with *-s,* *'s* is added.

   my two sisters' friends
   the four farmers' animals
   the children's pets
   our geese's feathers
   the mice's nest

Written Exercises

A. (Individual work. It is suggested that you look at each pupil's corrected first draft and make helpful suggestions before he writes the second draft.)

B. (Individual work. Check pupils' stories specifically for the points mentioned in Step 7: *Proofread and improve the story.* Those points are listed in Lesson Outline.)

Lesson 86

Purpose: To teach the use of apostrophes.

Oral Review:

1. List as many rules for using commas as you can.
   (a. Use commas to set off direct quotations.
   b. Use commas to separate words or phrases in a series.
   c. Use commas to separate two or more descriptive adjectives that modify the same noun, if it sounds right to say *and* between them.
   d. Use commas to set off appositives, nouns of direct address, and parenthetical elements.
   e. Use a comma before the conjunction in a compound sentence.
   f. Use commas correctly in letters and addresses.
   g. Use a comma after *yes* or *no* and after a mild interjection like *oh* or *well* when these words come at the beginning of a sentence.
   h. When an adverb phrase comes before the subject of a sentence, it is usually followed by a comma.)
2. List some common interjections. (oh, well, indeed)
3. Name some indefinite pronouns that are always singular. (each, either, neither, one, another, anybody, anyone, everybody, everyone, somebody, someone, nobody, no one)
4. Name some indefinite pronouns that are always plural. (both, few, several, many)
5. Name some indefinite pronouns that may be singular or plural. (some, any, none, all, most)

Lesson Introduction: Do apostrophes make a difference? Write the following sentence on the chalkboard, and have a student read it. All the punctuation marks are missing.

Well rest a little before cleaning the boys room

Study the possessive forms on this chart.

Singular	Singular Possessive	Plural	Plural Possessive
woman	woman's	women	women's
baby	baby's	babies	babies'
waitress	waitress's	waitresses	waitresses'
child	child's	children	children's

3. Apostrophes are not used to make the plural forms of nouns.

> **Incorrect:**
>> The <u>waitress's</u> served the cherry <u>pie's</u> to the <u>lady's</u>.

> **Correct:**
>> The <u>waitresses</u> served the cherry <u>pies</u> to the <u>ladies</u>.

However, apostrophes are used to make the plural forms of letters, digits, signs, and symbols.

4's   T's $'s   ?'s

Frank's *F*<u>'s</u> look like *7*<u>'s</u>, and his *r*<u>'s</u> look like *i*<u>'s</u>.

4. Apostrophes are used to make the possessive forms of indefinite pronouns that end with *one* or *body*. But they are not used to make the possessive forms of personal pronouns.

someone's	hers (*not* her's)
nobody's	ours (*not* our's)
everyone's	theirs (*not* their's)
anybody's	

Contractions

1. An apostrophe shows where one or more letters have been omitted in a contraction.

can't (can not)	I'll (I shall *or* I will)
don't (do not)	he'd (he had *or* he would)
we're (we are)	let's (let us)
they've (they have)	there's (there is)

Is the first word *well* or *we'll*? Does the room belong to one boy or several boys? It depends on the punctuation. In this lesson we will study the use of apostrophes.

Lesson Outline:

1. Apostrophes are used to make possessive forms.

   (1) The possessive case of most singular nouns is formed by adding *'s*. This includes most singular nouns that end with *s*. For a singular noun ending with a *zus* sound, only an apostrophe is added because *'s* would make the possessive form awkward to pronounce.

   (2) If a plural noun ends with *-s,* the possessive case is formed by adding only an apostrophe. If a plural noun does not end with *-s,* *'s* is added.

   (3) Apostrophes are not used to make the plural forms of nouns. But apostrophes are used to make the plural forms of numbers, letters, signs, and symbols.

   (4) Apostrophes are used to make the possessive forms of indefinite pronouns that end with *one* or *body*. But they are not used to make the possessive forms of personal pronouns.

2. Apostrophes are used to form contractions.

   (1) An apostrophe shows where one or more letters have been omitted.

   (2) Contractions must not be confused with possessive pronouns.

★ **EXTRA PRACTICE**
Worksheet 50 *(Apostrophes)*

2. Contractions must not be confused with possessive pronouns.

Contractions	Possessive Pronouns	
you're (you are)	your (belonging to you)	<u>your</u> book
they're (they are)	their (belonging to them)	<u>their</u> car
it's (it is *or* it has)	its (belonging to it)	<u>its</u> food
who's (who is)	whose (belonging to whom)	<u>whose</u> box

- Apostrophes are used to make possessive forms and contractions.
- Apostrophes are also used to make the plural forms of numbers, letters, signs, and symbols.

Class Practice

A. In the following sentences, tell where possessive forms could be used. Write the possessive forms on the chalkboard.
1. The servant of Abraham was sent to find a wife for Isaac.
2. The sister of Moses was Miriam.
3. The sisters of my mother are coming today.
4. I like the eggs of brown chickens best.
5. The teacher answered the questions of the children.
6. The coat of someone was left out on the playground.

B. Tell how to spell the missing words. Give an original sentence for each possessive word you spelled.

Singular	Singular Possessive	Plural	Plural Possessive
1. deer	——	——	——
2. wolf	——	——	——

C. Find the words that have mistakes in the use of apostrophes, and tell how to spell them correctly.
1. I found my pencil's beside Marthas seat.
2. Arent you're book's on anybodys desk?
3. Ive found them; theyre on the library shelves'.
4. I dont know why I put them they're.
5. Its good to have helpful friend's when your confused.

Lesson 86 Answers
Class Practice

A. 1. Abraham's servant
2. Moses' sister
3. mother's sisters
4. chickens' eggs
5. children's questions
6. someone's coat

B. (Words in italics are given in the pupil's text. Sentences will vary.)
1. *deer* deer's deer deer's
2. *wolf* wolf's wolves wolves'

C. 1. pencils, Martha's
2. Aren't, your, books, anybody's
3. I've, they're, shelves
4. don't, there
5. It's, friends, you're

Written Exercises

A. Copy and complete the chart.

Singular	Singular Possessive	Plural	Plural Possessive
1. pet	——	——	——
2. puppy	——	——	——
3. sheep	——	——	——

B. Rewrite these phrases, using possessive forms.
1. a track of a bear
2. the milk of several goats
3. problems of people
4. the love of Jesus
5. the gloves of somebody
6. the instructions for the waitresses

C. Write contractions for the following words.

1. I am	4. does not	7. was not
2. it is	5. they have	8. she will
3. we shall	6. he has	

D. Write the plural form of each item.

2   j $ #   5

E. Find the words that have mistakes in the use of apostrophes, and write those words correctly.
1. Alexs teacher couldnt make out several pupils ps and qs.
2. Theyre using Mothers scissors, but she wont care if theres a good reason.
3. Many people havent heard Jesus words of life.
4. Someones sweater was left outside; is it her's?
5. You're ds and ts shouldnt have loop's in them.
6. Octopus's have eight arm's, and squid's have ten.

Review Exercises

A. Write the simple subject of each sentence. Then write the correct word in parentheses, making sure it agrees with the word you wrote. [66]
1. Each day one of the students (watch, watches) the fox den.
2. Every one of the girls (pack, packs) (her, their) own lunch.
3. Each of the girls (comb, combs) (her, their) own hair.

Written Exercises

A. (Words in italics are given in the pupil's text.)

1. *pet*	pet's	pets	pets'
2. *puppy*	puppy's	puppies	puppies'
3. *sheep*	sheep's	sheep	sheep's

B. 1. a bear's track
2. several goats' milk
3. people's problems
4. Jesus' love
5. somebody's gloves
6. the waitresses' instructions

C. 1. I'm   5. they've
2. it's   6. he's
3. we'll   7. wasn't
4. doesn't   8. she'll

D. 2's, *j*'s, *$*'s, #'s, 5's

E. 1. Alex's, couldn't, pupils', *p*'s, *q*'s
2. They're, Mother's, won't, there's
3. haven't, Jesus'
4. Someone's, hers
5. Your, *d*'s, *t*'s, shouldn't, loops
6. Octopuses, arms, squids

Review Exercises

A. 1. one, watches
2. one, packs, her
3. Each, combs, her

4. Now all of the cleaning (is, are) finished.
5. All of the boys (is, are) glad they didn't have to help wash dishes.
6. Few of the women (like, likes) to drive the tractor.
7. Many (know, knows) how though.
8. Nobody (keep, keeps) his lunch in the room.

B. Copy each sentence, using correct capitalization and punctuation. [77, 80]
1. did you ever have a pet skink asked sara
2. no what is a skink asked susan
3. stephen replied it is a kind of striped lizard with an orange throat
4. is it true asked samuel that skinks drop their tails sometimes to get away from enemies
5. yes and young skinks have blue tails answered sara
6. sara said our pets eat ants gnats spiders and small moths

---

87. Hyphens, Colons, and Semicolons

In this lesson you will learn about three more punctuation marks. They are the hyphen (-), the colon (:), and the semicolon (;).

Hyphens

1. *Hyphens are used in writing compound number words from* twenty-one *through* ninety-nine.

    fifty-eight
    ninety-seven
    three hundred forty-five

2. *Hyphens are used in many compound words,* especially adjectives. Use your dictionary to be sure.

brother-in-law	great-grandchild	twice-mentioned
sisters-in-law	self-discipline	air-conditioned
great-grandfather	self-sealing	air-cooled
great-aunt	self-addressed	green-eyed

    All compound words that end with *in-law* are written with hyphens. Hyphens are also used in all *great-* compounds that

Lesson 87

Purpose: To teach the uses of hyphens, colons, and semicolons.

Oral Review:

1. How are apostrophes used? (to form possessive nouns, contractions, and the plural forms of numbers, letters, signs, and symbols)
2. Tell how to spell the following words as they are used in the sentences.
   a. David's   This is *David's* room.
   b. octopus's   An *octopus's* eight arms are lined with suction cups.
   c. Moses'   *Moses'* brother was Aaron.
   d. students'   All five *students'* lessons were finished.
   e. mice's   The field *mice's* food was seeds from the wheat field.
   f. you're   *You're* quite early today!

4. all, is
5. All, are
6. Few, like
7. Many, know
8. Nobody, keeps

B. (Corrections are underlined.)
1. "Did you ever have a pet skink?" asked Sara.
2. "No. What is a skink?" asked Susan.
3. Stephen replied, "It is a kind of striped lizard with an orange throat."
4. "Is it true," asked Samuel, "that skinks drop their tails sometimes to get away from enemies?"
5. "Yes, and young skinks have blue tails," answered Sara.
6. Sara said, "Our pets eat ants, gnats, spiders, and small moths."

---

   g. your   *Your* sister is here.
   h. it's   *It's* time to leave.
   i. its   Do you have *its* harness on right?
   j. their   *Their* stand opens at eight o'clock.
   k. they're   *They're* selling doughnuts today.
3. What helping verbs are used
   a. in the present perfect tense? (have *or* has)
   b. in the past perfect tense? (had)
   c. in the future perfect tense? (shall have *or* will have)
4. Give the three perfect tenses of the following verbs.
   a. find (have found, had found, will have found)
   b. think (have thought, had thought, will have thought)
   c. shut (have shut, had shut, will have shut)

refer to relatives. All compound words that begin with *self-* are hyphenated.

3. *A hyphen is used when it is necessary to divide a word between syllables at the end of a line of writing.* The following sentence shows examples of this.

> Sometimes it may be neces-
> sary to divide a word into syl-
> lables at the end of a line.

A word should be divided at the end of a line only when necessary. When you must divide a word, remember the following rules. Always use a dictionary when you are not sure.

a. Do not divide a one-syllable word.

> *not* sto-rm *or* cre-am

b. Divide only between syllables.

> ex-am-ples   care-ful-ly

c. Do not divide a word in such a way that a single letter is left at the beginning or end of a line.

> *not* husk-y *or* studi-o   *not* a-bundance *or* o-val

4. *A hyphen shows a series of connected verses.* The hyphen means "through." A comma shows a break in a series of verses.

> Jesse recited Psalm 119:1–8.
> Our Sunday school class memorized Hebrews 11:1–13, 32–34, 39.

Colons

1. *A colon is used after the greeting of a business letter.*

> Dear Sir: Dear Mr. Jones: Gentlemen:

2. *A colon is used for writing a time with numbers.* The colon is placed between the hour and the minute.

> 3:30 P.M.   9:22 in the evening   6:05 A.M.

3. *A colon is used to write Scripture references.* The colon is placed between the chapter and the verse.

> John 3:16   Colossians 3:12–16

Lesson Introduction: Write the following sentence on the chalkboard, using no punctuation. Ask students if they know what can be done to make this sentence easier to read.

> For our teams Jerry chose Nevin Jay Donald and
> Fred and I chose Harold Ray and Larry.

Point out that there is more than one possible way to use commas in this sentence. Also show how a semicolon makes the break between the parts of the compound sentence clearer.

> For our teams Jerry chose Nevin, Jay, Donald, and
> Fred; and I chose Harold, Ray, and Larry.
> For our teams Jerry chose Nevin Jay, Donald, and
> Fred; and I chose Harold Ray and Larry.
> For our teams Jerry chose Nevin, Jay Donald, and
> Fred; and I chose Harold Ray and Larry.

Today we will study some ways to use hyphens, colons, and semicolons.

Lesson Outline:

1. Use hyphens correctly.

(1) *Hyphens are used in writing compound number words from* twenty-one *through* ninety-nine.

(2) *Hyphens are used in many compound words,* especially adjectives.

   a. All compound words that end with *in-law* are written with hyphens.

   b. Hyphens are used in all *great-* compounds that refer to relatives.

   c. All compound words that begin with *self-* are hyphenated.

(3) *A hyphen is used when it is necessary to divide a word between syllables at the end of a line of writing.* The following rules apply.

   a. Do not divide a one-syllable word.

   b. Divide only between syllables.

Semicolons

1. *A semicolon is used between clauses in a compound sentence when no conjunction is used.* You know that a comma is not strong enough to hold two clauses together.

   Incorrect:
   > It had happened often before, this time it was more serious.
   > The lawyer asked Jesus a question, he learned more than he had expected.

   Correct:
   > It had happened often before; this time it was more serious.
   > The lawyer asked Jesus a question; he learned more than he had expected.

2. *A semicolon is also used between clauses in a compound sentence that does have a conjunction if commas are already used within one or more of the clauses.*

   > Esau begged, pleaded, and wept; but it was to no avail.
   > If we stop, they'll want us to stay for dinner, I'm sure; and we don't have time for that.

   Ordinarily, a comma and a conjunction are enough to join the clauses. But when commas are used between smaller units (words or phrases), semicolons are used between larger units (clauses).

- The hyphen is used in many compound words.
- The hyphen is used when it is necessary to divide a word between syllables at the end of a line.
- The colon is used after the greeting of a business letter, between the hour and the minute when a time is written with numbers, and between the chapter and the verse in a Bible reference.
- The semicolon is used to join clauses in a compound sentence when no conjunction is used. It is also used to join clauses in a compound sentence when a comma is already used within one or more of the clauses.

---

c. Do not divide a word in such a way that a single letter is left at the beginning or end of a line.

(4) *A hyphen shows a series of connected verses.* The hyphen means "through." A comma shows a break in a series of verses.

Teacher: In printed material, the short dash that means "through" is known as an en-dash (in distinction from the longer em-dash). But in handwritten and typewritten material, an en-dash and a hyphen are the same punctuation mark.

2. *Use colons correctly.*
   (1) *A colon is used after the greeting of a business letter.*
   (2) *A colon is placed between the hour and the minute when a time is written with numbers.*
   (3) *A colon is placed between the chapter and the verse in a Scripture reference.*

3. *Use semicolons correctly.*
   (1) *A semicolon is used between clauses in a compound sentence when no conjunction is used.* A comma is not strong enough to hold two clauses together.
   (2) *A semicolon is used between clauses in a compound sentence that does have a conjunction if commas are already used within one or more of the clauses.* Ordinarily, a comma and a conjunction are enough to join the clauses. But when commas are used between smaller units (words or phrases), semicolons are used between larger units (clauses). This is done to avoid confusion.

★ **EXTRA PRACTICE**
Worksheet 51 *(Hyphens, Colons, and Semicolons)*

Class Practice

A. Tell where these words may be divided between syllables at the end of a line of writing.

1. amidships
2. meaty
3. oversleep
4. ecliptic
5. oiliness
6. apothecary

B. Tell where hyphens, colons, and semicolons are needed in the following sentences.

1. He said that he had twenty two great uncles and great aunts.
2. She didn't list the sisters in law she said she didn't have time.
3. His brother in law sent a self addressed envelope with the order.
4. My great aunt recited Psalm 103 1 12 without a mistake.
5. In the family reunion, forty eight people gathered at 189 Walnut Street at 1 00 P.M.
6. My aunt brought celery, carrots, and cheese and her sister in law brought fruit.

Written Exercises

A. Write each word, using hyphens to show where it could be divided between syllables at the end of a line of writing. (Insert no hyphen if the word should not be divided.) Use a dictionary for help.

1. amendment
2. many
3. electrician
4. identification
5. realm
6. fascination

B. Copy these sentences, and add the missing hyphens, colons, and semicolons.

1. Twenty three great grandchildren sang for their great grandfather at 1 30 in the afternoon.
2. At my brother in law's self service station, he had one hundred seventy two customers in one day.
3. Every morning at 9 00, we recited Philippians 4 1 8.
4. He didn't recognize his sister in law he hadn't seen her for twenty four years.
5. His brothers in law are John, David, and Jonas and his sisters in law are Doreen and Mary.

Lesson 87 Answers
Class Practice

A.
1. amid-ships
2. meaty (no division allowed)
3. over-sleep
4. eclip-tic
5. oil-i-ness
6. apoth-e-cary

B. (Corrections are underlined.)
1. twenty-two, great-uncles, great-aunts
2. sisters-in-law;
3. brother-in-law, self-addressed
4. great-aunt, 103:1-12
5. forty-eight, Wal-nut Street, 1:00
6. cheese;, sister-in-law

Written Exercises

A.
1. amend-ment
2. many
3. elec-tri-cian
4. iden-ti-fi-ca-tion
5. realm
6. fas-ci-na-tion

B. (Corrections are underlined.)
1. Twenty-three great-grandchildren sang for their great-grandfather at 1:30 in the afternoon.
2. At my brother-in-law's self-service station, he had one hun-dred seventy-two customers in one day. (*Teacher:* In the pupil's text, *hundred* comes at the end of a line.)
3. Every morning at 9:00, we recited Philippians 4:1-8.
4. He didn't recognize his sister-in-law; he hadn't seen her for twenty-four years.
5. His brothers-in-law are John, David, and Jonas; and his sisters-in-law are Doreen and Mary.

C. Use numerals and abbreviations to write each time.

> **Example:** Half past five in the morning
> **Answer:** 5:30 A.M.

1. Thirteen minutes after nine in the evening
2. Thirty minutes before noon
3. A quarter to ten at night
4. Two minutes after midnight

D. Write two correct greetings for business letters.

E. Write two of your favorite Bible verses, with correct chapter and verse references.

Review Exercises

Copy each verb or verb phrase, and write whether its tense is *present, past, future, present perfect, past perfect,* or *future perfect.* [32–36]

1. At birth, a blue whale weighs about three tons.
2. The goose's eggs have hatched.
3. She chased away any intruder.
4. She had honked a warning in plenty of time.
5. We will stay away from the nest.
6. Before winter, the goslings will have flown south.

---

88. Chapter 7 Review

Class Practice

A. Give the meaning of each abbreviation.

1. Jan.	3. gal.	5. KJV	7. A.M.
2. oz.	4. min.	6. FBI	8. A.D.

B. Say *yes* or *no* to tell whether the following abbreviations may be used in general writing, such as letters, stories, and reports.

1. Mr.	3. Jr.	5. etc.
2. lb.	4. Aug.	6. B.C.

C. Give the postal service abbreviations for these states.

1. New Mexico	3. New York
2. Michigan	4. Minnesota

Lesson 88

Purpose: To review the concepts taught in Chapter 7.

C. 1. 9:13 P.M.
   2. 11:30 A.M.
   3. 9:45 P.M.
   4. 12:02 A.M.

D. (Sample answers.)

> Dear Sir: Gentlemen: Dear Madam:

E. (Individual answers.)

Review Exercises

1. weighs—present
2. have hatched—present perfect
3. chased—past
4. had honked—past perfect
5. shall stay—future
6. will have flown—future perfect

Lesson 88 Answers
Class Practice

A. 1. January
   2. ounce
   3. gallon
   4. minute
   5. King James Version
   6. Federal Bureau of Investigation
   7. before midday
   8. in the year of the Lord

B. 1. yes   4. no
   2. no   5. no
   3. yes   6. yes

C. 1. NM   2. MI   3. NY   4. MN

D. Identify each item set off by commas as an *appositive, a noun of direct address,* or a *parenthetical element.*
   1. Some turtles, strangely enough, live to be over one hundred years old.
   2. Barbara, did you know it takes a bullfrog tadpole three years to change into an adult?
   3. Guppies, little South American fish, are easy to raise, Barbara.
   4. They don't fight or get sick easily, I am told.
   5. Corydoras, a certain type of catfish, are good for keeping the gravel in an aquarium clean.

E. Tell which commas are not needed in the following sentences.
   1. The sea horse is a, small, mysterious, sea, creature.
   2. Two, antique, cuckoo clocks, struck the hour.
   3. Three, tall, eager young men stood ready to work.

F. Tell whether each sentence has a *direct quotation,* an *indirect quotation,* or *no quotation.* (All quotation marks have been omitted.)
   1. I have some pet cormorants said Hugo.
   2. Hugo said that his pets help him to fish!
   3. The Japanese fasten collars to the necks of these birds so that they don't swallow the fish they catch.
   4. These birds said Hugo help us to make a living.

G. Change each sentence so that it has an indirect quotation.
   1. "We are raising an orphan kangaroo," said Eric.
   2. "Whenever the joey wants her mother's pouch, she crawls into the sack we hung from the back fence," he said.
   3. Eric said, "We will use electric heating pads to keep the sack warm during cold weather."

H. Change each sentence so that it has a direct quotation.
   1. Eric said that he was sure their pet kangaroo would soon be ready to join other kangaroos in the wild.
   2. Eric said that she eats grasses and low shrubs.
   3. He said that kangaroos are natives of his country, Australia.

I. Tell how to spell the missing words.

Singular	Singular Possessive	Plural	Plural Possessive
1. camel	——	——	——
2. guppy	——	——	——
3. goose	——	——	——

D. 1. parenthetical element
   2. noun of direct address
   3. appositive, noun of direct address
   4. parenthetical element
   5. appositive

E. (Corrections are marked.)
   1. The sea horse is a, small, mysterious, sea, creature.
   2. Two, antique, cuckoo clocks, struck the hour.
   3. Three, tall, eager young men stood ready to work.

F. 1. direct quotation
   2. indirect quotation
   3. no quotation
   4. direct quotation

G. (Verb forms may vary.)
   1. Eric said that they are raising an orphan kangaroo.
   2. He said that whenever the joey wants her mother's pouch, she crawls into the sack they hung from the back fence.
   3. Eric said that they would use electric heating pads to keep the sack warm during cold weather.

H. (Verb forms may vary.)
   1. Eric said, "I am sure our pet kangaroo will soon be ready to join other kangaroos in the wild."
   2. Eric said, "She eats grasses and low shrubs."
   3. He said, "Kangaroos are natives of my country, Australia."

I. (Words in italics are given in the pupil's text.)
   1. *camel*   camel's   camels   camels'
   2. *guppy*   guppy's   guppies   guppies'
   3. *goose*   goose's   geese   geese's

J. On the chalkboard, write a phrase with a possessive form for each item below.

1. antlers of a moose
2. dish of the cats
3. tracks of the geese
4. bone of the dog

Written Exercises

A. Write correctly each word that should be capitalized.

1.
        the bumblebee
    i watched a striped bumblebee
        spin off into the air
    when he was finished with his lunch
        among the clover fair.

    god gives him nectar sweet to drink;
        he gives me milk and bread.
    he gives his creatures what they need,
        and by him we are fed!
                              —Edith Witmer

2. "o lord, to thee will i cry" (joel 1:19).
3. in the spring of 1896, henry ford tried out his first horseless carriage.
4. on june 16, 1903, the ford motor company began production of this sturdy, inexpensive american car.
5. the museum at greenfield village has several buildings about famous people, including president a. lincoln, noah webster, and the wright brothers.
6. the book *the times, the man, and the company* is about henry ford.
7. in 1922 some men from dearborn, michigan, wanted henry ford to run for president of the united states.
8. his father was william ford, and his mother was mary litogot.
9. father said, "please give this to mother."
10. mr. john b. chapman was the teacher at miller school, a small school in springwells township, michigan.

B. Copy this paragraph, adding the missing punctuation and capital letters.

    john deere was an american inventor he was born in 1804 in rutland vermont he was an excellent blacksmith after losing two shops by fire, he moved west in grand detour illinois he invented a steel plow that farmers badly needed soon he started a factory to make them it was

J. 1. a moose's antlers
   2. the cats' dish
   3. the geese's tracks
   4. the dog's bone

Written Exercises

A. 1.   **The Bumblebee**
       I, Spin, When, Among
       God, He, He, His, And, Him
   2. O, Lord, I, Joel
   3. In, Henry Ford
   4. On, June, Ford Motor Company, American
   5. The, Greenfield Village, President A. Lincoln, Noah Webster, Wright (Also accept *Brothers.*)
   6. The, *The Times, (the) Man, (and the) Company*, Henry Ford
   7. In, Dearborn, Michigan, Henry Ford, United States
   8. His, William Ford, Mary Litogot
   9. Father, Please, Mother
   10. Mr. John B. Chapman, Miller School, Springwells Township, Michigan

B. (Corrections are underlined.)
    John Deere was an American inventor. He was born in 1804 in Rutland, Vermont. He was an excellent blacksmith. After losing two shops by fire, he moved west. In Grand Detour, Illinois, he invented a steel plow that farmers badly needed. Soon he started a factory to make them. It was the beginning of one of the largest farm equipment factories in the United States.

the beginning of one of the largest farm equipment factories in the
united states

C. Copy each sentence or letter part, and add the missing capital letters
and punctuation marks.
1. 616 n johnson street   dear friend
    detroit mi 48216   sincerely yours
    jan 10 1893
2. mr and mrs taylors address is 867 south third street, springfield
    il 62703
3. who was the teacher of the apostle paul asked brother john
4. jason replied it was gamaliel
5. where in the Bible asked brother john can you read about this
6. it is written in acts 22:3 said gerald this verse also tells where
    paul was born

D. Write the correct abbreviations for these words. Use a dictionary if
you are not sure.
1. tablespoon	5. hour	9. after midday
2. quart	6. year	10. before Christ
3. foot	7. week	11. ounce
4. gallon	8. October	12. King James Version

E. Copy each word that needs a comma after it, and add the missing
comma.
1. The Ford Company the Chrysler Corporation and the General
    Motors Corporation in fact are leading car manufacturers in the
    United States.
2. Designing the product getting raw materials making the product and
    selling the product Mark are four main steps in manufacturing.
3. Well the Chrysler Corporation was a leader in some modern well-
    liked ideas like front-wheel drive Larry.
4. Yes more than one company has manufactured automobiles over
    the years but the competition has given customers better prod-
    ucts for less money.
5. In the 1870s Alexander Graham Bell invented the telephone.
6. After many demonstrations of his invention people finally became
    interested in the new instrument.

F. Write contractions for the following words.
1. they are	3. it is	5. we are
2. who is	4. I am	6. they have

C. (Corrections are underlined.)
1. 616 <u>N.</u> Johnson <u>Street</u>   <u>Dear</u> friend<u>,</u>
    <u>Detroit, MI</u> 48216   <u>Sincerely</u> yours<u>,</u>
    <u>Jan.</u> 10<u>,</u> 1893
2. <u>Mr.</u> and <u>Mrs. Taylor's</u> address is 867 <u>South</u>
    <u>Third Street</u>, Springfield, <u>IL</u> 62703.
3. <u>"Who</u> was the teacher of the apostle <u>Paul?"</u>
    asked <u>Brother John.</u> (Also accept *Apostle*.)
4. <u>Jason</u> replied<u>, "It</u> was <u>Gamaliel."</u>
5. <u>"Where</u> in the <u>Bible,"</u> asked <u>Brother John, "can</u>
    you read about <u>this?"</u>
6. <u>"It</u> is written in <u>Acts</u> 22:<u>3," said Gerald. "This</u>
    verse also tells where <u>Paul</u> was <u>born."</u>

D. (Some answers may vary.)
1. tbsp.	7. wk.
2. qt.	8. Oct.
3. ft.	9. P.M.
4. gal.	10. B.C.
5. hr.	11. oz.
6. yr.	12. KJV

E. 1. Company, Corporation, Corporation, fact,
2. product, materials, product, product, Mark,
3. Well, modern, drive,
4. Yes, years,
5. 1870s,
6. invention,

F.
1. they're	4. I'm
2. who's	5. we're
3. it's	6. they've

G. Find the words that have mistakes in the use of apostrophes, and write them correctly.
   1. Jasons brother read Jesus word's from Matthew 5 to us.
   2. The ladies purses are found on the second floor of Andys store.
   3. Someones paper had 5s that looked like Ss.

H. Copy each word, and place a hyphen between the syllables that could be divided at the end of a line of writing.
   1. abating   3. iguana
   2. periphery   4. immediately

I. Find each word that should have a hyphen or should be followed by a colon or semicolon. Write that word, and add the missing punctuation.
   1. When my great grandfather was twenty one years old, he came here from Germany.
   2. Sarah Jane's sister in law ordered thirty six self sealing envelopes.
   3. At 9 30 we recited 2 Corinthians 6 14 18.
   4. Dear Sir

      Please send me some information on your heavy-duty wagons a self addressed envelope is enclosed.

      Sincerely,
      Robert Martin

   5. Michael broke his leg he missed his step and fell out of a tree.
   6. Mark, John, and Justin went to see him and Glen, Gerald, and Daryl sent cards.

J. Rewrite this dialogue, adding necessary punctuation and dividing paragraphs properly.

   One day a young man came to where Jesus was teaching. Good Master, he asked, what shall I do to inherit eternal life? You know the commandments Jesus replied. Do not commit adultery. Do not kill. Do not steal. Do not lie. And honor your father and your mother. The young man answered I have always done all these things, ever since I was a boy. Jesus loved the young man very much. One thing remains for you to do He told him. Sell all your possessions; and come, follow Me. The young man said nothing and went sadly away. He was rich with many possessions.

G. 1. Jason's, Jesus', words
   2. ladies', Andy's
   3. Someone's, 5's, S's

H. 1. abat-ing
   2. pe-riph-ery
   3. igua-na
   4. im-me-di-ate-ly

I. (Corrections are underlined.)
   1. great-grandfather, twenty-one
   2. sister-in-law, thirty-six, self-sealing, enve-lopes
   3. 9:30, 6:14-18
   4. Sir:, wagons;, self-addressed
   5. leg;
   6. him;

J. (Corrections are underlined.)
   One day a young man came to where Jesus was teaching. "Good Master," he asked, "what shall I do to inherit eternal life?"

   "You know the commandments," Jesus replied. "Do not commit adultery. Do not kill. Do not steal. Do not lie. And honor your father and your mother."

   The young man answered, "I have always done all these things, ever since I was a boy."

   Jesus loved the young man very much. "One thing remains for you to do," He told him. "Sell all your possessions; and come, follow Me."

   The young man said nothing and went sadly away. He was rich with many possessions.

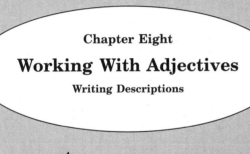

Chapter Eight

Working With Adjectives

Writing Descriptions

An
adjective is a
word that modifies a noun
or pronoun.

He hath made every thing beautiful in his time.

Ecclesiastes 3:11

Adjectives

Limiting Adjectives	Descriptive Adjectives
Which	**What Kind of**
Articles:	*Color:*
a, an, the	red, green,
Demonstrative	brown, pink
pronouns:	*Size:*
this, that,	tiny, huge,
these, those	high, long
Ordinal Numbers:	*Shape:*
first, second,	round, oval,
tenth, fiftieth	square, oblong
Interrogative and	*Taste:*
Relative Pronouns:	bitter, salty,
which, whose, what	spicy, sweet
Whose	*Sound:*
Possessive Nouns:	harsh, musical,
boy's, lady's,	shrill, loud
Paul's, Mary's,	*Touch:*
bird's, men's	rough, sharp,
Possessive Pronouns:	cold, soft
my, our, its,	*Traits:*
your, his,	kind, thoughtful,
her, their	lazy, angry
How Many	*Others:*
Cardinal Numbers:	late, swift,
two, seven,	Scottish, French
twelve, ninety	
Indefinite Pronouns:	
few, several,	
some, many	

Adjectives are words that describe, or modify, nouns and pronouns.

89. Adjectives

Adjectives are words that modify, or describe, nouns and pronouns. They tell *which, whose, how many,* and *what kind of.*

Adjectives can be placed in two general classes: *limiting adjectives* and *descriptive adjectives.* Limiting adjectives tell *which, whose,* and *how many.* They limit the meaning of nouns and pronouns in certain ways. There are several kinds of limiting adjectives.

1. The articles *a, an,* and *the* are limiting adjectives.
2. Demonstrative pronouns can be used as limiting adjectives to tell *which.*

   this   that   these   those

3. Ordinal numbers are used as limiting adjectives to tell *which. Ordinal* numbers show the *order* of things.

   third   sixth   twelfth

4. Some interrogative and relative pronouns can be used as limiting adjectives.

   which   whose   what

5. Possessive nouns are often used as limiting adjectives to tell *whose.*

   Harold's   boy's

6. Possessive pronouns are often used as limiting adjectives to tell *whose.*

   somebody's   my   their

7. Cardinal numbers are used as limiting adjectives to tell *how many. Cardinal* numbers are numbers like those on flash *cards.*

   two   seven   ten

8. Indefinite pronouns can be used as limiting adjectives to tell *how many.*

   many   several   few   every   other

Lesson 89

Purpose: To identify adjectives and to recognize their varieties.

Oral Review:

1. In what number words must hyphens be used? (in compound number words from twenty-one through ninety-nine)
2. Give some compound words that need hyphens. (words that begin with *self-* or *great-,* words that end with *in-law,* and words such as *twice-mentioned, green-eyed,* and *air-conditioned*)
3. What does a hyphen mean in a Scripture reference? (It means "through" and indicates a series of connected verses.)
4. Name the part of speech described.
   a. It takes the place of a noun. (pronoun)
   b. It modifies a verb, an adjective, or an adverb by telling *how, when, where,* or *to what degree.* (adverb)
   c. It modifies a noun or pronoun by telling *which, whose, how many,* or *what kind of.* (adjective)
   d. It is a connecting word that begins a phrase. (preposition)
   e. It is a word that joins words, phrases, or clauses in a sentence. (conjunction)
   f. It is a word that expresses strong feeling. (interjection)
   g. It names a person, place, thing, or idea. (noun)
   h. It can have present, past, or future tense. (verb)

Lesson Introduction: Ask students what flavor of ice cream they like best. Do they always choose plain vanilla, or do they like other flavors sometimes? Adjectives add "flavor" to our language. Even the words that describe flavors of ice cream are adjectives.

   chocolate ice cream
   cherry ice cream
   mint ice cream

Today we want to study limiting and descriptive adjectives.

Lesson Outline:

1. An adjective is a word that modifies, or describes, a noun or pronoun. It tells *which, whose, how many,* or *what kind of.*

2. Limiting adjectives tell which, whose, *and* how many. They limit the meaning of nouns and pronouns in certain ways.

   (1) The articles *a, an,* and *the* are limiting adjectives.
   (2) Demonstrative pronouns can be used as limiting adjectives to tell *which.*

      this   that   these   those

Descriptive adjectives tell *what kind of.* There are hundreds of descriptive adjectives. Here are some of them listed in groups.

color:	blue, orange, copper, green
size:	small, tiny, huge, wide
shape:	round, square, oval, triangular
taste:	sour, spicy, sweet, salty
sound:	harsh, shrill, quiet, harmonious
touch:	rough, cold, soft, fuzzy
traits:	kind, considerate, lazy, stubborn

Some descriptive adjectives are made from nouns by adding adjective suffixes. Here are some examples. Can you give the nouns from which they are formed?

-ish:	babyish, foolish, selfish, feverish
-like:	childlike, lifelike, cloudlike, Godlike
-ic:	historic, angelic, volcanic, Icelandic
-en:	woolen, earthen, wooden, silken

Nouns are often used before other nouns as descriptive adjectives.

<u>farm</u> animals   <u>shade</u> trees   <u>hand</u> soap   <u>garden</u> soil

Sometimes an adjective looks like a verb.

God made the <u>leaping</u> frogs and the <u>flying</u> birds.
Mother's garden is full of brightly <u>colored</u> flowers.

Leaping and *flying* are verb forms. But in the first example above, they describe *frogs* and *birds.* So they are used as adjectives. *Colored* is also a verb form. But in the second example, it describes *flowers.* So *colored* is an adjective in that sentence.

How can you tell whether a word is an adjective or another part of speech? You can tell by the way the word is used in a sentence. Whenever a word modifies a noun or pronoun by telling *which, whose, how many,* or *what kind of,* it is an adjective.

- An adjective modifies a noun or pronoun.

- A limiting adjective tells *which, whose,* or *how many.*

- A descriptive adjective tells *what kind of.*

---

(3) Ordinal numbers are used as limiting adjectives to tell *which.*

   first   second   third

(4) Some interrogative and relative pronouns can be used as limiting adjectives.

   which   whose   what

(5) Possessive nouns are often used as limiting adjectives to tell *whose.*

   Harold's   boy's

(6) Possessive pronouns are often used as limiting adjectives to tell *whose.*

   somebody's   our   your

   Some possessive pronouns are used only as limiting adjectives.

   my   your   her
   its   our   their

(7) Cardinal numbers are used as limiting adjectives to tell *how many.*

   one   two   three

(8) Indefinite pronouns can be used as limiting adjectives to tell *how many.*

   many   several   few
   every   other

3. Descriptive adjectives tell what kind of. Here are some examples of descriptive adjectives.

color:	pink, green, silver, red
size:	enormous, tiny, narrow, broad
shape:	circular, square, oval, triangular
taste:	bitter, spicy, sweet, salty, delicious
sound:	loud, musical, sweet, soft
touch:	smooth, warm, soft, fuzzy, rough
traits:	friendly, helpful, considerate, diligent

Some descriptive adjectives are made from nouns by adding adjective suffixes.

   selfish   childlike   historic   wooden

Nouns are often used before other nouns as descriptive adjectives. (*Teacher:* These are known as attributive nouns.)

<u>cherry</u> pie   <u>garden</u> tools   <u>gas</u> stoves

A descriptive adjective may look like a verb. (*Teacher:* These verb forms are participles.)

<u>galloping</u> horse   <u>walking</u> stick   <u>grown</u> men

4. An adjective can be identified by the fact that it modifies a noun or pronoun. Whenever a word modifies a noun or pronoun by telling *which, whose, how many,* or *what kind of,* it is an adjective.

★ **EXTRA PRACTICE**
Worksheet 52 *(Adjectives)*

Class Practice

A. The seven colors of the rainbow are red, orange, yellow, green, blue, indigo, and violet. Name five other colors.

B. Find the adjectives in these sentences. Tell whether each one is *limiting* or *descriptive*.
1. Bullfrogs hide in the cool mud at the bottom of the pond.
2. Out on the grassy bank, the plump bullfrog whips out his long tongue and snaps up a juicy insect.
3. Pointy or round, huge or tiny, speckled or plain, and green, blue, white, or brown eggs are found among the nine thousand different kinds of eggs that birds lay.

C. Tell whether each underlined word is an *adjective* or a *pronoun*. If it is an adjective, tell which word it modifies.
1. This is mine; that book is yours.
2. Several were found on that shelf.
3. Many people have read them.

Written Exercises

A. Copy all the adjectives in these sentences. Include the nouns and pronouns used as descriptive adjectives. Underline the limiting adjectives.
1. Common, ordinary insects are interesting creatures.
2. These insects live in our yards and vegetable gardens.
3. Some tiny insects hide in the tender, growing tips of young plants.
4. Other insects feed only in dark, shady areas.
5. Many brilliant butterflies flit about in the bright sunshine.
6. The huge beetles of tropical lands may have a length of six inches.

B. Write *adj.* or *pron.* for each underlined word. If it is an adjective, write the word it modifies.
1. Our pony is three years older than his.
2. That one is two years old.
3. His is younger than mine.
4. Their house is near ours.

C. List the eight kinds of limiting adjectives, and give two examples of each.

D. List all the personal pronouns that can be used as adjectives.

E. Write the definitions of cardinal and ordinal numbers, and write the first five of each.

Lesson 89 Answers
Class Practice
A. (Sample answers.)
pink, rose, maroon, peach, gold, ivory, turquoise, lilac, brown, tan, copper, bronze

B. 1. the—limiting; cool—descriptive; the—limiting; the—limiting
2. the—limiting; grassy—descriptive; the—limiting; plump—descriptive; his—limiting; long—descriptive; a—limiting; juicy—descriptive
3. Pointy, round, huge, tiny, speckled, plain, green, blue, white, brown—all descriptive; the—limiting; nine thousand—limiting; different—descriptive

C. 1. pronoun, pronoun, adjective—book, pronoun
2. pronoun, adjective—shelf
3. adjective—people, pronoun

Written Exercises
A. 1. Common, ordinary, interesting
2. These, our, vegetable
3. Some, tiny, the, tender, growing, young
4. Other, dark, shady
5. Many, brilliant, the, bright
6. The, huge, tropical, a, six

B. 1. adj.—pony; pron.
2. adj.—one
3. pron., pron.
4. adj.—house; pron.

C. (Examples will vary.)
1. *Articles:* a, an, the
2. *Demonstrative pronouns:* this, that, these, those
3. *Ordinal numbers:* first, second
4. *Interrogative and relative pronouns:* which, whose, what
5. *Possessive nouns:* John's, girl's,
6. *Possessive pronouns:* nobody's, my, your, their
7. *Cardinal numbers:* five, six
8. *Indefinite pronouns:* both, several, everyone, many

D. my, your, his, her, its, our, their

E. Cardinal numbers are number words that tell *how many.*
one, two, three, four, five

Ordinal numbers are number words that tell *which.*
first, second, third, fourth, fifth

Review Exercises

A. Write the three principal parts of each verb. Use *have* with the past participle. [30, 31]

1. attack   3. speak   5. forget
2. buy   4. wear

B. Copy these sentences, and label each word with one of the abbreviations shown.

noun—n.   verb—v.
pronoun—pron.   adjective—adj.

1. Grandmother gave me these two ripe peaches.
2. Six fluffy, yellow chicks hatched.

Review Exercises

A. 1. attack, attacked, (have) attacked
    2. buy, bought, (have) bought
    3. speak, spoke, (have) spoken
    4. wear, wore, (have) worn
    5. forget, forgot, (have) forgotten

B.
        n.   v. pron. adj. adj. adj.   n.
    1. Grandmother gave me these two ripe peaches.
        adj. adj.   adj.   n.   v.
    2. Six fluffy, yellow chicks hatched.

---

90. Predicate Adjectives

You have learned that adjectives are words that modify nouns and pronouns. They usually come just before the nouns they modify. However, an adjective may also come after a linking verb and modify the subject of the sentence. This is a *predicate adjective.*

> The air was <u>cold</u>.
> The apple pie tasted <u>delicious</u>.

In the first example above, the adjective *cold* comes after the linking verb *was* and modifies the subject *air.* We know that *cold* modifies *air* because it is sensible to say *cold air.* In the second example, *delicious* comes after the linking verb *tasted* and modifies the subject *pie.* We know that *delicious* modifies *pie* because it is sensible to say *delicious pie.*

Review the list of linking verbs. Be sure you know them by memory.

Forms of *be:*
    am, is, are, was, were, be, been, being

Verbs of sense:
    taste, feel, smell, sound, look, appear

Other linking verbs:
    grow, seem, stay, become, remain

Lesson 90

Purpose: To teach predicate adjectives.

Oral Review:

1. What parts of speech do adjectives modify? (nouns, pronouns)
2. What questions do limiting adjectives answer? (which, whose, how many)
3. What question do descriptive adjectives answer? (what kind of)
4. What kind of adjectives are the articles *a, an,* and *the*? (limiting adjectives)
5. What are some differences between direct quotations and indirect quotations?
    (a. A direct quotation repeats the exact words of a speaker. An indirect quotation does not.
    b. Quotation marks are used with a direct quotation, but not with an indirect quotation.
    c. The word *that* often comes before an indirect quotation.
    d. Some pronouns and verb forms may be different in an indirect quotation.)

Lesson Introduction: Ask students to list a few chores that they do each Saturday. Do you always do your work in the same order? For instance, do you always start with the cleaning, then prepare the food, and then do other things? Or when you do your homework in the evening, do you always start with math and then do English? It is good to have an orderly plan and follow it, but sometimes we like to change the order for variety.

We also like variety in sentences. Most adjectives come just before the nouns they modify. But sometimes an adjective comes after the noun; in fact, an adjective that modifies the subject may come after the verb. Such an adjective is a predicate adjective.

To find a predicate adjective in a sentence, first find the verb. If it is not a linking verb, your work is finished. There is no predicate adjective in the sentence.

If the verb can be a linking verb, see if it is followed by an adjective that modifies the subject. (Say the adjective before the subject to see if that makes sense.) If the adjective modifies the subject, it is a predicate adjective.

> We <u>finished</u> our work.
>> *Finished* cannot be a linking verb. There can be no predicate adjective.

> The cat's dish <u>was</u> <u>empty</u>.
>> *Was* can be a linking verb, and it is followed by the adjective *empty. Empty* modifies the subject because it is sensible to say *empty dish*. So *empty* is a predicate adjective.

> These ripe bananas <u>feel</u> <u>soft</u>.
>> *Feel* can be a linking verb, and it is followed by the adjective *soft. Soft* modifies the subject because it is sensible to say *soft bananas*. So *soft* is a predicate adjective.

An adjective in the predicate does not always modify the subject. It may modify a direct object, a predicate nominative, or some other word. Such an adjective is not a predicate adjective. It is a predicate adjective only if it modifies the subject.

> These are <u>soft</u> bananas.
>> *Soft* modifies the predicate nominative *bananas*. There is no predicate adjective in this sentence.

Some linking verbs may be used as either linking verbs or action verbs. How can you tell the difference? There are three tests that you can use.

Test 1: *Is the subject performing any action?* If so, the verb is an action verb and not a linking verb.

> We <u>smelled</u> the tulips.
>> (subject performs action; action verb)
> The tulips <u>smelled</u> fragrant.
>> (subject performs no action; linking verb)

In today's lesson we will study predicate adjectives.

Lesson Outline:

1. A predicate adjective comes after a linking verb and modifies the subject of the sentence.

2. The linking verbs include the forms of be and certain other verbs.

> **Forms of *be*:**
>> am, is, are, was, were, be, been, being

> **Verbs of sense:**
>> taste, feel, smell, sound, look, appear

> **Other linking verbs:**
>> grow, seem, stay, become, remain

3. A predicate adjective can be found by using certain steps.

> a. Look for the verb in the sentence. If it is not a linking verb, the sentence has no predicate adjective.

> b. If the verb can be a linking verb, see if it is followed by an adjective that modifies the subject. (Say the adjective before the subject to see if that makes sense.) If the adjective modifies the subject, it is a predicate adjective.

4. Not every adjective in the predicate is a predicate adjective. It is a predicate adjective only if it modifies the subject. It is not a predicate adjective if it modifies a direct object, a predicate nominative, or some other word in the predicate.

5. Some linking verbs may be used as either linking verbs or action verbs. Three tests can be used to tell the difference.

> **Test 1:** *Is the subject performing any action? If so, the verb is an action verb and not a linking verb.*

Test 2: *Can the verb be replaced by a form of* be? If the sentence still makes sense, the verb is a linking verb.

> The painters <u>appeared</u> tired.
>> (*The painters were tired* is sensible; linking verb.)

> The painters <u>appeared</u> today.
>> (*The painters were today* is not sensible; action verb.)

Test 3: *Is the verb followed by an adjective that modifies the subject?* If so, the adjective is a predicate adjective and the verb is a linking verb.

> The man <u>stayed</u> calm.
>> (*Calm man* is sensible; *calm* is a predicate adjective; *stayed* is a linking verb.)

> The man <u>stayed</u> there.
>> (*There man* is not sensible; no predicate adjective; no linking verb.)

A sentence can have more than one adjective in the predicate that modifies the subject. Such a sentence has a compound predicate adjective.

> Loren looked <u>happy</u> and <u>surprised</u>.

Remember that the main verb is the last word in a verb phrase. A form of *be* is a linking verb only if it is the main verb. Otherwise, it is a helping verb.

> The little house <u>has been</u> vacant.
>> *Been* is a linking verb followed by the predicate adjective *vacant*.

> The little house <u>has been standing</u> there for many years.
>> *Been* is a helping verb, not a linking verb.

- A predicate adjective follows a linking verb and modifies the subject of a sentence.

Test 2: *Can the verb be replaced by a form of* be? If the sentence still makes sense, the verb is a linking verb.

Test 3: *Is the verb followed by an adjective that modifies the subject?* If so, the adjective is a predicate adjective and the verb is a linking verb.

6. *A sentence can have more than one adjective in the predicate that modifies the subject.* Such a sentence has a compound predicate adjective.

7. *In a verb phrase, a form of* be *is a linking verb only if it is the main verb.* Otherwise it is a helping verb.

> have <u>been</u> (linking verb)
> <u>is</u> growing (helping verb)

★ **EXTRA PRACTICE**
Worksheet 53 *(Predicate Adjectives)*

Class Practice

A. Find each adjective, and tell whether it is a *predicate* adjective or some *other* adjective.
1. The problems on this page are easy.
2. The tornado damage may be severe.
3. This cardboard is tough.
4. The children were happy with their new sandbox.
5. The tired hikers were cold and hungry.
6. The grass grew tall and straight.

B. Tell whether each underlined word is an *action* verb or a *linking* verb. If it is a linking verb, also give any predicate adjective.
1. The water <u>looked</u> cold and deep.
2. We <u>looked</u> at the new books.
3. The flower soon <u>appeared</u> wilted.
4. The lost dog <u>appeared</u> suddenly.
5. Jonathan <u>became</u> David's friend.
6. Jonathan <u>became</u> upset because of Saul's words.

Written Exercises

A. Copy all the adjectives in these sentences. Write *P* after each predicate adjective.
1. We soon became tired.
2. The dogs on the front lawn sounded noisy.
3. All children should be kind.
4. The old building appeared large.
5. In this dim room, the cloth looks gray.
6. The little girl looked frightened and unhappy.
7. That water should taste cold and fresh.
8. Are you willing and obedient?
9. The old, dark prison cell felt cold.
10. The giants were great and strong.

B. Write *A* or *L* to tell whether each underlined verb is action or linking. Copy all the predicate adjectives.
1. The poplar trees <u>grew</u> quickly.
2. The poplar trees <u>grew</u> large.
3. Did you <u>look</u> at the bananas?
4. Those bananas <u>look</u> green.
5. We <u>tasted</u> the bean soup.

Lesson 90 Answers
Class Practice

A. 1. The—other; this—other; easy—predicate
   2. The—other; tornado—other; severe—predicate
   3. This—other; tough—predicate
   4. The—other; happy—predicate; their—other; new—other
   5. The—other; tired—other; cold—predicate; hungry—predicate
   6. The—other; tall—predicate; straight—predicate

B. 1. linking; cold, deep
   2. action
   3. linking; wilted
   4. action
   5. linking (*Friend* is a predicate nominative.)
   6. linking; upset

Written Exercises

A. 1. tired—P
   2. The; the; front; noisy—P
   3. All; kind—P
   4. The; old; large—P
   5. this; dim; the; gray—P
   6. The; little; frightened—P; unhappy—P
   7. That; cold—P; fresh—P
   8. willing—P; obedient—P
   9. The; old; dark; prison; cold—P
   10. The; great—P; strong—P

B. 1. A
   2. L, large
   3. A
   4. L, green
   5. A

6. The soup <u>tasted</u> spicy.
7. I <u>smelled</u> freshly baked cookies.
8. The room <u>smelled</u> fresh and clean.
9. Jason <u>felt</u> happy with his new bike.
10. Jason <u>felt</u> the smooth paint.

Review Exercises

Copy only the sentences that have direct quotations, and add the missing capital letters and punctuation marks. [77–80]

1. When did you get these peaches asked Sarah.
2. This morning said Mother on my way to the bank.
3. Mother said that we should not eat too many of the peaches.
4. Brian exclaimed they taste better than any I ever had before.
5. Do you like these peaches, which are very firm?

---

91. Diagraming Adjectives, and Using Appositive Adjectives

Adjectives usually come before the nouns they modify. Such an adjective may modify a subject, a direct object, an indirect object, the object of a preposition, or a predicate nominative.

> The <u>ancient</u>, <u>run-down</u> shed gave <u>the</u> <u>black</u> cat <u>a</u> <u>hiding</u> place.
> One of <u>those</u> <u>three</u> calves is <u>Susan's</u> calf.

In the first example above, *The, ancient,* and *run-down* modify the subject *shed; the* and *black* modify the indirect object *cat;* and *a* and *hiding* modify the direct object *place.* In the second example, *those* and *three* modify *calves,* the object of a preposition; and *Susan's* modifies *calf,* a predicate nominative. All these adjectives are diagramed on slanted lines beneath the nouns they modify.

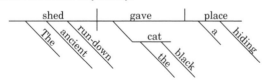

6. L, spicy
7. A
8. L, fresh, clean
9. L, happy
10. A

Review Exercises

1. "When did you get these peaches?" asked Sarah.
2. "This morning," said Mother, "on my way to the bank."
3. (not a direct quotation)
4. Brian exclaimed, "They taste better than any I ever had before!"
5. (not a direct quotation)

Lesson 91

Purpose: (1) To teach diagraming of adjectives. (2) To teach about adjectives in the appositive position.

Oral Review:

1. Adjectives modify what parts of speech? (nouns, pronouns)
2. Give the forms of *be.* (am, is, are, was, were, be, been, being)
3. What verbs other than *be* are sometimes used as linking verbs? (taste, feel, smell, sound, look, appear; grow, seem, stay, become, remain)
4. What is a predicate adjective? (an adjective that follows a linking verb and modifies the subject)
5. Complete this sentence: *An adjective in the predicate is a predicate adjective only if…* (follows a linking verb and modifies the subject)

Written Quiz:

1. Name the parts of speech that an adjective can modify.

   _____   _____

2. What four things can adjectives tell?

   _____   _____

   _____   _____

3. List the three articles. _____ _____ _____
4. A predicate adjective always follows what kind of verb? _____

Quiz Answers:

1. noun, pronoun
2. which, whose, how many, what kind of
3. a, an, the
4. linking

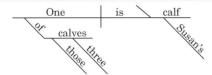

Adjectives may be put in other places in a sentence. For example, an adjective may follow a linking verb and modify the subject. Then it is a predicate adjective.

The pie was <u>tasty</u>.
The fruit punch was <u>cold</u>, <u>sweet</u>, and <u>delicious</u>.

Predicate adjectives are diagramed in the same way as predicate nominatives. A slanted line shows that the adjective in the predicate modifies the subject. If the predicate adjective is compound, the fork comes *after* the slanted line.

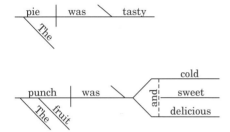

These are the two most common positions of an adjective: before the noun it modifies, and after a linking verb as a predicate adjective. But adjectives in these positions often receive little emphasis. For greater emphasis and better sentence variety, adjectives may also be placed directly after the nouns they modify. Such adjectives are in the *appositive* position. Appositive adjectives usually come in pairs joined by *and*.

Our dog, <u>keen</u> and <u>alert</u>, spotted the small animal.
Compare: Our keen, alert dog spotted the small animal.
(Adjectives receive less emphasis.)

Lesson Introduction: The way that words are arranged in a sentence can help to emphasize certain things. Compare the following sentences. In which one does the phrase *food, clothing, and shelter* receive more emphasis?

Food, clothing, and shelter are our three basic needs.
We have three basic needs: food, clothing, and shelter.

Now consider the following sentences. In which one do the adjectives receive more emphasis?

The tired, hungry children crowded around the table.
The children, tired and hungry, crowded around the table.

In today's lesson we will study adjectives that are used in this way.

Lesson Outline:

1. An adjective usually comes before the noun it modifies. Such an adjective is diagramed on a slanted line beneath the noun it modifies. The noun may be a subject, a direct object, an indirect object, the object of a preposition, or a predicate nominative. (*Teacher:* Adjectives that come before nouns are said to be in the attributive position.)

2. A predicate adjective follows a linking verb and modifies the subject. It is diagramed after a line that slants toward the subject, in the same way as a predicate nominative.

3. An adjective in the appositive position comes directly after the noun it modifies. Such adjectives usually come in pairs joined by *and*.

4. Appositive adjectives are set off by commas. A comma is placed just before the first adjective and right after the second adjective.

Appositive adjectives are set off by commas. A comma is placed just before the first adjective and right after the second adjective.

Adjectives in the appositive position are diagramed below the noun they modify, the same as other adjectives. The conjunction *and* is placed on a dotted line between the two adjectives.

- An adjective usually comes before the noun it modifies, and it is diagramed on a slanted line beneath that noun.

- A predicate adjective follows a linking verb and modifies the subject. It is diagramed on the base line after the verb, with a slanted line between the verb and the predicate adjective.

- Appositive adjectives directly follow the noun they modify. These adjectives usually come in pairs, and they are set off by commas. Appositive adjectives are diagramed on slanted lines beneath the noun they modify, with the conjunction on a dotted line between them.

Class Practice

A. Change each sentence by placing two adjectives in the appositive position. Tell where commas are needed.
   1. The large, white snowman had melted in the sun.
   2. The fresh, cold water quenched our thirst.
   3. Joseph's new, colorful coat was a gift from his father.

B. Diagram these sentences on the chalkboard. You need not diagram the words in italics.
   1. Dates, delicious and nourishing, are fruits *of a palm tree.*
   2. The afternoon treat, creamy and cold, tasted delicious.
   3. The gander is that large goose *under the maple tree.*

---

5. *Adjectives in the appositive position are diagramed below the noun they modify, the same as other adjectives.* The conjunction *and* is placed on a dotted line between the two adjectives.

★ **EXTRA PRACTICE**
   Worksheet 54 *(Diagraming Adjectives and Using Appositive Adjectives)*

Lesson 91 Answers
Class Practice

A. 1. The snowman, large and white, had melted in the sun.
   2. The water, fresh and cold, quenched our thirst.
   3. Joseph's coat, new and colorful, was a gift from his father.

B. 1.

   2.

   3.

C. Read each underlined adjective. Tell whether it comes *before* the noun it modifies, whether it is a *predicate* adjective, or whether it is an *appositive* adjective.

1. A bird, plump and brown, crouched under the evergreen bush.
2. Its eyes were beady and red.

Written Exercises

A. Rewrite each sentence, placing two adjectives in the appositive position. Use commas where they are needed.

1. The small, green fruit turns yellow as it ripens.
2. The tasty, nutritious treat was dates with peanut butter.
3. The Good Samaritan's deed showed pure, sincere love.

B. Copy each underlined adjective. After it, write *B* if it comes before the noun it modifies, *P* if it is a predicate adjective, or *A* if it is an appositive adjective.

1. The trees, well-tended and healthy, produce much fruit.
2. These dates, firm and chewy, taste sweet.
3. The farmer's frightened pigs ruined his new garden.
4. The old fence seemed weak at many places.

C. Diagram these sentences. Do not diagram the words in italics.

1. My dear younger sister drew me a pretty birthday card.
2. The morning sky grew dark and cloudy.
3. We watched the swans, calm and tranquil, *on the pond*.
4. A sudden, furious storm blew *over the plains*.
5. The poor dog, cringing and shivering, could *hardly* stay *on his feet*.

Review Exercises

Diagram these sentences.
1. She is a thoughtful girl.
2. Roses may be red or yellow.
3. Count the peacocks and the swans.
4. The potter made a bowl, but it broke.
5. Did you see that beautiful painting?

3.

4.

5.

C. 1. A—before; plump—appositive; brown—appositive; the—before; evergreen—before
2. Its—before; beady—predicate; red—predicate

Written Exercises

A. 1. The fruit, small and green, turns yellow as it ripens.
2. The treat, tasty and nutritious, was dates with peanut butter.
3. The Good Samaritan's deed showed love, pure and sincere.

B. 1. The—B; well-tended—A; healthy—A; much—B
2. These—B; firm—A; chewy—A; sweet—P
3. The—B; farmer's—B; frightened—B; his—B; new—B
4. The—B; old—B; weak—P; many—B

C. 1.

2.

3.

4.

5.

Review Exercises

1.

2.

92. Using Fresh Adjectives

Adjectives should add meaning and interest to sentences. However, many adjectives fail to do this because they are overused or misused. Here are some examples of overused, worn-out adjectives: *nice, big, great, real, awful,* and *funny.* There are adjectives with fresher, more vivid meanings that make writing clearer and more interesting. Study the following chart.

Overused Adjectives	More Meaningful Adjectives
awful:	dreadful, frightful, shocking, terrifying, horrible, alarming
bad:	harmful, unhealthy, hateful, faulty, evil, ungodly, painful, wrong
big:	huge, mountainous, impressive, bulky, enormous, important, massive
funny:	amusing, humorous, witty, absurd, laughable (Do not write *funny* when you mean *strange* or *unusual.*)
good:	helpful, excellent, profitable, valuable, useful, interesting
great:	huge, heavy, widespread, abundant, deep, extensive, strong, high (Do not write *great* when you mean *wonderful* or *excellent.*)
nice:	pleasant, agreeable, enjoyable, friendly, attractive, appealing
real:	actual, definite, certain, true, genuine, sure (Do not write *real* when you mean *severe* or *extreme.*)

It adds little meaning to call everything *great, real, awful,* or *nice* (or even *awful nice*!). Choose adjectives that describe your meaning more clearly. Learn to use adjectives that have fresh, vivid meanings. But where can you get them?

Lesson 92

Purpose: (1) To teach the need for fresh, vivid adjectives. (2) To show some ways to build vocabulary.

Oral Review:
1. How is an adjective diagramed when it comes before the noun it modifies? (on a slanted line beneath that noun)
2. How is a predicate adjective diagramed? (on the base line after the verb and after a line that slants toward the subject)
3. What are appositive adjectives? (adjectives that come right after the nouns they modify, usually in pairs)
4. What is a possessive noun? (a noun that shows possession or ownership)
5. A possessive noun is often used as what part of speech? (adjective)

Lesson Introduction: Ask the students if they have ever tasted stale bread. Do they like it? Do they prefer freshly baked bread? Why? Stale bread does not have a good taste, because it has lost its freshness.

Did you know that adjectives can become stale? Some adjectives lose their expressiveness just as old bread loses its flavor. This happens when the adjectives are used too often or when they are used with a wrong or unclear meaning. Today we want to learn how to use adjectives in a way that adds meaning and interest to sentences.

Lesson Outline:
1. Some adjectives are so overused that they have lost their freshness. They include words like *nice, big, great, real, awful,* and *funny.* There are adjectives with fresher, more vivid meanings that make writing clearer and more interesting. (See the chart in the lesson.)

Most of your vocabulary comes from what you read. If you do not read, you will not have a rich vocabulary. Pay attention to reading. Textbooks, readers, library books, and periodicals are good places to learn new words. Learn to use the words you are studying in vocabulary and spelling lessons. Notice the many words and phrases that capture your attention.

Do the same when you are listening to others speak. Notice what words they use to express themselves.

Develop the dictionary habit. Find the meanings of new words you meet. Synonym dictionaries are especially helpful.

Learn synonyms and antonyms. Synonyms are words with much the same meaning, such as *wonderful* and *marvelous*. Antonyms are words with opposite meanings, such as *common* and *unique*. Do not stop with learning just one synonym or antonym for a word; learn several if you can.

Try to choose the most suitable adjectives when you speak or write. You should be able to use more adjectives than *great, real, awful,* and *nice.*

- Adjectives with fresh, vivid meanings help to make writing clear and interesting. Textbooks, readers, library books, periodicals, and dictionaries are good helps for learning new words.

- Studying synonyms and antonyms will help to increase one's vocabulary.

Class Practice

A. Replace the underlined words with adjectives that are more descriptive. You may use words from the chart in the lesson.
   1. My wallet is made of <u>real</u> leather.
   2. The apples in that basket are <u>bad</u>.
   3. The drinking water here is <u>bad</u>.
   4. This is a <u>good</u> book on gardening.
   5. The tablet and pen set was a <u>good</u> gift.
   6. I made an <u>awful</u> mistake.

B. Give some synonyms and some antonyms for each adjective.
   1. smooth   2. fast

---

2. *Increasing one's vocabulary is helpful for choosing adjectives with fresh, vivid meanings.*
   a. Take notice of expressive adjectives in textbooks, readers, library books, and periodicals.
   b. Listen carefully for the descriptive words used by interesting speakers.
   c. Study synonyms and antonyms in regular dictionaries and in synonym dictionaries.

★ **EXTRA PRACTICE**
Worksheet 55 *(Original, Fresh Adjectives)*

Lesson 92 Answers
Class Practice
A. (Sample answers.)
   1. genuine, natural
   2. rotten, scabby, wormy
   3. impure, unhealthy, unsavory
   4. helpful, valuable, informative
   5. useful, suitable, appropriate
   6. foolish, costly, embarrassing

B. 1. **Synonyms:** level, sleek, glossy, glassy, polished, unwrinkled
      Antonyms: rough, uneven, coarse, rugged, prickly, lumpy, ribbed
   2. **Synonyms:** swift, rapid, brisk, quick, speedy, flying, fleet
      Antonyms: slow, sluggish, laggard, crawling, unhurried, leisurely

C. Supply fresh, descriptive adjectives to modify these nouns.

Example: children
Answer: noisy, merry, active, energetic, curious, helpful, playful

1. house
2. friend

Written Exercises

A. For each underlined word, write two adjectives that are more descriptive. You may use words from the chart in the lesson.
1. Ronald told some <u>funny</u> stories about his dog.
2. Eating applesauce on cereal seems <u>funny</u> to me.
3. The <u>big</u> stuffed mattresses were hard to move.
4. It looked like a <u>big</u> pile of dishes.
5. The teachers had a <u>big</u> problem to solve.
6. Her grandmother has a <u>nice</u> set of old china.
7. We had a <u>nice</u> school trip.
8. Mary is a <u>nice</u> lady.

B. Write the words that are more descriptive.
1. Yesterday was a (nice, sunny) day.
2. We had (a great, an enjoyable) time playing outside.
3. Last year on this date we had a (severe, real) snowstorm.
4. Sometimes the wind made (funny, strange) wailing sounds.
5. The storm left a (huge, big) drift right in front of our house.
6. We had (a difficult, an awful) time getting out of our driveway.
7. A (good, helpful) neighbor brought his tractor and opened our drive.

C. Write a synonym and an antonym for each of these adjectives. Be sure your answers are also adjectives.
1. curious   4. new
2. pleasant   5. sad
3. excited   6. enough

Review Exercises

Rewrite each expression, using a possessive form. [26]
1. the cart of the oxen   4. the pen of the calves
2. the tail of the ox   5. the game of the boys
3. the ears of the donkey   6. the book of my mother

C. (Sample answers. You may want to read these to your students to show them the possibilities.)
1. enormous, tiny, elegant, attractive, sturdy, symmetrical, magnificent, spacious, spotless, picturesque; dilapidated, run-down, rickety, ramshackle, crooked, rude, crude
2. loyal, helpful, hospitable, warm-hearted, affectionate, agreeable, pleasant, kind, cheerful, courteous, intelligent, quick-witted

Written Exercises

A. (Sample answers.)
1. amusing, humorous
2. odd, strange
3. large, bulky
4. huge, enormous
5. serious, difficult
6. attractive, delicate, fine
7. enjoyable, pleasant
8. agreeable, friendly, neighborly

B. 1. sunny
2. an enjoyable
3. severe
4. strange
5. huge
6. a difficult
7. helpful

C. (Sample answers.)

	Synonyms	**Antonyms**
1.	inquisitive, prying	indifferent, uninterested
2.	agreeable, delightful	unpleasant, disagreeable
3.	thrilled, enthusiastic	calm, bored
4.	fresh, recent, modern	old, ancient, antique
5.	cheerless, joyless, unhappy	happy, joyous, glad
6.	sufficient, adequate, ample	insufficient, inadequate, wanting

Review Exercises

1. the oxen's cart   4. the calves' pen
2. the ox's tail   5. the boys' game
3. the donkey's ears   6. my mother's book

Challenge Exercises

Supply five meaningful adjectives to modify each of these nouns.

1. table
2. toad
3. forest
4. squirrel

---

93. Writing Descriptions: Observing With Your Five Senses

In a description, a writer describes something he has seen, heard, or felt. A good description helps others to experience what the writer has experienced. Study the following paragraph.

> The old cabin drooped in the midmorning sun, heedless of our rare visit. The ancient roof, blackened by sun and rain, still reached from one gable to the other, but it sagged feebly in the center. Its wooden shingles wore a shabby growth of green moss like a patched coat. Much glass had disappeared from the windows, although some remained. A spider had patched one empty place with her flimsy web. The door still hung on one hinge, ready to fall flat in the next fresh breeze or from the push of any schoolboy. The stone walls still stood, but here and there the frost and wind had torn out the plaster from between the stones, leaving cracks large enough to put one's finger into. Close against one wall grew a few gorgeous orange poppies. If they felt sad or lonely, they did not show it. They smiled back at the sun as brilliantly as any poppies would do anywhere.

The paragraph above does not tell a story. It does not show a problem to be solved, nor does it include dialogue. It simply describes a scene.

If writing is to describe well, it must paint colorful pictures in the mind of the reader. A good writer of description must be observant. He depends mostly on his sight, but he also tells what he has heard, tasted, felt, or smelled.

How can you write about sounds? You might describe the noise of a city street—rumbling trucks, honking horns, and screeching brakes. The sounds of animals on a farm may be squealing pigs, quacking ducks, or

Challenge Exercises

(Sample answers.)

1. sturdy, expensive, well-made, oak, maple, kitchen, large, fine, antique, rugged, crude, rickety
2. brown, plump, striped, warty, quick, wet, young, large, small, croaking
3. deep, dark, inviting, cool, dense, tropical, redwood, immense, green, wet
4. sleek, saucy, chattery, pert, brown, red, bushytailed, swift

---

Lesson 93

Purpose: To teach the writing of descriptions based on careful observation.

Oral Review:

1. True or False?
   a. The title of a story should be long enough to give the main facts of the story. (false)
   b. The beginning of a story should arouse the reader's interest. (true)
   c. The middle of a story should describe the conflict. (true)
   d. A story should have dialogue only when it is necessary. (false)
   e. The ending of a story should tell in plain words what lesson the story teaches. (false)
2. In writing directions, what order should you use? (the order things are to be done)

3. In writing directions, what should you be careful to do? (Make sure the information is accurate. Write clearly so that the directions are simple to understand. Use transitional words like *first, second,* and *next.*)

Lesson Introduction: Have you ever gone through a hurricane? Did you ever experience the calm in the eye of a hurricane? Were you ever along to help on a cleanup crew after a hurricane?

Have you ever heard anyone describe what a hurricane is like? Have you ever heard or read a story by someone who was along on cleanup work?

We can learn many interesting and helpful things by reading what others have written about their experiences. Good descriptions help us to learn more about what others have seen. This lesson teaches some things that are helpful in writing good descriptions.

bleating sheep. Perhaps you are describing geese that are migrating. Does their excited honking sound like fifty people at a family reunion all talking at once?

In some cases you may describe how something tastes, smells, or feels. What flavors of candy did Aunt Mary make? Did the piece you sampled taste sweet, spicy, or tart? Did a sweet aroma come from the kitchen, or did it smell as if something had burned? A newly sanded board might feel smooth, while the bark on a tree might feel rough and scratchy. Be sure your five senses are alert as you create the picture. Use vivid, precise words that tell about colors, sounds, shapes, smells, sizes, and flavors.

The description of a cabin uses exact nouns and descriptive verbs. For example, it says *spider* and *poppies,* not just *bug, creature,* or *flowers.* It uses descriptive verbs like *sagged, drooped, torn, patched,* and *disappeared.*

Notice the difference in the following sentences.

Too vague and general:
> The <u>man</u> <u>arose</u> and <u>went</u> to the <u>barn</u> because his <u>animals</u> were <u>making</u> a lot of <u>noise</u>.

Much more descriptive:
> The <u>farmer</u> <u>hopped</u> out of bed and <u>raced</u> to the <u>barn</u> because his <u>pigs</u> were <u>squealing</u>, his <u>calves</u> were <u>bawling</u>, and his <u>turkeys</u> were <u>gobbling</u> in alarm.

The description of a cabin uses fresh, meaningful adjectives. Study the following lists. The first list shows examples from the description above. The second list shows less descriptive ways of writing the same thing.

More Descriptive	Less Descriptive
ancient roof	very old roof
shabby growth of green moss	green stuff
flimsy web	very weak web
fresh breeze	little wind
gorgeous poppies	nice flowers
large cracks	big holes

Remember not to use adjectives like *big, nice,* and *good* when you could use more exact words like *huge, pleasant, valuable, strong,* and *useful.* Use descriptive adjectives with nouns. For example, do not just

Lesson Outline:

1. A description simply describes a scene or a happening. It does not tell a story. It does not have conflict or dialogue.

2. A good description paints colorful pictures in the mind of the reader.

3. A good writer of description is observant and uses his five senses. The sense of sight is used most.

4. A good description uses exact nouns, verbs, and adjectives.

Exact nouns:
  Place: farm, town, city, park
  Worker: farmer, carpenter, plumber
  Plant: maple tree, cornstalk, blackberry bush

Exact verbs:
  Walk: trot, amble, stumble, pace
  Talk: mumble, chatter, encourage, whisper, shout

Exact adjectives:
  Big: huge, gigantic, towering
  Nice: pleasant, friendly, lovely

5. A good description uses spatial order. This is an orderly method of describing things as they are arranged in space. Various methods can be used.

> Begin at the top and move downward, or vice versa.
> Begin at the left and move right, or vice versa.
> Begin at the front and move back, or vice versa.
> Begin at the outside and move to the inside, or vice versa.
> Begin at a near point and move to a distant point, or vice versa.

say *the horse, the pig,* or *the grass* when you could say the *hardworking horse,* the *friendly old horse,* the *greedy little pig,* the *lush green grass,* or the *parched brown grass.*

A description should be arranged in a logical order. Notice the order in the following example, which describes an elephant. It begins with his trunk and ends with his tail.

> Do you know what an elephant looks like? His nose, called a trunk, looks like a large rubber hose hanging from his upper jaw. The tusks at the base of his trunk are like two ivory spears pointing forward, ready to fight any troublemaker. His ears look like huge fans, which he flaps to keep himself cool. The distance from the ground to the top of his back is about the same as from his trunk to his tail. He may be nine or ten feet tall. His back is broad and flat, a perfect place to sit for a ride. His legs, as thick as the trunk of a tree, are supported by round, flat feet. His tail is like a thin rope about three and one-half feet long. An elephant's tail is quite small compared to the rest of his body.

The order used in descriptions is called *spatial order,* or the order of space. Details may be given from top to bottom, from left to right, from front to back, from outside to inside, from near to far, or in the reverse order of any of these. The *kind* of order is not as important as having a *definite* order. Do not be haphazard in description—for example, first describing the trunk of an elephant, then his feet, then his tail, then his tusks, and then his back. Decide what order you will use, and stick to it.

- A good description paints colorful pictures in the mind of the reader.

- A good description uses exact nouns, verbs, and adjectives.

- A good description uses spatial order.

Class Practice

A. Give more exact nouns for the underlined words.
1. The hungry boy could hardly wait to eat the good food that he saw on the table.

Project idea: On the chalkboard, keep a list of striking, picturesque words and expressions from your textbooks or storybooks. Add more as you come across them in your own reading, and encourage the students to extend the list with colorful expressions from their reading. The expressions should stretch your students' imagination, but they must not kill interest by including words that are far above their level.

Lesson 93 Answers
Class Practice
A. (Sample answers.)
1. mashed potatoes, meat loaf, tossed salad, pumpkin pies, ice cream

2. <u>Certain toys</u> in the toy department caught the <u>child's</u> interest.
3. He described the <u>scenery</u> of Guatemala to us.

B. From the list, choose several suitable verbs that are more exact than the verb *went* in each sentence.

slithered	crashed	ambled	plodded
scuttled	sneaked	trotted	charged
crawled	pranced	squirmed	wriggled
stumbled	darted	waddled	scurried

1. The contented brown cow went down the path.
2. The fat old duck went toward the pond.
3. The surprised beetle went into the crack.
4. A shiny, brown-spotted snake went across the rock.
5. The hungry cat went through the tall grass.
6. The friendly white pony went up to the fence.

Written Exercises

A. Write three exact nouns or adjectives that could be used to replace each underlined word.
1. Eugene especially enjoyed watching the playful <u>animals</u> at the zoo.
2. Sister Mary read an <u>interesting</u> book to the class.
3. From the window of the hospital, we watched many <u>vehicles</u> jostling in the busy street below.

B. Write a more exact verb from the list for each underlined verb.

squirmed	soared	sailed	crawled
scurried	wallowed	slithered	bounded
floated	crashed	wriggled	glided
charged	rolled	hopped	

1. A wary rabbit <u>ran</u> across the lawn.
2. A frightened mouse <u>ran</u> under the cupboard.
3. The angry steer <u>went</u> through the fence.
4. A little pink worm <u>moved</u> through the mud.
5. A red-tailed hawk <u>flew</u> over the meadow.
6. The beautiful white swan <u>swam</u> across the water.
7. Two fat hogs <u>were</u> in the mudhole.

2. a. the realistic fire engine, the miniature tow truck, the farm collection, the baking set, the tiny toy oven, the new dictionary game
   b. the boy's, the girl's, John's, Mary's
3. steep mountains and smoking volcanoes, bumpy winding roads, small huts

B. 1. ambled, plodded
   2. waddled, scuttled
   3. scuttled, crawled, wriggled, squirmed, darted
   4. slithered, crawled, wriggled
   5. crawled, sneaked
   6. trotted, ambled, pranced

Written Exercises

A. (Sample answers.)
   1. otters, monkeys, bears, seals
   2. worthwhile, fascinating, exciting, intriguing
   3. cars, trucks, ambulances, taxis, motorcycles, bicycles

B. (Allow reasonable variation.)
   1. hopped, bounded
   2. scurried, wriggled
   3. charged, crashed
   4. slithered, wriggled, squirmed
   5. soared, sailed, floated
   6. glided, floated
   7. wallowed, rolled

C. Write a descriptive paragraph for one of the following. (About one hundred words.)

1. a storm
2. a woodland scene
3. a waterfall
4. a giraffe
5. inside a busy shop
6. inside a barn at milking time
7. a playground during recess
8. a kitchen on baking day

Review Exercises

Write the number of the better set of directions. Be ready to tell in class why it is better. [8, 17]

1. It is not hard to make a new friend if you follow a few simple steps. Introduce yourself to a friend. Of course you must look for a friend first. He may be the stranger who has come to your church. Give him your name and ask for his name. Show an interest in him by asking polite questions. Sooner or later you may hit upon a subject that is interesting to both of you, and you will not find it hard to talk. He may know someone that you know. Ask him about his church and school. Before you know it, you will have made a new friend. Perhaps you know someone with the same last name as his. Ask polite questions about his family. Early in the conversation, make him feel welcome by assuring him that you are glad to meet him.

2. It is not hard to make a new friend if you follow a few simple steps. First, look for a friend. He may be the stranger who has come to your church. Second, introduce yourself to him. Give him your name and ask for his name. Then make him feel welcome by assuring him that you are glad to meet him. Show an interest in him by asking polite questions. Perhaps you know someone with the same last name as his. Or he may know someone that you know. Ask him about his church and school. Ask polite questions about his family. Sooner or later you may hit upon a subject that is interesting to both of you, and you will not find it hard to talk. Before you know it, you will have made a new friend.

C. (Individual work.)

Review Exercises

Set 2 is better. (The steps are given in the order they should be done, and more transition words are used.)

94. Forms of Comparison for Adjectives

God is *great*. He is *greater* than the angels. He is the *greatest* Being of all, for He alone is God.

Most descriptive adjectives have three forms, or degrees, of comparison. In the paragraph above, the adjective *great* is used in all three degrees. *Great* is the *positive degree*. It describes without making a comparison. *Greater,* the *comparative degree,* compares God's greatness with the greatness of angels. *Greatest,* the *superlative degree,* compares His power with the power of all other beings. *Greatest* tells us that God is above all other beings in greatness.

The *positive degree* is the simplest form of an adjective. It is used to describe only one thing. It is not used to compare.

kind	hot	tiny
late	quiet	

The *comparative degree* is used to compare only two things. The comparative degree of one-syllable adjectives and a few two-syllable adjectives is made by adding *-er*. If necessary, double the final consonant or change the *y* to *i* before adding *-er*.

kinder	hotter	tinier
later	quieter	

The *superlative degree* is used to compare more than two things. The superlative degree of one-syllable adjectives and a few two-syllable adjectives is made by adding *-est*. Again, it may be necessary to double the final consonant or change a final *y* to *i* before adding *-est*.

kindest	hottest	tiniest
latest	quietest	

Study the following chart.

Positive	Comparative	Superlative
smooth	smoother	smoothest
glad	gladder	gladdest
busy	busier	busiest

For most adjectives with two or more syllables, the comparative and superlative forms are made by using the words *more* and *most* with the positive degree. This is done because words like *beautifuller* and *frightfullest* would be awkward to pronounce.

Lesson 94

Purpose: To teach the forms of comparison for adjectives, and their correct use.

Oral Review:

1. Why should one be careful about using words like *great, real, awful,* and *nice* in writing? (These are overused adjectives. Adjectives with fresher, more vivid meanings make writing clearer and more interesting.)

2. List some better adjectives for the following overused adjectives.
   a. funny (amusing, absurd, laughable, witty; *not* strange *or* unusual)
   b. nice (pleasant, agreeable, attractive, appealing, enjoyable, fine)
   c. real (actual, true, definite, genuine, certain, sure; *not* severe *or* extreme)

3. How can you become familiar with fresh, vivid adjectives? (by reading and listening; by using a dictionary, especially a synonym dictionary)

4. Name some capitalization rules that you have studied.
   (a. Capitalize the first word of every sentence, every direct quotation, and every line of poetry.
   b. Capitalize every personal name, with its initials and titles.
   c. Capitalize a title when it is used as a name.
   d. Capitalize *I* and *O* when they are used as words.
   e. Use proper capitalization in the heading, the greeting, the closing, and the signature of a letter.
   f. Capitalize a noun or pronoun that refers to God.
   g. Capitalize the names of days and months, but not seasons.
   h. Capitalize the first and last words and all important words in the title of a book, newspaper, magazine, song, story, or poem.
   i. Capitalize a common noun that is part of a proper noun.
   j. Capitalize an abbreviation made from a proper noun or used with a proper noun.
   k. Capitalize a proper adjective.)

Lesson Introduction: Is your grandfather very *old*? Do you know of anyone who is *older* than he? Who is the *oldest* person in your church? Being observant and noticing comparisons makes life interesting. Comparisons also make writing expressive and interesting.

Positive	Comparative	Superlative
wonderful	more wonderful	most wonderful
pleasant	more pleasant	most pleasant
durable	more durable	most durable

One common error when making comparisons is to use the superlative degree when only two things are compared.

Incorrect: Of the two boys, Harold is <u>oldest</u> but Henry is <u>tallest</u>.
Correct: Of the two boys, Harold is <u>older</u> but Henry is <u>taller</u>.

Another error is to use *more* and *most* with the *-er* and *-est* endings to form the comparative and superlative degrees.

Incorrect: Laurel is the <u>more faster</u> worker of the two girls.
Correct: Laurel is the <u>faster</u> worker of the two girls.

Incorrect:
Wednesday was the <u>most pleasantest</u> day of the whole week.
Correct:
Wednesday was the <u>most pleasant</u> day of the whole week.

A few common adjectives have irregular forms.

Positive	Comparative	Superlative
good	better	best
well	better	best
bad	worse	worst
ill	worse	worst
far	farther	farthest
much	more	most
many	more	most
little	less	least

Littler and *littlest* are also correct forms. *Littler* and *littlest* refer to size. *Less* and *least* refer to an amount.

The <u>littlest</u> puppy was sold for the <u>least</u> money.

Use a dictionary whenever you are not sure how to form the comparative and superlative degrees. In most dictionaries, if no forms of comparison are shown, they are formed in the usual way. Add *-er* or *-est* if the adjective has one syllable, and use *more* or *most* if the adjective has two or more syllables.

Lesson Outline:

1. Most descriptive adjectives have three degrees of comparison: positive degree, comparative degree, and superlative degree.

(*Teacher:* Adjectives that describe in an absolute sense do not have degrees of comparison. These include words like *perfect, correct, square, straight,* and *dead.* Instead of saying "more correct," one should say "more nearly correct.")

2. The positive degree is the simplest form. It is used to describe only one thing. It is not used to compare.

3. The comparative degree is used to compare only two things. The comparative degree of one-syllable adjectives and a few two-syllable adjectives is made by adding *-er.* For some adjectives, the final consonant must be doubled or the final *y* changed to *i* before adding *-er.*

4. The superlative degree is used to compare more than two things. The superlative degree of one-syllable adjectives and a few two-syllable adjectives is made by adding *-est.* For some adjectives, a final consonant must be doubled or a final *y* changed to *i* before adding *-est.*

5. For most adjectives with two or more syllables, the comparative and superlative forms are made by using the words **more** *and* **most** *with the positive degree.* Words like *wonderfuller* and *wonderfullest* would be awkward to pronounce.

6. One common error is to use the superlative degree when only two things are compared. Be especially careful with sentences that include the phrase "of the two" or "of the twins."

7. Another error is to use **more** *and* **most** *with the -er and -est endings to form the comparative and superlative degrees.* Expressions like *more better* and *most farthest* are not correct.

8. A few common adjectives have irregular forms of comparison. (See the chart in the lesson. Call attention to the alternate forms for *little.*)

9. A dictionary shows irregular comparative and superlative forms.

★ **EXTRA PRACTICE**
Worksheet 56 *(Forms of Comparison for Adjectives)*

- The positive degree of adjectives is used to describe without comparing.

- The comparative degree is used to compare two things. It is formed by adding -er or by using the word *more*.

- The superlative degree is used to compare more than two things. It is formed by adding -est or by using the word *most*.

- Do not use the superlative degree when only two things are compared. Do not use *more* and *most* with the -er and -est endings.

- Check a dictionary if you are not sure how to form the comparative and superlative degrees of an adjective.

Class Practice

A. Give the comparative and superlative forms of the descriptive adjectives in these sentences.
1. This tree is tall.
2. The little kitten is mine.
3. Irises are delicate flowers.
4. Father's chair is comfortable.
5. Good shoes cost much.
6. The old man raised some large pumpkins.

B. Tell what is wrong in each sentence. Read the sentences correctly.
1. These are the most smallest seeds I have ever seen.
2. James and William are both fast, but William is fastest.
3. Peas are the most early vegetable that we plant.
4. Of the two dogs, Scott is largest and strongest.
5. It was the terriblest sight I ever saw.
6. Alice is usually carefuller than Irene.

Written Exercises

A. Write the correct form of each word in parentheses.
1. We had (little) rain at school than we had at home.
2. Our north field has (many) rocks, but our south field has even (many) rocks.

Lesson 94 Answers
Class Practice
A. 1. taller, tallest
   2. littler, littlest
   3. more delicate, most delicate
   4. more comfortable, most comfortable
   5. better, best; more, most
   6. older, oldest; larger, largest

B. (Corrections are marked.)
1. These are the ~~most~~ smallest seeds I have ever seen.
2. James and William are both fast, but William is <u>faster.</u>
3. Peas are the ~~most~~ <u>earliest</u> vegetable that we plant.
4. Of the two dogs, Scott is <u>larger</u> and <u>stronger.</u>
5. It was the <u>most terrible</u> sight I ever saw.
6. Alice is usually <u>more careful</u> than Irene.

Written Exercises
A. 1. less
   2. many, more

3. Of all the hurricanes in 1992, Hurricane Andrew was the (bad) one.
4. The teacher gave (small) assignments on Bible school nights than on other nights.
5. He is the (tall) twelve-year-old I ever saw!
6. She has a soft voice, but it is (loud) than this at recess.
7. The weather today is (pleasant) than yesterday.
8. The painting of the autumn scene is (beautiful) than the painting of the winter scene.
9. Of the two girls, Maria is the (good) cook.
10. Of the twins, Ronald is (tall).
11. The people of Berea were (noble) than the people of Thessalonica because they put (much) effort into searching the Scriptures.
12. The Word of God is (precious) than silver or gold.

B. Write the positive, comparative, and superlative degrees of these adjectives. Give two sets of answers for number 7.

1. generous	4. rapid	7. little
2. dark	5. bad	8. marvelous
3. far	6. careful	

C. Choose any two adjectives in Part B, and use all three forms in sentences of your own. Underline the words you use. (You should underline six words altogether.)

Review Exercises

Copy and capitalize correctly. [20, 73, 74]

1.   **thanksgiving prayer**
    we thank thee for the morning light,
    for rest and shelter of the night,
    for health and food, for love and friends,
    for everything thy goodness sends.
                    —Author unknown

2. one wednesday in march, i read the poem "o god, our help in ages past," by isaac watts, to my class at lake view school.
3. do you know any poems written by the english poet elizabeth b. browning?
4. Next spring i hope to see mount st. helens in washington.

---

3. worst
4. smaller
5. tallest
6. louder
7. more pleasant
8. more beautiful
9. better
10. taller
11. nobler *or* more noble, more
12. more precious

B. 1. generous, more generous, most generous
2. dark, darker, darkest
3. far, farther, farthest
4. rapid, more rapid, most rapid
5. bad, worse, worst
6. careful, more careful, most careful
7. little, less, least; little, littler, littlest
8. marvelous, more marvelous, most marvelous

C. (Individual sentences.)

Review Exercises

(Corrections are underlined.)

1.   **Thanksgiving Prayer**
    We thank Thee for the morning light,
    For rest and shelter of the night,
    For health and food, for love and friends,
    For everything Thy goodness sends.

2. One Wednesday in March, I read the poem "O God, Our Help in Ages Past," by Isaac Watts, to my class at Lake View School.
3. Do you know any poems written by the English poet Elizabeth B. Browning?
4. Next spring I hope to see Mount St. Helens in Washington.

95. Prepositional Phrases as Adjectives

You have met many single words that are used as adjectives. A *prepositional phrase* can also be used as an adjective. Use the following steps to find a prepositional phrase in a sentence.

1. *Find the preposition.* Most prepositions are small, simple words like the ones listed below.

at	from	near	over	up
by	in	of	to	with
for	like	on	under	

For more prepositions, see the chart on page 508.

2. *Find the object of the preposition.* This is done by saying the preposition and asking *whom* or *what*. The object is always a noun or pronoun.

3. *The prepositional phrase includes all the words from the preposition to its object.* Any words in between are adjectives that modify the object. Not all phrases have adjectives.

   You may come <u>with me</u>.
   We went <u>to a large grocery store</u>.

Not all prepositional phrases are used as adjectives. Some act as adverbs. Compare the following sentences.

   The boy <u>in the car</u> is Thomas. (adjective telling *which* boy)
   The boy sat <u>in the car</u>. (adverb telling *where* he sat)

If a prepositional phrase is used as an adjective, it is called an *adjective phrase*. You can recognize an adjective phrase in three ways.

1. *An adjective phrase always modifies a noun or pronoun.*

   The giant <u>of Gath</u> saw someone <u>with a sling</u>.
   The phrase *of Gath* modifies the noun *giant*.
   The phrase *with a sling* modifies the pronoun *someone*.

2. *An adjective phrase usually tells* which *or* what kind *of about the word it modifies.*

   The boy <u>with red hair</u> is a visitor <u>from another country</u>.
   Which boy is a visitor? The phrase *with red hair* modifies the noun *boy* by telling *which*.

Lesson 95

Purpose: (1) To teach how to identify prepositional phrases used as adjectives. (2) To teach how to diagram adjective phrases.

Oral Review:

1. Tell how the following degrees of adjectives are used to compare.
   a. positive degree (It modifies without comparing.)
   b. comparative degree (It is used to compare only two things.)
   c. superlative degree (It is used to compare more than two things.)
2. Where can irregular forms of comparison be found? (in the dictionary)
3. What is the meaning of *learn*? (to gain knowledge)
4. What is the meaning of *teach*? (to give knowledge or instruction)

5. Give the correct past forms of the following verbs.
   a. tag (tagged, *not* tug)
   b. drag (dragged, *not* drug)
   c. drown (drowned, *not* drownded)
   d. attack (attacked, *not* attackted)
   e. burst (burst, *not* bursted *or* busted)
6. Which verb means "to be able to," *can* or *may*? (can)
7. Which verb means "to rest or recline," *lay* or *lie*? (lie)
8. Which verb means "to get up or go up," *raise* or *rise*? (rise)

Written Quiz:

1. Write the definition of an adjective. _____
   _____
   _____
   _____

What kind of visitor is he? The phrase *from another country* modifies the noun *visitor* by telling *what kind of.*

3. *An adjective phrase must come right after the word it modifies.*

The book <u>on the desk</u> is a gift <u>for my little sister</u>.

> The phrase *on the desk* comes right after *book* and tells *which.*
>
> The phrase *for my little sister* comes right after *gift* and tells *what kind of.*

An adjective phrase is diagramed beneath the noun or pronoun that it modifies. The preposition is diagramed on a slanted line, and its object goes on a horizontal line connected to it. Any adjectives go on slanted lines below the object of the preposition.

An adjective phrase can modify a subject, a direct object, an indirect object, a predicate nominative, or the object of a preposition. Study the following examples.

Adjective phrase modifying a subject:

The pictures <u>of the snowcapped mountains</u> are beautiful.

Adjective phrase modifying a direct object:

My white cat was watching the little birds <u>on the sunny lawn</u>.

2. Write the comparative and superlative forms of these adjectives.

a. good _____ _____
b. ill   _____ _____
c. wonderful _____ _____
d. busy   _____ _____
e. glad   _____ _____

Quiz Answers:

1. An adjective is a word that modifies a noun or pronoun by telling *which, whose, how many,* or *what kind of.* (Allow reasonable variation.)

2. a. better   best
    b. worse   worst
    c. more wonderful   most wonderful
    d. busier   busiest
    e. gladder   gladdest

Lesson Introduction: Suppose it is your birthday and your aunt has a box of beautiful gifts for you to choose from. Which will you choose?

> the large box <u>with shiny green paper</u>
> the small box <u>with sparkly blue paper</u>
> the box <u>with a good book</u>
> the soft package <u>of towels</u>
> the box <u>with pretty writing paper</u>
> the box <u>with a building set</u>

Can you tell which words make up the phrases that describe each *box* or *package* above? (Help students pick out the adjective phrases.) Today we will study adjective phrases like these.

Lesson Outline:

1. A prepositional phrase can be used as an adjective. Such a phrase is an adjective phrase.

2. A prepositional phrase can be found by using certain steps.

> (1) *Find the preposition.* Most prepositions are small, simple words; see the list in the lesson.
>
> (2) *Find the object of the preposition* by saying the preposition and asking *whom* or *what.* The object is always a noun or pronoun.
>
> (3) *The prepositional phrase includes all the words from the preposition to its object.* Any words in between are adjectives that modify the object, but not all prepositional phrases include adjectives.

3. A prepositional phrase used as an adjective can be recognized in three ways.

> (1) *An adjective phrase always modifies a noun or pronoun.*
>
> (2) *An adjective phrase usually tells* which *or* what kind of.
>
> (3) *An adjective phrase comes right after the word it modifies.*

Adjective phrase modifying an indirect object:
Jonathan gave the son <u>of Jesse</u> his sword.

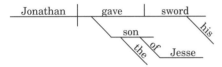

Adjective phrase modifying a predicate nominative:
France is a country <u>in Europe</u>.

Adjective phrase modifying the object of a preposition:
Saul came from the smallest tribe <u>of Israel</u>.

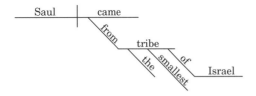

In the last example above, the prepositional phrase *from the smallest tribe* modifies the verb *came.* So this is an adverb phrase, not an adjective phrase. But the phrase *of Israel* modifies the noun *tribe,* so it is an adjective phrase.

- A prepositional phrase may be used as an adjective.

- A prepositional phrase includes a preposition, its object, and any adjectives that modify the object.

- An adjective phrase modifies a noun or pronoun.

---

4. An adjective phrase is diagramed beneath the noun or pronoun that it modifies. The preposition is diagramed on a slanted line, and its object goes on a horizontal line connected to it. Any adjectives go on slanted lines below the object of the preposition.

5. An adjective phrase can modify a subject, a direct object, an indirect object, a predicate nominative, or the object of a preposition.

★ **EXTRA PRACTICE**
Worksheet 57 *(Prepositional Phrases as Adjectives)*

Class Practice

A. Read each adjective phrase. Tell which noun it modifies.
1. That black spot in the sky is a flock of birds.
2. Grandfather gave the boys a bag of nuts on Monday.
3. Noah built an ark of gopher wood.
4. The grass in our yard looked greener after the rain.
5. The manager gave the foreman of the crew some instructions about the work.
6. The little birds in the nest in this tree are robins.
7. The boy with the coat of many colors was Joseph.
8. Hezekiah showed the visitors from Babylon his house of treasures.

B. Diagram sentences 1–5 of Part A at the chalkboard. You do not need to diagram adverb phrases.

C. Use these prepositional phrases as adjectives in sentences of your own. Be sure each one comes after a noun and tells *which* or *what kind of.*
1. by the shallow pool
2. with blue shutters

Written Exercises

A. Copy each adjective phrase, and write the noun it modifies.
1. The bridge over the creek was built by the men from the village.
2. That picture on the desk shows a bird with long yellow legs.
3. The dogs in the back yard would not be quiet last night.
4. One letter from my brother had news about the fierce storm in the West.
5. The man in the garden is my uncle.
6. This is a book about some tornadoes in Indiana.
7. Our song leader was a man from the valley across the mountain.
8. Eve was the mother of all living.
9. The disciples spoke the Word of God with boldness.
10. The second king of Israel was the son of Jesse.
11. We had heavy rains on the second day of school.
12. A stamp belongs in the upper right corner of an envelope.

Written Exercises

A. 1. over the creek—bridge; from the village—men
2. on the desk—picture; with long yellow legs—bird
3. in the back yard—dogs
4. from my brother—letter; about the fierce storm—news; in the West—storm
5. in the garden—man
6. about some tornadoes—book; in Indiana—tornadoes
7. from the valley—man; across the mountain—valley
8. of all living—mother
9. of God—Word
10. of Israel—king; of Jesse—son
11. of school—day
12. of an envelope—corner

Lesson 95 Answers
Class Practice

A. (Be sure to discuss the adverb phrases in these sentences.)
1. in the sky—spot; of birds—flock
2. of nuts—bag (*On Monday* is an adverb phrase that tells *when.*)
3. of gopher wood—ark
4. in our yard—grass (*After the rain* is an adverb phrase that tells *when.*)
5. of the crew—foreman; about the work—instructions
6. in the nest—birds; in this tree—nest
7. with the coat—boy; of many colors—coat
8. from Babylon—visitors; of treasures—house

B. 1.

2.

3.

4.

5.

C. (Sample sentences.)
1. The plump bullfrog by the shallow pool is singing.
2. My grandfather bought the house with blue shutters.

B. Diagram these sentences, including the prepositional phrases.
   1. Grandpa told us a story about his childhood days.
   2. The book with the blue cover is a collection of interesting poems.
   3. The first book on this shelf is a guide on birds.
   4. Six large crates of bananas were unloaded.
   5. Antarctica is the continent at the South Pole.
   6. The booklet at the left end of the shelf is a guide on insects.

C. Use these prepositional phrases as adjectives in sentences of your own. Be sure each one comes after a noun and tells *which* or *what kind of.*
   1. with brown braids
   2. with pink icing
   3. beside the dusty road
   4. across the river

Review Exercises

Write the correct verbs. [47–52]
   1. I might have (drowned, drownded) when I was accidentally (drug, dragged) into the water, but my brother had (taught, learned) me how to swim.
   2. The weather balloon (raised, rose) high into the air before it (burst, busted).
   3. (Let, Leave) me help you (lay, lie) those shelf papers in place.
   4. Brian often (tug, tagged) along with us, and we (let, left) him help us.
   5. We went away and (let, left) the dog in the barn, and he (laid, lay) down in the straw.
   6. (Can, May) I help you (set, sit) the glasses on the table?
   7. Father (raised, rose) the lawn mower blade a little.
   8. The wolf that had (attacked, attackted) the sheep has (laid, lain) in his den all day.
   9. Since Jeremy has been ill, he either (sets, sits) in the easy chair or (lays, lies) in bed.
   10. Grandfather (laid, lay) down his book and listened with interest to my little brother's amusing story.

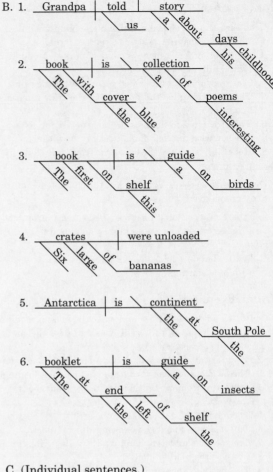

B. 1. Grandpa | told | story

C. (Individual sentences.)

Review Exercises

   1. drowned, dragged, taught
   2. rose, burst
   3. Let, lay
   4. tagged, let
   5. left, lay
   6. May, set
   7. raised
   8. attacked, lain
   9. sits, lies
   10. laid

96. Writing Descriptions: Using Comparisons

You have learned that a description is different from a story. A description does not have conflict or dialogue. Its purpose is to help the reader "see" what the writer has seen. A good description uses exact nouns, descriptive verbs, and fresh adjectives to paint colorful pictures in the mind of the reader. It is arranged in *spatial order,* or the order of space.

Using clear, exact words is not the only way to describe something. Another way is to describe by using comparisons. The sun may be described as setting in the western sky *like a huge orange ball.* We could say that a person was as excited *as a mother bird whose babies are out of the nest* or as uncomfortable *as a wet chicken.* We may say that a boy ran *like a scared rabbit* or worked *like a beaver.*

When we compare two things that really are not alike, and we use the word *like* or *as,* we are using a *simile* (sim′·ə·lē). A simile uses the word *like* or *as* to make an imaginative comparison. The Bible uses many similes. Study the following examples.

> "All flesh is <u>as grass</u>" (1 Peter 1:24).
> "The kingdom of heaven is <u>like to a grain of mustard seed</u>" (Matthew 13:31).
> "And he shall be <u>like a tree planted by the rivers of water</u>" (Psalm 1:3).

A *metaphor* is much like a simile, but it does not use *like* or *as.* A metaphor usually includes a form of *be: am, is, are, was,* or *were.* The following comparisons are metaphors. See how the first one is different from the simile in the paragraph above.

> The sun in the western sky <u>was a huge orange ball.</u>
> The stone walls <u>were soldiers standing erect and impressive.</u>

The comparison in a metaphor is not actually stated, but implied or understood. To say that a mountain *is an old man hovering over the village* or that the trees *were soldiers standing in straight rows* is to use a metaphor. The Bible contains many metaphors, as illustrated by the following examples.

> "The tongue <u>is a fire</u>" (James 3:6).
> "Ye <u>are the light of the world</u>" (Matthew 5:14).
> "Jesus said unto them, I <u>am the bread of life</u>" (John 6:35).

Lesson 96

Purpose: (1) To teach the use of comparisons in descriptions. (2) To teach the use of similes and metaphors. (*Previous experience:* Figurative language, without using the terms *simile* and *metaphor.*)

Oral Review:

1. How is a description different from a story? (A description does not tell a story. It does not show a problem to be solved; neither does it include dialogue. It simply describes a scene.)
2. Which of the five senses is used the most in descriptions? (sight)
3. Give words that are more exact than the following:
   a. building (barn, school, store, skyscraper)
   b. insect (bee, fly, moth, ant)
   c. worker (carpenter, farmer, clerk, nurse)
   d. went (darted, trotted, scampered, hurried)
   e. ran (raced, flew, charged, bounded)
4. Tell what is meant by describing something in spatial order. (describing something by giving details in the order of space, such as from top to bottom, from left to right, from front to back, or from outside to inside)
5. Why should you use more than one reference source when taking notes? (It helps to make your report more informative and interesting.)
6. How should you take notes as you find information? (Write only main ideas and key words.)
7. Why should you write plenty of notes? (It is easier to discard some notes than to go back through the reference books looking for more information.)

Lesson Introduction: Exact nouns, verbs, and adjectives are important in descriptions. But exact

Study the following paragraphs. The second one is much more descriptive because it uses a variety of exact nouns, verbs, and adjectives. It also uses some similes and metaphors.

A kind of fish that can fly lives in some oceans. Other sea animals may cause him to come up out of the water. How does he do it? First, he goes very fast under the water and starts moving up until he gets to the top. Then he goes a short way, he moves his tail, and he rises into the air. He uses his fins like wings by making them go apart, and he uses his tail to go right or left. He can stay in the air for a good while, and he can go a good distance before he comes down again. Then, by moving his tail, he can go right up again! Sometimes a flying fish goes into a boat. Then a person may have him for a meal because all flying fish are good to eat.

*   *   *   *   *

In warm oceans live several species of fish that can fly like model airplanes. Underwater enemies probably cause these fish to propel themselves out of the water. How does a flying fish fly? First, on an underwater runway, he swims upward faster and faster. When he reaches the surface, he skims along for a short distance. Finally with a flip of his powerful tail, he glides into the air. There he spreads his strong fins, which act as the wings of an airplane. His tail is the rudder that turns him to the right or left. His glistening scales shimmer in the sunlight for about one minute; he may travel one hundred fifty to one thousand feet before he hits the surface again. Then with another flip of his tail, he may go for a second cruise! The wind sometimes carries him high above the water. Once in a while, the flight of a flying fish ends on the deck of a boat. Then he may become a fine breakfast for some hungry sailor! All species of flying fish make tasty meals.

Both similes and metaphors are *figures of speech*. Both are imaginative comparisons between things that are really not similar. Not every comparison is a figure of speech. If you say that Charles ran as swiftly as Anthony, that is simply a comparison; it is not a simile.

- Comparisons help to make descriptions meaningful. A simile compares two unlike things by using the word *like* or *as*. A metaphor compares two unlike things by saying one thing is another thing.

---

words cannot always describe something clearly enough. Then it is helpful to describe by using comparisons. Illustrate by reading the following paragraphs to the pupils.

Do you know what an agouti (ə·gü tē) looks like? It is a small, furry animal with rounded ears. It has long legs, which it uses to run swiftly. It has a short tail or no tail at all. Agoutis live in dense forests from Mexico to Peru.

*   *   *   *   *

Do you know what an agouti looks like? It is a furry animal that looks much like a rabbit except that it has small, rounded ears. It has long legs, which it uses to run like a deer. Its tail, if it has one, is short like a rabbit's. Agoutis live in dense forests from Mexico to Peru.

The second paragraph is clearer because it uses comparisons. It tells *how small* an agouti is by comparing it to a rabbit. It tells *how swiftly* an agouti runs by comparing it to a deer. It compares an agouti's tail to a rabbit's tail. These comparisons give a much clearer mental picture of an agouti than is possible by using only the adjectives *small, furry, rounded, long,* and *short*.

In this lesson we will learn more about using comparisons in descriptions.

Lesson Outline:

1. A good description uses colorful, meaningful words to paint pictures in the reader's mind. It is arranged in spatial order, or the order of space. It may also use comparisons.

2. A simile compares two unlike things by using the word **like** *or* **as.**

Several species of <u>fish</u> that can fly <u>like model airplanes</u> live in warm oceans.
There the flying fish spreads his strong <u>fins,</u> which act <u>as the wings of an airplane.</u>

3. A metaphor compares two unlike things by saying one thing is another thing. A metaphor usually includes a form of *be: am, is, are, was,* or *were.*

The tail of the flying fish <u>is the rudder</u> that helps him turn in flight.
The <u>path</u> of the flying fish <u>is an underwater runway.</u>

Class Practice

A. Read the following paragraph. Pick out the descriptive nouns, verbs, and adjectives. Find the similes and the metaphors.

The grassy knoll lay just twenty feet from the peaceful stream, where small trout were breaking through the surface to catch unwary insects. Close by, but out of sight, sat a toad. He was a musician, singing for anyone who cared to listen. A trio of young maple trees was a canopy, shading half the knoll. Beside the stream, a margin of gravel and sand recorded that deer, raccoons, and various birds had been there earlier for a drink. A large black bird, like a guardian soldier, complained nervously that we had advanced too close to his nest. Already the sun was like a blazing torch, flooding us with strong heat and dazzling brightness.

B. Find each figure of speech in these sentences, and tell whether it is a *simile* or a *metaphor.*
1. The men worked like machines, their arms and legs moving in unison.
2. The duck led her little ones carefully over the grass like a school-teacher on a field trip.
3. The pile of cornhusks was a testimony to the hard work of the morning.
4. His Bible was his constant companion.
5. Her heart leaped within her like a terrified animal.

C. Complete the following similes and metaphors with ideas of your own.
1. He seemed to be as strong as . . .
2. The shop was as cluttered as . . .
3. He runs like . . .
4. Wise words are . . .
5. Kind and pleasant words are . . .
6. Words of an unkind talebearer are . . .

D. Tell how you would use spatial order to describe the following things.
1. an old barn
2. a garden
3. a large jet plane
4. a small town

Both similes and metaphors are figures of speech. A figure of speech is an imaginative comparison between two things that are essentially different. It is different from a simple comparison such as *a house like yours,* in which the things compared are actually similar.

(*Teacher:* Not all metaphors are in the form of "this thing equals that thing." In the paragraph about flying fish, for example, the sentence about an underwater runway actually says "on an underwater runway, he swims upward faster and faster." But that expression is true only in a figurative sense, so it is also considered a metaphor.)

★ **EXTRA PRACTICE**
Worksheet 58 (*Exact Words in Descriptions*)

Lesson 96 Answers
Class Practice

A. **Noun–adjective combinations:**
   grassy knoll, peaceful stream, small trout, unwary insects, young maple trees, margin of gravel and sand, large black bird, blazing torch, strong heat, dazzling brightness

Verbs:
   lay, breaking, catch, sat, singing, shading, recorded, complained, advanced, flooding

Similes:
   (bird) like a guardian soldier, (sun) like a blazing torch

Metaphors:
   (toad) was a musician, (trio of trees) was a canopy

B. 1. like machines, simile
   2. like a schoolteacher on a field trip, simile
   3. (pile of cornhusks) was a testimony, metaphor
   4. (Bible) was his constant companion, metaphor
   5. like a terrified animal, simile

C. (Sample answers. Encourage original figures of speech rather than trite expressions like "strong as an ox.")
   1. a man made of steel, an elephant
   2. a junkyard, a bachelor's cabin
   3. a fox, a cheetah
   4. goads (Ecclesiastes 12:11), a man's helper, like guideposts
   5. as a honeycomb (Proverbs 16:24), like a soothing balm, like cold lemonade on a warm day
   6. as wounds (Proverbs 18:8), swords, like briers

D. (Sample answers.)
   1. Begin with the outside from top to bottom: the roof, walls, windows, and doors. Continue with the inside of the upper story from left to right or from near to far. Describe the inside of the lower story in the same way.
   2. Begin with the fence surrounding it, and go to the gate. Tell next about the path through the middle, then describe things on the right side, and finally describe things on the left side.
   3. Begin with the outside from front to back; then describe the passenger compartment from front to back. The cockpit could be described last (as a climax).
   4. If there is only one main street, begin at the north and work toward the south. If there is more than one street, begin at the central square and work outward.

Written Exercises

A. Write whether each proverb contains a *simile* or a *metaphor*.
1. A merry heart doeth good like a medicine.
2. The righteous shall flourish as a branch.
3. The fear of the Lord is a fountain of life.
4. Counsel in the heart of a man is like deep water.
5. Children's children are the crown of old men.
6. The way of the slothful man is as an hedge of thorns.

B. Complete each sentence with a simile or metaphor of your own.
1. The mosquitoes buzzed around us like ...
2. The lone large tree looked like a ...
3. The Bible is a ...
4. The welcome news was like ...
5. The wind was howling like ...

C. Describe one of these things in a paragraph of about one hundred words. Use at least one simile and one metaphor in your paragraph.
1. an old barn
2. a mountain
3. a garden
4. a small town
5. a building site
6. a brisk October night
7. a stray cat or dog
8. a large jet plane
9. any big animal
10. a disorderly bedroom
11. a new snowfall
12. a dismal swamp

Review Exercises

These sentences review making an outline from notes. Write whether each one is *true* or *false*. [53]
1. The first step is to identify the main ideas in your notes.
2. The main ideas from all the reference sources should be grouped together.
3. The main ideas on your outline should be in the same order as you find them in your notes.
4. All the details in your notes should be included on your outline.
5. A good outline helps to give you a sense of direction for writing your report.

Written Exercises

A. 1. simile
2. simile
3. metaphor
4. simile
5. metaphor
6. simile

B. 1. a thousand little helicopters, an army of soldiers with bayonets
2. giant among dwarfs, skyscraper in a small town
3. map, guidebook, lamp, mirror, hammer, fire
4. a soothing balm, a refreshing breeze, a cold drink on a warm summer day
5. a pack of hungry wolves, a jet plane taking off

C. (Individual paragraphs.)

Review Exercises

1. true
2. true
3. false
4. false
5. true

97. Adjective Clauses

In Chapter 1 you learned that a clause is a group of words with a subject and a verb. In Chapter 6 you studied relative clauses, which are introduced by relative pronouns (*who, whom, whose, which, that*). The following sentences contain relative clauses in parentheses. In each sentence, the relative pronoun is in italics, the subject is underlined once, and the verb is underlined twice.

> Jesus welcomed the children (*who* <u>came</u> to Him).
> The man (*whose* <u>son</u> <u>was</u> sick) believed Jesus' words and returned home.
> The table (*that* <u>we</u> <u>bought</u>) looks like a sturdy one.

Relative clauses are also called *adjective clauses* because they modify nouns and pronouns. An adjective clause usually tells *which* or *what kind of.* In the following sentences, the underlined nouns are modified by the adjective clauses in parentheses.

> The <u>table</u> (that we bought) looks like a sturdy one.
> My uncle is the <u>man</u> (who sold it to us).
> We talked with the <u>girl</u> (whom you met in the hospital).

You know that an adjective phrase must come immediately after the word it modifies. The same is true of an adjective clause.

> **Correct:**   The man <u>who was born blind</u> could now see.
> **Incorrect:**   The man could now see <u>who was born blind</u>.

The second sentence is incorrect because the adjective clause is misplaced. The clause should come right after *man* because that is the word it modifies. Otherwise, the sentence is confusing. It sounds as if the man could see which person was born blind!

An adjective clause can modify a subject, an object, or a predicate nominative. It is not hard to tell which word it modifies because the clause comes right after that word. Study the following examples.

> **Adjective clause modifying a subject:**
> The <u>tree</u> (that Zacchaeus climbed) was a sycamore tree.

> **Adjective clause modifying a direct object:**
> Zacchaeus returned the <u>money</u> (that he had wrongfully taken).

Lesson 97

Purpose: To study *adjective clauses. (*Previous experience:* Relative clauses, without using the term *adjective clause.*)

Teacher: Many relative clauses begin with *that* or *which. That* usually introduces a restrictive clause, which restricts the meaning of the antecedent to a specific item and is not set off by commas. *Which* usually introduces a nonrestrictive clause, which gives nonessential information and is set off by commas. Restrictive and nonrestrictive clauses are introduced in grade 7 of this English series.

> **Restrictive:**
> We watered all the trees <u>that we planted yesterday.</u> (The sentence is not even true without the restrictive clause.)

> **Nonrestrictive:**
> We watered all those trees, <u>which we planted yesterday.</u> (*Trees* is already limited by *those.* The relative clause simply gives additional information.)

Which may also introduce a restrictive clause, especially if the antecedent is modified by a descriptive adjective (as in "the young tree which we had planted"). But in general, *that* introduces restrictive clauses, and *which* introduces nonrestrictive clauses.

Oral Review:
1. What parts of speech do adjective phrases modify? (nouns, pronouns)
2. What part of speech begins an adjective phrase? (preposition)
3. Give the nominative case pronouns. (I, you, he, she, it, we, they; *archaic:* thou, ye)

Adjective clause modifying an indirect object:
> Jesus showed <u>Zacchaeus</u> (who was a publican) His great love.

Adjective clause modifying the object of a preposition:
> Zacchaeus came down from the sycamore <u>tree</u> (which he had climbed).

Adjective clause modifying a predicate nominative:
> Zacchaeus was a short <u>man</u> (who climbed a tree).

An adjective clause is called a *dependent clause* because it depends on the rest of the sentence for its meaning. A dependent clause does not make sense if it stands alone as a simple sentence. A clause that does make sense by itself is called an *independent clause*. Study the following example.

> A bat swooped after the <u>rock</u> (that Dan had thrown).
> **Independent clause:**
>> A bat swooped after the rock. (sensible by itself)
> **Dependent clause:**
>> That Dan had thrown. (not sensible by itself)

You have learned about simple and compound sentences. A sentence with only one clause is a *simple sentence,* and a sentence with two independent clauses is a *compound sentence.* If a sentence has one independent clause and one dependent clause, it is a *complex sentence.* The examples below compare simple, compound, and complex sentences.

Simple sentence:
> <u>You</u> <u>should</u> not <u>get</u> too close to a bat.

Compound sentence:
> Bats' <u>teeth</u> <u>are</u> sharp, and some <u>bats</u> <u>carry</u> rabies.

Complex sentence:
> The <u>bat</u> (that <u>we</u> <u>took</u> to school) <u>had</u> a wing span of twelve inches.

The independent clause in a complex sentence can also be called the *main clause.* A main clause can stand alone as a simple sentence.

4. Give the objective case pronouns. (me, you, him, her, it, us, them; *archaic:* thee)
5. Nominative case pronouns can be used as what two sentence parts? (subject, predicate nominative)
6. Objective case pronouns can be used as what three sentence parts? (direct object, indirect object, object of a preposition)

Lesson Introduction: Suppose you are again looking at the packages your aunt brought for your birthday. Now which package do you want?

>> the package <u>that has something from the hard-ware store</u>
>> the package <u>that she got in the toy department</u>
>> the box <u>that smells like chocolate</u>
>> the package <u>which looks like a knitting kit</u>
>> the box <u>which rattles like old coins</u>

Clauses can be used as adjectives, just as phrases can. Can you pick out the clause that modifies the word *box* or *package* in each sentence? Today we will study adjective clauses.

Lesson Outline:

1. Adjective clauses are also called relative clauses because they begin with relative pronouns (who, whom, whose, which, that).

2. An adjective clause comes directly after the word it modifies.

3. An adjective clause can modify a subject, an object, or a predicate nominative.

Adjective clause modifying a subject:
> The <u>bird</u> (that I saw) was a hummingbird.

Adjective clause modifying a direct object:
> We watched the tiny <u>hummingbirds</u>, (which came to the trumpet vine).

Adjective clause modifying an indirect object:
> Grandmother gave <u>Nevin</u>, (who likes bird watching), a book on birds.

- A noun or pronoun may be modified by an adjective clause. An adjective clause is also called a relative clause because it begins with a relative pronoun (*who, whom, whose, which, that*).

- An adjective clause comes directly after the word it modifies.

- A sentence with an adjective clause is a *complex sentence*. A complex sentence contains one *independent clause* (main clause) and one *dependent clause*.

Class Practice

A. First read the dependent clause in each sentence. Then read only the independent (main) clause, and notice that it makes sense by itself.

1. A message from God came to Jonah, who was a prophet.
2. Nineveh, which was a wicked city, was in danger of God's judgment.
3. Jonah tried to flee to Tarshish, which was a faraway place.
4. The prophet was swallowed by a great fish that God had prepared.
5. The people to whom Jonah preached believed his message and repented.
6. Afterward Jonah learned an important lesson from a plant that God caused to grow.

B. Change each underlined word to a relative pronoun, and combine the two clauses into a complex sentence.

Example: I called the dog. <u>It</u> was lying in the lane.
Answer: I called the dog that was lying in the lane.

1. The man came to the door. <u>His</u> car was out of gasoline.
2. Father bought the black calves. He had admired <u>them</u> for some time.
3. The people ate supper at our house. <u>They</u> had visited our school.
4. The boys put on the shirts. My sister had ironed <u>them</u>.

Lesson 97 Answers
Class Practice

A. 1. who was a prophet; A message from God came to Jonah.
   2. which was a wicked city; Nineveh was in danger of God's judgment.
   3. which was a faraway place; Jonah tried to flee to Tarshish.
   4. that God had prepared; The prophet was swallowed by a great fish.
   5. to whom Jonah preached; The people believed his message and repented.
   6. that God caused to grow; Afterward Jonah learned an important lesson from a plant.

B. 1. The man whose car was out of gasoline came to the door.
   2. Father bought the black calves, which he had admired for some time.
   3. The people who had visited our school ate supper at our house.
   4. The boys put on the shirts that my sister had ironed.

Adjective clause modifying the object of a preposition:

I saw a picture of a ruby-throated hummingbird in this <u>book</u>, (which Grandmother gave).

Adjective clause modifying a predicate nominative:

Grandfather was a <u>carpenter</u> (whose work was well liked).

4. A sentence that contains an adjective clause is a **complex sentence.** The adjective clause is a *dependent clause,* and the rest of the sentence is an *independent clause* or a *main clause.*

★ **EXTRA PRACTICE**
Worksheet 59 *(Adjective Clauses)*

Written Exercises

A. Copy each adjective clause. Draw one line under the subject and two lines under the verb, and circle the relative pronoun. (Sometimes you will underline and circle the same word.)
 1. Disciples who worshiped the Lord were found in many cities.
 2. They believed the Word of God, which was preached to them.
 3. Some Christians whom Peter visited were at Lydda.
 4. Lydda, which was near the Great Sea, was the home of Aeneas.
 5. Peter healed Aeneas, who had palsy.
 6. He was a man who had been sick eight years.
 7. The power that healed him came from God.
 8. Many people who saw Aeneas turned to the Lord.

B. Change each underlined word to a relative pronoun. Then combine the two clauses into a complex sentence as in Class Practice, Part B.
 1. The book is ruined. <u>It</u> was left out in the rain.
 2. Frank Meese wrote us a letter. We met <u>him</u> last winter.
 3. The answers are not correct. You wrote <u>them</u> on your paper.
 4. The woman seemed very grateful. We had helped <u>her</u>.

Review Exercises

Write the correct pronouns. [61–64]
 1. (He, Him) and his three friends decided they would not eat the king's meat.
 2. Daniel said to the officer, "Please do not force (we, us) to eat the king's meat."
 3. For ten days the officer gave (they, them) the food they had requested.
 4. At the end of the ten days, Daniel and (they, them) looked healthier than the others.
 5. Soon (he, him) and (they, them) were found to be ten times better than the wisest men in Nebuchadnezzar's kingdom.
 6. (We, Us) boys will do what is right no matter how hard it may seem.
 7. The wisest man was (he, him).
 8. The Lord spoke to (he, him) in a dream.

Written Exercises

A. 1. (who) worshiped the Lord
 2. (which) was preached to them
 3. (whom) Peter visited
 4. (which) was near the Great Sea
 5. (who) had palsy
 6. (who) had been sick eight years
 7. (that) healed him
 8. (who) saw Aeneas

B. (Commas are not required at this point.)
 1. The book that was left out in the rain is ruined.
 2. Frank Meese, whom we met last winter, wrote us a letter.
 3. The answers that you wrote on your paper are not correct.
 4. The woman whom we had helped seemed very grateful.

Review Exercises

 1. He
 2. us
 3. them
 4. they
 5. he, they
 6. We
 7. he
 8. him

98. Diagraming Adjective Clauses

An adjective clause is a relative clause that modifies a noun or pronoun. Such a clause is diagramed below the main clause. A broken line connects the relative pronoun to its antecedent, which is the word that the clause modifies. No word is written on the connecting line; for the relative pronoun is the connecting word, and it also has a function within the relative clause.

I chose the game (that my aunt bought in the toy department).

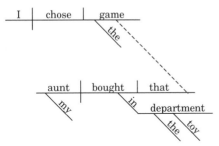

Adjective clauses can modify subjects, objects, or predicate nominatives. Study the following examples.

Adjective clause modifying a subject:

Saul (who had persecuted Christians) was converted.

```
Saul  |  was  |  converted

        who  |  had persecuted  |  Christians
```

7. What does a hyphen mean in a Scripture reference? (It means "through" and indicates a series of connected verses.)

Lesson 98

Purpose: To teach how to diagram sentences with adjective clauses.

Oral Review:

1. What parts of speech do adjective clauses modify? (nouns, pronouns)
2. With what part of speech does an adjective clause usually begin? (relative pronoun)
3. List the relative pronouns. (who, whom, whose, which, that)
4. Where in a sentence must an adjective clause be found? (right after the noun or pronoun it modifies)
5. How are apostrophes used? (to form contractions, possessive nouns, and the plural forms of numbers, letters, signs, and symbols)
6. In what number words must hyphens be used? (in compound number words from twenty-one through ninety-nine)

Written Quiz:

1. What parts of speech do adjectives modify?

   _____

2. What three things do limiting adjectives tell?

   _____

3. What do descriptive adjectives tell?

   _____

4. Underline the correct word: *The articles* a, an, *and the are* (limiting, descriptive) *adjectives.*

5. Match the degrees of comparison to their definitions.

   (1) positive
   (2) comparative
   (3) superlative

   _____ a. It is used to compare only two things.

   _____ b. It modifies without comparing.

   _____ c. It is used to compare more than two things.

Adjective clause modifying a direct object:
The apostles feared the man (who had persecuted them).

Adjective clause modifying a predicate nominative:
Barnabas was the man (who reassured them).

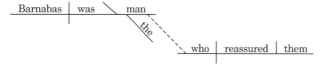

Relative pronouns may have different functions in relative clauses. They may be used as subjects, objects, predicate nominatives, or modifiers.

Subjects: who, which, that (nominative case)
Objects: whom, which, that (objective case)
Modifier: whose (possessive case)

Relative pronoun used as a subject:
This is the man <u>who</u> preached the Gospel boldly.

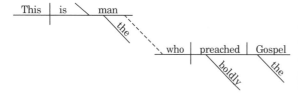

Quiz Answers:
1. nouns, pronouns
2. which, whose, how many
3. what kind of
4. limiting
5. a. (2)   b. (1)   c. (3)

Lesson Introduction: Read the following sentences to the class, and put their diagrams on the chalkboard. Explain that the first one is a simple sentence. The second one is a complex sentence with an adjective clause.

> We bought a children's magazine with colorful nature pictures.
> We bought a children's magazine that had colorful nature pictures.

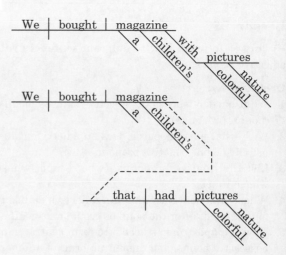

Note: A broken line may be curved if space is limited.

Relative pronoun used as a direct object:

This is the man <u>whom</u> the Lord stopped.

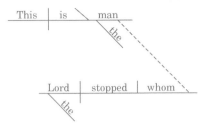

Relative pronoun used as a predicate nominative:

He was not the same man <u>that</u> he had been before.

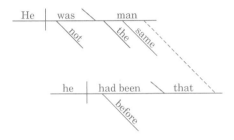

Relative pronoun used as a modifier:

He was a man <u>whose</u> heart had been changed.

Written Exercises *(continued)*

7.

8.

9.

10.

Today we want to learn how to diagram adjective clauses.

Lesson Outline:

1. An adjective clause is diagramed below the main clause. A broken line connects the relative pronoun to its antecedent, which is the word that the clause modifies. No word is written on the connecting line; for the relative pronoun is the connecting word, and it also has a function within the relative clause.

2. An adjective clause can modify a subject, an object, or a predicate nominative.

3. Relative pronouns may have different functions in relative clauses. They may be used as subjects, objects, predicate nominatives, or modifiers.

★ **EXTRA PRACTICE**

Worksheet 60 *(Diagraming Adjective Clauses)*

• An adjective clause is diagramed below the main clause. A broken line connects the relative pronoun to its antecedent, which is the word that the clause modifies.

Class Practice
Diagram the following sentences at the chalkboard.
1. Ananias helped Saul, who was blind.
2. Ananias, who trusted God, encouraged Saul.
3. Saul, who had been a persecutor, became a Christian.
4. Saul was preaching Jesus, whose followers he had joined.
5. The people who heard Saul were amazed.

Written Exercises
Diagram the following sentences. You do not need to diagram the underlined words.
1. Jewish rulers who were angry with Saul placed guards at the city gates.
2. His friends found a basket that was large enough to hold a man.
3. Saul was the man whom the apostles feared.
4. Barnabas was the one who brought Saul to the apostles.
5. The man whose former violence had frightened them was received gladly.
6. In Jerusalem Saul boldly preached Jesus, whom he was serving.
7. The Grecians who hated Saul were plotting against him.
8. Then Saul, who was a native of Tarsus, returned to his home town.
9. The Christians who had been persecuted now had rest.
10. Saul became a man whom the Lord used mightily.

Review Exercises
Copy these sentences, and add the missing commas, apostrophes, hyphens, colons, and semicolons. [81–87]
1. Marie bought them at a self service stand for ninety five cents.
2. The sessions begin at 9 00 A.M. and 2 00 P.M.
3. We memorized Psalm 119 1 8.
4. June made raisin cookies chocolate drops and pinwheels and Lisa made rolls doughnuts and bread.

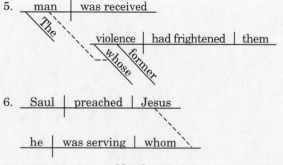

5.

6.

Numbers 7–10 are on page 431.

Review Exercises
(Corrections are underlined.)
1. Marie bought them at a self-service stand for ninety-five cents.
2. The sessions begin at 9:00 A.M. and 2:00 P.M.
3. We memorized Psalm 119:1-8.
4. June made raisin cookies, chocolate drops, and pinwheels; and Lisa made rolls, doughnuts, and bread.

Lesson 98 Answers
Class Practice

1.

2.

3.

4.

5.

Written Exercises

1.

2.

3.

4. Barnabas | was \ one

who | brought | Saul

5. All of Junes cookies were sold before lunch and most of Lisas bread was gone by evening.
6. Isnt her address Route 2 Box 114 Allentown Pennsylvania?

Challenge Exercises

Diagram the following sentences. They include adjective clauses that modify indirect objects and objects of prepositions.

Examples:

The king issued the command to Haman, who had made the suggestion.

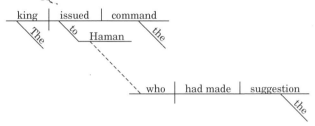

Haman gave Mordecai, whom he despised, a great honor.

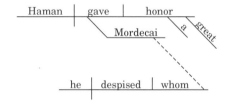

1. Esther made her request to Ahasuerus, who was greatly astonished.
2. The king gave Haman, who had plotted against the Jews, the punishment that he deserved.

5. All of June's cookies were sold before lunch, and most of Lisa's bread was gone by evening.
6. Isn't her address Route 2, Box 114, Allentown, Pennsylvania?

Challenge Exercises

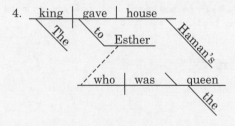

3. Ahasuerus gave Mordecai, who had saved his life, Haman's position.
4. The king gave Haman's house to Esther, who was the queen.

(Numbers 3–4 are on page 433.)

99. Chapter 8 Review

Class Practice

A. Give the definition of an adjective.

B. Tell whether each underlined word is an *adjective* or a *pronoun*. If it is an adjective, tell which word it modifies.
   1. We had <u>our</u> test yesterday.
   2. <u>That</u> was not a hard test.
   3. <u>This</u> question is about the planets.
   4. <u>Theirs</u> lasted about a half hour.

C. Replace the underlined words with more descriptive adjectives.
   1. Many deep-sea fish look <u>funny</u>.
   2. Raising produce is a <u>good</u> work.
   3. Aunt Mary usually makes <u>good</u> meals.
   4. We found some <u>real</u> bargains at the sale.

D. Give the comparative and superlative degrees of these adjectives.
   1. glad   3. ill   5. much
   2. late   4. pleasant   6. good

E. Tell which of the following paragraphs is a description. Discuss the descriptive words it uses.

   1.   Popcorn is easy to raise. To plant it, make rows in loose, rich soil and drop the popcorn kernels three at a place, about six inches apart. Keep the young plants well hoed. Popcorn ears are ready to pick when the husk is dry. After they are picked, let them dry until the kernels shell off easily. Then they are ready to pop.

   2.   Oily black smoke poured upward into the bright blue sky. From under the eaves, orange-red flames darted out eagerly, like angry serpents' tongues. The roaring fire was a savage, snarling giant. Weird, crackling explosions erupted from deep inside the old mill, which shivered and trembled in its agony. Far off in the village, the siren began to scream the alarm—hurry! hurry!

Lesson 99

Purpose: To review the concepts taught in Chapter 8.

Lesson 99 Answers
Class Practice

A. (Wording may vary.)
   An adjective is a word that modifies a noun or pronoun. It tells *which, whose, how many,* or *what kind of.*

B. 1. adjective, test
   2. pronoun
   3. adjective, question
   4. pronoun

C. (Sample answers.)
   1. odd, strange
   2. profitable, beneficial
   3. delicious, tasty
   4. excellent, outstanding

D. 1. gladder, gladdest
   2. later, latest
   3. worse, worst
   4. more pleasant, most pleasant
   5. more, most
   6. better, best

E. Paragraph 2 is a description. (Descriptive words are underlined in the paragraph below. Figurative language is in boldface. The expressions "darted out eagerly" and "shivered and trembled in its agony" are examples of the figurative device known as personification; but they are simply treated as descriptive words at this point.)

   2.   <u>Oily black</u> smoke <u>poured</u> upward into the <u>bright blue</u> sky. From under the eaves, <u>orange-red</u> flames <u>darted</u> out <u>eagerly</u>, **like angry serpents' tongues.** The <u>roaring</u> fire **was a savage, snarling giant.** <u>Weird, crackling explosions erupted</u> from deep inside the <u>old mill,</u> which <u>shivered and trembled in its agony.</u> Far off in the village, the siren began to <u>scream</u> the alarm—<u>hurry! hurry!</u>

Written Exercises

A. Copy all the descriptive adjectives. Write *P* after each predicate adjective and *A* after each appositive adjective.
  1. The hottest, swiftest planet is Mercury.
  2. Of all the planets, Venus is the brightest.
  3. Jupiter, large and bright, orbits the sun once every twelve years.
  4. Saturn with its huge rings appears beautiful.

B. Write the correct form of each word in parentheses.
  1. Uranus is a (large) planet, but Saturn is (large) than Uranus.
  2. Jupiter is the (large) of the eight planets.
  3. Of Saturn and Uranus, Uranus is (far) away from the sun.
  4. Of all the planets, Neptune is the (far) away from the sun.
  5. Sometimes Pluto is (close) to the sun than Neptune is.
  6. Rigel and Betelgeuse are (bright) stars in the constellation of Orion, but Betelgeuse is the (bright) of the two.
  7. Of all the stars, Sirius is the (bright).

Written Exercises

A. 1. hottest; swiftest
  2. brightest—P
  3. large—A; bright—A
  4. huge; beautiful—P

B. 1. large, larger
  2. largest
  3. farther
  4. farthest
  5. closer
  6. bright, brighter
  7. brightest

Saturn

PhotoDisc by Getty Images

C. Copy each adjective phrase. After it, write the noun it modifies.
1. Jacob gave Joseph a coat of many colors.
2. Joseph's brothers tended large flocks of sheep.
3. Soon a caravan of camels and merchants came along.

D. Copy each adjective clause, and underline the relative pronoun.
1. The brothers were jealous of the boy who had a coat of many colors.
2. The dreams which God sent to Joseph had a special meaning.
3. The dreams that made the brothers angry came true in Egypt.
4. The boy whom they hated became a leader in Egypt.
5. The brothers who had sold Joseph repented of their wickedness.

E. Diagram these sentences.
1. The Word of the Lord is pure.
2. Praise the Lord who created all things.
3. The Lord is merciful and gracious.
4. The moon, large and bright, is the ruler of the night.
5. The soft, silvery moonlight brightens the dark night.

F. Write a more descriptive verb to replace *looked* or *looked at* in each sentence.

gazed	peered	viewed	spied
stared	inspected	scanned	beheld

1. Moses sent twelve men, who <u>looked</u> on the land of Canaan for forty days.
2. If anyone <u>looked at</u> the serpent of brass, he lived.
3. Moses <u>looked at</u> the land of Canaan from a mountaintop.
4. John <u>looked</u> into the empty sepulcher.
5. When Jesus ascended, the disciples stood and <u>looked</u> toward heaven.

C. 1. of many colors, coat
2. of sheep, flocks
3. of camels and merchants, caravan

D. 1. <u>who</u> had a coat of many colors
2. <u>which</u> God sent to Joseph
3. <u>that</u> made the brothers angry
4. <u>whom</u> they hated
5. <u>who</u> had sold Joseph

E. 1.

2.

3.

4.

5.

F. (Answers may vary somewhat.)
1. spied
2. beheld
3. viewed
4. peered
5. gazed

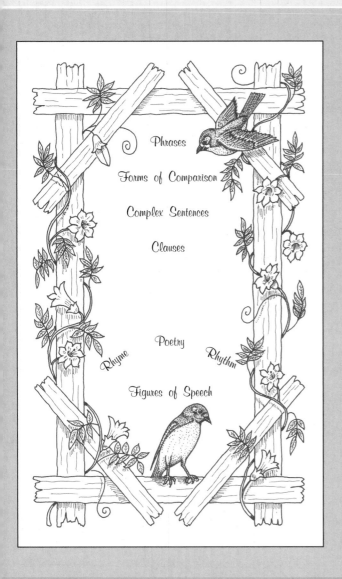

Phrases

Forms of Comparison

Complex Sentences

Clauses

Poetry

Rhyme   Rhythm

Figures of Speech

Chapter Nine

Working With Adverbs

Studying Poetry

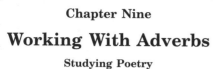

An
adverb is a
word that modifies a verb,
an adjective, or another
adverb.

Oh that men would praise the LORD for his goodness,
and for his wonderful works to the children of men!

Psalm 107:15

100. Poetry

There are two main types of literature: *prose* and *poetry*. Prose is written in sentences and paragraphs. Stories, reports, and descriptions are three examples of prose.

Poetry is writing put into a special form that is pleasing to hear. Poetry is not written in sentences and paragraphs, but in lines and stanzas. Each line of a poem begins with a capital letter. Study the following example.

Who Hath a Book

Who hath a book
   Has friends at hand,
And gold and gear
   At his command;
And rich estates,
   If he but look,
Are held by him
   Who hath a book.

Who hath a book
   Has but to read,
And he may be
   A king, indeed;
His kingdom is
   His inglenook—
All this is his
   Who hath a book.

—Wilbur D. Nesbit

Most poems make use of *rhyme*. Rhyming words have endings that sound alike, such as *right—might, sing—bring,* and *fine—combine.* In the poem above, every other line rhymes: *hand—command; look—book; read—indeed;* and *inglenook—book.*

Most poems also make use of *rhythm.* Rhythm is a regular pattern of accented and unaccented syllables, with a certain number of syllables in each line. In the poem above, each line has four syllables. The first and third syllables are unaccented, and the second and fourth syllables are accented.

    ˇ ′ ˇ ′
    Who hath a book
    ˇ ′ ˇ ′
    Has friends at hand,

Lesson 100

Purpose: To compare poetry with prose, and to promote appreciation for poetry.

Oral Review:

1. What is the purpose of a description? (to paint colorful pictures in the reader's mind by the use of exact words and colorful comparisons)
2. What kind of nouns should be used in descriptions? (exact nouns)
3. Tell which word in each pair is more exact and descriptive.
   a. insect, bee (bee)
   b. fresh, nice (fresh)
   c. went, galloped (galloped)
   d. big, huge (huge)
   e. pleasant, good (pleasant)

4. What is spatial order? (the order of space, as from top to bottom, from left to right, from front to back, or from outside to inside)
5. Tell whether each comparison is a simile or a metaphor.
   a. My dog is a chicken when he sees a skunk. (metaphor)
   b. He sat as still as a statue. (simile)
6. What are the three main parts of a story? (the beginning, the middle, and the ending)
7. What should each part of a story do? (The beginning should arouse the reader's interest. The middle should describe the story conflict. The ending should conclude the story by showing—not telling—the lesson that the story teaches.)

Lesson Introduction: Read the following selections to the students. Ask them which they like better, the paragraph or the poem.

It Couldn't Be Done

Once there was a hard job that needed to be done. Someone said the job was so hard that no one could do it. But just then a very brave and cheerful person came along. He said, "Maybe it can't be done, but I'm not going to say that until I try." He got at the job cheerfully and worked hard. He did not complain; in fact, he even sang as he worked. And sure enough, he did the job that no one thought could be done.

It Couldn't Be Done

Somebody said that it couldn't be done,
   But he with a chuckle replied
That "maybe it couldn't" but he would be one
   Who wouldn't say so till he'd tried.
So he buckled right in with the trace of a grin
   On his face. If he worried, he hid it.
He started to sing as he tackled the thing
   That couldn't be done, and he did it.

—Edgar A. Guest

Rhythm and rhyme work together to produce a certain feeling or mood. The even rhythm of this poem helps to give a feeling of study and thoughtfulness. The short lines add a feeling of happiness or thankfulness.

Poetry usually has more meaning packed into a few words than prose does. Poetry is rich and concentrated. The reader needs to meditate on the words to extract all their meaning and beauty. For example, the poem above says, "Who hath a book has friends at hand." What does this mean? As we read a good story, we live with the characters and share their struggles and their joys. We get to know them so well that they seem like familiar friends. We learn many things from the people in good stories, just as we learn many helpful things from being with good friends.

The poem also says that a person with a book has "gold and gear at his command." How might this be true? Many books have information that is as valuable as gold. If a book explains how to do something, it is as useful as gear (tools or equipment). The poem gives many other hints like this that stir our thinking.

Poetry makes special use of descriptive words and figurative language to stir the reader's imagination. Consider these lines: "And he may be a king, indeed; / His kingdom is his inglenook." Of course, having a book does not actually make the reader a king. What is meant by this figure of speech? If a person reads about a king, he identifies with the king and "rules" with him. Also, an inglenook (reading corner) with a wealth of good books is like a kingdom with a wealth of natural riches— all there for the reader to enjoy. These figures of speech are metaphors. Various kinds of figures of speech may be used in a poem.

Poetry is easier to memorize than prose. A poem can be set to music and sung with a group. The special beauty of poetry can affect our feelings and leave deep, meaningful impressions on us.

- Poetry is a special kind of writing arranged in lines and stanzas. Each line begins with a capital letter.

- Most poetry makes use of rhythm and rhyme.

- Good poetry is rich with meaningful, descriptive words and figurative language.

Today we want to study the difference between poetry and prose, and some things that make poetry beautiful.

Lesson Outline:

1. One main type of literature is prose. Prose is written in sentences and paragraphs. Stories, reports, and descriptions are examples of prose.

2. Another main type of literature is poetry. Poetry is written in lines and stanzas. Every line in a poem is capitalized.

3. Poetry is writing put into a special form that is pleasing to hear. It has a special beauty that affects our feelings. It is more easily memorized than prose. A poem can be set to music and sung with a group.

4. Most poems make use of rhyme. Rhyming words have endings that sound alike, such as *bring—fling, noon—tune,* and *emboss—across.*

5. Most poems also make use of rhythm. Rhythm is a regular pattern of accented and unaccented syllables, with a certain number of syllables in each line. Rhythm and rhyme work together to produce a certain feeling or mood.

6. Good poetry is rich with meaningful, descriptive words and figurative language. Poetry makes special use of descriptive words and figurative language to stir the reader's imagination.

(*Teacher:* When you give the assignment to plan and write a poem, why not write a poem yourself? Be a good example to your class.)

Class Practice

Read the poem below, and do these exercises.

1. Which lines rhyme in each stanza?
2. a. How many syllables are in lines 1, 3, 5, and 7?
   b. How many syllables are in lines 2, 4, 6, and 8?
3. Does each line begin with an accented syllable or an unaccented one?
4. What feelings does this poem give you?
5. This poem describes things according to some of the five senses.
   a. Tell which words describe things you can see.
   b. Tell which phrases describe things you can hear; things you can smell; something you can feel.
6. Find the phrase that speaks of a plant as doing something a person could do. What feeling does this phrase add to the poem?
7. The poet wrote, "I lost them yesterday" and "I cast them all away." What is the difference between *losing* one's worries and *casting* them away?
8. Why is it that "ill thoughts die and good are born" out in the fields?

Out in the Fields With God

The little cares that fretted me,
   I lost them yesterday,
Among the fields, above the sea,
   Among the winds at play;
Among the lowing of the herds,
   The rustling of the trees,
Among the singing of the birds,
   The humming of the bees.

The fears of what may come to pass,
   I cast them all away,
Among the clover-scented grass,
   Among the new-mown hay;
Among the husking of the corn,
   Where drowsy posies nod,
Where ill thoughts die and good are born—
   Out in the fields with God.

—Elizabeth Browning

Lesson 100 Answers
Class Practice

1. lines 1 and 3, 2 and 4, 5 and 7, 6 and 8
2. a. 8 syllables
   b. 6 syllables
3. an unaccented syllable
4. (Sample answers.)
   serious thinking, thankfulness for God's care, appreciation for the beauties of nature, peace
5. a. fields, sea, herds, trees, birds, bees, grass, hay, corn, posies
   b. **Things that can be heard:**
      winds at play
      lowing of the herds
      rustling of the trees
      singing of the birds
      humming of the bees
      Things that can be smelled:
      clover-scented grass
      new-mown hay
      Something that can be felt:
      winds at play
6. drowsy posies nod; It gives a feeling of restfulness and comfort.
7. Losing is unintentional, but casting is deliberate. The two phrases suggest that at first the poet simply forgot her worries as she enjoyed the beauties of God's creation. Then as she considered God's goodness, she deliberately cast her worries away.
8. As we consider the beauties of the great outdoors, "ill thoughts," such as worry, tend to fade away. In their stead are born noble thoughts of God's greatness and goodness.

Written Exercises

A. Read the poem below, and do these exercises.
1. Which words in this poem rhyme? Write them in pairs.
2. a. How many syllables are in the first line of the poem?
   b. How many syllables are in the second line?
   c. Does the whole poem follow this pattern in the number of syllables per line?
3. What feeling does this poem give to you?
4. In your own words, tell the main lesson of this poem.

Mr. Meant-To

Mr. Meant-To has a comrade,
　　And his name is Didn't-Do;
Have you ever chanced to meet them?
　　Did they ever call on you?

These two fellows live together
　　In the house of Never-Win,
And I'm told that it is shadowed
　　By the cloud of Might-Have-Been.
　　　　　　　　—Anonymous

B. Find a poem that you enjoy, and be prepared to read it in class. Your appreciation for this poem should help to prepare you for writing your own poem later in this chapter.

Review Exercises

Answer the following questions. [75, 79]
1. What are the three main parts of a story?
2. Which part of a story should describe the story conflict?
3. Which part should arouse the reader's interest?
4. Which part should conclude the story?
5. What is another term for conversation in a story?
6. In written conversation, when should you begin a new paragraph?

Written Exercises

A. 1. Didn't-Do and you; Never-Win and Might-Have-Been
2. a. 8 syllables
   b. 7 syllables
   c. yes
3. (Sample answers.)
   soberness, sadness, desire to avoid empty intentions
4. (Sample answers.)
   We must not only intend to do good things, but also be sure they get done.
   If we neglect things that we should do, we will lose a blessing.

B. (Individual work. Have pupils read their poems in class.)

Review Exercises

1. the beginning, the middle, and the ending
2. the middle
3. the beginning
4. the ending
5. dialogue
6. each time a different person begins to speak

Adverbs

Adverbs modify verbs, adjectives, and other adverbs.

How	When	Where	To What Degree
well	now	here	very
loudly	yesterday	there	almost
cheerfully	later	in	unusually
fast	soon	out	moderately
silently	usually	away	so
how	when	where	too
briefly	often	around	surely
softly	then	outside	rather
			quite
			partly

101. Adverbs

Adverbs are words that modify verbs, adjectives, and other adverbs. To remember the definition of adverbs, think of this statement: "Adverbs add to verbs." In this lesson you will study adverbs that modify verbs, and in the next lesson you will study adverbs that modify adjectives and adverbs.

Adverbs tell *how, when, where,* and *to what degree.*

They read the Bible stories <u>eagerly</u>.
(*Eagerly* tells *how* they read.)

Will you come <u>tomorrow</u>?
(*Tomorrow* tells *when* you will come.)

We climbed steadily <u>upward</u>.
(*Upward* tells *where* we climbed.)

Lesson 101

Purpose: (1) To define adverbs. (2) To teach that adverbs may be located in a variety of places.

Oral Review:
1. What connecting word joins an adjective clause to the main clause? (a relative pronoun)
2. Where must an adjective clause be placed in a sentence? (right after the noun or pronoun it modifies)
3. Where is an adjective clause diagramed? (beneath the main clause of the sentence)
4. On a sentence diagram, how is an adjective clause joined to the main clause? (by a broken line)
5. Name the eight parts of speech. (noun, pronoun, verb, adjective, adverb, preposition, conjunction, interjection)

Lesson Introduction: Adjectives modify nouns and pronouns. Adverbs do the same thing to verbs. Adverbs add color to our language. Listen to the following sentences with adverbs in them.

<u>Suddenly</u> the volcano spewed <u>out</u> fire, smoke, and lava.
The <u>unusually</u> heavy snowstorm stopped all traffic <u>indefinitely</u>.
We marveled at the <u>delicately</u> beautiful roses and daisies.
Rosa, a third grader, can paint <u>remarkably well</u>.

Learn to recognize adverbs and use them effectively.

Many adverbs end with *-ly*. They are formed by adding *-ly* to adjectives.

quiet—quietly   former—formerly
hasty—hastily   exceeding—exceedingly

The words *not, never, ever, almost, always, hardly, scarcely,* and *seldom* are always adverbs. These adverbs may come between the parts of a verb phrase. But they are not part of the verb phrase; they only modify it.

The cat <u>can</u> **never** <u>climb</u> down easily.
The car <u>had</u> **almost** <u>hit</u> a pole.

The words *how, when, where,* and *why* are also adverbs. These words ask *how, when, where,* and *why* rather than telling. When you answer questions beginning with these adverbs, you often use other adverbs.

<u>How</u> does he write?   He writes <u>well</u>.
<u>When</u> will they come?   They will come <u>tomorrow</u>.
<u>Where</u> are the children?   They are <u>here</u>.

If an adverb modifies a verb, it may be found at different places in a sentence. It may come just before or after the verb. It may come at the beginning of a sentence or at the end. The adverbs in the following sentences are in italics. The verbs they modify are underlined twice.

Harold *always* <u>sits</u> there.
The mower <u>works</u> better now.
Tomorrow we <u>shall work</u> harder.
Overhead, the wind <u>howled</u> fiercely.

An adverb is diagramed on a slanted line beneath the verb it modifies. This is true no matter where the adverb is in the sentence. In a sentence with *cannot*, the word *not* is an adverb and must be diagramed separately. If there is a contraction ending with *n't,* the *n't* is changed to *not* and diagramed separately.

Quietly the children entered the room.

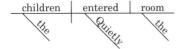

Lesson Outline:

1. Adverbs modify verbs by telling how, when, *and* where.

2. Many adverbs end with -ly. They are formed from adjectives.

3. The words not, never, ever, almost, always, hardly, scarcely, *and* seldom *are adverbs that may interrupt a verb phrase.* They are not part of the verb phrase; they only modify it.

4. The words how, when, where, *and* why *are also adverbs.* They ask *how, when, where,* and *why* rather than telling. When you answer questions beginning with these adverbs, you often use other adverbs.

<u>How</u> does she type? She types <u>swiftly</u>.

5. An adverb may be found at different places in a sentence. It may come just before or after the verb. It may come at the beginning of a sentence or at the end.

6. An adverb is diagramed on a slanted line beneath the verb it modifies. In the word *cannot, not* must be diagramed separately. In a contraction ending with *n't,* the *n't* is changed to *not* and diagramed separately.

★ **EXTRA PRACTICE**
Worksheet 61 *(Adverbs)*

I already saw a robin.

I cannot hear you well.
I can't hear you well.

- Adverbs modify verbs, adjectives, and other adverbs. They tell *how, when, where,* and *to what degree.*

- Many adverbs end with *-ly.*

- The words *not, never, ever, almost, always, hardly, scarcely,* and *seldom* are adverbs that may interrupt a verb phrase.

- An adverb may be found at different places in a sentence.

Class Practice

A. Tell which words are adverbs. Tell whether they tell *how, when,* or *where.* (Negative words like *not* and *hardly* tell *how. Never* tells *when.*)
  1. Come back here again soon.
  2. We should always live peaceably.
  3. We could not go anywhere.
  4. Eagerly the children came inside.
  5. The healed man had never walked before.
  6. Then I could scarcely see.
  7. How are new pencils made?

Lesson 101 Answers
Class Practice
A. 1. back—where; here—where; again—when; soon—when
  2. always—when; peaceably—how
  3. not—how; anywhere—where
  4. Eagerly—how; inside—where
  5. never—when; before—when
  6. Then—when; scarcely—how
  7. How—how

B. Read each sentence, putting the underlined adverb at the beginning of the sentence. Notice that it still modifies the verb.
1. The robin swallowed the worm <u>hungrily</u>.
2. The wild geese were honking <u>loudly</u>.
3. We went to the zoo <u>yesterday</u>.

C. Diagram the following sentences on the chalkboard.
1. I can't find my pen today.
2. The lost pen must surely be somewhere nearby.
3. Where should we work now?

Written Exercises

A. Copy each adverb, and write whether it tells *how, when,* or *where.* (Negative words like *not* and *hardly* tell *how. Never* tells *when.*)
1. Father carefully carried the burning rags outside.
2. We cannot find them anywhere.
3. The Lord will never leave us nor forsake us.
4. Afterward, the men earnestly discussed the matter.
5. Soon we shall be writing faster and better.
6. The settlers originally built the dam here.
7. Promptly, the old dog faithfully followed along.
8. A lazy person seldom works willingly.
9. Immediately the wind pulled the kite upward.
10. Finally the train moved forward again.
11. We could hardly finish the job sooner.

B. Diagram these sentences.
1. Later we shall carefully consider the results.
2. An owl was hooting mournfully nearby.
3. We cannot go there tomorrow.
4. The man patiently waited awhile.
5. I barely saw it there.
6. Why did you leave early?

C. Write four adverbs that tell how students should do their lessons.

D. Write four adverbs that tell when we do our lessons.

Review Exercises

Diagram the following sentences.
1. Do you always give the kittens table scraps?
2. See these lovely, small white snowdrops here!

B. 1. Hungrily the robin swallowed the worm.
2. Loudly the wild geese were honking.
3. Yesterday we went to the zoo.

C. 1.

2.

3.

Written Exercises

A. 1. carefully—how; outside—where
2. not—how; anywhere—where
3. never—when
4. Afterward—when; earnestly—how
5. Soon—when; faster—how; better—how
6. originally—when; here—where
7. Promptly—how or when; faithfully—how; along—where
8. seldom—when; willingly—how
9. Immediately—when; upward—where
10. Finally—when; forward—where; again—when
11. hardly—how; sooner—when

B. 1.

C. (Sample answers.)
diligently, promptly, carefully, neatly, conscientiously

D. (Sample answers.)
immediately, now, later, yesterday, today, tomorrow, then

Review Exercises

1.

2.

3. Rosa's favorite flowers are rhododendrons.

4. The flowers which we saw there yesterday were primroses and zinnias.

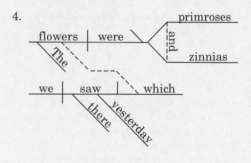

---

102. Adverbs of Degree

You know that "adverbs add to verbs." Adverbs can also modify adjectives and other adverbs. When they are used in this way, they are called *adverbs of degree* because they usually tell *to what degree*. These adverbs include words like *very, so, too, rather, quite, surely, partly, unusually,* and *extremely.*

> Wilbur tore the package open <u>too</u> hastily.
>> *Hastily* modifies *tore* by telling *how. Too* modifies *hastily* by telling *to what degree* Wilbur acted hastily.

> The barrel was <u>practically</u> empty.
>> *Empty* is a predicate adjective modifying *barrel. Practically* tells *to what degree* the barrel was empty.

An adverb of degree comes just before the word it modifies. So whenever you find two modifiers together, you must decide which word each one modifies. You can tell by saying each modifier with the word you think it may modify, and asking, "Is this sensible? Is it what the sentence really means?"

> Plants in the tundra grow <u>incredibly slowly</u>.
>> **Think:** Grow incredibly? No; *incredibly* does not modify *grow.*
>>
>> Grow slowly? Yes; *slowly* is an adverb modifying the verb *grow.*
>>
>> Incredibly slowly? Yes; *incredibly* is an adverb modifying *slowly.*

> Several <u>especially large</u> peaches had ripened.
>> **Think:** Especially peaches? No; *especially* does not modify *peaches.*
>>
>> Large peaches? Yes; *large* is an adjective modifying the noun *peaches.*
>>
>> Especially large? Yes; *especially* is an adverb modifying *large.*

Lesson 102

Purpose: To teach about *adverbs of degree. (*Previous experience:* Adverbs of degree called modifiers of adjectives and other adverbs.)

Oral Review:

1. What are the main things that adverbs tell? (how, when, where)

2. What words do adverbs modify? (verbs, adjectives, other adverbs)

3. What ending do many adverbs have? (*-ly*)

4. What adverbs may interrupt a verb phrase? (not, never, ever, almost, always, hardly, scarcely, seldom)

5. What are some differences between direct quotations and indirect quotations?

    (a. A direct quotation repeats the exact words of a speaker, but an indirect quotation does not.

    b. Quotation marks are used with a direct quotation, but not with an indirect quotation.

    c. The word *that* often comes before an indirect quotation.

    d. Some pronouns and verb forms may be different in an indirect quotation.)

Lesson Introduction: Did you ever consider how useful a pencil is? It can be used to do school lessons, jot down notes, make store lists, calculate math, draw lovely pictures, and do many more things. If there is a good eraser on it, it can be used to make corrections in spelling or math or to improve drawings or sketches. Pencils are sometimes used for unusual things like punching holes, making craft items, or doing science experiments. Who would want to be without a pencil?

Adverbs are also useful in more ways than one. They usually "add to verbs," but they can also modify

Father explained the reason, and we understood <u>fully then</u>.

Think: Understood fully? Yes; *fully* is an adverb modifying the verb *understood*.

Fully then? No; *fully* does not modify *then*.

Understood then? Yes; *then* is an adverb modifying *understood*.

Both adverbs modify the verb. There is no adverb modifying an adjective or another adverb.

Good writers use adverbs of degree sparingly, for these adverbs usually add little meaning to a sentence. This is especially true of adverbs like *very, really, surely,* and *awfully.* You will usually do better if you choose specific nouns, verbs, and adjectives to say exactly what you mean.

Poor: The rich man lived in an <u>awfully big house</u>.
Better: The rich man lived in a <u>mansion</u>.

Poor: Grandmother made a <u>really good</u> dinner.
Better: Grandmother made a <u>delicious</u> dinner.

Poor: The boys <u>ran very fast</u> to Father's truck.
Better: The boys <u>raced</u> to Father's truck.

- Adverbs of degree modify adjectives and other adverbs. They tell *to what degree.*

- Good writers use adverbs of degree sparingly.

Class Practice

A. Find each adverb of degree, tell which word it modifies, and tell what part of speech the modified word is.

1. In 1967, an unusually long train traveled about 150 miles in West Virginia.
2. Moving at twelve miles per hour, the five hundred coal cars and six engines traveled quite slowly.
3. It took twenty minutes for that very long train to pass by.
4. A person could count the cars rather easily.
5. A train that takes so much time to pass has too many cars!

adjectives and other adverbs. Learn how to recognize adverbs that modify adjectives and adverbs and how to use them correctly.

Lesson Outline:

1. Adverbs can modify adjectives and other adverbs. These adverbs are called *adverbs of degree* because they usually tell *to what degree.*

2. An adverb of degree comes just before the word it modifies. Whenever you find two modifiers together, you must decide which word each one modifies. You can tell by saying each modifier with the word you think it may modify, and asking, "Is this sensible? Is it what the sentence really means?"

Lesson 102 Answers
Class Practice

A. 1. Unusually, long, adjective
   2. Quite, slowly, adverb
   3. Very, long, adjective
   4. Rather, easily, adverb
   5. So, much, adjective
      Too, many, adjective

---

3. Good writers use adverbs of degree sparingly. It is usually better to choose specific nouns, verbs, and adjectives to say exactly what we mean. In particular, we must not overuse adverbs like *very, really, surely,* and *awfully.*

★ **EXTRA PRACTICE**
Worksheet 62 *(Adverbs of Degree)*

B. Give an adverb of degree for the blank. How many different ones can you think of?

> The wind was —— cold.

C. Replace the underlined words with more effective ones. Choose from the list below.

immaculate	dashed	rushed	rudely
spotless	scurried	surged	neatly
continually	sped	carelessly	frequently
thoroughly			

1. Loren and Mark <u>ran very fast</u> to the bus.
2. Joseph did his job <u>really badly</u>.
3. He did it <u>quite well</u> after Mother helped him.
4. The floor was <u>surely clean</u>.
5. Janelle visits her grandmother <u>quite often</u>.

Written Exercises

A. Copy each adverb of degree and the word it modifies.
1. Royal Gorge is spanned by an extremely high suspension bridge.
2. The Verrazano-Narrows bridge in New York is sixty feet longer than the very famous Golden Gate Bridge in San Francisco.
3. In winter, Alaskan seals swim amazingly far to warmer seas.
4. The unusually long round trip is about six thousand miles.
5. A Persian poet named Firdausi once wrote a poem with an extremely large number of verses.
6. The Persian sultan quite generously offered one gold piece for every verse that Firdausi wrote.
7. In thirty-five years, the very ambitious poet wrote sixty thousand verses.
8. His poem filled 2,084 pages in nine rather heavy books.
9. This exceptionally long poem, "Book of Kings," was a complete history of Persia.
10. The poet was quite unhappy when the sultan sent him sixty thousand pieces of silver instead of the more valuable gold pieces.
11. He was so upset that he quite foolishly gave away all the silver pieces.
12. Too many people are like this man; they depend almost entirely on earthly things to bring them happiness.

B. (Sample answers.)
extremely, unusually, especially, bitterly, surprisingly, rather, moderately, too, quite, surely, certainly, very

C. (If there is time, discuss the answers shown below and explain why they are better than some of the other choices. A few examples are given.)
1. dashed, sped (*Scurried* suggests running in short steps, as a mouse does. *Rushed* might be acceptable, but *rushed to the bus* sounds awkward.)
2. carelessly (*Rudely* suggests *impolitely.*)
3. neatly, thoroughly
4. immaculate, spotless
5. frequently (*Continually* might suggest that the visits are too frequent.)

Written Exercises

A. 1. extremely, high
2. very, famous
3. amazingly, far
4. unusually, long
5. extremely, large
6. quite, generously
7. very, ambitious
8. rather, heavy
9. exceptionally, long
10. quite, unhappy; more, valuable
11. so, upset; quite, foolishly
12. Too, many; almost, entirely

B. Write an adverb of degree for each blank. Do not use *very, really, surely,* or *awfully.*
1. The work went —— fast.
2. The road seemed —— long.
3. He spoke —— calmly.

C. Write a more effective word from the list to replace each underlined phrase.

pleasant	bulky	worn-out
friendly	immense	briskly
towering	antique	speedy
gigantic		

1. The <u>very big</u> skyscrapers in Malaysia became the world's tallest buildings in 1998.
2. The <u>very old</u> table sold for several hundred dollars.
3. Every morning we walked <u>very fast</u> to school.
4. Mrs. Rogers is a <u>very nice</u> old lady, and I like to visit her.
5. We had a <u>very fast</u> ride on the electric train.

Review Exercises

Copy the three sentences with direct quotations. Use correct capitalization and punctuation. [77–80]
1. how can a dog help a blind person asked mark
2. charles said that a dog is trained before it is given to a blind person
3. susan said the blind person must then be trained to work with the dog
4. each dog said jonathan learns to obey several simple commands
5. some of the commands are *forward, left, right, stop,* and *sit*

————————————

103. Diagraming Adverbs of Degree

Adverbs that modify adjectives or other adverbs are called adverbs of degree. An adverb of degree is diagramed beneath the word it modifies. But before you diagram a modifier, remember to say it with the other word to be sure it makes sense. Study the following examples.

Lesson 103

Purpose: To teach how to diagram adverbs of degree.

Oral Review:

1. Adverbs modify what parts of speech? (verbs, adjectives, other adverbs)
2. What do adverbs tell? (how, when, where, to what degree)
3. What do adverbs usually tell if they modify adjectives or other adverbs? (to what degree)
4. What caution should be taken with adverbs of degree? (Use adverbs of degree sparingly. It is usually better to use exact nouns, verbs, and adjectives.)
5. How can you find fresh, vivid adjectives? (by reading and listening; by using a dictionary, especially a synonym dictionary)

B. (Sample answers.)
1. amazingly, surprisingly, unusually
2. extremely, especially, unbearably
3. quite, rather (Words like *amazingly* and *surprisingly* may be used, but a combination like *surprisingly calmly* sounds awkward.)

C. (Allow reasonable variation.)
1. towering, gigantic, immense
2. antique
3. briskly
4. pleasant, friendly
5. speedy

Review Exercises

(Corrections are underlined.)
1. "<u>H</u>ow can a dog help a blind person<u>?</u>" asked <u>Mark.</u>
2. (indirect quotation)
3. <u>Susan</u> said<u>,</u> "<u>T</u>he blind person must then be trained to work with the dog<u>."</u>
4. "<u>E</u>ach dog<u>,</u>" said <u>J</u>onathan<u>,</u> "<u>l</u>earns to obey several simple commands.<u>"</u>
5. (no quotation)

————————————

6. Name the kind of pronouns in each of the following lists.
   a. I, you, he, she, it, we, they (personal pronouns, nominative case)
   b. my, mine, your, yours, his, her, hers, its, our, ours, their, theirs (personal pronouns, possessive case)
   c. me, you, him, her, it, us, them (personal pronouns, objective case)
   d. this, that, these, those (demonstrative pronouns)
   e. some, any, none, all, few, most, everyone, nobody (indefinite pronouns)
   f. who, whom, whose, which, that (relative pronouns)
   g. who, whom, whose, which, what (interrogative pronouns)
   h. thou, thee, thy, thine, ye (personal pronouns, archaic forms)

Adverb of degree modifying an adjective, which modifies a subject:

A partly finished sketch was found.

> **Think:**   Partly sketch? No; *partly* does not modify *sketch*.
> Finished sketch? Yes; *finished* modifies *sketch*.
> Partly finished? Yes; *partly* modifies *finished*.

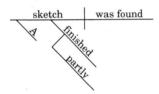

Adverb of degree modifying an adjective, which modifies a direct object:

Grandfather brought an unusually large watermelon.

> **Think:**   Unusually watermelon? No; *unusually* does not
> modify *watermelon*.
> Large watermelon? Yes; *large* modifies *watermelon*.
> Unusually large? Yes; *unusually* modifies *large*.

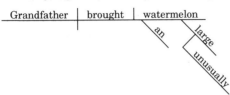

Adverb of degree modifying an adjective, which modifies a predicate nominative:

Your uncle is a rather tall man.

> **Think:**   Uncle is man? Yes; *man* is a predicate nominative.
> Rather man? No; *rather* does not modify *man*.
> Tall man? Yes; *tall* modifies *man*.
> Rather tall? Yes; *rather* modifies *tall*.

Lesson Introduction: What does a carpenter do when he wants to build a house? What do you do when you want to make an apron or a bird feeder? You use a plan or diagram to show how the different pieces fit together. Such diagrams help people to save much effort and get more done in less time.

Sentence diagraming is a way of arranging the words in a sentence so that we can see how they all fit together. It shows the structure and organization of a sentence. In today's lesson you will practice diagraming adverbs of degree.

Lesson Outline:

1. An adverb of degree is diagramed beneath the word it modifies.

2. An adverb of degree can modify an adjective or adverb in different parts of a sentence.

a. Adverb of degree modifying an adjective, which modifies a subject or a direct object

b. Adverb of degree modifying an adjective, which modifies a predicate nominative

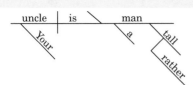

Adverb of degree modifying a predicate adjective:

Beth is feeling quite well again.

Think: Beth is well? Yes; *well* is a predicate adjective.
Feeling quite? No; *quite* does not modify the verb.
Quite well? Yes; *quite* modifies *well*.
Well again? This sounds reasonable, but *again* can
also be moved to another place in the sentence:
Beth is again feeling quite well.
So *again* must be a modifier of the verb.

Adverb of degree modifying another adverb:

The peaches will ripen very soon.

Think: Will ripen very? No; *very* does not modify *will ripen*.
Will ripen soon? Yes; *soon* modifies *will ripen*.
Very soon? Yes; *very* modifies *soon*.

Written Exercises, Part B *(Continued)*

6.

7.

8.

c. Adverb of degree modifying a predicate
adjective

d. Adverb of degree modifying another adverb

★ **EXTRA PRACTICE**
Worksheet 63 *(Diagraming Adverbs of Degree)*

• An adverb of degree is diagramed beneath the word it modifies.

Class Practice

Diagram these sentences at the chalkboard.
1. It is raining unusually fast now.
2. The old lantern was not very bright.
3. That star has a somewhat bluish color.
4. The remarkably short usher cordially greeted the visitors.
5. The little kittens became skilled mousers incredibly soon.

Written Exercises

A. Copy each adverb of degree and the word it modifies.
   1. Yesterday it rained unusually hard.
   2. Solomon was a very rich man.
   3. He was exceedingly wise, but he acted quite foolishly.
   4. It is rather uncertain whether Solomon repented.
   5. Gerald can write especially well.
   6. It is extremely cold at the South Pole.
   7. These partly cooked hamburgers are too raw.
   8. Why did you take them off so soon?
   9. The roses are surely beautiful this year.
   10. Only later, Charles grew seriously interested.

B. Diagram these sentences.
   1. Too many chickens are dying.
   2. How can Joel figure so accurately?
   3. The telephone rang almost immediately.
   4. A skyscraper is a very tall building.
   5. We are almost there now.
   6. It is quite cool today.
   7. A rather tall tree blew over.
   8. The boys left too soon.

Review Exercises

Write the kind of pronoun that each underlined word is: *personal, demonstrative, indefinite, interrogative,* or *relative.* Also write *archaic* for the archaic pronoun. [61–69]
   1. What kind of dog is it?

(Numbers 6–8 are on page 453)

Review Exercises
   1. interrogative

Class Practice

Written Exercises
A. 1. unusually, hard
   2. very, rich
   3. exceedingly, wise; quite, foolishly
   4. rather, uncertain
   5. especially, well
   6. extremely, cold
   7. partly, cooked; too, raw
   8. so, soon
   9. surely, beautiful
   10. Only, later; seriously, interested

B. 1.

   2.

2. <u>That</u> is a German shepherd.
3. The trainers are Mr. May and <u>he</u>.
4. <u>Both</u> are training dogs to help blind people.
5. The person <u>whom</u> you saw was blind from birth.
6. <u>Thou</u> shalt not put a stumbling block before the blind.

---

104. Rhythm in Poetry

Most poems have a regular pattern of accented and unaccented syllables. This is called rhythm. Different patterns of rhythm give different feelings or moods to poetry. Read the following lines. What feeling does the rhythm help to produce?

> Father, in my life's young morning,
> May Thy Word direct my way;
> Let me heed each gracious warning,
> Lest my feet should go astray.

In the poem above, each line begins with an accented syllable and alternates between one accented and one unaccented syllable. This pattern often gives a serious mood to a poem. Notice how the rhythm pattern is well suited to the lines above.

The accented syllables are the most important syllables in the pattern of rhythm. They are used to divide lines of poetry into units called feet. A *foot* of poetry contains one accented syllable and the unaccented syllables associated with it. Usually each line of poetry has the same number of syllables, or at least the lines follow a pattern in the number of syllables they have.

Accents in poetry usually follow the natural pattern of speech. One-syllable words are arranged so that the most important words are accented, and multisyllable words are arranged so that the accents fall on syllables normally accented. Study the four patterns of poetry and the examples given on the next page.

Lesson 104

Purpose: To teach four common varieties of rhythm.

Oral Review:

1. What are some differences between prose and poetry? (Prose is written in sentences and paragraphs; poetry is written in lines and stanzas. Most poetry has rhythm and rhyme, but prose does not. Poetry is usually more descriptive and expressive than prose.)
2. What is rhythm? (a regular pattern of accented and unaccented syllables)
3. How must every line of poetry begin? (with a capital letter)
4. Why do writers and speakers use outlines? (to organize their material)
5. Why do readers and listeners use outlines? (to help them remember what they read or hear)

2. demonstrative
3. personal
4. indefinite
5. relative
6. personal, archaic

6. What does an outline show? (a brief summary of a composition; the contents and organization of the material)

Lesson Introduction: Write the following poem on the chalkboard. Ask the students if they know which syllables are accented and which are not. Mark the syllables of the poem, first using one or two incorrect patterns. Try reading the poem according to wrong patterns, and show that they do not fit. Then show the correct pattern, and read the poem in correct rhythm.

> **The Wind**
> Who has seen the wind?
> Neither I nor you:
> But when the leaves hang trembling,
> The wind is passing through.
>
> Who has seen the wind?
> Neither you nor I:
> But when the trees bow down their heads,
> The wind is passing by.
> —Christina Rossetti

Today we want to study some common patterns of rhythm used in poetry.

The first rhythm pattern below is the *iambic* (ī·am′·bik) pattern. The iambic foot has one *unaccented* syllable followed by one *accented* syllable. This pattern is the most common one used in our language. Its light, cheerful rhythm is well suited to poems with a theme of joy or beauty. Study the following lines.

> ˘ ′ ˘ ′ ˘ ′ ˘ ′
> I wandered lonely as a cloud
> ˘ ′ ˘ ′ ˘ ′ ˘ ′
> That floats on high o'er vales and hills
> ˘ ′ ˘ ′ ˘ ′ ˘ ′
> When all at once I saw a crowd—
> ˘ ′ ˘ ′ ˘ ′ ˘ ′
> A host of golden daffodils.
> —William Wordsworth

The second rhythm pattern is the *trochaic* (trō·kā′·ik) pattern. The trochaic foot has one *accented* syllable followed by one *unaccented* syllable. (Iambic and trochaic patterns are opposite.) Trochaic rhythm is the pattern used in the first example of poetry in the lesson. This pattern is well suited to deep thoughts and sober words. It is also suited to feelings of earnestness and enthusiasm.

> ′ ˘ ′ ˘ ′ ˘ ′
> Courage, brother! Do not stumble,
> ′ ˘ ′ ˘ ′ ˘ ′
> Though thy path be dark as night;
> ′ ˘ ′ ˘ ′ ˘ ′ ˘
> There's a star to guide the humble—
> ′ ˘ ′ ˘ ′ ˘ ′
> Trust in God and do the right.

In the third pattern, each foot has two *unaccented* syllables followed by one *accented* syllable. This pattern gives the lines a light, flowing style.

> ˘ ˘ ′ ˘ ˘ ′ ˘ ˘ ′
> There's a land that is fairer than day,
> ˘ ˘ ′ ˘ ˘ ′ ˘ ˘ ′
> And by faith we can see it afar;
> ˘ ˘ ′ ˘ ˘ ′ ˘ ˘ ′
> For the Father waits over the way
> ˘ ˘ ′ ˘ ˘ ′ ˘ ˘ ′
> To prepare us a dwelling place there.

Lesson Outline:

1. Rhythm patterns give different feelings or moods to poems. Rhythm is a regular pattern of accented and unaccented syllables.

2. Accented syllables are used to divide lines of poetry into units called feet. The accented syllables are the most important syllables in the rhythm pattern.

  a. A foot of poetry contains one accented syllable and the unaccented syllables associated with it.

  b. Usually each line of poetry has the same number of syllables, or at least the lines follow a pattern in the number of syllables they have.

  c. Accents in poetry usually follow the natural pattern of speech. One-syllable words are arranged so that the most important words are accented, and multisyllable words are arranged so that the accents fall on syllables normally accented. (Slight irregularities are common.)

3. In the iambic rhythm pattern, each foot has one unaccented syllable followed by one accented syllable. This is a light, cheerful rhythm. (Iambic rhythm is also known as upbeat rhythm because in beating time, each foot begins with an upward motion of the hand. Note the connection between the mood of upbeat rhythm, and the informal use of *upbeat* to mean "cheerful; optimistic.")

> ˘ ′ ˘ ′ ˘ ′ ˘ ′
> A child should always say what's true,
> ˘ ′ ˘ ′ ˘ ′ ˘ ′
> And speak when he is spoken to,
> And behave mannerly at table;
> At least as far as he is able.
> —Robert Louis Stevenson

4. In the trochaic rhythm pattern, each foot has one accented syllable followed by one unaccented syllable. This rhythm has a heavier, more serious feeling. (Trochaic rhythm is also known as downbeat rhythm because in beating time, each foot begins with a downward motion of the hand.)

In the fourth pattern, each foot has one *accented* syllable followed by two *unaccented* syllables. (The third and fourth patterns are opposite.) The fourth pattern is well suited to a poem with a happy, delightful mood.

> ´ ˘ ˘ ´ ˘ ˘ ´ ˘ ˘ ´
> I am so glad that our Father in heav'n
>   ´ ˘ ˘ ´ ˘ ˘ ´ ˘ ˘ ´
>   Tells of His love in the Book He has giv'n;
> ´ ˘ ˘ ´ ˘ ˘ ˘ ´ ˘ ˘ ´
> Wonderful things in the Bible I see,
>   ´ ˘ ˘ ´ ˘   ˘ ´ ˘ ˘   ´
>   This is the dearest, that Jesus loves me.

A good poet makes careful use of rhythm to produce just the right mood for the message of his poem.

- Different patterns of rhythm give different feelings or moods to poetry.

- In the iambic pattern, each foot has one unaccented syllable followed by one accented syllable.

- In the trochaic pattern, each foot has one accented syllable followed by one unaccented syllable.

- In the third rhythm pattern, each foot has two unaccented syllables followed by one accented syllable.

- In the fourth rhythm pattern, each foot has one accented syllable followed by two unaccented syllables.

Class Practice

A. Tell what pattern of rhythm is used in each poem.

  1.   **What Bird Am I?**
      Largest of earth's birds am I,
        I have wings but cannot fly;
      To escape I run with speed,
        Sometimes swifter than a steed.

> ´ ˘ ´ ˘ ´ ˘ ´ ˘
> Children, do you love each other?
>   ´ ˘ ´ ˘ ´ ˘ ´
>   Are you always kind and true?
> Do you always do to others
>   As you'd have them do to you?

In lines 2 and 4, the last foot has only an accented syllable.

5. *The third rhythm pattern has two* unaccented *syllables followed by one* accented *syllable.* (*Teacher:* This is the anapestic pattern.)

> ˘ ˘ ´ ˘ ˘ ´ ˘ ˘ ´ ˘ ˘ ´
> Oh, the katydid says it as plain as can be,
> ˘ ˘ ´ ˘ ˘ ´ ˘ ˘ ´ ˘ ˘ ´
> And the crickets are singing it under the tree;
> In the aster's blue eyes you may read the same hint,
> Just as clearly as if you had seen it in print;
> And the corn sighs it, too, as it waves in the sun:
> That autumn is here, and that summer is done.
>   —Persis Gardiner

Lesson 104 Answers
Class Practice
A. 1. trochaic (This bird is the ostrich.)

---

  6. *The fourth rhythm pattern has one* accented ***syllable followed by two*** unaccented ***syllables.*** (*Teacher:* This is the dactylic pattern.)

> ´ ˘ ˘ ´ ˘ ˘   ´ ˘ ´
> Back of the loaf is the snowy flour,
> ˘   ´ ˘ ˘ ´ ˘ ´ ˘
> And back of the flour the mill,
> And back of the mill is the wheat and the shower,
> And the sun and the Father's will.
>   —Maltbie D. Babcock

The rhythm in this stanza has a number of irregularities.

★ EXTRA PRACTICE
Worksheet 64 *(Rhythm in Poetry)*

2.   **What Bird Am I?**
I am an early riser,
My call is loud and clear;
When Jesus was on trial,
I must have been quite near.

3.   **What Bird Am I?**
Harmless and gentle, the symbol of peace,
Used by the poor for their firstborn's release;
Jesus once said that His servants should be
Wise as the serpents and harmless as we.

4.   **With Your Might**
If you do with your might what your hand finds to do,
You will find work a pleasure and soon you'll be through;
If you murmur and whine and find ways to delay,
Not a thing will get done and you'll spoil the whole day.

B. On the chalkboard, mark the rhythm pattern of each line. Then tell
which line fits best for the last line of each poem.

1.   **A Snowfall**
When I awoke this morning,
   The sun was very bright.
I hurried to the window,
   Unconscious of the sight
That held my breath in rapture—

—————————————————
—Velma Orcutt

a. How white was everything in sight.
b. The secret of the night.
c. Snow had fallen in the night.

2.   **Diligence**
Do each task with diligence,
   Whether large or small;
What seems insignificant

—————————————————

a. May be the best job of all.
b. The best job may be of all.
c. May be best of all.

2. iambic (This bird is the rooster.)
3. fourth pattern (dactylic) (This bird is the dove.)
4. third pattern (anapestic)

B. 1. b (Mark lines with iambic pattern.)
   2. c (Mark lines with trochaic pattern.)

Written Exercises

A. Write the letter of the line that fits best for the last line of each stanza. Then copy the first line of the stanza, and mark the rhythm pattern.

1. There dwelt a miller, hale and bold,
    Beside the River Dee;
  He wrought and sang from morn till night,

    _____

    a. No other man as blithe as he.
    b. No lark more blithe than he.
    c. No one was as blithe as he.

2. Toiling through the changing seasons
    In the sunshine and the rain,
  Earnest prayer and faithful labor

    _____

    a. Yield a harvest of golden grain.
    b. Provide a wealth of golden grain.
    c. Yield a wealth of golden grain.

3. God gives the milk, but not the pail.
  God gives the wood, but not the nail.
  God gives the fish, but not the hook.
  God gives the food, but not the cook.
  He gives each one a task to do,

    _____

    a. And then the rest is up to you.
    b. All of the rest is dependent on you.
    c. All the rest is up to you.

4. One honest John Thompkins, a hedger and ditcher,
  Although he was poor, did not wish to be richer;
  For all such vain wishes in him were prevented

    _____

    a. Because he was always contented.
    b. He had a habit of being contented.
    c. By means of the habit of being contented.

Written Exercises

A. 1. b; There dwelt a miller, hale and bold,

2. c; Toiling through the changing seasons

3. a; God gives the milk, but not the pail.

4. c; One honest John Thompkins, a hedger and ditcher,

B. Name the rhythm pattern of each pair of lines (*iambic* or *trochaic*). Then write a line of your own to match that rhythm. Your line does not have to rhyme with the lines that are given. (This practice will be helpful when you write an original poem later in this chapter.)

1. God sent sparkling snow last night,
   Clean and spotless, pure and white . . .

2. My mother is so kind and true,
   She loves to help in all I do . . .

3. Spring is here, with March winds blowing,
   Bluebirds singing, flowers growing . . .

Review Exercises

Copy one wrong word in each sentence, and write the correct word beside it. [33]

1. Some outlines must have titles.
2. The main topics of an outline are marked with Arabic numerals.
3. Subtopics are marked with small letters.
4. Points are marked with Roman numerals.
5. A comma is placed after each numeral or capital letter that marks a division on the outline.
6. Each division of an outline should have at least three parts.

B. (Sample matching lines are given.)
1. trochaic; Oh, it's such a lovely sight.
2. iambic; She gives me cheer the whole day through.
3. trochaic; Raindrops falling, brooklets flowing.

Review Exercises
1. Some, All
2. Arabic, Roman
3. small, capital
4. Roman, Arabic
5. comma, period
6. three, two

105. Forms of Comparison for Adverbs

Adverbs have three degrees of comparison, the same as adjectives. They are the positive degree, the comparative degree, and the superlative degree.

Positive	Comparative	Superlative
fast	faster	fastest
swiftly	more swiftly	most swiftly

The positive degree shows no comparison. The comparative degree is used to compare *two* actions. The superlative degree is used to compare *more than two* actions.

Lesson 105

Purpose: To teach the forms of comparison for adverbs and their correct use.

Oral Review:

1. What is an adverb called if it modifies an adjective or another adverb? (adverb of degree)
2. Where is an adverb of degree diagramed? (beneath the word it modifies)
3. With what part of speech does an adjective clause usually begin? (relative pronoun)
4. List the relative pronouns. (who, whom, whose, which, that)
5. Where is an adjective clause diagramed? (beneath the main clause, with a broken line joining the relative pronoun to its antecedent)
6. Where in a sentence must an adjective clause be found? (right after the noun or pronoun it modifies)

Lesson Introduction: Have you ever been *far* away from home? What is the *farthest* you have ever gone? Would you like to go *farther*? How *high* have you ever climbed? Where have you climbed the *highest*? Have you been to the *lowest* spot in the United States? Is it *lower* than the area around the Dead Sea in Palestine? Have you ever gone *deep* into the water? What is the *deepest* you have ever been? Would you like to go *deeper*?

These questions contain forms of comparison for adverbs (and adjectives). In this lesson we will study the correct use of adverbs that compare.

Lesson Outline:

1. Adverbs have three degrees of comparison: the positive degree, the comparative degree, and the superlative degree.

2. The positive degree shows no comparison.

soon   carefully

For some short adverbs, the comparative and superlative degrees are formed by adding *-er* and *-est*.

Positive	Comparative	Superlative
deep	deeper	deepest
late	later	latest
high	higher	highest

But many adverbs end with *-ly*. For this reason, *more* and *most* are used to form the comparative and superlative degrees of most adverbs. The suffixes *-er* and *-est* are not used with many adverbs because words like *slowlier* and *carefulliest* would sound awkward. Check a dictionary if you are not sure whether *-er* and *-est* may be added.

Positive	Comparative	Superlative
slowly	more slowly	most slowly
carefully	more carefully	most carefully
easily	more easily	most easily
loudly	more loudly	most loudly

Exceptions:

early	earlier	earliest
lively	livelier	liveliest

Be careful to use the correct degree of comparison. Use the comparative degree for comparing two actions. Use the superlative degree for comparing more than two actions.

Incorrect: Of the two machines, this one runs <u>most slowly</u>.
Correct: Of the two machines, this one runs <u>more slowly</u>.

Incorrect: Roger runs the <u>fastest</u> of my two brothers.
Correct: Roger runs the <u>faster</u> of my two brothers.

Do not add *-er* to an adverb and also use *more* with it, or add *-est* and also use *most* with it.

Incorrect: Brian went <u>more farther</u> than Marcus did.
Correct: Brian went <u>farther</u> than Marcus did.

Some adverbs have irregular forms of comparison. Check a dictionary if you are not sure how to form the comparative and superlative degrees of an adverb.

3. *The comparative degree is used to compare only two actions.* It is formed by adding *-er* or by using the word *more*.

    sooner   more carefully

4. *The superlative degree is used to compare more than two actions.* It is formed by adding *-est* or by using the word *most*.

    soonest   most carefully

5. *Do not add the suffix* -er *or* -est *to most adverbs that end with* -ly.

    not "carefullier" *or* "carefulliest"
    Exceptions: earlier, earliest
                livelier, liveliest

6. *Be careful to use the correct degree of comparison.* The most common error is to use the superlative degree for comparing two things. Note especially sentences with the words like "of the two" or "of the twins."

**7. *Do not add* -er *to an adverb and also use* more *with it, or add* -est *and also use* most *with it.*

    not "more sooner" *or* "most soonest"
    not "more earlier" *or* "most earliest"

8. *Some adverbs have irregular forms of comparison.* Check a dictionary if you are not sure how to form the comparative and superlative degrees of an adverb.

Positive	Comparative	Superlative
well	better	best
badly	worse	worst
ill	worse	worst
little	less	least
much	more	most
far	farther	farthest

Positive	Comparative	Superlative
well	better	best
badly	worse	worst
ill	worse	worst
little	less	least
much	more	most
far	farther	farthest

Some words in the list above can be used as adjectives or adverbs. Their use in a sentence determines what part of speech they are.

- The positive degree of adverbs expresses no comparison.

- The comparative degree is used to compare two actions. It is formed by adding -er or by using the word *more*.

- The superlative degree is used to compare more than two actions. It is formed by adding -est or by using the word *most*.

- Do not use the superlative degree when only two actions are compared. Do not use *more* and *most* with the -er and -est endings.

- Check a dictionary if you are not sure how to form the comparative and superlative degrees of an adverb.

Class Practice

A. Give the comparative and superlative degrees of these adverbs.
   1. swiftly   3. soon   5. happily
   2. well   4. slowly   6. high

B. Tell how to correct the following sentences. Practice reading each one correctly.
   1. Of the twins, Marjorie works fastest.
   2. This pony walks slowlier than that one.
   3. She sings more softlier than her sister.
   4. The smallest boy talked the most loudliest of all.
   5. Brenda spoke the politeliest of all the girls.
   6. This cake pan should be floured the most lightly of the two.
   7. Which bakes most quickly, an oatmeal cake or a carrot cake?
   8. The peanut butter cookies baked the quickliest of all.

★ **EXTRA PRACTICE**
   Worksheet 65 *(Forms of Comparison for Adverbs)*

Lesson 105 Answers
Class Practice
A. 1. more swiftly, most swiftly
   2. better, best
   3. sooner, soonest
   4. more slowly, most slowly
   5. more happily, most happily
   6. higher, highest

B. (Corrections are underlined.)
   1. Of the twins, Marjorie works faster.
   2. This pony walks more slowly than that one.
   3. She sings more softly than her sister.
   4. The smallest boy talked the most loudly of all.
   5. Brenda spoke the most politely of all the girls.
   6. This cake pan should be floured the more lightly of the two.
   7. Which bakes more quickly, an oatmeal cake or a carrot cake?
   8. The peanut butter cookies baked the most quickly of all.

Written Exercises

A. Write the three degrees of comparison for each adverb.

1. warmly	5. ill	9. abundantly	13. perfectly
2. much	6. often	10. interestingly	14. little
3. hard	7. well	11. naturally	15. tenderly
4. softly	8. far	12. smoothly	16. richly

B. Write the correct form of each word in parentheses.
1. Read it (clearly) this time than you did the first time.
2. Lisa reads (well) this year than last year.
3. Joseph writes the (well) of all the pupils in his class.
4. Ronald worked (hard) than Robert, but Robert worked the (thoroughly) of the two.
5. Father worked the (hard) and (fast) of them all.
6. Mother can sew (swiftly) than the girls can.
7. The sinful woman loved Jesus (much) than Simon did.
8. Instead of calling (quietly) than before, Bartimaeus called even (loudly).

C. Write the correct words in parentheses.
1. Thistles grow (quicklier, more quickly) than garden vegetables.
2. Alma worked (neatlier, more neatly) than Sarah, even though Sarah worked (longer, more long).
3. Of all the boys in our class, David can jump the (higher, highest).
4. The rain started (sooner, more sooner) than we expected.
5. My arm hurt (terriblier, more terribly) than anything else I can remember.
6. Who picked strawberries (faster, fastest), June or Robin?
7. The Good Samaritan acted (neighborlier, more neighborly) than the priest or the Levite.
8. Peter and John ran toward Jesus' tomb, but John ran (faster, more faster).

Review Exercises

Copy the adjective clause in each sentence. After it, write the word the clause modifies, and put parentheses around it. [97]

Example: Many of the choices that Lot made were wrong.
Answer: that Lot made (choices)

1. The visitors whom Abraham entertained were angels.

Written Exercises

A. 1. warmly, more warmly, most warmly
2. much, more, most
3. hard, harder, hardest
4. softly, more softly, most softly
5. ill, worse, worst
6. often, oftener, oftenest
7. well, better, best
8. far, farther, farthest
9. abundantly, more abundantly, most abundantly
10. interestingly, more interestingly, most interestingly
11. naturally, more naturally, most naturally
12. smoothly, more smoothly, most smoothly
13. perfectly, more perfectly, most perfectly
14. little, less, least (*Littler* and *littlest* are adjective forms.)
15. tenderly, more tenderly, most tenderly
16. richly, more richly, most richly

B. 1. more clearly
2. better
3. best
4. harder, more thoroughly
5. hardest, fastest
6. more swiftly
7. more
8. more quietly, more loudly

C. 1. more quickly
2. more neatly, longer
3. highest
4. sooner
5. more terribly
6. faster
7. more neighborly
8. faster

Review Exercises
1. whom Abraham entertained (visitors)

2. The city that they came to visit was Sodom.
3. The woman who turned into a pillar of salt was Lot's wife.
4. The man whom the angels saved was Lot.
5. The little city to which Lot fled was Zoar.

2. that they came to visit (city)
3. who turned into a pillar of salt (woman)
4. whom the angels saved (man)
5. to which Lot fled (city)

---

106. Using *Good, Well,* and Negative Words

The words *good* and *well* are easily confused. *Good* is an adjective that modifies a noun or pronoun. Do not use it to modify a verb.

Correct: The farmer has a <u>good</u> horse.
Good modifies *horse.*

Incorrect: The horse works <u>good</u>.
The adjective *good* cannot modify the verb *works.*

Good may be used as a predicate adjective. Remember that a predicate adjective follows a linking verb and modifies the subject of a sentence.

Mother's apple pies are always <u>good</u>. (good pies)
The stories in this book are <u>good</u>. (good stories)

Well is usually an adverb that tells *how* something is done. *Well* can also mean "healthy," and then it is an adjective. But *good* must not be used as an adjective to mean "healthy."

Correct: The wire held <u>well</u>.
Well tells *how* the wire held.

Correct: Marcia is <u>well</u> again.
Well is a predicate adjective that means "healthy."

Incorrect: Grandmother has not been <u>good</u> ever since she had the flu.
Good must not be used to mean "healthy."

Negative words mean "not" or "almost not." Usually they change a

---

Lesson 106

Purpose: To teach the correct use of *good, well,* and negative words.

Oral Review:
1. Tell how the following degrees of adverbs are used to compare.
   a. positive degree (It modifies without comparing.)
   b. comparative degree (It is used to compare two actions.)
   c. superlative degree (It is used to compare more than two actions.)
2. How are the comparative and superlative degrees made for most adverbs that end with *-ly*? (by using the words *more* or *most*)
3. Give the comparative and superlative degrees of the following adverbs.
   a. well (better, best)
   b. ill (worse, worst)
   c. little (less, least)
   d. much (more, most)
   e. far (farther, farthest)

Lesson Introduction: Did you learn your English lesson *good* yesterday? Would you like to hear a *well* story? If you did*n't* have *no* good stories to tell, how many stories would you tell? Would you like it if your teacher could*n't hardly* think of any assignments to give in English? Would you like it better if the teacher *never* gave *no* homework?

All the previous sentences have mistakes in them. Today's lesson teaches the correct use of *good, well,* and negative words.

Lesson Outline:
1. Good is always an adjective that modifies a noun or pronoun. *Good* may come after a linking verb, as a predicate adjective that modifies the subject of a sentence.

sentence so that it has an opposite meaning. These are some common negative words.

no	never	neither	barely
not	nobody	nowhere	hardly
none	nothing		scarcely

Most negative words are adverbs or adjectives. A few, such as *none* and *nobody,* are pronouns. Some negative words are contractions formed by joining verbs with *not.*

isn't	haven't	couldn't	can't	won't

The contraction *ain't* is not a standard English word. Do not use it.

Do not use a *double negative.* That is, do not use two negative words to express one negative thought.

Incorrect: He <u>couldn't</u> find <u>no</u> eraser.
Correct: He <u>couldn't</u> find any eraser.
Correct: He could find <u>no</u> eraser.

Words like the following are not negative words. They may be used with negative words to express negative thoughts.

ever	anything	something
any	someone	

Often there are two ways to correct a sentence with a double negative. Study the examples below; the negative words are underlined.

Incorrect: I <u>hardly</u> <u>never</u> go.
Correct: I <u>hardly</u> ever go.
Correct: I <u>never</u> go.

Incorrect: He <u>didn't</u> see <u>nothing</u>.
Correct: He <u>didn't</u> see anything.
Correct: He saw <u>nothing</u>.

- *Good* is always an adjective.

- *Well* is usually an adverb that tells *how.* It is also an adjective that means "healthy."

- Use only one negative word to express a negative thought.

---

2. Well *is usually an adverb that tells* **how** *something is done.* **Well** *can also be an adjective that means "healthy."*

3. *Negative words mean "not" or "almost not."* Usually they change a sentence so that it has an opposite meaning.

    a. These are some common negative words.

no	nobody	barely
not	nothing	hardly
none	neither	scarcely
never	nowhere	

    b. Contractions with *not* are negative words.

isn't	couldn't	won't
haven't	can't	

    c. The contraction *ain't* is not a standard English word. Do not use it.

4. *Use only one negative word to express a negative thought.* Avoid expressions like "don't have no" and "can't hardly."

Words like the following are not negative words. They may be used with negative words to express negative thoughts.

ever	anything	something
any	someone	

(*Teacher:* Two negatives may be used together to express a positive thought, usually for a certain effect. This point is not taught at this level.

    I wouldn't do it for nothing!
      [I would do it for something.]
    I didn't tell them for no reason.
      [I did tell them for a reason.])

5. *Often there are two ways to correct a sentence with a double negative.*

    a. One negative word can be dropped.

Class Practice

A. Find the mistakes in the following sentences. Practice reading each sentence correctly.
1. The oranges didn't look well, but they tasted sweet.
2. Harvey works slowly, but he does his work good.
3. Titus was pale and didn't feel good.
4. The children sang good during the program at the old people's home.
5. My grades were well on my last two tests.

B. Correct each sentence in two ways.
1. We never take no money with us.
2. Thomas has hardly no potatoes to sell.
3. The baler doesn't scarcely work.
4. She doesn't have no brothers.

C. Read each sentence correctly. Use *barely, hardly,* or *scarcely* as the negative words.
1. I can't hardly hear him.
2. The boys barely never wash the dishes.
3. Hardly no snow fell in the valley.
4. There's not scarcely enough for everyone.

Written Exercises

A. Write the correct words in parentheses.
1. Cynthia is only in first grade, but she reads (good, well).
2. Aunt Fanny's pies are very (good, well).
3. Please clean your room (good, well).
4. Did your mother pack a (good, well) lunch for you?
5. Joel wrote a (good, well) story.
6. Grandmother is resting because she doesn't feel (good, well).
7. Your grades on these papers are (good, well).
8. A soft feather bed feels (good, well).

B. Rewrite each sentence correctly.
1. I haven't never seen a submarine.
2. He didn't know none of the answers.
3. I haven't seen nobody at their house all day.
4. We don't need no more paper now.

b. A negative word can be changed to a positive word, as *never* to *ever, nobody* to *anybody,* or *nothing* to *anything.*

  Incorrect: I couldn't feel nothing.
  Correct: I could feel nothing.
  Correct: I couldn't feel anything.

★ **EXTRA PRACTICE**
Worksheet 66 *(Good, Well,* and Negative Words)

Lesson 106 Answers
Class Practice
A. (Corrections are underlined.)
1. The oranges didn't look <u>good</u>, but they tasted sweet.
2. Harvey works slowly, but he does his work <u>well</u>.
3. Titus was pale and didn't feel <u>well</u>.
4. The children sang <u>well</u> during the program at the old people's home.
5. My grades were <u>good</u> on my last two tests.

B. 1. We never take money with us.
We take no money with us.
2. Thomas has hardly any potatoes to sell.
Thomas has no potatoes to sell.
3. The baler doesn't work.
The baler scarcely works.
4. She doesn't have any brothers.
She has no brothers.

C. 1. I can hardly hear him. *or* I hardly hear him.
2. The boys barely ever wash the dishes.
3. Hardly any snow fell in the valley.
4. There's scarcely enough for everyone.

Written Exercises
A. 1. well   5. good
2. good   6. well
3. well   7. good
4. good   8. good

B. (Two possibilities for most sentences.)
1. I have never seen a submarine.
I haven't ever seen a submarine.
2. He didn't know any of the answers.
He knew none of the answers.
3. I have seen nobody at their house all day.
I haven't seen anybody at their house all day.
4. We don't need any more paper now.
We need no more paper now.

5. We couldn't find the books nowhere.
6. We don't need nothing more to eat.
7. Nobody knew none of the answers.
8. I haven't had none of those papers.

C. Write each sentence correctly. Use *barely, hardly,* or *scarcely* as the negative words.
1. I can't scarcely see those small letters.
2. We can't hardly concentrate with so much noise.
3. We couldn't barely get our work finished on time.
4. I can't hardly wait until tomorrow.

Review Exercises

Write the correct form of each word in parentheses. [94, 105]
1. Of the two paintings, I like this one (well).
2. The tractor we have now is (powerful) than the one we had before.
3. God told Moses not to come (close) to the burning bush.
4. Moses went to Pharaoh, but Pharaoh made the people work (hard) than before.
5. In one plague, Egypt suffered the (bad) hailstorm in its history.

---

107. Prepositional Phrases as Adverbs

A *prepositional phrase* may be used to modify a verb. When it does this, it is an *adverb phrase*. A prepositional phrase includes a preposition, its object, and any adjectives that modify the object. Study the following example.

preposition   object
     ↓   ↓
Jesus went up the mountain and prayed.
　　Up the mountain is a prepositional phrase used as an adverb.
　　It tells *where* Jesus went.

5. We couldn't find the books anywhere.
　　We could find the books nowhere.
6. We don't need anything more to eat.
　　We need nothing more to eat.
7. Nobody knew any of the answers.
8. I haven't had any of those papers.
　　I have had none of those papers.

C. 1. I can scarcely see those small letters.
2. We can hardly concentrate with so much noise.
3. We could barely get our work finished on time.
4. I can hardly wait until tomorrow.

Review Exercises

1. better
2. more powerful
3. close (*or* closer)
4. harder
5. worst

Lesson 107

Purpose: (1) To teach how to identify prepositional phrases used as adverbs. (2) To teach how to diagram adverb phrases.

Oral Review:

1. What part of speech is the word *good*? (adjective)
2. When is *well* (*a*) an adjective? (*b*) an adverb? (*a.* when it means "healthy"; *b.* when it tells *how* about a verb)
3. What is a predicate adjective? (an adjective that follows a linking verb and modifies the subject)
4. List some common negative words. (no, not, none, never, nobody, nothing, neither, nowhere, barely, hardly, scarcely; contractions with *not*)
5. For what two words should the contraction *ain't* be used? (The contraction *ain't* is not a standard English word and should not be used.)
6. What rule should be followed when using negative

words? (Do not use two negative words to express one negative thought.)

Lesson Introduction: Ask students which sentences are more interesting and informative.

　　Uncle David went away.
　　Uncle David went to Canada.

　　Joel walked outside.
　　Joel walked on a trail in the woods.

　　The eggs were here.
　　The eggs were inside the nest in this bush.

Phrases often tell more than what single-word adverbs or adjectives can tell. Today we will learn about adverb phrases.

Lesson Outline:

1. A prepositional phrase that modifies a verb is an adverb phrase. An adverb phrase may tell *how, when, where, why,* or *to what degree.*

Review the common prepositions listed below. For more prepositions, see the chart on page 508.

across	behind	in	to
after	down	near	under
around	for	on	up
before	from	over	with

Review the following steps to find a prepositional phrase in a sentence.

1. *Find the preposition.*
2. *Find the object of the preposition.* This is done by saying the preposition and asking *whom* or *what.* The object is always a noun or pronoun.
3. *The prepositional phrase includes all the words from the preposition to its object.* Any words in between are adjectives that modify the object. Not all phrases have adjectives.

An adverb phrase may tell *how, when, where, why,* or *to what degree.* Like other adverbs, it may be found at different places in a sentence. It may come right after the verb, or it may be found at the beginning or end of the sentence.

Ronald came <u>on his bicycle</u>. (how)
<u>In the evening</u> Ronald came. (when)
Ronald came <u>to my house</u> after supper. (where)
Ronald came <u>for a tool</u>. (why)

Adverb phrases may also modify adjectives or other adverbs. When they do this, they usually tell *how.*

Store the cabbage separately <u>from the apples</u>.
     From the apples modifies the adverb *separately* by telling *how* to store the apples separately.

The sand was pure white <u>like fresh snow</u>.
     Like fresh snow modifies the adjective *white* by telling *how* white the sand was.

Review finding prepositional phrases in sentences. Call attention to the common prepositions listed in the lesson; then give the following steps.

(1) *Find the preposition.*
(2) *Find the object of the preposition* by saying the preposition and asking *whom* or *what.* The object is always a noun or pronoun.
(3) *The prepositional phrase includes all the words from the preposition to its object.* Any words in between are adjectives that modify the object. Not all phrases include adjectives.

2. An adverb phrase may be found at different places in a sentence. It may come right after the verb, or it may be found at the beginning or end of the sentence. (This is a general characteristic of adverbs.)

3. An adverb phrase may also modify an adjective or another adverb. When it does, it usually tells *how.*

---

4. An adverb phrase is diagramed beneath the word it modifies.

a. Adverb phrase modifying a verb:

b. Adverb phrase modifying a predicate adjective:

c. Adverb phrase modifying an adverb:

d. Sentence with several adverb phrases modifying the verb:

★ **EXTRA PRACTICE**
Worksheet 67 *(Prepositional Phrases as Adverbs)*

An adverb phrase is diagramed beneath the word it modifies.

Adverb phrase modifying a verb:

The sun shone brightly <u>in the afternoon</u>.

Adverb phrase modifying a predicate adjective:

The tree was full <u>of ripe peaches</u>.

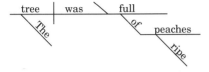

Adverb phrase modifying an adverb:

I will see you later <u>in the day</u>.

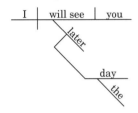

Sentence with several adverb phrases modifying the verb:

<u>On our trip</u>, we took pictures <u>in each state</u> <u>with our little camera</u>.

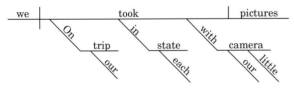

- A prepositional phrase may be used as an adverb.

- A prepositional phrase includes a preposition, its object, and any adjectives that modify the object.

- An adverb phrase modifies a verb, an adjective, or another adverb.

Class Practice

A. Read each adverb phrase. Tell which word it modifies, and what it tells about that word.
1. Trust in the Lord with all thine heart.
2. The ship will soon leave on a long voyage.
3. With a thud the book fell to the floor.
4. Nectarines are similar to peaches.
5. The weather was cold earlier in the month.
6. During the storm, a limb fell to the ground with a crash.

B. On the chalkboard, diagram the sentences in Part A.

Written Exercises

A. Copy each adverb phrase, and the verb, adjective, or adverb that it modifies.
1. After the storm, the boys floated around the pasture in a rowboat.
2. The rain was not noticed by the busy children.
3. We will move later in the year.
4. This bitter medicine is good for you.
5. In the afternoon the sun shone brightly.
6. I will look for Calicut on the map.
7. The baker baked the pies in an oven.
8. Mother made candy on the stovetop.
9. In our back yard we roasted hot dogs over a fire.
10. Did you put too many eggs into the cake?

B. Diagram these sentences.
1. In the evening the children gathered around the table.
2. My niece is afraid of dogs.
3. The workers became more tired by the minute.
4. After the Flood the ark rested on Mount Ararat.

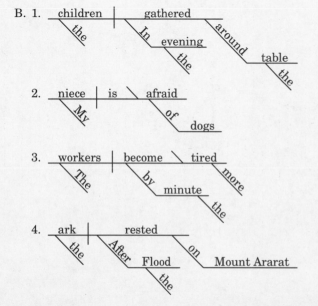

Lesson 107 Answers
Class Practice
A. 1. in the Lord, Trust, where
      with all thine heart, Trust, how
   2. on a long voyage, will leave, where
   3. With a thud, fell, how
      to the floor, fell, where
   4. to peaches, similar, how
   5. in the month, earlier, when
   6. During the storm, fell, when
      to the ground, fell, where
      with a crash, fell, how

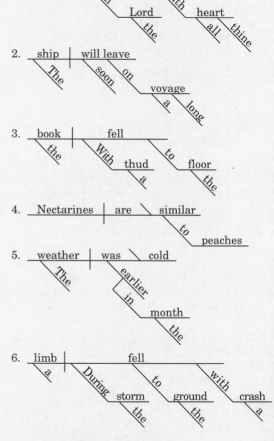

Written Exercises
A. 1. After the storm, floated
      around the pasture, floated
      in a rowboat, floated
   2. by the busy children, was noticed
   3. in the year, later
   4. for you, good
   5. In the afternoon, shone
   6. for Calicut, shall look
      on the map, shall look
   7. in an oven, baked
   8. on the stovetop, made
   9. In our back yard, roasted
      over a fire, roasted
   10. into the cake, Did put

Mount Ararat

Corel

5. You should get up earlier in the morning.
6. By evening the wind was roaring across the island at a high speed.

C. Write three sentences using prepositional phrases that tell *how,* *when,* and *where.*

Review Exercises

Diagram these sentences.
1. Clouds give us rain and shade.
2. Sometimes clouds trap heat that would otherwise escape from the earth.
3. Stratus clouds often bring rain or some other form of precipitation.
4. Those fluffy white clouds look especially beautiful.

---

108. Rhyme in Poetry

In many poems, the last word of one line rhymes with the last word of another line. These rhyming words add much to the beauty of good poetry. There are many different patterns of rhyme. In one common pattern, line 2 rhymes with line 4, line 6 rhymes with line 8, and so on. In another pattern, lines 1 and 2 rhyme, and lines 3 and 4 rhyme. In a third pattern, lines 1 and 3 rhyme, and lines 2 and 4 rhyme. These are just a few of the many patterns that are used.

Lesson 108

Purpose: (1) To teach the qualities of true rhyme. (2) To point out some qualities of Bible poetry.

Oral Review:
1. What is rhythm? (a regular pattern of accented and unaccented syllables)
2. Tell which pattern is iambic and which one is trochaic.
   a. It is the most commonly used pattern. (iambic)
   b. Each foot has one unaccented syllable followed by one accented syllable. (iambic)
   c. Each foot has one accented syllable followed by one unaccented syllable. (trochaic)
   d. It is well suited to a theme of joy or beauty. (iambic)
   e. It is well suited to deep thoughts and sober words. (trochaic)

C. (Individual work.)

Review Exercises

3. Describe two other patterns of rhythm.
   (a. The third pattern has two unaccented syllables followed by one accented syllable. This pattern gives poetry a light, flowing style.
   b. The fourth pattern has one accented syllable followed by two unaccented syllables. This pattern goes well with a happy, delightful mood in poetry.)
4. How is a description different from a story? (A description does not tell a story. It does not show a problem to be solved, neither does it include dialogue. It simply describes a scene.)

Study the different rhyming patterns shown below. The rhyming pattern is shown by using a different small letter for each set of rhyming words.

Faithfulness

Though a task may seem quite small,	a
Hardly worth your time at all,	a
Do it promptly, do it well;	b
Who is watching, none can tell.	b
Faithfulness in little things	c
Sure promotion with it brings.	c

What Bird Am I?

I often nest in buildings,	a
Against an eave or wall;	b
I come in early springtime	c
And leave again in fall.	b

Speak the Truth

Speak the truth!	a
Speak it boldly, never fear;	b
Speak it so that all may hear;	b
In the end it shall appear	b
Truth is best in age and youth.	a
Speak the truth.	a
Speak the truth!	a
Truth is beautiful and brave,	c
Strong to bless and strong to save;	c
Falsehood is a cowardly knave;	c
From it turn thy steps in youth—	a
Follow truth.	a

—Anonymous

Here are some rules for writing good rhymes in poetry.
1. The vowel sounds of the rhyming words or syllables must be the same.

5. Which of the five senses is used the most in descriptions? (sight)
6. Tell what is meant by describing something in spatial order. (describing something by giving details in the order of space, such as from top to bottom, from left to right, from front to back, or from outside to inside)

Lesson Introduction: Copy the following stanza on the chalkboard, using the words in italics. Read it with the class. Then change the underlined words to the words in parentheses, and read it again. Which way sounds better? Rhyming words add beauty to a poem, do they not?

Long, long ago before there was
    An earth or sky—just <u>emptiness</u> (space),
God made this world in which we live,
    A very pleasant <u>planet</u> (place).

This lesson teaches about rhyme in poetry, and it gives rules for writing good rhymes.

Lesson Outline:

1. The careful use of rhyme adds beauty to a poem.

    a. Rhyming words have endings that sound alike.

    b. Rhyming patterns are often shown by using a different small letter for each set of rhyming words.

2. Good rhyme in poetry requires following certain rules.

    (1) The vowel sounds of the rhyming words or syllables must be the same.

        <u>part</u>—<u>heart</u> and <u>loud</u>—<u>crowd,</u> but not <u>clap</u>—<u>shop</u> or <u>love</u>—<u>move</u>

    (2) The last consonant sound of the rhyming syllables must be the same.

        <u>bus</u>—<u>plus</u> and <u>dove</u>—<u>love,</u> but not <u>bus</u>—<u>rust</u> or <u>love</u>—<u>does</u>

Rhyming words: good—would (*but not* good—food)
teeth—sheath (*but not* teeth—death)

2. The last consonant sound of the rhyming syllables must be the same.

Rhyming words: let—get (*but not* let—step)
soar—store (*but not* soar—cord)

3. The beginning consonant sounds of the rhyming syllables must be different.

Rhyming words: night—light (*but not* night—knight)
morn—borne (*but not* morn—mourn)

Words like *night—knight* are homophones, not rhyming words.

Poetry is usually recognized by its rhyme, but this does not mean that all poetry rhymes. One example is Bible poetry, which is found in Job, Psalms, and Proverbs. Bible poetry does not have rhyme, but it is poetic in other ways.

Bible poetry can be written in lines and stanzas. It is full of descriptive words and rich meaning. Often two lines are similar, with the second line repeating the first one but using different words. Study the following lines from Psalm 119:103.

How sweet are thy words unto my taste!
Yea, sweeter than honey to my mouth!

These lines are beautifully descriptive. They rhyme in thought rather than sound. For this reason, Bible poems are true poetry in any language.

- The use of rhyme adds beauty to a poem.

- Rhyme is the matching of sounds at the ends of words or lines.

- Bible poetry is full of descriptive words and is rich in meaning.

---

(3) The beginning consonant sounds of the rhyming syllables must be different.

jay—hay and black—crack, but not dove—turtledove or maid—homemade

3. Bible poetry does not have rhyme. Many Bible poems are found in the Books of Job, Psalms, and Proverbs.

4. Bible poems have qualities that make them true poetry in any language.
a. They can be written in lines and stanzas.
b. They are full of descriptive words and rich meaning.
c. Often two lines are similar, with the second line repeating the first one but using different words.

Note: Some Bible poetry has rhythm and rhyme in the original language, but of course this is lost in translation.

★ **EXTRA PRACTICE**
Worksheet 68 *(Rhyme in Poetry)*

Class Practice

A. Give letters to tell which lines rhyme in the poems below. Follow the pattern in the lesson.

1. **The Old Lamp**

A lamp once hung in an ancient town,
    At the corner of a street,
Where the wind was keen, and the way was dark,
    And the rain would often beat;
And all night long, its light would shine
    To guide the travelers' feet.

The lamp was rough and plain and old,
    And the storm had beaten it sore;
'Twas not a thing one would care to show,
    Whate'er it had been before,
But no one thought what the lantern was,
    'Twas the light that, within, it bore.

                —Anonymous

2. **What We Give Away**

Love that is hoarded molds at last
    Until we know some day,
The only thing we ever have
    Is what we give away.

And kindness that is never used
    But hidden all alone
Will slowly harden till it is
    As hard as any stone.

It is the things we always hold
    That we will lose some day;
The only things we ever keep
    Are what we give away.

          —Author unknown

B. Look up Psalm 103. Discuss some of the descriptive words and phrases in the first few verses of this Bible poetry.

C. Look up Proverbs 4:1–4. Pick out the pairs of lines with similar thoughts in this Bible poetry.

Lesson 108 Answers
Class Practice

A. 1. abcbdb; efgfhf
   2. abcb; defe; ghih

B. (Suggested points for discussion.)

In verse 1, the word *bless* is packed with meaning. It means to praise God, honor Him, and obey Him. The phrase "all that is within me" is also full of meaning. How should we praise God? With everything we have!

Another meaningful word is *crowneth* in verse 4. This word suggests that God's blessings are bestowed upon us like a crown. It also suggests a climax. God does all the things described in the preceding phrases, and then—on top of everything else—He crowns us with "lovingkindness and tender mercies."

C. (Words with related thoughts are in parentheses.)

1. Hear, ye children, the instruction of a father,
And attend to know understanding.
    (Hear—attend, instruction—
    understanding)
2. For I give you good doctrine,
Forsake ye not my law.
    (doctrine—law)
3. For I was my father's son,
Tender and only beloved in the sight of my
mother.
    (father—mother)
4. He taught me also, and said unto me,
Let thine heart retain my words:
Keep my commandments, and live.
    (taught—said, retain—Keep, words—
    commandments)

Written Exercises

A. Study the following poem, and write which rhyming pattern is used in the first stanza: *aabb*, *abab*, or *abcb*. Then copy all the pairs of rhyming words.

I Saw God Wash the World

I saw God wash the world last night
    With His sweet shower on high;
And then when morning came, I saw
    Him hang it out to dry.

He washed each tiny blade of grass
    And every trembling tree;
He flung His showers against the hills
    And swept the billowy sea.

The white rose is a cleaner white,
    The red rose is more red,
Since God washed every fragrant face
    And put them all to bed.

There's not a bird, there's not a bee,
    That wings along the way,
But is a cleaner bird and bee
    Than it was yesterday.

I saw God wash the world last night;
    Ah, would He had washed me
As clean of all my dust and dirt
    As that old white birch tree!
            —William L. Stidger

Written Exercises

A. abcb
    high—dry; tree—sea; red—bed; way—yesterday;
        me—tree

B. Copy Psalm 23:1–3 in lines as in a poem. Write each verse in two lines, and begin each line with a capital letter. Follow the pattern shown below for Psalm 24:1, 2.

> The earth is the Lord's, and the fulness thereof;
> The world, and they that dwell therein.
> For he hath founded it upon the seas,
> And established it upon the floods.

C. Write a good rhyming word to fit in each blank.

The Fountain

1. Into the sunshine,
   Full of the light,
   Leaping and flashing
   From morn till ———!

2. Into the moonlight,
   Whiter than snow,
   Waving so flowerlike
   When the winds ———!

3. Into the starlight,
   Rushing in spray,
   Happy at midnight,
   Happy by ———!

4. Ever in motion,
   Blithesome and ———,
   Still climbing heavenward,
   Never aweary.

5. Full of a nature
   Nothing can tame,
   Changed every moment,
   Ever the ———;

6. Glorious fountain!
   Let my heart be
   Fresh, cheerful, constant,
   Upward like ———!

—James Russell Lowell

D. Choose a topic for writing a poem, and make a list of ideas that you might include in it. Here are some suggested topics.
1. Describe a winter scene just after a fresh snow.
2. Describe some of the kind things your mother does for you.
3. Describe your pet dog, kitten, or goldfish.
4. Describe the beauties of springtime.
5. Describe a thrilling bicycle ride down a steep hill.

Review Exercises

Choose and write the best answers. [93, 96]
1. A description usually (tells, does not tell) a story.
2. A description usually tells about a (scene, happening).
3. The sense of (sight, hearing) is used most in descriptions.
4. The word (*building, house*) is a more exact noun.

B. The Lord is my shepherd;
I shall not want.
He maketh me to lie down in green pastures:
He leadeth me beside the still waters.
He restoreth my soul:
He leadeth me in the paths of righteousness for his name's sake.

C. 1. night
2. blow
3. day
4. cheery
5. same
6. thee

D. (Individual work. Have pupils save their lists for later use in Lesson 112.)

Review Exercises

1. does not tell
2. scene
3. sight
4. *house*

5. The word (*ran, raced*) is a more exact verb.

6. The word (*wise, good*) is a more descriptive adjective.

7. The order of (time, space, importance) should be used in descriptions.

8. A (simile, metaphor) compares two unlike things by using the word *like* or *as.*

5. *raced*

6. *wise*

7. space

8. simile

---

109. Distinguishing Adverbs and Adjectives

How can you tell the difference between adverbs and adjectives? There are two tests that you can use.

The first test is to see what part of speech the word modifies. An adjective always modifies a noun or pronoun. An adverb always modifies a verb, an adjective, or another adverb.

> This engine starts <u>hard</u>.
> *Hard* modifies *starts,* which is a verb. So *hard* is an adverb.

> This factory makes <u>hard</u> candy.
> *Hard* modifies *candy,* which is a noun. So *hard* is an adjective.

> This soil is <u>hard</u> and <u>dry</u>.
> *Hard* and *dry* follow the linking verb *is* and modify the subject *soil. Hard* and *dry* are predicate adjectives.

A second test is to see what question the modifier answers. Adjectives tell *which, whose, how many,* and *what kind of.* Adverbs tell *how, when, where, why,* and *to what degree.*

> This engine starts <u>hard</u>.
> *Hard* tells *how* the engine starts, so *hard* is an adverb.

> This factory makes <u>hard</u> candy.
> *Hard* tells *what kind of* candy, so *hard* is an adjective.

> This soil is <u>hard</u> and <u>dry</u>.
> *Hard* and *dry* tell *what kind of* soil, so *hard* and *dry* are predicate adjectives.

Lesson 109

Purpose: To review the differences between adverbs and adjectives in order to distinguish them from each other.

Oral Review:

1. What do adjective clauses usually tell? (which, what kind of)

2. With what part of speech does an adjective clause usually begin? (relative pronoun)

3. What sentence part is a noun or pronoun that follows a linking verb and renames the subject? (predicate nominative)

4. What sentence part tells *who* or *what* the sentence is about? (subject)

5. What sentence part tells what the subject does or is? (predicate)

6. What sentence part receives the action of a transitive verb? (direct object)

7. What sentence part tells *to whom or what* or *for whom or what* the action of the verb is done? (indirect object)

8. What sentence part follows a linking verb and modifies the subject? (predicate adjective)

Lesson Introduction: Write the following sentences on the chalkboard. Ask students if they can tell whether the underlined words and phrases are adjectives or adverbs.

> James is a <u>diligent</u> worker. (adjective)
> James worked <u>diligently</u>. (adverb)

> My sister went <u>into the kitchen</u>. (adverb)
> The girl <u>in the kitchen</u> is my sister. (adjective)

Today we want to study the differences between adjectives and adverbs.

Remember that adverbs of degree modify adjectives or other adverbs. Test each modifier separately to see what part of speech it is.

Louann took the kettle <u>off</u> <u>too</u> <u>soon</u>.

Off modifies the verb *took* by telling *where*. *Off* is an adverb.

Too modifies the adverb *soon* by telling *to what degree*. *Too* is an adverb.

Soon modifies the verb *took* by telling *when*. *Soon* is an adverb.

He is an <u>especially</u> <u>courteous</u> <u>young</u> man.

Especially modifies the adjective *courteous* by telling *to what degree*. *Especially* is an adverb.

Courteous modifies the predicate nominative *man* by telling *what kind of*. *Courteous* is an adjective.

Young modifies the predicate nominative *man* by telling *what kind of*. *Young* is an adjective.

Many adverbs end with *-ly*. However, not all words that end with *-ly* are adverbs. Some *-ly* words tell *what kind of*. Study the following words that are often used as adjectives.

lonely	lovely	costly	brotherly
lowly	orderly	friendly	neighborly

How can you tell whether a word ending with *-ly* is an adjective or an adverb? Use the same two tests: See what part of speech the word modifies, and notice what question it answers.

The lady seemed <u>kindly</u> in her actions.

Kindly modifies the noun *lady* by telling *what kind of*. It is a predicate adjective. (*Seemed* is a linking verb because it can be replaced by a form of *be:* The lady *was* kindly in her actions.)

She spoke <u>kindly</u> to us.

Kindly modifies the verb *spoke* by telling *how,* so it is an adverb.

A prepositional phrase is either an adjective phrase or an adverb phrase. How can you tell the difference? Again, use the same two tests.

Lesson Outline:

1. One test for telling the difference between an adverb and an adjective is to see what part of speech the word modifies.

    a. An adjective modifies a noun or pronoun.

    b. An adverb modifies a verb, an adjective, or another adverb.

2. Another test for telling the difference between an adverb and an adjective is to see what question the word answers.

    a. Adjectives tell *which, whose, how many,* and *what kind of.*

    b. Adverbs tell *how, when, where, why,* and *to what degree.*

3. When several modifiers come together, each one must be tested separately. One may be an adverb modifying the verb, another may be an adjective modifying an object, and another may be an adverb of degree modifying an adjective or another adverb.

4. Not all words ending with -ly are adverbs. Some of them are adjectives. These words must be tested in the same way as other modifiers.

lonely	lovely	costly	brotherly
lowly	orderly	friendly	neighborly

5. A prepositional phrase can be tested just like a single-word modifier.

    a. What part of speech does the phrase modify?

    b. What question does the phrase answer?

That letter <u>on my desk</u> came today.
> The phrase *on my desk* modifies the noun *letter* by telling *which*. So *on my desk* is an adjective phrase.

I found a letter <u>on my desk</u>.
> The phrase *on my desk* modifies the verb *found* by telling *where*. So *on my desk* is an adverb phrase.

The position of a phrase within a sentence is another clue for deciding what kind of phrase it is. An adjective phrase must come *immediately after* the noun or pronoun that it modifies.

Adjective phrases:
> The paper <u>on the desk</u> is mine.
> John fed the calves <u>in the barn</u>.

An adverb phrase may be found almost anywhere in a sentence. It can often be moved to a different place without changing the meaning. Of course, if a prepositional phrase is at the beginning of a sentence, it must be an adverb phrase.

Adverb phrases:
> The boys worked <u>with all their might</u> yesterday.
> The boys worked yesterday <u>with all their might</u>.
>
> We visited awhile <u>after church</u>.
> <u>After church</u> we visited awhile.

The following sentence has an adverb phrase and an adjective phrase. Study this sentence and its diagram.

For devotions we read the parable <u>of the sower</u>.

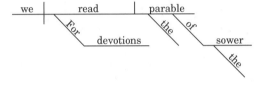

6. The position of a phrase within a sentence is another clue for deciding what kind of phrase it is.
> a. An adjective phrase must come *immediately after* the noun or pronoun that it modifies.
> b. An adverb phrase may be found almost anywhere in a sentence. It can often be moved to a different place without changing the meaning. (This is a general characteristic of adverbs.)

7. An adjective phrase may modify the object of a prepositional phrase just before it.
> One <u>of the hinges</u> <u>on the back door</u> needs repair.

★ **EXTRA PRACTICE**
Worksheet 69 (*Distinguishing Adverbs and Adjectives*)

An adjective phrase may modify the object of a prepositional phrase just before it. Study the following sentence and its diagram.

Fish live <u>beneath the surface</u> <u>of the water</u>.

>*Beneath the surface* modifies *live* by telling *where* fish live. So it is an adverb phrase.

>*Of the water* modifies *surface* by telling *what kind of* surface. So it is an adjective phrase.

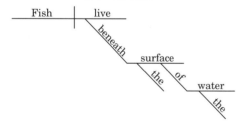

In the example above, you may think *beneath the surface* and *of the water* are both adverb phrases because both follow the verb. But the two tests show that the first is an adverb phrase and the second is an adjective phrase.

- One way to distinguish an adverb from an adjective is to see what part of speech the word or phrase modifies. An adjective modifies a noun or pronoun, but an adverb modifies a verb, an adjective, or another adverb.

- Another way to distinguish an adverb from an adjective is to see what question the word or phrase answers. An adjective tells *which, whose, how many,* or *what kind of;* but an adverb tells *how, when, where, why,* or *to what degree.*

- An additional way to distinguish an adverb phrase from an adjective phrase is to check the position of the phrase in a sentence. An adjective phrase comes directly after the noun or pronoun that it modifies, but an adverb phrase may be found almost anywhere in a sentence.

Class Practice

Look at each underlined word or phrase. Tell which word or words t modifies and what question it answers. Then tell whether it is used as an *adverb* or an *adjective*.

1. A jet is <u>fast</u>.
2. The bus came <u>late</u> again.
3. Sylvia can draw <u>well</u>.
4. Christians should practice <u>brotherly</u> kindness.
5. If you want to be known as a <u>friendly</u> person, you must act <u>friendly</u>.
6. We have not seen our cousins <u>from Alabama</u> <u>since last winter</u>.
7. Will we pay the toll <u>at the other side</u> of the bridge?
8. Get some water <u>at the faucet</u> in the kitchen.
9. How many verses <u>from the Bible</u> can you quote <u>by memory</u>?
10. <u>On the way home</u> we talked and sang.
11. The boy <u>in the wheelchair</u> can walk <u>with crutches</u>.
12. My grandfather walked <u>to school</u> <u>in his boyhood</u>.

Written Exercises

Write *adj.* or *adv.* to identify each underlined word or phrase.

1. The travelers walked <u>hurriedly</u>.
2. The <u>fresh</u> concrete soon became <u>hard</u>.
3. The farmers <u>of those days</u> worked <u>hard</u>.
4. That island is <u>almost</u> completely covered <u>with water</u>.
5. The crops are growing <u>well</u>.
6. The <u>old</u> car still runs <u>well</u>.
7. She has been feeling <u>quite</u> <u>well</u>.
8. A <u>beautiful</u> rainbow arched <u>across the sky</u>.
9. The Word <u>of God</u> will stand <u>forever</u>.
10. Your bouquet is <u>lovely</u>.
11. Such a trip would be <u>rather</u> <u>costly</u>.
12. The children <u>in the printer's shop</u> saw some huge rolls <u>of paper</u>.
13. <u>In the springtime</u> the shearers cut the thick fleece <u>off the sheep</u>.
14. The <u>old</u> people <u>in the nursing home</u> thanked us for coming.
15. Coal miners <u>of past days</u> worked <u>in dark and dangerous surroundings</u>.
16. Some coal lies <u>too</u> <u>deep</u> for surface mining.

Lesson 109 Answers
Class Practice

1. jet, what kind of, (predicate) adjective
2. came, when, adverb
3. can draw, how, adverb
4. kindness, what kind of, adjective
5. person, what kind of, adjective
   must act, how, adverb
6. cousins, which, adjective
   have seen, when, adverb
7. Will pay, where, adverb
   side, which, adjective
8. Get, where, adverb
   faucet, which, adjective
9. verses, what kind of, adjective
   can quote, how, adverb
10. talked (and) sang, where, adverb
11. boy, which, adjective
    can walk, how, adverb
12. walked, where, adverb
    walked, when, adverb

Written Exercises

1. adv.
2. adj., adj.
3. adj., adv.
4. adv., adv.
5. adv.
6. adj., adv.
7. adv., adj.
8. adj., adv.
9. adj., adv.
10. adj.
11. adv., adj.
12. adj., adj.
13. adv., adv.
14. adj., adj.
15. adj., adv.
16. adv., adv.

Review Exercises

Match the names of the sentence parts to the descriptions.

subject   direct object   predicate nominative
predicate   indirect object   predicate adjective

1. It tells *to whom or what* or *for whom or what* the action of the verb is done.
2. It follows a linking verb and renames the subject.
3. It receives the action of a transitive verb.
4. It tells *who* or *what* the sentence is about.
5. It follows a linking verb and modifies the subject.
6. It tells what the subject does or is.

110. Adverb Clauses

You know that a word or a phrase can be used as an adverb to tell *how, when, where,* or *why.* A *clause* can also be used as an adverb. Remember that a clause is any group of words with a subject and a predicate. In the following sentences, the underlined words are adverbs that tell *when.*

> Snow was falling <u>yesterday</u>. (single-word adverb)
> Snow was falling <u>on Monday</u>. (adverb phrase)
> Snow was falling <u>before we reached home</u>. (adverb clause)

Adverb clauses can answer questions other than *how, when, where, why,* and *to what degree.* They can also tell *how long, how much, in spite of what, under what condition,* and other things.

> Daniel was delivered <u>because he trusted in God</u>.
>   (modifies *was delivered* by telling *why*)

> We shall be rewarded <u>if we are faithful</u>.
>   (modifies *shall be rewarded* by telling *under what condition*)

An adjective clause begins with a relative pronoun and modifies a noun or a pronoun. But an adverb clause begins with a *subordinating conjunction,* and it modifies a verb, an adjective, or another adverb. Here are some common subordinating conjunctions.

Lesson 110

Purpose: To introduce *adverb clauses.

Oral Review:
1. What is a preposition? (a connecting word that begins a phrase)
2. What part of speech is the object of a preposition? (a noun or pronoun)
3. Prepositional phrases may be used as what parts of speech? (adjectives, adverbs)
4. What parts of speech may adverb phrases modify? (verbs, adjectives, adverbs)
5. What part of speech is the word *good*? (adjective)
6. When is *well* used as (a) an adjective? (b) an adverb? (a. when it means "healthy"; b. when it tells *how*)
7. Describe the following sentence parts.
   a. predicate adjective (an adjective that follows a linking verb and modifies the subject)
   b. predicate nominative (a noun or pronoun that follows a linking verb and renames the subject)
   c. direct object (a noun or pronoun that receives the action of a transitive verb)
   d. indirect object (a noun or pronoun that tells *to whom or what* or *for whom or what* the action of the verb is done)

Lesson Introduction: Write the following sentences on the chalkboard. Underline the adverbs, and point out that they all tell *when.*

> We mowed the lawn <u>yesterday</u>.
> We mowed the lawn <u>in the evening</u>.
> We mowed the lawn <u>before it rained</u>.

An adverb can consist of a single word, a phrase, or even a whole clause. In this lesson we will study adverb clauses.

after	before	until
although	if	when
as	since	where
because	unless	while

An adverb clause is a *dependent clause,* the same as an adjective clause. It cannot stand alone as a complete sentence. It depends on a *main clause* (an independent clause) for its meaning.

Dependent clause:
  If <u>we</u> <u>are</u> faithful. (cannot stand alone)

Main, or independent, clause: <u>We</u> <u>shall be rewarded</u>.

A sentence that contains a dependent clause and an independent clause is a *complex sentence.* The dependent clause may be an adverb clause or an adjective clause.

  We shall study <u>when recess is over</u>. (adverb clause)
  The boy <u>whom you saw</u> is my brother. (adjective clause)

To find an adverb clause in a sentence, look for a clause that begins with a subordinating conjunction. It may come before or after the main clause.

  The fluffy snowflake quickly melted <u>after it fell on my hand</u>.
  <u>After it fell on my hand</u>, the fluffy snowflake quickly melted.

An adverb clause is set off by a comma when it comes before the main clause. Notice how this is done in the sentence above.

- An adverb clause is a clause that modifies a verb, an adjective, or an adverb. Adverb clauses may tell *how, when, where, why,* and *to what degree,* as well as *how long, how much, in spite of what, under what condition,* and other things.

- An adverb clause begins with a subordinating conjunction, such as *after, although, as, because, before, if, since, unless, until, when, where,* and *while.*

- A sentence with an adverb clause is a complex sentence.

- An adverb clause may be found before or after the main clause in a sentence.

Lesson Outline:

1. An adverb clause is a clause that modifies a verb, an adjective, or an adverb. It may tell *how, when, where, why,* and *to what degree,* as well as *how long, how much, in spite of what, under what condition,* and other things. (*Teacher:* Only adverb clauses that modify verbs are taught in this lesson.)

2. An adverb clause begins with a subordinating conjunction. An adverb clause is a dependent clause that depends on a main clause (an independent clause) for its meaning. Here are some common subordinating conjunctions.

after	because	since	when
although	before	unless	where
as	if	until	while

3. A sentence with an adverb clause is a complex sentence.

4. An adverb clause may come before or after the main clause in a sentence.

5. When an adverb clause comes at the beginning of a sentence, it is set off by a comma.

Class Practice

A. First read the adverb clause in each sentence. Then read the main clause.
 1. The old stairs creaked as we went up.
 2. The disciples felt sad because Jesus would leave them soon.
 3. Although dark clouds covered the sky, we received no rain.
 4. Leave the pan on the stove until the water boils.
 5. Things do not always happen as we had planned.
 6. Do not rejoice when your enemy falls.

B. Read the adverb clauses in Part A again. Tell which words they modify, and what questions they answer.

C. Use these adverb clauses in sentences of your own. Begin the second sentence with the adverb clause, and write it correctly on the chalkboard.
 1. where the catfish were biting   2. unless we fix it soon

Written Exercises

A. Copy each adverb clause, and underline the subordinating conjunction.

 Example: As we drove through Wyoming, we saw some buffaloes.
 Answer: <u>As</u> we drove through Wyoming

 1. I have not seen Uncle Wilbur's since they moved to Illinois.
 2. Put all these tools away where they belong.
 3. Because you have carelessly damaged the book, you must pay for it.
 4. The girls washed the windows until they sparkled.
 5. If a horse is not thirsty, it will not drink much water.
 6. The wash dries faster when a breeze is blowing.

B. Copy each adverb clause. Also copy the verb or verb phrase that each clause modifies.

 Example: King Nebuchadnezzar was startled when he saw four
             men in the furnace.
 Answer: when he saw four men in the furnace, was startled

 1. Daniel was serving Nebuchadnezzar when the king had a frightening dream.
 2. The king told his dream when Daniel came.

Lesson 110 Answers
Class Practice

A. 1. as we went up; The old stairs creaked.
 2. because Jesus would leave them soon; The disciples felt sad.
 3. Although dark clouds covered the sky; we received no rain.
 4. until the water boils; Leave the pan on the stove.
 5. as we had planned; Things do not always happen.
 6. when your enemy falls; Do not rejoice.

B. 1. as we went up, creaked, when
 2. because Jesus would leave them soon, felt, why
 3. Although dark clouds covered the sky, received, in spite of what
 4. until the water boils, Leave, how long
 5. as we had planned, do happen, how
 6. when your enemy falls, Do rejoice, when

C. (Sample sentences.)
 1. We moved to the deeper pool where the catfish were biting.
 2. Unless we fix it soon, this engine will be beyond repair.

Written Exercises

A. 1. <u>since</u> they moved to Illinois
 2. <u>where</u> they belong
 3. <u>Because</u> you have carelessly damaged the book
 4. <u>until</u> they sparkled
 5. <u>If</u> a horse is not thirsty
 6. <u>when</u> a breeze is blowing

B. 1. when the king had a frightening dream, was serving
 2. when Daniel came, told

3. After Daniel was silent for a long time, he explained the dream.
4. As Nebuchadnezzar was boasting one day, a voice spoke from heaven.
5. The people drove Nebuchadnezzar from the palace because he acted like an animal.
6. After Nebuchadnezzar had his right mind again, he honored the King of heaven.

C. Write complex sentences of your own, using these dependent clauses. Begin sentences 1 and 2 with the adverb clause, and sentences 3 and 4 with the main clause.
1. before anyone could stop him
2. if you do not know the answer
3. because we were late
4. although I had not seen it

Review Exercises

A. Write the correct words in parentheses. [106]
1. Marilyn can write (good, well).
2. Jonathan is feeling quite (good, well) again.
3. This book about foxes is (good, well).
4. We had not seen (none, any) of the girls.
5. We hadn't seen (none, any) of the boys either.
6. I (can, can't) hardly see where we are going.

B. Write the correct word for each sentence. Also write whether that word is a *direct object*, an *indirect object*, a *predicate nominative*, or a *predicate adjective*. [64, 106]
1. Mother gave (we, us) girls the directions.
2. Sarah brought (she, her) to us.
3. The song leader is (he, him).
4. This pie tastes (good, well).
5. Father told (we, us) boys the story.

———————————

3. After Daniel was silent for a long time, explained
4. As Nebuchadnezzar was boasting one day, spoke
5. because he acted like an animal, drove
6. After Nebuchadnezzar had his right mind again, honored

C. (Individual sentences.)

Review Exercises

A. 1. well
   2. well
   3. good
   4. any
   5. any
   6. can

B. 1. us—indirect object
   2. her—direct object
   3. he—predicate nominative
   4. good—predicate adjective
   5. us—indirect object

111. Diagraming Adverb Clauses

You know how to diagram a single word used as an adverb. It is placed on a slanted line beneath the word it modifies.

The visitors arrived late.

An adverb phrase is also diagramed beneath the word it modifies.

The visitors arrived after midnight.

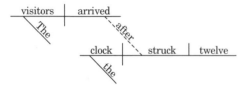

Likewise, an adverb clause is diagramed beneath the word it modifies. A broken line is drawn from the word (usually the verb) that the clause modifies, to the verb in the adverb clause. The subordinating conjunction is placed on the broken line.

The visitors arrived after the clock struck twelve.

The last diagram above shows how the main clause and the adverb clause are related. The main clause contains the main thought of the sentence, and the adverb clause modifies the verb in the main clause by telling *when*.

When you diagram a sentence with an adverb clause, you must recognize which part of the sentence is the main clause and which part is

7. An adjective clause usually begins with what part of speech? (relative pronoun)
8. Where in a sentence must an adjective clause be found? (right after the noun or pronoun it modifies)

Lesson Introduction: Diagram the following sentences on the chalkboard.

We mowed the lawn <u>yesterday</u>.

We mowed the lawn <u>in the evening</u>.

We mowed the lawn <u>before it rained</u>.

Adverbs are diagramed beneath the words they modify, whether they are single words, phrases, or clauses. Today we will learn how to diagram adverb clauses.

Lesson Outline:

An adverb clause is diagramed beneath the main clause of a sentence.

   a. Decide which part of the sentence is the adverb clause and which part is the main clause.
   b. Diagram the main clause.
   c. Diagram the adverb clause in its proper place beneath the main clause.
   d. Draw a broken line from the word (usually the verb) that the adverb clause modifies, to the verb in the adverb clause. Write the subordinating conjunction on the broken line. (Only adverb clauses that modify verbs are taught at this level.)

★ **EXTRA PRACTICE**
Worksheet 70 *(Adverb Clauses)*

Lesson 111

Purpose: To teach *how to diagram adverb clauses.

Oral Review:
1. What parts of speech do adverb clauses modify? (verbs, adjectives, adverbs)
2. What do adverb clauses tell? (how, when, where, why, to what degree, how long, how much, in spite of what, under what condition)
3. a. An adverb clause begins with what part of speech? (subordinating conjunction)
   b. List some subordinating conjunctions. (after, although, as, because, before, if, since, unless, until, when, where, while)
4. What is a plural noun? (a word that names more than one person, place, thing, or idea)
5. How are most plural nouns spelled? (by adding *-s*)
6. Give the better verb: *Measles (is, are) a contagious disease.* (is)

the adverb clause. Look for a subordinating conjunction, such as *after, although, as, because, before, if, since, unless, until, when, where,* and *while.* Then find the rest of the adverb clause, being sure it includes a subject and a verb. Diagram the main clause first, and then diagram the adverb clause as shown in the lesson.

> • An adverb clause is diagramed beneath the main clause. The subordinating conjunction is written on the broken line that connects the modified word in the main clause to the verb in the adverb clause.

Class Practice

Diagram these sentences on the chalkboard.
1. After Sandra ate her breakfast, she gathered the eggs.
2. Tonight we will work until the sun sets.
3. We saw you before you saw us.
4. When you come, she will be ready.

Written Exercises

A. Copy each adverb clause, and underline the subordinating conjunction. Also copy the word or phrase that the adverb clause modifies.
1. God gave Abraham a son as He had promised.
2. If You had been here, Lazarus would not have died.
3. While the farmer slept, an enemy sowed weed seeds in his field.
4. Before the lamp of God went out, Samuel lay down to sleep.
5. He ran to Eli several times because he heard a voice.
6. After Samuel went back again, the Lord called him.
7. In those days the word of the Lord was precious because the Lord did not frequently speak to anyone.
8. Wherever Jesus leads, we will follow.

B. Diagram these sentences.
1. We traveled slowly because it was very foggy.
2. The children sang because they were happy.
3. He asked for money when he saw Peter and John.

Lesson 111 Answers
Class Practice

Written Exercises

A. 1. <u>as</u> He had promised, gave
2. <u>If</u> You had been here, would have died
3. <u>While</u> the farmer slept, sowed
4. <u>Before</u> the lamp of God went out, lay
5. <u>because</u> he heard a voice, ran
6. <u>After</u> Samuel went back again, called
7. <u>because</u> the Lord did not frequently speak to anyone, was
8. <u>Wherever</u> Jesus leads, will follow

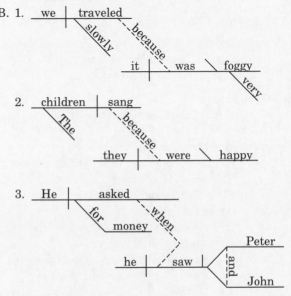

4. The lame man was healed when Peter lifted him up.
5. Many people believed in Jesus after this happened.
6. When Jesus spoke, the leprosy departed from the man.

Review Exercises

A. Write the plural form of each word. [22, 23]
1. key   6. alto
2. town   7. hero
3. bus   8. gentleman
4. leaf   9. tooth
5. safe   10. child

B. Write the better words in parentheses. [23]
1. Measles (is, are) a disease that can cause serious harm.
2. Leon's new trousers (is, are) dark blue.
3. Where (is, are) the scissors?

C. Diagram these sentences, which have adjective clauses. [98]
1. The bird book, which Father gave me, was helpful.
2. Mother served the ice cream that Grandmother brought.
3. The people who helped us live in Dalton.

---

112. The Special Language of Poetry

Good poetry often uses figures of speech. You studied similes and metaphors in Lesson 96. Poems also contain similes, metaphors, and other figures of speech.

A simile is a figure of speech comparing two things that are not really alike, with the use of *like* or *as*. The similes in the following poems are underlined.

Words

Words are <u>like kites</u>—
    We send them away
On the wing of the air
    When we speak or we pray.

Lesson 112

Purpose: (1) To teach the use of figurative language in poetry: similes, metaphors, and *personification. (2) To promote appreciation for poetry.

Oral Review:

1. What is rhyme? (the matching of sounds at the ends of words or lines)
2. What are some rules for good rhymes?
   (a. The vowel sounds of the rhyming words or syllables must be the same.
   b. The last consonant sound of the rhyming syllables must be the same.
   c. The beginning consonant sounds of the rhyming syllables must be different.)
3. What poetic qualities does Bible poetry have?
   (a. It can be written in lines and stanzas.
   b. It is full of descriptive words and rich meaning.

Review Exercises

A. 1. keys   6. altos
    2. towns   7. heroes
    3. buses   8. gentlemen
    4. leaves   9. teeth
    5. safes   10. children

B. 1. is
    2. are
    3. are

C.

c. Often two lines are similar, with the second line repeating the first one but using different words.)
4. What are some reasons for writing friendly letters? (to visit with someone you do not see often; to give help or encouragement to someone who is not with you; to give or accept an invitation; to thank someone for a favor shown)

Words fly away
>For good or for ill,
But we can't pull them in,
>Like kites, at our will.

Winter Blanket

The snow is <u>like a blanket</u> that
>God spreads across the land,
Where wheat and oats and barley sleep,
>Awaiting spring's command.

The first poem shows a comparison between words and kites: both words and kites go flying through the air. It also shows a contrast: we can pull kites back in, but we cannot do that with words. The second poem compares snow to a blanket that is spread across the land while crops "sleep" under it. These comparisons are so fitting that we can easily understand what the poems mean.

A metaphor is much like a simile, but the word *like* or *as* is not used. The metaphors in the following poems are underlined.

I Am Jesus' Little Lamb

<u>I am Jesus' little lamb,</u>
Ever glad at heart I am;
For my Shepherd gently guides me,
Knows my need, and well provides me,
Loves me every day the same,
Even calls me by my name.
>—Henrietta Louisa von Hayn

Thy Word Have I Hid in My Heart

<u>Thy Word is a lamp</u> to my feet,
<u>A light</u> to my path alway;
To guide and to save me from sin,
And show me the heavenly way.
>—Ernest O. Sellers

5. Name the five parts of a friendly letter. (heading, greeting, body, closing, signature)
6. Compare friendly letters and business letters.
   a. What additional part does a business letter have? (inside address)
   b. How are the greetings punctuated differently? (A comma follows the greeting of a friendly letter. A colon follows the greeting of a business letter.)

Lesson Introduction: When we compare two unlike things that are similar in a certain way, we use a figure of speech. Good poems use many figures of speech. The Bible also uses figures of speech. Listen to the following comparisons.

>The Lord God is a sun and shield.
>The tongue is a fire.
>All flesh is as grass.
>The kingdom of heaven is like to a grain of mustard seed.

How is the Lord a sun? The sun gives us light and warmth. We could not live without the sun. Since we know these things about the sun, we can understand the Lord better by comparing Him to the sun. By the light of His Word, the Lord shows us how to live and how to reach heaven. Our hearts are warmed by His love. He gives eternal life to those who trust and obey Him.

Figures of speech make ideas more clear and meaningful. Today we want to study several different figures of speech and some poems that use them.

Be on Guard
Guard well your thoughts,
For they are seeds
For lovely blooms
Or ugly weeds.

Guard well your words,
For they have power
To cheer and bless
Or wound and mar.

"I am Jesus' little lamb" because He tenderly cares for me. "Thy Word is a lamp" because it shows us the right way to go. "Thoughts are seeds" because they grow into words and deeds. Again, the comparisons are well suited to the thoughts in the poems.

In another figure of speech, the characteristics of a person or animal are applied to an inanimate object (neither person nor animal). This is called *personification*. Study the following lines from the poem "Columbus."

They sailed. They sailed. Then spake the mate:
"This mad sea shows his teeth tonight;
He curls his lips, he lies in wait,
With lifted teeth as if to bite;
Brave Admiral, say but one good word.
What shall we say when hope is gone?"
The words leaped like a leaping sword:
"Sail on! sail on! sail on! and on!"
—Joaquin Miller

These lines speak of the mad sea showing his teeth, curling his lips, and lying in wait as if to bite. Of course, the sea never actually does these things. It does not even have teeth or lips. But if one imagines the raging sea to be a vicious animal, the personification is truly fitting.

A poet often uses words that suggest the sounds of what they refer to. For example, the word *smooth* is a smooth-sounding word. The word *purr* sounds like the noise made by a contented kitten, and *pitter, patter* sounds like raindrops on a windowpane. Study the underlined examples in the following stanzas.

Lesson Outline:

1. Good poetry has many figures of speech.

    a. A simile compares two unlike things by using *like* or *as*.

    b. A metaphor makes a comparison without using *like* or *as*.

    c. Personification applies the characteristics of a person or an animal to an inanimate object.

2. Various methods are used to give poetry a pleasing sound.

    a. Words are used that suggest the sounds they describe. These are imitative words like *buzz, hiss, crash,* and *bang*. (*Teacher:* This poetic device is called *onomatopoeia* [on·ə·mat·ə·pē·ə]. The term is not taught at this level.)

    b. Several words beginning with the same sound are placed close together. One example is the line "In the *rifted rock* I'm *resting*." (*Teacher:* This poetic device is called *alliteration*. The term is not taught at this level.)

The Barnyard Chorus

The cows are singing bass notes
    As they raise their heads and <u>moo</u>,
The hens are <u>clucking</u> alto to their brood;
The mourning doves sing tenor
    With a harmonizing <u>coo</u>,
The pigs <u>squeal</u> high soprano for some food.

What a racket, what a <u>babble</u>,
    As the turkeys add their <u>gabble</u>,
The gander <u>honks</u>, the mule starts to <u>bray</u>;
Then the rooster adds his <u>crowing</u>,
    So I think that I'll be going,
And listen to their music—far away!

—Viola Jacobson Berg
From *Pathways for the Poet*, copyright 1977
Reprinted by permission of Baker Book House
Company

The Waters of Lodore

And <u>rushing</u> and <u>flushing</u> and <u>brushing</u> and <u>gushing</u>,
And <u>flapping</u> and <u>rapping</u> and <u>clapping</u> and <u>slapping</u>,
And <u>thumping</u> and <u>plumping</u> and <u>bumping</u> and <u>jumping</u>,
And <u>dashing</u> and <u>flashing</u> and <u>splashing</u> and <u>clashing</u>;
And so never ending, but always descending,
Sounds and motions forever and ever are blending,
All at once and all o'er, with a mighty <u>uproar</u>:
And this way, the water comes down at Lodore.

—Robert Southey

In the first example above, many words are so much like animal sounds that we can almost hear the clamor of a barnyard. The second example has many words that suggest the sound of rushing water, and this helps us to "hear" the roaring waterfall.

The sound of words can make poetry beautiful in other ways. You have already studied rhyme, in which words with the same ending sound are placed close together. Words with the same *beginning sound* can also be placed close together to make poetry sound pleasing. Notice how this is done in the example below.

Light After Darkness

Light after darkness, gain after loss,
Strength after weakness, <u>crown</u> after <u>cross</u>,
Sweet after bitter, hope after fears,
Home after wandering, praise after tears.

<u>Sheaves</u> after <u>sowing</u>, <u>sun</u> after rain,
Sight after mystery, <u>peace</u> after <u>pain</u>;
Joy after sorrow, calm after blast,
Rest after weariness, sweet rest at last.

Near after distant, <u>gleam</u> after <u>gloom</u>,
<u>Love</u> after <u>loneliness</u>, <u>life</u> after tomb;
<u>After</u> long <u>agony</u>, rapture of bliss;
Right was the pathway leading to this!

—Frances R. Havergal

Words with similar beginning sounds may have similar meanings, such as *blessing and bliss* or *peace and pleasure*. They may have opposite meanings, such as *crown after cross, peace after pain,* and several other examples in the poem above. The words may not be related at all, such as *after long agony*. In any case, words with similar beginning sounds add to the beauty and appeal of poetry.

- Good poetry has many figures of speech.
  a. A simile compares two unlike things by using *like* or *as*.
  b. A metaphor makes a comparison without using *like* or *as*.
  c. Personification applies the characteristics of a person or an animal to an inanimate object.

- Various methods are used to give poetry a pleasing sound.
  a. Words are used that suggest the sounds they describe.
  b. Several words beginning with the same sound are placed close together.

Class Practice

Tell what figures of speech are used in the poetry below. Tell how the sound of the words makes the lines pleasing to hear.

1. Amidst the storm they sang,
        And the stars heard, and the sea;
    And the sounding aisles of the dim woods rang
        To the anthem of the free.

2. Thy Word is like a garden, Lord,
    With flowers bright and fair;
                        —Edwin Hodder

3. The Lord is my Shepherd, I shall not want;
        He maketh me down to lie
    In pastures green, He leadeth me
        The quiet waters by.

4. **Drop a Pebble in the Water**
    Drop a pebble in the water,
        Just a splash, and it is gone;
    But there's half-a-hundred ripples,
        Circling on and on and on,
    Spreading, spreading from the center,
        Flowing on out to the sea;
    And there is no way of telling
        Where the end is going to be.

    Drop a word of cheer and kindness,
        Just a flash and it is gone;
    But there's half-a-hundred ripples
        Circling on and on and on,
    Bearing hope and joy and comfort
        On each splashing, dashing wave
    Till you wouldn't believe the volume
        Of the one kind word you gave.
                        —Author unknown

Written Exercises

A. Write whether each line contains an example of a *metaphor*, a *simile*, or *personification*.
    1. Clouds like floating shadows
    2. When spring was in her youth

Lesson 112 Answers
Class Practice

(Extra discussion ideas are included with the answers.)

1. a. personification: the stars heard, and the sea
    b. similar beginning sounds: storm, sang; stars, sea
    c. imitative words: sang, sounding, rang
2. a. simile: Word is like a garden
    b. similar beginning sounds: flowers, fair
3. metaphor: The Lord is my Shepherd
4. a. imitative words: splash, splashing
        (The words *flash* and *dashing* rhyme with *splash* and *splashing*. This gives a special effect.)
    b. metaphor or personification:
        Bearing hope and joy and comfort
        On each splashing, dashing wave
    c. The words *Spreading, spreading* and *Circling on and on and on* give the feeling of waves spreading infinitely.

Written Exercises

A. 1. simile
   2. personification

3. The blue sky is the temple's arch
4. The ocean looketh up to heaven
5. Blessings like a shower of gold
6. The sands of time are diamond sparks

B. Copy the words with similar beginning sounds that help to make each stanza pleasing to the ear.

1.   **The Valley of Silence**

    I walk down the valley of silence,
        Down the dim, voiceless valley alone;
    And I hear not the fall of a footstep
        Around me—save God's and my own,
    And the hush of my heart is as holy
        As hovers where angels have flown.

2.   **The Lark**

    O'er fell and fountain sheen,
    O'er moor and mountain green,
  O'er the red banner that blazons the day,
    Over the cloudlet dim,
    Over the rainbow's rim,
  Musical jewel, soar, singing away!

C. Finish the similes and metaphors.
1. The boys were as noisy as ———.
2. As quick as ———, the deer disappeared.
3. The tall tree stood like ———.
4. Her words were smoother than ———, but deceit was in her heart.
5. The pleasant little girl was a ———, and her friendly brother was a ———.
6. Words are ———.

D. Write an original poem of at least eight lines. Use your notes from Lesson 108. Your poem should include at least one figure of speech and one of the methods that make poetry pleasing to hear, as introduced in this lesson.

Review Exercises

Find one mistake in each numbered line. If it is an error of capitalization, write the word correctly. If it is an error of punctuation, write the word before the error and add the correct punctuation. [63]

3. metaphor
4. personification
5. simile
6. metaphor

B. 1. down—dim; voiceless—valley; fall—footstep; hush—heart—holy—hovers
    2. fell—fountain; moor—mountain; banner—blazons; rainbow's—rim; soar—singing

C. (Sample answers.)
1. a troop of Indians, a flock of turkeys
2. a flash, lightning
3. a guard, a statue
4. butter, oil
5. ray of sunshine, springtime breeze
6. arrows, like water

D. (Individual work. Writing a poem is a major assignment, so the pupils should be allowed several days to do this part. Read each poem to the class, *including the one you wrote.* Do not tell who the authors are. Let the students figure that out for themselves.)

1.
2.
3.
4. Dear Brent
5.   I am so sorry to hear that you broke your leg. we are praying
6. that you will be better soon. Im hoping to see you back in school
7. before long
8.
9.

         *   *   *   *   *

10.
11.
12.

13. Crafts Especially For Boys
14. 504 Crescent Ave
15. Eugene, Or 97401

16. Dear Sirs,

17.   I am interested in the book *Building bluebird Houses.*
18. please send me information on how I can order it.

19.
20.

Route 1, box 3310
Newark DE 19702
april 5, 20—

Sincerely
mark

855 East King st.
Newville, pa 17241
July 10 20—

Sincerely:

John bowens

Review Exercises

1. Box
2. Newark,
3. April
4. Brent,
5. We
6. I'm
7. long.
8. Sincerely,
9. Mark
10. St.
11. PA
12. 10,
13. for
14. Ave.
15. OR
16. Sirs:
17. Bluebird
18. Please
19. Sincerely,
20. Bowens

---

113. Simple, Compound, and Complex Sentences

NO

    Sentences may be simple, compound, or complex, according to their structure. How can you tell which is which? One help is to use sentence formulas as you studied earlier. *S* stands for the subject, *V* stands for the verb, and + stands for a conjunction.

    1. *A simple sentence has only one skeleton.*

        Some <u>planets</u> | <u>shine</u> brightly in the night sky.
        S | V = simple sentence

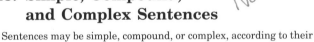

Lesson 113

Purpose: To review and compare simple, compound, and complex sentences.

Oral Review:

1. What parts of speech do adjectives modify? (nouns, pronouns)
2. What do adverbs modify? (verbs, adjectives, other adverbs)
3. What do adjectives tell? (which, whose, how many, what kind of)
4. What do adverbs tell? (how, when, where, to what degree)
5. What do adverb clauses tell? (how, when, where, why, to what degree, how long, how much, in spite of what, under what condition)
6. With what part of speech does an adverb clause begin? (subordinating conjunction)

Lesson Introduction: Write the following sentences on the chalkboard. Ask students to pick out the sentence skeletons. Can they identify the simple sentence, the compound sentence, and the complex sentence?

    Ants are insects.
    Ants are insects, but spiders are arachnids.
    Spiders are not insects because spiders have eight legs.

Today we will study simple, compound, and complex sentences.

Lesson Outline:

    1. Sentences may be simple, compound, or complex, according to their structure.

    2. One help to distinguish between simple, compound, and complex sentences is to use sentence formulas.

A simple sentence may have a compound subject or a compound verb, but it is still a simple sentence.

> The <u>sun</u> | <u>rises</u> and <u>sets</u> faithfully every day. (compound verb)
> S | V + V = simple sentence

> <u>Mercury</u> and <u>Venus</u> | <u>are</u> closest to the sun. (compound subject)
> S + S | V = simple sentence

2. *A compound sentence has two skeletons joined by a conjunction.*

> <u>Mars</u> | <u>reflects</u> a reddish color, **and** <u>Jupiter</u> | <u>shows</u> bands of red, yellow, and brown on its surface.
> S | V + S | V = compound sentence

3. *A complex sentence has two skeletons joined by a conjunction.*

> A five-mile-deep <u>canyon</u> | <u>was discovered</u> on Mars **after** <u>satellites</u> | <u>took</u> pictures there.
> S | V + S | V = complex sentence

The formulas for compound and complex sentences are the same. How can you tell the difference between them? The main way is to see what kind of conjunction is used to join the two clauses.

1. *The two clauses of a compound sentence are joined by a* coordinating conjunction.

Coordinating conjunctions:

and	but	or	for	nor	yet

> Mars reflects a reddish color, <u>and</u> Jupiter shows bands of red, yellow, and brown on its surface. (compound sentence)

> Jupiter is beautiful, <u>but</u> it would not be a good place to live. (compound sentence)

2. *The two clauses of a complex sentence are joined by a* subordinating conjunction *or a* relative pronoun.

Subordinating conjunctions: (used to introduce adverb clauses)

after	because	since	when
although	before	unless	where
as	if	until	while

(1) *A simple sentence has only one skeleton.* It is a simple sentence even though it may have a compound subject or a compound predicate.

> S | V = simple sentence
> S + S | V = simple sentence
> S | V + V = simple sentence

(2) *A compound sentence has two skeletons joined by a conjunction.*

> S | V + S | V = compound sentence

(3) *A complex sentence has two skeletons joined by a conjunction.*

> S | V + S | V = complex sentence

3. One way to distinguish a compound sentence from a complex sentence is to see what kind of conjunction is used to join the clauses.

(1) *The two clauses of a compound sentence are joined by a* coordinating conjunction. *The most common coordinating conjunctions are* and, but, or, for, nor, *and* yet.

(2) *The two clauses of a complex sentence are joined by a* subordinating conjunction *or a* relative pronoun.

a. Subordinating conjunctions include *after, although, as, because, before, if, since, unless, until, when, where,* and *while.* These are used to introduce adverb clauses.

b. The relative pronouns are *who, whom, whose, which,* and *that.* These are used to introduce adjective clauses.

A five-mile-deep canyon was discovered on Mars <u>after</u> satellites took pictures there. (complex sentence with adverb clause)

<u>Before</u> close-up pictures were taken, scientists knew little about the surface of Mars. (complex sentence with adverb clause)

Relative pronouns: (used to introduce adjective clauses)

who   whom   whose   which   that

Venus is the planet <u>that</u> shines brightly as an evening or a morning star.
(complex sentence with adjective clause)

We should praise God, <u>who</u> made the beautiful, fascinating planets for His glory.
(complex sentence with adjective clause)

Another way to tell the difference between a compound and a complex sentence is to study the clauses of each sentence.

1. *A compound sentence is made of two independent clauses.* Remember that an independent clause makes sense by itself. Either clause in a compound sentence can stand alone as a complete sentence.

   Compound sentence:
   Mars reflects a reddish color, and Jupiter shows bands of red, yellow, and brown on its surface.

   Clauses standing alone:
   Mars reflects a reddish color. (complete sentence)

   And Jupiter shows bands of red, yellow, and brown on its surface. (complete sentence; *and* is a transitional word)

2. *A complex sentence is made of one independent clause and one dependent clause.* The independent clause is a complete sentence by itself, but the dependent clause is not.

   Complex sentences:
   A five-mile-deep canyon was discovered on Mars after satellites took pictures there.
   Mars has polar caps that appear white from the earth.

4. Another way to distinguish a compound sentence from a complex sentence is to study the clauses of each sentence.

   (1) *A compound sentence is made of two independent clauses.* Either clause in a compound sentence can stand alone as a complete sentence.

   (2) *A complex sentence is made of one independent clause and one dependent clause.* The independent clause is a complete sentence by itself, but the dependent clause is not.

★ **EXTRA PRACTICE**
Worksheet 71 *(Simple, Compound, and Complex Sentences)*

Clauses standing alone:
    A five-mile-deep canyon was discovered on Mars.
        (complete)
    After satellites took pictures there.
        (not complete; *after* is not a transitional word)
    Mars has polar caps. (complete)
    That appear white from the earth. (not complete)

- A simple sentence has only one skeleton. A compound or complex sentence has two skeletons joined by a conjunction.

- The two clauses of a compound sentence are joined by a coordinating conjunction. The two clauses of a complex sentence are joined by a subordinating conjunction or a relative pronoun.

- A compound sentence is made of two independent clauses. A complex sentence is made of one independent clause and one dependent clause.

Class Practice

A. Tell whether each underlined word is a *coordinating conjunction,* a *subordinating conjunction,* or a *relative pronoun.*
   1. Ostriches cannot fly, <u>but</u> they can run very fast.
   2. This is one mother bird <u>that</u> uses solar energy to incubate her eggs.
   3. The ostrich does sit on her eggs <u>when</u> the sun does not shine.
   4. Young ostriches are hard to spot <u>because</u> the color of their feathers matches the desert sand.

B. Tell whether each underlined clause is *dependent* or *independent.* If it is dependent, tell whether it is an *adjective clause* or an *adverb clause.*
   1. A young ostrich lies very still <u>when an enemy comes near.</u>
   2. When blowing desert sands partly cover a motionless ostrich, <u>he may appear to be hiding his head in the sand.</u>
   3. <u>The ostrich closes his eyes</u> so that an enemy cannot easily spot him.
   4. The special instincts <u>that God gave the ostrich</u> help it.

Lesson 113 Answers
Class Practice
A. 1. coordinating conjunction
   2. relative pronoun
   3. subordinating conjunction
   4. subordinating conjunction

B. 1. dependent, adverb clause
   2. independent
   3. independent
   4. dependent, adjective clause

C. Tell whether each sentence is *simple, compound,* or *complex.*
   1. A mother ostrich is not really deserting her chicks when she runs away from them.
   2. She is leading the enemy away from her hidden chicks.
   3. The ostrich has no understanding of her own, but God has given her special instincts.

D. On the chalkboard, write the formulas for the sentences in Part C.

Written Exercises

A. Write whether each underlined clause is *dependent* or *independent.* If it is dependent, write whether it is an adjective clause (*adj.*) or an adverb clause (*adv.*).
   1. The children of Israel cried to the Lord <u>when the Midianites came against them</u>.
   2. <u>Gideon was threshing wheat by the winepress</u> when the angel of the Lord came to him.
   3. God wanted to use Gideon for greater work <u>because Gideon was already working faithfully</u>.
   4. Twenty-two thousand men <u>who were fearful</u> returned home.

B. Write whether each underlined word is a *coordinating conjunction,* a *subordinating conjunction,* or a *relative pronoun.*
   1. The earth around the fleece was dry, <u>but</u> Gideon wrung a bowlful of water out of the fleece.
   2. Gideon knew that God would save Israel <u>because</u> the fleece was dry on the second morning.
   3. On the second day, the ground <u>that</u> was around the fleece was wet with dew.
   4. Gideon was ready to go <u>after</u> he knew that God would be with him.

C. Write whether each sentence is *simple, compound,* or *complex.*
   1. The Lord gave another special sign to Gideon.
   2. Gideon asked his servant to go with him, and they crept to the edge of the Midianite camp.
   3. A Midianite was telling his dream when Gideon came near.
   4. In his dream a cake of barley bread tumbled into the camp of the Midianites, and the rolling cake overturned one of the tents.
   5. Another soldier explained the meaning of the dream.
   6. Gideon worshiped the Lord after he heard the interpretation.

C. 1. complex
   2. simple
   3. compound

D. 1. S | V + S | V = complex sentence
   2. S | V = simple sentence
   3. S | V + S | V = compound sentence

Written Exercises

A. 1. dependent, adv.
   2. independent
   3. dependent, adv.
   4. dependent, adj.

B. 1. coordinating conjunction
   2. subordinating conjunction
   3. relative pronoun
   4. subordinating conjunction

C. 1. simple   4. compound
   2. compound   5. simple
   3. complex   6. complex

7. He divided his three hundred men into three groups, and then he stationed them around the Midianite camp.
8. Gideon and his men blew the trumpets, broke the pitchers, and raised a battle cry.

Review Exercises

Diagram the following sentences.
1. When Gideon's men blew the trumpets, the Midianites were greatly frightened.
2. The whole host cried out and fled in panic.
3. God helped Gideon because Gideon obeyed God.

---

114. Chapter 9 Review

Class Practice

A. Give the definition of an adverb.

B. Give the three degrees of comparison for each modifier.
1. fast   4. little   7. well   9. easily
2. swiftly   5. early   8. far   10. ill
3. late   6. lively

C. For each underlined phrase, give a word or phrase that is more effective.
1. The teacher is reading a <u>really good</u> book to us.
2. The weather was <u>really awful</u> yesterday.
3. My grandmother was <u>very bad</u> again yesterday.
4. We saw an <u>awfully hot</u> fire last night.
5. That car went <u>very fast</u> past our house.

D. Tell whether each underlined word, phrase, or clause is used as an *adverb* or an *adjective*. Also tell which word each one modifies, and what question the modifier answers.
1. We wanted to make handprints in the new concrete, but it was already <u>hard</u>.
2. The crank on the old car turned <u>hard</u>.
3. Jennifer is a <u>friendly</u> girl.
4. The book <u>on the table</u> is for you.

Lesson 114

Purpose: To review the concepts taught in Chapter 9.

7. compound
8. simple

Review Exercises

1.

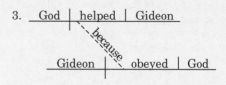

2.

3.

Lesson 114 Answers
Class Practice

A. An adverb is a word that modifies a verb, an adjective, or another adverb. It tells *how, when, where,* or *to what degree.*

B. 1. fast, faster, fastest
2. swiftly, more swiftly, most swiftly
3. late, later, latest
4. little, less, least
5. early, earlier, earliest
6. lively, livelier, liveliest
7. well, better, best
8. far, farther, farthest
9. easily, more easily, most easily
10. ill, worse, worst

C. (Sample answers.)
1. interesting, informative, fascinating
2. stormy, extremely cold, hot and humid
3. quite ill, in much pain
4. blazing, raging, roaring
5. sped, flew, raced

D. 1. (predicate) adjective, it, what kind of
2. adverb, turned, how
3. adjective, girl, what kind of
4. adjective, book, which

5. I put the book about ships <u>on the living room table</u>.

6. Sister Janice tacks a box of tissues on the side <u>of her desk</u>.

7. The tissues <u>that she put on the table</u> are for everyone.

8. Several students became curious <u>when Sister Jane placed a box on the table</u>.

E. Read the poem below, and do these exercises.

1. Find the similes in the poem.

2. Find one metaphor.

3. Find some words that are close together, which begin with the same sound.

4. Find one example of personification.

5. Find some words that imitate the sounds they describe.

The Village Blacksmith

Under a spreading chestnut tree
　　The village smithy stands;
The smith, a mighty man is he,
　　With large and sinewy hands,
And the muscles of his brawny arms
　　Are strong as iron bands.

His hair is crisp and black and long,
　　His face is like the tan;
His brow is wet with honest sweat,
　　He earns whate'er he can,
And looks the whole world in the face,
　　For he owes not any man.

Week in, week out, from morn till night,
　　You can hear his bellows blow;
You can hear him swing his heavy sledge
　　With measured beat and slow,
Like a sexton ringing the village bell
　　When the evening sun is low.

And children coming home from school
　　Look in at the open door;
They love to see the flaming forge,
　　And hear the bellows roar,
And catch the burning sparks that fly
　　Like chaff from a threshing floor.

5. adverb, put, where

6. adjective, side, which

7. adjective, tissues, which

8. adverb, became, when

E. 1. strong as iron bands
　　face is like the tan (*Teacher:* "The tan" may be a solution for tanning leather.)
　　Like a sexton ringing the village bell
　　Like chaff from a threshing floor.

2. the flaming forge of life *or* its sounding anvil

3. (Sample words are underlined.)
　　Under a spreading chestnut tree
　　　　The village <u>smithy</u> <u>stands</u>;
　　The smith, a <u>mighty</u> <u>man</u> is he,
　　　　With large and sinewy hands,

　　<u>Week</u> in, <u>week</u> out, from morn till night,
　　　　You can hear his <u>bellows</u> <u>blow</u>:
　　You can hear him <u>swing</u> his heavy <u>sledge</u>
　　　　With measured beat and slow,

　　Thus at the <u>flaming</u> <u>forge</u> of life
　　　　Our <u>fortunes</u> must be wrought;

4. looks the whole world in the face
　　(The world does not really have a face.)

5. blow, ringing, roar

Toiling, rejoicing, sorrowing,
    Onward through life he goes;
Each morning sees some task begun,
    Each evening sees it close;
Something attempted, something done,
    Has earned a night's repose.

Thanks, thanks to thee, my worthy friend,
    For the lesson thou hast taught!
Thus at the flaming forge of life
    Our fortunes must be wrought;
Thus on its sounding anvil shaped
    Each burning deed and thought!
                              —Henry W. Longfellow

Written Exercises

A. Copy all the adverbs. Write whether each one tells *how, when, where,* or *to what degree.*

1. We are happiest when we work cheerfully.
2. I usually sweep the floors first.
3. The tide rose unusually high there yesterday.
4. Does she speak Spanish well?
5. We have not often met here.

Written Exercises

A. 1. cheerfully—how
   2. usually—when; first—when
   3. unusually—to what degree; high—where; there—where; yesterday—when
   4. well—how
   5. not—how; often—when; here—where

B. Copy each adverb of degree. After it, write the word that it modifies.
1. This manual on repairing small engines is surely helpful.
2. After James studied the rules of good penmanship, he learned to write quite well.
3. Before he studied, he felt that writing neatly was too difficult.
4. We arrived at our friends' house rather early.
5. Mother said that she had brought too many doughnuts.

C. Write the correct forms in parentheses.
1. Of the two cars, this one runs (more, most) quietly.
2. On our school hike this year, we hiked (more farther, farther) than we did last year.
3. We hiked (farthest, fartherest) of all two years ago.
4. Today we arrived at school (more early, earlier) than yesterday.
5. The horse walked (more slowly, slowlier) yesterday.
6. Grandfather seems (more well, better) this week than last week.
7. I like to read Janet's stories; she writes (good, well).
8. Marilyn is a (good, well) seamstress.
9. It is (good, well) that you are here on time.
10. I couldn't see (anything, nothing) on the shelves.
11. I didn't hear (any, no) birds singing in the woods.
12. Carolyn said she hadn't (ever, never) seen such a tall giraffe before.

D. Write each sentence correctly, using *barely, hardly,* and *scarcely.*
1. Brian couldn't hardly see that sign.
2. We hadn't barely made it on time.
3. I couldn't scarcely see anything through his telescope.

E. Copy each adverb clause, and underline the subordinating conjunction. Also copy the word or phrase that each clause modifies.
1. Jacob grieved because Joseph had disappeared.
2. The brothers were afraid when Joseph spoke roughly to them.
3. They feared even more after Joseph revealed his identity.
4. Although the brothers had acted wickedly, God was caring for them.
5. After Joseph tested his brothers, he assured them of his forgiveness.

B. 1. surely, helpful
2. quite, well
3. too, difficult
4. rather, early
5. too, many

C. 1. more
2. farther
3. farthest
4. earlier
5. more slowly
6. better
7. well
8. good
9. good
10. anything
11. any
12. ever

D. 1. Brian could hardly see that sign.
2. We had barely made it on time.
3. I could scarcely see anything through his telescope.

E. 1. <u>because</u> Joseph had disappeared, grieved
2. <u>when</u> Joseph spoke roughly to them, were
3. <u>after</u> Joseph revealed his identity, feared
4. <u>Although</u> the brothers had acted wickedly, was caring
5. <u>After</u> Joseph tested his brothers, assured

F. Diagram these sentences.
1. Soon the water of our creek rose quite high.
2. It rose over the banks of the creek.
3. The wheat field was flooded after it had rained for several hours.
4. The sheaves in that field are rather wet.
5. After the storm passed, the men went out to the wheat field.

G. Copy the first line of each poem, and mark the rhythm pattern. Then write the correct words for numbers 5 and 6.

1.
Swans
These fair birds when full-grown are a beautiful sight,
They have long necks and feathers of pure, sparkling white;
Though quite often on ponds or in gardens they're seen,
They are listed with those whom God's Word calls unclean.

2.   ### Who Has Seen the Wind?
Who has seen the wind?
    Neither I nor you.
But when the leaves hang trembling,
    The wind is passing through.

Who has seen the wind?
    Neither you nor I.
But when the trees bow down their heads,
    The wind is passing by.
                              —Christina G. Rossetti

3.   ### The Sparrow
My relatives are numerous,
    We're found most ev'rywhere;
But God the Father feeds us all
    And keeps us in His care.

4.   ### The Eagle
High on the crags of the mountain I nest,
For I fly far without stopping to rest;
Swift is my flight and my wings are so strong,
On my broad back I can carry my young.
Sometimes this picture is used to compare
How our great God for His children doth care.

F. 1. (diagram)
2. (diagram)
3. (diagram)
4. (diagram)
5. (diagram)

G. 1. These fair birds when full-grown are a beautiful sight,
2. Who has seen the wind?
3. My relatives are numerous,
4. High on the crags of the mountain I nest,

5. The rhythm pattern in number 2 is (iambic, trochaic).
6. The rhythm pattern in number 3 is (iambic, trochaic).

H. Write the pairs of rhyming words in the poems of Part G.

_____

5. trochaic
6. iambic

H. 1. sight—white; seen—unclean
2. you—through; I—by
3. ev'rywhere—care
4. nest—rest; strong—young; compare—care
   (*Strong—young* is optional, since the rhyme
   is not exact.)

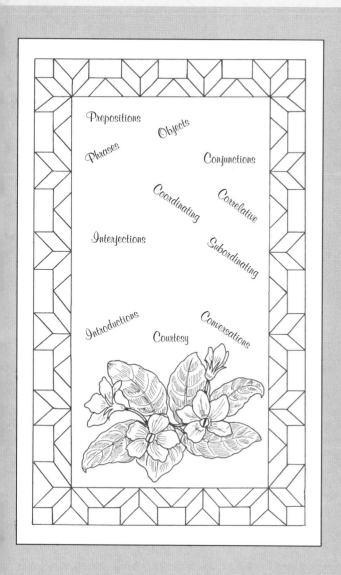

Prepositions
Objects
Phrases
Conjunctions
Coordinating
Correlative
Interjections
Subordinating
Introductions
Conversations
Courtesy

Chapter Ten

Using Prepositions, Conjunctions, and Interjections

Communicating Orally

A preposition is a connecting word that begins a prepositional phrase.
A conjunction is a word that joins words, phrases, or clauses.
An interjection is a word that expresses strong feeling.

Sound speech, that cannot be condemned.

Titus 2:8

Common Prepositions

aboard	before	except	off	under
about	behind	for	on	underneath
above	below	from	over	until
across	beneath	in	past	unto
after	beside	inside	since	up
against	between	into	through	upon
along	beyond	like	throughout	with
among	by	near	to	within
around	down	of	toward	without
at	during			

115. Prepositions

A *preposition* is a connecting word that begins a *prepositional phrase*. It shows the relationship between its *object* and some other word in the sentence.

preposition   object
↓   ↓

A bird flew <u>over the lake</u>.

   (*Over* shows the relationship between *flew* and *lake*.)

Most prepositions are simple, basic words. Study the chart above. You do not need to memorize the list, but you should become thoroughly familiar with the common prepositions. Many words in the list may also be used as adverbs or conjunctions. But a preposition always begins a phrase, and it always has an object.

There are other prepositions that are not on the list. You can easily recognize those if you are familiar with the most common prepositions. A dictionary will tell you whether a word can be used as a preposition.

A preposition is always the first word of a prepositional phrase. A prepositional phrase includes the preposition, its object, and any adjectives that modify the object. The object of a preposition is the noun or pronoun at the end of the phrase. Here is another sentence with a prepositional phrase.

Lesson 115

Purpose: To teach the recognition of prepositions and prepositional phrases.

Oral Review:

1. What do adjectives modify? (nouns, pronouns)
2. What parts of speech do adverbs modify? (verbs, adjectives, adverbs)
3. What do adjectives tell? (which, whose, how many, what kind of)
4. What do adverbs tell? (how, when, where, to what degree)
5. What do adverb clauses tell? (how, when, where, why, to what degree, how long, how much, in spite of what, under what condition)
6. What is a run-on error? (the mistake of writing two or more sentences together without the proper punctuation between them)
7. In what number words must hyphens be used? (in compound number words from twenty-one through ninety-nine)
8. Give three instances when a colon is used. (after the greeting of a business letter, between the hour and minute when writing a time with numbers, between the chapter and verse in a Scripture reference)
9. Give two instances when a semicolon is used. (to join clauses in a compound sentence when no conjunction is used; to join clauses in a compound sentence when a conjunction is used, if a comma is used within one or more of the clauses)

Lesson Introduction: Write the following sentence on the chalkboard. Ask, "Does this sentence make sense without a word in the blank?"

   The car drove ——— the road.

preposition adjectives object
↓   ↓ ↓   ↓
Joseph told Pharaoh the meaning <u>of his two dreams</u>.

Use the following steps to find a prepositional phrase in a sentence.

1. *Find the preposition.*
2. *Find the object of the preposition by saying the preposition and asking* whom *or* what. The answer is the object; it is always a noun or pronoun.
3. *The prepositional phrase includes all the words from the preposition to its object.* Any words in between are adjectives that modify the object. Not all prepositional phrases have adjectives.

Use these steps to find the prepositional phrase in this sentence.

Sing unto the Lord a new song.

Think: 1. The preposition is *unto.*
2. Unto *whom*? The object is *Lord.*
3. The prepositional phrase is *unto the Lord.*

Prepositional phrases can be used as adjectives to modify nouns and pronouns. An adjective phrase comes immediately after the noun that it modifies.

The flowers <u>along the road</u> are poppies. (modifies *flowers*)
Finally we reached the top <u>of the hill</u>. (modifies *top*)

Prepositional phrases can be used as adverbs to modify verbs, adjectives, and other adverbs. Adverb phrases tell *how, when, where, why,* and *to what degree.* An adverb phrase may be found at various places in a sentence.

The visitors arrived yesterday <u>before noon</u>.
The visitors arrived <u>before noon</u> yesterday.
<u>Before noon</u> yesterday, the visitors arrived.
(In every sentence, *before noon* tells *when* the visitors arrived.)

A prepositional phrase is diagramed beneath the word it modifies. The preposition is written on a slanted line, and its object goes on a horizontal line connected to it. Any adjectives go on slanted lines below the object of the preposition.

The sentence needs a word to show the relationship between *drove* and *road.* The part of speech that does this is the preposition. Have the students turn to the list of prepositions and give suggestions for the blank.

Lesson Outline:

1. A preposition is a connecting word that begins a prepositional phrase. It shows the relationship between its object and another word in the sentence. Most prepositions are simple, basic words, as shown on the chart on page 508.

2. A prepositional phrase includes the preposition, its object, and any adjectives that modify the object.

3. The object of a preposition is the noun or pronoun at the end of the phrase. Every preposition has an object that the preposition connects to another word in the sentence.

4. Use the following steps to find a prepositional phrase in a sentence.

(1) *Find the preposition.*
(2) *Find the object of the preposition by saying the preposition and asking* whom *or* what. The object is always a noun or pronoun.
(3) *The prepositional phrase includes all the words from the preposition to its object.* Any words in between are adjectives that modify the object. Not all prepositional phrases include adjectives.

5. A prepositional phrase may be used as an adjective to modify a noun or pronoun. An adjective phrase comes immediately after the noun it modifies.

Sing unto the Lord a new song.

If a prepositional phrase has a compound object, the objects are diagramed on a fork.

We looked for strawberries and raspberries.

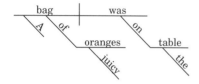

The object of a preposition cannot be the subject of a sentence. Make sure you choose the right word for the subject when it is followed by a prepositional phrase.

A <u>bag</u> (of juicy oranges) <u>was</u> (on the table).

Sometimes more than one phrase modifies the same word.

Several trees fell across the road during the storm.

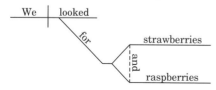

6. A prepositional phrase may be used as an adverb to modify a verb, an adjective, or another adverb. An adverb phrase may come at the beginning of the sentence, in the middle, or at the end.

7. A prepositional phrase is diagramed beneath the word it modifies. The preposition is placed on a slanted line, its object goes on a horizontal line connected to it, and any adjectives go on slanted lines below the object of the preposition.

  a. If a prepositional phrase has a compound object, the compound object is diagramed on a fork.

  b. If a prepositional phrase comes after the subject, be sure to choose the right word for the subject. The subject is never the object of a preposition.

  c. If more than one prepositional phrase modifies the same word, each phrase is diagramed under that word.

  d. If a prepositional phrase modifies the object of another preposition, it is diagramed beneath the object of the first preposition.

8. Do not confuse prepositions and adverbs. A preposition begins a phrase. An adverb stands alone.

They went <u>up</u>.
They went <u>up the elevator</u>.

★ **EXTRA PRACTICE**
Worksheet 72 *(Prepositions)*

Sometimes a prepositional phrase modifies the object of another preposition. Study the following sentence.

The sun was shining <u>through a crack</u> <u>in the wall</u>.

In the sentence above, the two phrases work together to tell *where*. *Through a crack* is an adverb phrase. *In the wall* is an adjective phrase that tells *which* about the noun *crack*. The second phrase does not directly modify the verb, for the sun was not shining *in the wall*!

Because *in the wall* modifies *crack,* it is diagramed below that word. It is not placed directly below the verb.

The sun was shining through a crack in the wall.

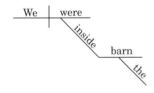

Do not confuse prepositions and adverbs. A preposition begins a phrase, but an adverb stands alone. Compare the following sentences and their diagrams.

We were inside.

We were inside the barn.

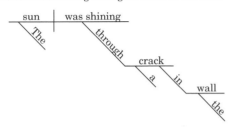

Written Exercises, Part B

B. 1.

(*Wise* may be an adjective.)

2.

(*For Christ* may be diagramed under *way.*)

3.
4.
5.

6.

- A preposition is a connecting word that begins a prepositional phrase. The object of a preposition is a noun or pronoun.

- A prepositional phrase may be used as an adjective to modify a noun or pronoun.

- A prepositional phrase may be used as an adverb to modify a verb, an adjective, or another adverb.

Class Practice

A. Read each prepositional phrase. Tell what kind of phrase it is, and which word it modifies.
  1. My cousins from Illinois arrived after midnight.
  2. At first Uncle Ben's lived across the river.
  3. Brother John calmly read from the book in his hands.
  4. James was working on the window near the chimney.
  5. We received several letters from Aunt Mary since last month.

B. Write the prepositional phrases from numbers 1–3 in Part A on the chalkboard. Underline each preposition, and put parentheses around each object.

C. Diagram the following sentences on the chalkboard.
  1. The weasel lined its den with dry grass for the winter.
  2. These flowers are for Grandfather and Grandmother.
  3. The first book on the shelf was about ships.
  4. The chipmunk in the back yard has dived into its hole.

Written Exercises

A. Copy the prepositional phrases. Write whether each one is an *adjective* or an *adverb*.
  1. A journey of forty days was before them.
  2. By the end of June, we had finished.
  3. Lot beheld all the plain of Jordan.
  4. We memorized from the books of Psalms and Proverbs.
  5. Philip went down to the city of Samaria.
  6. The angel of the Lord sent him toward the south.
  7. A man of Ethiopia was reading from Isaiah.

Lesson 115 Answers
Class Practice

A. 1. from Illinois, adjective, cousins
      after midnight, adverb, arrived
   2. At first, adverb, lived
      across the river, adverb, lived
   3. from the book, adverb, read
      in his hands, adjective, book
   4. on the window, adverb, was working
      near the chimney, adjective, window
   5. from Aunt Mary, adverb, received
      since last month, adverb, received

B. 1. <u>from</u> (Illinois), <u>after</u> (midnight)
   2. <u>At</u> (first), <u>across</u> the (river)
   3. <u>from</u> the (book), <u>in</u> his (hands)

C.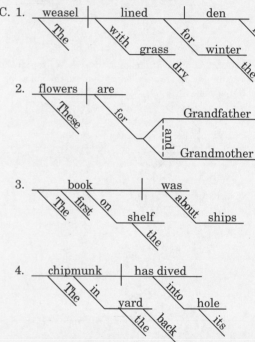

Written Exercises

A. 1. of forty days, adjective; before them, adverb
   2. By the end, adverb; of June, adjective
   3. of Jordan, adjective
   4. from the books, adverb; of Psalms and Proverbs, adjective
   5. to the city, adverb; of Samaria, adjective
   6. of the Lord, adjective; toward the south, adverb
   7. of Ethiopia, adjective; from Isaiah, adverb

8. In the days of King Josiah, God spoke to Jeremiah.
9. Jesus taught with authority.
10. God is with us.

B. Diagram the following sentences.
   1. The wise men rejoiced with exceeding joy.
   2. John prepared the way for Christ.
   3. At the Jordan, he baptized the people.
   4. Jesus came into Galilee.
   5. Beside the Sea of Galilee, He taught the people.
   6. The angel of the Lord descended from heaven.

C. Write two original sentences in which the simple subjects are modified by prepositional phrases. Then write two original sentences in which the verbs are modified by prepositional phrases.

Review Exercises
Copy each sentence, and add the missing punctuation marks. [77–87]
   1. Raccoons eat young grass shoots earthworms frogs salamanders turtles fish and insects in the spring and they eat strawberries cherries blackberries and wild grapes in the summer and fall.
   2. One of their favorite foods is corn they especially like the kernels that are almost ripe.
   3. The raccoons break down the cornstalks by climbing them and they usually taste a few bites from every ear.
   4. Theyre also especially fond of sugar cane sweet potatoes peanuts and buckwheat.
   5. We found thirty three ruined cornstalks in my great uncles garden this morning.
   6. Proverbs 12 10 is a verse about being kind to animals.
   7. Sister Lois said Finish memorizing Exodus 20 1 17 by Monday.

---

116. Using Prepositions Correctly

It is easy to make mistakes in using certain prepositions, especially if they are similar in spelling or meaning. A dictionary is helpful in learning the actual meanings and uses of troublesome prepositions. But

---

8. In the days, adverb; of King Josiah, adjective; to Jeremiah, adverb
9. with authority, adverb
10. with us, adverb

(Part B is on page 511.)

C. (Individual sentences.)

Review Exercises
(Corrections are underlined.)
   1. Raccoons eat young grass shoots, earthworms, frogs, salamanders, turtles, fish, and insects in the spring; and they eat strawberries, cherries, blackberries, and wild grapes in the summer and fall.
   2. One of their favorite foods is corn; they especially like the kernels that are almost ripe.
   3. The raccoons break down the cornstalks by climbing them, and they usually taste a few bites from every ear.
   4. They're also especially fond of sugar cane, sweet potatoes, peanuts, and buckwheat.
   5. We found thirty-three ruined cornstalks in my great-uncle's garden this morning.
   6. Proverbs 12:10 is a verse about being kind to animals.
   7. Sister Lois said, "Finish memorizing Exodus 20:1–17 by Monday."

Lesson 116

Purpose: To teach correct usage of specific problem prepositions.

Oral Review:
1. What is a preposition? (a connecting word that begins a prepositional phrase)
2. What part of speech is the object of a preposition? (a noun or pronoun)
3. What part of speech are the words between the preposition and its object? (adjectives)
4. A prepositional phrase can be used as what parts of speech? (adjective, adverb)
5. Answer these questions about capitalization.
   a. Which word in every sentence should be capitalized? (the first word)
   b. Which words in a poem should be capitalized? (the first word of every line)
   c. When should a word like *street* or *river* be capitalized? (when it is part of a proper noun)
   d. When should the pronouns *He* and *Him* be capitalized? (when they refer to God)
   e. What one-letter words are always capitalized? (*I* and *O*)
   f. Which words should be capitalized in the title of a book, story, or poem? (the first word, last word, and every important word)

Lesson Introduction: Read the following sentences to the students, and see if they can identify the errors.

> Divide the candy <u>between</u> all the children.
> Peter jumped <u>in</u> the water and swam ashore.
> Blueberries are a little different <u>than</u> huckleberries.
> We shelled peas <u>in back of</u> the house.
> He sits <u>besides</u> me in school.

most people need study and practice to use them correctly. Learn the following rules for the proper use of prepositions.

1. *In* refers to location. *Into* refers to movement from one location to another.

   Incorrect: The mother cat climbed <u>in</u> the box with her kittens.
   Correct: The mother cat climbed <u>into</u> the box with her kittens.
   Correct: The mother cat was <u>in</u> the box with her kittens.

2. *Except* is a preposition that means "not including." *Accept* is a verb that means "to receive."

   Incorrect: Everyone is here <u>accept</u> Jean.
   Correct: Everyone is here <u>except</u> Jean.
   Correct: I will gladly <u>accept</u> your advice.

3. *Between* refers to only two objects. *Among* refers to more than two.

   Incorrect: The village was hidden <u>between</u> many hills.
   Correct: The village was hidden <u>among</u> many hills.
   Correct: The village was located <u>between</u> the mountain and the lake.

4. *Beside* means "by the side of." *Besides* means "in addition to."

   Correct: Come and sit <u>beside</u> me.
   Correct: Two girls, <u>besides</u> Carol, went along.

5. Do not use *at* or *on* when you mean *to*. We do not talk *at* people or listen *on* them; we talk *to* them and listen *to* them.

   Incorrect: I was talking <u>at</u> my neighbor.
   Correct: I was talking <u>to</u> my neighbor.

   Incorrect: You should listen <u>on</u> your older sister.
   Correct: You should listen <u>to</u> your older sister.

6. Do not use the preposition *of* for the verb *have*. Do not say *could of, should of, would of,* and *must of* for *could have, should have, would have,* and *must have.*

   Incorrect: It must <u>of</u> rained during the night.
   Correct: It must <u>have</u> rained during the night.

Where is Anthony <u>at</u>?
Doesn't anyone know where he went <u>to</u>?
What fell off <u>of</u> the roof?

Each of the sentences above has a mistake in the use of prepositions. Today we will study some rules about using prepositions correctly.

Lesson Outline:

   1. When prepositions are similar in spelling or meaning, be careful to use the correct one.
   (1) *In* refers to location. *Into* refers to movement from one location to another.
   (2) *Except* is a preposition that means "not including." *Accept* is a verb that means "to receive."
   (3) *Between* refers to only two objects. *Among* refers to more than two. (*Teacher:* The second syllable in *between* is related to *twain* and *two.*)

   (4) *Beside* means "by the side of." *Besides* means "in addition to."
   (5) Do not use *at* or *on* when you mean *to*. We do not talk *at* people or listen *on* them; we talk *to* them and listen *to* them.
   (6) Do not use the preposition *of* for the verb *have*. Do not say *could of, should of, would of,* or *must of.*
   (7) Do not say *different than.* Say *different from.*
   (8) Do not say *in back of* for *behind.*

   2. Avoid using unnecessary prepositions.
   (1) Do not use *of* with *off, inside,* or *outside.*

      off the porch, *not* off of the porch
      inside the house, *not* inside of the house

   (2) Do not use *at* or *to* with *where.*

      Where is my glove? *not* Where is my glove at?
      Where are you going? *not* Where are you going to?

   (3) Do not use *with* after *over.*

      after the test was over, *not* after the test was over with

   3. A sentence may end with a preposition if it is needed to complete the meaning. Such a sentence is correct, even though it ends with a preposition. The preposition is needed because the meaning is not complete without it.

★ **EXTRA PRACTICE**
Worksheet 73 *(Using Prepositions Correctly)*

7. Do not say *different than.* Say *different from.*

    Incorrect: This is <u>different than</u> that one.
    Correct: This is <u>different from</u> that one.

8. Do not say *in back of* for *behind.*

    Incorrect: We went <u>in back of</u> the house.
    Correct: We went <u>behind</u> the house.

Do not use unnecessary prepositions. Study the following examples.
1. Do not use *of* with *off, inside,* or *outside.*

    Incorrect: Some calves are outside <u>of</u> their pen.
    Correct: Some calves are outside their pen.

    Incorrect: Try to keep them off <u>of</u> the lawn.
    Correct: Try to keep them off the lawn.

2. Do not use *at* or *to* with *where.*

    Incorrect: Where did you buy that shovel <u>at</u>?
    Correct: Where did you buy that shovel?

    Incorrect: Where are we going <u>to</u> for dinner?
    Correct: Where are we going for dinner?

3. Do not use *with* after *over.*

    Incorrect: The meeting was soon <u>over with</u>.
    Correct: The meeting was soon <u>over</u>.

A preposition usually comes before its object. But sometimes the object comes before the preposition. This is especially common with the pronouns *what, whom, which,* and *that.*

    <u>What</u> were you talking <u>about</u>?
    This is the shovel <u>which</u> I was digging <u>with</u>.

These sentences can often be reworded, with the words in their normal positions. Compare these sentences with the ones above.

    <u>About what</u> were you talking?
    This is the shovel <u>with which</u> I was digging.

As you can see, it is not always wrong to have a preposition at the end of a sentence. Sometimes the preposition is needed because the meaning is not complete without it. Compare the following sentences

Review Exercises *(Lesson 123 answers)*

1.

2.

3.

4.

(From the trees may be diagramed under the verb.)

5.

6.

7.

8.

9.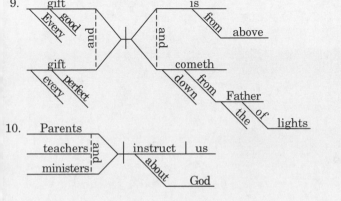

10.

with the previous ones. The meaning of each one is incomplete because a needed preposition is missing.

Incomplete: What were you talking?
Incomplete: This is the shovel which I was digging.

- When prepositions are similar in spelling or meaning, be careful to use the correct one.

- Do not use *of* for *have.* Do not use unnecessary prepositions.

- A sentence may end with a preposition if it is needed to complete the meaning.

Class Practice

Read these sentences correctly. Sometimes you simply need to leave words out. Not all the sentences contain mistakes.

1. Where will the visitors stay at tonight?
2. We are all here accept Charles.
3. We would of seen them go if we could of been there on time.
4. The money was divided between the four brothers.
5. Where are all the children running to?
6. Gerald fell off of the wagon and got hurt.
7. Rover is different than the other dog we had.
8. He has sneaked in the house again.
9. This is the machine that she sewed the purses with.
10. When he talks at you, you should listen on him.
11. After the test was over with, we played ball in back of the school.
12. Please put the bicycles inside of the barn.
13. She must of wanted to sit besides her mother.
14. Whom are you traveling with?

Written Exercises

Write the headings *Mistakes* and *Corrections.* Under *Mistakes,* write the words that should be omitted or changed in the sentences. Beside the wrong words, write any corrected words under *Corrections.* (Some sentences have only words that should be omitted. They will not have words under *Corrections.*)

Lesson 116 Answers
Class Practice
(Corrections are marked.)

1. Where will the visitors stay ~~at~~ tonight?
2. We are all here <u>except</u> Charles.
3. We would <u>have</u> seen them go if we could <u>have</u> been there on time.
4. The money was divided <u>among</u> the four brothers.
5. Where are all the children running ~~to~~?
6. Gerald fell off ~~of~~ the wagon and got hurt.
7. Rover is different <u>from</u> the other dog we had.
8. He has sneaked <u>into</u> the house again.
9. This is the machine that she sewed the purses with. (correct)
10. When he talks <u>to</u> you, you should listen <u>to</u> him.
11. After the test was over ~~with,~~ we played ball <u>behind</u> the school.
12. Please put the bicycles inside ~~of~~ the barn.
13. She must <u>have</u> wanted to sit <u>beside</u> her mother.
14. Whom are you traveling with? (correct)

Examples: a.   Where did you get that drink at?
              b.   Jerry sat among Samuel and me.

Answers: **Mistakes**   **Corrections**
              a.   at
              b.   among   between

1. Divide the candy among you two girls.
2. All the frogs accept one jumped off of the bank and in the water.
3. After the lesson was over with, we took a quiz.
4. John fell off of the roof; he should of been more careful.
5. The children hid between all the trees in back of the house.
6. Does anyone know where Richard is at now?
7. This pretty picture came off of a calendar.
8. Ruth went in Boaz's field to gather grain among all the other reapers.
9. This secret is only among you and me.
10. You should listen on your teacher.
11. James came in the house and sat down besides the stove.
12. Come to the telephone; your brother wants to talk at you.
13. Everyone accept Jane was there before.
14. The place where we went to is hundreds of miles away.
15. I hope my friend sits here besides me.
16. The car was parked in back of a large tree.
17. This test is different than the other one we had.
18. I'll be glad when it is over with.
19. The children sat between the many flowers in the grass.
20. Where are you staying at?

Review Exercises

Copy each adverb clause, and underline the subordinating conjunction. Also copy the verb that the clause modifies. [110]

Example: Lot fled from Sodom before the Lord destroyed the city.
Answer: <u>before</u> the Lord destroyed the city, fled

1. Lot was taken captive when Sodom was defeated.
2. Although Lot had taken the best land, Abraham rescued him.
3. Melchizedek met Abraham after he had defeated the kings.
4. Abraham would not accept the spoils when the king of Sodom offered them to him.

Written Exercises

Mistakes	Corrections
1. among	between
2. accept	except
of	
in	into
3. with	
4. of	
of	have
5. between	among
in back of	behind
6. at	
7. of	
8. in	into
9. among	between
10. on	to
11. in	into
besides	beside
12. at	to
13. accept	except
14. to	
15. besides	beside
16. in back of	behind
17. than from	
18. with	
19. between	among
20. at	

Review Exercises

1. <u>when</u> Sodom was defeated, was taken
2. <u>Although</u> Lot had taken the best land, rescued
3. <u>after</u> he had defeated the kings, met
4. <u>when</u> the king of Sodom offered them to him, would accept

117. Making an Introduction

An introduction helps people who are strangers to get acquainted. Knowing how to introduce people will help you to make friends more easily. The Bible says, "A man that hath friends must shew himself friendly" (Proverbs 18:24). It also says, "Be ye kind one to another" (Ephesians 4:32).

Introducing people that you know can be enjoyable if you follow the rules. There are six main rules for making introductions.

1. To introduce a younger person and an older person, say the older person's name first.

   > "Father, this is my friend Roy."
   > "Roy, this is my father."

2. To introduce a man and a woman or a boy and a girl of about the same age, say the woman's or girl's name first.

   > "Sister Hannah, this is Brother John."
   > "Brother John, this is Sister Hannah."

3. To introduce two boys, two girls, two men, or two women of about the same age, say either name first.

   > "James, this is my cousin Mark Weaver."
   > "Mark, this is my friend James Martin."

4. To introduce anyone to your mother, say "Mother" first.

   > "Mother, meet my teacher, Sister Mary."
   > "Sister Mary, this is my mother."

5. To introduce one person to a group, say the person's name first.

   > "Mark, this is the sixth grade class."
   > "This is my friend Mark Hoover from Missouri."

6. To introduce yourself to a stranger, say "Hello" and give your name. Sometimes you will be alone with another person whom you do not know. A good thing to do then is to walk up, smile, and say "Hello. My name is —— ——. I don't think we have ever met before."

Speak names clearly when you make an introduction. Let your voice and manner show your pleasure in what you are doing. It is also a good idea to add a bit of information about the one whom you are introducing.

Lesson 117

Purpose: To teach the rules for proper introductions.

Oral Review:

1. Answer these questions to show how much you remember about introductions.
   a. When you introduce an older person and a younger person, whose name should you say first? (the older person's name)
   b. When you introduce a man and a woman, whose name should you say first? (the woman's name)
   c. If you were to introduce your mother to the president of the United States, whose name should you say first? ("Mother")
   d. What should you do when you are with a stranger and no one introduces you? (Introduce yourself.)

2. Paragraphs may be written in spatial order, the order of time, or the order of importance. Tell which kind of order is most suitable for the following kinds of writing.
   a. a set of directions (order of time)
   b. a description (spatial order)
   c. a story (order of time)
   d. giving several reasons for something (order of importance)

3. Why should you use more than one reference source when you take notes for a report? (It helps to make your report more informative and interesting.)

4. Why should the notes for a report be organized? (so that the report will be orderly and meaningful)

5. Why should you keep your notes after you have made your outline? (You may need them when you want to add meaningful details to your report.)

Lesson Introduction: Have you ever been to a strange church? About the time you were worrying about how you would find the Sunday school class, a kind friend came along and showed you the way. After church he introduced himself to you and then introduced you to his friends. How did you feel? Relieved? Happy? Then you should do the same thing when strangers come to your church.

In making introductions, the most important thing to remember is to be courteous, respectful, and gracious. The rules for making introductions will help you in this. Today we will study those rules.

Lesson Outline:

1. To introduce a younger person and an older person, say the older person's name first.

2. To introduce a man and a woman or a boy and a girl of about the same age, say the woman's or girl's name first.

If possible, tell about something that you know both persons are interested in, to help them get started in conversation.

> "Laura, this is Carrie Martin. Carrie lived in Guatemala for three years, and she came back only two weeks ago."

When you are introduced to someone, it is a good idea to repeat his name at once. If you have heard it wrong, your mistake can be corrected right away. Repeating the name will also help you to remember it.

> "I'm glad to meet you, Carrie. Are you going back to Guatemala very soon?"

- Be courteous, respectful, and gracious when you make introductions.

- Say an older person's name before a younger person's.

- Say a woman's name before a man's.

- Say either name first when introducing two men, two women, two boys, or two girls of about the same age.

- Always say "Mother" first.

- When introducing one person to a group, say the person's name first.

- Introduce yourself to a stranger when no one else does it for you.

Class Practice

A. Tell which rule in the lesson applies to each introduction.
1. Hello. My name is Susan White. What is yours?
2. Jason, this is my Sunday school class.
3. Father, this is my friend Frank.
4. Donna, this is my cousin Darla.
5. Mother, this is Sister Mary, my teacher.

B. Tell whose name should be said first in the following introductions. Also tell what you might say in each case. You may use real names.
1. Your teacher who is a woman, and your uncle
2. Your mother and your Bible school teacher
3. Your brother and a boy who is his age
4. Yourself and a stranger

---

3. To introduce two boys, two girls, two men, or two women of about the same age, say either name first.

4. To introduce anyone to your mother, say "Mother" first.

5. To introduce one person to a group, say the person's name first.

6. To introduce yourself to a stranger, say "Hello" and give your name. Sometimes you will be alone with another person whom you do not know. A good thing to do then is to walk up, smile, and say "Hello. My name is ———— ————. I don't think we have ever met before."

7. Speak names clearly when you make an introduction.

Lesson 117 Answers
Class Practice
A. 1. Rule 6
2. Rule 5
3. Rule 1
4. Rule 3
5. Rule 4

B. (Sample introductions.)
1. your teacher's name; "Sister Ruth, this is my uncle John Martin. Uncle John, this is my teacher, Sister Ruth Miller."
2. "Mother"; "Mother, this is Brother Mark Sensenig, my Bible school teacher. Brother Mark, this is my mother."
3. either name; "James, this is my friend Ronald Smith. Ronald, this is my brother James."
4. your own name; "Hello. My name is ———— ————. May I ask your name?"

---

8. Add a bit of information about the one whom you are introducing. If possible, tell about something that you know both persons are interested in, to help them get started in conversation.

9. When you are introduced to someone, repeat his name at once. If you heard it wrong, your mistake can be corrected right away. Repeating the name will also help you remember it.

5. Your cousin and your classmates
6. Your younger brother and your Sunday school teacher

C. Make an introduction in class, using real names. You may get ideas from Part B.

Written Exercises

Write what you might say in the following introductions. You may use real names.

1. Your sister and a girl who is her age
2. Your teacher who is a man, and your aunt
3. Your cousin and your Bible school class
4. Your mother and a friend from school
5. Yourself and a stranger
6. Your grandfather and a neighbor man about your father's age

Review Exercises

A. Write the names of the two rhythm patterns you have studied. [104]

B. Read the poem below, and do these exercises. [104, 108, 112]
   1. Copy the first line, mark the rhythm, and name the rhythm pattern.
   2. Copy all the pairs of rhyming words.
   3. Copy the simile in the first line.
   4. Personification is used in this poem.
      a. What prepositional phrase describes the appearance of each wave?
      b. What are three verbs that tell what the waves did?

Twilight at Sea
The twilight hours, like birds, flew by,
   As lightly and as free;
Ten thousand stars were in the sky,
   Ten thousand on the sea;
For every wave, with dimpled face,
   That leaped upon the air,
Had caught a star in its embrace,
   And held it trembling there.
          —Amelia Welby

5. your cousin's name; "Charles, this is the sixth grade class. This is my cousin Charles Good."
6. your teacher's name; "Brother Philip, this is my younger brother David. David, this is my Sunday school teacher, Brother Philip Weaver."

C. (Class activity.)

Written Exercises
(Individual answers.)

Review Exercises

A. iambic, trochaic

B. 1. The twilight hours, like birds, flew by;
      iambic pattern
   2. by—sky; free—sea; face—embrace; air—there
   3. like birds
   4. a. with dimpled face
      b. leaped, caught, held

118. Coordinating Conjunctions

A conjunction is a word that joins words, phrases, or clauses in a sentence. A conjunction is often called a *connector* because it connects various sentence parts.

A *coordinating conjunction* joins sentence parts of parallel structure. Words are joined to words, phrases to phrases, and clauses to clauses.

> Oranges **and** bananas were sold at the stand.
> (single words joined by *and*)

> The sparrow flew around the room **and** out the window.
> (phrases joined by *and*)

> I just had it yesterday, **but** now I cannot find it.
> (clauses joined by *but*)

When you use coordinating conjunctions, be careful to join only sentence parts that are parallel. Perhaps the most common mistake is to join words to phrases. Study the following examples.

Incorrect: The dog ran around the room **and** outside.
(phrase joined to word)

Correct: The dog ran around the room **and** out the door.
(phrase joined to phrase)

Correct: The dog ran around the room, **and** then he ran outside. (clause joined to clause)

Incorrect: A car slid across the road, into a guardrail, **and** hit a tree. (phrases joined to word)

Correct: A car slid across the road, into a guardrail, **and** into a tree. (three parallel phrases)

Correct: A car slid across the road and into a guardrail, **and** then it hit a tree. (phrase joined to phrase, and clause joined to clause)

The main coordinating conjunctions are *and, but, or, for, nor,* and *yet*. *So* can be used as a coordinating conjunction when it means *therefore*. Coordinating conjunctions can show various relationships, as shown below.

Continuation or addition:
Pennsylvania has beautiful rivers **and** mountains.
Mary and Edith washed the dishes **and** swept the floors.
Children should not talk back, **nor** should they pout.

Lesson 118

Purpose: To teach coordinating and *correlative conjunctions.

Oral Review:

1. Where in a sentence must an adjective phrase be placed? (right after the word it modifies)
2. Does an adverb phrase always come immediately after the word it modifies? (No; it may be found at various places in a sentence.)
3. What parts of speech do adverb clauses modify? (verbs, adjectives, adverbs)
4. What do adverb clauses tell? (how, when, where, why, to what degree, how long, how much, in spite of what, under what condition)
5. With what part of speech does an adverb clause begin? (subordinating conjunction)

Lesson Introduction: Did you ever see a yoke of oxen? Did you know that if two animals are yoked together, it works best if they both have equal strength? Two strong oxen work together better than one strong one and one weak one. Two oxen of the same size work together better than one large one and one small one. Of course it doesn't work well either if one ox pulls forward while the other holds back!

A coordinating conjunction is somewhat like a yoke that holds two animals together. Coordinating conjunctions join words, phrases, or clauses of *equal* function and structure. Today we will learn more about coordinating conjunctions.

Contrast:
David sinned, **but** he repented.
God warned Solomon, **yet** he fell into idolatry.

Choice or option:
I'm sure they were raccoons **or** opossums.
Go to the bus stop now, **or** you will be late.

Cause and effect:
We had recess inside, **for** it was raining.
It was raining, **so** we had recess inside.

A comma is placed before a conjunction that joins two independent clauses in a compound sentence.

Cover the plants carefully, or the frost will ruin them.

Correlative conjunctions are connecting words used in pairs.

either—or   neither—nor
both—and   not only—but also

Correlative conjunctions also join sentence parts of parallel structure, the same as coordinating conjunctions. Study the following examples.

We hoe **either** in the morning **or** in the evening.
Both Jesus **and** His disciples were Galileans.
Neither you **nor** I can fully understand God's great love.
Not only petroleum **but also** coal is scarce in some places.

When using *not only—but also,* as correlative conjunctions, be sure to include all the words in the pair. Do not omit the word *also.*

Incorrect: We had **not only** pie **but** cake for dessert.
Correct: We had **not only** pie **but also** cake for dessert.

Sometimes *or, either-or,* or *neither-nor* is used with two subjects, one singular and one plural. Then the verb should agree with the subject that is nearer to it.

Either the dog **or** the kittens were fed. (plural)
Either the kittens **or** the dog was fed. (singular)

Neither the door **nor** the windows are securely closed. (plural)
Neither the windows **nor** the door is securely closed. (singular)

Lesson Outline:
1. A conjunction is a word that joins words, phrases, or clauses in a sentence.

2. A coordinating conjunction joins sentence parts of parallel structure.
   a. Coordinating conjunctions should join only parallel sentence parts—words to words, phrases to phrases, and clauses to clauses. It is not correct to join unparallel parts, such as words and phrases.
   b. The main coordinating conjunctions are *and, but, or, for, nor,* and *yet. So* is a coordinating conjunction when it means *therefore.*

3. A comma is placed before a conjunction that joins two independent clauses in a compound sentence.

4. Correlative conjunctions are connecting words used in pairs.

either—or   neither—nor
both—and   not only—but also

5. Correlative conjunctions also join sentence parts of parallel structure.

6. When using **not only—but also** *as correlative conjunctions, be sure to include all the words in the pair.* Do not omit the word *also.*
(*Teacher:* The combination "not only…but" is correct in sentences like the following examples.

I was not only tired but sick.
Solomon was not only a wise king but a king wiser than any other.

In these sentences, the words after *but* serve to intensify the thought of the preceding noun or adjective, and they are heavily emphasized in speaking.

- A conjunction is a word that joins words, phrases, or clauses in a sentence.

- A *coordinating conjunction* joins sentence parts of parallel structure. It must not be used to join a word to a phrase.

- *Correlative conjunctions* are connecting words used in pairs.

- Correlative conjunctions also join sentence parts of parallel structure.

Class Practice

A. Tell which words are conjunctions. Tell whether they join *words, phrases,* or *clauses.*
   1. A large tan-and-white cat was hunting in the meadow.
   2. The children raised corn in their garden and in the field.
   3. One cow stood on the road and bawled.
   4. Both the hired man and the boys chased her back in.
   5. Father will leave either in the morning or after lunch.
   6. We wanted to plant corn, but it rained.

B. Tell how to correct these sentences so that the parts joined are parallel.
   1. Our cousins will come today or in the morning.
   2. The shoes were not under the bed, the dresser, or in the closet.
   3. Be of good cheer and brave.
   4. Father is outside or in the basement.
   5. The ball flew across the yard, over the road, and hit the barn.

C. Tell how to correct the following sentences.
   1. We learned not only the capital but the shape of each state.
   2. Either the pills or the injection are helpful.
   3. Neither the mother nor her girls was helpless when it came to cooking.
   4. We found the recipe and made the dough but Mother baked the bread.
   5. The cats or the dog dig holes in the flower beds.

Not only is not part of a correlative conjunction in such a construction; it is simply a combination of modifiers equal to *not just* or *not merely*.)

7. When or, either—or, *or* neither—nor *is used with two subjects, one singular and one plural, the verb should agree with the subject that is nearer to it.*

★ EXTRA PRACTICE
Worksheet 74 *(Coordinating Conjunctions)*

Lesson 118 Answers
Class Practice
A. 1. and, words
   2. and, phrases
   3. and, words
   4. Both—and, words
   5. either—or, phrases
   6. but, clauses

B. 1. Our cousins will come today or tomorrow.
   2. The shoes were not under the bed, under the dresser, or in the closet.
   3. Be cheerful and brave.
   4. Father is outside the house or in the basement.
      or Father is outside or downstairs.
   5. The ball flew across the yard, over the road, and into (against) the barn.
      or The ball flew across the yard and over the road, and then it hit the barn.

C. (Corrections are underlined.)
   1. We learned not only the capital but <u>also</u> the shape of each state.
   2. Either the pills or the injection <u>is</u> helpful.
   3. Neither the mother nor her girls <u>were</u> helpless when it came to cooking.
   4. We found the recipe and made the dough<u>,</u> but Mother baked the bread.
   5. The cats or the dog <u>digs</u> holes in the flower beds.

Written Exercises

A. Copy the conjunctions. Write whether they join *words, phrases,* or *clauses.*
1. Uncle David is a carpenter and farmer.
2. Mother bought new shoes for John, but they do not fit him.
3. This cake is for lunch or for supper.
4. Both you and I can use this.
5. We will shop either on Friday or on Saturday.
6. The deer looked at us for a little, but soon it ran into the woods.

B. Rewrite these sentences so that the parts joined are parallel.
1. They read loudly and in a distinct manner.
2. We usually pray in the morning, at noon, and evening.
3. The owl flew silently and with great swiftness.
4. We ran downhill and into the woods.
5. Swiftly and with skill, the nurse cleaned the boy's wounds.
6. We should be respectful to our teachers, our ministers, and respect our parents.

C. Rewrite the following sentences correctly.
1. Neither Father nor the boys has ever been there.
2. Either you boys or Susan were helping us.
3. Pick not only the beans but the peas.
4. We got three bushels of beans and they got four bushels of peas.
5. The storm brought not only rain but hail.
6. We gathered a bucket full of hailstones and Mother made ice cream.

Written Exercises

A. 1. and, words
2. but, clauses
3. or, phrases
4. Both—and; words
5. either—or; phrases
6. but, clauses

B. 1. They read loudly and distinctly.
2. We usually pray in the morning, at noon, and in the evening.
3. The owl flew silently and swiftly.
4. We ran down the hill and into the woods.
5. Swiftly and skillfully, the nurse cleaned the boy's wounds.
6. We should be respectful to our teachers, (to) our ministers, and (to) our parents.

C. (Corrections are underlined.)
1. Neither Father nor the boys <u>have</u> ever been there.
2. Either you boys or Susan <u>was</u> helping us.
3. Pick not only the beans but <u>also</u> the peas.
4. We got three bushels of beans<u>,</u> and they got four bushels of peas.
5. The storm brought not only rain but <u>also</u> hail.
6. We gathered a bucket full of hailstones<u>,</u> and Mother made ice cream.

Review Exercises

Diagram the following sentences.

1. Harold repaired the roof of the shed while Jacob painted the trim around the windows.
2. Yesterday we picked some pretty yellow daffodils for Grandmother and Grandfather.
3. The purple lilacs by the side of the house smell rich and sweet.
4. The boy who was here today is my cousin.

---

119. Subordinating Conjunctions

Conjunctions are in two main classes: *coordinating conjunctions* and *subordinating conjunctions.* Something that is subordinate is in a lower class, or it is dependent on something else. A subordinating conjunction introduces a dependent clause. A dependent clause cannot stand alone as a main clause can.

Subordinating conjunctions join clauses of *unequal* rank in a sentence. They do not join words or phrases, as coordinating conjunctions do. They are used only to join dependent clauses to independent clauses.

There are more subordinating conjunctions than coordinating conjunctions. Some common subordinating conjunctions are listed here.

after	if	until
although	since	when
as	than	where
because	though	while
before	unless	

Some words in the list above may also be used as adverbs or prepositions. They are subordinating conjunctions only when they connect two clauses.

Subordinating conjunctions introduce adverb clauses that tell *how, when, where,* or *why.*

Do unto others <u>as you would have them do to you</u>. (tells *how*)
<u>After I did the right thing</u>, I felt better. (tells *when*)
I will go <u>where you go</u>. (tells *where*)
<u>Since you are not ready</u>, we must go without you. (tells *why*)

Review Exercises

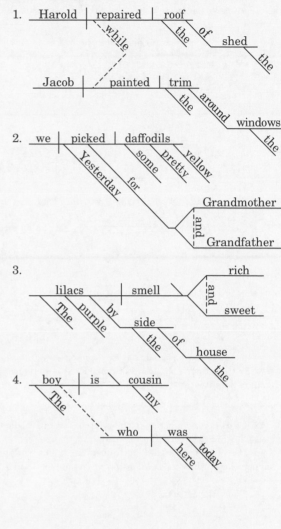

Lesson 119

Purpose: To teach subordinating conjunctions.

Oral Review:

1. What is a conjunction? (a word that joins words, phrases, or clauses in a sentence)
2. What kind of sentence parts are joined by coordinating conjunctions? (words, phrases, or clauses of parallel structure)
3. (*a*) Define correlative conjunctions. (*b*) Give some examples of them. (*a.* connecting words that are used in pairs; *b.* both—and, either—or, neither—nor, not only—but also)
4. What is meant when it is said that the subject and verb of a sentence must agree? (If the subject is singular, the verb must be singular. If the subject is plural, the verb must be plural.)
5. What part of speech is the word *good*? (adjective)
6. When is *well* (*a*) an adverb? (*b*) an adjective? (*a.* when it tells *how* about a verb; *b.* when it means "healthy")
7. List some common negative words. (no, not, none, never, nobody, nothing, neither, nowhere, barely, hardly, scarcely; contractions with *not*)
8. What rule should be followed when using negative words? (Do not use two negative words to express one negative thought.)

Lesson Introduction: A coordinating conjunction is somewhat like a yoke that joins two oxen of equal strength. But a subordinating conjunction is more like the hitch between a tractor and a wagon. The wagon cannot move on its own; it must be connected to the tractor with a hitch. However, the tractor is not worth much without a wagon or some other implement, for what work could it do? So the hitch is a very important part.

Since an adverb clause functions as an adverb, the entire clause is diagramed as an adverb. It is placed on its own base line below the word it modifies.

After the hammer hit his thumb, he was more careful.

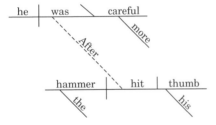

We could hardly see because it was very foggy.

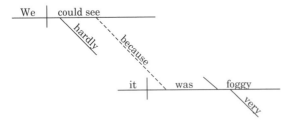

When *as* or *than* is used to state a comparison, it is followed by a clause rather than a single word. Consider this sentence. Which pronoun in parentheses is correct?

Elizabeth is not as tall as (I, me).

Since *as* is a conjunction in this sentence, it must be followed by a clause having a subject and a verb. But where is the verb? It is the word *am*. (The verb is not stated, but understood.) The sentence is really saying, *Elizabeth is not as tall as I am*. So the nominative case *I* must be used.

Consider the following sentence, which uses the conjunction *than*.

They came sooner than (we, us).

In this lesson we will study subordinating conjunctions. These conjunctions connect dependent (subordinate) clauses to independent (main) clauses. A subordinating conjunction shows the relationship between the two clauses. It is an important part of speech because the meaning of the sentence depends on it.

Lesson Outline:

1. Subordinating conjunctions join clauses of unequal rank in a sentence. They are called subordinating conjunctions because they introduce dependent clauses (which are of subordinate rank). Subordinating conjunctions do not join words or phrases of parallel structure as coordinating conjunctions do. They join only clauses.

2. There are more subordinating conjunctions than coordinating conjunctions. (See the list in the lesson.) Some of these conjunctions may also be adverbs or prepositions. They are conjunctions only when they connect two clauses.

3. Subordinating conjunctions introduce adverb clauses that tell **how, when, where, or why.**

4. An adverb clause is diagramed below the word it modifies.

5. When **as or than** *is used to state a comparison, it is followed by a clause rather than a single word. If a pronoun follows* **as or than,** *it is the subject and must be in the nominative case.*

Elizabeth is not as tall as I (am).
They could run faster than we (could run).

(*Teacher:* The objective case is correct in some elliptical constructions like this. It depends on what is meant, as shown by the following examples.

I know John better than he (knows him).
I know John better than (I know) him.

At this level, only nominative case pronouns are used after *as* or *than*.)

★ **EXTRA PRACTICE**
Worksheet 75 (*Subordinating Conjunctions*)

This sentence means, *They came sooner than <u>we came</u>*. So the nominative case *we* must be used.

- A *subordinating conjunction* joins clauses of *unequal* rank in a sentence. The clause it introduces in an adverb clause.

- When *as* or *than* is used to state a comparison, it is followed by a clause rather than a single word. If a pronoun follows *as* or *than*, it is the subject and must be in the nominative case.

Class Practice

A. Tell which words are subordinating conjunctions. Read the clause that each one introduces.
1. While the boys waited, they studied their Bible lessons.
2. He came before I did.
3. Jesus departed to a mountain after He sent the multitude away.
4. When the lame man saw Peter and John, he asked for money.
5. A lamp shines more brightly than a candle does.

B. On the chalkboard, diagram sentences 1–4 in Part A.

C. Read each sentence, using the correct pronoun. Also tell what verb is understood.
1. These trees are not as tall as (they, them).
2. She can write more neatly than (I, me).
3. Can you type as fast as (she, her)?
4. Saul was not as brave as (he, him).
5. God is wiser than (we, us).

Written Exercises

A. Copy the subordinating conjunctions in these sentences.
1. When we plant a garden, we look forward to the harvest.
2. The motor stopped because the electricity went off.
3. Since we oiled the sewing machine, it works fine.
4. Venus travels around the sun faster than Mars does.
5. Unless we work faster, we will not finish on time.
6. We should bale the hay after it is dry.
7. If it rains, the hay will be ruined.
8. When the mailman comes, he might bring us a letter.

Lesson 119 Answers
Class Practice
A. (Subordinating conjunctions are underlined.)
1. <u>While</u> the boys waited
2. <u>before</u> I did
3. <u>after</u> He sent the multitude away
4. <u>When</u> the lame man saw Peter and John
5. <u>than</u> a candle does

B. 1.

2.

3.

3.

C. (Elliptical verbs are in parentheses.)
1. they (are)
2. I (can write)
3. she (can type)
4. he (was)
5. we (are)

Written Exercises
A. 1. When   5. Unless
   2. because   6. after
   3. Since   7. If
   4. than   8. When

B. Diagram these sentences.
1. These apples should be picked when they are ripe.
2. While we were waiting, he was studying.
3. Farmers rode their machines as the horses pulled them.
4. The fields were very dry before the rain came.
5. Because his leg was broken, the boy walked with crutches.

C. Choose a fitting subordinating conjunction for each short blank, and supply a main clause of your own for the long blank. Write the whole sentence.
1. —— Marcus looked up from his work, ————.
2. —— I realized what was happening, ————.
3. —— the rain stopped, ————.

D. Write the correct pronoun for each sentence. Also write the verb that is understood, and put parentheses around it.

Examples: a. He can work faster than (I, me).
   b. We did not arrive as soon as (they, them).
Answers: a. I (can work)
   b. they (arrived)

1. Our parents have more experience than (we, us).
2. Did you miss as many days of school as (I, me)?
3. John declared that Jesus was greater than (he, him).
4. I cannot sew as well as (she, her).
5. We were later than (they, them).

Review Exercises

A. These sentences contain adjective clauses, which are introduced by relative pronouns rather than subordinating conjunctions. Copy each adjective clause, and underline the relative pronoun. [97]
1. He is the man whom Father saw.
2. My brother sold the chairs that he sanded.
3. They came from the lady whose house Father remodeled.
4. The dog that barked the loudest ran away first.
5. Andrew read the short note, which the teacher left on his desk.
6. Dr. Alvin L. Punt, who teaches at Smith College, has experimented with plant diseases.
7. John telephoned the man whose wallet he had found.
8. Only those who have a license may drive on the road.

B. 1.

2.

3.

4.

5.

C. (Individual sentences.)

D. 1. we (have)
2. I (missed)
3. he (was)
4. she (can sew)
5. they (were)

Review Exercises

A. 1. <u>whom</u> Father saw
2. <u>that</u> he sanded
3. <u>whose</u> house Father remodeled
4. <u>that</u> barked the loudest
5. <u>which</u> the teacher left on his desk
6. <u>who</u> teaches at Smith College
7. <u>whose</u> wallet he had found
8. <u>who</u> have a license

B. Write the correct words in parentheses.

1. Most of the girls (know, knows) their verses.
2. None of the milk (is, are) sour.
3. Most of the children usually (choose, chooses) the colorful posters.
4. No one (bring, brings) (his, their) lunch anymore.
5. None of the boys (is, are) ready yet.
6. Many of the children (walk, walks) to our school.
7. Cousin Ann sews very (good, well).
8. Aunt Sarah surely makes (good, well) candy.
9. Mark doesn't feel (good, well).
10. I haven't told (nobody, anybody) the secret.
11. Gerald and Ben don't have (none, any) at all.
12. I hardly had (no, any) time to finish.

B. 1. know
    2. is
    3. choose
    4. brings, his
    5. are
    6. walk
    7. well
    8. good
    9. well
    10. anybody
    11. any
    12. any

120. Avoiding Misplaced Phrases and Clauses

When phrases and clauses are used as modifiers, they may be put at various places in a sentence. But you must be careful, or you may put them in the wrong place—with absurd or confusing results. Be sure that your sentences say what you mean for them to say.

An adjective phrase must be placed immediately after the noun or pronoun that it modifies.

Misplaced: The car ran into a post <u>without brakes</u>.
Correct: The car <u>without brakes</u> ran into a post.

Misplaced: Sister Anna brought a book for the boy <u>in a paper bag</u>.
Correct: Sister Anna brought a book <u>in a paper bag</u> for the boy.

An adjective clause must also be placed immediately after the noun or pronoun that it modifies.

Misplaced: The tree house is in that tree <u>which the boys built</u>.
Correct: The tree house <u>which the boys built</u> is in that tree.

Lesson 120

Purpose: To teach the proper placement of modifying phrases and clauses.

Oral Review:

1. Which preposition refers to movement from one location to another, *in* or *into*? (into)
2. Which preposition refers to only two objects, *between* or *among*? (between)
3. Should you say *different than* or *different from*? (different from)
4. Instead of saying *in back of the house,* what should you say? (behind the house)
5. In the following expressions, tell which prepositions are unnecessary.
   a. inside of the barn (of)
   b. where he is going to (to)
   c. the pen that I write with (correct)
   d. where my cap is at (at)
   e. after the test was over with (with)
   f. the girl I was speaking to (correct)
6. What is a transitive verb? (a verb that passes action to a receiver)
7. What two kinds of voice do verbs have? (active, passive)
8. a. Which voice should you use most in writing? (active voice)
   b. When is it desirable to use the passive voice? (The passive voice may be used for variety. It may also be used when the doer of an action is unknown or unimportant.)

Lesson Introduction: Read the following sentences to the class. Ask, "Do these sentences sound right?"

The boy sat patiently in his chair with a broken leg.

We took the shoe to the shoe repairman with the loose tongue.

Misplaced: He sold the table to his uncle <u>that he just made</u>.
Correct: He sold the table <u>that he just made</u> to his uncle.
Correct: He sold his uncle the table <u>that he just made</u>.

In the last sentence above, notice that the phrase *to his uncle* is changed to an indirect object. This is another useful way to correct some sentences with misplaced modifiers.

An adverb phrase may come immediately after the word it modifies, but it may also be found at other places in a sentence. Always be sure it is in a place where it clearly modifies the word you intend.

I received a package <u>from my grandmother</u> <u>in the mailbox</u>.

Both *from my grandmother* and *in the mailbox* are adverb phrases that modify *received*. But the second phrase could seem like an adjective phrase that tells which grandmother. Surely your grandmother was not in the mailbox! And if the phrases are exchanged, the sentence seems to say that the mailbox was from your grandmother.

I received a package <u>in the mailbox</u> <u>from my grandmother</u>.

The best and clearest way is to put one phrase at the beginning of the sentence.

<u>In the mailbox</u> I received a package <u>from my grandmother</u>.

Here are several more sentences with misplaced adverb phrases.

Misplaced: I saw the children playing softball <u>through the window</u>.
Correct: <u>Through the window</u> I saw the children playing softball.
Misplaced: I read about the earthquake that destroyed many homes <u>in our church paper</u>.
Correct: I read <u>in our church paper</u> about the earthquake that destroyed many homes.

Do not place an adverb phrase between two verbs when it could logically modify either one.

Mother said <u>on Wednesday</u> she would pack my lunch.

Does this sentence mean that Mother *said* something on Wednesday, or that she *would pack* something on Wednesday? It could mean either. Compare the following, corrected sentences.

Rodney saw an elephant with a long trunk on his school trip.
Sister Miriam said on Monday we will have a test on adverbs.
Mother served some new potatoes from the garden that we baked for supper.

These sentences have phrases and clauses that are misplaced. Today we want to learn how to avoid this problem.

Lesson Outline:

1. An adjective phrase must be placed immediately after the noun or pronoun it modifies. It will give the wrong meaning if it comes after another noun or pronoun in the sentence.

2. An adjective clause must also be placed immediately after the word it modifies.

Misplaced:
    Rachel gave the package to her aunt <u>that she had just wrapped</u>.

Correct:
    Rachel gave the package <u>that she had just wrapped</u> to her aunt.

Correct:
    Rachel gave her aunt the package <u>that she had just wrapped</u>.

Note the use of an indirect object in the second correction.

On Wednesday Mother said she would pack my lunch.
Mother said she would pack my lunch on Wednesday.

> - An adjective phrase or clause must be placed immediately after the noun or pronoun that it modifies.
> - An adverb phrase must be put in a place where it clearly modifies the word intended.

Class Practice

Decide where the misplaced phrases or clauses belong. Read each sentence correctly.

1. The train stopped and let the people off with two steam locomotives.
2. She sent her granddaughter a card that had measles.
3. The girl went to the doctor with severe headaches.
4. School was closed because of the storm by the principal.
5. We watched the geese flying south through our binoculars.
6. The man bought several dozen ears of corn with a gold watch.
7. Martha wrote a letter while she traveled on a piece of notebook paper.
8. In the clothes basket I saw the wet laundry and hung it up.
9. My teacher said on Monday she would give the test.
10. Mother said on my birthday we would have a picnic.
11. The auctioneer sold the chair to the wealthy lady that was two hundred years old.
12. That chocolate cake was baked by Nancy which was so delicious.
13. We helped the Martins to clean the house on Railroad Avenue that they had recently bought.
14. We bought a new table from the carpenter with a hardwood top.

Written Exercises

Rewrite these sentences, putting the misplaced phrases or clauses where they belong.

1. John wrote a note while he waited on a piece of scrap paper.
2. I saw the dessert that Mother had made in the refrigerator.
3. My uncle told me on my birthday he would take us to the zoo.
4. The boy came slowly down the stairs with a broken leg.

3. An adverb phrase must be put in a place where it clearly modifies the word intended.

   a. An adverb phrase may be put at various places in a sentence. Always be sure it is in a place where it clearly modifies the word you intend.

   b. Do not place an adverb phrase between two verbs when it could logically modify either one.

   My sister said on Monday she would take me to school.

★ EXTRA PRACTICE

Worksheet 76 (*Avoiding Misplaced Phrases and Clauses*)

Lesson 120 Answers
Class Practice

(Corrections are underlined.)

1. The train with two steam locomotives stopped and let the people off.
2. She sent her granddaughter that had measles a card.
   or She sent a card to her granddaughter that had measles.
3. The girl with severe headaches went to the doctor.
4. School was closed by the principal because of the storm.
5. Through our binoculars we watched the geese flying south.
6. The man with a gold watch bought several dozen ears of corn.
7. Martha wrote a letter on a piece of notebook paper while she traveled.
8. I saw the wet laundry in the clothes basket and hung it up.
9. On Monday my teacher said she would give the test.
   or My teacher said she would give the test on Monday.
10. Mother said we would have a picnic on my birthday
    or On my birthday Mother said we would have a picnic.
11. The auctioneer sold the chair that was two hundred years old to the wealthy lady.
12. That chocolate cake which was so delicious was baked by Nancy.
13. We helped the Martins to clean the house that they had recently bought on Railroad Avenue.
14. We bought a new table with a hardwood top from the carpenter.

Written Exercises

(Corrections are underlined. Some variation is acceptable, as long as the phrases and clauses clearly modify the words intended.)

1. John wrote a note on a piece of scrap paper while he waited.
2. In the refrigerator I saw the dessert that Mother had made.
3. My uncle told me he would take us to the zoo on my birthday.
   or On my birthday my uncle told me he would take us to the zoo.
4. The boy with a broken leg came slowly down the stairs.

5. Brother Daniel told us about pioneers who used oxen in history class.
6. The motorist was fined for violating a traffic law by the judge.
7. The teacher read us a story about some missionaries from the church papers.
8. The boy found a blacksnake that was wearing a straw hat.
9. Sarah passed chips to her friends on paper plates.
10. He shot the bear just before it reached him with his gun.
11. Janice saw a fisherman catch a huge trout from her bicycle.
12. That man is the father of the baby girl in the black suit.
13. Father said on Wednesday he wanted to begin planting.
14. Grandmother said on my birthday she would send me a book.
15. Gerald bought a whistle at the department store that cost four dollars.
16. She gave a can of juice to each student that weighed sixteen ounces.
17. The museum bought a book from the antique man that was three hundred years old.
18. A motorist stopped me who wanted directions.

Review Exercises

A. Write *yes* or *no* to tell whether each underlined verb is transitive. If it is transitive, write its direct object. [38]
1. Hornets <u>chew</u> wood to make the paper for their nests.
2. Strangely enough, the paper nest <u>is</u> waterproof!
3. Honeybees <u>lose</u> their stingers, but hornets do not.
4. That hornet's nest <u>looks</u> unusually big.
5. A hornet <u>stings</u> sooner than a wasp or a bee.
6. A hornet is the farmer's friend because it <u>eats</u> harmful insects.

B. Write whether each sentence is in the active or passive voice. [55]
1. She was stung by a hornet.
2. A hornet does inject a venom into the wound.
3. The venom causes a very painful sting.
4. That large nest was built by hornets.
5. Each nest is used only one summer.

C. Copy and capitalize correctly. [73, 74]
1. barbara said, "every wednesday in the fall and winter, i go to see my spanish teacher, miss viola n. monteroso, who lives in millersville, pennsylvania."

---

5. <u>In history class</u> Brother Daniel told us about pioneers who used oxen.
6. The motorist was fined <u>by the judge</u> for violating a traffic law.
7. <u>From the church papers</u>, the teacher read us a story about some missionaries.
8. The boy <u>that was wearing a straw hat</u> found a blacksnake.
9. Sarah passed chips <u>on paper plates</u> to her friends.
10. He shot the bear <u>with his gun</u> just before it reached him.
11. <u>From her bicycle</u> Janice saw a fisherman catch a huge trout.
12. That man <u>in the black suit</u> is the father of the baby girl.
13. Father said he wanted to begin planting <u>on Wednesday</u>.
    or <u>On Wednesday</u> Father said he wanted to begin planting.
14. Grandmother said she would send me a book <u>on my birthday</u>.
    or <u>On my birthday</u> Grandmother said she would send me a book.
15. Gerald bought a whistle <u>that cost four dollars</u> at the department store.
16. She gave a can of juice <u>that weighed sixteen ounces</u> to each student.
17. The museum bought a book <u>that was three hundred years old</u> from the antique man.
18. A motorist <u>who wanted directions</u> stopped me.

Review Exercises

A. 1. yes, wood
   2. no
   3. yes, stingers
   4. no
   5. no
   6. yes, insects

B. 1. passive
   2. active
   3. active
   4. passive
   5. passive

C. (Corrections are underlined.)
   1. <u>B</u>arbara said, "<u>E</u>very <u>W</u>ednesday in the fall and winter, <u>I</u> go to see my <u>S</u>panish teacher, <u>M</u>iss <u>V</u>iola <u>N</u>. Monteroso, who lives in <u>M</u>illersville, <u>P</u>ennsylvania."

2.   **to remember**
find out what god would have you do,
    and do that little well;
for what is great and what is small,
    this only he can tell.

—Author unknown

---

2.   **To Remember**
<u>F</u>ind out what <u>G</u>od would have you do,
    <u>A</u>nd do that little well;
<u>F</u>or what is great and what is small,
    <u>T</u>his only <u>H</u>e can tell.

121. Courtesy in Conversation

We all enjoy talking with our friends. We want to exchange news and express our opinions. We want to encourage each other to keep doing right. Even when we have nothing spectacular to say, we can still find something worthwhile to talk about!

We enjoy talking with some friends more than with others. One reason may be that they have such interesting things to say. But there may be another reason. Perhaps we enjoy talking with them because they *listen* so well!

One of the most important rules in good conversation is to listen carefully. The Bible says, "Let every man be swift to hear, slow to speak, slow to wrath" (James 1:19). By being more ready to listen than to speak, we will also follow the verse that says, "In honour preferring one another" (Romans 12:10).

When someone is talking to you, listen with interest and follow his train of thought. Do not just wait quietly until it is your turn to speak. Of course you would not interrupt another person who is talking, but that is not enough. You must take a real interest in what he is saying. How few of us do this really well!

Part of good listening is asking questions and talking about things that are of interest to others. This is not difficult because friends naturally share common interests. Guide the topic into areas where your friends feel at ease. Then you will learn more about them and their interests. Do not be selfish and talk only about yourself or the things that happen to you. And of course you must not boast about your own accomplishments. Learn to be interested in others, and take pleasure in their successes.

Another important rule is to speak kindly. One familiar Bible command is "Be ye kind" (Ephesians 4:32). Another command is "Speak not

Lesson 121

Purpose: To give some guidelines for courtesy in conversation.

Oral Review:

1. Answer these questions to show how much you already know about courtesy in conversation.
    a. What are the most important rules in conversation? (Listen carefully and speak kindly.)
    b. If you must disagree, how should you do it? (kindly)
    c. In a conversation, how can you show your interest in others? (by asking polite questions; by being interested in them)
2. a. When you introduce an older person and a younger person, whose name should you say first? (the older person's name)
    b. When you introduce a boy and a girl, whose name should you say first? (the girl's name)
    c. If you were to introduce your mother to the governor of your state, whose name should you say first? ("Mother")
    d. What might you do and say when you are with a stranger and no one introduces you? (Walk up to him, smile, and say "Hello. My name is ——— ———. May I ask your name?")
3. List several ways of developing a paragraph. (by using details, by using examples and illustrations, by using comparison or contrast)
4. When you write a paragraph showing *similarities* between two things, you are developing the paragraph by ———. (comparison)
5. When you write a paragraph showing *differences* between two things, you are developing the paragraph by ———. (contrast)

evil one of another" (James 4:11). Never speak *to* others or *about* others in a way that you would not want them to speak.

Do not be eager to criticize, correct, or contradict the things others say. That is like throwing dirt into the machinery! When you need to disagree with someone, be kind and considerate. Do not boldly challenge him or rudely contradict him, and do not get into an argument with him. You may say something like "Some people believe differently about that" or "Could it be that it is like this?" When you agree with what someone says, tell him so. Be positive about areas of agreement, and do not emphasize differences.

Use correct, clear English when you speak. Do not talk too rapidly or too loudly. Do not use pronouns without antecedents ("They say . . .") or other vague, general expressions ("Everyone thinks . . ."). Do not assume that people will know what you mean unless you express yourself clearly.

Courtesy in conversation is not based on keeping a set of rules. In fact, too much concern about "the proper rules" will make you uneasy and self-conscious (thinking mostly about yourself). But if you take a sincere interest in other people, your conversations with them will be truly enjoyable.

- The most important rules in good conversation are to listen carefully and to speak kindly.

- Ask polite questions, and show that you are interested in others.

- When you need to disagree, do it kindly.

- Use correct, clear English when you speak.

Class Practice

Answer these questions.
1. According to the lesson, what are the most important rules in conversation?
2. What are some things we should not do in conversation?
3. Why do we enjoy talking with some friends more than with others?
4. When you are speaking, what are some things that will make you hard to understand?

Lesson Introduction: The Bible says, "Be not forgetful to entertain strangers" (Hebrews 13:2). We need to learn and practice courtesy in our conversations with other people. Even our good friends would still be strangers if we had never engaged in conversation with them. God rewards those who obey the Bible. When we practice courtesy in talking with other people, both they and we will usually enjoy the conversation.

Lesson Outline:

1. The most important rules in good conversation are to listen carefully and to speak kindly.

2. Ask polite questions, and show that you are interested in others. Learn to talk about things that are interesting to other people. Do not be selfish and talk only about yourself or the things that happen to you.

Lesson 121 Answers
Class Practice
1. Listen carefully and speak kindly.
2. Do not be selfish and talk only about yourself or the things that happen to you. Do not be eager to criticize, correct, or contradict the things that others say.
3. probably because they listen so well
4. speaking too fast; failing to use clear, correct English; using expressions that are not specific enough

---

3. When you need to disagree, do it kindly. Do not be eager to criticize, correct, or contradict the things that others say. Perhaps you could say "Some people think differently about that" or "Could it be that it is like this?"

4. Use correct, clear English when you speak. Do not talk too rapidly or too loudly. Do not use pronouns without antecedents, or other expressions that are not specific.

5. If there is someone in the group who has little to say, how might you encourage him to say more?

6. When someone is obviously wrong in what he is saying, what should you *not* do? What should you do?

Written Exercises

Write three polite questions that you might ask the following persons.

1. Your friend who just came back from visiting British Columbia.
2. Your friend who is in bed with a broken leg.
3. Your friend who has a new baby brother or sister.
4. A cousin your age who just moved to a new area and is visiting at your house.

Review Exercises

A. Write *true* or *false*. [50, 53]

1. When you take notes, you should use more than one reference source.
2. Knowing how to arrange notes in outline form will probably be valuable to you later in life.
3. Your outline should include main ideas from all your reference sources.
4. You should arrange the main ideas on your outline in the order you found them.
5. There is only one right way to arrange the order of your main ideas.
6. Your outline should include all the details that are in your notes.

B. Write the parts of speech described in these sentences.

1. It may be limiting or descriptive.
2. It modifies a verb, adjective, or adverb.
3. It takes the place of a noun.
4. It shows action or being.
5. It tells *which, whose, how many,* or *what kind of.*
6. It modifies a noun or pronoun.
7. It names a person, place, thing, or idea.
8. It is a connecting word that begins a phrase.
9. It may be an article (*a, an, the*).
10. It tells *how, when, where,* or *to what degree.*

5. Ask him questions about things he is interested in.

6. Do not be overly eager to correct him. Do not boldly challenge him or rudely contradict him. Avoid getting into an argument with him.

Kindly ask him if he is sure about what he is saying. Say something like "I thought it was this way" rather than "You're all wrong."

Written Exercises

(Sample answers.)

1. What did you enjoy most about your trip?
   Did you meet any new friends (or a certain person you both know)?
   Did you have pleasant weather on your trip?
   Did you see any wild animals?

2. How are you feeling today?
   Have you had much pain?
   What do you do to pass the time?
   How long will you need to wear your cast?

3. Does he look like you?
   Does he sleep well at night?
   Have you helped much in taking care of him?
   Does he seem to have any special likes or dislikes?

4. How large is your property? What is your house like?
   Do you have a good place for a garden?
   What special features does your property have (such as woods, a creek, or a pond)?
   What is the name of your new school? How many students are in your class at school?

Review Exercises

A. 1. true
   2. true
   3. true
   4. false
   5. false
   6. false

B. 1. adjective
   2. adverb
   3. pronoun
   4. verb
   5. adjective
   6. adjective
   7. noun
   8. preposition
   9. adjective
   10. adverb

C. Diagram the following sentences.
1. The sun is the nearest star.
2. The sun rotates on its axis.
3. Do not look at the sun without special protection for your eyes.
4. Some telescopes project the sun's image onto a screen.
5. Others have special sun filters.

122. Interjections

An *interjection* is a word that expresses strong feeling. It is not used as a subject, predicate, object, modifier, or any other sentence part. So we say that an interjection is not related to the rest of the sentence. It is an independent word.

An interjection usually comes at the beginning of a sentence. Some common interjections are listed below.

| ah | ha | oh | well | whew |
| alas | ho | ouch | what | why |

There are many interjections, but not all of them are proper to use. Words like *hello* and *good-bye* may be used as interjections in sentences. But it is not proper to use interjections that express anger or contempt. It is also improper to use interjections that are slang words or to use a common word as an interjection that has nothing to do with the normal meaning of the word. We should use only those interjections that are suitable for God's people.

The Bible uses several interjections. The words *lo* and *behold* are interjections used to call attention to something or to express wonder or surprise. *Amen* expresses agreement or approval. *Alas* shows sorrow, pity, or concern. The interjection *ah* is a synonym for *oh*. It expresses feelings such as astonishment, grief, or desire.

"Lo, I come to do thy will, O God" (Hebrews 10:9).
"Behold, he that keepeth Israel shall neither slumber nor sleep" (Psalm 121:4).
Gideon said, "Alas, O Lord GOD! for because I have seen an angel of the Lord face to face" (Judges 6:22).3

An interjection that is spoken with strong expression is followed by

C. 1. [diagram: The sun | is \ star; modifiers: The, the, nearest]

2. [diagram: The sun | rotates; on axis, its]

3. [diagram: (you) | Do look; not, at sun the, without protection the special, for eyes]

4. [diagram: Some telescopes | project | image the sun's; onto screen a]

5. [diagram: Others | have | filters sun special]

Lesson 122

Purpose: To teach interjections.

Oral Review:
1. Can a dependent clause stand alone as a sentence? (no)
2. With what part of speech does an adjective clause begin? (relative pronoun)
3. With what part of speech does an adverb clause begin? (subordinating conjunction)
4. What parts of speech do adverb clauses modify? (verbs, adjectives, adverbs)
5. What do adverb clauses tell? (how, when, where, why, to what degree, how long, how much, in spite of what, under what condition)
6. Name the six tenses. (present tense, past tense, future tense, present perfect tense, past perfect tense, future perfect tense)

7. Give the six tenses for the verb *come*. (come, came, will come, have come, had come, will have come)

Lesson Introduction: Write the following sentence, and ask a student to diagram it on the chalkboard. Tell him to diagram all the words he knows how to do. If he does not know how to diagram the interjection, tell him that he should know how after today's class.

Well, this is a surprise!

The word *well* is an interjection. Today we will see what interjections are and how to diagram them.

an exclamation point. The word after the interjection is capitalized as the first word of a new sentence.

Ouch! Did I step on a nail?
Hello! Come on in.

An interjection that is spoken mildly is followed by a comma. The word after the comma does not begin with a capital letter unless it is normally capitalized.

Oh, it feels cool in the shade.
Well, I don't know the answer yet.
Say, did you see the clock?

Since an interjection is not related to the rest of the sentence, it is diagramed on a separate line.

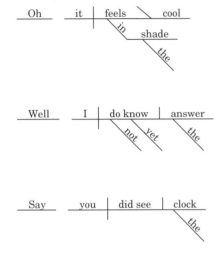

• An interjection is a word that expresses strong feeling. It is not used as a sentence part, but is an independent word.

• A strong interjection is followed by an exclamation point. A mild interjection is followed by a comma.

Lesson Outline:

1. An interjection is a word that expresses strong feeling.

2. An interjection is not related to the rest of the sentence. It is not used as a subject, predicate, or any other sentence part; but it stands alone as an independent word.

3. There are many interjections, but not all of them are proper to use. Words like *hello* and *good-bye* may be used as interjections in sentences. But it is not proper to use interjections that are slang words. It is also improper to use a common word (like *boy* or *man*) as an interjection that has nothing to do with the normal meaning of the word. We should use only those interjections that are suitable for God's people.

4. The Bible uses several interjections.

  a. The words *lo* and *behold* are interjections used to call attention to something or to express wonder or surprise.

  b. *Amen* expresses agreement or approval.

  c. *Alas* shows sorrow, pity, or concern.

  d. The interjection *ah* is a synonym for *oh*. It expresses feelings such as astonishment, grief, or desire.

5. A strong interjection is followed by an exclamation point. A mild interjection is followed by a comma.

6. An interjection is diagramed on a line separate from the rest of the sentence.

★ **EXTRA PRACTICE**
Worksheet 77 *(Interjections)*

Class Practice

A. Read each interjection, and tell whether it should be followed by a *comma* or an *exclamation point*. Also tell whether the next word should begin with a *small letter* or a *capital letter*.
1. Ouch my finger was in the way.
2. Oh what a beautiful sunset that is.
3. Well the job is finally completed.
4. Hello do come in.

B. Diagram these sentences at the chalkboard.
1. What! Haven't you finished yet?
2. Why, there is your lost key!
3. Alas! The axhead was borrowed.
4. Behold, it is floating.

Written Exercises

A. Copy each interjection, and put a comma or an exclamation point after it. Write *yes* or *no* to tell whether the next word should be capitalized.
1. Well it's time to leave for church.
2. Whew it is windy tonight.
3. Why this is a wonderful surprise!
4. What this must be where the chickens are getting out.
5. Oh look at that gurgling spring of water.
6. Lo in her mouth was an olive leaf.
7. Alas the great city of Babylon has been destroyed.

B. Diagram these sentences.
1. Hello. My name is Jonathan.
2. Say! Can you answer this question?
3. Well, show me the problem.
4. Ouch, this needle is sharp!
5. Why, here is the book that I had lost.
6. Lo, mine eye hath seen all this.

Review Exercises

A. Write the tense of each underlined verb or verb phrase. [32–36]

present	past	future
present perfect	past perfect	future perfect

Lesson 122 Answers
Class Practice
A. (Answers may vary.)
1. Ouch, exclamation point, capital letter
2. Oh, comma, small letter
3. Well, comma, small letter
4. Hello, exclamation point, capital letter

B. 1.

2.

3.

4.

Written Exercises
A. (Allow reasonable variation.)
1. Well, no
2. Whew! yes
3. Why, no
4. What! yes
5. Oh, no
6. Lo, no
7. Alas! yes

B. 1.

2.

3.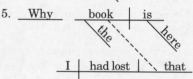

4.

5.

6.

1. I <u>see</u> a ruby-throated hummingbird on the clothesline.
2. I <u>saw</u> one sipping nectar from our trumpet vine yesterday.
3. I <u>have seen</u> several of them.
4. I <u>had</u> not <u>known</u> that they live in this area.
5. The Lord willing, we <u>shall see</u> you next Wednesday.
6. I am quite sure that <u>I shall have finished</u> before you return.

B. Rewrite each sentence, putting the misplaced phrase or clause where it belongs. [120]
1. The lonely old lady watched the happy children with sad eyes.
2. The car is in this garage that was wrecked.
3. My grandmother bought me the book at the bookstore that I wanted.
4. My mother said on Monday she hopes to bake pies.

C. Diagram these sentences. [111]
1. The garden looked greener after it had rained.
2. The bus had left before I got there.
3. When Christians pray, God hears them.
4. While they are yet speaking, I will hear.

---

123. Review of the Parts of Speech

There are eight parts of speech altogether: *noun* (n.), *pronoun* (pron.), *verb* (v.), *adjective* (adj.), *adverb* (adv.), *preposition* (prep.), *conjunction* (conj.), and *interjection* (interj.). Be sure you know their definitions and abbreviations.

A **noun** is a word that names a person, place, thing, or idea.
A **pronoun** is a word that takes the place of a noun.
A **verb** is a word that shows action or being.
An **adjective** is a word that modifies a noun or pronoun. A limiting adjective tells *which, whose,* or *how many.* A descriptive adjective tells *what kind of.* The articles *a, an,* and *the* are also adjectives.
An **adverb** is a word that modifies a verb, an adjective, or another adverb. It tells *how, when, where,* or *to what degree.*

Lesson 123

Purpose: To review the parts of speech.

Oral Review:
1. What is an interjection? (a word that expresses strong feeling)
2. Is an interjection used as a sentence part? (no)
3. What punctuation mark follows (*a*) a strong interjection? (*b*) a mild interjection? (*a.* an exclamation point; *b.* a comma)
4. Give the nominative case pronouns. (I, you, he, she, it, we, they; *archaic:* thou, ye)
5. Give the objective case pronouns. (me, you, him, her, it, us, them; *archaic:* thee)

Review Exercises
A. 1. present   4. past perfect
   2. past   5. future
   3. present perfect 6. future perfect

B. 1. With sad eyes the lonely old lady watched the happy children.
   2. The car that was wrecked is in this garage.
      or In this garage is the car that was wrecked.
   3. At the bookstore my grandmother bought me the book that I wanted.
   4. On Monday my mother said she hopes to bake pies.
      or My mother said she hopes to bake pies on Monday.

C.

Lesson Introduction: Write the following sentence on the chalkboard. Have the students tell you how to label the parts of speech. Help them if they have trouble.

interj. pron. v.   adj. pron. conj. adj.   n.   v.
Well, I am glad you and your sister arrived
adv. prep. n.
here on time.

This sentence includes all the parts of speech. In today's lesson we will review the eight parts of speech.

A **preposition** is a connecting word that begins a prepositional phrase.

A **conjunction** is a word that joins words, phrases, or clauses.

An **interjection** is a word that expresses strong feeling.

The *parts of speech* are not always the same as the *parts of a sentence*. As a sentence part, a noun may be a subject, direct object, predicate nominative, indirect object, or object of a preposition. But as a part of speech, it is a noun no matter how it is used. The same is true of a pronoun.

There is less difference for the other parts of speech. For example, an adjective or an adverb is called the same whether we mean a sentence part or a part of speech. Compare the labels above the following sentences.

Sentence parts labeled:

v.   sub. adj.   d.o.   prep. adj.   o.p.

Hear ye the word of the Lord.

Parts of speech labeled:

v.   pron. adj.   n.   prep. adj.   n.

Hear ye the word of the Lord.

When you are told to label the parts of speech in a sentence, you should follow the second pattern shown above.

Generally, you can tell by looking at a word whether it is a noun or a verb or some other part of speech. But remember, the way a word is used in a sentence determines its part of speech. Sometimes you must think carefully to know for sure what part of speech a word is. Be especially careful in the following cases.

1. *Some words can be used as prepositions or adverbs.* A preposition always begins a phrase. An adverb stands alone. So you should say the word and ask *whom* or *what*. If there is no noun or pronoun to answer the question, the word must be an adverb.

We went <u>down</u> in the morning.
   Think: Down *what*? There is no noun or pronoun to answer the question. *Down* is an adverb.

They went <u>down</u> the stairs.
   Think: Down *what*? The answer is *stairs. Down* is a preposition.

Lesson Outline:

1. Be sure you know the definitions and abbreviations of the eight parts of speech.

  a. A *noun* (n.) is a word that names a person, place, thing, or idea.

  b. A *pronoun* (pron.) is a word that takes the place of a noun.

  c. A *verb* (v.) is a word that shows action or being.

  d. An *adjective* (adj.) is a word that modifies a noun or pronoun. A limiting adjective tells *which, whose,* or *how many.* A descriptive adjective tells *what kind of.* The articles *a, an,* and *the* are also adjectives.

  e. An *adverb* (adv.) is a word that modifies a verb, an adjective, or another adverb. It tells *how, when, where,* or *to what degree.*

  f. A *preposition* (prep.) is a connecting word that begins a prepositional phrase.

  g. A *conjunction* (conj.) is a word that joins words, phrases, or clauses.

  h. An *interjection* (interj.) is a word that expresses strong feeling.

2. The parts of speech are not always the same as the parts of a sentence. As a sentence part, a noun or pronoun may be a subject, a direct object, a predicate nominative, an indirect object, or the object of a preposition. As a part of speech, it is a noun or pronoun no matter how it is used. But words like adjectives and adverbs are called adjectives and adverbs whether we mean parts of speech or parts of a sentence.

3. You cannot always tell what part of speech a word is just by looking at the word itself. The way the word is used in a sentence determines its part of speech.

  (1) *Some words can be used as prepositions or adverbs.* A preposition always begins a phrase. An adverb stands alone.

  (2) *Sometimes a word that is normally a noun or pronoun is used as an adjective.* An adjective modifies a noun or pronoun. A noun or pronoun stands alone.

  (3) *Sometimes a word that is usually an adjective is used as a noun.* It is an adjective

2. *Sometimes a word that is normally a noun or pronoun is used as an adjective.* Be sure the word is not used as a modifier before you decide that it is a noun or a pronoun.

> That was a delicious <u>cherry</u>. (names a thing; noun)
> Mother made a delicious <u>cherry</u> pie. (modifies *pie;* adjective)
>
> <u>Each</u> child brings his own glove. (modifies *child*; adjective)
> <u>Each</u> brings his own glove. (stands alone; pronoun)

3. *Sometimes a word that is usually an adjective is used as a noun.*

> The <u>rich</u> and the <u>poor</u> meet together.
> A word to the <u>wise</u> is sufficient.

We normally expect the underlined words to be used as adjectives. However, in these sentences they do not modify other words. Rather, the words *rich, poor,* and *wise* all name people. So they are nouns in these sentences.

What is the best way to label the parts of speech in a sentence? Begin the same way you do when you diagram. First, find all the verbs and label them. Then find all the nouns and pronouns, and label them. Next, find all the adjectives and adverbs. Then look for prepositional phrases, and label the prepositions. Last of all, label the conjunctions and interjections.

- You should know the definitions and abbreviations of all the eight parts of speech.

- You cannot always tell what part of speech a word is just by looking at the word itself. The way the word is used in a sentence determines its part of speech.

Class Practice

A. Name the eight parts of speech, and write their abbreviations on the chalkboard.

B. Name the parts of speech described here.
1. It modifies a verb, adjective, or adverb.
2. It modifies a noun or pronoun.
3. It is a connecting word that begins a phrase.

only when it modifies a noun or pronoun. It is a noun if it is used by itself to name a person, place, or thing.

4. To label the parts of speech in a sentence, follow much the same order as for diagraming sentences.
  a. First, label the verbs.
  b. Second, label all the nouns and pronouns.
  c. Third, label the adjectives and adverbs.
  d. Fourth, find the prepositional phrases and label the prepositions.
  e. Last of all, label the conjunctions and interjections.

★ **EXTRA PRACTICE**
Worksheet 78 *(Review of the Parts of Speech)*

Lesson 123 Answers
Class Practice
A. noun (n.), pronoun (pron.), verb (v.), adjective (adj.), adverb (adv.), preposition (prep.), conjunction (conj.), interjection (interj.)

B. 1. adverb
   2. adjective
   3. preposition

4. It joins words, phrases, or clauses.
5. It expresses strong feeling.
6. It names a person, place, thing, or idea.
7. It can be limiting or descriptive.
8. It takes the place of a noun.
9. It shows action or being.
10. It may be an article (*a, an,* or *the*).
11. It tells *how, when, where,* or *to what degree.*
12. It tells *which, whose, how many,* or *what kind of.*

C. Tell whether each underlined word is a *preposition, adverb,* or a *conjunction.*
   1. <u>After</u> the crisis was <u>over</u>, we all came <u>back</u> <u>to</u> our seats <u>and</u> breathed a sigh of relief.
   2. <u>During</u> the night, the tree came <u>down</u> <u>across</u> the road.

D. Name the part of speech for each word.
   1. Well, bring your question here to me.
   2. The chocolate sundae, cold and creamy, tasted refreshing on that warm day.
   3. Jesus healed the blind and the lame.

Written Exercises

In all these exercises, you may use abbreviations for the parts of speech.

A. Write whether each underlined word is a *noun,* a *pronoun,* or an *adjective.*
   1. <u>His</u> <u>papers</u> are here. <u>Mine</u> are over there.
   2. <u>That</u> <u>boy</u> <u>who</u> is standing must be <u>your</u> <u>brother.</u>
   3. <u>Many</u> are called, but <u>few</u> are chosen.
   4. The <u>meek</u> shall inherit the <u>earth.</u>

B. Write whether each underlined word is a *preposition,* an *adverb,* or a *conjunction.*
   1. The lid came <u>off</u> <u>as</u> we drove <u>around</u> the corner.
   2. This is different <u>from</u> ours, <u>but</u> we like it anyway.
   3. The cows were <u>inside</u> the barn <u>before</u> the storm came <u>up.</u>
   4. Walter tore <u>up</u> his paper. (Be careful!)

C. Copy each sentence, and label the parts of speech.
   1. Whew! That was hard work.
   2. Well, either you or I must do it soon.

4. conjunction
5. interjection
6. noun
7. adjective
8. pronoun
9. verb
10. adjective
11. adverb
12. adjective

C. 1. After—conjunction; over—adverb; back—adverb; to—preposition; and—conjunction
   2. During—preposition; down—adverb; across—preposition

D. 1.
   interj. v. adj. n. adv. prep. pron.
   Well, bring your question here to me.

   2.
   adj.   adj.   n.   adj. conj. adj.   v.
   The chocolate sundae, cold and creamy, tasted
   adj.   prep. adj. adj. n.
   refreshing on that warm day.

   3.
   n.   v.   adj. n. conj. adj. n.
   Jesus healed the blind and the lame.

Written Exercises

A. 1. adj., n., pron.
   2. adj., n., pron., adj., n.
   3. pron., pron.
   4. n., n.

B. 1. adv., conj., prep.
   2. prep., conj.
   3. prep., conj., adv.
   4. adv.

C. 1.
   interj. pron. v. adj. n.
   Whew! That was hard work.

   2.
   interj. conj. pron. conj. pron. v.   v. pron. adv.
   Well, either you or I must do it soon.

3. The red-and-orange butterfly flitted daintily from one fragrant flower to another.
4. Swiftly and skillfully, the blacksmith put a new shoe on the horse.
5. Jesus helped the sad, the sick, and the sinful.
6. We pray in the morning, at noon, and in the evening.
7. Today we shall wash, and tomorrow we shall iron.
8. This is the man whom you seek.

Review Exercises

Diagram these sentences.

1. A calculator is a small but useful machine.
2. The left margin should always be straight.
3. Some fruit from the basket was lying at the side of the road.
4. The deer were eating apples from the trees during the night.
5. After the storm, the rescuers helped the needy and the homeless.
6. Before the rain started, the boys closed their window.
7. We finally have a cherry tree that produces good fruit.
8. Heaven and earth shall pass away, but My words shall not pass away.
9. Every good gift and every perfect gift is from above, and cometh down from the Father of lights.
10. Parents, teachers, and ministers instruct us about God.

---

124. Chapter 10 Review

Class Practice

A. Give the definition of a preposition.

B. Read these sentences, correcting the errors.
1. I talked at the stranger that visited our class on Sunday.
2. I listened at what he said about his home and school.
3. All his cows were Holsteins accept one.
4. One Jersey cow stood among two Holsteins.
5. A new house is being built besides our house.
6. Their new porch is different than ours.
7. In back of the house is a garden.
8. Among the two houses is a large lawn.

Lesson 124

Purpose: To review the concepts taught in Chapter 10.

3. The red-and-orange butterfly flitted daintily
   adj. adj. conj. adj.   n.   v.   adv.
   from one fragrant flower to another.
   prep. adj.   adj.   n.   prep. pron.
4. Swiftly and skillfully, the blacksmith put a new
   adv. conj.   adv.   adj.   n.   v. adj. adj.
   shoe on the horse.
   n. prep. adj. n.
5. Jesus helped the sad, the sick, and the sinful.
   n.   v.   adj. n. adj. n. conj. adj. n.
6. We pray in the morning, at noon, and in the
   pron. v. prep. adj.   n.   prep. n.   conj. prep. adj.
   evening.
   n.
7. Today we shall wash, and tomorrow we shall iron.
   adv. pron. v.   v.   conj.   adv.   pron. v.   v.
8. This is the man whom you seek.
   pron. v. adj. n. pron. pron. v.

(Review Exercises are on page 515.)

Lesson 124 Answers
Class Practice

A. A preposition is a connecting word that begins a prepositional phrase.

B. (Corrections are marked.)
1. I talked <u>to</u> the stranger that visited our class on Sunday.
2. I listened <u>to</u> what he said about his home and school.
3. All his cows were Holsteins <u>except</u> one.
4. One Jersey cow stood <u>between</u> two Holsteins.
5. A new house is being built <u>beside</u> our house.
6. Their new porch is different <u>from</u> ours.
7. <u>Behind</u> the house is a garden.
8. <u>Between</u> the two houses is a large lawn.

9. Inside of this closet is an ironing board.
10. The treat was for the boys who helped outside of the house.
11. I should of brought more.
12. We gave a scrapbook to the sick girl with glossy white pages.
13. The boy lay on the bed with a broken leg all day long.
14. I received some fruit from my cousin in a basket.
15. The minister led the devotional at school from Guatemala.
16. Father said on Saturday we would go to the sale.
17. From the refrigerator I packed the basket with leftovers.
18. There was not only peach pie but cherry pie.
19. Either the two boys or the one girl clean the floors on Saturday.
20. Either Mary or the boys scrubs the tank every morning.
21. The book was about explorers that the teacher read aloud.
22. Yesterday I gave my report to my teacher that was several pages long.
23. Slowly and with care, the farmer backed the truck toward the loading ramp.
24. He unloaded the hogs, loaded some calves, and some goats.
25. The marble rolled down the steps, across the floor, and disappeared down the register.

C. Tell how the following introductions should be improved.

1. Introducing yourself to a stranger:

   "Hello! What is your name?
   Where are you from?"

2. Introducing your classmate to your father.

   "Samuel, this is my father."
   "Father, this is my classmate Samuel."

3. Introducing your classmate to your cousin the same age.

   "Samuel, this is my cousin Raymond."
   "Raymond, this is my classmate Samuel."

D. Answer these questions.

1. What are the most important rules in conversation?
2. What are some things we should not do in conversation?
3. If there is someone in the group who has little to say, how might you encourage him to say more?
4. When someone is obviously wrong in what he is saying, what should you *not* do? What should you do?

9. Inside ~~of~~ this closet is an ironing board.
10. The treat was for the boys who helped outside ~~of~~ the house.
11. I should <u>have</u> brought more.
12. We gave a scrapbook <u>with glossy white pages</u> to the sick girl.
13. The boy <u>with a broken leg</u> lay on the bed all day long.
14. <u>From my cousin</u> I received some fruit in a basket.
15. The minister <u>from Guatemala</u> led the devotional at school.
16. Father said we would go to the sale <u>on Saturday</u>.

    or <u>On Saturday</u> Father said we would go to the sale.
17. I packed the basket with leftovers <u>from the refrigerator</u>.
18. There was not only peach pie but <u>also</u> cherry pie.
19. Either the two boys or the one girl <u>cleans</u> the floors on Saturday.
20. Either Mary or the boys <u>scrub</u> the tank every morning.
21. The book <u>that the teacher read aloud</u> was about explorers.
22. Yesterday I gave my report <u>that was several pages long</u> to my teacher.
23. Slowly and <u>carefully</u>, the farmer backed the truck toward the loading ramp.
24. He unloaded the hogs, loaded some calves, and <u>loaded</u> some goats.
25. The marble rolled down the steps, across the floor, and ~~disappeared~~ down the register.

    or The marble rolled down the steps <u>and</u> across the floor, and <u>then it</u> disappeared down the register.

C. 1. When introducing yourself to a stranger, say your own name first.
2. When introducing a younger person and an older person, say the older person's name first.
3. Add a bit of information about the one whom you are introducing. If possible, tell about something you know both persons are interested in, to help them get started in conversation.

D. 1. Listen carefully and speak kindly.
2. Do not interrupt another person who is speaking. Do not be eager to criticize, correct, or contradict what others say. Do not talk too rapidly or too loudly. Do not use pronouns without antecedents, or other expressions that are not specific. Do not assume that people know what you mean unless you express yourself clearly.
3. Ask polite questions to show your interest in him.
4. Do not be overly eager to correct him. Do not boldly challenge him or rudely contradict him. Avoid getting into an argument with him.

   Kindly ask him if he is sure about what he is saying. Say something like "I thought it was this way" rather than "You're all wrong."

Written Exercises

A. Copy each prepositional phrase. Underline the preposition, and put parentheses around the object of the preposition.
   1. Who came down to the river and saw the baby in the basket?
   2. What brave girl came from her hiding place and spoke to the princess?

B. Copy each dependent clause, and underline the subordinating conjunction that introduces it.
   1. Since the baby needed a nurse, the princess gave him to his mother.
   2. Moses' mother gave him back to the princess after several years had passed.
   3. Although Moses was raised in the king's palace, he chose to identify with the people of God.
   4. Moses led his people out of Egypt when he became a man.

C. Copy each sentence, and label the parts of speech.
   1. What! All the doughnuts that we made have been sold already.
   2. Mother had made dozens of doughnuts for the market, but they were sold before noon.
   3. In life we must accept the bad with the good.

D. Diagram the following sentences.
   1. The boy in first grade and the boy in third grade are brothers.
   2. Before they came here, they lived in New York.
   3. What! Is the man who spoke first your brother?
   4. Well, I hadn't seen him for a long time.

E. Write whose name should be said first in the following introductions.
   1. Your father and your classmate
   2. Your aunt and your teacher who is a man
   3. Your mother and your teacher who is a woman
   4. Your friend from another state and several friends from your Sunday school class
   5. Yourself and a stranger

Written Exercises

A. 1. <u>to</u> the (river), <u>in</u> the (basket)
   2. <u>from</u> her hiding (place), <u>to</u> the (princess)

B. 1. <u>Since</u> the baby needed a nurse
   2. <u>after</u> several years had passed
   3. <u>Although</u> Moses was raised in the king's palace
   4. <u>when</u> he became a man

C. 1.
   interj. adj. adj.   n.   pron. pron. v.   v.
   What! All the doughnuts that we made have
   v.   v.   adv.
   been sold already.
   2.
   n.   v.   v.   n.   prep.   n.   prep. adj.
   Mother had made dozens of doughnuts for the
   n.   conj. pron. v. v.   prep.   n.
   market, but they were sold before noon.
   3.
   prep. n. pron. v.   v.   adj. n. prep. adj. n.
   In life we must accept the bad with the good.

D. 1.
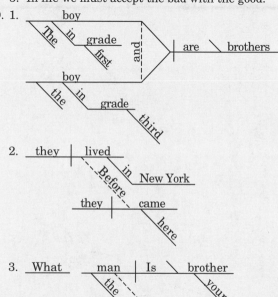

E. 1. "Father"
   2. your aunt's name
   3. "Mother"
   4. your friend's name
   5. your own name

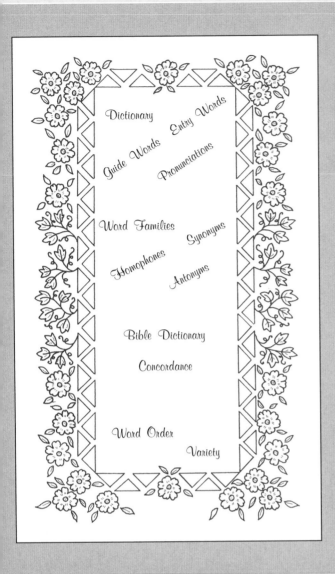

Dictionary

Guide Words   Entry Words

Pronunciations

Word Families   Synonyms

Homophones   Antonyms

Bible Dictionary

Concordance

Word Order

Variety

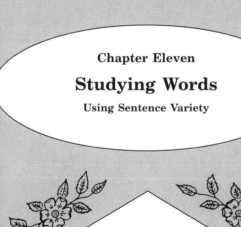

Chapter Eleven

Studying Words

Using Sentence Variety

The
dictionary
helps us to use words
correctly.

A word fitly spoken is like apples of gold in pictures of silver.

Proverbs 25:11

125. Using the Dictionary

The dictionary is like a valuable servant. It quickly provides us with information on the pronunciations, spellings, and meanings of words. Learn to use this handy servant well.

The *entry words* in a dictionary are in boldface and are listed in alphabetical order. When entry words begin with the same letter, they are alphabetized by the second letter. *Element* comes before *erupt* because *el* comes before *er*. When the first two letters are alike, words are alphabetized by the third letter, and so forth. *Anchor* comes before *angry* because *anc* comes before *ang*. *Grope* comes before *group* because *grop* comes before *grou*.

Guide words at the top of the page show the first and last entry words on that page. The guide word at the left is the same as the first entry word on the page, and the guide word at the right is the same as the last word on the page. All the words on that page must come alphabetically between the guide words. See the sample dictionary page below.

Alberta   **audience**

Al ber ta (al ber′tə), *n.* a province in western Canada.

al li ga tor (al′ə gā tər), *n.* 1. a large, thick-skinned reptile that looks much like a crocodile. 2. leather made from the skin of an alligator.

an nounce (ə nouns′), *v.* make known publicly; proclaim. **an nounced, an nounc ing.** —**an nounc′er** *n.*

an nounce ment (ə nouns′ mənt), *n.* something made known publicly; a proclamation.

a pos tro phe (ə pos′trə fē), *n.* a punctuation mark (′) used to show possession, to indicate omitted letters, or to form certain plurals: *dog's, we'll, 6's.*

ap pear (ə pir′), *v.* 1. come into view; become visible. 2. seem: *The corn appears to be growing well.* 3. come before a public audience; present oneself: *The governor is to appear in town next week.*

ap proach (ə prōch′), *v.* 1. move toward and come near to, in distance or time: *The plane approached the airport. We are approaching winter.* —*n.* 2. the act

of coming nearer: *the approach of spring.* 3. a way by which to reach (something); access: *The approach to the house was overgrown with weeds.* 4. method of dealing with a task or problems: *Your approach seems reasonable.*

ap prove (ə prüv′), *v.* 1. consider favorably; be pleased with. 2. agree to; consent to: *The board approved the plans.* **ap proved, ap prov ing.**

ar riv al (ə rī′vəl), *n.* 1. the act of arriving; the coming to a place: *the arrival of the visitors.* 2. a person or thing that arrives: *a bench for late arrivals.*

as sist (ə sist′), *v.* give help to; aid.

at tempt (ə tempt′), *v.* 1. put forth effort to accomplish; try; endeavor. —*n.* 2. an effort to accomplish; a trying.

at tic (at′ik), *n.* the story between the ceiling and the roof of a building.

au di ence (ô′dē əns), *n.* 1. a group of listeners. 2. a

After each entry word is a *phonetic spelling*. The phonetic spelling uses special symbols to show the correct pronunciation of the entry word. It shows the pronunciation of the word according to the pronunciation key.

The *pronunciation key* in the front of the dictionary shows the meaning of each pronunciation symbol. Many dictionaries also have a short pronunciation key at the bottom of each page. Each symbol in the pronunciation key stands for one particular speech sound.

Lesson 125

Purpose: To teach about alphabetical order and pronunciation aids in a dictionary.

Important Note: Check your school's supply of Bible concordances and dictionaries for Lesson 127. If necessary, you might ask pupils to bring copies from home so that every student has a copy of each book for his own use.

Oral Review:

1. Name the part of speech described.
   a. It is a connecting word that begins a phrase. (preposition)
   b. It can be limiting or descriptive. (adjective)
   c. It takes the place of a noun. (pronoun)
   d. It shows action or being. (verb)
   e. It joins words, phrases, or clauses. (conjunction)
   f. It expresses strong feeling. (interjection)
   g. It tells *which, whose, how many,* or *what kind of.* (adjective)
   h. It may be an article (*a, an,* or *the*). (adjective)
   i. It modifies a verb, adjective, or adverb. (adverb)
   j. It modifies a noun or pronoun. (adjective)
   k. It names a person, place, thing, or idea. (noun)
   l. It tells *how, when, where,* or *to what degree.* (adverb)

2. What is a possessive noun? (a noun that shows possession or ownership)

3. How is a possessive noun usually written? (with an apostrophe and -*s*)

4. A possessive noun is often used as what part of speech? (adjective)

5. Nominative case pronouns can be used as what two sentence parts? (subject, predicate nominative)

6. Objective case pronouns can be used as what three sentence parts? (direct object, indirect object, object of a preposition)

Lesson Introduction: The first dictionaries were made hundreds of years ago by Greeks and Romans. But they defined only the more difficult Latin words; they did not define all the words in the language. An English schoolteacher made the first English dictionary in 1604. However, this dictionary contained only the hardest words of the English language. Later, some men decided they would like dictionaries that included more English words instead of only the hard words. They also wanted their dictionaries to set the standard for good usage in English. The first one that included most of the English words was published in 1721 in England. In 1806 Noah Webster published a small school dictionary in the United States. He wanted a dictionary that had the words used by people in the United States. Webster's dictionaries were frequently revised, and today we still use Webster's dictionaries.

Special symbols and diacritical marks are used in the pronunciation key because the English language has more sounds than letters. An upside-down *e* (ə) is called the *schwa* symbol. Diacritical marks include the bar or macron to show long vowels (such as ā), and one or two dots to show various other vowel sounds.

The phonetic spelling shows how the word is divided into syllables. Sometimes the syllable divisions in the entry word are different from the divisions in the phonetic spelling. This is because the entry word shows the *written* syllable divisions, but the phonetic spelling shows the *spoken* syllable divisions.

Written syllable divisions: morn·ing
Spoken syllable divisions: môr′·ning

Accent marks are used to show which syllables are stressed. Some words have a *primary* and a *secondary* accent. Usually a heavy accent mark shows that a syllable receives heavy stress. A lighter accent mark shows that a syllable receives medium stress. Unaccented syllables are not marked at all. Check your particular dictionary to see how it shows accent.

math′·ə·mat′·iks

If a word has more than one correct pronunciation, more than one pronunciation is shown. If only one syllable of a word has two correct pronunciations, the rest of the word may not be repeated in the second pronunciation. Study the following example.

garage (gə·räzh′, räj′)

You cannot always tell from the spelling how an English word should be pronounced. Do not just guess at the pronunciation of unfamiliar words that you meet in reading. Use your dictionary and find out for sure!

- *Entry words* in a dictionary are in boldface and are listed in alphabetical order.
- *Guide words* at the top of a dictionary page show the first and last entry words on that page.
- *Phonetic spellings* use special symbols to show the correct pronunciation of entry words.

Lesson Outline:

1. The entry words in a dictionary are in boldface and are listed in alphabetical order. When entry words begin with the same letter, they are alphabetized by the second letter. When the first two letters are alike, words are alphabetized by the third letter; and so forth.

2. Guide words at the top of the page show the first and last entry words on that page. The guide word at the left is the same as the first entry word on the page, and the guide word at the right is the same as the last word on the page. All the words on that page must come alphabetically between the guide words.

3. The phonetic spelling uses special symbols to show the correct pronunciation of the entry word. It is found immediately after the entry word.

4. The pronunciation key in the front of the dictionary shows the meaning of each pronunciation symbol. Many dictionaries also have a short pronunciation key at the bottom of each page. Each symbol in the pronunciation key stands for one particular speech sound.

5. Special symbols and diacritical marks are used in the pronunciation key because the English language has more sounds than letters.
   a. An upside-down *e* (ə) is called the *schwa* symbol.
   b. Diacritical marks include the bar or macron to show long vowels, and one or two dots to show various other vowel sounds.

6. The phonetic spelling shows how the word is divided into syllables. The entry word shows the *written* syllable divisions, but the phonetic spelling shows the *spoken* syllable divisions.

7. Accent marks are used to show which syllables are stressed. A syllable that receives a *primary accent* (heavy stress) is shown with a heavy accent mark. A syllable that receives a *secondary accent* (medium stress) is shown with a lighter accent mark. Unaccented syllables are not marked at all.

(*Teacher:* Accent marks are usually placed after accented syllables. In a few dictionaries, they are placed before accented syllables.)

8. If a word has more than one correct pronunciation, more than one pronunciation is shown. If only one syllable of a word has two correct pronunciations, the rest of the word may not be repeated in the second pronunciation.

★ EXTRA PRACTICE
Worksheet 79 *(Dictionary Practice)*

Class Practice

A. Tell how you would pronounce these words. Your teacher may tell you to check the dictionary if you are wrong.
1. aerie   2. draught   3. chaos   4. malefactor

B. Read each phonetic spelling, and tell how the word is actually spelled.
1. līk   4. krēm   7. krīm
2. lik   5. shō   8. shü
3. nir'·sī'·tid   6. nē'·kap'   9. kwil'·ting

C. Tell whether each entry word would be found on a dictionary page with the guide words *object* and *old*.
1. ocean   3. oily   5. olive
2. obey   4. office   6. odd

Written Exercises

A. Make a single list with all these words in alphabetical order.

scarf   scurry   scene   seal   scroll
scrape   scour   scythe   scare   shuffle

B. Write *yes* or *no* to tell whether each entry word would be found on a dictionary page with the guide words *scoop* and *scuff*.
1. scorn   4. scrape   7. scurry   10. scour
2. scene   5. scythe   8. septic   11. seal
3. scare   6. scroll   9. scotch   12. screw

C. Write these words in syllables as shown in the entry words. Then mark the primary and secondary accents as shown in the phonetic spellings.
1. declarative   3. imperative   5. interrogative
2. exclamatory   4. recognize   6. opportunity

D. Copy each word, and write the phonetic spelling after it. Include the syllable divisions and the accent marks.
1. plateau   2. enumerate   3. symmetrical

Review Exercises

A. Rewrite each phrase, using a possessive form. [26]
1. the paws of the raccoon
2. the tails of the deer
3. the antlers of the moose
4. the food of the gulls
5. the wings of the moth

Lesson 125 Answers

Class Practice

A. (Meanings are given for added interest.)
1. er·ē, ar·ē, ir·ē (an eagle's nest; a lofty position)
2. draft, dräft (draft—an alternate spelling)
3. kā·os (a very great confusion)
4. mal·ə·fak·tər (evildoer; criminal; antonym of *benefactor*)

B. 1. like   4. cream   7. crime
   2. lick   5. show   8. shoe
   3. nearsighted   6. kneecap   9. quilting

C. 1. yes   4. yes
   2. no   5. no
   3. yes   6. yes

Written Exercises

A. scare   scroll
   scarf   scurry
   scene   scythe
   scour   seal
   scrape   shuffle

B. 1. yes   7. no
   2. no   8. no
   3. no   9. yes
   4. yes   10. yes
   5. no   11. no
   6. yes   12. yes

C. (Accents may vary according to dictionaries used.)
1. de·clar·a·tive
2. ex·clam·a·to·ry
3. im·per·a·tive
4. rec·og·nize
5. in·ter·rog·a·tive
6. op·por·tu·ni·ty

D. (Phonetic symbols may vary according to dictionaries used.)
1. plateau, pla·tō
2. enumerate, i·n(y)ü·mə·rāt
3. symmetrical, si·met·ri·kəl

Review Exercises

A. 1. the raccoon's paws
   2. the deer's tails
   3. the moose's antlers
   4. the gulls' food
   5. the moth's wings

B. Write the correct pronouns. [61–64]

1. Kendra and (she, her) were feeding bread crusts to the sea gulls.
2. (We, Us) girls picked up many colorful rocks.
3. Give (she, her) the one with white crystals.
4. Take Sandra and (they, them) to the big rocks.
5. These are for Grandmother and (he, him).
6. It was (they, them) at the door.

B. 1. she
   2. We
   3. her
   4. them
   5. him
   6. they

---

126. Spellings and Meanings in the Dictionary

The dictionary shows the correct spellings of words. If you cannot find a word in the dictionary, you probably do not know how to spell it. Think of other ways the word might be spelled, and keep looking. If you still cannot find it, you may need to ask someone to help you.

A few words have more than one correct spelling. If the alternate spellings are close together in alphabetical order, the more common spelling is used for the entry word and the other one is shown as an alternate spelling. See the entry for *fulfill* below. If the two spellings are not close together, each spelling is shown as a separate entry word, and the entry for the less common spelling refers you to the more common spelling. See the entry for *sceptic* below.

ful·fill or **ful·fil** (fŏol·fil′), *v.* To carry out, as a promise.

scep·tic (skep′·tik), *n.* Skeptic.

The dictionary shows irregular plural forms of nouns. It does not show plural forms for words such as *cup* and *glass,* because they are formed by simply adding *-s* or *-es.* But it does show irregular plural forms such as *calves* and *women.* To find an irregular plural form, look up the singular form of the word. The plural form is shown after the entry word, usually with the abbreviation *pl.*

calf (kaf), *n., pl.* **calves**

wom·an (wŏom′·ən), *n., pl.* **wom·en**

The dictionary also shows irregular verb forms. If only one past form is shown, the same spelling is used for the past form and the past

---

Lesson 126

Purpose: To teach about spellings, meanings, and *usage labels in a dictionary.

Oral Review:

1. Answer the following questions about the dictionary.
   a. How are the entry words listed? (in alphabetical order)
   b. What are guide words? (words at the top of each page, which show the first and last entry words on that page)
   c. What is a phonetic spelling? (a spelling that uses phonetic symbols to show the pronunciation of a word)
   d. What does the pronunciation key show? (the meaning of each pronunciation symbol)
2. With what part of speech does an adjective clause usually begin? (relative pronoun)
3. List the relative pronouns. (who, whom, whose, which, that)
4. Where in a sentence must an adjective clause be placed? (right after the noun or pronoun that it modifies)
5. With what part of speech does an adverb clause begin? (subordinating conjunction)
6. What parts of speech do adverb clauses modify? (verbs, adjectives, adverbs)
7. What do adverb clauses tell? (how, when, where, why, to what degree, how long, how much, in spite of what, under what condition)

Lesson Introduction: Suppose you were setting out to make the first dictionary. Where would you start? How would you make sure you got all the words that should be in the dictionary? No one even knows exactly how many words are in the English language! Would you include the names of all the participle. If two past forms are shown, the first is the past form and the second is the past participle.

> **bring** (bring), *v.* **brought**

> **grow** (grō), *v.* **grew, grown**

The dictionary shows irregular forms of comparison for adjectives and adverbs. If you look up *large,* you may not see *larger* and *largest,* because these are regular forms. But if you look up *ill,* you will also see *worse* and *worst* because these are irregular forms of comparison.

One of the main purposes of a dictionary is to give the meanings of words. If a word has more than one meaning, only one entry word is shown and the different meanings are given. The definitions are usually numbered. Read the definitions for the word *crane* in the illustration below.

> **crane** (krān), *n.* 1. A tall wading bird. 2. A machine for moving
> heavy objects.

Can you find two cranes in this picture?

Sometimes two or more words come from different sources, but they happen to have the same spelling. Then they have separate entries because each one is actually a different word. See the examples below.

> **bark¹** (bärk), *n.* The tough outside covering of a tree.
> [from Scandinavian *börkr*]
> **bark²** (bärk), *n.* The short, sharp cry of a dog.
> [from Old English *beorcan*]
> **bark³** (bärk), *n.* A kind of sailing ship.
> [from Italian *barca*]

A dictionary shows what part of speech a word is. Notice how this is done in the examples in this lesson. *Calf* and *woman* are nouns (*n.*), and *bring* and *grow* are verbs (*v.*).

plants and animals? (There are over 750,000 names of insects alone!) What about the thousands of proper nouns, such as geographical names? Besides, new words are constantly being devised for new inventions and discoveries. And because of modern travel and communication, words are constantly being borrowed from other languages. Dictionary editors face the challenging task of finding words and deciding which ones to include.

People have gone through all this work, and today we have dictionaries that are full of useful information. In this lesson we will learn about some more things that a dictionary shows.

Lesson Outline:

1. The dictionary shows the correct spellings of words. If you cannot find a word in the dictionary, think of other ways the word might be spelled, and keep looking.

   a. If there is more than one correct spelling, the dictionary will show the other spelling with the entry word or as a separate entry word.

   b. The dictionary shows irregular plural forms of nouns.

   c. The dictionary shows irregular verb forms. If only one past form is shown, the same spelling is used for the past form and the past participle. If two past forms are shown, the first is the past form and the second is the past participle.

   d. The dictionary shows irregular forms of comparison for adjectives and adverbs.

2. The dictionary shows the meanings of words.

   a. If a word has more than one meaning, only one entry word is shown and the different meanings are given. The definitions are usually numbered.

   b. Sometimes two or more words come from different sources, but they happen to have the same spelling. Then they have separate entries because each one is actually a different word.

3. The dictionary shows what part of speech a word is. Many words can be used as more than one part of speech.

Dictionaries also give *usage labels* to certain words. Four common labels are *informal, slang, dialectal,* and *archaic.* God has given us language for the purpose of sharing ideas with others. So it is important that we use words in such a way that others clearly understand what we mean.

Informal words are common in everyday use but are not proper in formal writing. They include expressions like *mike* for "microphone" and *elbow grease* for "hard physical effort."

Slang words were first used by people trying to invent clever new ways of saying things. They are not suitable for God's people to use, because many slang words have hidden evil meanings. Using *guy* for "person," *dough* for "money," and *chow* for "food" is slang and not proper English.

Dialectal words are used mainly by people living in certain areas. One example is the word *reckon,* whose standard meaning is "to consider or count." The dialectal meaning of *reckon* is "to suppose or guess." Other words with dialectal meanings are *poke,* meaning "sack," and *all,* meaning "all gone." We should avoid dialectal words in most writing because they may not be clear to the reader.

Archaic words are old words no longer in general use. They include words like *conversation* for "manner of life," *careful* for "anxious," and *chapman* for "merchant." We are especially interested in the archaic words used in the King James Bible.

- A dictionary shows the correct spellings and meanings of words.
- A dictionary shows what part of speech a word is.
- A dictionary gives usage labels to certain words.

Class Practice

A. Use a dictionary to find two different meanings for each word. Give the part of speech for each meaning.

1. drill	3. right	5. steep
2. fine	4. wrench	6. rung

B. Answer these questions. If the answer is *no,* tell what the underlined word means.
1. Can a <u>staff</u> publish a paper?
2. Can a person ride a <u>mount</u>?

---

4. **The dictionary gives usage labels to certain words.**
   a. *Informal* words are common in everyday use but are not proper in formal writing.
   b. *Slang* words were first used by people trying to invent clever new ways of saying things. Slang words should be avoided because many of them have hidden evil meanings.
   c. *Dialectal* words are used mainly by people living in certain areas. Dialectal words should be avoided in most writing because they may not be clear to the reader.
   d. *Archaic* words are old words no longer in general use. We are especially interested in the archaic words used in the King James Bible.

★ EXTRA PRACTICE
Worksheet 80 *(More Dictionary Practice)*

Lesson 126 Answers
Class Practice
A. (Sample answers.)
1. a. *n.* A tool for boring holes.
   b. *n.* A farm implement for planting grain.
   c. *n.* An activity that is done to practice something.
2. a. *adj.* Very thin.
   b. *adj.* Excellent.
   c. *n.* Money paid as a punishment for wrongdoing.
3. a. *adj.* Fair; just; lawful.
   b. *adj.* The opposite of left.
   c. *adv.* According to fact or truth.
4. a. *n.* A tool for turning bolts.
   b. *n.* A violent, twisting pull.
   c. *v.* To twist or pull violently.
5. a. *adj.* Having a sharp slope; almost vertical.
   b. *v.* To soak, as tea leaves.
   c. *v.* To be deeply involved.
6. a. *v.* Past participle of *ring.*
   b. *n.* A crosspiece between the legs of a chair.
   c. *n.* A crosspiece in a ladder, used as a step.

B. 1. yes (A staff may be a group of people.)
   2. yes (A mount may be a horse.)

3. Is <u>heartwood</u> shaped like a heart?
4. Can a <u>pointer</u> bark?
5. Can a <u>thunderbolt</u> hold two materials together?
6. Is <u>Phoebe</u> the name of a bird and a name for a girl?
7. Is any group of men a <u>council</u>?
8. Could a sack of feed fall <u>plump</u> beside you?

Written Exercises

A. Write the plural form of each word.
  1. policeman   2. handkerchief   3. secretary   4. zero

B. Write the present form, past form, and past participle of each verb.
  1. strive   2. dig   3. awake   4. forbid

C. Write the three forms of comparison for each adjective or adverb.
  1. early   2. good   3. much   4. far

D. Write the other correct spelling for each word.
  1. sizable   2. slue   3. counselor   4. pickax

E. Write the letter of the correct meaning for each underlined word in the sentences below. Choose from the meanings given. (You will not write all the letters.)
  a. Something that is heard.
  b. A long, wide body of water joining two larger bodies of water.
  c. To cause something to make a noise.
  d. To dive swiftly.
  e. Free from defect or disease.

1. The priests <u>sounded</u> the trumpets.
2. We should be thankful for <u>sound</u> minds.
3. The whale <u>sounded</u> several times.
4. We rowed across the <u>sound</u>.

  f. A class in school.
  g. A slope.
  h. To check and give a score to.
  i. To place in classes; sort.
  j. To make smooth and level.

5. My teacher will <u>grade</u> the papers tomorrow.
6. I am in the sixth <u>grade</u>.
7. The workmen will <u>grade</u> the new road next week.
8. Samuel was <u>grading</u> eggs all morning.

3. no. Heartwood is the wood in the center, or heart, of a tree.
4. yes (A pointer may be a kind of dog.)
5. no. A thunderbolt is a flash of lightning and the thunder that follows it.
6. yes
7. no. A council is a group of people who give advice or make decisions.
8. yes (*Plump* may mean "heavily and suddenly.")

Written Exercises

A. 1. policemen
   2. handkerchiefs
   3. secretaries
   4. zeroes *or* zeros

B. 1. strive, strove *or* strived, striven *or* strived
   2. dig, dug, dug
   3. awake; awoke *or* awaked; awaked, awoken, *or* awoke
   4. forbid, forbade *or* forbad, forbidden *or* forbid

C. 1. early, earlier, earliest
   2. good, better, best
   3. much, more, most
   4. far, farther, farthest

D. 1. sizeable
   2. slew *or* slough
   3. counsellor
   4. pickaxe

E. 1. c   5. h
   2. e   6. f
   3. d   7. j
   4. b   8. i

F. Write two different meanings for each word.
   1. season   2. watch   3. switch

G. Write the part of speech for each underlined word, as it is used in that sentence. You may use abbreviations.
   1. On Thursday we boarded the <u>train</u> at Sugarcreek.
   2. <u>Train</u> up a child in the way he should go.
   3. The queen of Sheba came to Jerusalem with a very great <u>train</u>.
   4. Were you ever at the <u>train</u> museum?
   5. What is the <u>charge</u> for crossing this bridge?
   6. That hardware store <u>charges</u> high prices for tools.
   7. When the ram <u>charged</u>, the boys clambered quickly up a tree.
   8. Baby Jonathan is my special <u>charge</u> today.

Review Exercises

Copy the dependent clauses. Write whether each one is used as an adjective (*adj.*) or an adverb (*adv.*). Write which word the clause modifies. [97, 110]
   1. The bird that you hear is a mockingbird.
   2. He was still singing after we went to bed.
   3. The boy who was parking cars is the janitor's son.
   4. Before the meeting started, the parking lot was filled.
   5. The boys could not go inside before they had finished their job.
   6. The minister who spoke tonight was from Wisconsin.

---

127. Using a Bible Concordance and a Bible Dictionary

The Bible is the most important book we can study. But sometimes we need help in studying the Bible. We may want to know where a certain verse is found. Or we may need additional information to help us understand what a certain verse means. Two books that provide this kind of help are a Bible concordance and a Bible dictionary.

A *concordance* is useful for finding verses in the Bible that contain a certain word. You may have a concordance in the back of your Bible, but that is a very small, limited one. There are other concordances that are larger and more extensive. *Strong's Exhaustive Concordance* is a very good, complete concordance.

F. (Sample answers.)
   1. a. One of the four regular divisions of the year.
      b. Any period of time.
      c. To add something that improves flavor.
   2. a. To look at attentively.
      b. A person or persons who guard something.
      c. A small timepiece.
   3. a. A slender stick used for whipping.
      b. To whip; strike.
      c. A device for changing the direction of something or for making or breaking a connection.

G. 1. n.   5. n.
   2. v.   6. v.
   3. n.   7. v.
   4. adj.   8. n.

Review Exercises
   1. that you hear, adj., bird
   2. after we went to bed, adv., was singing
   3. who was parking cars, adj., boy
   4. Before the meeting started, adv., was filled
   5. before they had finished their job, adv., could go
   6. who spoke tonight, adj., minister

Lesson 127

Purpose: To teach the use of a Bible concordance and a Bible dictionary.

Oral Review:
1. When does a dictionary show:
   a. the plural forms of nouns? (when they are spelled irregularly)
   b. the past forms of verbs? (when they are spelled irregularly)
   c. the forms of comparison for adjectives? (when they are spelled irregularly)
2. Give the usage label for each kind of word.
   a. Old words no longer in general use. (archaic)
   b. Words common in everyday use but not proper in formal writing. (informal)
   c. Words used mainly by people living in certain areas. (dialectal)
   d. Words first used by people trying to invent clever new ways of saying things. (slang)
3. Name the three principal parts of verbs. (present, past, past participle)
4. Give the principal parts of the following verbs.
   a. leave (leave, left, [have] left)
   b. ride (ride, rode, [have] ridden)
5. Give the meanings of the following verbs.
   a. lay (to put or place [something])
   b. raise (to cause [something] to go up or grow up)
   c. learn (to gain knowledge)
   d. teach (to give knowledge or instruction)
6. Give the correct past tense of each verb.
   a. tag (tagged, *not* tug)
   b. drag (dragged, *not* drug)
   c. drown (drowned, *not* drownded)
   d. attack (attacked, *not* attackted)
   e. burst (burst, *not* bursted *or* busted)

The entry words in a concordance are arranged in alphabetical order, as in a dictionary. Under each entry word are references showing where the word is found, and beside each reference is the phrase that contains the word. The references are listed in the order of the books of the Bible. If you want to find references only from the Book of Psalms, you would find the section with verses from Psalms.

Suppose you are making a scrapbook page for someone who is sick, and you want to find the reference for the verse "He careth for you." Which entry word should you find: *he, careth, for,* or *you*? Choose *careth,* the least common word in the verse, and look it up. There you will see several phrases from different references. The first is Deuteronomy 11:12: "which the Lord thy God *c* for." (The *c* stands for *careth.*) Keep looking until you find the phrase with the words you want. The reference you are looking for is 1 Peter 5:7.

Perhaps you want to find a longer verse like "Behold, what manner of love the Father hath bestowed upon us." Which word should you look up this time? You could find *behold, love,* and *Father,* but these are very common words in the Bible. You would probably need to go through many references before you found the right one. But if you look up *manner* or *bestowed,* you will find your verse much more easily because these words are less common. *Bestowed* has the fewest references of all, so you will find the verse most quickly if you look under *bestowed.* (The reference is 1 John 3:1.)

A *Bible dictionary* gives information about people, places, things, and customs of the Bible. Entry words are arranged in alphabetical order, as in a dictionary, and information is given about each item.

Perhaps you want to know if it ever snows in Jerusalem. You could look in a Bible dictionary for the information. Find the word *Jerusalem* as you would in a dictionary, using the guide words. Under *Jerusalem* are several subtitles. Look for one on weather or climate. There you will find that in the wintertime the lowest temperature is about 25 degrees. Sometimes as much as one foot of snow falls in Jerusalem, but it usually does not last long.

Or suppose you want to write a report about an animal of the Bible, such as the bear. So you look up *bear* in a Bible dictionary. There you may find a note that says, "See Animal Kingdom." So you turn to *A* and find the entry *Animal Kingdom.* The names of Bible animals are listed alphabetically under this entry word.

Bible concordances and Bible dictionaries are not perfect as the Bible is. We must carefully compare these reference books with the Bible

Lesson Introduction: Ask the pupils if they would like to guess how many verses are in the Bible. There are 31,102 in all! What would they do if they wanted to find a particular verse but had no idea of where it was? It would be very much like looking for a needle in a haystack. But with a concordance, the job becomes so simple that it can usually be done in a matter of seconds or minutes. Can we imagine all the hours that went into making a Bible concordance? We should be truly thankful for this valuable reference book. Today we will learn how to use a Bible concordance and a Bible dictionary.

Lesson Outline:

1. A Bible concordance shows words from the Bible, along with references that contain those words.

　　a. The entry words in a concordance are arranged in alphabetical order, as in a dictionary. Under each entry word are references showing where the word is found. Beside each reference is the phrase that contains the word. The references are listed in the order of the books of the Bible.

　　b. To use a concordance, look up one of the less common words in the verse you want to find. You will find the verse more quickly in this way because there will be fewer references to read through.

2. A Bible dictionary gives information about people, places, things, and customs of the Bible.

　　a. Entry words are arranged in alphabetical order, as in a dictionary, and information is given about each item.

　　b. Sometimes an entry word will refer you to another word or section in the book.

tself because any other book may not always be accurate. However, these reference books will be a great help in studying the Bible if we use them wisely.

> - A Bible concordance shows words from the Bible, along with references that contain those words.
> - A Bible dictionary gives information about people, places, things, and customs of the Bible.

Class Practice

A. Use a concordance to find the reference for each verse.
1. When it is evening, ye say, It will be fair weather: for the sky is red.
2. As the clay is in the potter's hand, so are ye in mine hand.
3. Man looketh on the outward appearance, but the LORD looketh on the heart.
4. The effectual fervent prayer of a righteous man availeth much.
5. I will go before thee, and make the crooked places straight.
6. There is one God, and one mediator between God and men, the man Christ Jesus.

B. Do the following exercises.
1. Look up *train* in a concordance.
   a. How many references are given?
   b. Which books of the Bible contain this word?
2. Look up *train* in a Bible dictionary.
   a. What meanings does the word have?
   b. Does any meaning have the idea of a row of cars, as on a railroad?
3. Look up *bath* in a Bible dictionary.
   a. To what does the word refer?
   b. How does it compare with an English gallon?

Written Exercises

A. Write the reference for each verse, using a concordance.
1. The steps of a good man are ordered by the LORD: and he delighteth in his way.
2. Let every one of us please his neighbour for his good to edification.
3. Keep thy heart with all diligence; for out of it are the issues of life.

Lesson 127 Answers
Class Practice
A. 1. Matthew 16:2
2. Jeremiah 18:6
3. 1 Samuel 16:7
4. James 5:16
5. Isaiah 45:2
6. 1 Timothy 2:5

B. (Answers are based on *Strong's Concordance* and *Unger's Bible Dictionary*.)
1. a. three
   b. 1 Kings, Proverbs, Isaiah
2. a. In 1 Kings 10:2, *train* refers to the caravan that came with the queen of Sheba. In Proverbs 22:6, *train* has to do with teaching a child to do right. In Isaiah 6:1, *train* refers to the long, trailing part of a king's robe.
   b. no
3. a. the largest of liquid measures, equal to the ephah
   b. The bath is equal to seven and one-half gallons.

Written Exercises
A. 1. Psalm 37:23
2. Romans 15:2
3. Proverbs 4:23

4. Watch ye, stand fast in the faith, quit you like men, be strong.
5. I have learned, in whatsoever state I am, therewith to be content.
6. Before they call, I will answer; and while they are yet speaking, I will hear.

B. Look up *hail* in a concordance.
1. Write the reference for the following verse.

> "Hast thou entered into the treasures of the snow? or hast thou seen the treasures of the hail?"

2. How many references from the Book of Psalms are given?
3. How many different books of the Bible contain this word?

C. Look up *bees* in a Bible dictionary. Then do the following exercises.
1. Write two references of verses that mention bees or honey.
2. Write two interesting facts about bees in Palestine.

   Suggestions:
   Wild bees in Palestine
   Where wild bees make their homes
   How many bees are in Palestine today

3. From the Book of Proverbs, give one caution about eating honey.

D. Read about one or more of the following subjects in a Bible dictionary, and write two interesting facts that you discover.

potter	threshing floor	Dead Sea
fishing	wine press	Bethlehem

Review Exercises

A. Write the three principal parts of each verb. Use *have* with the past participle. [31]
1. ride
2. send
3. draw
4. come
5. begin
6. put

B. Write the correct verbs. [47–52]
1. When the dog (set, sat) on the sidewalk and would not move, it (raised, rose) a question in his master's mind.
2. The dog had been (taught, learned) to protect his blind owner from danger.
3. Some workmen had (digged, dug) a deep hole just the day before, and steam was (raising, rising) from it.

4. 1 Corinthians 16:13
5. Philippians 4:11
6. Isaiah 65:24

B. (Answers are based on *Strong's Concordance*.)
1. Job 38:22
2. six
3. ten

C. (Answers are based on *Unger's Bible Dictionary*.)
1. (Any two.)
   1 Samuel 14:25, 26; Deuteronomy 32:13; Psalm 81:16; Matthew 3:4; Deuteronomy 1:44; Psalm 118:12 (Other answers also possible.)
2. Wild bees are especially plentiful in the wilderness of Judea. They are very fierce and dangerous to man.
   The bees sometimes live in trees, but they generally make their homes in cracks of rocks.
   Wild bees are not as plentiful in Palestine today as they may have been in earlier times. But an enormous number of domesticated bees are raised.
3. Do not eat too much honey (Proverbs 25:16, 27).

D. (Individual answers.)

Review Exercises

A. 1. ride, rode, (have) ridden
2. send, sent, (have) sent
3. draw, drew, (have) drawn
4. come, came, (have) come
5. begin, began, (have) begun
6. put, put, (have) put

B. 1. sat, raised
2. taught
3. dug, rising

4. A water pipe had (burst, busted), but the workers had not (set, sat) barriers around it.

5. The faithful dog would not (let, leave) his master fall in to be (drowned, drownded).

6. The grateful owner patted the dog and (let, left) him have a juicy bone.

7. Later the dog (laid, lay) the chewed bone in the garden.

8. It has (laid, lain) there ever since.

9. The dog wanted to (let, leave) the house for a walk, but his master (laid, lay) down to rest awhile.

10. (Can, May) I pet your dog?

11. Please do not pet the dog while he is working, or you may be (attacked, attackted).

12. The dog (drug, dragged) his master home because he wanted a juicy bone.

13. The master decided that he must (learn, teach) the dog a lesson.

14. The dog should (have, of) obeyed his master's command.

Challenge Exercises

In *Strong's Concordance,* each Bible reference is followed by a number. By using that number, you can turn to the dictionaries in the back of the concordance and find the original Hebrew or Greek word used in that reference. (The Old Testament was written in Hebrew, and the New Testament in Greek.) The dictionaries give the root meanings of the Hebrew and Greek words.

1. In 1 Samuel 25:25, Abigail said, "Nabal is his name, and folly is with him." Why did she say that? (Find *Nabal* in the Hebrew dictionary.)

2. Find the Greek word that is translated *comfortless* in John 14:18. Which of the following English words comes from that Greek word?
   a. grief   b. orphan   c. forsake

3. Find the Greek word that is translated *offences* in Matthew 18:7. Which of the following English words comes from that Greek word?
   a. insult   b. confusion   c. scandal

4. When Jesus said "Verily, verily" (as in John 10:1), He used the word from which the English word ———— comes.
   a. solemn   b. amen   c. behold

---

4. burst, set
5. let, drowned
6. let
7. laid
8. lain
9. leave, lay
10. May
11. attacked
12. dragged
13. teach
14. have

Challenge Exercises

1. The name *Nabal* comes from the Hebrew words for "fool," "foolish," and "folly."
2. b. orphan
3. c. scandal
4. b. amen

128. Sentence Variety in Paragraphs

Good writers make careful use of sentence variety in their paragraphs. You have already studied declarative, interrogative, imperative, and exclamatory sentences, as well as simple, compound, and complex sentences. You have also studied different kinds of word order in sentences. So you should be well prepared to use sentence variety in paragraphs.

Study the sentences below. All four of them express admiration for a beautiful sunset. Notice how the same thought can be stated in the four different kinds of sentences.

> That sunset is beautiful. (declarative)
> Look at that beautiful sunset. (imperative)
> Have you ever seen such a beautiful sunset? (interrogative)
> What a beautiful sunset that is! (exclamatory)

The following sentences use the three different kinds of word order. Which one expresses the thought in the most interesting and forceful way?

> The lively heifers <u>charged through the fence</u>. (normal word order)
> <u>Through the fence charged</u> the lively heifers. (inverted word order)
> <u>Through the fence</u> the lively heifers <u>charged</u>. (mixed word order)

Normal word order makes statements in a plain, simple manner. That is why normal order is used most often. Inverted or mixed word order tends to catch the reader's attention more because it is different. When you write paragraphs, try to use an inverted or mixed sentence once in a while. This serves two purposes. First, it provides sentence variety. Second, it emphasizes the thought in that particular sentence.

Short sentences can sometimes be combined to make a compound sentence and thus add variety to a paragraph. In the following part of a paragraph, all the sentences are short and choppy. Notice how awkward this sounds.

> Henry threw the ball. David caught it. Then David began running toward the end of the playground. Robert ran after him. Soon David threw the ball back to Henry. . . .

Lesson 128

Purpose: To teach sentence variety in paragraphs.

Oral Review:

1. What are the most important rules in conversation? (Listen carefully, and speak kindly.)
2. How should one disagree when necessary? (kindly)
3. How can you show your interest in others in conversation? (by asking polite questions and listening carefully)
4. List several ways of developing a paragraph. (by giving convincing details, by using examples and illustrations, by using comparison or contrast)
5. If you develop a paragraph by showing similarities between two people, places, things, or ideas, what method are you using? (comparison)
6. If you develop a paragraph by showing differences between two people, places, things, or ideas, what method are you using? (contrast)

Lesson Introduction: Read the following paragraphs to the students. Ask them which one sounds better.

> Saul told the Israelites that anyone who ate any food all day would be cursed. They were in battle. They came to a woods. Honey was dripping onto the ground. All the people were faint with hunger. They were afraid to eat any honey because of Saul's oath. Jonathan had not heard the oath. He dipped the end of his rod into some honeycomb and ate it. Jonathan felt strengthened to go on in the battle.

> *   *   *   *   *

> Saul told the Israelites that anyone who ate any food all day would be cursed. At this time they were in battle. They came to a woods, and there they found honey dripping onto the ground. All the people were faint with hunger. But they were afraid to eat any honey because

The sentences are more readable if some of them are joined into compound sentences.

> Henry threw the ball, and David caught it. Then David began running toward the end of the playground. Robert ran after him, and David soon threw the ball back to Henry....

Of course, not all short sentences should be combined to make them compound. Rather, you should combine sentences in a way that makes your writing flow smoothly and naturally.

Simple sentences can sometimes be changed to complex sentences by the use of adjective and adverb clauses.

> I ate three sandwiches. I was quite hungry.
> I ate three sandwiches because I was quite hungry.
>   (adverb clause)
>
> I ate three sandwiches. I enjoyed them very much.
> I ate three sandwiches, which I enjoyed very much.
>   (adjective clause)

Complex sentences are especially valuable because they clearly show the relationship between two ideas. Using complex sentences properly can be a complex problem! But with study and practice, you will be able to make these sentences a natural part of your writing. Soon you will find it hard to write without using complex sentences.

A paragraph should have some longer sentences and some shorter sentences. Of course, making some sentences compound or complex will automatically make some sentences longer. But short sentences are also needed for variety. Short sentences do not waste words. They get right to the point. Short sentences also sound more like natural conversation.

Read the two following paragraphs. Which one do you like better?

> Fossils are the remains of plants or animals that lived long ago. Most scientists agree that they were laid down by flood waters. Fossils are found all over the world. Many fossils of ocean animals have been found even on top of high mountains. They have been discovered on Mount Everest, the highest mountain in the world. They are convincing evidence of a worldwide flood. We know that the Bible account of Noah and the Flood is true, even without any special natural evidence. Fossils are an interesting evidence that God has given for us to observe.

> *   *   *   *   *

... of Saul's oath. Jonathan had not heard the oath. So he dipped the end of his rod into some honeycomb and ate it. After this he felt strengthened to go on in the battle.

The second paragraph sounds better because it has a variety of sentences. "Variety is the spice of life." Learn how to use sentence variety when writing paragraphs.

Lesson Outline:

1. Good writers make careful use of sentence variety in paragraphs.

2. Declarative, interrogative, imperative, and exclamatory sentences can be used for variety in paragraphs. Often the same thought can be stated in all four kinds of sentences.

3. Normal, inverted, and mixed word order can be used for sentence variety.

   a. Sentences in normal word order express thoughts in a plain, simple way.

   b. Sentences in mixed or inverted word order provide sentence variety, and they also emphasize the thought in a particular sentence.

4. Simple, compound, or complex sentences can be used for sentence variety. This method also produces variety in the length of sentences.

★ EXTRA PRACTICE
Worksheet 81 *(Sentence Variety in Paragraphs)*

What are fossils? They are the remains of plants or animals that lived long ago. How were fossils formed? Most scientists agree that they were laid down by flood waters. Fossils are found all over the world. Even on top of high mountains, many fossils of ocean animals have been found. They have been discovered on Mount Everest, the highest mountain in the world. Are they not convincing evidence of a worldwide flood? We know that the Bible account of Noah and the Flood is true, even without any special natural evidence. But fossils are an interesting evidence that God has given for us to observe.

Do you like the second paragraph better? Can you tell why? What kinds of sentence variety does it have?

Of course, sentence variety must be used carefully. We should usually avoid writing paragraphs in which all the sentences follow the same pattern. But neither should we write paragraphs filled with all kinds of unusual sentences. Variety is like spice. A little spice improves the flavor, but too much spice ruins the cake!

- Good writers make careful use of sentence variety in paragraphs.

- Declarative, interrogative, imperative, and exclamatory sentences can be used for variety in paragraphs.

- Normal, inverted, and mixed word order can be used for sentence variety.

- Simple, compound, and complex sentences can be used for sentence variety. This method also produces variety in the length of sentences.

Class Practice

A. The following paragraph contains only declarative sentences in normal word order. Tell how to improve the sentence variety in the following ways.
   1. Change sentence *c* to mixed word order.
   2. Change sentence *e* to an exclamatory sentence with inverted word order.
   3. Tell which other sentence should be an exclamatory sentence.

Lesson 128 Answers
Class Practice
A. 1. At the Jordan, they cut down trees to make lumber for a new house.
   2. Into the river flew the axhead!
   3. sentence *h* (The iron axhead floated!)

^aThe sons of the prophets wanted to build a new house near the Jordan River. ^bThey asked Elisha the prophet to go with them. ^cThey cut down trees to make lumber for a new house at the Jordan. ^dOne of the servants was using a borrowed ax to fell a beam. ^eThe axhead flew into the river. ^fBut Elisha cut a stick and threw it into the water. ^gThe servant must have had a great surprise then. ^hThe iron axhead floated. ⁱElisha told him to take it out of the water, and he obeyed.

B. The following paragraph contains only simple sentences. Tell how to improve the sentence variety in the following ways.
1. Join sentences *a* and *b* into a complex sentence with an adjective clause.
2. Join sentences *d* and *e* into a complex sentence with an adverb clause. Begin with the transitional word *However.*
3. Join sentences *f* and *g* into a compound sentence.

^aMother thanked Brother Nathan. ^bHe had changed the tire. ^cThen she climbed in and started the engine. ^dShe put the car in gear. ^eIt did not move. ^fShe pressed the accelerator. ^gStill the car would not budge. ^hWhat could be the matter? ⁱSuddenly Mother realized that the emergency brake was on! ^jWith a sheepish smile, she released the brake and drove away.

Written Exercises

A. The paragraph below contains only declarative sentences. Improve the sentence variety in the following ways. (Write only the sentences that would be changed.)
1. Rewrite sentence *b* as an imperative sentence.
2. Rewrite sentence *c* as an interrogative sentence.
3. Rewrite sentence *g* as an exclamatory sentence.

^aA polar bear seems to like the cold. ^bYou should consider, for example, that he does not hurry to a warm cave as other bears do when cold weather comes. ^cYou may wonder how he stands the cold and wet. ^dGod has created the polar bear with layers of fat under his skin and with air spaces in his fur to keep him warm. ^eHis oily fur keeps him dry even when he swims under the icy water to hunt for his dinner. ^fHe has fur on the bottom of his feet to help him walk on ice without slipping. ^gIt is no wonder that the polar bear does not mind the cold.

B. 1. Mother thanked Brother Nathan, who had changed the tire.
2. However, when she put the car in gear, it did not move.
3. She pressed the accelerator, but still the car would not budge.

Written Exercises

A. 1. Consider, for example, that he does not hurry to a warm cave as other bears do when cold weather comes.
2. How does he stand the cold and wet?
3. No wonder the polar bear does not mind the cold!

B. The following paragraph contains many short, choppy sentences. Improve the sentence variety in the following ways. (Write the entire paragraph.)

1. Join sentences *a* and *b* into a complex sentence with an adverb clause. Move *long ago* to the beginning of the sentence.
2. Join sentences *c* and *d* into a compound sentence.
3. Join sentences *f* and *g* into a complex sentence with an adjective clause.
4. Move *immediately* to the beginning of sentence *h*.
5. Join sentences *i* and *j* into a complex sentence with an adverb clause. Begin the sentence with *when*.
6. Join sentences *k* and *l* into a compound sentence.
7. Join sentences *m* and *n* into a compound sentence. Move *soon* to the beginning of the sentence.
8. Rewrite sentence *o* as an exclamatory sentence, beginning with *how*.

   *a*An old man met a band of robbers long ago. *b*He was riding through the forests of Poland. *c*The robbers took all his valuables. *d*Then they asked if he had given them everything. *e*He said that he had. *f*But soon afterward he remembered some gold. *g*It was sewed in the hem of his robe. *h*He hurried back immediately and looked for the robbers. *i*He found them. *j*He told them that he had not been truthful. *k*He offered the gold to them. *l*They would not take it. *m*One robber soon went and brought back the old man's wallet. *n*Others brought back his horse and other valuables. *o*The man was very glad that he had been so honest.

Review Exercises

Write the correct phrase for each description. [21, 24, 27]

   developing by contrast
   developing by comparison
   developing with details
   developing with examples and illustrations

1. Paragraph development by showing similarities between two persons, places, things, or ideas.
2. Paragraph development by showing differences between two persons, places, things, or ideas.
3. Paragraph development by using an incident.

B. (Wording may vary somewhat.)

   Long ago an old man met a band of robbers while he was riding through the forests of Poland. The robbers took all his valuables, and then they asked if he had given them everything. He said that he had. But soon afterward he remembered some gold that was sewed in the hem of his robe. Immediately he hurried back and looked for the robbers. When he found them, he told them that he had not been truthful. He offered the gold to them, but they would not take it. Soon one robber went and brought back the old man's wallet, and others brought back his horse and other valuables. How very glad the man was that he had been so honest!

Review Exercises

1. developing by comparison
2. developing by contrast
3. developing with examples and illustrations

4. Paragraph development by giving a series of steps, such as showing the things to do in starting a stamp collection.

5. Paragraph development by describing American farm life in relation to European farm life.

4. developing with details

5. developing by comparison (or contrast)

---

129. Synonyms, Antonyms, and Homophones

The English language has a great variety of words. When you were only six years old, you probably knew three or four thousand English words already. However, as you continue to read, you recognize that there are many English words that you still need to learn. Your vocabulary grows mostly from speaking and reading, but you can help it to grow with word study. Learn pairs of synonyms and antonyms as an aid to vocabulary growth. Learn to distinguish between homophones to overcome one kind of spelling problem.

Synonyms are words with similar meanings. Two synonyms may be very close in meaning, but they never have exactly the same meaning. They cannot always be used in the same way. For example, *cheap* and *inexpensive* are synonyms. Which word would you use to describe something you want to sell? You might say, "Buy these; they are cheap." But *cheap* can mean "of poor quality." So if you are selling a well-made product, you should rather say, "Buy these; they are inexpensive."

Here are several more pairs of synonyms.

purpose—reason   drive—propel   enough—sufficient

Antonyms are words with opposite or nearly opposite meanings. Sometimes we can make a meaning clearer by using an antonym to tell what something is *not*. Some antonyms are words like *huge* and *tiny*. Other antonyms are formed by adding a prefix such as *un-* or *dis-* to a word. In this way we can form antonyms like *buckle—unbuckle* and *order—disorder*.

Here are several more pairs of antonyms.

arrive—depart   giant—dwarf   ordinary—special

Lesson 129

Purpose: To teach about synonyms, antonyms, and homophones (formerly called homonyms).

Oral Review:

1. What reference book can you use to find a Bible verse that contains a certain word? (a Bible concordance)

2. What reference book can you use to find information about people, places, things, and customs of the Bible? (a Bible dictionary)

3. Give three ways that apostrophes are used. (to form possessive nouns; to form contractions; to form the plurals of numbers, letters, signs, and symbols)

4. Which preposition refers to movement from one location to another, *in* or *into*? (into)

5. Which preposition refers to only two objects, *between* or *among*? (between)

6. Which is correct: "This one is *different than* that one" or "This one is *different from* that one"? (different from)

7. Tell which of the following prepositions are unnecessary.
   a. after the test was over with (with)
   b. the pen that I write with (correct)
   c. inside of the barn (of)
   d. Where are you going to? (to)
   e. Whom were you speaking to? (correct)

Lesson Introduction: Write the following words on the chalkboard.

noisy   thunderous   deafening

All these words are synonyms for *loud,* but none of them have exactly the same meaning. Which one would fit best in each of the following sentences?

True synonyms and antonyms are the same part of speech. Study the following examples.

Synonyms:
> joy—gladness (nouns), *but not* rejoice (verb)
> begin—start (verbs), *but not* first (adjective)
> gentle—mild (adjectives), *but not* mildness (noun)

Antonyms:
> joy—grief (nouns), *but not* grieve (verb)
> begin—finish (verbs), *but not* last (adjective)
> gentle—harsh (adjectives), *but not* roughness (noun)

Homophones are words that are pronounced alike, but their spellings and meanings are different. It takes care and thought to spell homophones correctly, but this is important so that you communicate the right idea.

> The (rumors, roomers) usually come during the summer.
> (*Rumors* usually come at any time of the year. Most likely the correct word is *roomers*.)

> I'll go (by, buy) that store.
> (Not many people can so easily *buy* a store. Most likely the correct word is *by*.)

Here are several more pairs of homophones.

ant—aunt	flee—flea	maze—maize
bin—been	guessed—guest	nay—neigh
cellar—seller	hour—our	oar—ore
die—dye	lane—lain	pale—pail

Some homophones come in sets of three or four.

air, heir, ere, e'er	heel, heal, he'll
burro, burrow, borough	I'll, isle, aisle
dew, do, due	meat, meet, mete
gnu, knew, new	right, write, rite, wright

In some sets of homophones, one word is a contraction. Be sure to use the correct word. Think of the words a contraction stands for when you use it.

> your—you're (*You're* means "you are.")
> its—it's (*It's* means "it is" or "it has.")

The children were ——— in their play.
The noise of the jackhammer was ———.
The water made a ——— roar as it cascaded over the steep cliff.

Read the following sentences to the students. Ask them how to spell the underlined words.

> I <u>sent</u> some of the new ten-<u>cent</u> rose <u>scent</u> to my friend Rose.
> Grandpa is <u>too</u> old <u>to</u> <u>load</u> those <u>two</u> sacks of <u>flour</u>.

Studying synonyms, antonyms, and homophones will help to make you aware of the great variety of meanings in words.

Lesson Outline:

1. Synonyms are words with similar meanings. Two synonyms may be very close in meaning, but they never have exactly the same meaning. They cannot always be used in the same way.

2. Antonyms are words with opposite meanings. True synonyms and antonyms are the same part of speech.

3. Homophones are words that are pronounced alike, but their spellings and meanings are different.
  a. Some homophones come in sets of three or four.

> air, heir, ere, e'er
> burro, burrow, borough

whose—who's (*Who's* means "who is" or "who has.")
aisle—isle—I'll (*I'll* means "I shall" or "I will.")
there—their—they're (*They're* means "they are.")

Use synonyms, antonyms, and homophones carefully. Check a dictionary when you are not sure of the spelling or meaning of a word.

• Synonyms are words with similar meanings.

• Antonyms are words with opposite meanings.

• Homophones are words that are pronounced alike, but their spellings and meanings are different.

Class Practice

A. Tell whether these pairs of words are *synonyms, antonyms,* or *homophones.*
1. unite—divide
2. rye—wry
3. region—area
4. sight—cite
5. convince—persuade
6. center—edge

B. Tell which words are incorrect. Tell how to spell each one correctly.
1. The break on my bicycle doesn't holed.
2. A bare usually has a short tale or none at all.
3. Last winter hour neighbors gave us slay rides.
4. Save that peace of construction paper; we don't want to waist it.
5. Harry tolled me that the bells were wringing because of a fire.

Written Exercises

A. Copy each word, and write the matching synonym.
1. brief   raise
2. dwelling   warped
3. bent   residence
4. consume   short
5. elevate   lowly
6. humble   devour

Lesson 129 Answers
Class Practice
A. 1. antonyms   4. homophones
   2. homophones   5. synonyms
   3. synonyms   6. antonyms

B. 1. break—brake; holed—hold
   2. bare—bear; tale—tail
   3. hour—our; slay—sleigh
   4. peace—piece; waist—waste
   5. tolled—told; wringing—ringing

Written Exercises
A. 1. brief—short
   2. dwelling—residence
   3. bent—warped
   4. consume—devour
   5. elevate—raise
   6. humble—lowly

b. In some sets of homophones, one word is a contraction. Think of the words a contraction stands for when you use it.

   your—you're (you are)
   its—it's (it is, it has)

Use this memory device: <u>Syn</u>onyms have <u>sim</u>ilar meanings. <u>Ant</u>onyms have <u>anti</u>- (opposite) meanings. <u>Hom</u>ophones <u>hum</u> alike.

★ EXTRA PRACTICE
Worksheet 82 *(Synonyms, Antonyms, and Homophones)*

B. Copy each word, and write the matching antonym.

1. reckless	shorten
2. lengthen	sturdy
3. question	careful
4. frail	depart
5. simple	complex
6. arrive	answer

C. Write a homophone for each word.

1. blew   3. plane   5. steak
2. steel   4. wait   6. groan

D. Write whether the words in each pair are synonyms (*S*), antonyms (*A*), or homophones (*H*).

1. construct—build   5. eyelet—islet
2. clime—climb   6. shorten—abbreviate
3. pause—resume   7. rough—smooth
4. serious—sober   8. knead—need

E. Write the homophones that properly complete these sentences.
1. These (to, too, two) girls went (to, too, two) the city (to, too, two).
2. He made a (rye, wry) face.
3. The snow was (pact, packed) between the buildings.
4. Many people yield to the temptation of (pried, pride).
5. A full-grown (mail, male) lion has a (main, mane) around his neck.
6. The little boat moved by means of a large (sale, sail).
7. This (gored, gourd) is shaped like a (pair, pear).
8. How many inches have you (groan, grown) since last summer?

Review Exercises

A. Copy each sentence, and add the missing punctuation marks. [77–87]
1. In fact were taking twenty eight visitors to our great uncles house.
2. Yes Marie well sing for him and then well recite John 14 1 6 for him.
3. Soon after 12 00, theyll serve the meal.
4. Mother said, Martha will bring the bread butter and jelly and Marie will bring the potatoes meat and peas.
5. My great grandfather John Lane will be ninety four years old tomorrow.
6. In the early days a printer had to keep his *p*s and *q*s straight the *p*s could easily come out as *q*s.

B. 1. reckless—careful
   2. lengthen—shorten
   3. question—answer
   4. frail—sturdy
   5. simple—complex
   6. arrive—depart

C. 1. blue   4. weight
   2. steal   5. stake
   3. plain   6. grown

D. 1. S   5. H
   2. H   6. S
   3. A   7. A
   4. S   8. H

E. 1. two, to, too
   2. wry
   3. packed
   4. pride
   5. male, mane
   6. sail
   7. gourd, pear
   8. grown

Review Exercises

A. (Corrections are underlined.)
1. In fact, we're taking twenty-eight visitors to our great-uncle's house.
2. Yes, Marie, we'll sing for him, and then we'll recite John 14:1-6 for him.
3. Soon after 12:00, they'll serve the meal.
4. Mother said, "Martha will bring the bread, butter, and jelly; and Marie will bring the potatoes, meat, and peas."
5. My great-grandfather, John Lane, will be ninety-four years old tomorrow.
6. In the early days, a printer had to keep his *p*'s and *q*'s straight; the *p*'s could easily come out as *q*'s.

B. Copy the incorrect words. If other words should be used instead, write the correct words beside them. [116]

1. My book is different than yours, accept for the first chapter.
2. After we are inside of the building, June will sit besides me.
3. The lawn mower is in back of the house.
4. The three bullfrogs on the bank leaped in the water.
5. Where is your book at?
6. After art class was over with, they shared the pictures between all the girls in the class.

B. 1. than—from; accept—except
2. of; besides—beside
3. in back of—behind
4. in—into
5. at
6. with; between—among

---

130. Word Families

Have you ever met a stranger who guessed your last name before you even told him? Perhaps he said, "I can tell what family you belong to." The reason he could do this is that people in the same family are alike in many ways. They tend to look alike, and they have similar ways of talking and acting.

Words come in families too. If you become acquainted with several words in a *word family,* you can recognize other words in that family. With practice, you will sometimes be able to guess the meaning of a completely new word simply because you are acquainted with its "relatives."

People in the same family have the same last name. Words in the same family also have the same "last name." That is, they have the same *root* or basic word element. You can improve your vocabulary by studying words in groups according to their roots. If you know the meaning of a root, you can recognize more words in the same word family.

For example, the word *number* comes from the Latin root *numer,* which means "number." The following words have the same root, so they are in the same word family. How many of these words do you recognize?

numeral	numerable	innumerable	numerator
enumerate	numerical	numerous	numberless

The Latin root *vari* means "different." The following words are in the *vari* family. Can you see how they are related in meaning?

vary	variation	variable
various	variety	invariable

Lesson 130

Purpose: To teach the *study of related words as a means of expanding one's vocabulary.

Oral Review:

1. What are synonyms? (words with similar meanings)
2. What are antonyms? (words with opposite meanings)
3. What are homophones? (words with the same pronunciation but different spellings and meanings)
4. What is an interjection? (a word that expresses strong feeling)
5. What is a conjunction? (a word that joins words, phrases, or clauses in a sentence)
6. What is a divided quotation? (a quotation that is separated into two parts by explanatory words)
7. When does the second part of a divided quotation begin with a capital letter? (when it begins a new sentence or is capitalized for another reason)

8. What are some differences between direct quotations and indirect quotations?
   (a. A direct quotation repeats the exact words of a speaker. An indirect quotation does not.
   b. Quotation marks are used with a direct quotation, but not with an indirect quotation.
   c. The word *that* often comes before an indirect quotation.
   d. Some pronouns may be different in an indirect quotation.
   e. Some verb forms may be different in an indirect quotation.)

Roots may appear at different places in words. The root *graph* means "to write." Notice the various places where this root is found in the following words.

graphite   stenographer   photograph

Many words are formed by using prefixes and suffixes to change or add to the meanings of roots. If you know the meaning of the root and of the prefix or suffix, you can often tell the meaning of the word. For example, the root *port* means "to carry." The table below shows what happens when various prefixes are added to this root.

Prefix	New Word	New Meaning
ex- (out)	export	to carry out
im- (in)	import	to carry in
re- (back)	report	to carry back
de- (away)	deport	to carry away
trans- (across)	transport	to carry across

This chart shows what happens when suffixes are added to the root *port*.

Suffix	New Word	New Meaning
-able (able)	portable	able to be carried
-er (one who)	porter	one who carries
-age (act of)	portage	act of carrying

Sometimes both a prefix and a suffix are added to a root.

Prefix and Suffix	New Word	New Meaning
re- (back) -er (one who)	reporter	one who carries back
trans- (across) -ation (act of)	transportation	act of carrying across

Here are some members of another word family.

simple	simplify	simplification
simply	simplicity	simplistic

Simple is an adjective that means "having one part." The suffix *-ly* changes it to an adverb that means "in a simple way," and *-ify* changes it to a verb that means "to make simple." *Simplicity* is a noun that means "the state of being simple," and *simplification* is a different noun that

Lesson Introduction: Discuss Matthew 1:23 with the pupils. Call attention to the name for Jesus as given in the verse, and ask what the name means. Show how it is made of three parts: *em* (with), *manu* (us), and *el*. Which part of *Emmanuel* means "God"? (*el*) What other names in the Bible have this root?

Samuel ("asked of God")
Daniel ("God is my judge")
Elijah ("My God is Jehovah")
Eli ("God is high")

New words are still made in this way. Simple words and word parts are combined in various ways to make bigger words. Today we will learn some interesting things about this, and see how words are related to each other.

Lesson Outline:

1. A word family is a group of words with the same root. Roots are the basic elements of words. They may appear at different places in words.

2. Prefixes and suffixes give different meanings to words in the same family. Knowing the meanings of roots, prefixes, and suffixes helps to unlock the meanings of new words.

3. The study of word families will help to increase your vocabulary. It is easier to learn several words of the same family together than to learn only one new word at a time. A dictionary is helpful for distinguishing the individual words in a word family.

means "the act of making simple." *Simplistic* is another adjective, but this word means "overly simple."

You can easily see that it is *simpler* to learn these six words together than to learn them one by one! A dictionary will introduce you to the individual "members" in a word family. It will give the part of speech for each word, along with its meaning. This will help you to avoid confusing "twins" like *simplicity* and *simplification,* which do not mean the same at all, even though both are nouns. You will learn all these things and more as you become acquainted with the whole family.

Exploring the meanings of roots, prefixes, and suffixes is a fascinating study. Do not miss the interesting discoveries that you can make by studying word families.

- A word family is a group of words with the same root. Prefixes and suffixes give different meanings to words in the same family.

- The study of word families will help to increase your vocabulary.

Class Practice

A. Give the root of each word family. Use a dictionary to find the meaning of the root, and also to find other words in that family.
   1. hydrant, dehydrate, hydraulic, hydrophobia
   2. endure, during, durable, durum
   3. ire, irritate, irritable, irascible

B. Look up the following prefixes and suffixes in your dictionary. Tell what they mean, and give examples of words that have them.
   1. dis-   4. -less
   2. pre-   5. -er
   3. mis-   6. -ish

C. Tell what the following words mean by the clues given.
   1. The root *don* means "give," and the suffix *-or* means "one who."
      a. What does *donor* mean?
      b. How are the words *donate* and *donee* related?
      c. Two other forms of *don* are *dose* and *dote*. What is a dose?
      d. The prefix *anti-* means "against." What is an *antidote*?

Lesson 130 Answers
Class Practice

A. 1. hydr = water (hydroplane, hydrofoil, anhydrous)
   2. dur = hard (durability, duration, endurable, perdurable)
   3. ir = anger (irate, irritation, irritative)

B. 1. not; opposite (dishonest, discontent, disobey, disunity)
   2. before (prefix, predawn, preschool, predict)
   3. wrong (misspell, misbehave, misinterpret, mislead)
   4. without (careless, fruitless, toothless, sinless)
   5. one who (baker, teacher, farmer, writer)
   6. like; with the bad qualities of (foolish, childish, selfish)

C. (This part is intended mainly as a matter of interest. Simply have students give their ideas; then tell them the answers. Write other words from the same word family on the chalkboard.)
   1. a. one who gives
      b. To *donate* is to give something. A *donee* is a person to whom something is given.
      c. something that is given (usually a certain amount of medicine)
      d. something that is given to work against something else, like a poison

2. The prefix *in-* means "in," the root *habit* means "dwell," and the suffix *-ant* means "one who."
   a. What is an inhabitant?
   b. What other words do you know that are related to *inhabitant*?

Written Exercises

A. Do these exercises with words from the same families. Check a dictionary to make sure your answers are correct.
   1. The root *cav* means "hollow."
      a. What word with this root names a large hollow space underground?
      b. The prefix *con-* means "with." The surface of a *concave* lens has (a hollow, an outward bulge).
      c. The suffix *-ity* means "condition of." If your tooth has a "condition of being hollow," it has a ———.
      d. The prefix *ex-* means "out." The suffix *-ate* means "to make." The suffix *-or* means "one who." If your father wants to call "one who makes a hollowed-out place," he will call an ——— cav ———.
   2. The root *circ* means "round" or "around."
      a. A *circle* is a ——— figure.
      b. A *circuit* is a trip or a line ——— something.
      c. The prefix *circum-* comes from the *circ* root. The root *spec* means "look." If a person is *circumspect,* he carefully does what?
      d. *Solar* means "of the sun." What is a *circumsolar* path?
      e. Find and write four more words that begin with *circu-* or *circum-*.

B. Write the correct word for each question by using the meanings given. You may use your dictionary.
   1. The root *geo* means "earth" or "land." Some words with this root are *geometry, geographer, geothermal,* and *geomagnetic.*
      a. The root *graph* means "to write." Which word means "one who writes about the earth"?
      b. Which word has to do with the earth's magnetism?
      c. The root *metr* means "measure." Which word names a branch of mathematics that deals with measures?
      d. Which word refers to heat from the earth?

2. a. one who dwells in (a certain place)
   b. habit—customary practice (activity in which one "dwells")
      habitable—place where one is able to dwell
      habitat—place where an animal normally dwells
      habitation—dwelling place

Written Exercises

A. (Some answers may vary.)
   1. a. cave *or* cavern
      b. a hollow
      c. cavity
      d. excavator
   2. a. round
      b. around
      c. looks around
      d. a path around the sun (like that of the planets)
      e. (Sample answers.) circular, circulate, circulation, circumference, circumstance, circumstantial, circumvent, circumscribe

B. 1. a. geographer
      b. geomagnetic
      c. geometry (This term referred originally to the measuring of land.)
      d. geothermal

2. The root *ped* means "foot." Some words with this root are *pedal, pedestrian, biped, centipede,* and *millipede.*
   a. The prefix *bi-* means "two." Which word names a creature with two feet?
   b. The prefix *centi-* means "hundred." Which word names a creature with a hundred feet? (It actually has from 15 to 170 pairs of legs.)
   c. The prefix *milli-* means "thousand." Which word names a creature that is supposed to have a thousand feet? (It actually has no more than 115 pairs of legs.)
   d. Which word names a lever or treadle that is operated by foot?
   e. Which word names a person traveling on foot?

C. Write original sentences using three new words that you learned by studying word families in this lesson.

Review Exercises

A. Copy the three sentences with direct quotations, and add the missing punctuation marks and capital letters. [77, 80]
   1. On Sunday said Galen we saw fourteen deer in our garden
   2. Yes and one buck was white Andrew exclaimed
   3. Paul said it must have been an albino
   4. Albino animals are born without the usual coloring in their skin.
   5. My teacher said that a true albino is all white with pink eyes.

B. Write whether each underlined word is a *preposition,* a *conjunction,* or an *interjection.* You may use abbreviations. [115–122]
   1. <u>What</u>! Did you see two hyenas <u>and</u> a leopard <u>in</u> the game park?
   2. <u>Well</u>, four lions were running <u>after</u> a zebra, <u>but</u> it got away.

Challenge Exercises

For each word, write what part of speech it is. Then write three other words of that family, and name their parts of speech.
   1. respond   2. ample   3. reality

---

2. a. biped
   b. centipede
   c. millipede
   d. pedal
   e. pedestrian

C. (Individual answers.)

Review Exercises

A. (Corrections are underlined.)
   1. <u>"</u>On Sunday<u>,"</u> said Galen<u>,</u> <u>"</u>we saw fourteen deer in our garden.<u>"</u>
   2. <u>"</u>Yes<u>,</u> and one buck was white<u>!"</u> Andrew exclaimed<u>.</u>
   3. Paul said<u>,</u> <u>"</u>It must have been an albino.<u>"</u>
   4. (no quotation)
   5. (indirect quotation)

B. 1. interj., conj., prep.
   2. interj., prep., conj.

Challenge Exercises

(Sample related words.)
   1. verb; respondent—adjective, noun; responder—noun; response—noun; responsive—adjective; responsible—adjective; responsibility—noun
   2. adjective; ampleness—noun; amply—adverb; amplify—verb; amplification—noun; amplitude—noun
   3. noun; real—adjective, adverb, noun; realism—noun; realistic—adjective; realize—verb; really—adverb; unreal—adjective; surreal—adjective

131. Chapter 11 Review

Class Practice

A. Look up the following words. Give several different meanings for each one. Tell what part of speech goes with each meaning.
1. bid
2. pen
3. peep
4. shy

B. Tell whether these pairs are *synonyms, antonyms,* or *homophones.*
1. nose—knows
2. aromatic—odorless
3. exasperation—annoyance
4. one—won

C. Tell which words are spelled incorrectly. Tell how to correct each one.
1. Jerry spoke in a courtious manor.
2. We sang in the hauls of the hospitel.
3. The right answer was guest by the last guessed.
4. Weal serve the desert for lunch.

D. Look up the following prefixes and suffixes in the dictionary. Tell what they mean, and give examples of words that begin with each prefix.
1. dis-
2. re-
3. -ment
4. -ous

E. Answer these questions about reference books.
1. What reference book would you use to find where in the Bible the following sentence is found? Which word would you look up?

   "But ask now the beasts, and they shall teach thee."

2. What reference book would you use to find how many men named James are mentioned in the New Testament, and what each one did?
3. What reference book would you use to find where Bethel was located?

F. Tell how to improve the sentence variety in the following paragraphs.
1. The sentences in the following paragraph are all in normal word order. Tell how to change sentence *b* to mixed word order, and sentence *d* to inverted word order.

Lesson 131

Purpose: To review the concepts taught in Chapter 11.

Lesson 131 Answers
Class Practice

A. (Sample answers.)
1. a. verb: to issue an order
   b. verb: to request to come; invite
   c. noun: an offer
   d. noun: a statement of what one will give or take for something
   e. noun: an invitation
2. a. noun: a tool used in writing with ink
   b. noun: a small yard for farm animals
   c. verb: to write
   d. verb: to shut in
3. a. verb: to look through a small hole or crack
   b. noun: a look through a small hole or crack
   c. noun: the cry of a young bird or chicken
   d. verb: to make the sound of a young bird or chicken
   e. noun: the first glimpse
4. a. adjective: bashful; uncomfortable in company
   b. adjective: easily frightened away
   c. verb: to move aside suddenly, as in fright
   d. verb: to throw swiftly

B. 1. homophones
   2. antonyms
   3. synonyms
   4. homophones

C. 1. courtious—courteous; manor—manner
   2. hauls—halls; hospitel—hospital
   3. guest—guessed; guessed—guest
   4. Weal—We'll; desert—dessert

D. 1. not, opposite of; discontent, disentangle, disable, disagree
   2. back, again; return, reprint, replace, rewrite
   3. act of; condition of
   4. full of; having

E. 1. Bible concordance; beasts
   2. Bible dictionary
   3. Bible dictionary

F. 1. By touching an object, you can tell if it is hot or cold, hard or soft, rough or smooth, wet or dry.
   When you stroke the fur of a cat, you receive a pleasant sensation.

*a*The sense of touch is a wonderful gift from God. *b*You can tell if an object is hot or cold, hard or soft, rough or smooth, wet or dry, by touching it. *c*If you put your fingers against your throat and sing, you can feel the quiver of your vibrating vocal cords. *d*You receive a pleasant sensation when you stroke the fur of a cat. *e*If you prick yourself with a pin, you feel pain. *f*You know how hard to grip a paper cup because you can feel the pressure of your fingers against it. *g*The sense of touch helps us in many ways.

—Lester Showalter

2. The following paragraph contains all simple sentences. Tell how to join each pair of underlined sentences into a compound or complex sentence.

The mink is a brown, furry animal with pointed ears and bright eyes. <u>He looks appealing. He is a fierce hunter.</u> He finds much of his food like crayfish, frogs, and minnows in the water. On land he finds mice, muskrats, rabbits, and snakes to eat. <u>He has a bad reputation among farmers. He sometimes steals chickens from them.</u>

3. The following paragraph contains all declarative sentences. Tell how to change the paragraph so that it has at least one interrogative sentence, one imperative sentence, and one exclamatory sentence.

*a*It was a topsy-turvy Saturday. *b*First of all, my alarm clock didn't ring and I overslept. *c*I awoke to hear Mother telling me to get up immediately. *d*"The chimney is clogged, and the wood stove is smoking!" she said. *e*You can imagine how I hurried then. *f*I wondered what would happen next. *g*Soon Father had extinguished the fire in the stove, but not before the whole house was full of white, choking smoke. *h*Instead of doing what we had planned that day, Mother and I washed bedding, curtains, and clothes until the lines were full and we were tired out. *i*I am glad that not every day is like that one.

2. He looks appealing, but he is a fierce hunter.
    or Although he looks appealing, he is a fierce hunter.
   He has a bad reputation among farmers, for he sometimes steals chickens from them.
    or He has a bad reputation among farmers because he sometimes steals chickens from them.

3. (Sample changes are underlined.)
    a<u>What a topsy-turvy Saturday it was!</u> *b*First of all, my alarm clock didn't ring and I overslept. *c*I awoke to hear Mother telling me to get up immediately. *d*"The chimney is clogged, and the wood stove is smoking!" she said. *e*<u>Imagine how I hurried then.</u> *f*<u>What would happen next?</u> *g*Soon Father had extinguished the fire in the stove, but not before the whole house was full of white, choking smoke. *h*Instead of doing what we had planned that day, Mother and I washed bedding, curtains, and clothes until the lines were full and we were tired out. *i*<u>How glad I am that not every day is like that one!</u>

Written Exercises

A. For each entry word, write *yes* or *no* to tell whether you would find it on a dictionary page with the guide words *Joab* and *Jonah*.
1. John 3. Joash 5. Johanan
2. Jezreel 4. Jordan 6. Joel

B. Divide these words into syllables, and mark the accents.
1. solidify 2. facility 3. intertwine

C. Copy each word, and write the phonetic spelling beside it. Include the accent marks.
1. photographic 3. misdemeanor
2. competent 4. liquefaction

D. Write the plural form of each word.
1. ratio 4. medley
2. proof 5. novelty
3. spoonful 6. radius

E. Write the forms of comparison for these adjectives and adverbs.
1. many 3. bad
2. hardy 4. energetic

F. Write the other correct spelling for each word.
1. jailor 2. helixes

G. Write the part of speech that each underlined word is. Use a dictionary if you need help.
1. There is a small <u>spring</u> in the woods behind our house.
2. These plants <u>spring</u> from seeds blown here by the wind.
3. This is a <u>spring</u> flower; it blooms in early May.
4. The ninety-year-old lady is still quite <u>spry</u>.

H. Write the root of each word family. Then write another word with that root.
1. thermal, thermometer, thermograph
2. vitamin, vitality, revitalize
3. vision, supervision, visualize, visible

I. Rewrite one of the paragraphs in Part F of Class Practice, making the suggested improvements.

Written Exercises

A. 1. yes 4. no
   2. no 5. yes
   3. yes 6. yes

B. 1. so·lid·i·fy
   2. fa·cil·i·ty
   3. in·ter·twine

C. (Phonetic symbols may vary.)
   1. photographic, fō·tə·graf·ik
   2. competent, kom·pi·tənt
   3. misdemeanor, mis·di·mē·nər
   4. liquefaction, lik·wə·fak·shən

D. 1. ratios 4. medleys
   2. proofs 5. novelties
   3. spoonfuls 6. radii *or* radiuses

E. 1. more, most
   2. hardier, hardiest
   3. worse, worst
   4. more energetic, most energetic

F. 1. jailer 2. helices

G. 1. noun
   2. verb
   3. adjective
   4. adjective

H. (Sample related words.)
   1. *therm(o);* thermostat, thermoelectric
   2. *vita;* vital, vitalism
   3. *vis;* visit, visibility

I. (You may wish to specify which paragraph is to be rewritten. See suggested answers in Class Practice.)

132. Final Review

Class Practice

A. Name the part of speech described.
1. It modifies a verb, adjective, or adverb.
2. It modifies a noun or pronoun.
3. It is a connecting word that begins a phrase.
4. It joins words, phrases, or clauses.
5. It expresses strong feeling.
6. It names a person, place, thing, or idea.
7. It can be limiting or descriptive.
8. It takes the place of a noun.
9. It shows action or being.
10. It may be an article (*a, an, the*).
11. It tells *how, when, where,* or *to what degree.*
12. It tells *which, whose, how many,* or *what kind of.*

B. Say the verbs in each group.
1. The twenty-three helping verbs.
2. The most common linking verbs.
3. Verbs of sense used as linking verbs.
4. Other linking verbs.

C. Say the three principal parts of each verb.
1. bring   4. raise
2. come   5. set
3. reach   6. tear

D. Say each verb in the tense shown in parentheses.
1. freeze (simple past)   4. buy (future perfect)
2. keep (present perfect)   5. dig (simple present)
3. list (simple future)   6. begin (past perfect)

E. Tell whether each sentence is *declarative, interrogative, imperative,* or *exclamatory.* Also tell whether it is *simple, compound,* or *complex.* (All punctuation has been omitted.)
1. Who came to Bethany after Lazarus died
2. Roll away the stone
3. Jesus called Lazarus and he came forth
4. What a great miracle that was

Lesson 132 Answers
Class Practice

A. 1. adverb
2. adjective
3. preposition
4. conjunction
5. interjection
6. noun
7. adjective
8. pronoun
9. verb
10. adjective
11. adverb
12. adjective

B. 1. am, is, are, was, were, be, been, being
have, has, had
do, does, did
may, might, must
can—could, shall—should, will—would
2. am, is, are, was, were, be, been, being
3. taste, feel, smell, sound, look, appear
4. grow, seem, stay, become, remain

C. 1. bring, brought, (have) brought
2. come, came, (have) come
3. reach, reached, (have) reached
4. raise, raised, (have) raised
5. set, set, (have) set
6. tear, tore, (have) torn

D. 1. froze   4. will have bought
2. have kept   5. dig
3. will list   6. had begun

E. 1. interrogative, complex
2. imperative, simple
3. declarative, compound
4. exclamatory, simple

Lesson 132

Purpose: To give a final review of English concepts taught this school year.

F. Name the kind of pronouns in each set. Choose from this list.

demonstrative	personal—nominative case
indefinite	personal—objective case
interrogative	personal—possessive case
relative	

1. this, that, these, those
2. I, you, he, she, it, we, they
3. my, mine, your, yours, his, her, hers, its, our, ours, their, theirs
4. some, any, none, all, most, each, either, one, nobody, anyone, anybody, both, few, several, many
5. who, whom, whose, which, what
6. me, you, him, her, it, us, them
7. who, whom, whose, which, that

G. Give the correct words.
1. A good description is developed by (chronological order, spatial order, the order of importance).
2. The three main parts of a story include all the following except (the beginning, the conflict, the middle, the ending).
3. The title of a story should *not* (be short, be interesting, give away the outcome, arouse the reader's curiosity).
4. The extra part of a business letter is the (heading, inside address, greeting, body, closing, signature).
5. Paragraphs can be developed in all the following ways except (by using details, by using examples and illustrations, by using comparison or contrast, by using rhyme and rhythm).
6. "For pleasures are like poppies spread,
   You seize the flower, its bloom is shed."

   a. These lines follow the (iambic: ˘ ΄ ˘ ΄, trochaic: ΄ ˘ ΄ ˘) rhythm pattern.
   b. The figure of speech in the first line is (a simile, a metaphor, personification).
   c. One thing that makes the lines sound appealing is (words with similar beginning sounds, words that suggest the sounds they refer to).

Written Exercises

A. Write the parts of speech for the underlined words.
1. Myron <u>and</u> John will be choosing the new songs <u>tomorrow</u>.

F. 1. demonstrative
   2. personal—nominative case
   3. personal—possessive case
   4. indefinite
   5. interrogative
   6. personal—objective case
   7. relative

G. 1. spatial order
   2. the conflict
   3. give away the outcome
   4. inside address
   5. by using rhyme and rhythm
   6. a. iambic: ˘ ΄ ˘ ΄
      b. a simile
      c. words with similar beginning sounds

Written Exercises
A. 1. conjunction, adverb

2. Will the <u>service</u> be held <u>in</u> the morning?
3. <u>Oh</u>, the singing <u>sounded</u> beautiful!
4. <u>We</u> sang several <u>new</u> songs.

2. noun, preposition
3. interjection, verb
4. pronoun, adjective

B. Identify the underlined words as follows: direct object (*DO*), indirect object (*IO*), object of a preposition (*OP*), predicate nominative (*PN*), predicate adjective (*PA*), or appositive adjective (*AA*).
1. Paul and Barnabas were <u>missionaries</u> in the early days.
2. They preached the <u>Gospel</u> at every opportunity.
3. Many of the Gentiles were quite <u>ignorant</u>.
4. The apostles taught <u>them</u> the truth.
5. Paul, bold and <u>courageous</u>, was not afraid of suffering.
6. Please read the story to <u>me</u>.

B.	1. PN	4. IO
	2. DO	5. AA
	3. PA	6. OP

C. Write whether each group of words is a sentence (*S*), a fragment (*F*), or a run-on error (*R*).
1. Long ago my great-grandmother washed with a washboard.
2. Finally bought her a washing machine.
3. She was quite pleased now she no longer had to scrub by hand.
4. The children were helping to wash.
5. By turning a great wheel by hand.

C.	1. S	4. S
	2. F	5. F
	3. R	

D. Write *yes* or *no* to tell whether the underlined words should be capitalized.
1. on a <u>sunday</u> morning
2. one day last <u>spring</u>
3. with <u>uncle</u> James
4. this Sunbeam <u>mixer</u>
5. David, the <u>king</u> of Israel
6. Jesus and <u>his</u> disciples
7. the song "Abide <u>with</u> Me"
8. an interesting <u>scottish</u> custom

D.	1. yes	5. no
	2. no	6. yes
	3. yes	7. yes
	4. no	8. yes

E. Write the best words for these sentences.
1. Several (boy's, boys') projects are finished.
2. The first (minister's, ministers') topic was on loving others.
3. Show kindness to the one (who, whom) asks you to go one mile by going with him two miles.
4. Did the man (who, whom) you helped seem surprised by your kindness?
5. The horse (who, that) had run away was caught by my brother.
6. The (chair's rungs, rungs of the chair) were broken.
7. (This, This here) job looks endless.
8. (Them, Those) girls worked determinedly.
9. It was (we, us) children who finished the job.
10. It must have been John and (they, them).

E.
1. boys'
2. minister's
3. who
4. whom
5. that
6. rungs of the chair
7. This
8. Those
9. we
10. they

11. Mother and (she, her) cleaned the rooms.
12. Brother Andrew took Paul and (they, them) to church.
13. (It's, Its) time to give the kitten (it's, its) milk.
14. (They're, Their) mother was waiting for them.
15. He (could, couldn't) scarcely see to drive down the mountain.
16. We didn't have (no, any) visitors at church.
17. My pet kitten is (laying, lying) on the rug.
18. Please (raise, rise) the window a bit.
19. Because of the dry weather, the price of corn will (raise, rise).
20. The boys usually (set, sit) with their fathers in church services.
21. Father (let, left) me help with the plowing.
22. Please (let, leave) the dolls at home.
23. My brother (taught, learned) me how to beat time for this song.
24. (Can, May) we please see your pictures?
25. Of the two girls, Judith is (taller, tallest).
26. This is the (baddest, worst) storm we've had this summer.
27. This snail crawls (more slowly, slowlier) than I imagined it would.
28. The frogs jumped (off, off of) the bank and (in, into) the water.
29. You should (except, accept) a gift graciously.
30. Please divide the cookies evenly (between, among) the two of you.
31. No one was there (beside, besides) the Owen family.
32. I want to talk (to, at) Aunt Miriam before she leaves.
33. I should (of, have) brought my grandfather along to see you.
34. These peaches taste different (from, than) the peaches on the other tree.
35. The peach orchard is (in back of, behind) the house.
36. Where is the new (shovel, shovel at)?
37. I saw it just (outside, outside of) the door.
38. We can hardly wait until this job is (over, over with).
39. What were you (talking, talking about)?
40. The evening was (nice, pleasant) and cool.

F. Write the subjects, and then write the correct words in parentheses.
1. None of the children (was, were) idle.
2. Both of the girls (wash, washes) dishes.
3. Some of the mothers (prepare, prepares) fruit for the meeting.

11. she
12. them
13. It's, its
14. Their
15. could
16. any
17. lying
18. raise
19. rise
20. sit
21. let
22. leave
23. taught
24. May
25. taller
26. worst
27. more slowly
28. off, into
29. accept
30. between
31. besides
32. to
33. have
34. from
35. behind
36. shovel
37. outside
38. over
39. talking about
40. pleasant

F. 1. None, were
2. Both, wash
3. Some, prepare

4. Elizabeth and Lois (don't, doesn't) have paring knives.
5. Father or Mother (sharpen, sharpens) the knives.
6. There (was, were) several dull knives already.
7. (Here's, Here are) the sharpeners.
8. Henry (don't, doesn't) go to that school.

G. Write the word that receives the action of each verb. Then write whether the voice of the verb is *active* or *passive*.
1. A widow was helped by Elijah.
2. Elijah raised her son to life.
3. Elijah was protected by God.
4. God sent ravens to feed Elijah.

H. Copy each underlined item, and add the punctuation mark that should be used after it.
1. <u>Yes</u> a package has arrived for <u>Joan</u> my sister.
2. Janice, Sandra, and June helped Miss <u>Taylor</u> but Dawn, Louise, and Kristen helped <u>Mrs</u> Smith.
3. We found several old barrels in the <u>attic</u> in the <u>garage</u> and in the basement.
4. My <u>great</u> grandfather quoted Psalm <u>119</u> <u>1</u> 8 by memory.
5. <u>Self</u> denial is an important <u>virtue</u> no one can be Jesus' disciple without it.
6. Dear Sirs

   I will not be able to keep my appointment of <u>2</u> 00 on March 12.
7. <u>Boys</u> hurry <u>inside</u> it's going to rain.

I. Write whether each underlined item is an *adjective* or an *adverb*.
1. We hit the nails <u>hard</u> to get them into the <u>hard</u> wood.
2. The lady <u>in the kitchen</u> is my grandmother.
3. My grandfather is visiting <u>in the living room</u>.
4. The big truck, <u>which we had loaded</u>, broke down.
5. They had just finished moving in the furniture <u>when it began to snow</u>.

J. Label the words in each pair as synonyms (*S*), antonyms (*A*), or homophones (*H*).
1. silence—quietness
2. plane—plain
3. brightness—dimness
4. knew—new
5. flammable—fireproof

4. Elizabeth (and) Lois, don't
5. Father (or) Mother, sharpens
6. knives, were
7. sharpeners, Here are
8. Henry, doesn't

G. 1. widow, passive
   2. son, active
   3. Elijah, passive
   4. ravens, active

H. (Corrections are underlined.)
1. Yes, Joan,
2. Taylor; Mrs.
3. attic, garage,
4. great- 119: 1-
5. Self- virtue;
6. Sirs: 2:
7. Boys, inside:

I. 1. adverb, adjective
   2. adjective
   3. adverb
   4. adjective
   5. adverb

J. 1. S   4. H
   2. H   5. A
   3. A

Name _____   (*English 6, Lesson 1*)

Worksheet 1

Sentences and Fragments

A. Write *S* or *F* in the first blank to tell whether each group of words is a sentence or a fragment. If it is a fragment, write a letter in the second blank to tell what is missing. The first two have been done for you.

  a. Missing a subject   c. Missing a subject and a predicate
  b. Missing a predicate   d. Missing a helping verb

__F__   __d__   1. The twins wearing eyeglasses now.

__S__   _____   2. Eyeglasses were invented sometime in the 1200s.

__F__   __b__   3. The name of the inventor.

__F__   __a__   4. Is not known for certain.

__S__   _____   5. He may have invented the first pair for himself.

__S__   _____   6. The inventor of eyeglasses was probably a glass blower.

__F__   __b__   7. People with poor eyesight.

__F__   __a__   8. Had no way to read or do fine work.

__F__   __d__   9. Grandfather taking aspirin for his arthritis.

__F__   __b__   10. Physicians of ancient times.

__F__   __c__   11. From the bark of a willow tree.

__S__   _____   12. Powder from the bark of a willow tree was used for pain.

__F__   __a__   13. Helped but irritated the stomach.

__S__   _____   14. Charles Gerhardt produced the first man-made aspirin powder in 1853.

__F__   __a__   15. Was later made into tablets.

__F__   __b__   16. In 1915 the Bayer company in Germany.

__S__   _____   17. Later, companies all over the world began to make it.

__F__   __a__   18. Kills pain, reduces fever, and cuts down swelling.

B. From the fragments above, choose one that needs a subject, one that needs a predicate, one that needs a subject and a predicate, and one that needs a helping verb. Make complete sentences from the four fragments you chose.   (Individual sentences.)

_____

_____

_____

_____

_____

_____

Name _____

Worksheet 2
The Predicate of a Sentence

A. Underline all the words below that could be used as action verbs.

<u>taste</u>	<u>tear</u>	<u>boast</u>	lilies	<u>bless</u>	birds	beautiful
<u>tease</u>	<u>give</u>	heart	early	the	old	<u>answer</u>
<u>honor</u>	pure	<u>obey</u>	<u>make</u>	angry	<u>keep</u>	read

B. List the forms of *be*. _____am_____ _____is_____ _____are_____ _____was_____

_____were_____ _____be_____ _____been_____ _____being_____

C. Write the "sometimes linking verbs" given in Lesson 2. _____taste_____ _____feel_____

_____smell_____ _____sound_____ _____look_____ _____appear_____

D. List the helping verbs in groups.

__am__ __is__ __are__ __was__ __were__ __be__ __been__ __being__ ;

__have__ __has__ __had__ ; __do__ __does__ __did__ ; __may__ __might__ __must__ ;

__can__ — __could__ , __shall__ — __should__ , __will__ — __would__

E. What does the predicate of a sentence do? _____

_____It tells what the subject does or is._____

F. Draw two lines under the simple predicate. Draw parentheses around the complete predicate. The first two have been done for you.

1. God (<u>is</u> my high tower.)

2. People (<u>can see</u> far around from a high tower.)

3. A firefighter (<u>looks</u> for fires from a high tower.)

4. He (<u>is</u> safe there.)

5. God (<u>can keep</u> us safe from trouble.)

6. We (<u>must trust</u> in the Lord.)

7. The Lord (<u>knows</u> all about us.)

8. Every person (<u>should speak</u> the truth in love.)

9. Foolish words (<u>tear</u> down much good.)

10. Cheryl (<u>said</u> it softly and kindly.)

11. That story (<u>sounds</u> interesting.)

12. They (<u>have sung</u> a hymn for the grandmother.)

13. We (<u>can help</u> with that song.)

14. The big black berries (<u>tasted</u> sweet and tangy.)

15. He (<u>may bring</u> his new book along.)

16. These flowers (<u>do smell</u> fragrant!)

17. The pretty blue dress (<u>appeared</u> fresh and clean.)

Name _____   *(English 6, Lesson 3)*

Worksheet 3
The Subject of a Sentence

A. What does the subject of a sentence tell? _____

    ___It tells *who* or *what* the sentence is about._____

B. What part of speech is the simple subject? It can be a _____noun_____ or a ____pronoun____ .

C. Write the definition of a noun. _____

    ___A noun is a word that names a person, place, thing, or idea._____

D. List the subject pronouns. ___I___ ___you___ ___he___ ___she___ ___it___ ___we___ ___they___

E. List the three steps for finding the skeleton of a sentence.

    1. ___Find the simple predicate._____

    2. ___Say *who* or *what* about the predicate._____

    3. ___Say the subject and predicate together to be sure they make sense.___

F. Draw one line under each simple subject. Put parentheses around the complete subject. The first two have been done for you.
    1. (<u>We</u>) didn't see you coming.
    2. (The little red <u>barn</u>) will soon be finished.
    3. (Our <u>grandfather</u>) is building it.
    4. (My <u>sister</u>) was watching on Saturday.
    5. (<u>I</u>) can carry the smaller boards.
    6. (The huge maple <u>tree</u>) was blown down.
    7. (The little black <u>kitten</u>) climbed onto the roof.
    8. (<u>They</u>) painted the new barn red.
    9. (The new <u>roof</u>) is covered with black shingles.
    10. (A pleasant young <u>nurse</u>) bandaged my finger.

G. Draw two lines under the simple predicate, and one line under the simple subject. Draw a dividing line between the simple subject and the simple predicate. The first two have been done for you.

    1. <u>We</u> | <u>were sitting</u> in a circle.

    2. <u>Carl</u> | <u>was telling</u> an exciting story.

    3. <u>He</u> | <u>had been</u> to faraway places.

    4. <u>You</u> | <u>would know</u> by the pictures in the book.

    5. A fierce <u>lion</u> | <u>had charged</u> out of the jungle.

    6. Carl's <u>helpers</u> | <u>saved</u> him from the lion.

    7. The <u>people</u> | <u>wanted</u> Bibles very badly.

    8. <u>They</u> | <u>listened</u> attentively to messages from the Bible.

Name _____

Worksheet 4
More About Subjects and Predicates

A. Fill in the blanks with some common prepositions.   (Answers will vary.)

_____   _____   _____   _____

_____   _____   _____   _____

_____   _____   _____   _____

B. Put parentheses around any prepositional phrase in the complete subject. Underline the simple predicate with two lines and the simple subject with one line. Draw a dividing line between the complete subject and the complete predicate.

1. Great Britain | ruled Canada until 1867.

2. The United States | borders Canada.

3. Fur traders (from Europe) | explored Canada in the 1600s.   (Also accept *Fur traders.*)

4. The two official languages (of Canada) | are English and French.

5. The Rocky Mountains (in western Canada) | are a great scenic attraction.

6. The peaks (of many mountains) | are covered with snow.

7. This mountain range (of North America) | is similar to the Swiss Alps.
   (Also accept *mountain range.*)

8. The Ocean of Storms | is really a flat plain on the moon.

9. Galileo Galilei | thought the plains were oceans.

10. They | were given ocean names because of this misconception.

11. The morning glories | were blooming on the trellis.

12. The Great Salt Lake Desert | lies in northwestern Utah.

13. A hot plate | is a special cooking appliance.

14. The full moon | shone brightly.   (Also accept *full moon.*)

15. The speeding driver | was finally stopped by the police.

16. The spark plugs (in your engine) | should be replaced.

17. The bushes (in the yard) | have been trimmed.

18. The Statue of Liberty | stands on Liberty Island in the New York Harbor.

19. Our class | will not be visiting there this year.

20. You | have never seen them.

21. We | can often see those mountain peaks in the distance.

22. I | can hardly wait for it.

23. The Mount of Olives | stands just east of Jerusalem.

24. The Sea of Galilee | is often mentioned in the Gospels.

Name _____   *(English 6, Lesson 6)*

Worksheet 5

Sentences and Clauses

A. In each blank, write *C* if the group of words is a clause, or *N* if it is not a clause. If it is a clause, draw two lines under the simple predicate, and one line under the simple subject.

   __N__   1. Yesterday about noon.

   __C__   2. Since <u>we</u> <u>knew</u> it.

   __C__   3. Because <u>he</u> <u>told</u> us.

   __C__   4. <u>You</u> <u>can do</u> it tomorrow.

   __N__   5. Up in the haymow.

   __C__   6. When <u>it</u> <u>is finished</u>.

   __C__   7. Before <u>you</u> <u>came</u>.

   __N__   8. In the yard behind the bush.

   __C__   9. <u>We</u> <u>saw</u> you in the front yard.

B. In each blank, write *S* if the group of words is a sentence, or *F* if it is a fragment.

   __F__   1. After the settlers moved in.

   __F__   2. When the Indians roamed the land.

   __S__   3. France wanted to claim the land.

   __S__   4. Because of John Cabot's voyage, England had a claim to North America.

   __S__   5. Jacques Cartier was the first explorer for France.

   __F__   6. Did you bring?

   __F__   7. When Samuel de Champlain came.

   __F__   8. Because Quebec was at a narrow place on the river.

   __S__   9. It became a large town.

   __S__ 10. Samuel de Champlain was the founder of Quebec.

   __F__ 11. Since both countries had claimed the land.

   __S__ 12. Some wars broke out.

   __F__ 13. So that it could be settled.

   __F__ 14. Because the French helped the Algonquin Indians.

   __S__ 15. The Iroquois were enemies to the French ever after that.

   __F__ 16. When the French and Indian War broke out.

Name _____

Worksheet 6
The Four Sentence Types

A. Write the definition for each sentence type. Also tell what end punctuation should be used with each one.   (Wording may vary.)

1. declarative _____

    A declarative sentence states a fact and ends with a period.

2. interrogative _____

    An interrogative sentence asks a question and ends with a question mark.

3. imperative _____

    An imperative sentence gives a command or request and ends with a period.

4. exclamatory _____

    An exclamatory sentence expresses strong feeling and ends with an exclamation point.

B. Write the abbreviations *dec., int., imp.,* or *exc.* to tell whether each sentence is declarative, interrogative, imperative, or exclamatory. (All the exclamatory sentences have special word order.) Also add the correct end punctuation.

dec. 1. China has the largest population of any country in the world.

int. 2. Do one-fifth of the people in the world live in China?

exc. 3. What a large country it is!

int. 4. Does its history really go back 3,500 years?

dec. 5. China covers over one-fifth of Asia.

int. 6. Does China have any large cities?

dec. 7. It has several of the largest cities in the world.

exc. 8. How interesting this study is!

dec. 9. You should tell us some more stories about it.

dec. 10. Many false religions are taught in China.

dec. 11. Communism took over in 1949.

int. 12. Had China ever been friendly with Russia?

int. 13. Are they friends now?

imp. 14. Check this history book.

exc. 15. Oh, how much the people do need the Word of God!

imp. 16. Let the Gospel light shine out.

Name _____   *(English 6, Lesson 10)*

Worksheet 7
Diagraming Sentence Skeletons

A. List the three steps for finding a sentence skeleton.

1. Find the _____verb_____.

2. Ask _____*who or what*_____ about the verb.

3. Say __the subject and verb together to be sure they make sense_____.

B. Diagram the skeletons of the following sentences in the space below.
1. Is the cardinal your state bird?
2. What a cheery song he sings!
3. A crest of feathers appears as a peaked cap on top of his head.
4. The cardinal is the state bird of North Carolina.
5. Look at that brown female on her nest.
6. Cardinals do not migrate in winter.
7. Feed cardinals in the wintertime with sunflower seeds and safflower seeds.
8. Safflower seeds are a favorite food of cardinals.
9. I have never seen a cardinal here in California.
10. The babies eat insects, grains, and seeds.

1. cardinal | Is

2. he | sings

3. crest | appears

4. cardinal | is

5. (you) | Look

6. Cardinals | do migrate

7. (you) | Feed

8. seeds | are

9. I | have seen   10. babies | eat

Name _____

Worksheet 8
Compound Subjects and Predicates

Diagram the skeletons of the following sentences.
1. South America and Central America have some interesting animals in their tropical rain forests.
2. One unusual animal is the three-toed sloth.
3. Have you ever seen or read about one?
4. Look up into this cecropia tree and see the sloth in the top branches.
5. He crawls around very slowly and eats the leaves of the cecropia tree.
6. He swims very well but never walks.
7. What an interesting creature he is!
8. He does not move very swiftly.
9. He hangs upside down most of the time and may live in the same tree all his life.
10. He grips tree branches with his long claws and sleeps upside down in the tree.
11. His long gray hair and the green algae on it give him a greenish gray color.
12. The mother and her baby stay together a long time.

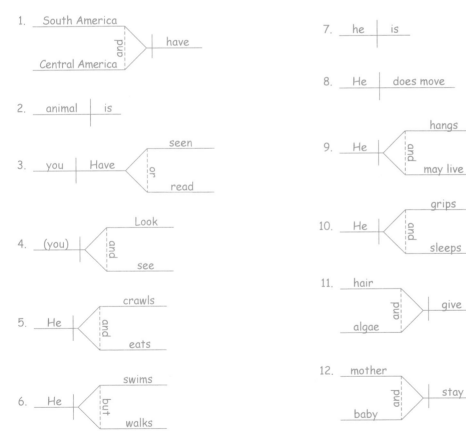

Name _____   (*English 6, Lesson 12*)

Worksheet 9
Compound Sentences

A. Combine the following sentences to make compound sentences. Be sure to use suitable conjunctions.

1. The song of a mourning dove sounds sad. That is its normal call. _____

    The song of a mourning dove sounds sad, but that is its normal call.

2. Baby mourning doves look much like their parents. Their tails are shorter. They have a more grayish color.

    Baby mourning doves look much like their parents, but their tails are shorter, and they
    have a more grayish color.

3. Come quickly. You may not see this mourning dove. _____

    Come quickly, or you may not see this mourning dove.

B. Add the missing commas to the compound sentences. Then diagram the skeleton of each sentence in the space below. (*Mourning dove* is a noun phrase.)

1. The sky grows lighter, and the sun pushes its first orange beams over the hills.
2. Another night has ended, and the mourning doves call softly one to another.
3. The female goes for breakfast, and the male takes over the nest.
4. He sits dutifully on the nest and appears solemn and intelligent.
5. Cracked grain, weed seeds, and many other seeds are the food of mourning doves.
6. The mother partly digests the seeds and feeds them to the babies.
7. The baby mourning doves thrive on this partly digested food, and soon they eat raw grain and seeds.
8. Their nests are made crudely, and sometimes the eggs fall through the cracks!
9. People sometimes mistake mourning doves for passenger pigeons, but those pigeons are now extinct.

(*Teacher:* If a student has unusual difficulty, have him underline each simple subject once and each simple predicate twice before diagraming. Also have him write the formula for each sentence.)

1. sky | grows and sun | pushes

2. night | has ended and mourning doves | call

3. female | goes and male | takes

4. He | sits and appears

5. grain / seeds / seeds and | are

6. mother | digests and feeds

7. mourning doves | thrive and they | eat

8. nests | are made and eggs | fall

9. People | mistake but pigeons | are

Name _____

Worksheet 10
Avoiding Run-on Errors

A. Write the following sentences correctly. If two sentences are run together without a comma or a conjunction, use a capital letter and correct end punctuation. If two sentences have only a comma between them, use a comma and a suitable conjunction.   (End punctuation may vary.)

1. An elephant weighs two hundred pounds when it is born what a big baby that is when it is grown, it weighs up to six tons.

   <u>An elephant weighs two hundred pounds when it is born. What a big baby that is! When</u>

   <u>it is grown, it weighs up to six tons.</u>

   _____

2. Look at that tall giraffe it has a very long neck, its legs are long too a giraffe is the tallest but not the heaviest animal an adult giraffe may weigh two thousand pounds, an African elephant may weigh twelve thousand pounds.

   <u>Look at that tall giraffe! It has a very long neck, and its legs are long too. A giraffe is the</u>

   <u>tallest but not the heaviest animal. An adult giraffe may weigh two thousand pounds,</u>

   <u>but an African elephant may weigh twelve thousand pounds.</u>

   _____

B. Before each sentence, write *C* for correct or *RO* for run-on error.

   <u>RO</u>   1. Birds are interesting creatures people have always been fascinated by them.

   <u>RO</u>   2. Many birds have beautiful colors, they have inspired many poets and painters.

   <u>C</u>   3. Birds sing sweet songs, and many lonely persons have been cheered by them.

   <u>C</u>   4. I heard it clearly; I'm sure it was a cardinal.

   <u>C</u>   5. Grandmother gave me the book, and I use it often.

   <u>RO</u>   6. Food is hard to find in winter, some birds migrate to warmer places where food is plentiful.

   <u>C</u>   7. Some birds migrate, but others stay in one area all year.

   <u>RO</u>   8. Many return north in spring, there they build their nests.

   <u>C</u>   9. Ducks and gulls live along shores and swim in the water.

   <u>C</u>   10. He may be fast, but his work is not accurate.

   <u>RO</u>   11. Mary swept the floor, Karen mopped it.

   <u>C</u>   12. We must cover these plants; they may freeze.

Name _____   *(English 6, Lesson 15)*

Worksheet 11

Word Order in Sentences

A. Write *N, I,* or *M* to tell whether each sentence is written in normal, inverted, or mixed word order.

   __N__   1. Most spiders can make five different kinds of silk.

   __I__   2. On its body are several spinnerets.

   __M__   3. With them, a spider spins its silk.

   __N__   4. The silk may be dry or sticky.

   __M__   5. How does the spider keep from sticking to his own web?

   __N__   6. Oil keeps the spider from sticking fast.

   __I__   7. In the corner was a triangular web.

   __M__   8. Out rushed the spider and captured the fly.

   __N__   9. Spiders have sharp, hollow fangs connected to poison glands.

   __M__ 10. With their fangs, spiders seize and paralyze their prey.

B. Rewrite the following sentences, changing the word order as the directions say. The words in italics are noun phrases (to help you with Part C below).
  1. Change to mixed word order.
    a. The spider spun a funnel web in the tall grass. _____

       In the tall grass the spider spun a funnel web.

    b. The *water spider* can live underwater in its air bubble web for several months.

       For several months the water spider can live underwater in its air bubble web.

       or In its air bubble web the water spider can live underwater for several months.

  2. Change to inverted word order. (Begin each sentence with an adverb phrase.)
    a. The spider's nest was in a folded leaf.

       In a folded leaf was the spider's nest.

    b. The biggest tarantulas live in South American jungles. _____

       In South American jungles live the biggest tarantulas.

  3. Change to normal word order.
    a. In the doorway was a *spider web*.   A spider web was in the doorway.

    b. In a flower hid the *crab spider*.   The crab spider hid in a flower.

C. On other paper, diagram the skeleton of each sentence in Part B.

1. a.	spider	spun		b.	water spider	can live
2. a.	nest	was		b.	tarantulas	live
3. a.	spider web	was		b.	crab spider	hid

Name _____

Worksheet 12
Unity and Coherence in a Paragraph

A. Write the following sentences in correct order and in proper paragraph form. Be sure to write the topic sentence first. Leave out the sentence that does not belong.
   1. Next, tie a thin nylon string to each hole.
   2. Hang your wind chimes on the porch where you can enjoy their pleasant music.
   3. Get some lightweight seashells, and tap a small hole in the top of each one.
   4. The shells should hang close enough together that they hit each other lightly.
   5. If you put a seashell to your ear, it sounds like ocean waves.
   6. How would you like to make a set of wind chimes?
   7. Then tie the loose end of each string to a stick.

   How would you like to make a set of wind chimes? Get some lightweight seashells, and tap a

   small hole in the top of each one. Next, tie a thin nylon string to each hole. Then tie the loose

   end of each string to a stick. The shells should hang close enough together that they hit each

   other lightly. Hang your wind chimes on the porch where you can enjoy their pleasant music.

   Sentence that does not belong: 5. If you put a seashell to your ear, it sounds like ocean waves.

B. Write the following sentences in paragraph form. Begin with the topic sentence, and arrange the reasons from the least important to the most important. Add the following transitional words at suitable places: *first, second, also, most important.* Do not write the sentences that should be left out.
   1. Raising hamsters is an interesting hobby.
   2. Another important reason is that regular chores help me to learn self-discipline.
   3. There are several reasons that I am thankful for chores to do.
   4. I like to ride my bicycle to the barn.
   5. The exercise is good for my muscles.
   6. Doing chores gives me practice in being obedient to my parents.
   7. I learn much about animals when I do chores.
   8. Doing chores helps to bring in money for my family.

   (Transitional words are underlined. Allow reasonable variation in the placement of transitional words and in the order of the sentences.)

   There are several reasons that I am thankful for chores to do. First, the exercise is good

   for my muscles. Second, doing chores helps to bring in money for my family. I also learn much

   about animals when I do chores. Another important reason is that regular chores help me to

   learn self-discipline. Most important, doing chores gives me practice in being obedient to

   my parents.

   Sentences that do not belong: 1. Raising hamsters is an interesting hobby. 4. I like to ride my bicycle to the barn.

Name _____   (English 6, Lesson 19)

Worksheet 13
Recognizing Nouns

A. Write the definition of a noun.

_____A noun is a word that names a person, place, thing, or idea._____

_____

B. Underline only the words that could be used as nouns.
1. seek	4. <u>title</u>	7. loved	10. stun
2. loud	5. teach	8. <u>braid</u>	11. <u>question</u>
3. <u>voyage</u>	6. <u>timber</u>	9. <u>cloth</u>	12. nor

C. Make nouns from these words by adding *-ness, -ion, -ity,* or *-ment.* Use a dictionary if you are not sure of the correct spelling.

1. pay _____payment_____   5. clean _____cleanness_____

2. pure ___pureness *or* purity___   6. revise _____revision_____

3. rigid ___rigidness *or* rigidity___   7. appoint _____appointment_____

4. good _____goodness_____   8. navigate _____navigation_____

D. Underline the 41 nouns in these paragraphs. (*Alexander the Great* is a noun phrase.)

   <u>Alexander the Great</u>, it seems, was born with <u>determination</u>. When he was a young <u>boy</u>, he tamed a wild <u>horse</u> that no other <u>person</u> dared to ride! The <u>dream</u> of his <u>life</u> was to conquer the <u>world</u>. With his <u>armies</u> he charged across the <u>land</u> like a <u>goat</u> with a single, powerful <u>horn</u>, as <u>Daniel</u> had prophesied. His <u>armies</u> swept eastward into <u>Asia</u> and all the <u>way</u> to <u>India</u>. Then he conquered the <u>lands</u> of <u>Egypt</u> and <u>Persia</u>. He gave the <u>name</u> of <u>Alexandria</u> to sixteen <u>cities</u>.

   But <u>pride</u> and <u>immoderation</u> spoiled his <u>life</u>. <u>Alexander</u> lost his <u>temper</u> and had his best <u>friend</u> killed. He was only thirty-three <u>years</u> old when he died of a <u>fever</u> caused by <u>drunkenness</u>. His <u>determination</u> had helped to unite the known <u>world</u> of his <u>day</u> and prepare it for the <u>time</u> when <u>Jesus</u> would come to <u>earth</u>. <u>Alexander</u> had conquered the <u>world</u>; but if he lost his <u>soul</u>, what did it profit him?

E. List nouns as described below.   (Individual answers.)
   1. Three names of forest animals. **Example:** squirrel

   _____

   2. Three nouns that have to do with gardening. **Example:** seeds

   _____

   3. Three names of transportation vehicles. **Example:** bicycle

   _____

Name _____

Worksheet 14
Proper Nouns

A. Write the definition of a proper noun.

___A proper noun is the name of a specific person, place, or thing._____

_____

B. Write two proper nouns for each common noun given below.
   (Answers will vary. Check for correct capitalization.)

1. king   _____   _____

2. mother   _____   _____

3. mountain   _____   _____

4. lake   _____   _____

5. pet   _____   _____

C. Underline each word that is not capitalized but should be.

1. The song "god of our strength" was written by fanny jane crosby.

2. We think of september, october, and november as autumn months.
   (*Name* may also be underlined.)

3. One of jesus' last instructions was to baptize in the name of the father, the son, and the holy ghost.

4. My grandparents flew from seattle, washington, to chicago, illinois, and from there to pittsburgh, pennsylvania.

5. President warren g. harding kept a pen of turkeys at the white house.

6. Mr. dwight david eisenhower was named after his grandfather, president dwight d. eisenhower.

7. The people of japan observe a holiday called constitution day.

8. Bethel mennonite church had bible classes every monday, wednesday, and friday evening for three weeks.

9. In the armenian mountains is lake van, a salty lake with no outlet.

10. About halfway between the black sea and the caspian sea is lake sevan.

11. Lake sevan is fed by thirty streams; but its only outlet is the zanga river, which empties into the araxes river.

12. In california and nevada is a national park called death valley.

13. We went with james e. martin to look at a ford truck and a dodge car.

14. Would you rather study the spanish language or the german language?

15. Which do you prefer, carnation milk or pensupreme ice cream?

Name _____   *(English 6, Lesson 21)*

Worksheet 15
Details in Paragraphs

A. Underline the topic sentence of the paragraph that is properly developed with details.

1.   <u>I would rather have a cat than a dog for a pet.</u> Cats are more graceful than dogs, and they are usually more affectionate and loyal than dogs. Cats can also catch mice better. They can do interesting things that dogs cannot do, like climbing trees. Cats do not get hurt as easily as dogs. When a cat falls, it almost always lands on its feet. You may have dogs; I prefer cats.

2.   I would rather have a cat than a dog for a pet. There are many different kinds of cats. Two of the largest kinds are tigers and lions. All cats are good hunters. Domestic cats are small cats that live with people. Some favorite breeds are Siamese and Persian. In the United States and Canada, about 42 million cats are kept as pets.

B. Briefly list five details that support the topic sentence of the better paragraph in Part A above.
                                                                            (Wording will vary.)

1. _Cats are more graceful._____

2. _Cats are more affectionate and loyal._____

3. _Cats can catch mice better._____

4. _Cats do interesting things like climbing trees._____

5. _Cats do not get hurt as easily._____

C. Choose one of the following topic sentences. Write a paragraph that uses details correctly. (If you want to use a topic sentence of your own, first get it approved by your teacher.)   (Individual work.)

1. Dogs are better pets than cats.
2. I had an interesting school day.
3. Raising cantaloupes is hard work, but it is a worthwhile job.

_____

_____

_____

_____

_____

_____

_____

_____

_____

_____

_____

Name _____

Worksheet 16
Examples and Illustrations in Paragraphs

A. Write *1* before the paragraph that is developed with only one extended example or illustration. Write *2* before the paragraph that is developed with several examples or illustrations.

   _1_   1. <u>Mosquito bites can be dangerous.</u> In some parts of the world, mosquitoes spread a serious disease called malaria. A mosquito bites someone who has malaria. Then it bites someone else, and that person also catches the disease. Every year millions of people get sick from malaria and other diseases carried by mosquitoes.

   _2_   2. <u>Some insects are helpful to man.</u> Bees make wax and delicious honey. Ladybugs eat aphids and other harmful insects on fruit trees. Termites help to keep the world clean by eating out the insides of old, dead trees. Praying mantises eat flies and other pests. Silkworms spin a special kind of thread that can be woven into beautiful cloth. Even the butterflies help man by displaying some of the beauty and wonder of God's creation.

B. Underline the topic sentences of the paragraphs in Part A above.

C. For each topic sentence, write *X* before two sentences that contain good examples or illustrations to support that topic sentence.
1. Maple trees are useful in several ways.

   _____   a. Sugar maples and silver maples are two kinds of maple trees.

   _X_   b. Maple syrup is made from the sap of maple trees.

   _____   c. Maple seeds have wings that look like airplane propellers.

   _X_   d. The wood of maple trees makes good hardwood lumber.

2. Some Bible prophets suffered when they spoke the Word of God.

   _____   a. Long before King Cyrus was born, Isaiah spoke of him by name.

   _X_   b. Zechariah was stoned to death at King Joash's command.

   _X_   c. Jeremiah was beaten and put in the stocks.

   _____   d. The people of Nineveh repented when Jonah preached.

3. A Christian father has many responsibilities.

   _X_   a. He must train his children and be a good example to them.

   _____   b. Ministers must be good examples to the congregation.

   _X_   c. He needs to provide naturally and spiritually for his family.

   _____   d. Children should greatly appreciate their Christian parents.

Name _____   *(English 6, Lesson 25)*

Worksheet 17
Plural Nouns

A. Write the plural form of each word.

1. team	teams		14. soprano	sopranos	
2. enemy	enemies		15. assembly	assemblies	
3. leaf	leaves		16. belief	beliefs	
4. patio	patios		17. potato	potatoes	
5. class	classes		18. volcano	volcanoes *or* volcanos	
6. foot	feet		19. radius	radii *or* radiuses	
7. trout	trout		20. swine	swine	
8. basis	bases		21. cupful	cupfuls	
9. larva	larvae *or* larvas		22. manservant	menservants	
10. woman	women		23. sister-in-law	sisters-in-law	
11. notebook	notebooks		24. toothache	toothaches	
12. vice-president	vice-presidents		25. great-grandmother	great-grandmothers	
13. master builder	master builders		26. surgeon general	surgeons general	

B. Above each underlined noun, write *S* for singular or *P* for plural.

1. The team^S made a hobby^S of studying extra facts^P in mathematics^S.

2. The flock^S of sheep^P followed its shepherd^S.

3. Our family^S works together in the garden^S.

4. The bad news^S is that my cousins^P have measles^S.

5. Take the scissors^P to the lady^S who is mending the trousers^P.

6. We saw several deer,^P a few salmon,^P and a trout^S at the lake.^S

7. Use the tweezers^P to get the splinters^P out of your foot.^S

8. The maidservant^S lost a goose^S from the flock.^S

C. Underline the correct verbs.
1. Our team usually (win, <u>wins</u>).
2. Measles (<u>is</u>, are) a dangerous disease.
3. Our families (<u>enjoy</u>, enjoys) singing together.
4. The news (<u>was</u>, were) encouraging.
5. The two classes (<u>visit</u>, visits) the Bible school every year.
6. Our class (paint, <u>paints</u>) murals sometimes.
7. The flock (<u>was</u>, were) helpless without a shepherd.
8. The assembly (learn, <u>learns</u>) a new song every Friday.

Worksheet 18
Possessive Nouns

A. Rewrite these expressions, using possessive forms.

1. the books of the teacher _____the teacher's books_____
2. the books of the teachers _____the teachers' books_____
3. the miracles of Jesus _____Jesus' miracles_____
4. the room of the children _____the children's room_____
5. the room of the child _____the child's room_____
6. the hole of the mouse _____the mouse's hole_____
7. the hole of the mice _____the mice's hole_____
8. the nest of the bird _____the bird's nest_____
9. the nest of the birds _____the birds' nest_____

B. Improve the following expressions.

1. the roof's tiles _____the tiles of (on) the roof_____
2. the window's cracks _____the cracks of (in) the window_____
3. the car's paint _____the paint of (on) the car_____
4. the house's walls _____the walls of the house_____

C. Fill in the missing words.

Singular	Singular Possessive	Plural	Plural Possessive
1. sister	sister's	sisters	sisters'
2. wife	wife's	wives	wives'
3. baby	baby's	babies	babies'
4. monkey	monkey's	monkeys	monkeys'
5. ox	ox's	oxen	oxen's
6. goose	goose's	geese	geese's
7. deer	deer's	deer	deer's
8. fox	fox's	foxes	foxes'

D. Write original sentences to illustrate all the forms that you wrote for *sister* in Part C above.
   (Individual work.)

_____

_____

_____

Name _____   *(English 6, Lesson 29)*

Worksheet 19
Verbs

A. Write the definition of a verb. _____

_____A verb is a word that shows action or being._____

B. List the forms of *be*. _____am_____ _____is_____ _____are_____ _____was_____

_____were_____ _____be_____ _____been_____ _____being_____

D. List the helping verbs in groups.

_____have_____ _____has_____ _____had_____

_____do_____ _____does_____ _____did_____

_____may_____ _____might_____ _____must_____

_____can_____ — _____could_____ , _____shall_____ — _____should_____ , _____will_____ — _____would_____

D. Underline the ten verbs that show physical action.

long	<u>drag</u>	<u>sing</u>	might
<u>break</u>	road	<u>raise</u>	<u>speak</u>
desk	<u>build</u>	thorn	<u>write</u>
<u>drink</u>	<u>float</u>	<u>explain</u>	hard

E. Underline the ten verbs that show mental action.

<u>know</u>	<u>suppose</u>	would	<u>dream</u>
discuss	<u>consider</u>	<u>remember</u>	must
freeze	dash	<u>enjoy</u>	<u>believe</u>
<u>learn</u>	<u>realize</u>	handle	<u>appreciate</u>

F. Underline all the verbs and verb phrases in these sentences.
   1. The wind <u>is blowing</u>, and the snow <u>is falling</u> fast.
   2. It <u>had been snowing</u> all night.
   3. Timothy <u>was reading</u> this book.
   4. Laura <u>may have been</u> here yesterday.
   5. Grandmother <u>had</u> always <u>kneaded</u> the bread.
   6. Mary <u>has</u> not <u>drawn</u> this picture.
   7. Louise <u>has</u> surely <u>done</u> a good job.
   8. The wren <u>has</u> often <u>built</u> its nest here.
   9. We <u>should</u> not <u>have forgotten</u> it.
   10. The ocean waves <u>roared</u> and <u>crashed</u> on the rocky shore.
   11. The robin <u>has been singing</u> in the tree.
   12. The nine lepers <u>did</u> not <u>thank</u> Jesus.
   13. Only one <u>came</u> back and <u>thanked</u> Him.
   14. <u>Do</u> not <u>forget</u>; <u>thank</u> God today.
   15. A thankful person <u>is</u> a joyful person.

Name _____

Worksheet 20
Principal Parts of Verbs

A. Write the missing principal parts.

First (Present)	Second (Past)	Third (Past Participle)
1. like	liked	(have) liked
2. carry	carried	(have) carried
3. stay	stayed	(have) stayed
4. tag	tagged	(have) tagged
5. teach	taught	(have) taught
6. go	went	(have) gone
7. buy	bought	(have) bought
8. bring	brought	(have) brought
9. come	came	(have) come
10. freeze	froze	(have) frozen
11. drag	dragged	(have) dragged
12. reach	reached	(have) reached

B. Write the correct form of each verb in parentheses, using the second or third principal part. Use the third principal part only if there is a helping verb in the sentence. Underline each helping verb.

1. Jeremiah _____spoke_____ the words of the Lord. (speak)

2. Baruch the scribe _____read_____ God's words to the people in the temple. (read)

3. Baruch <u>had</u> _____written_____ the words for Jeremiah. (write)

4. He _____wrote_____ the words on a scroll. (write)

5. King Jehoiakim _____sent_____ for the scroll. (send)

6. The king _____threw_____ the scroll into the fire. (throw)

7. He <u>had</u> _____cut_____ the scroll in pieces with his penknife. (cut)

8. The angry king _____tried_____ to find Jeremiah and Baruch. (try)

9. The Lord <u>had</u> _____hidden_____ His faithful servants. (hide)

10. God _____told_____ Jeremiah and Baruch to write the same words on another scroll. (tell)

11. They _____added_____ many more words besides. (add)

12. God <u>had</u> _____spoken_____ all the additional words. (speak)

13. Later the king of Babylon _____came_____ with his armies. (come)

14. He destroyed Jerusalem just as the Lord <u>had</u> _____said_____. (say)

Name _____

Worksheet 21
More Principal Parts

A. Underline the main verb in each sentence. Then write the second and third principal parts of the main verb. Use *have* with the past participle.

1. We <u>write</u> the names.   ___wrote___   ___(have) written___

2. They <u>do</u> God's will.   ___did___   ___(have) done___

3. He <u>knows</u> about them.   ___knew___   ___(have) known___

4. They <u>see</u> three birds.   ___saw___   ___(have) seen___

5. He <u>reads</u> a letter.   ___read___   ___(have) read___

6. She <u>gives</u> the answer.   ___gave___   ___(have) given___

7. Mother <u>sings</u> a song.   ___sang___   ___(have) sung___

8. He <u>speaks</u> to me.   ___spoke___   ___(have) spoken___

9. Saul <u>travels</u> to Damascus.   ___traveled___   ___(have) traveled___

10. A bright light <u>shines</u>.   ___shone___   ___(have) shone___

11. Ananias <u>inquires</u> about Saul.   ___inquired___   ___(have) inquired___

12. The Lord <u>calls</u> Saul to Himself.   ___called___   ___(have) called___

B. Write the correct form of each verb in parentheses, using the second or third principal part. Use the third principal part only if there is a helping verb in the sentence. Underline each helping verb.

1. Nobody <u>has</u> ___come___ yet. (come)

2. I ___thought___ we were late. (think)

3. Somebody <u>has</u> ___taken___ it. (take)

4. He ___stole___ away in the darkness. (steal)

5. I <u>have</u> ___spoken___ to him about it. (speak)

6. <u>Have</u> you ___torn___ your dress? (tear)

7. <u>Has</u> she ___drunk___ her juice? (drink)

8. I ___chose___ you to help me. (choose)

9. It <u>has</u> ___broken___ into hundreds of pieces. (break)

10. I ___liked___ the story about the honest Indian. (like)

11. We always ___burned___ the leaves. (burn)

12. The baby ___cried___ himself to sleep. (cry)

13. They ___reported___ every one of their problems. (report)

14. They <u>have</u> ___slipped___ in the back door. (slip)

15. The lovely singing ___attracted___ the crowds. (attract)

Name _____

Worksheet 22
Verb Tenses

A. These verbs are in the present tense. Write the five other tenses for each one: simple past, simple future, present perfect, past perfect, and future perfect.

1. buy ___bought, will buy, have bought, had bought, will have bought___

2. ring ___rang, will ring, have rung, had rung, will have rung___

3. sink ___sank, will sink, have sunk, had sunk, will have sunk___

4. go ___went, will go, have gone, had gone, will have gone___

5. come ___came, will come, have come, had come, will have come___

6. sleep ___slept, will sleep, have slept, had slept, will have slept___

7. bring ___brought, will bring, have brought, had brought, will have brought___

8. swim ___swam, will swim, have swum, had swum, will have swum___

B. Write the verb tenses indicated in parentheses. Be sure to use the correct helping verbs.

1. Two boys ___had broken___ through the thin ice. (past perfect of *break*)

2. The students ___chose___ their seats. (simple past of *choose*)

3. John said, "I ___had finished___ the job before lunch." (past perfect of *finish*)

4. Jewel ___has memorized___ her verses. (present perfect of *memorize*)

5. Before school closes, you ___will have learned___ ninety Bible verses. (future perfect of *learn*)

6. The Lord ___will keep___ those who trust in Him. (simple future of *keep*)

7. We ___have done___ the work. (present perfect of *do*)

8. After this purchase, Jerry ___will have bought___ six hammers for the workers. (future perfect of *buy*)

Name _____

Worksheet 23
Diagraming Direct and Indirect Objects

Diagram the skeletons, direct objects, and indirect objects.
1. Kenneth and Kurvin caught two bass.
2. Kathleen brought Mother and Father a new catalog.
3. I told Karen and Karla about the lost broom.
4. Keith and Karl will direct traffic and park cars.
5. Eli Whitney invented the cotton gin.
6. Joel planned the route for the trip to Canada.
7. Kathy gave the teacher a box of cookies.
8. Kay read the children a story and a poem.
9. Kendall gave Grandfather a box of handkerchiefs, and Kendra gave Grandmother a bouquet.
10. Brother Kurtis taught his students a new song.

Name _____

Worksheet 24
Outlining

Write a topical outline from the following composition.   (Sample outline below.)

The Marys of the New Testament

The first Mary in the New Testament was the mother of Jesus. She was from the tribe of Judah. Mary and Joseph traveled to Bethlehem, where Jesus was born. She was at the wedding in Cana where Jesus turned the water into wine. At His crucifixion, Jesus told the disciple John to take care of her. This Mary was among those who were praying in the upper room in Jerusalem after Jesus had ascended.

The second Mary was Mary Magdalene. Jesus had cast seven devils out of her. She and some other women were with Jesus and the disciples in Galilee, and they ministered to Him. Mary Magdalene was often with Mary, the mother of Jesus. She was the first to see Jesus after He rose from the dead.

The third Mary was the sister of Lazarus. Mary, Martha, and Lazarus often invited Jesus to their house. Jesus said Mary had chosen that good part, when she sat at Jesus' feet. Jesus called for Mary when He came to raise Lazarus from the dead. This Mary anointed Jesus' feet. She used a very costly ointment and wiped His feet with her hair. Jesus said she had done this in honor of His burial.

The fourth Mary is mentioned in the Book of Acts. She was the mother of Mark. She was also a sister to Barnabas. The Christians were praying at this Mary's house when Peter was freed from prison.

The fifth Mary is mentioned in the Book of Romans. She is spoken of as one who greatly helped the apostle Paul and other Christians.

The Marys of the New Testament

I. Mary, the mother of Jesus
  A. Was from the tribe of Judah
  B. Traveled to Bethlehem, where Jesus was born
  C. Was at wedding in Cana
  D. Was cared for by John after Jesus' crucifixion
  E. Prayed with the disciples in the upper room
II. Mary Magdalene
  A. Had seven devils cast out
  B. Ministered to Jesus in Galilee
  C. Was often with Mary, the mother of Jesus
  D. Was the first to see the risen Lord
III. Mary, the sister of Lazarus
  A. Had Jesus as a regular guest
  B. Chose to sit at Jesus' feet
  C. Was called for by Jesus after Lazarus died
  D. Anointed Jesus' feet
    1. Used costly ointment
    2. Did this in honor of His burial
IV. The fourth Mary
  A. Is mentioned in the Book of Acts
  B. Was the mother of Mark and a sister to Barnabas
  C. Had a prayer meeting at her house when Peter was in prison
V. The fifth Mary
  A. Is mentioned in the Book of Romans
  B. Helped the apostle Paul and other Christians

Name _____

Worksheet 25

Diagraming Predicate Nominatives and Predicate Adjectives

Diagram the sentence skeletons, predicate nominatives, and predicate adjectives.
1. Brother Martin will be the visiting speaker.
2. His message was inspirational.
3. My great-grandparents were immigrants from Germany.
4. Aunt Mary is a good seamstress.
5. Grandmother's homemade bread always tastes delicious.
6. The fern has grown much larger.
7. These books about birds and flowers are mine.
8. This book about fish looks quite interesting.
9. The potatoes tasted burnt.
10. Sister Lois and Sister Eunice will be the teachers of the preschool classes in Sunday school.

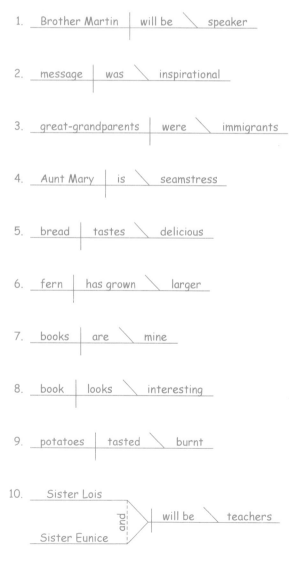

Name _____

Worksheet 26
Diagraming Review

Diagram the skeletons, direct objects, indirect objects, predicate nominatives, and predicate adjectives.

1. We smelled the smoke from the bonfire.
2. The smoke smelled strong.
3. Soon the smoke appeared above the trees.
4. We tasted Aunt Jennie's green tomato pies.
5. They taste sweet and spicy.
6. Peggy has become a good cook.
7. Aunt Martha grew Mother some ivy plants.
8. We looked upstairs and downstairs for it.
9. The blanket looks old and worn.
10. I have felt the quilt, and it feels soft and fluffy.

1.

2.

3.

4.

5.

6.

7.

8.

9.

10.

Name _____   *(English 6, Lesson 49)*

Worksheet 27
Lay—Lie, Raise—Rise, and *Set—Sit*

A. Fill in the principal parts of each verb.

Present	Past	Past Participle
1. lay	laid	(have) laid
2. lie	lay	(have) lain
3. raise	raised	(have) raised
4. rise	rose	(have) risen
5. set	set	(have) set
6. sit	sat	(have) sat

B. Cross out each wrong word, and write the correct word above it. Not every sentence needs a correction.

Example: Lay up treasure in heaven, for your heart ~~lays~~ **lies** where your treasure is.

1. Jacob ~~lay~~ **laid** his right hand on the head of Ephraim.

2. When Jesus came, Lazarus had ~~laid~~ **lain** in the grave four days already.

3. Martha went to Jesus, but Mary ~~set~~ **sat** in the house.

4. Balaam blessed the Israelites and said, "He lay down as a lion; who shall stir him up?"

5. Even though war should ~~raise~~ **rise** against me, I shall not fear.

6. The Lord will raise a protection for me.

7. Hannah and her husband had ~~rose~~ **risen** up early to worship at the house of the Lord.

8. Arise, shine, for the glory of the Lord has ~~raised~~ **risen** upon you.

9. The Lord ~~rose~~ **raised** up judges for the children of Israel.

10. The Lord said to Isaiah, "Set a watchman in the watchtower."

11. The people ~~set~~ **sat** down on the grass in groups at Jesus' command.

12. How many baskets full of leftover bread and fish were ~~setting~~ **sitting** there?

C. In the space below, diagram the subjects, verbs, and direct objects of sentences 1, 6, 9, and 11 in Part B. Be sure to use the correct verb forms on your diagrams.

1. Jacob | laid | hand

9. Lord | raised | judges

6. Lord | will raise | protection

11. people | sat

Name _____

Worksheet 28
Let—Leave

A. Fill in the principal parts of each verb.

Present	Past	Past Participle
1. let	let	(have) let
2. leave	left	(have) left

B. Write *let* or *leave* for each definition.

____leave____   1. To depart or go away from

____let____   2. To allow or permit

C. Cross out each wrong word, and write the correct word above it. Not every sentence needs a correction.

1. Jesus foretold that the enemies of Israel would not ~~let~~ **leave** one stone of the temple upon another.

2. His prophecy was fulfilled years later when Roman soldiers destroyed Jerusalem and left the temple in ruins.

3. If a man takes your coat, ~~leave~~ **let** him have your cloak also.

4. Jesus ~~left~~ **let** the children come unto Him.

5. Do you know why God does not ~~leave~~ **let** us have everything we want?

6. Boaz said, "Let her glean even among the sheaves."

7. ~~Leave~~ **Let** me know when this job is finished.

8. Mother ~~leaves~~ **lets** me read when my work is finished.

9. The sun has ~~raised~~ **risen**, and the grass has withered.

10. Christ has ~~rose~~ **risen** from the dead, and He has become the firstfruits of them that slept.

11. Solomon ~~rose~~ **raised** money by taxing the people heavily.

12. Jesus said, "Destroy this temple, and in three days I will raise it up again."

13. The Bible story book is sitting on the top shelf.

14. We will ~~set~~ **sit** on the couch and read it together.

Name _____   (English 6, Lesson 52)

Worksheet 29
Troublesome Verbs

A. Fill in the principal parts of each verb.

Present	Past	Past Participle
1. tag	tagged	(have) tagged
2. drag	dragged	(have) dragged
3. drown	drowned	(have) drowned
4. attack	attacked	(have) attacked
5. burst	burst	(have) burst

B. Write *teach, learn, can,* or *may* for these definitions.

    teach   1. To give knowledge or instruction

    learn   2. To gain knowledge

    may   3. To be permitted to

    can   4. To be able to

C. Cross out each wrong word, and write the correct word above it. Not every sentence needs a correction.

1. In the days of Jehoshaphat, the Levites went through the cities of Judah and ~~learned~~ taught the people the Book of the Law.

2. The kingdoms around Judah learned the fear of the Lord.

3. Jehoshaphat was not ~~attackted~~ attacked by the kingdoms around him.

4. The disciples ~~drug~~ dragged the net full of fishes to the shore where Jesus was.

5. Jesus said that it would be better for one to be ~~drownded~~ drowned in the depth of the sea than to keep a little one from believing in Him.

6. Jeremiah said that the people had turned away from God, had broken their yoke, and had ~~busted~~ burst their bonds.

7. Jesus left the earth, but He will return again.

8. Our teacher does not ~~leave~~ let us whisper in school.

9. He ~~lets~~ leaves his books at school when he goes home.

10. Will you let him stay alone?

11. Please do not ~~leave~~ let Rover come into the house.

12. Leave your muddy boots on the porch.

13. Let the visitors come in.

14. "~~Can~~ May I play outside?" asked Martha.

15. Rhoda can read simple Bible stories now.

Name _____

Worksheet 30
Subject and Verb Agreement

A. Underline the correct words.

1. A (<u>singular</u>, plural) word refers to only one.

2. A (singular, <u>plural</u>) word refers to more than one.

3. A noun that ends with -*s* is usually (singular, <u>plural</u>).

4. A verb that ends with -*s* is usually (<u>singular</u>, plural).

5. The contraction (*don't, <u>doesn't</u>*) is used with singular subjects.

B. Underline the subjects of the following sentences. Also underline the correct words in parentheses that must agree with the subjects. (In open compounds such as *Baltimore oriole,* students may not have the first word underlined.)

1. There (is, <u>are</u>) <u>birds</u> that do not build nests at all.

2. The <u>cowbird</u> and the <u>cuckoo</u> (<u>lay</u>, lays) their eggs in other birds' nests.

3. (Here's, <u>Here are</u>) some <u>nests</u> that look like braided baskets.

4. The <u>Baltimore oriole</u> (don't, <u>doesn't</u>) make an ordinary nest; his nest is like a hanging cradle.

5. The <u>weaverbird</u> (do, <u>does</u>) actually weave his nest.

6. A <u>swift</u> or a <u>swallow</u> (<u>was</u>, were) flying around overhead.

7. The <u>nest</u> of those swallows (don't, <u>doesn't</u>) fall off the wall.

8. (<u>There's</u>, There are) a <u>kingfisher</u> from Borneo who builds his nest inside the hive of certain bees.

9. Some <u>enemies</u> of the kingfisher (is, <u>are</u>) afraid of the bees.

10. A <u>beach</u> or a <u>marsh</u> (<u>is</u>, are) the home of some crabs that dig burrows in the ground.

11. <u>Sand crabs</u> and <u>fiddler crabs</u> (<u>run</u>, runs) with a sideways motion.

12. <u>Crabs</u> in the sand (is, <u>are</u>) hard to see.

13. Their quick <u>movements</u> and protective <u>color</u> (<u>make</u>, makes) them seem to disappear before your eyes.

14. There (is, <u>are</u>) many <u>crabs</u> that people can eat.

15. <u>Blue crabs</u> with their delicious taste (is, <u>are</u>) a prized seafood.

16. There (<u>is</u>, are) also a green <u>crab</u>.

17. (There's, <u>There are</u>) some <u>hermit crabs</u> that live in empty snail shells.

18. A <u>hermit crab</u> (don't, <u>doesn't</u>) have a shell of his own.

19. A <u>snail</u> or another <u>hermit crab</u> in a shell (<u>is</u>, are) sometimes killed by an invading hermit crab.

Name _____   *(English 6, Lesson 58)*

Worksheet 31
Active and Passive Voice

A. In each sentence, draw two lines under the verb (or verb phrase) and one line under the word that receives the action of the verb. Then write *A* for active or *P* for passive in the blank.

   P   1. Zacharias was visited by an angel.

   A   2. God sent Gabriel to Zacharias.

   P   3. A sign was given to Zacharias.

   A   4. Zacharias had seen a vision from God.

   A   5. For many days he could not speak a single word.

   A   6. God gave a son to Elisabeth and Zacharias.

   A   7. Zacharias wrote the baby's name on a writing tablet.

   P   8. The news of the birth was spread though the hill country.

   A   9. Many people hid the strange tidings in their hearts.

   A   10. John taught many truths about right living.

   P   11. Their hearts were prepared for Jesus' coming.

   P   12. John was dressed in raiment of camel's hair.

   P   13. He was filled with the Holy Spirit.

   A   14. He preached repentance to the people.

   A   15. He showed Jesus to them.

   P   16. Jesus was baptized by John.

   P   17. Some men were sent to John.

   A   18. They asked questions about his calling.

   A   19. John gave humble answers.

   A   20. He always gave the honor to Jesus.

B. Change each sentence to the active voice.
1. All kinds of people were preached to by John.

    John preached to all kinds of people.

2. Many people were baptized by John in the Jordan River.

    John baptized many people in the Jordan River.

Worksheet 32
Friendly Letters

A. Read the letter below. What is its purpose?

  to give an invitation

B. Write the names of the letter parts in the blanks. Then underline each small letter that should be capitalized, and add the missing punctuation.

  heading   1.   316 apple street
                                         wasco, or 97065
                                         march 10, 20—

  greeting   2. dear jesse,
         ,   greetings from oregon!
                 "in all thy ways acknowledge him, and he shall direct thy paths." this
             is one of the verses in proverbs that we learned in school recently.

  body   3.   mother said that i may invite your family to our house the first sunday in
             april. special meetings are planned for that weekend, and we are expecting
             many visitors from neighboring communities. please let us know soon if you
             can come. i surely hope you can!

  closing   4.   sincerely,

  signature   5.   brian warren

C. Correctly address the "envelope" below. Use the name and address in Part B for the receiver's address, and your own return address.

  _____
      (Pupil's return address.)
  _____

                    BRIAN WARREN

                    316 APPLE STREET

                    WASCO OR 97065

Name _____   *(English 6, Lesson 64)*

Worksheet 33
Using Pronouns Correctly

Underline the correct pronouns. In each blank, write *S, PN, DO, IO,* or *OP* to tell whether the pronoun is a subject, predicate nominative, direct object, indirect object, or the object of a preposition.

_DO_   1. William Rittenhouse helped (they, <u>them</u>).

_S_   2. (<u>He</u>, Him) built the first paper mill in Germantown.

_PN_   3. It was (<u>they</u>, them) who helped after the flood.

_IO_   4. The builders gave him and (I, <u>me</u>) a lift.

_S_   5. He and (<u>they</u>, them) built

_IO_   (he, <u>him</u>) a new mill.

_S_   6. (<u>We</u>, Us) mothers supplied

_DO_   (they, <u>them</u>) with old linen rags.

_S_   7. His workers and (<u>he</u>, him) pounded the rags in mortars with hammers.

_OP_   8. Then the workers added other materials to (they, <u>them</u>).

_OP_   9. Laying out the mixture was a job for (we, <u>us</u>) boys.

_OP_   10. It was hard work for the boys and (he, <u>him</u>).

_PN_   11. It was (<u>we</u>, us) boys and

_PN_   (<u>he</u>, him) who rebuilt the water wheel.

_PN_   12. The ministers were Rittenhouse and (<u>he</u>, him).

_IO_   13. He preached (they, <u>them</u>) a good sermon.

_OP_   14. They were kind to me and (they, <u>them</u>).

_IO_   15. The older girls brought (we, <u>us</u>) younger girls water.

_DO_   16. The mothers helped (we, <u>us</u>) older girls.

_IO_   17. Father told the girls and (we, <u>us</u>) the story.

_OP_   18. The lesson was good for (we, <u>us</u>)

_OP_   and (they, <u>them</u>).

_DO_   19. I told Mother and (she, <u>her</u>).

_DO_   20. He crowneth (thou, <u>thee</u>) with loving-kindness and tender mercies.

_S_   21. O Lord my God, (<u>Thou</u>, Thee) art very great.

_DO_   22. All Thy works shall praise (Thou, <u>Thee</u>), O Lord.

Name _____

Worksheet 34
More Practice With Pronoun Usage

Underline the correct pronouns. In the blank write *S, PN, DO, IO,* or *OP* to tell whether the pronoun is a subject, predicate nominative, direct object, indirect object, or the object of a preposition.

DO 1. A rabid dog attacked a boy and bit (he, <u>him</u>) fourteen times.

S 2. (<u>He</u>, Him) was named Joseph Meister.

PN 3. The boy was (<u>he</u>, him).

S 4. Soon (<u>he</u>, him) would be very sick.

DO 5. Joseph's parents took (he, <u>him</u>) to Louis Pasteur.

PN 6. It was (<u>he</u>, him) who developed a rabies vaccine.

S 7. (<u>He</u>, Him) had already vaccinated sheep against anthrax.

PN 8. The scientist was (<u>he</u>, him).

OP 9. Joseph went with (they, <u>them</u>) to Paris.

DO 10. Pasteur met the parents and (he, <u>him</u>).

IO 11. He gave (they, <u>them</u>) a welcome.

DO 12. Please help (we, <u>us</u>) if you can.

S 13. (<u>He</u>, Him) hesitated to use the new rabies vaccine.

OP 14. No human had yet received it from (he, <u>him</u>).

DO 15. Two other men encouraged (he, <u>him</u>).

PN 16. The doctors were (<u>they</u>, them).

S 17. (<u>They</u>, Them) pointed out that the boy had no other chance.

IO 18. You might provide (we, <u>us</u>) the answer.

OP 19. Finally he listened to (they, <u>them</u>).

IO 20. Pasteur gave (he, <u>him</u>) treatments with the vaccine.

S 21. In several weeks (<u>he</u>, him) recovered.

OP 22. What joy it brought to (they, <u>them</u>)!

PN 23. The first known survivor of rabies is (<u>he</u>, him).

IO 24. Pasteur had done (he, <u>him</u>) a great service, and Joseph Meister was very thankful.

S 25. Later (<u>he</u>, him) served at the Pasteur Institute.

PN 26. The gatekeeper was (<u>he</u>, him).

S 27. (<u>He</u>, Him) was loyal to Louis Pasteur the rest of his life.

Name _____   *(English 6, Lesson 65)*

Worksheet 35
Practice With Pronouns

A. Write the answers in complete sentences.
   1. What is a pronoun?

   _____*A pronoun is a word that takes the place of a noun.*_____

   _____

   2. What is an antecedent?

   _____*An antecedent is the noun for which a pronoun stands.*_____

   _____

B. Above the underlined words, write personal pronouns that would be suitable to replace them. Write one pronoun for each word group.
   1. <u>My mother and I</u> **We** prepared a meal for <u>the Jacobson family</u> **them**.
   2. <u>Lisa and you</u> **You** should take <u>this bread</u> **it** to <u>Mrs. Carter</u> **her**.
   3. <u>Uncle Mervin</u> **He** gave <u>this book</u> **it** to <u>my brother and me</u> **us**.

C. Underline each pronoun, and draw an arrow from the pronoun to its antecedent.

   1. Sarah made a dress for Janice, but <u>it</u> was too big for <u>her</u>.

   2. Robert caught several fish, but <u>he</u> said <u>they</u> were not large enough.

   3. David wrote in the Psalms, "Save <u>me</u>, O God, by <u>thy</u> name, and judge <u>me</u> by <u>thy</u> strength.

D. Write *N, O,* or *P* in the blanks to tell whether the underlined pronouns are nominative, objective, or possessive case.

   __N__ 1. <u>They</u> lived in the highlands of Germany with

   __P__   <u>their</u> relatives.

   __N__ 2. It was <u>we</u> boys in sixth grade who reported

   __P__   on <u>its</u> geography.

   __N__ 3. O Lord, <u>Thou</u> hast searched me

   __O__   and known <u>me</u>.

   __P__ 4. Whither shall I go from <u>Thy</u> Spirit,

   __N__   or whither shall <u>I</u> flee from Thy presence?

Name _____

Possessive, Demonstrative, and Indefinite Pronouns

A. Read each set of pronouns. Write *singular* if those pronouns are always singular, *plural* if they are always plural, or *either* if they are either singular or plural.

____plural____ 1. both, few, several, many

___singular___ 2. each, either, neither, one, another, anybody, anyone, everybody, everyone, somebody, someone, nobody, no one

____either____ 3. some, any, none, all, most

B. Underline the correct words in parentheses.

1. (<u>Your</u>, You're) flower book has (<u>its</u>, it's) name listed.

2. (Your, <u>You're</u>) turning the pages too fast.

3. (Its, <u>It's</u>) listed several pages farther back.

4. (Their, <u>They're</u>) found in the section on purple flowers.

5. (Them, <u>Those</u>) flowers grow in the desert.

6. (<u>Those</u>, Them there) lupines grow wild in the Arctic.

7. (<u>This</u>, This here) marigold grows in forests.

8. (<u>These</u>, These here) pansies look like (<u>hers</u>, her's).

9. (<u>Ours</u>, Our's) are not as colorful as (<u>those</u>, those there).

10. Hundreds of morning glories grow in (<u>their</u>, they're) fields.

C. Underline the correct words in parentheses. When you underline a verb, also underline the subject that it must agree with.

1. <u>Both</u> of the flower beds (<u>need</u>, needs) weeding.

2. <u>Neither</u> of these books (list, <u>lists</u>) the daffodil.

3. <u>Some</u> of the flowers (<u>grow</u>, grows) better in shady places.

4. <u>Each</u> of the flowers on this page (bloom, <u>blooms</u>) in August.

5. <u>Few</u> (has, <u>have</u>) flowers in December.

6. <u>Everybody</u> (want, <u>wants</u>) to bring (<u>his</u>, their) teacher a bouquet.

7. <u>Nobody</u> in our class (own, <u>owns</u>) a greenhouse.

8. <u>Many</u> (has, <u>have</u>) hotbeds in (his, <u>their</u>) gardens.

9. <u>All</u> of the students (<u>plant</u>, plants) marigolds for (his, <u>their</u>) mothers.

10. <u>All</u> of the potting soil (<u>is</u>, are) used up.

Name _____   *(English 6, Lesson 67)*

Worksheet 37
Business Letters

A. Read the letter below. What is its purpose?

_____Its purpose is to get information (a catalog)._____

B. Write the names of the letter parts in the blanks. Then underline each small letter that should be capitalized, and add the missing punctuation.

____heading____ 1.   742 north hudson street
                                       boston, ma 24351
                                       may 22, 20—

inside address 2. rod and staff publishers, inc.
                    highway 172
_____   crockett, ky 41413

___greeting___ 3. gentlemen:

____body____ 4.   i am interested in your books and periodicals. please send me a catalog.

___closing___ 5.   sincerely,

__signature__ 6.   lillian justin

C. Correctly address the "envelope" below to send the letter in Part B.

Lillian Justin
742 North Hudson Street
Boston, MA 02113

ROD AND STAFF PUBLISHERS INC
HIGHWAY 172
CROCKETT KY 41413

Name _____

Worksheet 38
Possessive, Demonstrative, Indefinite, and Interrogative Pronouns

A. Before each group of pronouns, write the letter of the kind that it is.

a. personal—nominative case
b. personal—objective case
c. personal—possessive case
d. personal—archaic

e. demonstrative
f. indefinite
g. interrogative

___e___   1. this, that, these, those

___g___   2. who, whom, whose, which, what

___b___   3. me, you, him, her, it, us, them

___d___   4. thou, thee, thy, thine, ye

___c___   5. my, mine, your, yours, his, her, hers, its, our, ours, their, theirs

___f___   6. some, any, none, all, most, each, either, one, nobody, anyone, anybody, both, few, several, many

___a___   7. I, you, he, she, it, we, they

B. In the blanks, write *adj.* or *pro.* to tell how each underlined word is used. If it is an adjective, draw an arrow from the adjective to the word it modifies.

___adj.___   1. That dolphin is a playful one.

___pron.___ 2. That was interesting to watch.

___adj.___   3. Each sloth hung upside down on his own tree branch.

___pron.___ 4. Each eats leaves from the tree.

___adj.___   5. Whose drawing of a bat is this?

___adj.___   6. What kind of food does the hyrax eat?

___pron.___ 7. What is another name for a coney?

___adj.___   8. Bless the Lord, O my soul, and forget not all His benefits.

___adj.___   9. Who forgiveth all thine iniquities; who healeth all thy diseases.

___pron.___ 10. Son, thou art ever with me, and all that I have is thine.

C. Underline the correct words in parentheses.

1. (Its, It's) good that (there, they're) here.

2. (Your, You're) speaking with (their, they're) daughter.

3. (Your, You're) cat is watching a blue jay out (there, they're).

4. (Its, It's) nest is in that tree.

Name _____   *(English 6, Lesson 69)*

Worksheet 39
Relative Pronouns

A. Write *I* or *R* to tell whether each underlined pronoun is interrogative or relative.

   I   1. <u>Who</u> was the first European to see Australia?

   R   2. The man <u>who</u> discovered Australia also sailed around Antarctica.

   I   3. <u>What</u> are the main characteristics of reptiles?

   R   4. The person with <u>whom</u> you talked was my cousin.

   R   5. The horse <u>that</u> they saw was a runaway.

   I   6. <u>Whom</u> did you meet?

   R   7. The flowers <u>which</u> never bloomed were asters.

B. Underline each relative pronoun, and draw an arrow from the pronoun to its antecedent. Put parentheses around the clause each relative pronoun introduces.

    Example: The farm (<u>that</u> he bought) had been his grandfather's.

1. The man (<u>who</u> helped you) was my uncle.

2. It is my sister's ducks (<u>that</u> you see.)

3. The lady (<u>whom</u> you met) was here last week.

4. We watched the elephant (<u>that</u> could do tricks.)

5. The person (to <u>whom</u> you spoke) was grateful.

6. I felt sorry for the mother (<u>whose</u> baby was crying.)

7. The customer (<u>whom</u> you served) was pleased with our products.

8. May I talk with the secretary (<u>who</u> waited on me yesterday?)

9. The worker (<u>whom</u> you saw) is new here.

10. The interesting book, (<u>which</u> you just read,) was written by a teacher.

11. My grandfather was the carpenter (<u>who</u> built this barn.)

12. Hezekiah was a king (<u>whom</u> God gave a miraculous sign.)

Name _____

Worksheet 40
Using Relative Pronouns

A. Write *N, O,* or *P* in the blanks to tell whether the underlined pronouns are nominative, objective, or possessive case.

   O   1. The girl to <u>whom</u> I spoke was my classmate.

   O   2. Of all the boys here, the only boy <u>whom</u> I know is Brian.

   N   3. The man <u>who</u> laid the new floor said he was here before.

   P   4. I gave a new tablet to the girl <u>whose</u> pen I borrowed.

   N   5. The yellow house <u>which</u> is on Apple Street was sold.

   N   6. The boy <u>that</u> usually sets up the chairs is absent.

   P   7. The man <u>whose</u> truck is parked here will move it.

   N   8. The children <u>that</u> usually fetch the milk have not come yet.

   O   9. The house of <u>which</u> I spoke was green.

B. Underline the correct pronouns. In each blank, write *S, DO, IO,* or *OP* to tell whether the pronoun is a subject, direct object, indirect object, or object of a preposition.

   OP   1. The girl of (who, <u>whom</u>) I spoke was very young.

   S   2. The boy (<u>who</u>, whom) planted the corn was paid.

   DO   3. The man (who, <u>whom</u>) I paid yesterday has come back.

   IO   4. Moses was the man (who, <u>whom</u>) God gave the Law.

   DO   5. A song leader (who, <u>whom</u>) I know well is coming tonight.

   S   6. We met the minister (<u>who</u>, whom) had preached last Sunday.

   OP   7. The people to (who, <u>whom</u>) he spoke had listened eagerly.

   OP   8. Mother called the lady with (who, <u>whom</u>) Alice was staying.

C. Underline the correct pronoun in each sentence. Write *P, A,* or *O* in the blank to tell whether the pronoun refers to a person, animal, or object.

   P   1. We talked with the man (<u>who</u>, which) was standing there.

   P   2. The boy and girl (<u>whom</u>, which) we saw are his children.

   A   3. The bear (whom, <u>that</u>) they were feeding was their pet.

   O   4. Father sawed down a tree (which, <u>whose</u>) bark was falling off.

   P   5. Martha picked up the baby (<u>that</u>, which) had just awakened.

   O   6. The flowers (who, <u>which</u>) are blooming there are zinnias.

Name _____   *(English 6, Lesson 73)*

Worksheet 41
Using Capital Letters

Underline each small letter that should be capitalized.

1. jesus said, "blessed are the poor in spirit: for theirs is the kingdom of heaven."

2. for devotions my father read what solomon wrote in proverbs: "righteousness exalteth a nation; but sin is a reproach to any people."

3. grandfather martin taught us by example the saying benjamin franklin wrote: "early to bed and early to rise, makes a man healthy, wealthy, and wise."

4. brother joseph, our teacher, read the saying that benjamin franklin wrote: "laziness travels so slowly that poverty soon overtakes him."

5. uncle alvin led a song that was written by harriet b. stowe.

6. "do tell us, mother!" the children cried.

7. "oh, i know c. a. miller quite well," said uncle george.

8. whose mother made him a new coat every year?

9. samuel's mother was a faithful woman.

10. in proverbs 8:32 Wisdom says, "now therefore hearken unto me, o ye children: for blessed are they that keep my ways."

11.   **god's word**
    there is a lamp whose steady light
    guides the poor traveler in the night;
    'tis god's own Word! Its beaming ray
    can turn a midnight into day.
    —Author unknown

12. dear aunt mary,

13. sincerely yours,
    joseph stuart

14. 114 church street
    moundridge, ks 67107
    march 4, 20—

Name _____

Worksheet 42
More Capital Letters

Underline each small letter that should be capitalized.

1. o my soul, bless thou jehovah,
    all within me bless his Name;
   bless jehovah and forget not
    all his mercies to proclaim.
    —Author unknown

2. "bless the lord, o my soul: and all that is within me, bless his holy name" (Psalm 103:1)

3. "with my whole heart have i sought thee: o let me not wander from thy commandments" (Psalm 119:10)

4. sing about jesus who died to save,
   who for my soul his life he gave;
   sing, for he's reigning above the grave,
    sing about him, yes, sing about him.
    —Author unknown

5. last spring there was a great flood in lancaster, pennsylvania.

6. lansdale christian school was closed on wednesday.

7. have you read the book *the call of the north country*?

8. you should read the book *come to the south and help us.*

9.   **spring song**
   wild geese are winging,
   late snows cease clinging,
   march winds keep flinging
    winter's debris.

   no longer sleeping,
   crocus starts peeping,
   bright color creeping
    for all to see.

   robins are singing,
   high nests are swinging,
   children come bringing
    bluebells for me.

   everything growing,
   new life is showing.
   what joy in knowing,
    springtime is free!

Name _____

Worksheet 43
Capital Letters in Proper Nouns and Proper Adjectives

Underline each small letter that should be capitalized.

1. j. h. sammis wrote the song "trust and obey" after he heard a story by d. b. towner in brockton, massachusetts.

2. a young man from the town had said at a meeting, "i am going to trust, and i am going to obey."

3. mr. sankey invited mr. g. c. needham to stay with him one summer when mr. sankey was living at cohasset, massachusetts.

4. even though mr. needham had never written a song before, he wrote words for a tune that mr. ira d. sankey had composed.

5. mr. g. c. needham objected, but ira insisted that he write the words.

6. mr. needham wrote a song called "from the riven rock there floweth."

7. mr. w. h. doane asked mrs. van alstyne, also known as fanny j. crosby, to write a poem for a tune that he had composed.

8. when mrs. van alstyne heard the tune, she exclaimed, "why, it says, 'safe in the arms of jesus'!"

9. timothy weber, jr., lives near saskatoon, a large city in saskatchewan, canada.

10. the rock river begins in wisconsin and flows southwest into illinois and into the mississippi river at rock island.

11. if polish people come from poland and the chinese come from china, where do the danish come from?

12. dr. trovolsky was a russian, but dr. shuber was a german.

13. monte rosa, on the swiss and italian border, is the highest mountain peak in the pennine alps.

14. kurnool is an indian city just southwest of hyderabad, another city of india.

15. holstein, a region in northwest germany, is located just south of the jutland peninsula.

16. jersey is an island in the english channel.

17. st. peter port is on guernsey, another island in the english channel.

18. my brother-in-law raises jersey cows and guernsey cows, but i like the milk from holstein cows best of all.

Worksheet 44
End Punctuation

A. Cross out each small letter that should be capitalized, and write a capital letter above it. Also add the missing punctuation.   (Allow variation in the use of exclamation points.)

1. **I**n the days of our great-great-grandfathers, farmers of the Schleswig-Holstein region of Germany raised Holstein cattle. **T**hese cattle have black and white coats. **M**ilk from Holstein cattle is not rich in butterfat. **H**owever, Holstein cows produce more milk than any other kind of cattle.

2. **M**r. **H**enry sells all the milk produced by **I**van, **J**r. **H**is store opens at 8:00 **A**. **M**. **H**e also sells cream, butter, and cottage cheese.

3. **I**s the store open until 9:00 **P**. **M**.? **W**hat! **Y**ou have only twenty minutes left. **Q**uickly take this list and buy the things for **M**rs. **B**rown. **Y**ou may not be able to finish in time.

B. Write the correct abbreviation for each word. Use a dictionary if you are not sure.

(Some answers may vary.)

1.	pint	pt.	7.	November	Nov.
2.	mile	mi.	8.	Tuesday	Tues.
3.	year	yr.	9.	Wednesday	Wed.
4.	foot	ft.	10.	Doctor	Dr.
5.	pound	lb.	11.	et cetera	etc.
6.	Sunday	Sun.	12.	after midday	P.M.

C. Write the postal service abbreviations for the following states.

1.	Idaho	ID	6.	Wyoming	WY
2.	Maryland	MD	7.	Tennessee	TN
3.	Illinois	IL	8.	Washington	WA
4.	Colorado	CO	9.	North Dakota	ND
5.	Indiana	IN			

Name _____   *(English 6, Lesson 78)*

Worksheet 45
Direct and Indirect Quotations

A. Write whether each sentence has a direct quotation (*D*), an indirect quotation (*I*), or no quotation (*N*). There are no quotation marks to help you.

___I___ 1. Jesus said that the disciples should let the little children come to Him.

___N___ 2. The disciples had tried to send the children away.

___D___ 3. Jesus said suffer the little children, and forbid them not, to come unto Me.

___D___ 4. Jesus said for of such is the kingdom of heaven.

___D___ 5. The lawyer asked who is my neighbor?

___I___ 6. Jesus said that the priest and the Levite did not stop to help.

___D___ 7. Jesus said when the Samaritan saw the wounded man, he had compassion on him.

___I___ 8. The Good Samaritan said that he would pay the extra expenses at the inn when he came back.

B. Rewrite each sentence so that it has a direct quotation.

1. Mother said that Sarah and Rhoda would make the bread.

   Mother said, "Sarah and Rhoda will make the bread." _____

   _____

2. Sister Joan said that our reports are due on Monday.

   Sister Joan said, "Your reports are due on Monday." _____

   _____

C. Rewrite each sentence so that it has an indirect quotation.

1. Sister Joyce told us, "Give your drawings to me by next week."

   Sister Joyce told us that we should give our drawings to her by next week. _____

   or Sister Joyce told us to give our drawings to her by next week. _____

2. Farmer John told us, "You may use my tractor to plow your garden."

   Farmer John told us that we may use his tractor to plow our garden. _____

   _____

Name _____

Worksheet 46
Using Dialogue in Stories

Write *P* before each sentence where a new paragraph should begin. Add the missing quotation marks. In at least three places where *said* is used, cross out *said* and write a more expressive word above it.

"Where's Anita?"

Deborah Joy recalled Father's parting words. "Deborah Joy, you are thirteen years old, so you should be able to take care of the younger ones while we are gone."

After her evening work was finished, she hurried to get her book *Year of Doubt.* "I think I'll go outside to read," she decided. She climbed into the old apple tree. The minutes passed. Suddenly Deborah Joy jumped. "Where's Anita?" she ~~said~~ *wondered.* "Well, I'm sure she's over there with the boys. I simply have to find out what happens to Lois Ann next." She kept on reading, unaware of the time.

Awhile later, Mother and Father came home. Deborah Joy jumped up and ran to the orchard. "Boys, where is Anita?" she ~~said~~ *asked.* P"Isn't she with you?" "No, I haven't seen her for a long time," Gerald ~~said~~ *replied.* He looked startled. P"Oh! Please come help!" Deborah Joy ~~said~~ *exclaimed* frantically. Father, Mother, and the boys joined in the search. In the attic, in the basement, in the barn—everywhere they could think of.

Finally Deborah Joy entered the barn for the second time. There was Anita in the haymow! "Oh, Anita! Here you are!" ~~said~~ *exclaimed* Deborah Joy. P"Look, baby kittens!" was Anita's only comment. P"You were told to watch Anita while we were gone, Deborah Joy," Father told her later. "For one week you may not read storybooks, to help you remember to take your responsibilities more seriously."

A sober girl climbed the steps to bed that night. How thankful she was that Anita was safe!

Name _____   (English 6, Lesson 80)

Worksheet 47
More Practice With Direct Quotations

Underline each small letter that should be capitalized. Add the missing punctuation marks.

1. "the oxen were plowing, and the asses were feeding beside them," said the messenger.

2. he continued, "the Sabeans fell upon them and took them away, and killed all the servants."

3. the messenger said, "i alone escaped to tell you."

4. "the fire of God fell from heaven," said another servant. "all the sheep and the other servants were killed."

5. another servant said, "the Chaldeans have taken the camels and killed the servants."

6. "i am the only one left to tell you," he continued.

7. "while your children were feasting," said a fourth messenger, "a great wind blew down the house, and i am the only one that escaped."

8. job said, "the lord gave, and the lord hath taken away."

9. "blessed be the Name of the lord," he added.

10. eliphaz said, "behold, happy is the man whom god correcteth."

11. "how forcible are right words!" job exclaimed.

12. "how long," said bildad, "shall the words of thy mouth be like a strong wind?"

13. "my days are swifter than a running messenger," said job. "they flee away."

14. zophar asked, "canst thou by searching find out god?"

15. "but ask now the beasts," said job. "they shall teach thee."

16. "ask the birds, and they shall tell thee," he continued.

17. "who knoweth not that the hand of the lord hath made all this?" asked job.

18. elihu said, "surely god will not do wickedly."

(or the lord asked, "job, where were you . . .")

19. the lord asked job, "where were you when i laid the foundations of the earth?"

20. "i know that Thou canst do everything," job answered. "no thought can be kept from Thee."

21. "because ye have not spoken of Me the thing that is right, as My servant job hath," the lord said to eliphaz the temanite, "My wrath is kindled against thee and thy two friends."

22. "my servant job shall pray for you," said the lord.

Name _____

Worksheet 48
Using Commas in Sentences

A. Write whether each word or phrase set off by commas is an appositive (*A*), a noun of direct address (*D*), or a parenthetical element (*P*).

___A___ 1. The rhinoceros, a large grassland animal, has one horn.

___D___ 2. The arctic hare, Jean, also wears a white coat.

___A___ 3. That great jumper, the kangaroo, comes from Australia.

___P___ 4. Of course, the white coat of the polar bear helps to keep it from being seen by its prey.

B. Add the missing commas and end punctuation.

1. The elephant, a faithful worker, wrapped his trunk around his owner, lifted him, and placed him high on his back.

2. The prairie dog, a small, squirrel-like animal, digs underground tunnels in the grasslands of western North America.

3. The frog snapped out his tongue, caught the fly, and swallowed it.

4. The six white, dainty flowers added a pleasing sparkle to the bouquet.

5. Henry Ford, the determined inventor, was trying out his new gasoline engine in his wife's kitchen.

6. The kitchen light dimmed, the sink shook, the engine coughed and roared, and flames shot from the exhaust.

7. The huge brown bear ambled to the water's edge, slapped out a fish with one paw, and ate it.   (A comma may be placed after *huge.*)

8. Wash the dishes, sweep the floors, and mow the lawn, Sara, while we are gone.

9. The little ant, as you can see, is an orderly, diligent insect.

10. The queens, drones, housekeepers, and soldiers work together to keep the ant colony running smoothly.

11. A large, tropical ant nest, believe it or not, may extend forty feet below the surface of the ground.

12. By the way, that old, tall grandfather clock still works.

Name _____   *(English 6, Lesson 84)*

Worksheet 49
More Practice With Commas

A. Add the missing commas.

1. Noah warned the people to repent, but they did not believe him.

2. It rained forty days and forty nights, but Noah and his family were safe.

3. After many days, the ark rested on top of a mountain.

4. Noah waited awhile, and then he sent out a raven.

5. He sent out a dove two times, but she came back because she could not find a place to rest.

6. The dove did not return the next time, and Noah knew it was time to leave the ark.

7. Noah offered a sacrifice to God as soon as his family left the ark, and God accepted it.

8. God promised that He would never send another flood to cover the whole earth, and He gave the rainbow for a sign.

B. Add the missing commas to this letter.

Box 115, Woodland Road

Southdale, MN 55420

May 29, 20—

Dear Brian,

Greetings in Jesus' Name. Oh, I wish you could have seen what I saw on Saturday. We went to a zoo where you drive on roads that go right into the cages of the animals. Yes, ostriches, lamas, and other animals came right up to our car windows and looked in at us! You must come and see my pictures. When we were in the monkey area, Mother said, "What! Are those monkeys going to climb right up on our car?" Well, sure enough, they did! I don't think I'll ever forget that experience. Come and see us soon.

Your friend,

Mervin Wadel

Name _____

Worksheet 50
Apostrophes

A. Fill in the chart.

Singular	Singular Possessive	Plural	Plural Possessive
1. waitress	waitress's	waitresses	waitresses'
2. ostrich	ostrich's	ostriches	ostriches'
3. lady	lady's	ladies	ladies'
4. raccoon	raccoon's	raccoons	raccoons'
5. deer	deer's	deer	deer's

B. Rewrite these phrases, using possessive forms.

1. the den of the bear   the bear's den
2. the food of the squirrels   the squirrels' food
3. the spots of the leopard   the leopard's spots
4. the path of the rabbits   the rabbits' path
5. the howl of the wolf   the wolf's howl

C. Write contractions for the following words.

1. can not __can't__   4. who is __who's__   7. it is __it's__
2. I am __I'm__   5. will not __won't__   8. you are __you're__
3. they are __they're__   6. he is __he's__

D. Write the plural forms.

1. 3 __3's__   3. T __T's__   5. $ __$'s__
2. # __#'s__   4. m __m's__   6. Z __Z's__

E. Add the missing apostrophes.

1. Somebody's hat was left in the men's anteroom.
2. You're supposed to take their charts upstairs.
3. Who's doing Mary's chart?
4. All Mary's 8's are backward, but her 6's are beautiful.
5. Remember to use the $'s and #'s on your math problems.
6. They've used several elephants' tusks to make carvings.

Name _____   (English 6, Lesson 87)

Worksheet 51
Hyphens, Colons, and Semicolons

A. Write each word, placing hyphens between only the syllables that could be divided at the end of a line of writing.

1. identical   _____iden-ti-cal_____   4. luncheon   _____lunch-eon_____

2. subsidiary   _____sub-sid-i-ary_____   5. oversimplify   _____over-sim-pli-fy_____

3. saddlebag   _____sad-dle-bag_____   6. heavenly   _____heav-en-ly_____

B. Add the missing hyphens, colons, and semicolons.

1. Bees, ants, beetles, crickets, and grasshoppers are insects; but spiders, ticks, and scorpions are arachnids.

2. Jenny recited Proverbs 4:7, Hebrews 13:17, and 1 Corinthians 3:11; and June recited Romans 15:2, John 3:16, and 1 Corinthians 16:14.

3. By memory, our class recited 1 Corinthians 13:1–6 last Sunday; and we said 1 Corinthians 13:7–13 this Sunday.

4. My great-grandfather had sixty-two grandchildren.

5. In 1902, a man named Willis Carrier invented an air-conditioning device almost by accident.

6. Mr. Carrier made an air-cooling machine to keep the moisture out of a printing plant; the printers couldn't be sure their colors would come out right in a damp room.

7. Hard study requires self-discipline.

8. Dear Sirs:

   I am returning these shoes because the size is too small. Please send me a pair in size 9.

Sincerely,

Robert Hall

C. In each blank, write numerals and abbreviations to write the time given.

Example: Half past eight in the morning. (8:30 A. M.)

_____10:15 A.M._____   1. Fifteen minutes after ten in the morning.

_____11:30 P.M._____   2. Thirty minutes before midnight.

_____4:45 A.M._____   3. A quarter to five in the morning.

_____12:02 P.M._____   4. Two minutes after noon.

Name _____

Worksheet 52
Adjectives

A. Draw one line under each limiting adjective, and two lines under each descriptive adjective.

1. Moses' rod was a symbol of God's power.

2. Daniel was taken to Babylon during the third year of Jehoiakim's reign.

3. Jesus' first miracle was done in a small town.

4. Fill the waterpots with water.

5. The shepherd searched for one lost sheep.

6. Sheep know the shepherd's voice.

7. The blind man was begging for his food.

8. The disciples' ship was tossing on the stormy sea.

9. A little lad brought five loaves and two small fish for his lunch.

10. People sat on the green grass.

11. The fragments filled twelve baskets.

12. Take these ten loaves to your brothers in Saul's army.

13. Egyptians saved corn during their seven good years.

14. Christ arose on the first day of the week.

15. God is a great King above all gods.

16. A wise son maketh a glad father.

17. The foolish man built his house on soft sand.

18. A grievous disease killed many Egyptians' cattle.

B. Write *adj.* (adjective) or *pron.* (pronoun) for each underlined word. If the word is an adjective, underline the word that it modifies.

   adj.   1. That animal is an antelope.

  pron.   2. That is a gazelle.

   adj.   3. Those answers can be found in the last paragraph.

  pron.   4. These are in the first paragraph.

  pron.   5. This is the last one.

   adj.   6. That boy studies his lessons well.

   adj.   7. Each boy carried one large box.

  pron.   8. Each was a diligent worker.

Name _____   (English 6, Lesson 90)

Worksheet 53
Predicate Adjectives

A. Underline all the adjectives in these sentences. Write *P* above each predicate adjective.

1. The warm fall weather has been pleasant.

2. January is a cold, frosty, winter month.

3. The designs on the frosted windows are beautiful.

4. This old map looks interesting.

5. Many Indians were friendly.

6. An elephant's trunk is quite strong.

7. No two snowflakes are alike.

8. The little brown dog was friendly.

9. His few words were meaningful.

10. The little kittens are soft and cuddly.

11. These peas from our garden are fresh.

12. Harold's scissors are too small for his large hands.

13. The stranger looked cheerful.

14. Those pies smell good.

B. Write *A* or *L* in the blank before each sentence to tell whether the verb is action or linking. Underline all the predicate adjectives.

___L___   1. That pineapple cake looks good.

___A___   2. We looked everywhere for the lost book.

___A___   3. We tasted the banana cake.

___L___   4. The orange cake tasted delicious.

___L___   5. These hyacinths are sweet and fragrant.

___A___   6. We smelled the spicy cake baking.

___L___   7. The little children appear drowsy.

___A___   8. He suddenly appeared around the corner.

___L___   9. The bananas will become riper.

___L___   10. You have grown much kinder.

___L___   11. Surely you can stay dry with that raincoat.

___A___   12. Please stay with us another day.

Name _____

Worksheet 54

Diagraming Adjectives and Using Appositive Adjectives

A. Rewrite each sentence, placing two adjectives in the appositive position. Use commas where they are needed.

1. The white, fluffy snow blew into deep drifts. _____

   <u>The snow, white and fluffy, blew into deep drifts.</u> _____

2. The shiny, sharp knife cut the meat easily. _____

   <u>The knife, shiny and sharp, cut the meat easily.</u> _____

3. The cold, ripe apples were refreshing. _____

   <u>The apples, cold and ripe, were refreshing.</u> _____

4. The fresh, tasty buns were eaten before long. _____

   <u>The buns, fresh and tasty, were eaten before long.</u> _____

B. Underline all the adjectives Write *P* above each predicate adjective, and *A* above each appositive adjective.

1. <u>Proven</u> remedies, <u>old</u> or <u>new</u>, are always <u>useful</u>.
      A   A   P

2. The <u>picnic</u> dinner was <u>delicious</u>.
                  P

3. Are you <u>attentive</u> and <u>obedient</u>?
           P   P

4. <u>Those</u> cedars, <u>tall</u> and <u>stately</u>, are on <u>their</u> property.
              A   A

5. The people, <u>tired</u> but <u>happy</u>, gathered for worship.
            A   A

C. Diagram these sentences in the space below.

1. Ants are small, but they are diligent.
2. The women, young and old, were sewing.
3. Those flowers are beautiful.
4. They were giants, great and tall.
5. The water, cold and fresh, tasted good.

Name _____   *(English 6, Lesson 92)*

Worksheet 55
Original, Fresh Adjectives

A. In each blank, write a more descriptive adjective that could replace the underlined word. See the chart in the lesson. Use a different adjective each time.   (Sample answers.)

1. Throw these <u>bad</u> apples out.   *rotten, scabby, wormy*

2. Too much candy is <u>bad</u> for your teeth.   *unhealthy, harmful*

3. We had a <u>nice</u> evening with our friends from church.   *pleasant, enjoyable*

4. Laurel is a <u>nice</u> friend.   *pleasant, agreeable, kind*

5. I'm sorry I can't go, but I have a <u>big</u> job to do.   *important, demanding*

6. We watched a <u>big</u> earthmover as it traveled down our highway.   *enormous, huge*

7. We had an <u>awful</u> storm last night.   *frightening, terrifying, destructive*

8. The news that Miriam broke both legs was <u>awful</u> to hear.   *dreadful, shocking*

9. Howard found an arrowhead with a <u>funny</u> shape.   *strange, unusual*

10. We worked in some <u>real</u> heat on that day in July.   *extreme, oppressive*

B. Write a synonym and an antonym for each adjective. Be sure your answers are also adjectives.
   (Sample answers.)

	Synonym	**Antonym**
1. enormous	*huge, mountainous, massive*	*tiny, little, minute*
2. unhealthy	*sickly, ailing, frail*	*healthy, well, sound*
3. enjoyable	*pleasant, agreeable, appealing*	*unpleasant, disagreeable, distasteful*
4. true	*genuine, actual, authentic*	*false, deceitful, dishonest*
5. strong	*vigorous, powerful, durable*	*weak, feeble, flimsy*
6. valuable	*precious, costly, expensive*	*useless, worthless, unprofitable*

Name _____

Worksheet 56
Forms of Comparison for Adjectives

A. Write the comparative and superlative degrees of these adjectives.

1. good   _____better_____   _____best_____
2. bad   _____worse_____   _____worst_____
3. swift   _____swifter_____   _____swiftest_____
4. tiny   _____tinier_____   _____tiniest_____
5. ill   _____worse_____   _____worst_____
6. many   _____more_____   _____most_____

B. Write the correct form of each word in parentheses.

_____best_____ 1. Timothy is the (good) tenor singer in our class.

_____heaviest_____ 2. Your book bag is the (heavy) one of all.

_____tall_____ 3. King Saul was a (tall) young man.

_____wisest_____ 4. Solomon was the (wise) man that ever lived.

_____meekest_____ 5. Moses was the (meek) man on earth.

_____busier_____ 6. She is (busy) today than she was yesterday.

_____younger_____ 7. Of the two girls, Rhoda is (young).

_____swifter_____ 8. Of the two sewing machines, this one is (swift).

_____coldest_____ 9. The day we left was the (cold) day of the winter.

_____lowest_____ 10. The (low) spot on earth is around the Dead Sea.

_____bright_____ 11. That (bright) star is Vega.

more content 12. The baby seems (content) in the playpen than in the crib.

more expensive 13. The blueberries were (expensive) than the cherries.

_____highest_____ 14. Mount Everest is the (high) mountain in the world.

C. Cross out the incorrect words. If other words should be used instead, write the corrections above them.

1. Our home is ~~more far~~ farther from school than from church.

2. Of the two boys, Galen is the ~~tallest~~ taller.

3. Melvin can run ~~more~~ faster than Marlin.

4. Cherry pie tastes ~~gooder~~ better than peach pie.

5. The weather is even ~~worser~~ worse this Saturday than last Saturday.

Name _____   (English 6, Lesson 95)

Worksheet 57
Prepositional Phrases as Adjectives

A. Underline each adjective phrase, and draw an arrow from the phrase to the noun it modifies.

1. The car beside the road has a flat tire.

2. Mark has a new pony with a white mane.

3. The closet under the stairway is small.

4. A minister from Ohio preached this morning.

5. The girl with red hair sits near the front.

6. My cousin is the girl in the blue dress.

7. The boy on horseback is our neighbor.

8. The baby in the basket was Moses.

9. The star in the east shone brightly at Jesus' birth.

10. This book is a story about life in Canada.

11. The little lad with the lunch was not selfish.

12. The disciples of Jesus were obedient.

B. Diagram these sentences.
1. Daniel spilled the can of green paint.
2. The house with white siding is ours.
3. He is a teacher in that small school.
4. The words of a talebearer are hurtful.
5. The young boy in the temple was Jesus.
6. Our trust in God is firm.

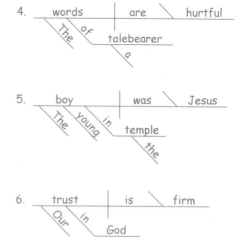

Worksheet 58
Exact Words in Descriptions

A. Underline the adjective in parentheses that describes the noun more specifically. Use a dictionary to find the meaning of any adjective that is not familiar to you.

1. (<u>fertile</u>, good) soil
2. a (mean, <u>vicious</u>) dog
3. (<u>rough</u>, bad) roads
4. (pretty, <u>dainty</u>) ferns
5. (<u>strenuous</u>, hard) work

6. a (good, <u>worthwhile</u>) book
7. a (nice, <u>courteous</u>) guest
8. (nice, <u>luscious</u>) grapes
9. a (large, <u>spacious</u>) room
10. a (<u>frosty</u>, cold) morning

B. Write a more descriptive word from the following list to replace each underlined word or phrase.

good	tiny	raging	true	sunny
extreme	dreadful	sloppy	pleasant	careless

<u> extreme </u> 1. My little brother was in <u>real</u> danger.

<u>pleasant *or* sunny</u> 2. It was a <u>nice</u> morning.

<u> dreadful </u> 3. The boys saw a <u>bad</u> accident.

<u> raging </u> 4. During the storm the wind was <u>very strong</u>.

<u>sloppy *or* careless</u> 5. Someone did an <u>awful</u> job of painting that house.

<u> tiny </u> 6. Fourteen people live in that <u>very little</u> house.

C. Rewrite the following description. Replace the underlined words or phrases with more exact nouns, verbs, and adjectives. Choose from the list below. (Answers may vary somewhat. Changes are underlined.)

chickadee	spied	hiked
spicy and sweet	were floating	scooped
the pine needles	piles of gray tapioca	a bluebird
like springtime	big, bubbly masses	frog
his spring song	our back lane to the pond	Timothy

My brother Timothy and I <u>went</u> down <u>to a nice spot on our place</u>. <u>Big bunches</u> of <u>some kind of</u> eggs <u>were there</u> on the water. They looked like <u>something else</u>. <u>One of us put</u> some into a jar. Then we walked into the woods. It smelled <u>nice</u> in there. The sun was shining on <u>some brown things</u> on the ground, and they smelled <u>good</u>. We heard a <u>bird</u> singing <u>a nice tune</u>. On our way home, I <u>saw</u> <u>another bird</u> sitting on the fence.

<u> My brother Timothy and I hiked down our back lane to the pond. Big, bubbly masses of frog</u>

<u> eggs were floating on the water. They looked like piles of gray tapioca. Timothy scooped</u>

<u> some into a jar. Then we walked into the woods. It smelled like springtime in there. The sun</u>

<u> was shining on the pine needles on the ground, and they smelled spicy and sweet. We heard</u>

<u> a chickadee singing his spring song. On our way home, I spied a bluebird sitting on the fence.</u>

Name _____   *(English 6, Lesson 97)*

Worksheet 59
Adjective Clauses

A. Put parentheses around each adjective clause. Draw an arrow from the clause to the word it modifies.

1. The man (who spoke these proverbs) was Solomon.

2. A mother (whose son is wise) is a happy mother.

3. He (that walketh with wise men) shall be wise.

4. They (which hunger and thirst after righteousness) shall be filled.

5. We love the Lord, (who has done so much for us.)

6. God, (who is rich in mercy,) has blessed us greatly.

7. The heart of him (that hath understanding) seeketh knowledge.

8. Happy is the man (that findeth wisdom.)

9. The testimonies (which thou hast commanded) are righteous and very faithful.

10. There is a way (that seemeth right unto a man,) but the end thereof are the ways of death.

11. Great peace have they (which love Thy law.)

12. He (who is greedy of gain) troubleth his own house.

13. A man (that hath friends) must show himself friendly.

14. He (that is slow to anger) is better than the mighty.

15. They (that sow in tears) shall reap in joy.

B. Combine each pair of sentences by using an adjective clause.

> **Example:** Here is the book. I bought it for you.
> **Answer:**   Here is the book that I bought for you.

1. Here is the pencil. I want it.

   Here is the pencil that I want.

2. He is the man. We met his son.

   He is the man whose son we met.

3. She is the one. She is going with us.

   She is the one who is going with us.

Name _____

Worksheet 60
Diagraming Adjective Clauses

Diagram the following sentences.

1. He who loves God will love his brother.
2. The disciple who recognized Jesus was John.
3. John was the disciple whom Jesus loved.
4. The net which had caught many fish was unbroken.
5. They who love God's law have great peace.
6. I am the man whom you are seeking.
7. Philip, whose four daughters prophesied, was an evangelist.
8. Those who are merciful shall obtain mercy.
9. They visited the brother who was ill.
10. He is the one whose son is my friend.
11. She is the nurse who helped us.
12. They will sing the song that I like

Name _____   *(English 6, Lesson 101)*

Worksheet 61
Adverbs

A. Underline the adverbs. Write *1* above the ones that tell *how*, *2* above the ones that tell *when*, and *3* above the ones that tell *where*. (Negative words like *not* and *hardly* tell *how*.)   (Allow reasonable variation.)

1. The sun is shining here today.

2. How did you get there, and when did you arrive?

3. The bus seldom comes late.

4. The travelers walked hurriedly.

5. Come back again soon.

6. The visitors may park their cars here.

7. Our freezer has always worked well.

8. Tomorrow we must do our chores quickly.

9. This river often rises considerably.

10. Hungrily the robin swallowed the worm.

11. Already it is raining fast.

12. Sometimes an earthquake shakes violently.

13. Then Zacchaeus received Jesus joyfully.

14. Nebuchadnezzar once looked proudly over Babylon.

B. Diagram these sentences in the space below.
1. Pick the beans carefully again.
2. How are your rabbits doing today?
3. Finally the train moved forward again.
4. How are pencils made now?

Name _____

Worksheet 62
Adverbs of Degree

A. Underline each adverb of degree, and draw an arrow from it to the word it modifies.

   1. Those <u>exceedingly</u> tall trees are sequoias.

   2. The autumn leaves are <u>especially</u> colorful.

   3. The river rose <u>unusually</u> high.

   4. The neighbor who helped was <u>quite</u> friendly.

   5. A <u>completely</u> full bucket of milk was spilled.

   6. The cookie jar is <u>almost</u> empty already.

   7. Uzziah acted <u>rather</u> foolishly.

   8. A skyscraper is <u>extremely</u> tall.

   9. We should leave <u>almost</u> immediately.

   10. Perhaps we stayed <u>too</u> long.

B. In each blank, write a more effective word for the underlined word. Choose from the following list. Do not use any word more than once.   (Answers may vary somewhat.)

actually	certainly	beautifully	unusually
entirely	neatly	completely	surprisingly
extremely	intensely	exceedingly	uncomfortably

<u>extremely, exceedingly</u>   1. The students worked <u>very</u> hard.

<u>extremely, uncomfortably</u> 2. The old woods trail was <u>very</u> rough.

<u>certainly</u>   3. The doughnuts were <u>surely</u> delicious.

<u>intensely</u>   4. Last January in Maine, it was <u>awfully</u> cold.

<u>unusually, surprisingly</u>   5. The Morrises were <u>awfully</u> late.

<u>entirely, completely</u>   6. Fred was <u>surely</u> lost in the maze of city streets.

Name _____   (*English 6, Lesson 103*)

Worksheet 63
Diagraming Adverbs of Degree

Diagram these sentences in the space below.
1. It was uncomfortably cold there.
2. A modern jet travels exceedingly fast.
3. Mary Lynn always writes quite neatly.
4. Motorists should never drive too fast.
5. The colorful sunset is especially beautiful tonight.
6. The children are unusually quiet today.
7. A boil can be intensely painful.
8. The attendance is unusually low tonight.
9. The climate of tropical lowlands is extremely warm.
10. Gwen's letters are certainly interesting and informative.
11. Your completely clear directions saved us much time.
12. There we saw many beautifully carved pieces.

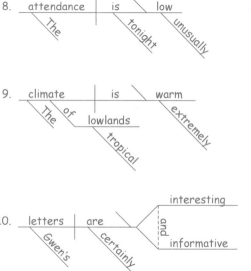

(*Certainly* may be diagramed under *interesting* or just before the compound predicate adjective.)

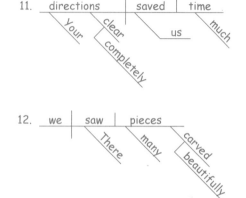

Name _____

(*English 6, Lesson 104*)

Worksheet 64

Rhythm in Poetry

A. Mark the rhythm pattern in the first line of each poem.

1.   **Do Not Stand Idle**

/ ˘ ˘ / ˘ ˘ / ˘ ˘ /
Do not stand idle, there's work to be done;
Don't make excuses, we need ev'ryone;
When all are willing the labor to share,
How it will lighten the load that we bear.

Think of Jerusalem's broken-down wall,
When Nehemiah came calling for all
Who had a mind to work—who would not stop
Until that wall was repaired to the top!

2.   **A Kitten**

˘ / ˘ / ˘ / ˘ /
A kitten isn't very big,
    She doesn't need much care:
A dish of milk, a mouse or two,
    A pillow or a chair.

But if you hold her gently,
    And softly stroke her fur,
She'll start her little motor,
    And she'll purr,
            and purr,
                and purr!

3.   **The Owl**

/ ˘ / ˘ / ˘ /
Folks who hear my call at night
    Often say it causes fright;
The impression that I'm wise
    Comes from seeing my big eyes.

4.   **I Am Nearing the Port**

˘ ˘ / ˘ ˘ / ˘ ˘ / ˘ ˘ /
I am nearing the port, I will soon be at home,
    And the voyage of life will be o'er;
And beneath the high arches of heaven's bright dome
    I shall dwell with my friends gone before.

B. Underline the correct words.
    1. The rhythm pattern of poem 2 above is (iambic, trochaic).
    2. The rhythm pattern of poem 3 above is (iambic, trochaic).

Name _____   *(English 6, Lesson 105)*

Worksheet 65
Forms of Comparison for Adverbs

A. Write the comparative and superlative degrees of each adverb.

1. well   _____better_____   _____best_____
2. close   _____closer_____   _____closest_____
3. quickly   _____more quickly_____   _____most quickly_____
4. much   _____more_____   _____most_____
5. ill   _____worse_____   _____worst_____
6. quietly   _____more quietly_____   _____most quietly_____
7. early   _____earlier_____   _____earliest_____
8. far   _____farther_____   _____farthest_____

B. In each blank, write the correct form of the adverb in parentheses.

____closer____   1. We are (close) to our goal today than we were yesterday.

____better____   2. Your paper today was done (well) than the paper you did yesterday.

___farthest___   3. Of all the pupils, we have to walk the (far).

__more wisely__   4. Be sure to use your time (wisely) this morning than you did yesterday morning.

more heartily   5. The students in sixth grade sing (heartily) than the students in seventh grade.

__more loudly__   6. The later it became, the (loudly) the baby cried.

__most slowly__   7. Of all the cows in the herd, this one walks (slowly).

__more easily__   8. When the men put the refrigerator on rollers, they could move it (easily) than before.

C. Underline the correct words in parentheses.
  1. Who arrived (<u>earliest</u>, most earliest) of all the students?
  2. We have to drive (<u>farther</u>, more farther) now than we did before.
  3. I think he works (<u>harder</u>, more harder) than some who get higher grades.
  4. If we go that way, we will probably get there (later, <u>latest</u>) of all.
  5. This road was torn up (more badly, <u>worse</u>) than the other road.

Name _____

Good, Well, and Negative Words

A. Underline the correct words in parentheses.
1. Your book report was (<u>good</u>, well).
2. I'm glad my baby brother is behaving so (good, <u>well</u>) this morning.
3. This iced tea tastes (<u>good</u>, well) on a hot day.
4. My grandmother had flu, but she is feeling (good, <u>well</u>) again.
5. It's hard to keep from worrying when Grandma isn't (good, <u>well</u>).
6. There aren't (<u>any</u>, none) of those cookie bars left.
7. I didn't see (<u>anyone</u>, no one) at the nurse's station.
8. We (<u>could</u>, couldn't) scarcely see through the thick forest.
9. It seemed no boys (<u>could</u>, couldn't) be found to do the evening chores.
10. I don't see (<u>any</u>, none) that are correct.

B. Rewrite each sentence correctly in two ways.
1. I don't have none of those sheets.

   I don't have any of those sheets.

   I have none of those sheets.

2. We couldn't see no one at the desk.

   We couldn't see anyone at the desk.

   We could see no one at the desk.

3. The mailman didn't put nothing into our mailbox.

   The mailman didn't put anything into our mailbox.

   The mailman put nothing into our mailbox.

C. Write each sentence correctly, using *barely, hardly,* and *scarcely.*
1. We can't hardly lift that heavy desk.

   We can hardly lift that heavy desk.

2. It seemed that we weren't scarcely moving.

   It seemed that we were scarcely moving.

3. I don't have barely enough money to buy the book.

   I have barely enough money to buy the book.

Name _____   *(English 6, Lesson 107)*

Worksheet 67
Prepositional Phrases as Adverbs

A. Underline each adverb phrase. Draw an arrow from the phrase to the word or phrase it modifies.

1. John Sutter built a sawmill in California.

2. In a stream some men found shiny yellow specks.

3. The men had found gold in the area!

4. Soon many eager men journeyed over the Rocky Mountains for gold.

5. Some adventurous people took ships around South America.

6. A good route across Panama was needed for a shorter trip.

7. In 1882, a canal was started across Panama by a Frenchman.

8. But too many mosquitoes lived in the swamps, and the project could not be completed.

9. After some time, President Theodore Roosevelt was attracted by the idea.

10. The United States made an agreement with Panama in 1903.

11. Many workers from the United States went to Panama and worked on the canal.

12. A renowned doctor wiped out yellow fever in Panama.

13. He had wiped it out in Cuba after the Spanish-American War.

14. Mosquitoes live in swampy places, so the men drained the swamps.

15. In a few years, the canal was completed.

16. The *SS Ancon* was the first ship that made a complete trip through the canal.

17. Now many ships cross Panama through the canal.

18. They carry many things between the Atlantic and Pacific oceans.

B. On other paper, diagram numbers 1–6 of Part A.   (Numbers 3–6 are on page T–649)

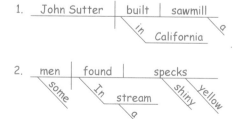

Name _____

Worksheet 68
Rhyme in Poetry

A. Underline each pair of rhyming words, and connect them with a line. The first pair is done for you.

1. **In October**

    There's a brightness in October:
      She has skies of azure blue,
    Harvest gold and frosts of silver,
      Painted leaves of crimson hue.

    There's a crispness in October:
      Feel her pleasant, nippy breeze,
    Bursting seedpods, dropping apples,
      Rustling fodder, swaying trees.

    There's a beauty in October:
      From each garden plot and field,
    We have filled our shelves and freezers,
      Barns and cribs with harvest yield.

    How we love each hour and minute
      Of these bright October days.
    Joyfully we lift our voices
      In the great Creator's praise.

2. **Butterfly**

    I see a yellow butterfly.
    He flits down low, then soars so high!
      He's like a dancing, flashing flower;
      I love to watch him by the hour!
    God made his colors, gave him wings,
    All decked with scallops, dots, and rings!
    —Edith Witmer

3. **Chase Away Drizzles**

    When it drizzles and drizzles,
      If we cheerfully smile,
    We can make the weather,
    By working together,
      As fair as we choose in a little while.
    For who will notice that clouds are drear
    If pleasant faces are always near,
    And who will remember that skies are gray
    If he carries a happy heart all day?

B. Match the numbers of the stanzas above to their rhyming patterns. There is one extra pattern.

   __2__ aabbcc   _____ ababcdcd   __3__ abccbddee   __1__ abcb

3. men │ had found │ gold │ The │ in │ the │ area

4. men │ journeyed │ many │ eager │ Soon │ over │ the │ Rocky Mountains │ for │ gold

5. people │ took │ ships │ Some │ adventurous │ around │ South America

6. route │ was needed │ A │ good │ across │ Panama │ for │ trip │ a │ shorter

Name _____

(English 6, Lesson 109)

Distinguishing Adverbs and Adjectives

In each blank, write *adj.* or *adv.* to tell what part of speech the underlined word or phrase is.

adj.   1. The freshly poured concrete became <u>hard</u> soon.

adv.   2. The men worked <u>hard</u> all day.

adj.   3. The visitor felt <u>lonely</u>.

adj.   4. The bread was <u>hard</u> and dry.

adv.   5. Leon felt so dizzy that he couldn't walk <u>straight</u>.

adj.   6. A carpenter works with many <u>straight</u> lines.

adj.   7. The fence <u>around the school yard</u> needs to be repaired.

adv.   8. The children played tag <u>in the yard</u>.

adv.   9. We will not go <u>into the house</u> before suppertime.

adj.   10. The tree <u>beside the road</u> fell during the storm.

adj.   11. The frost made a lovely pattern <u>of ice</u> on the window.

adv.   12. <u>In Bible times</u>, people often wrote their names

adj.   at the beginning <u>of their letters</u>.

adj.   13. For devotions we read about the miracles <u>of Jesus</u>.

adv.   14. Our belief is based <u>on the teaching</u> of the Bible.

adv.   15. The second shelf was filled <u>with books</u>.

adv.   16. We will move <u>in the spring</u> of next year.

adj.   17. Elijah stayed with a widow <u>of Zarephath</u>.

adj.   18. The sign <u>along the road</u> showed that we were going the right way.

adv.   19. The children were working diligently <u>on that afternoon</u>.

adj.   20. We took umbrellas along because of the dark clouds <u>in the sky</u>.

adv.   21. Mother took a meal <u>to the family</u> whose barn burned.

adj.   22. The story <u>in this book</u> happened in Switzerland.

adv.   23. This flashlight would shine <u>brightly</u> if it had new batteries.

adv.   24. After the lad gave his lunch <u>to Jesus</u>, many people were fed.

Name _____

Worksheet 70
Adverb Clauses

A. Put parentheses around each adverb clause. Underline the conjunction, and draw an arrow from it to the word that the clause modifies.

1. (<u>Although</u> the rain was pouring down,) the Rebers left for the zoo.

2. (<u>After</u> several hours had passed,) the storm finally was over.

3. (<u>When</u> the sun came out again,) they saw many animals in outdoor cages.

4. (<u>Since</u> it rained,) the grass looks greener.

5. I have not found the basket (<u>since</u> it rained.)

6. I will send the directions (<u>after</u> I hear from you.)

7. I swept the floor (<u>before</u> she washed the dishes.)

8. I will go later (<u>unless</u> you are ready now.)

9. Nevin will leave (<u>when</u> Larry comes.)

10. You may use my lawn mower (<u>if</u> you fill it with gasoline.)

11. (<u>If</u> the sun shines,) the snowman will melt.

12. Fresh green moss grows well here (<u>because</u> a creek flows nearby.)

13. It is dark and cool here (<u>because</u> there are large pine branches overhead.)

14. Three little mice scurried into their hole (<u>when</u> a large cat came by.)

B. Diagram numbers 1–6 of Part A.

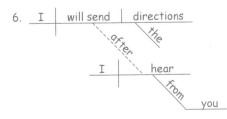

(In outdoor cages may be diagramed under saw.)

Name _____

Worksheet 71
Simple, Compound, and Complex Sentences

A. Underline the dependent clause in each sentence. Write *adj.* or *adv.* in the blank to tell whether it is an adjective clause or an adverb clause.

__adj.__ 1. That maple tree, <u>which still has its leaves</u>, was planted by Grandfather.

__adj.__ 2. Neighbors helped the family <u>whose basement was flooded</u>.

__adv.__ 3. <u>When Jesus comes</u>, we will rejoice.

__adv.__ 4. We love Him <u>because He first loved us</u>.

__adj.__ 5. Jesus' death on Calvary is proof <u>that He loves us</u>.

__adv.__ 6. The people in Galilee received Jesus <u>because they had seen His miracles</u>.

B. Underline the word that connects the two clauses in each sentence. Write *C, S,* or *R* in the blank to tell whether the connecting word is a coordinating conjunction, a subordinating conjunction, or a relative pronoun.

__R__ 1. A nobleman <u>whose</u> son was sick came to Jesus.

__C__ 2. The man believed Jesus' word, <u>and</u> his son was healed immediately.

__S__ 3. <u>Because</u> Jesus healed a man on the Sabbath, the Jews found fault with Him.

__R__ 4. God is the One <u>who</u> made heaven and earth.

__C__ 5. Abraham pleased God, <u>but</u> Lot was selfish.

__R__ 6. He <u>that</u> hateth his brother is in darkness.

C. Write the letter of the correct formula for each sentence.

   a. S | V = simple sentence
   b. S | V + S | V = compound sentence
   c. S | V + S | V = complex sentence

__b__ 1. Blue whales look like huge fish, but they are mammals.

__c__ 2. Whales come to the surface from time to time for air because they have lungs.

__a__ 3. God gave blue whales some unusual characteristics.

__c__ 4. The blue whale eats plankton, which he strains out of the seawater with the thin, brush-like plates in his mouth.

__a__ 5. These plates are called baleen or whalebone.

__b__ 6. Blue whales are the largest animals in the world, yet they eat some of the tiniest animals in the world.

Name _____

Worksheet 72
Prepositions

A. Find the prepositional phrases. Underline each preposition, and put parentheses around each object.

   Example: You will find the broom <u>beside</u> the (refrigerator).

   1. We parked <u>between</u> two other (cars) <u>along</u> the (street.)

   2. All the cows <u>except</u> (Buttercup) are lying <u>beyond</u> the (stream.)

   3. The ball bounced back <u>to</u> (Vernon) after he threw it <u>against</u> the (wall.)

   4. They always keep their tractor <u>under</u> a (roof) <u>during</u> a (storm.)

   5. <u>By</u> (evening,) the hay bales should all be <u>inside</u> the (barn.)

   6. A load <u>of</u> (bales) was parked <u>beside</u> the (road.)

   7. Our neighbor boy rode past <u>on</u> his (horse.)

   8. There are several time zones <u>throughout</u> the (country.)

   9. Two <u>of</u> my (friends) were <u>aboard</u> the (plane.)

   10. Airplanes often fly <u>above</u> the (clouds.)

   11. She keeps all her dishes <u>except</u> the (bowls) <u>near</u> the (sink.)

   12. Will we pay the toll <u>at</u> the other (side) <u>of</u> the (bridge?)

   13. We have not seen our cousins <u>from</u> (Missouri) <u>since</u> last (winter.)

   14. We looked <u>for</u> some pretty (flowers) <u>among</u> the (weeds.)

   15. The plants were created <u>before</u> the (animals.)

   16. Esau pleaded <u>with</u> his (father) <u>for</u> a (blessing.)

   17. <u>After</u> twenty (years) <u>at</u> the (home) <u>of</u> (Laban,) Jacob returned <u>to</u> (Canaan.)

   18. The false prophets called <u>to</u> (Baal) <u>from</u> (morning) <u>until</u> (evening.)

   19. Jonah called <u>upon</u> the (Lord) when he was <u>inside</u> the (whale.)

   20. The Bible teaches us <u>about</u> (life) <u>after</u> (death.)

   21. David put a stone <u>into</u> his (sling) and ran <u>toward</u> (Goliath.)

   22. <u>From</u> the (temple) Hezekiah <u>prayed</u> to (God.)

B. Write four different prepositions that could fit in each blank.   (Sample answers.)
   1. Thomas found an old coin ——— the chest.

   ___in___   ___inside___   ___beneath___   ___under___   (on, beside, above)

   2. The flowers ——— the house are tulips.

   ___near___   ___beside___   ___along___   ___behind___   (around)

Name _____   *(English 6, Lesson 116)*

Worksheet 73
Using Prepositions Correctly

Cross out each incorrect word. If another word should be used instead, write the correct word above it. Not every sentence needs a correction.

1. Mother was listening ~~on~~ to Lynn while Lynn was talking ~~at~~ to Aunt Martha on the telephone.

2. The frogs always jump ~~in~~ into the pond when we walk ~~in back of~~ behind them.

3. Everyone was here ~~accept~~ except Anita.

4. Uncle David would not ~~except~~ accept pay for his work on our house.

5. We divided the cookies ~~between~~ among the six children.

6. You may sit here ~~among~~ between Mary and me or ~~besides~~ beside Joy.

7. We had nothing ~~beside~~ besides apples for lunch.

8. This textbook is different ~~than~~ from the one we had last year.

9. We put the fudge ~~among~~ between the two layers of the cake.

10. It was so warm that I was glad when the meeting was over ~~with.~~

11. Mother is inside ~~of~~ the house.

12. Whom are you working with?   (no correction needed)

13. Please stay off ~~of~~ the wet paint.

14. I was busy and did not see where the boys went ~~to.~~

15. Where did you put your paintbrush ~~at?~~

16. You must ~~of~~ have gotten my brush.

17. I should ~~of~~ have brought a brush; then I could ~~of~~ have helped.

18. The brush I painted with was a good one.   (no correction needed)

Name _____

Worksheet 74
Coordinating Conjunctions

A. Underline the coordinating and correlative conjunctions. Write whether they join words (*W*), phrases (*P*), or clauses (*C*).

_W_   1. The wild roses, pink <u>and</u> dainty, are blooming again.

_P_   2. Did you catch this bass in the creek <u>or</u> in the pond?

_W_   3. <u>Either</u> a robin <u>or</u> a thrush is singing that beautiful song.

_C_   4. The young boy was small, <u>but</u> he was strong.

_W_   5. The sheepskin blanket was soft <u>and</u> warm.

_W_   6. He is <u>neither</u> a farmer <u>nor</u> a carpenter.

_P_   7. Did you eat in the house <u>or</u> in the yard?

_W_   8. <u>Not only</u> eggs <u>but also</u> chickens are sold there.

_C_   9. We sold produce, <u>and</u> they sold baked goods.

_W_ 10. Bring <u>either</u> an umbrella <u>or</u> a raincoat.

B. Underline the correct words so that parallel sentence parts are joined.

1. Swiftly and (<u>silently</u>, in silence) the owl flew through the night sky.

2. Uncle John will leave (tomorrow, <u>on Thursday</u>) or on Friday.

3. The balloon floated over the trees, into the sky, and (disappeared, <u>out of sight</u>).

4. We swept the living room, the dining room, and (<u>the kitchen</u>, swept the kitchen).

5. Then we mopped the floors, washed the walls, and (the windows, <u>washed the windows</u>).

C. Add the missing commas.

1. An oriole's song sounds somewhat like a robin's, but the oriole's song is louder and more bell-like.

2. The silver pouchlike nest swings and sways in every breeze, but the baby birds are perfectly safe inside.

D. Underline the correct words in parentheses.

1. A mother oriole uses not only milkweed fibers, hair, and grapevine bark (but, <u>but also</u>) yarn.

2. Either the orioles or the robin (take, <u>takes</u>) the purple yarn that Mother hangs on the clothesline.

3. Either the white yarn or the milkweed fibers (<u>give</u>, gives) that nest an unusual texture.

Name _____

Worksheet 75
Subordinating Conjunctions

Put parentheses around each dependent clause, and underline the subordinating conjunction that introduces it.

Example: I hope I am here (<u>when</u> the cocoons hatch).

1. One butterfly had hatched (<u>before</u> the children got to school.)

2. Its wings looked small and crumpled (<u>after</u> it hatched.)

3. (<u>As</u> the children watched,) the newly hatched butterfly began pumping its wings.

4. The butterfly must pump its wings (<u>because</u> they are not dry and strong.)

5. The wrinkles disappear (<u>after</u> the butterfly fans its wings awhile.)

6. (<u>When</u> the children put the butterfly outside,) it sat there for a long time.

7. We will watch (<u>until</u> the butterfly flies away.)

8. The butterfly flew away (<u>after</u> a few hours passed.)

9. They were fat green caterpillars with gold dots (<u>when</u> Ronald had first brought them.)

10. (<u>When</u> each chrysalis was spun,) it was silky green with golden dots.

11. (<u>After</u> they finished spinning,) they did not change for a long time.

12. They will not hatch (<u>before</u> they are fully developed.)

13. (<u>If</u> you do not know what kind it is,) look it up in the butterfly book.

14. The children decided they were monarch butterflies (<u>after</u> they had looked it up.)

15. The first butterfly flew away (<u>while</u> the children watched the second one hatch.)

16. (<u>As</u> the second one opened,) a swallowtail butterfly also started coming out of its chrysalis.

17. They hatch in the spring (<u>unless</u> they have died during the winter.)

18. I have not seen any (<u>since</u> you let yours go.)

19. They are not (<u>where</u> we left them.)

20. (<u>Because</u> it is late,) we will omit the science quiz.

Name _____

Worksheet 76
Avoiding Misplaced Phrases and Clauses

Underline each misplaced phrase or clause. Draw an arrow to show where it belongs in the sentence.

Example: We bought an old chair from the trader <u>that was made of iron</u>.

1. Nevin gave a package to his great-aunt <u>that weighed three pounds</u>.

2. The boy went to the doctor <u>with the sore throat</u>.

3. Grandmother gave cookies to the children <u>with nuts</u>.

4. The teacher said <u>on Monday</u> we would give book reports.
   (or The teacher said we would give book reports <u>on Monday</u>.*)*

5. Robert saw a large black dog <u>on his way to school</u>.

6. The report was given <u>about the earthquake</u> by the boys <u>in California</u>.
   (like this: The report <u>about the earthquake in California</u> was given by the boys.*)*

7. Julia saw a drawing done by Gloria <u>on the wall</u>.

8. That photograph is the one Jacob took <u>on the first page of the photo album</u>.

9. The speaker from British Columbia told us about logging <u>in the afternoon</u>.

10. The deer jumped over the fence <u>with a graceful bound</u>.

11. The tall boy caught a muskrat <u>which had a blue shirt</u>.

12. The man bought a new fan <u>with a brown suit</u>.

13. The diagrams interested the students <u>that are on the bulletin board</u>.

14. The train stopped and unloaded the cattle <u>with twenty cars</u>.

15. The boy received several cards <u>with a broken leg</u>.

16. A priest could not serve in the tabernacle <u>with a lame foot or a crippled hand</u>.

17. I read about the missionary who went to West Virginia <u>in my new book</u>.

18. The chickens were fed and watered by my sister <u>in the chicken house</u>.

19. My brother was punished when the expensive tool was lost <u>by my father</u>.

20. There is a letter from your cousin <u>in the mailbox</u>.

21. We learned about the migration of birds <u>in science class</u>.

22. He caught the two white rabbits that had been running around in the woods <u>with his trap</u>.

23. The teachers saw the maintenance crew mowing the lawn <u>from the window</u>.

24. <u>In the creek</u> I saw that the water was dangerously high.

Name _____   *(English 6, Lesson 122)*

Worksheet 77
Interjections

A. Underline each interjection, and add the missing punctuation after it. Also underline the first letter of the next word if it should be capitalized.

1. Oh! there's a rattlesnake in the path!

2. Why, I didn't see that other patch of blueberries.

3. What! don't we have extra scissors?

4. Say, did you hear what happened to Jason?

5. Alas! he fell in and could not get out.

6. Why, I must have forgotten all about it.

7. Oh, what a beautiful sunset it is!

8. Ouch! that must have been a live coal.

9. Behold, what manner of man is this, that even the wind and the sea obey Him!

10. Ho, every one that thirsteth, come ye to the waters.

11. Lo, they are written in the book of the kings of Israel and Judah.

12. "Ah, Thou that destroyest the temple and buildest it in three days, save Thyself," said Jesus' enemies.

B. Diagram these sentences.
   1. Whew! The water in this mountain stream is cold!
   2. Say, do you know the way to the Zion Church?
   3. Ouch! I pinched my finger in the door.
   4. Well, those primroses certainly look beautiful.

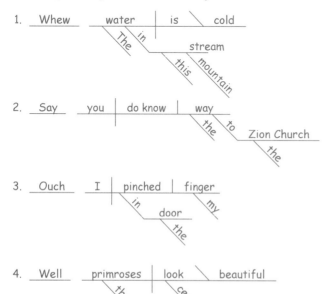

Name _____

Worksheet 78
Review of the Parts of Speech

A. Write the abbreviation for each part of speech described below.

____v.____ 1. It shows action or being.

____n.____ 2. It names a person, place, thing, or idea.

____prep.____ 3. It is a connecting word that begins a phrase.

____adj.____ 4. It tells *which, whose, how many,* or *what kind of.*

____conj.____ 5. It joins words, phrases, or clauses.

____adj.____ 6. It modifies a noun or pronoun.

____adj.____ 7. It may be limiting or descriptive.

____adv.____ 8. It modifies a verb, adjective, or adverb.

____interj.____ 9. It expresses strong feeling.

____pron.____ 10. It takes the place of a noun.

____adj.____ 11. It may be an article (*a, an,* or *the*).

____adv.____ 12. It tells *how, when, where,* or *to what degree.*

B. Above each word, write the abbreviation for the part of speech.

   interj. v. adv. adj.   n.   v.   v. prep. adj.   n.   conj. pron. v.   v.
1. Oh! See how the weeds have grown in my garden since I was gone.

   prep. adj. adj.   n.   prep.   n.   adj.   n.   v.   n.   adj. conj. adj. prep. adj. adj.   n.
2. In the new settlement in Paraguay, the workers had water, cold and fresh, from a new well.

   interj. adj.   n.   v.   adv. prep. adj. adj.   n.   conj.   v.   prep. adj.   n.   adv. (*or* adj.)
3. Alas! A kitten fell down into the new well and landed on a ledge inside.

   adv. adj. adj.   n.   v.   adv. conj.   v.   adj. adj.   n.
4. Soon a young man climbed down and rescued the poor kitten.

   adj.   n.   v. adj. n.   conj. pron. v.   adv. v.   adj. adj.   n.   adj.   n.
5. The girls set a trap, but they did not catch the large lizard that way.

   interj.   conj.   adj.   adj.   n.   v.   adj. adj.   n.   pron.   v.   pron. v.   n.
6. What! When the American girl tasted the lizard meat, she thought it was chicken.

   n.   v.   adj.   n.   adj.   n.   conj. adj.   n.   conj. pron.   v.   adj.   n.
7. Jesus healed the blind, the deaf, and the lame, and He raised the dead.

Name _____   (*English 6, Lesson 125*)

Worksheet 79
Dictionary Practice

A. Make a sentence by writing these words in alphabetical order. Use correct capitalization and punctuation.

with, to, weekly, Samuel, stamps, Uncle, sent, Yvonne, several, Vincent

_____Samuel sent several stamps to Uncle Vincent weekly with Yvonne._____

_____

B. Write *X* before each entry word that you would find on a dictionary page with the guide words *bear* and *coney.*

_____ 1. cuckoo	_____ 6. cormorant
___X___ 2. chameleon	___X___ 7. caterpillar
_____ 3. badger	_____ 8. bat
___X___ 4. beetle	___X___ 9. cockatrice
___X___ 5. camel	

C. Write the phonetic spelling of each word. Include the syllable divisions and accent marks.
(Phonetic symbols may vary.)

1. picturesque _____pik′·chə·resk′_____

2. typhoon _____tī·fün′_____

3. buoyant _____boi′·ənt_____

4. querulous _____kwer′·(y)ə·ləs_____

5. hypothesis _____hī·poth′·i·sis_____

D. Write the correct spelling for each phonetic spelling.

1. ir	_____ear_____	5. thôt	_____thought_____
2. snēz	_____sneeze_____	6. tekst	_____text_____
3. slīt	_____slight_____	7. gärd	_____guard_____
4. brüd	_____brood_____	8. frāt	_____freight_____

Name _____

Worksheet 80
More Dictionary Practice

A. Write the plural form of each word.

   1. gentleman   _____gentlemen_____   3. chassis   _____chassis_____

   2. bucketful   _____bucketfuls_____   4. igloo   _____igloos_____

B. Write the second and third principal parts of each verb, as shown in the dictionary.

   1. shrink   _____shrank *or* shrunk_____   _____(have) shrunk *or* (have) shrunken_____

   2. tear   _____tore_____   _____(have) torn_____

   3. spin   _____spun_____   _____(have) spun_____

   4. tread   _____trod_____   _____(have) trodden *or* (have) trod_____

C. Write the forms of comparison for these adjectives and adverbs.

   1. good   _____better_____   _____best_____

   2. ill   _____worse_____   _____worst_____

   3. far   _____farther_____   _____farthest_____

D. Write the other correct spelling for each word.

   1. encyclopedia _____encyclopaedia_____   3. woolly   _____wooly_____

   2. infold   _____enfold_____   4. indorse   _____endorse_____

F. Write the letter of the best meaning for each underlined word.

patch	**land**
a. a piece used to mend a hole	e. ground; soil
b. a small piece of ground	f. country; region
c. to mend a hole	g. to bring to solid ground
d. to assemble quickly	h. to arrive

   ___c___ 1. The road workers were <u>patching</u> the highway.

   ___b___ 2. Gerald was working in the potato <u>patch</u>.

   ___d___ 3. The traveler <u>patched</u> together a shelter for the night.

   ___a___ 4. Mother needs to put a <u>patch</u> on these trousers.

   ___g___ 5. The pilot safely <u>landed</u> the damaged airplane.

   ___h___ 6. Philip broke his leg and <u>landed</u> in the hospital.

   ___e___ 7. This is good <u>land</u> for farming.

   ___f___ 8. We are thankful to live in a <u>land</u> of freedom.

Name _____   *(English 6, Lesson 128)*

Worksheet 81
Sentence Variety in Paragraphs

A. Improve the paragraph below by the following directions.
1. Combine sentences *b* and *c* into a compound sentence. _____

    They had been out fishing all night, but they caught nothing. _____

2. Change sentence *d* to mixed word order. _____

    In the morning the disciples did not recognize Jesus standing on the seashore. _____

3. Combine sentences *f* and *g* into a complex sentence. _____

    Imagine their astonishment when they caught 153 great fishes without breaking the net! _____

4. Change sentence *i* to inverted word order. (Begin with *over.*) _____

    Over a fire were laid fish and bread. _____

   [a]Jesus surprised His disciples early one morning by the Sea of Galilee. [b]They had been out fishing all night. [c]They caught nothing. [d]The disciples did not recognize Jesus standing on the seashore in the morning. [e]He told them to cast the net on the right side of the ship. [f]Imagine their astonishment. [g]They caught 153 great fishes without breaking the net! [h]They came to shore and saw that breakfast was ready. [i]Fish and bread were laid over a fire. [j]"Come and dine," Jesus called the disciples. [k]They knew by this time that it was Jesus.

B. The following paragraphs contain all declarative sentences. Rewrite the paragraphs on the blanks below or on other paper. Change at least three sentences to imperative sentences. Also rewrite one underlined sentence as an interrogative sentence, and one as an exclamatory sentence.

   Trapping raccoons requires skill and know-how. First, you must have some good traps. Then you must choose a good place to set your traps. If the raccoons are eating your sweet corn, you should set a trap right in the sweet corn row. You should wear gloves to set your traps. Raccoons are smart, and they won't come near a trap that has your scent on it.

   You can also set traps in other places where raccoons travel. <u>You may wonder what kind of bait to use.</u> One good kind is fish. You should dig a shallow hole in a good place, bait your trap with fish, and set it in the hole. Then you should brush some dirt over the trap with a whisk broom. You should check your traps every day. <u>You may not believe it, but you will probably get some raccoon skins.</u>

(Sample paragraphs; changed sentences underlined.)

   Trapping raccoons requires skill and know-how. First, you must have some good traps. Then

   you must choose a good place to set your traps. If the raccoons are eating your sweet corn,

   set a trap right in the sweet corn row. You should wear gloves to set your traps. Raccoons are

   smart, and they won't come near a trap that has your scent on it.

   You can also set traps in other places where raccoons travel. What kind of bait should you

   use? One good kind is fish. Dig a shallow hole in a good place, bait your trap with fish, and

   set it in the hole. Then brush some dirt over the trap with a whisk broom. Check your traps

   every day. Believe it or not, you will probably get some raccoon skins!

   _____

Name _____

Worksheet 82

Synonyms, Antonyms, and Homophones

A. Match the synonyms.

    c   1. mistake   a. mixture

    a   2. combination   b. display

    d   3. discern   c. error

    b   4. flaunt   d. perceive

B. Match the antonyms.

    d   1. noisy   a. neat

    a   2. disorderly   b. cheerful

    c   3. sound   c. sickly

    b   4. discontent   d. silent

C. Match the homophones.

    c   1. knew   a. meet

    b   2. hole   b. whole

    d   3. straight   c. new

    a   4. meat   d. strait

D. Write whether the words in each pair are synonyms (*S*), antonyms (*A*), or homophones (*H*).

    A   1. flammable, fireproof   A   5. brightness, dimness

    H   2. lee, lea   S   6. material, substance

    S   3. lie, falsehood   A   7. fearful, brave

    H   4. he'll, heal   H   8. night, knight

E. Underline the homophones that properly complete these sentences.

1. (Your, <u>You're</u>) invited (<u>to</u>, too, two) be our (<u>guest</u>, guessed) today.
2. On the way (hear, <u>here</u>) we drove (passed, <u>past</u>) many orchards.
3. (There, <u>Their</u>, They're) (to, too, <u>two</u>) rocking chairs both (creek, <u>creak</u>).
4. Do you (<u>know</u>, no) the (hole, <u>whole</u>) verse by memory?
5. (Its, <u>It's</u>) (to, <u>too</u>, two) cold to remain outside for long.
6. (Right, <u>Write</u>) the date at the top of (<u>your</u>, you're) paper.
7. The man took out a (lone, <u>loan</u>) to (by, <u>buy</u>) a (<u>new</u>, knew) car.
8. The (led, <u>lead</u>) in my pencil (<u>breaks</u>, brakes) (to, <u>too</u>, two) often.
9. A pigeon suddenly (<u>flew</u>, flu, flue) out of the (flew, flu, <u>flue</u>).
10. Aunt Martha was (dying, <u>dyeing</u>) some clothes (<u>blue</u>, blew).

Progressing With Courage

Chapter 1 Test   Score _____

Name _____ Date _____

A. Write the definition of each word, as used in studying English.

1. sentence _____

    _A sentence is a group of words that expresses a complete thought._____

2. skeleton _____

    _A skeleton is a simple subject and a simple predicate together._____

3. clause _____

    _A clause is a group of words that has a skeleton (or a subject and a verb)._____

(3 points)

B. Write the name of the sentence type described by each sentence: *declarative, interrogative, imperative,* or *exclamatory.*

____declarative____   4. It states a fact and ends with a period.

____exclamatory____   5. It expresses strong feeling and ends with an exclamation point.

____interrogative____   6. It asks a question and ends with a question mark.

____imperative____   7. It gives a command or request and ends with a period.

____imperative____   8. The subject is *you,* but it is not usually stated.

____declarative____   9. It is either true or false.

____exclamatory____   10. It may have its own special form, such as the skeleton coming at the end.

(7 points)

C. Write whether each sentence is *declarative, interrogative, imperative,* or *exclamatory.* Also add the correct end punctuation.

____interrogative____   11. Are most of the people in South America Indians?

____declarative____   12. Some of the countries have mostly white people.

____imperative____   13. Look it up in an encyclopedia.

____exclamatory____   14. What a large number of people live there!

(4 points)

D. Describe each group of words by writing *S* for sentence or *F* for fragment in the first blank. If it is a fragment, in the second blank write the letter that tells why it is a fragment. Choose from the letters below.

a. Subject is missing.

b. Predicate is missing.

c. Both subject and predicate are missing.

d. Helping verb is missing.

e. It has a subject and predicate, but thought is incomplete.

f. Direct object is missing.

<u>F</u> <u>d</u> 15. My uncle living in Arizona.

<u>F</u> <u>c</u> 16. Down the trail in one day.

<u>F</u> <u>b</u> 17. Mountains and plateaus.

<u>F</u> <u>a</u> 18. Make up more than half the country.

<u>F</u> <u>e</u> 19. Because so many Indians live there.

<u>F</u> <u>f</u> 20. Every day we are finding.

<u>S</u> <u> </u> 21. Because my pictures didn't come back in time, I couldn't show them to my friends.

(7 points)

E. Put parentheses around any prepositional phrase in the complete subject. Draw two lines under the simple predicate, and one line under the simple subject. Draw a dividing line between the complete subject and the complete predicate. (Count 2 points for each skeleton and 1 point for each prepositional phrase in the complete subject.)

22. Blue-green <u>algae</u> | <u>are</u> a kind of bacteria.

23. <u>Lakes</u> (with this algae) | <u>look</u> bluish green.

24. <u>Algin</u> | <u>is made</u> from brown algae.

25. <u>It</u> | <u>is</u> often <u>used</u> in ice cream, mayonnaise, and other products.

26. The <u>Statue of Liberty</u> | <u>was</u> a gift from France.

27. <u>Sister Julia</u> | <u>will</u> not <u>be teaching</u> this class tomorrow.

28. <u>Hot dogs</u> | <u>are</u> an American food.

29. <u>Some</u> (of our foods) | <u>are</u> Italian.

(18 points)

F. Write *T* if the sentence is true and *F* if the sentence is false.

___T___   30. A good story is written about a problem someone or something had.

___F___   31. Variety in sentence beginnings and lengths will confuse your reader.

___T___   32. Written directions must be given even more clearly than spoken directions.

___F___   33. *Which, whose,* and *how many* are the main facts you must tell in a story. (The main facts are *who, what, when, where, why,* and *how.*)

___F___   34. If you are not sure of the directions you are writing, you should make your best guess.

___T___   35. Making a list of steps before you write directions will help you to keep things in order.

(6 points)

Total points: 45

Progressing With Courage

Chapter 2 Test   Score _____

Name _____ **Date** _____

A. Write six common conjunctions.

_____and_____   _____but_____   _____or_____   _____for_____   _____nor_____   _____yet_____

(2 points)

B. Do the following things with the sentences below.

   a. Write the formula for each sentence. Use *S* for each simple subject, *V* for each verb (simple predicate), + for each conjunction, and | to divide subjects and predicates.
   b. Be sure each formula tells whether the sentence is simple or compound.
   c. Add commas where they are needed in the sentences.

(Count 2 points for each formula and 1 point for each comma.)

1. Grizzly bears have long claws, and they dig out squirrels and mice with them.

   Formula: _S | V + S | V = compound_____

2. Some children and even grownups are overly frightened of these bears.

   Formula: _S + S | V = simple_____

3. White hairs grow in their brown coats and give them a grizzled (gray-streaked) appearance.

   Formula: _S | V + V = simple_____

4. Some people called them grizzled bears, but others called them silvertip bears.

   Formula: _S | V + S | V = compound_____

(10 points)

C. Correct the run-on errors by following the directions in parentheses.

5. (Add the missing period after each sentence. Cross out each incorrect small letter, and write a capital letter above it.)

   The leopard is an excellent climber. $\overset{H}{\text{h}}$e is strong enough to carry loads heavier than himself. $\overset{H}{\text{h}}$e often stores his kill in the fork of a tree.

6. (Write a suitable conjunction in each blank, and add the missing commas where they belong.)

    a. One leopard was caught in a trap, he bent the iron jaw back with his free paw and got away! _____ but _____

    b. Leopards' coats vary in shades from tan to black, every leopard has his own individual pattern of spots. _____ and _____

7. (Add a semicolon to each sentence.)

    a. A few leopards are black ; their spots are hard to see.

    b. Albinos are white leopards ; they are even rarer than black leopards.

(5 points)

D. Write *normal, inverted,* or *mixed* to tell in what order each sentence is written.

_____ inverted _____ 8. In Africa are many wild leopards.

_____ mixed _____ 9. Almost from the beginning, leopard cubs learn about hunting.

_____ normal _____ 10. They stalk their mother's moving tail.

_____ mixed _____ 11. Was the black leopard actually hunting his food in broad daylight?

(4 points)

E. Rewrite sentences 12 and 14 in mixed word order. Rewrite sentence 13 in inverted word order.

12. The crafty leopard chased his tail for a while.

    For a while the crafty leopard chased his tail.

13. A curious deer came closer and closer.

    Closer and closer came a curious deer.

14. The leopard had a fine meal soon.

    Soon the leopard had a fine meal.

(3 points)

F. Diagram the sentence skeletons. (Count ½ point for each simple subject or simple predicate.)

15. The Chesapeake Bay divides Maryland almost exactly in half.

Chesapeake Bay | divides

16. Down the mountainside came Moses.

Moses | came

17. Is the post office on this street?

post office | is

18. On the next street is one.

one | is

19. Drop your letters into this slot.

(you) | Drop

20. I was not looking for it and almost missed it.

21. At Greenfield Village in Dearborn, Michigan, you can see museums of Thomas A. Edison's laboratory and the Wright Brothers' bicycle shop.

you | can see

22. Craft shops at Greenfield Village display early American tools.

shops | display

23. Minneapolis and St. Paul are twin cities.

24. Minneapolis lies just across the Mississippi River from St. Paul but is larger than St. Paul.

25. Minneapolis has twenty-two lakes within the city limits, and its name means "City of Lakes."

Minneapolis | has   and   name | means

26. Was Peter casting a net or mending a net?

(15 points)

G. Read the paragraph below, and write *X* before the best topic sentence. Then write *B* before the topic sentence that is too broad, and write *N* before the topic sentence that is too narrow.

   __B__   27. There are some beautiful national parks in the western United States.

   __N__   28. How the Badlands got its name is an interesting story.

   __X__   29. The Badlands region of the western United States is a beautiful, interesting place.

Wind and water have cut the hills and valleys into strange shapes. Some of the stones and clay are very colorful. The Badlands in South Dakota was given that name because it was poor farmland and was difficult to travel through. It did not get its name from the wild characters who sometimes lived there. President Theodore Roosevelt visited the Badlands of North Dakota in 1884. He liked the area so much that he stayed there for two years.

(3 points)

H. Underline the topic sentence and four transitional words in this paragraph. Cross out two sentences that do not belong.

<u>In 1681 William Penn received a piece of wilderness in payment for a debt.</u> King Charles II had owed William's father a large sum of money, and the father had died. <u>So</u> the king now owed the money to William. <u>But</u> William Penn was a Quaker, and the Quakers were persecuted at that time. ~~Other people who disagreed with the Church of England were also persecuted.~~ <u>Therefore</u> William asked to be paid with land in America, where there was freedom of religion. ~~He paid the Indians for the land because he wanted to be fair to them.~~ <u>For</u> he wanted to have a place where people could worship God freely, even though the land was a wilderness!

(7 points)

I. Number the sentences below in the correct order. Be sure to mark the topic sentence first.

   __2__   30. First, my friends are all from Christian homes.

   __5__   31. Above all, in a Christian school I learn many things about God and His Word.

   __3__   32. Second, my teacher is a Christian who tries to help me do what is right.

   __4__   33. Our textbooks also teach what is right according to the Bible, rather than teaching men's ideas.

   __1__   34. There are several reasons why I am glad I go to a Christian school.

(2 points)

J. Would the paragraph for Part I be written in the order of *time* or the order of *importance*?

      __importance__

(1 point)

Total points: 52

Progressing With Courage

Chapter 3 Test   Score _____

Name _____ **Date** _____

A. Write the definition of a noun. <u>A noun is the name of a person, place, thing, or idea.</u>

_____

(1 point)

B. Change each word to a noun by adding the suffix *-ness, -ion, -ity,* or *-ment.*

<u>payment</u> 1. pay   <u>donation</u> 3. donate

<u>greatness</u> 2. great   <u>scarcity *or* scarceness</u> 4. scarce

(4 points)

C. Underline the nouns in these sentences.

5. In <u>Proverbs</u> the <u>Bible</u> says, "A <u>man</u> that hath <u>friends</u> must shew himself friendly."

6. You can ruin a <u>friendship</u> with unkind <u>words.</u>

7. If a <u>person</u> has showed <u>unkindness</u>, he should offer an <u>apology</u> and ask <u>forgiveness.</u>

(10 points)

D. Write *M, F, N,* or *C* to tell whether the gender of each noun is masculine, feminine, neuter, or common.

_F_ 8. princess   _C_ 11. traveler

_C_ 9. servant   _M_ 12. grandfather

_N_ 10. temple

(5 points)

E. Underline each word that should be capitalized because it is a proper noun.

13. The <u>grand coulee dam</u>, the largest concrete dam in the <u>united states</u>, is found in the state of <u>washington.</u>

14. The king of <u>england</u> gave <u>pennsylvania</u> to <u>william penn</u> in 1681.

15. This state has ports on the <u>delaware river</u> and on <u>lake erie.</u>

16. The <u>declaration</u> of <u>independence</u> was signed in <u>independence hall</u> in <u>philadelphia.</u>

(11 points)

F. Underline each word that should be capitalized because it is a proper adjective.

   17. This <u>hershey</u> chocolate comes from the world's largest chocolate factory.

   18. Candy was first made by ancient <u>egyptian</u> and <u>indian</u> people.

   19. Mr. Taylor sells <u>brach's</u> candy and <u>schwan's</u> ice cream.

(5 points)

G. Write the plural form of each noun.

   20. handful   <u>handfuls</u>

   21. mother-in-law   <u>mothers-in-law</u>

   22. police officer   <u>police officers</u>

(3 points)

H. Rewrite these expressions, using possessive forms.

   23. the chairs of the men   <u>the men's chairs</u>

   24. the books of the girls   <u>the girls' books</u>

   25. the story of the chief   <u>the chief's story</u>

   26. the pen of the sheep   <u>the sheep's pen</u>

   27. the eggs of the goose   <u>the goose's eggs</u>

(5 points)

I. Fill in the chart.

Singular	Singular Possessive	Plural	Plural Possessive
28. boy	boy's	boys	boys'
29. alto	alto's	altos	altos'
30. family	family's	families	families'
31. calf	calf's	calves	calves'
32. larva	larva's	larvae *or* larvas	larvae's *or* larvas'

(15 points)

J. Read the paragraphs below, and do these exercises. (Count 2 points for each *X* and 2 points for the topic sentence.)

33. Decide which paragraph is better. Write *X* in the blank before that paragraph, and underline the topic sentence.

34. Write *X* before the phrase that tells how the better paragraph is developed.

_____ a. by giving details in the order of time

___X___ b. by giving examples or illustrations

_____ c. by giving comparisons or contrasts

___X___ **Paragraph A:**

New Mexico has many interesting places to visit. In Santa Fe you can see the Palace of the Governors, the oldest public building in the United States. The state also has many Indian pueblos, which are houses built like apartments on the sides of cliffs or hills. Carlsbad Caverns National Park has many caves from which bats fly in large masses. You can even visit a Mennonite publishing house in New Mexico.

_____ **Paragraph B:**

New Mexico has many interesting places to visit. Many tourists go there. You should take time off and go see the state. My family was in the state once to visit some relatives. We had car trouble there. The engine did not run smoothly, and a mechanic finally found a bad spark plug wire. We really had an enjoyable time in New Mexico.

(6 points)

K. Read the paragraph below, and do these exercises.

35. Write *X* before the correct answers.

    a. This paragraph is developed mainly by

    _____ comparisons.   __X__ contrasts.

    b. Which method is used in this paragraph?
       _____ (1) All the points about the first thing are given, and then all the points about the
                    second thing.
       __X__ (2) The comparisons or contrasts are given in turns, point by point.

36. Underline the sentence that ties the end of the paragraph to the beginning.

37. Write briefly two of the comparisons or contrasts used in the paragraph. (Any two; wording will vary.)

    a. _Pushing a lawn mower gives more exercise than washing dishes._____

       _Dishes are done inside the house, but mowing is done outside._____

    b. _Dishes must be done more often than mowing._____

       _It is easier to see how much mowing was done than how many dishes were washed._____

   Mowing the lawn is more rewarding than washing the dishes. You get much more exercise when
you push a lawn mower than when you wash dishes. Dishes are done inside the house, but mowing
is done outside where you get plenty of fresh air. Dishes must be done every day; mowing has to be
done only once or twice a week. After the dishes are washed and put away, it is hard to tell just
how much work you have done. A nicely mowed lawn clearly shows how much you have accomplished! <u>I would rather mow the lawn than wash the dishes almost any day</u>.

(5 points)

Total points: 70

Progressing With Courage

Chapter 4 Test   Score _____

Name _____ Date _____

A. Write the definition of a verb.   <u>*A verb is a word that shows action or being.*</u>

(1 point)

B. Match by writing one letter in each blank. Some letters will be used more than once.

      a. direct object   c. predicate adjective

      b. indirect object   d. predicate nominative

  <u>d</u>   1. A word that renames the subject.

  <u>a</u>   2. A word that receives action.

 <u>c d</u>   3. A word that follows a linking verb.

 <u>a b</u>   4. A word that follows an action verb.

  <u>c</u>   5. A word in the predicate that describes the subject.

  <u>b</u>   6. A word that follows an action verb and tells *to whom or what* or *for whom or what*.

(8 points)

C. Write the missing principal parts.

First (Present)	Second (Past)	Third (Past Participle)
7. tag	tagged	(have) tagged
8. study	studied	(have) studied
9. fall	fell	(have) fallen
10. bring	brought	(have) brought
11. buy	bought	(have) bought

(5 points)

D. Write the missing tenses.

Simple Present	Simple Past	Simple Future
12. break	broke	will break
13. forget	forgot	will forget
14. ring	rang	will ring

Simple Present	Present Perfect	Past Perfect	Future Perfect
15. go	have gone	had gone	will have gone
16. run	have run	had run	will have run
17. grow	have grown	had grown	will have grown

(6 points)

E. Underline each verb or verb phrase. In the blank, write the letter showing the tense of the verb.

a. present   c. future   e. past perfect
b. past   d. present perfect   f. future perfect

__c__   18. I <u>shall clean</u> the room tomorrow.

__f__   19. They <u>will have arrived</u> by then.

__e__   20. Matthew <u>had done</u> the work before noon.

__c__   21. We <u>shall read</u> the Bible every morning.

__b__   22. We <u>sang</u> that song yesterday.

__d__   23. Julia <u>has made</u> the dress.

__d__   24. The students <u>have finished</u> this lesson.

__f__   25. The service <u>will have begun</u> before then.

(8 points)

F. Write the verb tenses indicated in parentheses. Be sure to use the correct helping verbs.

26. (past tense of *keep*) They _____kept_____ the sick children inside.

27. (future tense of *take*) They _____will take_____ the tables back to school.

28. (past perfect tense of *think*) He _____had thought_____ it was his.

29. (present perfect tense of *buy*) Father _____has bought_____ the tools we need.

30. (future perfect tense of *come*) Before we finish, they _____will have come_____.

(5 points)

G. Diagram the skeletons, direct objects, indirect objects, predicate nominatives, and predicate adjectives of the following sentences.

31. Galen tore up the old papers and threw them
(3 pt.) away.

32. He will surely have arrived by then!
(2 pt.)

33. The roses smell sweet, and the carnations smell
(6 pt.) spicy.

34. My teacher has always been Brother Jonathan.
(3 pt.)

35. These plants certainly have grown
(3 pt.) tall.

36. Take Grandmother these pies.
(4 pt.)

37. Give Glenn and Gerald some cookies
(4 pt.) and milk.

(25 points)

H. Follow the directions for completing the outline below.

   (1) Write these items as main topics where they belong. Make them parallel with the other main topics.

      Animals found in the oceans   Animals seen in the tropics

   (2) Write these points where they belong.

      camel   octopus   spider monkey
      penguin   killer whale

Kinds of Animals

I. Animals of the polar regions

   A. Polar bear

   B. _____ Penguin _____

   C. Arctic hare

   D. Arctic loon

II. _____ Animals of the oceans _____

   A. Starfish

   B. _____ Octopus _____

   C. Whales

      1. Blue whale

      2. _____ Killer whale _____

   D. Jellyfish

III. Animals of the deserts

   A. _____ Camel _____

   B. Cactus wren

IV. _____ Animals of the tropics _____

   A. Monkeys

      1. _____ Spider monkey _____

      2. Woolly monkey

   B. Parrot

   C. Tiger

(7 points)

I. Write *T* for true or *F* for false.

   _F_   38. An oral book report should be written out and read to the audience.

   _T_   39. The setting is the place and time of a story.

   _T_   40. A book report should include the main events of the story.

   _F_   41. A book report should also give the outcome of the story.

   _F_   42. A book report should simply tell what the story is about, without giving a personal opinion of the book.

(5 points)

Total points: 70

Progressing With Courage

Chapter 5 Test   Score _____

Name _____ **Date** _____

A. Match these verbs to the meanings and descriptions below. You will use some letters more than once.

a. lay	e. set	i. can
b. lie	f. sit	j. may
c. raise	g. let	k. teach
d. rise	h. leave	l. learn

___i___ 1. To be able to   ___l___ 5. To gain knowledge

___d___ 2. To get up or go up   ___f___ 6. To rest or be seated

___g___ 3. To allow or permit   ___b___ 7. To rest or recline

___j___ 4. To be permitted to   ___h___ 8. To depart or go away from

   ___c___ 9. To cause (something) to go up or grow up

   ___k___ 10. To give knowledge or instruction

   _a, e_ 11. To put or place (something) (2 answers)

   _a, c, e_ 12. Verbs that can have a direct object (3 answers)
   (*also* g, h, k, l)

   ___g___ 13. Main verb that is always followed by another verb form   *(16 points)*

B. Underline the correct words in parentheses. In numbers 14–16, also underline the direct object if there is one.

14. Wayne (<u>raised</u>, rose) the <u>blind</u> and saw that the moon had (raised, <u>risen</u>, rose).

15. The glasses are still (setting, <u>sitting</u>) where we had (<u>set</u>, sat) <u>them</u>.

16. Mother (<u>laid</u>, lay) the <u>carpet</u> in the yard, and it has (laid, <u>lain</u>) there ever since.

17. The dog has not (<u>dragged</u>, drug) it away.

18. Father (<u>let</u>, left) me help him.

19. We (let, <u>left</u>) the tools and supplies there.

20. Jean (<u>tagged</u>, tug) you, so you are it.

21. The large bubble (bursted, <u>burst</u>) after it floated up several feet.

22. Aphids have (attackted, <u>attacked</u>) my rosebushes.

23. My aunt (<u>taught,</u> learned) me how to raise these flowers.

(16 points)

C. Underline the subjects in these sentences. Then underline the verbs in parentheses that agree with the subjects.

24. A <u>porcupine</u> in the woods (don't, <u>doesn't</u>) have to be speedy.

25. (There's, <u>There are</u>) many sharp <u>quills</u> in his tail ready to protect him.

26. The disturbed <u>porcupine</u> (strike, <u>strikes</u>) the attacker with his tail.

27. The <u>hooks</u> on each quill (<u>work</u>, works) their way deep into the skin.

28. (Here's, <u>Here are</u>) two <u>mothers</u> with their prickly babies.

29. At birth, the <u>baby</u> (don't, <u>doesn't</u>) weigh much more than one pound.

30. A <u>branch</u> (or) a whole <u>tree</u> (<u>is</u>, are) sometimes killed when a porcupine eats the bark.

(7 points)

D. Follow these directions for the sentences below.

(1) Draw two lines under each simple predicate, and one line under the word that receives the action of the verb.

(2) In the first blank before each sentence, write *DO* or *S* to tell whether the receiver of the action is the direct object or the subject.

(3) In the second blank, write *A* for active voice or *P* for passive voice.

<u>S</u> <u>P</u> 31. One day five thousand <u>people</u> <u>were fed</u> by Jesus.

<u>DO</u> <u>A</u> 32. One lad <u>had</u> not <u>forgotten</u> his <u>lunch</u>.

<u>S</u> <u>P</u> 33. His <u>lunch</u> <u>was given</u> to Jesus.

<u>DO</u> <u>A</u> 34. Jesus <u>gave</u> <u>thanks</u> for the food.

<u>DO</u> <u>A</u> 35. The disciples <u>distributed</u> the <u>food</u>.

<u>S</u> <u>P</u> 36. Twelve <u>baskets</u> of leftover food <u>were gathered</u>.

(12 points)

E. Rewrite each sentence as indicated. Do not change the voice of the verb.

37. Change to past tense.
   The children are brought by the mothers.

   The children were brought by the mothers.

38. Change to future tense.
   The mothers are sent away by the disciples.

   The mothers will be sent away by the disciples.

   (2 points)

F. Rewrite these sentences in the passive voice.

39. Jesus rebuked the disciples.

   The disciples were rebuked by Jesus.

40. Jesus blessed the little children.

   The little children were blessed by Jesus.

   (2 points)

G. Rewrite these sentences in the active voice.

41. Many people were healed by Jesus.

   Jesus healed many people.

42. The world is still touched by Jesus' love.

   Jesus' love still touches the world.

   (2 points)

H. Answer these questions about writing reports. (Answers should include the following ideas.)

43. Why should you take notes from several reference sources?

   to help make the report more informative and interesting

44. Why should you write plenty of notes?

   so that you have plenty of ideas to choose from

   or so that you do not have to go back later and look for more information

45. What is the purpose of an outline?

    <u>to organize the material in a report</u>

    _____

46. After you write the first draft of your report, you should try to improve it. What is one improvement that you can make in the way the sentences are written?

    <u>variety in sentence lengths</u>

    <u>variety in sentence types</u>

    <u>or variety in the word order of sentences</u>

(8 points)

Total points: 65

Progressing With Courage

Chapter 6 Test

Score _____

Name _____ Date _____

A. Write the answers.

1. What is a pronoun? <u>a word that takes the place of a noun</u>

2. What is an antecedent? <u>the noun for which a pronoun stands</u>

3. Which case of pronouns must be used for subjects and predicate nominatives?

   <u>nominative case</u>

4. Which case of pronouns must be used for direct and indirect objects? <u>objective case</u>

(4 points)

B. Before each group of pronouns, write the letter of the kind that it is. You will not use all the letters.

a. personal—nominative case
b. personal—objective case
c. personal—possessive case
d. personal—archaic
e. demonstrative

f. definite
g. indefinite
h. interrogative
i. imperative
j. relative

<u>e</u>   5. this, that, these, those

<u>b</u>   6. me, you, him, her, it, us, them

<u>j</u>   7. who, whom, whose, which, that

<u>c</u>   8. my, mine, your, yours, his, her, hers, its, our, ours, their, theirs

<u>d</u>   9. thou, thee, thy, thine, ye

<u>g</u>   10. some, any, none, all, most, each, either, one, nobody, anyone, anybody, both, few, several, many

<u>a</u>   11. I, you, he, she, it, we, they

<u>h</u>   12. who, whom, whose, which, what

(8 points)

C. Underline each pronoun, and draw an arrow from the pronoun to its antecedent.

13. Mother baked the bread, and then she sent it to Mrs. Johnson.

14. The girl whom Susan met last week called her from Missouri.

(4 points)

D. Underline the pronoun in each sentence below, and then follow these directions.
(Count 2 points for each sentence.)

(1) In the first blank, write *1, 2,* or *3* to tell whether the pronoun is first, second, or third person.

(2) In the second blank, write *M, F, N,* or *C* to tell whether the pronoun is masculine, feminine, neuter, or common gender.

<u>1</u> <u>C</u> 15. We were watching a goldfinch.

<u>3</u> <u>F</u> 16. Mother and she had filled the feeder.

<u>3</u> <u>M</u> 17. A goldfinch is small, and his feathers are bright yellow.

(6 points)

E. Underline the pronoun in each sentence below, and then follow these directions.
(Count 2 points for each sentence.)

(1) In the first blank, write *S* or *P* to tell whether the pronoun is singular or plural in number.

(2) In the second blank, write *N, O,* or *P* to tell whether the pronoun is in the nominative, objective, or possessive case.

<u>S</u> <u>O</u> 18. Thistle seeds were in the feeder for him.

<u>P</u> <u>N</u> 19. Were you boys watching too?

<u>S</u> <u>P</u> 20. Be not wise in thine own eyes.

(6 points)

F. Underline the correct pronoun for each sentence. In the blank, write *S, PN, DO, IO,* or *OP* to tell whether the pronoun is a subject, predicate nominative, direct object, indirect object, or object of a preposition.

<u>PN</u> 21. The artists were Nina and (she, her).

<u>IO</u> 22. Kevin gave (we, us) boys a diagram for a birdhouse.

<u>S</u> 23. The swallows and (they, them) eat many harmful insects.

<u>DO</u> 24. The same idea struck (we, us) three boys at the same time.

<u>S</u> 25. (We, Us) girls typed up the lists for them.

_OP_   26. In (Thou, <u>Thee</u>), O Lord, do I put my trust.

_S_   27. The Lord, (<u>who</u>, which) made heaven and earth, cares for you.

_OP_   28. The man to (who, <u>whom</u>) I spoke showed me the directions.

_DO_   29. The lady (who, <u>whom</u>) I called responded promptly.

_S_   30. The dog (who, <u>which</u>) is my pet came from Germany.

(10 points)

G. Underline the correct words in parentheses.

31. (Its, <u>It's</u>) time to go; they will soon be (<u>there</u>, they're).

32. (Your, <u>You're</u>) not too late to go with us to (<u>their</u>, they're) house.

33. (<u>Its</u>, It's) house is made of twigs and bark.

34. (<u>Your</u>, You're) book has pictures of house wrens.

35. (Their, <u>They're</u>) my favorite kind of birds.

(7 points)

H. On the blank, write *adj.* or *pron.* to tell how each underlined word is used. Draw an arrow from each underlined adjective to the word it modifies.

adj.   36. <u>That</u> birdhouse was made for bluebirds.

pron.   37. <u>This</u> is the one Kendall made.

pron.   38. <u>Whose</u> is this one?

adj.   39. <u>Whose</u> drawing of an octopus is this?

pron.   40. <u>Each</u> of those drawings was made by a sixth grader.

adj.   41. <u>Each</u> student drew his own.

adj.   42. <u>His</u> drawings are excellent.

(7 points)

I. Underline the correct words in parentheses. When you underline a verb, also underline the subject that it must agree with.

43. <u>Both</u> of the girls (<u>help</u>, helps) in the garden.

44. <u>Each</u> of the boys (use, <u>uses</u>) a hoe.

45. <u>Some</u> of the fertilizer (<u>is</u>, are) gone.

46. <u>Some</u> of the children (is, <u>are</u>) here already.

47. <u>Everyone</u> (study, <u>studies</u>) from (<u>his</u>, their) own book.

48. <u>Neither</u> of the girls (<u>has</u>, have) (<u>her</u>, their) own ruler.

(8 points)

J. Follow the directions below.
(Count 1 point each for the six letter parts, 2 points for capitalization, and 2 points for punctuation.)
(1) Write the names of the letter parts in the blanks.
(2) Underline six small letters that should be capitalized.
(3) Cross out three unnecessary punctuation marks, and add three missing punctuation marks.

49. _____heading_____

631 Orange Street

Altamont, TN, 37301

march 2, 20—

50. _____inside_____
_____address_____

Nature Magazine

37, Maple street

Lakeview, Ca 92353

51. _____greeting_____

gentlemen:

52. _____body_____

I learned about your magazine from a friend who likes it very much. Please send me a free sample copy.

53. _____closing_____

sincerely,

54. _____signature_____

Maria schrock,

(10 points)

Total points: 70

Progressing With Courage

Chapter 7 Test   Score _____

Name _____ Date _____

A. Underline each small letter that should be capitalized.
(Count 2 points for each sentence and 4 points for number 3.)

1. did you know that india ink did not originally come from india, but from china?

2. louis braille invented the braille reading system when he was only fifteen years old!

3.   **god cares**

   god cares for me. i know not why

   his eyes should see each time i cry,

      nor why he stoops to make me glad;

      but he's the best friend i have had!

   i know not why he cares to show

   his love to me, but this i know

      he is my god! i love him too!

      i'll please him by the things i do.

   —Edith Witmer

4. "but thou, o lord, art a shield for me; my glory, and the lifter up of mine head" (Psalm 3:3).

5. the queen of england, queen elizabeth, gave some english noblemen land in the country of ireland.

6. the first u.s. five-cent stamp had a picture of mr. benjamin franklin on it.

7. your father will build it for grandmother next spring in may.

8. have you read *fisherman andy and the brown pelican?*

(18 points)

B. In each blank, write *D, I,* or *N* for direct quotation, indirect quotation, or no quotation. (All quotation marks have been omitted.)

   I   9. Ronald said that tares look very much like wheat.

   D   10. Sister Julia said you will find information on tares in the Bible dictionary.

   N   11. A poisonous variety of darnel is the most common kind of tare.

(3 points)

C. Cross out each small letter that should be capitalized, and write a capital letter above it. Also add the missing punctuation marks. (Count 2 points for each number.)

12. "*W*~~w~~hat king brought gold, silver, ivory, apes, and peacocks to *J*~~j~~erusalem every three years asked?" *S*~~s~~iste*r* *M*~~m~~ary.

13. *B*~~b~~en answered, "*I*~~i~~t was *S*~~s~~olomon."

14. "*W*~~w~~hat a rich and wise king he must have been!" exclaimed *R*~~r~~honda.

15. *J*~~j~~eremiah said, "*B*~~b~~ehold, *I*~~i~~ cannot speak, for *I*~~i~~ am a child."

16. "*B*~~b~~e not afraid of their faces," said the *L*~~l~~ord. "*I*~~i~~ am with thee."

17. "*T*~~t~~hou shalt go," said the *L*~~l~~ord, "to all that *I*~~i~~ shall send thee."

18. *D*~~d~~ear *U*~~u~~ncle *J*~~j~~ohn,

   Y~~y~~ours truly,

19. 1211 *M*~~m~~aple *A*~~a~~venue

   A~~a~~ustin, *TX*~~tx~~ 78702

   A~~a~~ug. 3, 20—

(16 points)

D. Add the missing commas.

20. You must read it, copy it, and repeat it several times.

21. Before starting, you must crush ten graham crackers.

22. Oh, the last load, a box of old books, was especially interesting.

23. Sister Angela, stay and have supper with us.

24. Yes, your problem, my dear friend, is a very common one.

25. As you know, the old roof must first be removed, Alvin.

(6 points)

E. Write the correct abbreviation for each word.

26. dozen   doz.   30. September   Sept.

27. mile   mi.   31. pound   lb.

28. Monday   Mon.   32. Mister   Mr.

29. before midday A.M.   33. Junior   Jr.

(8 points)

F. Add the missing apostrophes.

34. Jonathan's brother mowed the two neighbors' lawns.

35. We'll show you someone's paper that has neat 2's and 3's.

36. The two bears' tracks were easily seen in the farmer's field.

(3 points)

G. Add the missing hyphens, colons, and semicolons.

37. His brother–in–law has twenty–one nieces and nephews.

38. Our great–grandfathers were men of self–discipline.

39. We memorized John 14:1–14.

40. At 5:30 we'll take my great–aunt to the airport; she will fly to Washington from there.

41. Daisies, marigolds, and asters are beautiful; but roses, lilies, and violets are still my favorite flowers.

(5 points)

H. Change these sentences so that they have direct quotations.

42. Mother said that we may plant the asters now. _____

   Mother said, "You may plant the asters now." _____

43. Father said that he would help us with our work. _____

   Father said, "I will help you with your work." _____

(4 points)

I. Change these sentences so that they have indirect quotations.

44. Marlin said, "I would like to watch Henry fix it." _____

   Marlin said that he would like to watch Henry fix it. _____

45. James said, "I will bring you some water." _____

   James said that he would (will) bring me (us) some water. _____

(4 points)

J. Fill in the chart.

Singular	Singular Possessive	Plural	Plural Possessive
46. lion	lion's	lions	lions'
47. baby	baby's	babies	babies'
48. sheep	sheep's	sheep	sheep's

(3 points)

K. Rewrite each phrase, using a possessive form.

49. the ladders of the salmon _____ the salmon's ladders _____

50. the fur of the fox _____ the fox's fur _____

51. the tails of the monkeys _____ the monkeys' tails _____

52. the needles of the ladies _____ the ladies' needles _____

(4 points)

L. Write *P* before each sentence that should begin a new paragraph. Add the missing punctuation.
(Count 1 point for each paragraph.)

It was the first day of school. "You must be Joel Martin, is that right?" the teacher, Sister Marie, asked a small boy in the first row. P"Yes," he replied, "I am." P"Is your father Howard Martin?" she inquired. P"Yes," he answered. P"When is your birthday, Joel?" she asked. "I need to write this information in my book." P"March 9," he responded. P Then she asked, "What year?" P Joel frowned slightly and then said, "Every year, I think."

(8 points)

Total points: 82

Progressing With Courage

Chapter 8 Test

Score _____

Name _____ Date _____

A. Answer the following questions about adjectives.

1. What two parts of speech do adjectives modify?

   _____nouns_____   _____pronouns_____

2. What four things do adjectives tell?

   _____which_____   _____how many_____

   _____whose_____   _____what kind of_____

   (3 points)

B. Write *adj.* or *pron.* to tell whether each underlined word is an adjective or a pronoun.

   __pron.__ 3. <u>Mine</u> is not here.

   __adj.__ 4. <u>Your</u> order has not come in yet.

   __adj.__ 5. <u>This</u> box is for James.

   __pron.__ 6. You may take <u>those.</u>

   (4 points)

C. In each blank, write a more descriptive adjective for the underlined word. Choose from the list below. (More than one word may be correct.) (Do not accept *real, awful,* or *great.*)

severe	bulky	valuable	stormy
difficult	extensive	awful	great
neat	real	useful	attractive

   ____severe, stormy____   7. The explorers ran into <u>bad</u> weather near the South Pole.

   ____attractive, neat____   8. Your drawing of the buildings on the farm is <u>nice.</u>

   ____valuable, useful____   9. The tool set you gave was a <u>good</u> gift.

   ____difficult, extensive____   10. Repairing the old buildings on the farm was a <u>big</u> job.

   (4 points)

D. Write the comparative and superlative degrees of the following adjectives.

11. happy _____happier_____ _____happiest_____

12. bad _____worse_____ _____worst_____

13. many _____more_____ _____most_____

14. wonderful ____more wonderful____ ____most wonderful____

15. late _____later_____ _____latest_____

(5 points)

E. Write the correct form of each word in parentheses.

_____younger_____ 16. Brenda is (young) than Beverly.

_____less_____ 17. The fields produced (little) wheat this year than last year.

_____tallest_____ 18. He is the (tall) man in our church.

_____worst_____ 19. It was the (bad) earthquake ever recorded.

(4 points)

F. Underline the descriptive adjectives. If a sentence has a predicate adjective or an appositive adjective, write *P* or *A* in the blank before the sentence.

_____ 20. Abraham saw three strangers from his <u>tent</u> door.

__P__ 21. Abraham was <u>kind</u>, and he invited the strangers to stay.

__A__ 22. Sarah, <u>willing</u> and <u>obedient</u>, prepared the meal.

_____ 23. The <u>heavenly</u> visitors brought a <u>solemn</u> message of judgment on Sodom.

_____ 24. Abraham made a <u>long</u>, <u>earnest</u> request for mercy on the people of Sodom.

__P__ 25. But the <u>wicked</u> city was <u>ripe</u> for God's judgment.

(10 points)

G. Underline each adjective phrase, and draw an arrow from the phrase to the word it modifies.

26. The man <u>on the biggest camel</u> was their leader.

27. Unload the bundles <u>of the smallest camel</u> first.

28. The men <u>in the caravan</u> sold merchandise <u>from many countries</u>.

4 points)

H. Put parentheses around each adjective clause, and underline the word that it modifies.

29. The <u>judge</u> (who went with Barak) was Deborah.

30. The Israelites fought against <u>Sisera,</u> (who was the enemy captain.)

31. The Israelites feared this <u>man,</u> (whose soldiers had iron chariots.)

32. Jael was the <u>woman</u> (who received the honor of defeating Sisera.)

33. God delivers <u>those</u> (who obey and trust Him.)

(5 points)

I. Diagram the following sentences.

34. The sunshine, warm and bright, cheered the cold, weary travelers.
(5 pt.)

35. The night had been cold and damp.
(3 pt.)

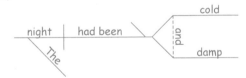

36. The children in the group were given milk from the farm.
(5 pt.)

37. All the children that could help worked in the garden.
(6 pt.)

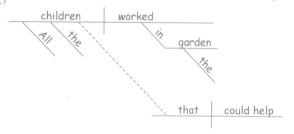

(19 points)

J. The verb *shook* would fit in all the following sentences. Write a more descriptive verb for each sentence.
(Answers may vary somewhat.)

flapped	shivered	vibrated	swayed
trembled	shuddered	fluttered	rattled

_____shivered_____ 38. Jonathan ——— in the chilly wind.

___flapped, fluttered___ 39. The clean wash ——— in the breeze.

_____swayed_____ 40. The tree branches ——— to and fro.

_____trembled_____ 41. The Israelites ——— when they heard the voice of God.

(4 points)

K. Read the description below, and do these exercises.

42. In sentence *a*, underline an exact noun and a descriptive adjective that comes just before it. Do the same in sentence *b*. (Be careful not to underline limiting adjectives.)

43. In sentence *c*, underline an exact verb and two descriptive adverbs that come right after it.

44. Underline the two comparisons used in this description.   *(And around may also be underlined.)*

ᵃA whirligig is a kind of beetle that lives in quiet ponds and streams. ᵇIts front legs have long claws, and its back legs are shaped like paddles. ᶜThis beetle whirls swiftly around and around in all directions on the surface of the water. ᵈThat is how it got its name; it spins just like a whirligig or pinwheel in a strong wind.

(5 points)

Total points: 67

Progressing With Courage

Chapter 9 Test   Score _____

Name _____ **Date** _____

A. Write the definition of an adverb, telling what parts of speech it can modify and what questions it can answer.

   An adverb is a word that modifies a verb, an adjective, or another adverb. It tells *how, when,*

   where, or *to what degree.*

                                                                              (2 points)

B. Write the comparative and superlative degrees of these adverbs.

   1. well _____ better _____   _____ best _____

   2. far _____ farther _____   _____ farthest _____

   3. ill _____ worse _____   _____ worst _____

   4. early _____ earlier _____   _____ earliest _____

   5. swiftly _____ more swiftly _____ _____ most swiftly _____

                                                                              (5 points)

C. For each sentence, write a word or phrase that gives a better description than the underlined words do. Choose from the list below. (Not all the answers are good choices.)

   | destructive | quite awful | immense | awfully chilly |
   | really tall | surely great | bitterly cold | skilled |

   _____ destructive _____ 6. The last hurricane in Florida was <u>very bad.</u>

   _____ immense _____ 7. The new skyscraper will be <u>very big.</u>

   _____ skilled _____ 8. Both eighth grade girls are <u>very good</u> seamstresses.

   _____ bitterly cold _____ 9. The weather was <u>very cold</u> on the day we drove by Lake Michigan.

                                                                              (4 points)

D. Write whether each underlined word, phrase, or clause is an adjective (*adj.*) or an adverb (*adv.*).

   adj. 10. The ice cream is too <u>hard</u> to dip.

   adv. 11. He always studies <u>hard</u> for tests.

adj. 12. You can do better work if you have an <u>orderly</u> desk.

adj. 13. The first book <u>on the top shelf</u> belonged to my great-grandfather.

adv. 14. Please set these dishes <u>on the table</u>.

adj. 15. This is the book <u>that I borrowed from the library</u>.

adv. 16. I must pay a fine <u>if I do not return it in time</u>.

(7 points)

E. Underline the correct words in parentheses.

17. It is (<u>good</u>, well) to see you again.

18. Father couldn't find (<u>anything</u>, nothing) wrong with the engine.

19. Peter does (more well, <u>better</u>) in math this year than he did last year.

20. Aunt Marie is a (<u>good</u>, well) cook.

21. I haven't had (<u>any</u>, none) of her doughnuts for a long time.

22. Of the two ponies, Ginger trots (<u>faster</u>, fastest).

23. You arrived (most early, <u>earliest</u>) of all.

24. Glenn has the (<u>farthest</u>, fartherest) of all to walk to school.

25. I (<u>can</u>, can't) scarcely tell the twins apart.

26. We hardly (<u>ever</u>, never) shop on Friday evening.

(10 points)

F. Write S, Cd, or Cx to tell whether each sentence is simple, compound, or complex.

_S_ 27. Jacamars are colorful tropical birds.

_Cd_ 28. A jacamar's bill is long, black, and sharply pointed, and its tail is long.

_S_ 29. The top of its head, its neck, its back, and its tail feathers are a shiny green.

_Cx_ 30. Jacamars do not migrate as many other birds do.

_Cd_ 31. They usually stay in tropical forests, but sometimes they are seen in the open country.

_Cx_ 32. Jacamars feed on large insects that they catch.

(6 points)

G. Diagram the following sentences.

33. Because the weather was unusually cold, we didn't go to the zoo yesterday.
(7 pt.)

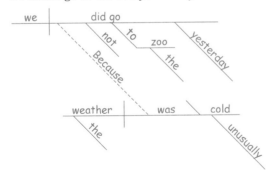

34. The van that you saw was not ours.
(6 pt.)

35. He became quite ill after he ate the green apple.
(6 pt.)

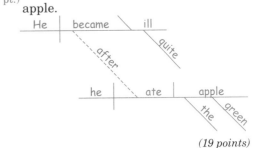

(19 points)

H. Write the number of the correct rhythm pattern for each poem.

Pattern 1 (iambic) ˘ ′ ˘ ′   Pattern 3 ˘ ˘ ′ ˘ ˘ ′

Pattern 2 (trochaic) ′ ˘ ′ ˘   Pattern 4 ′ ˘ ˘ ′ ˘ ˘

___4___ 36. How do you like to go up in a swing,
          Up in the air so blue?
          Oh, I do think it the pleasantest thing
          Ever a child can do!

          —Robert Louis Stevenson

___1___ 37. A careful boy I want to be,
          A little brother follows me;
          I do not dare to go astray,
          For fear he'll go the selfsame way.

___2___ 38. Leaves were budding,
          Birds were singing,
          Fawns were feeding,
          Spring was springing.

___3___ 39. There's a city of light 'mid the stars, we are told,
          Where they know not a sorrow or care;
          And the gates are of pearl and the streets are of gold,
          And the building exceedingly fair.

          (4 points)

I. Find the rhyming words in Part H, and copy them in pairs.

40. (36) __swing—thing; blue—do__   42. (38) __singing—springing__

41. (37) __be—me; astray—way__   43. (39) __told—gold; care—fair__

(4 points)

J. Identify the poetic device used in each line by writing the correct letter in the blank.

  a. simile   d. words that suggest the sound they refer to
  b. metaphor   e. words with similar beginning sounds
  c. personification

__a__   44. Noiselessly as the springtime

__e__   45. In the rifted rock I'm resting

__b__   46. The storm is a trumpet

__c__   47. The waves lie sleeping in their cradle

__a__   48. Clouds like wreaths of purest snow

__d__   49. The patter and the tinkle of the rain

(6 points)

Total points: 67

Progressing With Courage

Chapter 10 Test   Score _____

Name _____ **Date** _____

A. Underline the prepositions, and put parentheses around their objects.

  1. The sun is 93 million miles away <u>from</u> the (earth.)

  2. If the earth were much closer <u>to</u> the (sun,) everything <u>on</u> the (earth) would burn up.

  3. If the sun were too far away, all the water would turn <u>into</u> (ice.)

  4. God made the distance <u>between</u> the (earth) and the (sun) just right <u>for</u> (us.)

                                                                    (6 points)

B. Cross out the wrong words. If other words are needed, write the corrections above them.

  5. Did you talk <s>at</s> ^to^ the visitors this morning?

  6. Go <s>in</s> ^into^ that shed and get some baskets.

  7. They were all broken <s>accept</s> ^except^ one.

  8. They divided the leftover cookies <s>among</s> ^between^ the two families.

  9. This new edition is different <s>than</s> ^from^ the old one.

  10. We park <s>in back of</s> ^behind^ the house.

  11. On Sunday morning I sat <s>besides</s> ^beside^ Jennifer.

  12. After the service was over <s>with,</s> I talked to my friends.

  13. Where were you <s>at</s> for dinner?

  14. I could <s>of</s> ^have^ come, but we were late.

                                                                    (10 points)

C. Underline the correct words so that parallel sentence parts are joined.

  15. Always speak kindly and (<u>courteously</u>, with courtesy).

  16. Brother Luke has been in Mexico, in Guatemala, and (Honduras, <u>in Honduras</u>).

  17. Will he come home tonight or (<u>tomorrow</u>, in the morning)?

  18. The bird flew from the cage, around the room, and (outside, <u>out the door</u>).

                                                                    (4 points)

D. Put parentheses around each dependent clause, and underline the subordinating conjunction that introduces it.

19. (<u>After</u> the sun went down,) the bats poured out of the cave entrance.

20. (<u>Because</u> she saw a spider,) she shouted for help.

21. Her brother kindly removed the offensive creature (<u>while</u> she watched.)

22. (<u>Although</u> she hates spiders,) she does not hate mice.

23. Mice look appealing (<u>when</u> they are not inside the house.)

(5 points)

E. Underline the correct words. In the blank after each sentence, write the verb that is understood.

24. The other pupils did not come as soon as (<u>we</u>, us). _____ came _____

25. No one else in school is as tall as (<u>he</u>, him). _____ is _____

26. Mary made a better choice than (<u>she</u>, her). _____ made _____

(3 points)

F. Underline each misplaced phrase or clause, and draw an arrow from it to the place where it belongs. (Pupils may have marked a different phrase or clause to be moved, which is also correct if the resulting sentence is clear.)

27. Julie gave the letter to the mailman <u>that she had just typed</u>.

28. The teacher read about the discovery of America <u>during story time</u>.

29. I received a new book <u>from my aunt</u> in that box.
    (or <u>In that box</u> I received a new book from my aunt.)

30. Father said <u>on Saturday</u> we might go to Grandfather's house.
    (or <u>On Saturday</u> Father said we might go to Grandfather's house.)

31. I gave a card to my cousin <u>with a border of roses around the edge</u>.

(5 points)

G. In each pair, underline the name you should say first when making an introduction.

32. a younger person and an <u>older person</u>

33. a man and a <u>woman</u> about the same age

34. a boy and a <u>girl</u> about the same age

35. your teacher and your <u>mother</u>

36. <u>yourself</u> and a stranger

(5 points)

H. Write *X* before the better introduction in each pair.

___X___ 37. a. Uncle Paul, this is my friend John. John, this is my uncle Paul, who has a large stamp collection. He brought it with him. I know you have collected some stamps too, John.

_____ b. John, this is my uncle Paul. Uncle Paul, this is my friend John.

_____ 38. a. Martha, this is Mary Brown. Mary, this is Martha Martin.

___X___ b. Martha, this is Mary Brown, my first cousin. Mary, this is Martha Martin, my class-mate. She likes to collect quilt patterns, Mary. Maybe she can give you an idea of what to put on the quilt you are embroidering.

(2 points)

I. Write *T* for true or *F* for false.

___T___ 39. One of the most important rules in conversation is to listen carefully.

___T___ 40. You should show interest in what the other person is saying.

___F___ 41. You should avoid asking the other person for information about himself.

___F___ 42. If someone makes a mistake in conversation, you should correct him immediately.

___T___ 43. You should use correct, clear English when you speak.

___T___ 44. You should put more emphasis on points of agreement than on points of disagreement.

___T___ 45. You should avoid talking too rapidly or too loudly.

___F___ 46. Courtesy in conversation is based on keeping a set of rules.

(8 points)

J. Above each word, write the abbreviation for the part of speech that it is.

     interj. pron.   adv.   v.   adj.
47. Well, that certainly is mysterious.

     n.   conj. adj.   n.   v. adj.   n. prep.   n.   prep. adj.   n.
48. Sunspots and solar flares are two kinds of storms on the sun.
(*Solar flares* may be considered a compound noun.)

(17 points)

K. Diagram these sentences.

49. Sirius and Arcturus are two very bright stars.
(4 pt.)

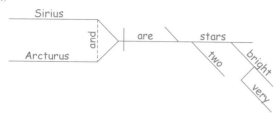

50. When you view the constellation of Orion, you see Rigel.
(7 pt.)

51. What! Antares must be an extremely large star.
(4 pt.)

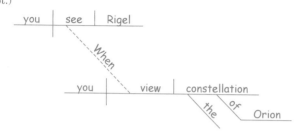

(15 points)

Total points: 80

Progressing With Courage

Chapter 11 Test   **Score** _____

Name _____ **Date** _____

A. Before each entry word, write *yes* or *no* to tell whether you would find it on a dictionary page with the guide words *Pharisee* and *Philistine*.

  __yes__ 1. Philip   __yes__ 4. Philippian

  __no__ 2. Petra   __no__ 5. Pharaoh

  __no__ 3. Phoebe   __yes__ 6. Philadelphia

(6 points)

B. Write the letter of the best meaning for each underlined word.

    a. to give an order   d. a price or expense

    b. to blame; accuse   e. a duty; responsibility

    c. to rush at; attack

  __c__ 7. The angry dog <u>charged</u> at the intruder.

  __e__ 8. Taking care of the baby was my only <u>charge</u> that morning.

  __b__ 9. The young man was <u>charged</u> with speeding.

  __d__ 10. Father thought the mechanic's <u>charge</u> was quite high.

(4 points)

C. Name the part of speech for each underlined word in Part B above.

11. (7) _____verb_____   13. (9) _____verb_____

12. (8) _____noun_____   14. (10) _____noun_____

(4 points)

D. Write the letter of the best reference source to use for finding the answer to each question.

    a. dictionary   b. Bible concordance   c. Bible dictionary

   __b__   15. What is the reference for the verse "As cold waters to a thirsty soul, so is good news from a far country"?

   __a__   16. Is it acceptable to use *galore* in formal writing?

   __c__   17. When the Bible mentions the coney, what animal is it referring to?

   __a__   18. Which spelling is correct, *arguement* or *argument*?

   __c__   19. How was frankincense used in Bible times?

   __b__   20. How often is the word *kingdom* used in the Book of Matthew?

(6 points)

E. Write whether each description tells about synonyms (*S*), antonyms (*A*), or homonyms (*H*).

   __A__   21. They are words with opposite or nearly opposite meanings.

   __S__   22. They are words with similar meanings.

   __A__   23. They may be formed by using prefixes like *un-* and *dis-*.

   __H__   24. They are words that are pronounced alike, but their spellings and meanings are different.

(4 points)

F. Write whether the words in each pair are synonyms (*S*), antonyms (*A*), or homonyms (*H*).

   __S__   25. enough—sufficient   __H__   28. throne—thrown

   __A__   26. arrive—depart   __A__   29. capture—release

   __H__   27. aloud—allowed   __S__   30. purpose—reason

(6 points)

G. Underline the incorrect words.

31. She <u>guest</u> that the boy had forgotten his proper <u>manors</u>.

32. The <u>dessert</u> shall rejoice and blossom as a <u>rows</u>.

33. I have never <u>scene</u> storm damage <u>worser</u> than this.

34. The prison <u>sell</u> was <u>bear</u> except for a cot.

(4 points)

H. Before each word family, write the letter of the word that also belongs in that family. You will not use all the letters.

    a. simply   c. innumerable   e. photograph

    b. invariable   d. verify

_c_   35. numeral, numerator, enumerate, numerical

_b_   36. various, variety, varied, variable

_e_   37. graph, graphite, autograph, stenographer

_a_   38. simple, simplicity, simplify, simplistic

(4 points)

I. Write *X* before the paragraph that has better sentence variety.

_X_   39.   [a]How delighted we were! [b]There in Mother's flower garden flitted a beautiful yellow-orange butterfly. [c]It flew gracefully from flower to flower, and it took little sips of nectar here and there. [d]My father, mother, little sister, and I watched it for a long time. [e]What kind could it be? [f]When we looked in the butterfly book, we learned that it was an orange sulphur. [g]We had a very enjoyable time watching this interesting little part of God's creation.

_____   40.   [h]It was delightful. [i]A beautiful yellow-orange butterfly flitted in Mother's flower garden. [j]It flew gracefully from flower to flower. [k]It took little sips of nectar here and there. [l]My father, mother, little sister, and I watched it for a long time. [m]We wondered what kind it was. [n]We looked in the butterfly book. [o]It was an orange sulphur. [p]We had a very enjoyable time watching this interesting little part of God's creation.

(1 point)

J. In Part I above, how is sentence variety used in the better paragraph? Find sentences that illustrate the following methods, and write the letters of the sentences in the blanks. You will not use all the sentences. One letter should be written two times.

_e_   41. interrogative sentence   _a, e, or f_ 44. mixed word order

_a_   42. exclamatory sentence   _c_   45. compound sentence

_b_   43. inverted word order   _f_   46. complex sentence

(6 points)

Total points: 45

Progressing With Courage

Final Test

Score _____

Name _____ Date _____

A. Name the parts of speech for the underlined words.

1. ^a_Jesus_ visited Mary and Martha ^b_often._

   a. _____nouns_____   b. _____adverb_____

2. Martha ^a_worked_ and worried, ^b_but_ Mary listened to Jesus.

   a. _____verb_____   b. _____conjunction_____

3. ^a_Oh,_ she learned ^b_wonderful_ lessons at Jesus' feet.

   a. _____interjection_____   b. _____adjective_____

4. ^a_We_ too can learn ^b_from_ His Word.

   a. _____pronoun_____   b. _____preposition_____

(8 points)

B. Read the items in italics, and write the correct letters in the blanks below them.

   Jesus taught His followers many lessons.

   ___a___ 5. The verb *taught* is (a) transitive. (b) not transitive.

   ___b___ 6. The word *followers* is (a) a direct object. (b) an indirect object.

   James and John became Jesus' disciples.

   ___b___ 7. The word *became* is (a) an action verb. (b) a linking verb.

   ___a___ 8. The word *disciples* is a (a) predicate nominative. (b) direct object.

   The Word of the Lord was preached to us.

   ___b___ 9. The voice of the verb is (a) active. (b) passive.

   ___b___ 10. The word *us* is (a) a direct object. (b) the object of a preposition.

   The Bible, precious and eternal, shows the way to heaven.

   ___a___ 11. The words *precious* and *eternal* are (a) appositive adjectives. (b) predicate adjectives.

   ___a___ 12. The word *way* is (a) a direct object. (b) an indirect object.

Love wielded pick and carried pack
And bent to heavy loads the back.

____a____ 13. The rhythm pattern of these lines is (a) iambic: ˘ ′ ˘ ′. (b) trochaic: ′ ˘ ′ ˘.

____b____ 14. The figure of speech in these lines is (a) a simile. (b) personification.

____a____ 15. One thing that makes the lines sound appealing is (a) words with similar beginning sounds. (b) words that suggest the sounds they refer to.

(11 points)

C. What kind of sentence is each of these? Answer by writing two letters: one from group *a–d* and one from group *e–g*. (All punctuation has been omitted.)

a. declarative   e. simple
b. interrogative   f. compound
c. imperative   g. complex
d. exclamatory

_c_ _g_ 16. Provide food that these people may eat

_b_ _e_ 17. How can we feed so many

_a_ _f_ 18. One boy had food but it was a very small amount

_d_ _e_ 19. How greatly the food was multiplied

(8 points)

D. Write *X* before each phrase in which the underlined word should be capitalized.

_____ 20. during early <u>summer</u>   __X__ 22. the song "Bring Them <u>in</u>"

__X__ 21. a visit with <u>grandfather</u>   _____ 23. a new Ford <u>tractor</u>

(4 points)

E. These sentences test your skill in using verbs. Underline the best words in parentheses.

24. None of the girls (was, <u>were</u>) finished with their jobs early.

25. Both of the boys (<u>help</u>, helps) Father in the barn.

26. Jason and Joel (<u>do</u>, does) the milking every evening.

27. John or James (feed, <u>feeds</u>) the pigs.

28. Here (<u>is</u>, are) a nest of kittens.

29. Two of the balloons have (<u>burst,</u> bursted).

30. (Here's, <u>Here are</u>) some wild raspberry bushes.

31. Martha (don't, <u>doesn't</u>) have very many in her bucket.

32. My calf is (laying, <u>lying</u>) in the shade.

33. I hope they do not (<u>raise,</u> rise) the price.

34. If it rains much more, the water in the creek will (raise, <u>rise</u>).

35. We usually (set, <u>sit</u>) with our mothers in church.

36. Mother (<u>let</u>, left) me help with the washing.

37. In a fire drill, please (let, <u>leave</u>) your possessions behind.

38. Can you (<u>teach,</u> learn) me how to get the right pitch for a song?

39. (Can, <u>May</u>) I please borrow this book?

(16 points)

F. These sentences test your skill in using other parts of speech. Underline the best words in parentheses.

40. The two (girl's, <u>girls'</u>) Bibles are on the shelf.

41. Our first grade (<u>teacher's,</u> teachers') desk is in this room.

42. The (pump's handle, <u>handle of the pump</u>) is curved.

43. (Who, <u>Whom</u>) did you see at church?

44. The girl (<u>who</u>, whom) bakes the bread is my cousin.

45. The man (<u>who</u>, which) led the singing is from Indiana.

46. It was (<u>we</u>, us) boys who picked them.

47. It must have been Uncle Ben and (<u>they,</u> them) who helped us.

48. Aunt Susan and (<u>she</u>, her) canned the peaches.

49. We helped Mother and (they, <u>them</u>).

50. (You're, <u>Your</u>) mother is waiting for you.

51. I (<u>can</u>, can't) hardly make it in time.

52. He didn't have (no, <u>any</u>) reason to be late.

53. (<u>It's</u>, Its) time to feed the calves.

54. Of the two boys, Ronald is (<u>taller,</u> tallest).

55. This is one of the (<u>most beautiful,</u> beautifullest) gardens around.

56. This machine works (<u>more swiftly</u>, swiftlier) than the other one.

57. The runaway car crashed (in, <u>into</u>) a tree.

58. Everyone (<u>except</u>, accept) Mary was here.

59. Divide this candy (between, <u>among</u>) the three of you.

60. Please sit here (<u>beside</u>, besides) me.

61. I want to talk (<u>to</u>, at) my former schoolteacher before she leaves.

62. I would (of, <u>have</u>) asked a few questions if I had known.

63. These tulips are different (<u>from</u>, than) the ones we had last year.

64. We planted the new flowers (in back of, <u>behind</u>) the house.

65. Please keep (<u>off</u>, off of) the wet paint.

66. Where will we be (<u>staying</u>, staying at)?

67. I'll be glad when this test is (<u>over</u>, over with).

68. This is the part that I had (trouble, <u>trouble with</u>).

69. Sister Rose read (a good, <u>an inspiring</u>) story to us.

(30 points)

G. In each blank, write the letter of the tense for the underlined verb.

    a. simple present   d. present perfect
    b. simple past   e. past perfect
    c. simple future   f. future perfect

   _e_   70. Judas <u>had betrayed</u> Jesus that night.

   _f_   71. Before the cock crows, Peter <u>will have denied</u> Jesus three times.

   _b_   72. Jesus <u>rose</u> on the first day of the week.

   _d_   73. Jesus <u>has risen</u> from the dead.

   _c_   74. Jesus <u>will come</u> again.

(5 points)

H. Add the two missing punctuation marks to each sentence.

75. Uncle Daniel brought Ernest, Ray, and Kendall; and Uncle Elmer brought Justin, Clair, and Wilford.

76. Revelation 4:4 speaks of twenty–four elders sitting around the throne in heaven.

77. My great–uncle plans to be here by 3:00 tomorrow afternoon.

78. We'll have to keep looking; we cannot finish this job without it.

(8 points)

I. Write whether each underlined item is an adjective (*adj.*) or an adverb (*adv.*).

79. We drove the horses ᵃhard until we came to a ᵇsteep hill.

   a._____adv._____   b. _____adj._____

80. The books ᵃon the top shelf will be moved ᵇto the back room.

   a._____adj._____   b. _____adv._____

81. The shelves ᵃthat Father built were polished ᵇuntil they shone.

   a._____adj._____   b. _____adv._____

(6 points)

J. Write whether the words in each pair are synonyms (*S*), antonyms (*A*), or homonyms (*H*).

___A___ 82. fearful—brave   ___A___ 84. center—edge

___H___ 83. groan—grown   ___S___ 85. convince—persuade

(4 points)

Total points: 100

Index

A

R

Raise, rise, 212–213

Reference books

Bible dictionary, 555–557

concordance, 555–557

dictionary, 548–549, 551–553

Regular nouns, 107–108

Regular verbs, 137–138

Relative clauses, 305–307

Relative pronouns, 305–307, 309–310, 392, 393, 429–432

Reports

book, 197–199

drafts, 248–250, 252–253

outlining for, 167–169, 234–238

proofreading, 252–253

taking notes, 198, 219–224

using reference books, 219–224

writing, 248–250, 252–253

Review Exercises

action verbs, 17, 33, 251, 308, 347, 371

active and passive voice, 269, 308, 356–357, 532

adjective clauses, 463–464, 488, 528, 555

adjectives, 467, 485, 529

adverb clauses, 517, 555

adverbs, 64, 467, 485, 529

agreement of subjects and verbs, 24, 257, 272–273, 304–305, 312–313, 380–381, 488, 529

apostrophes, 432–433

archaic pronouns, 325, 454–455

be, forms of, 33, 72

book reports, 315

business letters, 337, 494–495

capitalization, 177, 197, 341, 345, 381, 400, 415, 451, 494–495, 532–533, 573

clauses, 57, 463–464, 488, 517, 528, 539, 555

coherence, 107, 115–116, 128, 155, 226, 280, 352–353

colons, 432–433

commas, 98, 197, 341, 372, 432–433

comparisons, 467

complete sentences, 28–29, 41, 45, 57, 76

compound sentences, 98, 115–116, 123, 197, 341

conjunctions, 98, 197, 341, 573

declarative sentences, 60, 72, 76, 103–104, 285

demonstrative pronouns, 296, 312–313, 325, 344, 454–455

descriptions, 476–477

diagraming, 60, 84, 112–113, 123, 136–137, 189, 192–193, 211, 218–219, 234, 247–248, 290–291, 361, 403, 447–448, 471, 488, 500, 524–525, 536, 539, 543

directions, writing, 68, 107, 170–171, 185–186, 411

direct objects, 189, 192–193, 211, 234, 247–248, 269, 290–291, 308, 347, 356–357, 361, 482, 485, 532

direct quotations, 381, 400, 451, 573

end punctuation, 60, 76, 103–104, 197, 285, 341, 381, 451, 494–495, 573

exact words, 476–477

exclamatory sentences, 60, 76, 103–104, 285

figures of speech, 476–477, 520

fragments, sentence, 28–29, 41, 45, 76

friendly letters, 337, 494–495

gender of nouns, 110